# HOW TO clean just about EVERYTHING

## CLEANING SECRETS THAT SAVE TIME, MONEY AND EFFORT!

READER'S DIGEST

## NOTE

The information in this book has been carefully researched, and all efforts have been made to ensure accuracy and safety. Neither the author nor Reader's Digest (Australia) Pty Limited assumes any responsibility for any injuries suffered or damages or losses incurred as a result of following the instructions in this book. Before taking any action based on information in this book, study the information carefully and make sure that you understand it fully. Test any new or unusual cleaning method before applying it broadly, or on a highly visible or valuable area or item. The mention of any product or web site in this book does not imply an endorsement. All product names and web sites mentioned are subject to change and are meant to be considered as general examples rather than specific recommendations.

# A WORD BEFORE YOU RUSH OFF TO CLEAN THE HOUSE...

For years I put up with filmy looking drinking glasses. It's not that I'm dim-witted, but like most people, I'm a creature of habit. The glasses came out of the dishwasher with a residue that seemed etched into the surface. No amount of scrubbing or dishwashing detergent could remove it. But it seemed a shame to throw out a set of perfectly good drinking glasses. It was much simpler to just keep using them—and to stop inviting friends over for dinner.

Then one day as I was wandering through a kitchen supplies warehouse, I spied a 5-litre container of distilled white vinegar, enough to take a bath in. And something clicked—this stuff is acetic acid, a powerful and versatile cleaner that can attack, among a million other things, grimy deposits and filmy residues. While it might seem absurd to try to clean a cupboardful of glasses with a regular-sized bottle of white vinegar, this tanker of it had serious potential. And it didn't cost much, either.

When I hauled the 'vat' of vinegar into the kitchen, my wife rolled her eyes—the same look I get when I start spritzing around the house, testing some new recipe for a home-brewed cleaner. But her scepticism soon turned to delight. I filled a large plastic bowl with vinegar and dunked our glasses into it two or three at a time. When I removed them after a few minutes, they looked brand new.

I know I wasn't breaking any new ground. If I had really given it a thought, I could have worked out this solution ages ago. But it took stumbling across a cheap source of bulk vinegar to spark my imagination, and a small corner of my life has been changed forever.

My hope is that, as you read this book, you'll have thousands of similar revelations. Hundreds of experts have been interviewed for this book and we've sifted through wheelbarrow loads of research to turn it into the ultimate household cleaning book. You'll be amazed at how easy it is to clean everything you own using only readily available tools and materials. There's even a surprisingly simple step-by-step 'ZAP' system for thoroughly cleaning your entire house in the least amount of time. With this advice in hand, your surroundings will sparkle, your possessions will last longer, your family will be healthier and you'll save tons of money. Get to it!

**Jeff Bredenberg**

# contents

# 1 a clean home

# 1 The right attitude to cleaning

You know a person with a serious cleaning habit, when they wake up for their morning run and it is still pitch black. They run two blocks down to the local school's oval, where they run a few kilometres before sunrise. On their first few laps around the oval, however, they do an unusual thing—they throw the students' non-recyclable water bottles, soft-drink cans and potato-chip bags into rubbish bins. They pick up forgotten sportswear out of the dewy grass and hang them on the benches to dry. They don't expect any recognition for the tidy-up job. At best, they think, some PE teacher might be wondering who this mysterious clean-up person is.

The cleaning fanatic's one moment of 'recognition' does come, however, when they snatch a jacket out of the grass and head off to hang it on a bench. Another early-morning runner pops out of the darkness, exclaiming, 'Hey, that's my jacket!'.

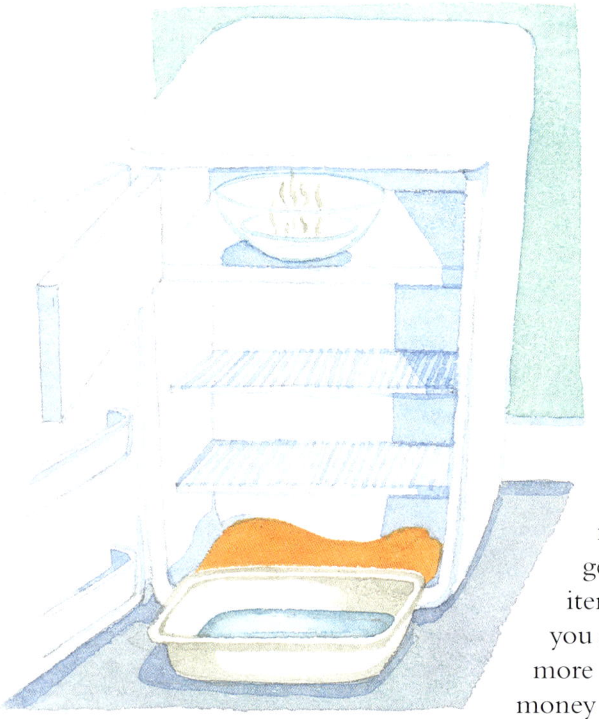

Fridge cleaning is always easier if you don't keep putting it off.

**There are two morals to our story:** firstly, you'll find cleaning is most effective and least bothersome when it's done as a regular part of your everyday life. Secondly, if you do anything to the point of obsession, even cleaning, you're going to end up in trouble.

The majority of people (the cleaning fanatic being part of the minority) see cleaning as an odious chore that can't be avoided, but all too easy to put off for another day. We're here to convince you of the opposite: that if you have the right attitude to cleaning and its benefits, cleaning becomes something that is much easier to accomplish.

**Take a thoughtful, even laid-back, approach to cleaning.** This book covers the full spectrum of topics related to cleaning—from smart routines and the right gear to handling unexpected messes and cleaning specific items. But underlying it all is one key idea: the more savvy you are about cleaning—the more you know about it and the more organised you are about it—the less effort, time and money you will have to spend actually doing it.

Later, in Chapter 6, you'll find a fail-safe, tried-and-true system for cleaning your house. ZAP (zoned attack plan) is a truly time-saving strategy for weekly house cleaning. It is a super-efficient plan that eliminates double work and lets you get your house spick-and-span with the least amount of effort. ZAP knocks hours off your cleaning time, and makes house cleaning almost fun. But first let's take a broader view of cleaning.

## THE THREE KINDS OF CLEANING

**WE'LL GET INTO** THE DETAILS OF WHAT WE CALL 'THE RIGHT ATTITUDE TO CLEANING': THE MIND-SET THAT WORKS BEST FOR EASIER, FASTER, MORE EFFECTIVE CLEANING. BUT FIRST, TO UNDERSTAND THIS MINDSET, IT'S IMPORTANT TO UNDERSTAND WHAT THE THREE CATEGORIES OF CLEANING ARE.

Wipe up spills immediately, to prevent any further damage.

**Immediate cleaning** prevents small, easy-to-clean-up messes from becoming big, tough messes. Let's say that after cooking dinner, your stovetop has a few spatters of grease on it. You could leave it—it's scarcely noticeable. But if you take a minute to wipe the stove with a sponge or cloth every time you use it, the job will take only seconds, the stove will be restored to pristine condition, and you'll prevent what could eventually become a multi-layered build-up requiring hours of remedial attention.

In the immediate cleaning mode, you clean up messes as soon as they happen. Otherwise, messes accumulate, stains and grime set in, and your family learns that a dirty house is acceptable.

**Maintenance cleaning** is done regularly, but not necessarily often. This kind of cleaning can be put on a schedule. For example, you could decide to clean the shower once a week (perhaps even set the day) and wash the curtains twice a year. Maintenance cleaning can be organised in a written plan. Or it can be simple habits, like always cleaning the kitchen immediately after dinner is done.

**Remedial cleaning** covers cleaning after long periods of neglect, such as tackling the fridge after a year's growth of drips and spills have accumulated on the bottom shelf. That kind of remedial cleaning is preventable. You can avoid it by taking immediate steps or following maintenance routines—it saves time and energy in the long run. Remedial cleaning also includes what you do after a disaster, major or minor, such as a flood or a pet accident on the carpet.

The big danger is that remedial cleaning can easily become abusive cleaning. That happens when a mild cleaner fails to budge the dirt, so stronger and more abrasive cleaners and tools are called into service. Abusive cleaning often does more damage than the original dirt did.

Simple solutions

### Contain and maintain

Cleaning tasks fall into three main categories. Here are some examples.

**Immediate**

- Towelling off the shower recess after each time it is used.
- Having family members remove their shoes at the front and back door.
- Washing dishes immediately after using them, rather than stacking them up.

**Maintenance**

- Spraying the shower recess with soap scum remover once a week.
- Vacuuming all the dirt that family members track inside each week.
- Making sure all dishes, glasses and cooking gear are cleaned up each night before bedtime.

**Remedial**

- Spending hours scrubbing away a year's worth of soap scum and mildew.
- Vacuuming whenever your friends make jokes about the dust build-up.
- Wasting your Sunday scrubbing hardened food from the week's dishes and pots so you have something to cook with.

## PLANNING FOR A CLEAN LIFE

**PART OF THE** PHILOSOPHY BEHIND 'THE RIGHT ATTITUDE TO CLEANING' IS TO CLEAN THINGS IMMEDIATELY OR AT LEAST TO A REGULAR MAINTENANCE SCHEDULE, SO THAT YOU ALMOST NEVER HAVE TO DO ANY REMEDIAL CLEANING. HERE ARE SOME EASY WAYS TO ACHIEVE THIS.

**Always focus on the benefits of cleaning**, as there are many.

- A feeling of being in control instead of out of control.
- Renewed pride in your environment.
- A healthier, safer home.
- More and better time with your family.
- A more active social life.
- Reduced stress.

If you hate cleaning and organising, why not try to change your attitude? Look for the beauty and value in those activities. Yogis have long taught the value of doing simple chores such as cleaning. They describe the benefits of 'karma yoga', or being in a meditative state of awareness as you clean or garden as being calming, focusing and centring. The idea is to let go of your mental clutter—the bad family dynamics, the bills that need paying, your dispute with your boss—and focus on the job at hand. Be in the moment.

Even without the yoga philosophy, cleaning can help you to be more serene. If you're under a lot of stress, doing something mundane and methodical, such as cleaning, can often be very therapeutic and calming. It's a back-to-basics kind of feeling.

Simple solutions

### Getting help

If you love being well organised but just can't seem to get there, a pro can set you firmly on the right path. Professional organisers help people with wardrobes, files, kitchens, store rooms, garages, garden sheds, entire houses, offices and businesses.

How can an organiser help you? Organisers are flexible and work in various ways. They may help you make a plan and leave you to carry it out, work with you for as long as you like or even do the job for you. They charge from $60 and up per hour, depending on the nature of the job and the experience of the professional. Prices vary from city to city, too, and the service may not always be available outside the major cities. In an initial visit, the organiser will estimate how long the job will take and how much it will cost.

Type 'professional organiser' and the name of your city into your web search engine and see what you can find.

If you don't want or can't find the services of a professional organiser, you might just need a really good professional cleaner to get you kick-started on your new regime. Check the *Yellow Pages* for listings.

**Treat cleanliness as a value that your whole household shares.** If you are always the sole cleaner of the home, then what are you teaching everyone else? That they can be messy, and someone else will take care of it. Instead, make it a family job to keep your home clean. And make them proud of it.

Part of this means giving children cleaning chores beginning at an early age. When they're very young, they'll enjoy it because they're working with you. Later they may come to see the chores as onerous, but if they've been well trained, they'll do them anyway. Explaining how to train children to do chores is simple; the actual training process is less so. But what it really comes down to is insisting that the children do what you've asked them to do: no excuses from them, no idle threats from you. One day they'll thank you for the training and discipline.

## EXPERT ADVICE

### HOW CHILDREN LEARN TO CLEAN

How do you begin to teach children to pick up after themselves, clean their belongings, do the washing and clean the house? After all, it's something they really do need to learn before adulthood.

An easy way to begin is to start early. When a child is about 18 months old, put a rag and a spray bottle in their hands and teach them how to clean something a child can easily reach and appreciate—say, a toy truck. As the children grow, their cleaning reach is extended until eventually they know how to clean the whole house, and by the time they are 18, they know how to take care of themselves.

**Build cleaning routines** and procedures into your everyday life. This may be the single most important thing for achieving the spick-and-span home you have dreamed about. It means making your bed every morning (and teaching your kids to do it too). It's always wiping your feet at the door; putting dishes directly into the dishwasher; having a mail-sorting routine that puts bills, catalogues, coupons and correspondence immediately into their right place. With well-established routines like this, you can keep the time spent house cleaning to a minimum.

**Have strategies for keeping your home both clean and neat.** Neat means benchtops are clear, coats are hung up, clutter is under control. Clean means the floors aren't muddy, the corners aren't cobwebby, the doors aren't smudgy. While the two often go hand in hand, it is possible to have a messy home that's clean, or a neat home that's dirty. Neatening and cleaning need not happen together. But it's certainly easier and faster to clean a room that is neat.

**Understand the special cleaning requirements** of the things you own. What materials are your carpets, furniture, appliances, curtains and clothes made of? The more you know about materials, the better you'll be able to clean them. When you make purchasing decisions, take into consideration how the items should be cleaned.

**Don't despair at messes,** but rather, see the order and cleanliness that can emerge from them. Visualising the result in advance is one powerful tool for the right attitude to cleaning. Before-and-after pictures are very motivating and energising. But when you're still in the 'before' stage, you have no 'after' picture to inspire you. By visualising, you can make one.

Pick a spot in the house that bothers you because it's dirty or disorganised. Conjure up an image of order or cleanliness. You might even draw a picture, or write a description.

Take visualisation a step further and create a small clutter-free area, just to see how it feels. Pick a desk or table that has bothered you and put all the stuff on it into a box. For the moment, don't worry about sorting it. After the table or desk is clear, dust it, wash it if it needs it and just savour the feeling: clean and orderly!

# 2 Ten golden rules of cleaning

Your primary goal in cleaning is to remove dirt, whether it be in your home (inside or outside) or on your garments. But you do need to determine at what cost. Surely you don't want to injure yourself. Surely you don't want to damage the very thing you're trying to clean. And surely you want to get it done as quickly and with as little effort as possible. Stick to the following ten golden rules, and you will achieve safe, effective cleaning that attacks the problem early and with the least amount of effort.

## 1 • CLEAN IT UP SOONER RATHER THAN LATER

**Spills and stains are generally much easier to clean up** when you attack them right away. When you treat that tomato sauce splatter on your dress shirt without delay, for example, it offers little resistance. If you wait until the next day, you'll have a permanent-looking red polka dot stain that you'll expend a lot more cleaning solution and time getting out. Similarly, clothing or carpet stains are easiest to remove when they're fresh. The longer you wait, the more chance the stain has to set and become more difficult to remove.

The rare exception to this rule is mud that has been tracked onto your carpet. Mud is easiest to clean when you've let it dry first. Wait until it's bone dry and crumbly; then just vacuum it up.

## 2 • CLEAN FROM THE TOP DOWN

**Don't fight gravity when you clean.** You'll lose. Working from high to low almost always works better in cleaning situations.

When you're cleaning the entire house, always start on the top floor and work your way down. This will avoid tracking through the rooms you have already thoroughly cleaned.

When you're cleaning a room, first remove the cobwebs from the ceiling and cornices. Then dust the ceiling fan and light fixtures, followed by window frames and wall hangings. Moving downwards, work on the furniture, skirting boards and floors. This ensures that any dust shaken loose from high up does not settle on something you've already cleaned below, so you don't have to dust the room twice.

Similarly, when you clean windows and mirrors, start up high and work your way down, because your cleaner, obeying gravity, will drip down. This saves you elbow grease and time.

The rare exception to this rule is wall washing. If you start at the top when you're washing a wall in your home, dirty water will drip onto the lower areas you haven't cleaned yet, making streaks that will be tough to remove.

## 3 • THINK DRY, THEN WET

**When you're cleaning a room,** start with the cleaning jobs that require dry methods (dusting, sweeping and vacuuming, for example). Then move on to wet methods (using an all-purpose cleaner and glass cleaner, mopping and such like). This way, there will be less dirt floating around in the room to cling to wet surfaces.

To maximise dust removal, brush your furniture before vacuuming the floor.

## 4 • START WITH THE LEAST HARMFUL APPROACH

**Use your gentlest cleaning methods first** and move up to more aggressive techniques only if necessary. And know your materials well enough so that you will stop your cleaning efforts before you do any damage. It is better to suffer the small spot on your stovetop, for example, than to ruin the surface with steel wool.

## 5 • LET TIME DO THE WORK FOR YOU

**A little time management trick** will make your cleaning easier and faster. When you organise your approach to a cleaning task, remember to spray on your cleaning chemicals first and then find another little job to do while the cleaner does its dirty work. If you're cleaning in the kitchen, for example, spray your cleaner on the bench-tops and appliances, then occupy yourself with removing old food from the fridge while the cleaner soaks in. When you come back to wipe the cleaner off, there will be little or no scrubbing to do.

## 6 • CARRY YOUR SUPPLIES WITH YOU

**Carry your core cleaning products with you.** This will save you from making multiple trips around the house looking for the right tools and cleaners. Pick up one of these accessories at a home improvement shop or hardware shop:

- A cleaning caddy—a plastic or rubber carrier with a handle and compartments for holding your gear.
- A sturdy, large plastic bucket with a good handle.
- A small-cleaning trolley.
- An apron with roomy pockets.

Put all your cleaning supplies into the receptacle you're chosen from above, including clean rags, paper towels and a rubbish bag for emptying wastebaskets, and cart it with you from room to room. If your house has more than one floor, keep a fully stocked caddy on each level.

Don't overburden your carrier with specialty products that are needed for only one job around the house. Store toilet bowl cleaner, for example, under the bathroom sink.

## 7 • WHEN IN DOUBT, TEST FIRST

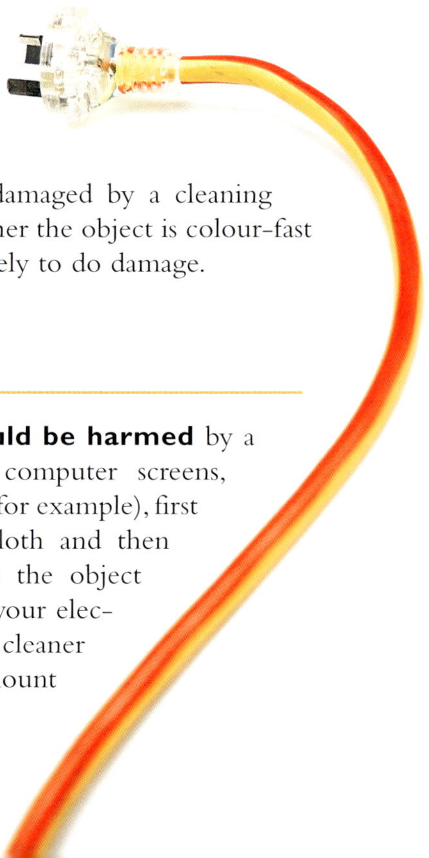

**Before you use a new cleaning technique or product,** test the method on an inconspicuous area of the object you're cleaning. This rule also applies when you first clean an object that is delicate and might be damaged by a cleaning compound. Testing will show you whether the object is colour-fast and whether the cleaning method is likely to do damage.

## 8 • USE CLEANING LIQUIDS SPARINGLY

**When you clean an item that could be harmed** by a liquid cleaning product (electronics, computer screens, framed artwork or framed photographs, for example), first spray the cleaner on your cleaning cloth and then wipe. Don't spray cleaner directly on the object you're cleaning. Cleaner dripping into your electronics could do them damage, and cleaner dripping into a frame and soaking the mount could harm your artwork.

## 9 • READ THE INSTRUCTIONS

**You would have heard this before,** but the makers of all of those wonderful furnishings in your home do know best how to clean them. And the makers of your cleaning products know best how to use them. So when at all possible, follow the manufacturer's instructions when cleaning anything. This goes for everything from toasters to silk blouses and Doonas to blinds. File the instructions and cleaning tips that come with any new appliance, rug or other household item. Don't remove those care labels that come on clothes, linens and any other potentially washable objects. They are there for a purpose.

## 10 • PROTECT YOURSELF

**Last but not least, take care of yourself.** Many of the cleaning products you use contain acid, bleach, abrasives and other ingredients that can damage your eyes, skin, nose and even your lungs. So make sure your cleaning kit includes a pair of rubber gloves and protective safety glasses. If it's not too hot, wear old long pants or tracksuit pants and an old long-sleeved shirt to cover your arms in case of spatters from cleaning products. Cover your hair with a scarf or baseball cap.

To protect your nails, a good trick is to dab a line of petroleum jelly underneath your nails to keep out dirt. And dot more on your cuticles to keep them from drying out, roughening and splitting from the continual exposure to harsh cleaning chemicals.

It is important that you don't let your cleaning products get mixed together. Some chemical combinations, chlorine bleach and ammonia, for example, will produce poisonous gases. As an extra safety precaution when you're using cleaning chemicals, make sure the room you're in is properly ventilated.

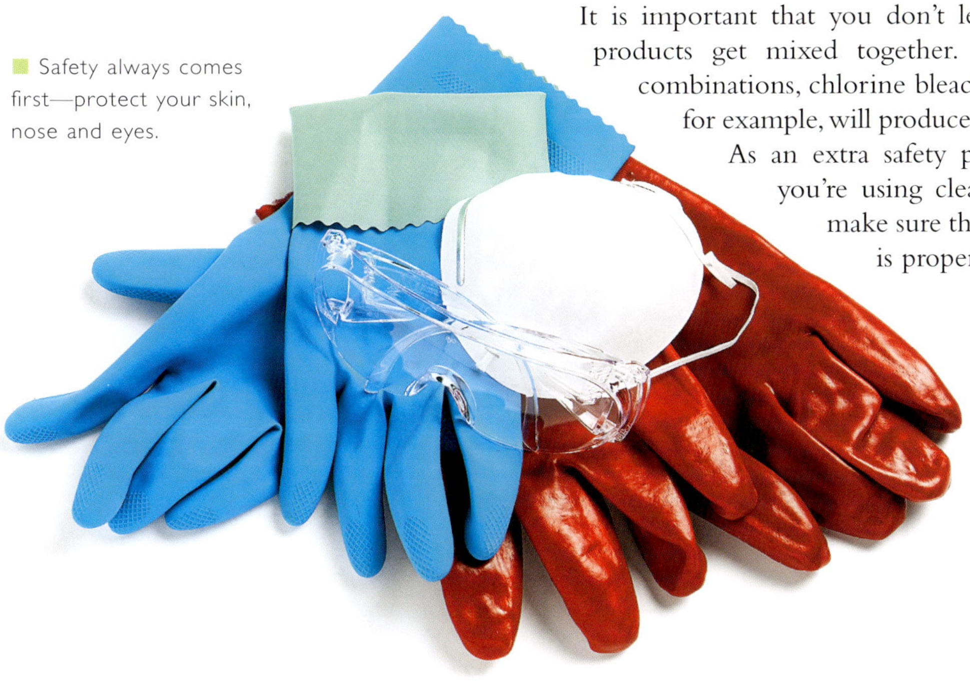

Safety always comes first—protect your skin, nose and eyes.

# 3 Stopping dirt at the door

The best way to avoid cleaning up dirt is not allowing it into your house in the first place. As we all know from the 'ounce of prevention' saying, it's easier to head off a problem than to fix it after the damage is done. So learn to stop dirt in its tracks.

## GET DIRT ON THE MAT

**ACTUALLY, WHAT YOU** WANT TO DO IS STOP THE DIRT IN YOUR TRACKS—SPECIFICALLY, ON THE SOLES OF YOUR SHOES. USE DOORMATS AT EVERY ENTRANCE TO YOUR HOME, INSIDE AND OUT. REMEMBER THAT MOST OF THE GRIME IN YOUR HOME COMES FROM THE OUTSIDE, THE BULK OF IT COMING IN ON PEOPLE'S FEET UNNOTICED.

**Choosing the right doormats** will cut down on the time you spend looking for and cleaning dirt. People coming into the house need to walk across the doormats and, in doing so, give the dirt on their shoes the brush-off (see below left). The heavy-duty mats that retail stores, supermarkets and hospitals use to keep dirt at bay are a terrific choice here. Typically doormats can be purchased in hardware shops and home improvement shops.

Doormats for outside your door are usually made of a vegetable fibre, such as coir matting, or rubber- or vinyl-backed synthetic turf. Inside doormat choices come in different materials, such as nylon or olefin (polypropylene) with either vinyl or rubber backing. The indoor variety is available in several dark, dirt-defying colours to coordinate with your particular decor. A doormat should be long enough so that both of a person's feet walk across it before entering the house, and the width no wider than the door itself. The mat should never impede the door's movement, either.

To stop dirt in its tracks, invest in a doormat for all doors outside.

**Floor mats are also a good idea** near high-traffic or spill-prone areas such as the kitchen sink, the fridge, the bath and the toilet. Clean-ups are much easier when all you have to do is clean a mat instead of the floor. Just think of all the stuff that gets dripped on the floor in front of the sink or the fridge, for example.

**Doormats need minimal maintenance.** Just haul them outside occasionally and give them a good shake and also give them a once-over with the vacuum cleaner now and then.

**When mats are really grimy,** hose them down and scrub them with a squirt of dishwashing liquid in warm water. Rinse and allow them to thoroughly air-dry. Another method is a wet and dry vacuum or an upholstery shampoo to freshen them. Make sure your mats are completely dry before you put them back on the floor. Moisture caught underneath the mats

could damage your floors. When your mats get threadbare, replace them—worn mats don't do their job as well as new ones.

**To reduce the amount of dirt entering your house,** limit the number of entrances that are used. This way, you'll cut down on the places where people and pets can bring dirt in. And if most people enter your house through an entrance or hall with an easy-wipe floor, a lot of grime can be quickly cleaned up and not distributed to the rest of the house.

**An even better idea** though is to make your house a shoeless zone for everyone. Encourage family members, guests and friends to remove their shoes just inside the entrance. Provide a decorative basket or some other receptacle where people can place their shoes. Keep some stylish, fresh, 'house' slippers (ones that never go outside) on hand for guests if they are uncomfortable about being 'shoeless' inside your house.

## DESIGN TO REDUCE GRIME

**IT'S NOT EVERY** DAY THAT YOU GET TO BUY NEW FURNITURE OR REDECORATE THE KITCHEN OR BATHROOM. BUT WHEN YOU DO, CHOOSE YOUR SURFACES WISELY.

**Easy-care decorating choices abound.** For example, there are a number of wax-free, easy-care floors to choose from. For benchtops in the kitchen or bathroom, you'll find that solid surfaces—those that have few or no seams, don't have indentations and are impervious to spills and marks—are remarkably easy to keep clean.

Over time, many blinds, curtains and other window coverings become magnets for dust and cobwebs. Instead of buying materials that catch dust, choose fabrics treated with a stain-and-dust-resistant finish, or treat the fabric yourself with a product such as Scotchgard fabric protector, following package instructions.

**To childproof a child's bedroom, a playroom or the kitchen,** use a good quality low-sheen or semi-gloss scrubbable paint (available from paint shops) on the walls. It may cost a bit more than other brands, but texta and crayon will wipe right off it.

Instead of making a mess of a family room wall by taping and tacking children's artwork to it, you can have a full-wall gallery in your home without the damage. Just cover the wall in a magnetic paint (available from paint shops) and use magnets to post the work of your budding Michelangelos.

**Patterns and designs camouflage dirt and grime,** whereas solid colours hide very little. And it's also important not to forget your pets when you redecorate. If you have a black Labrador retriever or another dark-haired breed, for example, light-coloured surfaces may not be the wisest choice.

**If concrete or mortar joints haven't been sealed,** they can slough off bits of sand and concrete dust onto surrounding surfaces. To keep this grime at bay, look for a concrete sealer, available from hardware shops, paint shops and home improvement shops.

## PREVENTIVE MEASURES IN THE KITCHEN

**WHEN YOU HAVE** COOKED A MEAL, YOUR KITCHEN SHOULD NOT LOOK LIKE A DEMOLITION SITE.

**To keep airborne grease and such away from benchtops,** turn on the exhaust fan when you're cooking on the stovetop.

**To cut down on splattering sauces and other messes,** use big pots and pans, with their lids on. When you deep-fry, sauté or cook foods that spit, line kitchen benches around your stove with newspapers or paper bags, cut open to extend them. (Always keep these papers away from any heat source.)

**For oven splatters** from a pie or casserole bubbling over, sprinkle the stains with salt (see below) to keep the smoke down and to make your eventual clean-up job much easier.

**To protect the fabric on kitchen chairs,** which is always under assault, especially from children spilling porridge and ice-cream, have the fabric laminated for easy wiping. If you have removable cushions on your chairs, have just one side laminated. The easy-wipe side is for everyday use, and the other side is for special occasions. To find someone to laminate fabric for you, consult a fabric shop or go through an interior designer.

As a quick, temporary measure, you can sprinkle oven splatters with salt.

★★★

EXPERT ADVICE

### FIRST THINGS FIRST

Apply products that keep surfaces from getting grimy only after you've cleaned them. For example, lemon oil works wonders in preventing soil build-up on shower doors, but you have to clean the doors of mildew, soap scum and other gunk before applying it. The same applies for fabrics, as the spray-on fabric protectors that repel stains and spills, such as melted cheese (see below), also require that the fabric be clean before you apply the protectant.

Spills, such as melted cheese, are easily cleaned if the garment is effectively protected with a fabric protector.

## CLEAR THE AIR

**YOUR AIRCONDITIONING SYSTEM** IS ANOTHER LABOUR-FREE WAY TO KEEP DIRT OUT OF YOUR HOME. IF YOU THINK ABOUT IT, SOONER OR LATER EVERY MOLECULE OF AIR IN YOUR HOUSE MUST PASS THROUGH THE DUCTWORK SYSTEM YOU HAVE FOR HEATING AND COOLING.

**Keep the airconditioning filter** clean, so it functions effectively. Replace the filter at least twice a year to prevent airborne grime from spreading all over the house. Switch filters as often as once a month if the filter collects lots of dust during the heating and cooling seasons.

**If your ducts are clogged with dust and debris,** or if you can see mould building up in there, call in a professional duct cleaner, who will clear everything out with a high-powered vacuum. (See 'Choosing an air-duct cleaning service', on page 367.) Your ducts may get particularly grimy if you've done work that throws around a lot of dust (such as sanding wooden floors or renovating), or if you frequently use a fireplace or wood stove.

**Make sure your windows and doors are sealed tightly.** Some utility companies will inspect your home without charge to determine whether you have any cracks where heat or airconditioned air could be seeping out—which also means that dirt could be creeping in through the same cracks.

## KEEP TOOLS CLEAN

**DIRTY CLEANING TOOLS** NOT ONLY MAKE YOUR JOB MORE DIFFICULT, THEY CAN MAKE YOU LOSE HEART AS WELL. IF THINGS DON'T LOOK BETTER WHEN YOU'VE MADE A BIG CLEANING EFFORT, WHY BOTHER IN THE FIRST PLACE?

**Worn-out cleaning tools**—sponges, mops, squeegees and such—are a waste of time. They make you work harder to get the job done. Dirty cleaning tools are worse, because they're actually counter-productive—they smear grime and germs all over the things you're trying to clean. Here's how to maintain your tools:

- Throw out cleaning tools as soon as they look chewed-up and tired.
- Regularly wash cleaning rags in your washing machine, using detergent, hot water and ½ cup of white vinegar or a scoop of an in-wash booster, such as Napisan In Wash Booster, to remove stains and freshen their scent.
- Wash your cellulose sponges—which are great at soaking up germs and offending odours—in the washing machine or even in the top rack of your dishwasher.
- Replace the bag in your vacuum cleaner at least once a month—more often if you have pets that shed. Vacuum bags need air inside to suck properly, so make sure you change them when they are two-thirds full. Remember to keep the vacuum brushes clean, too.

## CLOSE YOUR DOORS

**IT MIGHT SEEM** SO OBVIOUS THAT IT BARELY NEEDS REPEATING, BUT IT REALLY IS WORTH REMEMBERING THAT A CLOSED DOOR IS YOUR FIRST LINE OF DEFENCE WHEN WAGING YOUR CLEANING BATTLES.

**Dirt just likes to travel.** It's happiest when it can roam freely all over your home, hiding in those nooks and crannies where it's the most labour-intensive to find and remove.

So stop dirt at the borders. That is, habitually keep your doors, drawers, cabinets, wardrobes and other barriers closed. This will help keep dirt out and in the open, where your vacuum cleaners and cleaning cloths will be able to deal with it more readily.

If you're working on a messy, dust-producing project in the house, keep the doors to the room you're working in closed. Better yet, hang protective plastic across the door and any air vents to confine the dust to one room.

Periodically wash screens and other dirt-trapping window coverings (plantation shutters, venetian blinds and the like) to keep dirt at hand. Remember that dirt loves company and acts as a powerful magnet for more.

## TIDY PET HABITS

**THE WHOLE FAMILY** JUST ADORES YOUR BIG, BOOFY LABRADOR, BUT BOY, DOES HE ADD TO THE DAILY AND WEEKLY CLEANING CHORES. MUDDY PAW PRINTS IN AND OUT OF THE KITCHEN DOOR, WATER SLOPPED FROM HIS DRINKING BOWL, PET HAIR GATHERING IN EVERY CORNER AND ON THE RUGS AND SOFA.

**Keeping your dogs and cats clean** will definitely reduce the amount of dirt they can bring into your house. The following preventive maintenance tips will help:

- Station a clean rag by the door that your pet uses so that muddy, wet paws and claws can be wiped off before your beloved animal makes unsightly tracks through the house.
- Once a week, take your dog outside and give its fur a good going-over with the type of brush recommended for its coat (see below). Do this well away from the house, so that the tufts won't tumble inside.
- The miracle way to lift pet hair from furniture and other surfaces is to wipe with a damp sponge or cloth—the hair will gather in clumps and is easy to pick up. An alternative is to use one of those special rubber brushes with nubs on it that is intended for grooming cats (available from pet shops).
- Nothing beats your vacuum cleaner or a powerful hand-held vacuum for pulling pet hair out of your rugs and carpets.

Brush your dog outside regularly to reduce the build-up of pet hair inside.

## rules of the game

HAIRY SOLUTIONS

- To reduce dirt coming into your home, keep your pets clean.
- Have a rag handy—near the door—to wipe muddy, wet paws and claws.
- Brush down your dog or cat once a week outside.
- Lift hair from furniture and other surfaces with a damp sponge or cloth, or use a vacuum cleaner.

# 4 Clearing out clutter

Where has our hoarding instinct come from? Is it a reaction against Pandora, from Greek mythology, when on opening a box the gods had given her, she boldly decreed, 'Let there be clutter!', and thereupon unleashed all manner of ills upon the world? Or perhaps we inherited a hoarding instinct from our primitive ancestors, who saved and stored whatever they could because they had so little. And what little they had was subject to attack by the elements, predators and plunderers.

'Don't put it down, put it away'. This anti-clutter mantra could provide the inspiration that you need.

In modern times, the hoarding gene is about as useful as the eat-till-you're-stuffed gene—and has similar effects.

Whatever the cause, there's clutter everywhere. Clutter happens to all of us, and we need to ask ourselves would life be better not surrounded by this clutter?

You've probably heard the saying, 'Don't put it down, put it away'. If following that advice solves your clutter problem, you're lucky. The greater problem comes if there is no 'away'. To quote another old saying, 'If there is no place for everything, how can everything be in its place?'.

## WHAT IS CLUTTER?

**THERE IS NO** SINGLE DEFINITION OF CLUTTER, AS ONE PERSON'S CLUTTER IS ANOTHER'S DELIGHT. BUT PEOPLE WHO HELP OTHERS DE-CLUTTER THEIR SURROUNDINGS AGREE ON A FEW PRINCIPLES.

**Here are some basic ideas about clutter:**

- It is anything that bothers you and interferes with your well-being because it is disorganised, messy or chaotic.
- It can consist of things you don't love or don't use—such as unfinished projects—and too many objects in too small a space.
- It makes you feel overwhelmed, smothered, not in control of your space, victimised, scattered or unfulfilled.
- It may be a symptom of a lack of clarity about who you are and what your life is about.
- It is like the static on a radio. It's a distraction and an interference that doesn't allow you to focus on what is important.
- Clutter is stressful.

**The first step in getting rid of clutter** is making the decision either to accept clutter and stop complaining about it—or to do something about it, and do it now!

**The benefits of removing clutter include these:**

- You will find that cleaning up is easier.
- Your desk, table, room or house will look cleaner.
- You'll have more time for things that are important to you.
- You'll feel better.

EXPERT ADVICE

### DO YOU NEED DE-CLUTTER THERAPY?

There are two types of people who live amid clutter day after day. Some lack organising skills, and others are surrounded by clutter for deeper psychological reasons.

Helping the first group is easy. Show them the sense of storing all of the Christmas decorations in one place instead of scattered all over the house, and the penny will drop. Once they learn the skills behind organising themselves and their home, they become de-clutter experts.

The second group is more difficult. They may have deep-seated reasons for cluttering, going back to childhood—such as a feeling of deprivation or insecurity. Having lots of stuff around them may give them a feeling of fake prosperity that is needed for their day-to-day survival.

## CONFRONT YOUR CLUTTER

**LOOKING AT CLUTTER** TYPICALLY MAKES PEOPLE FEEL PARALYSED AND OVERWHELMED, BUT LUCKILY THE PROCESS OF GETTING RID OF IT IS ACTUALLY QUITE SIMPLE.

**Organising your home,** office, files, desk or anything else comes down to three steps.

- Eliminate the things you don't need, want, use or love.
- Categorise what remains by grouping similar things together.
- Organise the categories by having a place for everything and everything in its place.

**Whatever system of organisation you come up with** should fulfill three requirements. The system should be:

- Beautiful, in the sense that it makes you happy to look at it and is a pleasure to work in it.
- Functional, because such beauty without function is meaningless.
- Easy for the user to maintain.

A well-organised wardrobe makes life so much easier.

## ANALYSE YOUR CLUTTER

**ONCE YOU'VE DECIDED** TO DO SOMETHING ABOUT YOUR CLUTTER, BEGIN BY ANALYSING THE CLUTTER CLUSTERS. MAKE A LIST OF THEM. IF YOU HAVE TROUBLE DOING THAT OFF THE TOP OF YOUR HEAD, THEN GO FROM ROOM TO ROOM AND MAKE A NOTE OF ANY CLUTTER YOU ENCOUNTER. THEN GROUP THE ITEMS INTO CATEGORIES.

**Paper is a major clutter category.** If you have clutter, some of it is almost certainly paper. What is your specific pattern of creating paper clutter—unread newspapers and magazines, newspaper clippings, old mail, children's school papers, notes or lists, or all of the above?

**Clothing is another common clutter factor.** Is your problem that clothes aren't organised, or is it that you're chronically unable to get rid of things that no longer fit, are out of style, are worn out or are never worn for some reason?

**After these two categories,** clutter patterns look like the many tributaries of a large river—they're all over the map. Some common kinds are clutter related to home office space, pets, books, videos and CDs, electronics, hobbies, children's toys and kitchen utensils.

**Before you begin your clutter attack,** recognise that the feeling of being overwhelmed goes with the territory, and don't let it stop you. Break the job into small parts, because each tiny part that you conquer will lift your spirits.

To pick a starting point, find the area that bothers you the most. If it's a large area, like the garage or garden shed, pick one tiny part—let's say a cabinet you've stored there. Now pick one tiny part of that—a single drawer (it seems more manageable this way).

Or maybe your most irritating area is the kitchen table, where you can hardly find space to eat because of all the papers and other stuff. Pick a pile from one corner of the table.

## USE A CLEANING SYSTEM

**GO TO WORK** ON YOUR CHOSEN AREA USING A CLEANING SYSTEM—BASED ON HOW URGENTLY THINGS NEED TO BE CLEANED. IN OTHER WORDS, IT'S A SYSTEM OF SETTING AND CATEGORISING PRIORITIES.

**A cleaning system for clutter** includes categories for:

- Discarding
- Keeping
- Taking action

**When applying a cleaning system,** your discard pile may include items to be dumped, donated, sold or recycled. Items to keep may be papers to file, clothing to hang up or sports equipment to put away. Things to take action on might include bills to pay, library books or videos to return, or purchases to exchange. A cleaning system can be applied to any kind of clutter or potential clutter, including incoming mail, piles of paper and boxes of stuff stored away.

**Make your judgments quickly.** Don't linger over items. Be ruthless. Depending on how old your pile is, you've managed without some items for weeks, months or years. So think clearly and realise you can probably do without them forever.

EXPERT ADVICE

### BLENDING TWO HOUSEHOLDS

Remarriage creates special clutter challenges. People bring more stuff—including children and their gear, as well as pets—to second marriages, and putting two households together isn't always easy.

In these circumstances, both parties should make a written inventory of household goods. It's easier to decide on paper what to weed out and what to keep, and it may well open up communication about any hidden assumptions.

People who remarry are not the only ones who need help with merging possessions. It may be difficult, but university room-mates, house mates and even household guests need to know something about organising and respecting another person's space.

**If you have things you are going to keep** and want to store away, such as children's clothing that will be handed down to younger children in a few years, sort and label them well. For example, have separate boxes for '1–2 years', '3–4 years' and so on. Don't mix everything together and create a future nightmare when you want to find something and put your hands on it quickly.

**If you have a lot of sentimental memorabilia,** ask yourself whether there is some other way to keep it. Instead of saving your daughter's science project, for example, take a photo of her with the project (and perhaps a close-up of the project) and throw the project away. Keep photo albums and scrapbooks up-to-date, well labelled and accessible.

## REDUCE INCOMING CLUTTER

**EVEN BEFORE YOU** HAVE COMPLETED YOUR HOME ORGANISATION PLAN, TAKE STEPS TO REDUCE INCOMING CLUTTER. VIEW YOUR CLUTTER AS AN OVERFLOWING BATH AND TURN OFF THE TAP.

**For less clutter in your life,** here are some steps to consider:

- Focus more on doing and being in your life, not having.
- Whenever you're tempted to buy something, decide whether your buying impulse falls into the 'worthwhile' or 'future clutter' category. Like the right marriage partner, the worthwhile items will be just as worthwhile if you wait.
- Buy cloth shopping bags and use them to cut down on the plastic and paper bags you bring home.
- Stop the subscriptions to magazines that you somehow never get around to reading.
- Instead of buying things that you'll use just once or rarely ever, consider renting them.

Simple solutions

### Throw a de-cluttering party

If you want some outside help but don't want to hire a professional organiser, enlist a friend to help you with de-cluttering.

Meet every week or so, with one of you taking two or three boxes of clutter to the other's house. Go through your clutter together, and use your cleaning system and a timer to move quickly through the items. Allot around 30 minutes to each box. After two to three hours, celebrate over dinner.

A trusted friend is the best choice for a de-clutter companion, because spouses and other family members are more likely to be judgmental. The idea is to create a festive atmosphere in which to help each other 'see what's absurd' in the mess. And it's important to laugh with, not at, each other.

# 5 Advice on laundry

Thanks to automatic machines that do all the washing and drying for you, laundry day has changed drastically over the past century. Instead of boiling wash water in a big black kettle or a copper, scrubbing clothes against a corrugated washboard, squeezing the water out with a hand-cranked wringer and hanging the clothes on a line to dry, today you simply toss the clothes and a measured amount of detergent into a machine and flip a switch, then toss them into a dryer and flip another switch. It's an easy, quick way to get clean, fresh-smelling clothes.

For optimum results, check out all the fabric care options on your washing machine.

Doing the laundry used to be a tough job: the dirtier the clothes, the harder you scrubbed. But as machines, fibres and fabrics have evolved over the years, so have laundry products and techniques. Today, laundering is mostly a mental exercise, a matter of deciphering the hieroglyphics of care label symbols, keeping up with the latest new-and-improved laundry products, recognising the differences between fabric types and understanding the chemistry behind stain-removal techniques.

Everyone has clothes to clean. Not everyone cleans them as well as they could. They wing it or get by on the bare minimum. This chapter will help you do a better, more thorough job on your laundry. You'll be more knowledgeable, more confident and more efficient. Your clothes will be cleaner, brighter, fresher and longer lasting.

## SORTING YOUR CLOTHES

SORTING CLOTHES SHOULD BE EASY. DARKS GO IN ONE PILE, AND WHITES IN ANOTHER. THAT'S A GOOD START, BUT IF YOU REALLY WANT TO DO IT RIGHT—AND KEEP YOUR CLOTHES LOOKING THEIR BEST—ALSO SORT BY SIMILAR FABRICS AND DIRT LEVEL.

**Sorting by colour.** Separate whites from colours and light colours from dark colours. When in doubt, read care labels. If the label in a particular garment says to wash separately, that is because the dye colours will run. Even tiny amounts of dye can transfer to other fabrics, making the clothes look discoloured and dingy.

**Sorting by soil.** Separate heavily soiled or greasy items from lightly soiled ones. Lightly soiled clothes will pick up the extra soil and grease, making whites look grey or yellow and colours look dull.

**Sorting by construction and material.** Separate out clothes that are loosely knit or woven and clothes that have delicate trimmings or unfinished seams that can fray. Wash those on a shorter cycle that features more gentle agitation. Also separate lint producers, such as fleecy tracksuits, chenille items, new towels and flannel pyjamas, from lint attractors, such as corduroys, synthetic blends and dark things.

## ROUTINE PREP WORK

**WHILE LAUNDRY PREP** WORK IS NOT AS EXTENSIVE (AND TIRESOME) AS, SAY, PAINTING PREP WORK, IT IS IMPORTANT FOR GETTING THE CLEANEST CLOTHES. A FEW ROUTINE STEPS BEFORE STARTING—LIKE REMOVING CRAYONS FROM YOUR CHILD'S POCKET—CAN PREVENT A LAUNDRY DISASTER.

**Empty all the pockets.** Remove lipstick, lip balm, paper (especially tissues), sweets, nails and crayons—plus anything else hidden away in pants and jackets. Keep a small brush handy, so you can brush dirt and lint out of cuffs.

Make sure you get those crayons out of pockets before washing garments.

**Close zippers and Velcro.** Open zippers can get caught on things and closing Velcro prevents it from getting matted (and losing its staying power) with lint and thread.

**Bag your hose.** Put pantihose and items with long ties in a laundering bag to keep them from snagging and tearing.

## STAIN REMOVAL

**IT'S ALWAYS BEST** TO TRY TO REMOVE STAINS WHEN THEY ARE FRESH. BUT IF CLOTHES ARE STAINED, YOU NEED TO ADDRESS THIS BEFORE WASHING. IF YOU LET THEM PASS THROUGH A WASHING CYCLE (OR THE DRYER), THE STAINS MAY BECOME PERMANENT. IF YOU TREAT THEM BEFOREHAND WITH THE RIGHT STAIN-REMOVAL SOLUTION, YOU STAND A GOOD CHANCE OF REMOVING THE STAINS FOR GOOD. HERE'S A LOOK AT SOME GENERAL TIPS FOR STAIN REMOVING, BUT FOR MORE DETAILED TECHNIQUES SEE 'STAINS', ON PAGE 328.

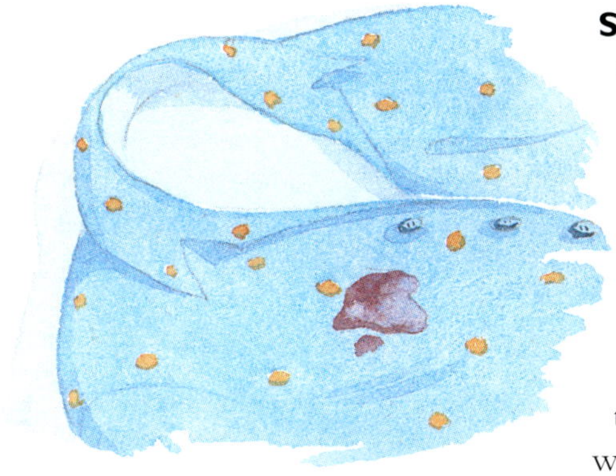

For the best results, pre-treat stains before washing.

**Soak protein stains in cold water.** These stains include egg, milk, faeces, urine, blood and the like. Soak for half an hour, and then run the stain under cold water, gently rubbing the fabric together with your hands to loosen the stain. Avoid warm or hot water, which can cook the proteins, setting the stain permanently.

**Pre-treat oil and grease stains** with liquid laundry detergent or pre-treatment spray. Apply the detergent or spray, such as Preen or Frend, directly to the stain.

**Soak tannin stains,** such as coffee, tea, soft drinks and jam, for half an hour in a solution of 1 teaspoon of liquid laundry detergent (preferably one containing enzymes) per 2 litres of warm water. Do not use soap or a soap-based product, as soap can make the tannin stain harder to remove.

**After washing,** check to see whether the stain has gone. If it hasn't, do not dry—heat can permanently set the stain. Try again to remove the stain and then repeat washing.

## WASHING TIPS

**THE INVENTION OF** THE AUTOMATIC WASHING MACHINE WAS TO HOUSEHOLD CLEANING WHAT THE PETROL-POWERED MOWER WAS TO LAWN CARE—REVOLUTIONARY. THE AUTOMATIC WASHING MACHINE ACCOMPLISHES WHAT ONCE TOOK HOURS OF SKIN-SCALDING, BACK-BREAKING WORK. AND THE MACHINE DOES IT BETTER. IT GETS CLOTHES CLEANER AND TREATS THEM MORE GENTLY. TODAY, MACHINES, AND ESPECIALLY THE NEW GENERATION OF FRONT-LOADERS, ARE MORE EFFICIENT THAN EVER.

**Evenly distribute clothes in a top-loading washing machine.** The spin cycle relies on a balanced load. Never wrap sheets or long garments around the agitator post. That can tear fabric and jam the machine. The best loads are ones that mix small and large items—for example, sheets mixed with hand towels and socks.

**Don't overload the washing machine.** The wash cycle depends on clothes rubbing together to remove the soil. If the machine is too full, the clothes will not have enough space to rub together. Powdered detergent may not have room to adequately dissolve, and you may end up with clumps of powdered detergent stuck on your clothes. Moreover, there must be enough free-flowing water to carry away the soil removed from the clothes. Make sure you check your washing machine's manual for the recommended maximum load.

**Pick the right setting.** Most clothes, of course, are OK with the normal or regular setting. Use the gentle or delicate setting (typically shorter agitation and spinning cycles) for lingerie, loose knits, washable woollens and rayon fabrics. The permanent press setting usually has normal agitation but includes a cool-down rinse to reduce wrinkling.

Simple solutions

### All things bright

Sometimes household bed linen and tea towels can start to look a bit dingy after repeated washing. Or despite your best efforts, they end up with stains of varying sorts. Try this simple recipe for brightening them up again. In an empty 2-litre plastic bottle, mix 250 ml of mild dishwashing liquid, 1.5 litres of hot water, 60 ml of ammonia and 60 ml of methylated spirits. Use 60 ml of the solution in a hot wash cycle. You may need to repeat the process to complete the rejuvenation. Make sure that you cap the remainder of the solution tightly and label the bottle.

**Choose the right water temperature.** The hot cycle draws directly from your household hot-water supply. Warm is either a 50:50 or 40:60 hot and cold water mix. Cold draws directly from the cold water line. Each of these can vary greatly depending on the distance of your water heater from your washing machine and on the season. (Incoming cold water, for example, can range from near freezing in winter to 27 °C in summer.) When using the hot or warm cycle, run a hot-water tap in a nearby sink until the hot water fills the pipes. This way you will cut down on the amount of cold water that inadvertently mixes in with the hot in the washing machine. As a general guide:

- *Hot (48 °C to 50 °C):* Use for whites and colour-fast fabrics and heavily soiled clothes (such as underwear and nappies). Hot water is

## Front-loading washing machines

Front-loading washing machines have been around for a while. And they haven't exactly caused a laundry equipment revolution. Most people still use top-loading models with a central agitating post. But attitudes are changing.

Although slightly more expensive, the new models have many advantages. They're more efficient, in some cases using only a third of the amount of water standard washing machines use. That not only saves water, but it also saves the power needed to heat it. Front-loaders clean as well, if not better, than top-loaders. And the tumbling action is gentler on clothes.

However, there are disadvantages as well. Front-loading washing machines call for different kinds of detergents—ones that are low foaming—to prevent excess suds that can impede the crucial tumbling (soil-removing) action of the clothes. In addition, there is less water to rinse the detergent away. If you have purchased one of these new front-loading machines, make sure that you use a detergent specially suited for it.

needed to kill bacteria. When starting a hot-water load, make sure your water heater has had a chance to replenish its hot-water supply after being exhausted by family showers and dishwashing.

- ***Warm (40 °C):*** Use for non-colour-fast fabrics, moderately soiled loads, synthetics, wrinkle-free fabrics, knits, silks and woollens.
- ***Cold:*** Use for dark or bright colours that you know will bleed and for lightly soiled loads. Use a powdered detergent that is specially formulated for cold water, or use liquid detergent. If you live in an area where the natural temperature of the cold-water tap is especially cold, you might need to add a small amount of hot water, even to a 'cold' wash, for best results.

Save energy and peg out your washing whenever possible.

**Use the right detergent for the job.** Most wash loads will use general-purpose detergents. But, use light-duty detergents for washing lightly soiled and delicate fabrics. Liquid detergents work better in cold water and on oily stains, whereas powders are especially good for removing ground-in dirt and clay.

**Add the right amount of detergent.** Even though this sounds obvious—you just scoop up the powder (or fill the cap with liquid) and toss it in—you may need to vary the amount of detergent you use. The main cause of clothes coming out yellow, grey and dingy is not using enough detergent.

Always check your owner's manual for the recommendations about detergent usage specific to your machine. If you have a larger load, heavy soil or harder water, you will need to use more detergent.

**Soften your water.** If you have hard water, meaning there is an excess of calcium, magnesium and other minerals present in your water, you will have a laundry handicap that you'll need to counteract. These minerals react with soaps, reducing their effectiveness and forming a sticky curd that is hard to remove from fabrics. In addition, detergents that contain silicate or carbonate builders can react with the minerals to leave insoluble deposits on your clothes. If your clothes come out of the wash looking grey and dingy and feeling rough, you may have a hard-water problem. (Other symptoms of hard water are rings around your bathtub, white residue around taps and drains, and soaps and shampoos that don't seem to lather well.) Contact your water supplier or a water-treatment specialist for advice on testing your water's mineral content.

To soften hard water (often a problem for home owners who use bore water as opposed to municipal water), you can install a water-softening system to solve the problem. For a temporary solution, add a water-softening product, such as Calgon, available from supermarkets, directly to the wash or rinse cycle.

## LAUNDRY EXTRAS

**ALONG WITH DETERGENTS,** THE LIST OF LAUNDRY PRODUCTS DESIGNED FOR MORE SPECIFIC USES IS GROWING: ALL-FABRIC BLEACHES, SOFTENERS AND BOOSTERS, FOR EXAMPLE. AT LEAST ONE CENTURY-OLD PRODUCT—BLUE—IS MAKING A COMEBACK, TOO. HERE'S A LOOK AT SOME LAUNDRY EXTRAS.

**Bleaches** come in two varieties:

- Chlorine bleach (sometimes labelled as sodium hypochlorite).
- All-fabric bleach (containing sodium percarbonate, hydrogen peroxide or some other chlorine substitute).

**Chlorine bleach** is the most effective whitener and sanitiser, but we all know how strong chlorine bleach is. It can fade or alter the colour of fabrics and can weaken fibres.

As a general rule, never pour full-strength liquid chlorine bleach directly into a washing machine load. Always dilute it or dispense it through a machine's bleach dispenser, following the instructions found on the bleach container. Don't soak cottons in a bleach solution for more than 15 minutes. (If the stain remains after 15 minutes, that means it's not going to go away.) And don't use chlorine bleach on silk, wool, spandex, polyurethane foam, rubber or anything with rubber or spandex elastic in it.

**All-fabric bleaches** are not as harsh as chlorine bleaches and may be safe for colours. At the same time, they are not as powerful or fast-acting as a chlorine bleach.

**Enzyme pre-soaks** are good for loosening and removing troublesome stains, especially protein stains (milk, egg, urine and faeces), before the wash cycle. When added to the wash cycle, they act like boosters to improve the washing ability.

**Pre-wash stain removers** are often spray products containing some combination of concentrated detergents, alcohol, mineral spirits or enzymes. These products are especially good for removing oily or greasy stains from synthetic fibres.

Specialised laundry products can make your washdays a breeze.

**Blue** is an old-fashioned product that is actually used to make whites whiter. It's not a bleach (so it's environmentally friendly). In effect, blue is just that—blue dye. When white fabric is new, it contains blue colouring (invisible to the naked eye) that makes the white brighter. After repeated washings, the blue colouring is removed, leaving whites with a yellowish tint. By adding blue to your wash, you replace the microscopic blue pigment, and your whites look new again. (See 'The laundry blues' box, below, for a bit of the history of bluing.)

**Detergent boosters,** as the name suggests, help detergents do their job by increasing stain- and soil-removal action, altering the pH of water and brightening clothes.

**Water softeners and conditioners** are quick fixes if you have hard water. When added directly to the wash or rinse cycle of your machine, both of these products will soften the water, making the detergent work more effectively.

## The laundry blues

A century ago, everyone who did laundry knew about blue. It was how you got whites really white. But, thanks to the washing machine, modern detergents and bleaches, blue was nearly forgotten—until recently. Today, some environmentally conscious consumers are rediscovering the virtues of blue, which they consider an ecologically sound alternative to bleach.

Blue works very simply. Instead of removing dirt or bleaching it white, blue, known as an optical whitener, adds the slightest hint of blue to your whites, making them look brighter and whiter. Most white clothes start out with blue tints that have been added, but those tints fade after repeated washings, sometimes making whites look yellow and dingy. Blue, which is basically a fine blue iron powder in a water suspension, is a safe and easy way to add back the blues. (Nevertheless, as with other laundry products, it shouldn't be swallowed and should always be kept out of the reach of children.)

Everybody in the 1920s and '30s knew about blue and they knew how to use it. In the old days, special bluing tubs were set up beside the rinse tub. Today, you dilute a few drops of blue with water and add it either to the wash cycle or to the final rinse cycle. A lot of people think that if a little is good, a lot is better. With blue, that's just not true.

Blue is an old-fashioned bargain, too. A single bottle of the highly concentrated stuff, which costs only a few dollars, can last a year or more.

**Fabric softeners** come in liquid that you add to the final rinse cycle of your wash load or in sheets that you add to the dryer. These products make fabrics softer and fluffier, reduce static cling and wrinkling, and make ironing easier. However, if overused, fabric softeners can reduce the absorbency of towels and nappies. Dryer sheets, if overused, can leave oily looking splotches on medium-coloured items.

**Starches, fabric finishes and sizings** are used either in the final rinse or after drying. They stiffen fabrics, making them look crisp and fresh. These products tend to make ironing easier and fabric less susceptible to soil and stains.

## SPEED DRYING

**LIKE THE WASHING** MACHINE, THE AUTOMATIC DRYER HAS MADE LIFE MUCH EASIER FOR MODERN FAMILIES. DRYERS MEAN DRY CLOTHES IN WINTER, ON RAINY DAYS AND IN CROWDED CITIES, WHERE LINE SPACE IS AT A PREMIUM. DRYING YOUR CLOTHES ON A CLOTHES LINE IS CERTAINLY BETTER FOR THE ENVIRONMENT, BUT WHEN YOU DO NEED TO USE THE DRYER, THERE ARE TRICKS THAT CAN HELP YOU DRY CLOTHES WITHOUT WRINKLING OR DAMAGING THEM.

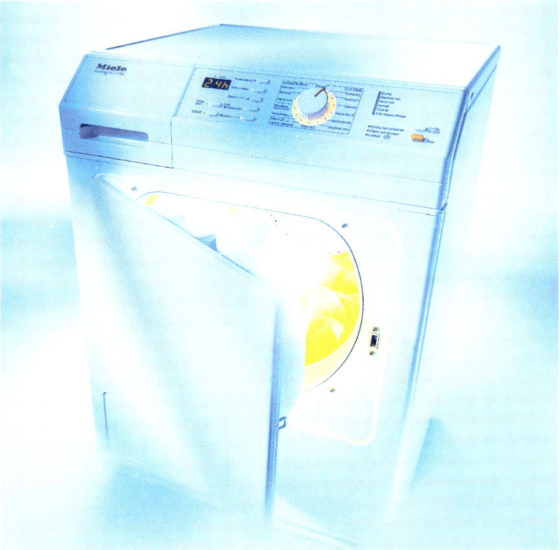

■ Always follow the fabric guidelines to get the best results from your dryer.

**Check clothes for stains before drying.** If you overlook a stain that the washing machine failed to remove, you could set it permanently by drying it. If you find a stain, treat the stain and re-wash.

**Shake damp pieces before drying.** This loosens them and helps them dry faster and more completely. Pull out anything that you want to hang on the clothes line.

**Don't overload the dryer.** A dryer needs airflow to do its work properly. Clothes that are bunched up in a dryer will take longer to dry and will wrinkle more easily.

**Don't under-load the dryer.** Believe it or not, a nearly empty dryer doesn't work as well as one that is fuller (but not too full). The tumbling effect is reduced in dryers with small loads, and that prolongs the drying period. If you must dry a small load, find a few towels that are already clean and dry and of a colour similar to the wet clothes, and throw them into the dryer to improve the process.

**Use the right setting.** Most dryers have automatic settings:
- *Regular*, for loads made up mostly of all-cotton fabrics.
- *Permanent press*, for synthetics.
- *Cool* or *Low*, for lingerie, hand washables, washable woollens, and heat-sensitive items marked 'tumble dry—*Low*'.

The permanent press cycle typically features a cool-down period after the drying is completed to reduce wrinkling.

**Avoid overdrying.** Leaving clothes in the dryer too long causes shrinkage, static build-up and wrinkling. Overdrying actually sets wrinkles, making them hard to remove.

**To reduce wrinkling,** remove items from the dryer as soon as they are dry. And don't let them lie in a heap in the basket. Hang them up or fold them as soon as possible. Remove permanent press items while they are damp and hang them on a rustproof hanger. Close buttons and press-studs, straighten creases and brush out any wrinkles.

**Clean the lint filter after each use.** This not only improves air-flow, which makes the dryer work better (and less drying time means you use less electricity), but it also reduces the chance of a dryer fire.

**Use a laundry bag for drying nylon hosiery.** It will protect those delicate items from getting ladders and holes.

**For items that call for flat drying,** such as jumpers, squeeze out excess water (but don't wring, or you may cause wrinkling). Roll the garment in a clean, dry towel to absorb water. Then shape and lay out flat on a dry towel or drying rack.

## rules of the game

DRYER ETIQUETTE

- Check that stains on garments have been removed before going into the dryer, as heat from the dryer can permanently set the stain.
- For the best drying results, don't overload or under-load the dryer.
- Sort your garments by their different fabrics and use the right fabric setting for drying these garments.
- Clean the lint filter after each use.

## PRESSING ISSUES

**THE GOAL FOR** MOST PEOPLE IS TO DO AS LITTLE IRONING AS POSSIBLE. ON THE OTHER HAND, MOST PEOPLE LIKE THE RESULTS THAT IRONING GIVES THEM—CRISP, UNWRINKLED SHIRTS AND TROUSERS WITH RESPECTABLE CREASES. HOW ELSE TO EXPLAIN THE EXPLOSION OF PERMANENT PRESS AND IRON-FREE FABRICS? SOMETIMES YOU HAVE TO IRON, HOWEVER, AND WHEN YOU DO, YOU WANT TO BE EFFECTIVE. HERE'S HOW, PLUS A TIP OR TWO FOR MAKING THE JOB EASIER.

**Wash and dry your clothes correctly.** Follow the previous advice for reducing wrinkles before your clothes get near the ironing board. Chief among that advice is not to overload your dryer and don't overdry your clothes. Sometimes all you need to do is smooth a garment with your hands and fold it or hang it and put it away. Dry things well, and you will cut your ironing time down considerably.

Special drip-dry pegs don't any leave marks on your clothes.

**Try touch-up ironing.** Instead of giving a garment the full going-over, you might just have to run your iron quickly over collars and cuffs. That may be enough to make them look more respectable.

**Read care labels.** They will tell you what the best technique is for ironing a particular garment.

**Keep your equipment handy and easy to use.** Don't pile boxes in front of your ironing board or leave the cords of your iron in a tangle. The set-up hassles will discourage you from ironing the next time. And the next time. And the next.

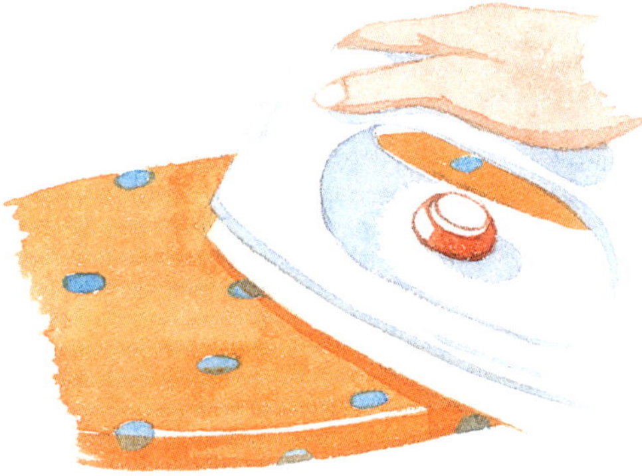

Keep your iron and board clean, and have an allotted space for them so they are always handy.

**Keep your ironing board and iron clean.** Otherwise, you might stain clothes the next time you iron them.

**Sort items by ironing temperature.** Start with fabrics that require a low ironing temperature, such as silks and synthetics, and move on to high-temperature items, such as cottons and linens.

**Iron clothes while they are still damp.** This will make the job easier, since wrinkles are not as set in the fabric. Hang your garments up immediately to help them stay fresh and pressed.

**To keep wrinkling to a bare minimum,** start ironing with small areas, such as cuffs, collars and sleeves, and then work your way to the larger areas. Iron lengthwise on the fabric, as this will help prevent the fabric from stretching.

**Never iron stains.** The heat will set the stains permanently.

## The miracle of nanotechnology

Imagine you're at a dinner party having a great time when a stray elbow bumps your glass of merlot and wine splashes into your lap onto your white dress. You don't panic. You don't cry. There's no need for soda water, no soaking and blotting and more soaking and blotting. You simply wipe the spill off your dress with a paper towel and ask for a refill. No, you're not wearing some racy new rubber suit. You're wearing stain-resistant clothing made possible through nanotechnology.

Scientists are now using nanotechnology, which is the manipulation of materials on an atomic or molecular scale, to treat certain natural and synthetic textiles so they become stain-, wrinkle- and waterproof. One way is by coating a fabric's fibres with microscopic liquid-repelling nanowhiskers (billions of atoms in structures that look like hairs or whiskers). Each whisker measures 10 nanometres long. (Nano- means 'billionth', so a nanometre equals one billionth of a metre.) To understand how small that is—a single grain of sand measures 100,000 nanometres across—makes you realise what we are dealing with here.

The application of nanotechnology to textiles works better than the older method of stain-proofing fabrics—coating them with a special layer of fabric protector such as Scotchgard. Such treatments wear off and make fabric stiff, even shiny. Fibres that have been altered molecularly don't change. Neither does the feel of the fabric. You can't even tell there's a stain-resistant treatment on it. That is, until a spill hits it. Then, because the nanowhiskers create a barrier of air around the fabric fibres, the spill simply beads up and rolls off or waits patiently to be removed.

Developed by a company called Nano-Tex, which licenses its techniques to manufacturers, nanotech-textile products are already on the market in the United States, under brand names such as Lee, Gap, Eddie Bauer and Land's End. The next breakthrough from Nano-Tex are clothes that don't absorb odours.

## KNOW YOUR FABRIC

**NOT ALL FABRICS** ARE ALIKE, AND NOT ALL FABRICS CAN BE CLEANED THE SAME WAY. ALTHOUGH YOU SHOULD ALWAYS CHECK THE CARE LABEL IN A PARTICULAR GARMENT, HERE ARE TIPS FOR CLEANING SOME OF THE MOST COMMON FABRICS.

**Acetate.** Used often in linings because it does not pill or suffer from static cling, acetate is also made into dresses, suits and sportswear. Most acetates are dry-clean only, but some are washable. For the washable variety, you typically hand wash in warm water with mild suds. (Don't soak coloured items.) Do not wring the item dry. Instead, lay it flat to dry. While it's still damp, press it inside out with a cool iron. If you are finishing the right side, use a pressing cloth. When removing stains from acetate, never use acetone or a nail-polish remover that contains acetone. The acetone will dissolve the fibres.

**Acrylic.** Known for its ability to draw moisture away from the body, acrylic is a popular material for socks, as well as other clothing items. Garments made from acrylic can be washed or dry-cleaned. Generally, you should machine wash, using a warm-water setting. Add a fabric softener during the final rinse. Acrylics are heat-sensitive, so tumble dry at a low temperature. To avoid wrinkling, remove from the dryer as soon as dry. When hand washing is required, as with delicate items, use warm water and a mild detergent. Rinse and gently squeeze out the water, smooth out the garment and dry on a rustproof hanger. Lay jumpers and knits flat to dry with a clean towel underneath. For ironing, use a moderately warm iron.

**Alpaca.** Made from the fine, soft hair of the alpaca, a cousin of the llama, alpaca is gaining in popularity as a substitute for wool. Nearly all alpaca can be dry-cleaned, and some can be gently washed. Woven items should be dry-cleaned, whereas knitted garments, such as jumpers, should be washed by hand in cool water with a mild, undyed soap or shampoo. Don't twist or wring. Lay them out flat to dry, pressing with a dry towel to remove excess water. Touch-up with a cool iron as needed.

**Cashmere.** A fine wool made from the undercoat of the cashmere goat, cashmere is as soft as it is expensive. Most cashmere can be dry-cleaned, and some can be gently washed. Most woven cashmere requires dry-cleaning to retain its shape. But knitted cashmere, such as jumpers, can—and should—be hand washed. Careful washing helps them retain their lustre and loft. Use a natural, undyed soap and cool water. Move the jumper around in the cool water for a few minutes. Rinse repeatedly—until the rinse water is clear. Lay out the jumper to dry, pressing it with a dry towel to remove excess water. If you need to touch it up with an iron, do so carefully, using a pressing cloth.

**Cotton.** By far, cotton is the most widely used fibre found in today's wardrobes. Since not even boiling hurts the fibres, cotton can be machine washed in high temperatures using any good detergent. You can use chlorine bleach safely on cotton whites (but never soak for more than 15 minutes, since the bleach will break down the fibres) and all-fabric bleach on dyed cottons. Cotton is an absorbent fibre and requires lots of drying time. Because it wrinkles easily, it often requires pressing. Use a hot steam iron.

**Linen.** Linen is made from flax, one of the oldest textile fibres. (It dates back to at least 5000 BC!) Today, you can wash some varieties of linen, but others should be dry-cleaned. Sometimes it's up to you. Linen has a natural pectin that keeps it stiff and crisp. Washing removes the pectin, making it softer. If you prefer crisp linen, then have your linen dry-cleaned. Otherwise, machine wash it in warm water and tumble dry. It tends to wrinkle and often requires pressing. Use a steam iron on medium or high heat.

**Nylon.** The second-most common synthetic after polyester, and the strongest fibre available, nylon is relatively easy to care for. It can be machine washed in warm water. To reduce static cling, add a dryer sheet to the dryer and remove clothes from the dryer as soon as they have finished drying. If you need to iron nylon, use a warm iron.

**Polyester.** Strong, durable, shrink- and wrinkle-resistant, polyester is a miracle fibre, the most common of the synthetic fibres. It does tend to take on oily stains easily, however. In general, polyester is easy to clean, which helps account for its popularity. Most polyester items can be washed or dry-cleaned. Wash in warm water and tumble dry at a low temperature setting. To prevent pilling and snagging, turn knits inside out. To reduce static cling, use a dryer sheet (see below) and remove garments as soon as they have dried. When ironing, use a moderately warm iron.

EXPERT ADVICE

WHAT IS IT?

These days, all clothing is required to carry a composition and care label—so you know exactly how you should care for it. But this hasn't always been the case, and you may have no idea of how to clean older, or antique, garments. If in doubt, seek expert advice, especially from a reputable drycleaner, before you simply hurl it into the washing machine and do irreparable damage.

Throw in a dryer sheet with your wet polyesters to reduce static cling.

**Ramie.** A vegetable fibre similar to flax, ramie comes from the stem of a shrub that originated in Asia. The fibres are strong (but they have low twisting and bending strength), do not shrink and have a lustrous appearance. Much like linen, ramie can be machine washed in warm water and tumble dried or dry-cleaned. It tends to wrinkle and often requires pressing. Use a steam iron on medium or high heat.

**Rayon.** Developed in 1910, rayon was the first synthetic fibre. Originally, most rayon was dry-clean only, but there are now washable rayons on the market. Check the care label for any rayon garment you're unsure of. Dry-clean-only rayon that gets wet (even in the rain) can bleed dyes, shrink and grow stiff. Washable rayon is typically hand wash only. (Since it loses up to 50 per cent of its strength when wet, rayon can be destroyed easily by the agitating action of most washing machines.) Wash in lukewarm or cool suds, squeezing the suds through the fabric and rinse. Never wring or twist rayon. Shake out or smooth the garment and hang it on a rustproof hanger to dry. Lay jumpers flat to dry. While the garment is still damp, iron inside out on low heat. For finishing on the right side, use a pressing cloth.

**Silk.** Made from protein fibre produced by the silkworm (the finest silk fibre is produced by worms that eat mulberry leaves), this ancient material connotes fabulous wealth and exotic locales. It is expensive and must be treated accordingly. Most silk is dry-clean only, since laundry detergents can harm silk. If the care label says that hand washing is OK, use a mild soap and lukewarm water. Never use bleach with silk. When ironing, iron inside out on low heat.

## Drying a woollen jumper

1 Trace your wool jumper's shape before washing (see below).

2 To remove excess water roll the jumper in a towel (see below right) and then pull back into shape to dry.

**Spandex.** Developed in the late 1950s, spandex is lightweight, durable and known for being flexible. That's why it turns up in swimming costumes, pantihose and tights. (Lycra is simply a brand name for spandex.) You can machine or hand wash spandex. Don't use chlorine bleach, however. Either let it drip-dry or put it in a dryer on a low setting. When ironing spandex, use a low temperature setting and iron in swift strokes, never letting the iron linger in one spot.

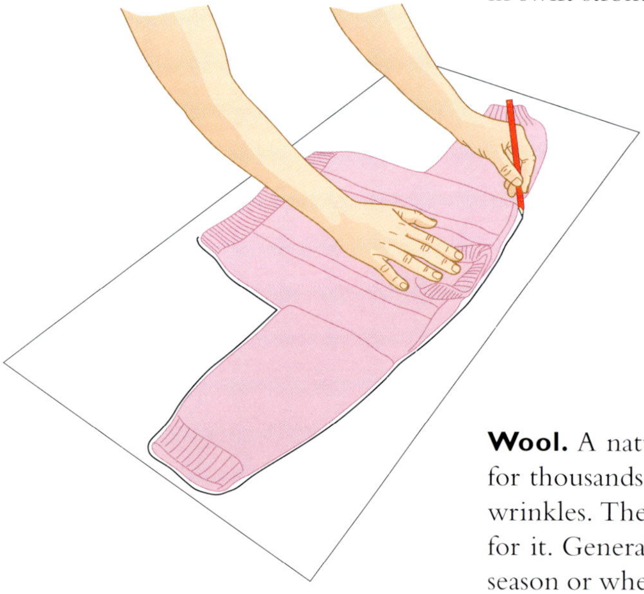

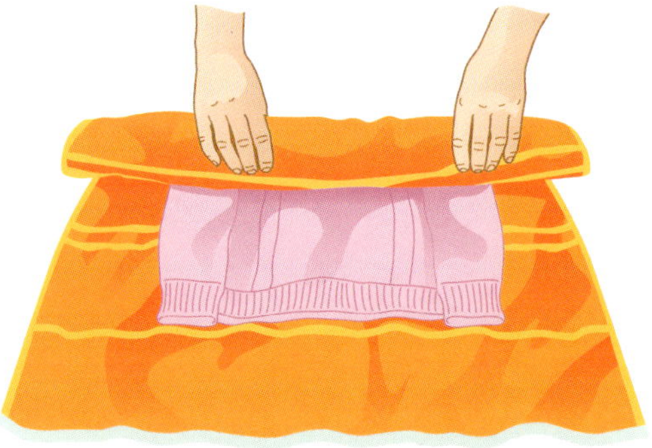

**Wool.** A natural fibre that comes from sheep, wool has been around for thousands of years. It is known for its warmth and ability to shed wrinkles. There are many types of wool and different ways to care for it. Generally speaking, you should dry-clean wool at least once a season or when needed. You can also hand wash wool. Since wool loses its shape when wet, when washing a wool jumper, first lay the jumper out on a piece of clean paper and trace the shape (see 1, above left). You'll use this for laying the jumper out while drying. Use warm water and a mild detergent that contains no bleach. Don't soak. Rinse well. To dry, roll the jumper in a clean towel and squeeze out excess water (see 2, above). Put a piece of plastic over the pattern you made, to prevent dyes from the paper from bleeding onto the jumper. Pat the jumper out to fit the shape. Smooth out wrinkles. If the item needs pressing, use light steam and a press cloth.

## Label tips

Nowadays, all clothing sold in Australia and New Zealand must carry a composition and care label that follows the International Textile Care Labelling code. They might scratch your neck occasionally, but these labels give instructions for the best way to care for a garment, including how to properly clean, dry and iron, and what techniques and products you should avoid. However, the symbols used to denote the various cleaning processes can be baffling to people not in the fashion industry. Here's a handy explanation of them.

## Washing

### Machine wash

- normal
- permanent press/wrinkle resistant
- gentle/delicate
- hand wash

**Warning signs**

- do not wash
- do not wring

### Water temperature

- ••• hot (50 °C to 95 °C)
- •• warm (30 °C to 45 °C)
- • cold/cool (0 °C to 25 °C)

### Bleach

- any bleach (when needed)
- only non-chlorine bleach (when needed)

**Warning sign**

- do not bleach

## Dry-cleaning

### Dry-clean: normal cycle

- dry-clean
- Ⓐ any solvent
- Ⓟ any solvent except trichloroethylene
- Ⓕ petroleum solvent only

### Professionally dry-clean

- reduce moisture
- short cycle
- no steam finishing
- low heat

**Warning sign**

- do not dry-clean

## Drying

### Tumble dry

- dry
- normal
- permanent press/wrinkle resistant
- gentle/delicate

### Heat setting

- high
- medium
- low
- ● no heat/air

### Special instructions

- line dry/hang to dry
- drip-dry
- dry flat
- dry in the shade

**Warning signs**

- do not tumble dry
- do not dry (*used with do not wash*)

## Ironing

### Iron: dry or steam

- iron
- high
- medium
- low

**Warning signs**

- do not iron
- no steam

# PROBLEMS AND SOLUTIONS

**SOMETIMES CLOTHES JUST** DON'T TURN OUT RIGHT. HERE ARE SOME COMMON PROBLEMS AND THE MOST LIKELY SOLUTIONS TO THESE PROBLEMS.

**Your clothes come out grey or yellow.** You may need to increase the amount of detergent in the next load, use a detergent booster or increase the temperature of the wash water. However, the grey could be from dye that has bled from darks to lights, suggesting you need to sort better. Try blue added to the wash load—it sometimes corrects greying in white fabrics.

**You notice detergent residue on clothes.** Your powdered detergent isn't dissolving properly. Make sure the loads aren't too full. Use liquid detergent with cold-water cycles. Try letting the washing machine fill with water, adding the detergent and then adding the clothes. If the problem is caused by hard water, you may need to add a water-softening product in the next load. To remove hard-water residue from clothes, soak them in a solution of 1 cup of white vinegar per 4 litres of warm water. Rinse and re-wash.

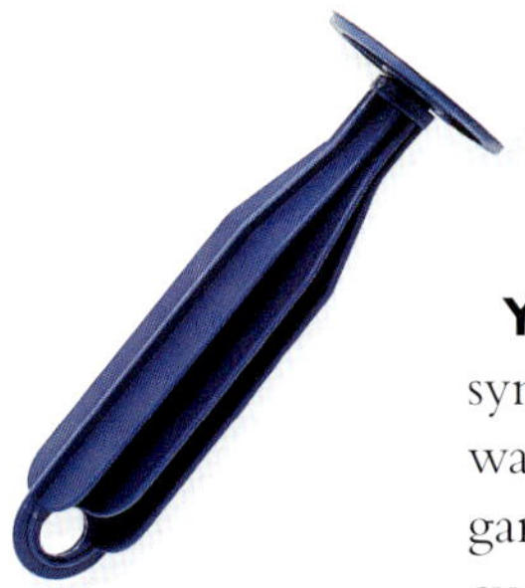

Use a lint roller to remove lint that builds up on garments in the washer and dryer.

**If there's a lot of lint on your clothes,** you probably need to sort better. Separate the lint producers, such as fleecy tracksuits, chenille items, new towels and flannel pyjamas, from lint attractors, such as corduroys, synthetic blends and dark fabric. To remove the lint, use a lint roller (see left) or pat with the sticky side of masking or packing tape. Check to make sure pockets are empty of tissues and other paper before you wash. Make sure the washer and dryer lint filters are clean.

**You have a problem with pilling.** This is most common among synthetic fabrics. Try turning synthetic clothing inside out before washing. (Pilling is caused by abrasion of fibres, and by turning a garment inside out it cuts down on abrasion during the wash and dry cycles.) You can also wash your synthetics all together in a gentler, shorter cycle. Using a liquid detergent will help. To remove pills, snip them off with a battery-powered pill remover (available from sewing shops and discount retailers), or pull the fabric tight over a curved surface and carefully shave the pills off with a safety razor.

Simple solutions

### That shrinking feeling

The unthinkable has happened and you have shrunk your favourite wool jumper. While you can't always reverse the process, it's worth trying this remedy before you throw the jumper away. In a bucket, make up a lukewarm solution of Fullers Earth (from hardware shops) with water, following the packet instructions. Soak the jumper for 30 minutes, roll in a towel to remove excess water, then lay the jumper flat on another towel and keep gently stretching it to shape as it dries. Epsom salts (100 g in a bucket of lukewarm water) can also be used to relax wool fibres in the same way.

# The ZAP cleaning system

ZAP! your weekly house cleaning is done, top to bottom. Professional housekeepers say you need two things to do a speedy but thorough job of cleaning your home: focus and organisation.

**FOCUS** For the 3 hours or even more that you're going to spend cleaning your home from top to bottom, don't be distracted. Don't dawdle over the magazines that you should be throwing out into the recycling bin. And don't watch TV when you should be dusting the windowsills in the living room.

A clean and tidy house is like a breath of fresh air. Enjoy the benefits of being focused and organised in your cleaning.

**ORGANISATION** In other words, you need a plan for cleaning your house—to establish a pattern, to lock into a rhythm. That's when you reach your maximum efficiency.

To achieve this, we do have a system for you—the Zoned Attack Plan (ZAP). It's called this, because it reflects the system of concentrating your cleaning on one portion of your home at a time. It is the ultimate time-saving strategy for weekly house cleaning.

A place for everything and everything in its place; to achieve this, invest in some storage boxes.

## DON'T WASTE A MOMENT

**BEFORE WE GET** TO THE SPECIFICS OF HOW TO ZAP YOUR HOME, WE NEED TO ESTABLISH SOME TIME-SAVING GROUND RULES.

**Clean from left to right and top to bottom** in each room. A systematic, clockwise approach to a room eliminates a lot of retracing of steps. And a top to bottom system lets gravity work for you and avoids duplication of effort. You don't want the dust from your window ledges falling on a freshly polished table, for example.

**Keep cleaning supplies together and close at hand** to make every movement count. Interrupting the bathroom cleaning to track down window cleaner slows your momentum.

**Deal with the clutter in your home separately.** De-cluttering can be very time consuming, and if you combine it with cleaning, you'll be seriously slowed down. This approach assumes you'll lay down the law with other family members: no clothes strewn about the bedroom, for example; no dishes left in the sink; and no newspapers covering the family room floor.

**Move furniture towards the centre** of the room when it's time to dust. This way, the dust from the architraves, sills and such will settle to the floor, where it's easy to vacuum up. Once the perimeter of the room is vacuumed, you can push furniture back into place and vacuum the rest of the room.

**Set a deadline** for completing your cleaning. Knowing up front how much time you'll spend cleaning can make the list of chores less daunting, and also keep you on the move.

### Maid to order

We all need a break from house cleaning once in a while. When you're ready for some professional help, either for yourself or as a gift to a loved one, following these guidelines will ensure a trouble-free experience:

- Decide whether you want to hire a cleaning service or a single cleaner. Cleaning services typically dispatch teams of two to four, who complete the work more quickly. Solo cleaners will often take on tasks that the cleaning services avoid, such as washing laundry, doing the dishes and picking up clutter.
- Ask for references from current and former clients. Call those people and find out what they liked and disliked about the service provided.
- Ask the company whether they conduct background checks on their employees and what type of insurance they carry to cover damage or theft.
- Before you hire anyone, decide what they'll clean, how long they'll be in your home and whether they'll bring their own cleaning tools or use yours. (They typically clean when you're not around, so you won't be there to supervise.)
- If there are items you don't want cleaning people to touch, such as the frame of an original oil painting or a family heirloom, discuss those issues in advance.

Discuss the price up-front—is it a set fee or an hourly rate, and if it's the latter, how long will it take? Can you pay extra for additional chores, such as window cleaning? Expect to pay more for the first visit, because the cleaning required usually makes up for months or years of house cleaning neglect and the cleaners will need to spend significantly more time than they will on subsequent visits.

**Learn to multi-task.** If you absolutely must answer the telephone while you're cleaning, at least use this chat time to do some low-concentration tasks, such as cleaning windows, polishing a table or loading the dishwasher. Get a cordless phone and a headset (important for your neck) and work while you talk.

**Don't turn on the TV.** You'll end up getting distracted and waste time. Instead, entertain yourself with up-beat music to keep energised and to get the cleaning done more quickly. This will also have the added bonus of making cleaning seem less of a chore.

A sock on one hand makes dusting easy while lifting objects with your other hand.

**Use both hands** while cleaning. Dust or wipe furniture surfaces with one hand while lifting objects with the other. Scrub benchtops with a cloth in each hand. Squirt spray cleaner with one hand and wipe the surface with the other.

**Pull an old, clean cotton sock over your dusting hand** and lift objects with the other hand as you clean (see left). If you have arthritis or problems with your hand dexterity, it's helpful to wear a rubber glove on the hand you use for lifting objects to increase your grip.

## Cleaning schedules

Ideally you should polish your silver each and every week. But, we know that's not really achievable in the real world, so here's how often you should perform cleaning tasks that are not part of the weekly ZAP routine.

**Every day**

- Put things away when you finish using them.
- Wash dishes, wipe kitchen benchtops, clean-up stove spills and empty rubbish as needed.
- Squeegee showers after use to prevent mineral deposits, soap scum and mildew.
- Wipe sinks.
- Make beds and straighten rooms.

**Twice a week**

- Dust-mop hardwood floors to prevent scratching from dirt.
- Put away clutter.
- Vacuum if you live in a dusty region or have children and pets that track in lots of dirt. Otherwise, weekly vacuuming should suffice.

**Once a month**

- Wipe or vacuum skirting boards and blinds.
- Sweep the garage (and remove cobwebs), veranda and paths.
- Vacuum upholstered furniture with the brush attachment.
- Clean ceiling fixtures in one room per month (rotate).
- Wash throw rugs.
- Dust ceiling fans.

**Every three months**

- Polish wood furniture.
- Remove cobwebs from ceiling corners, stairwells and such.
- Change or clean airconditioner filters (less frequently in low-use seasons).
- Clean the oven (monthly if grunge builds up quickly).

**Every six months**

- Wash windows inside and out. Do this quarterly for windows near work spaces (the kitchen sink or a desk, for example).
- De-clutter storage areas in the attic and garage.
- Vacuum, flip and rotate mattresses.
- Polish silver.
- Air out pillows.

**Once a year**

- Move heavy furniture to clean behind and underneath.
- Vacuum rug pads and the backs of large rugs.
- Clean curtains and carpets.
- Turn large rugs 180 degrees to even out wear.
- Wash walls.
- Clean chandeliers.

Simple solutions

## Size versus numbers

If you have a big family and a small house, you'll be cleaning more often, as key items will get a lot more use. Conversely, if you live alone in a big house, you can clean less often. It all comes down to how often any particular feature of the house gets used. This rundown will help you figure it all out:

- **Bathroom basins:** scrub after 30 uses.
- **Doormats:** clean after 25–30 foot wipes in damp climates. In drier climates, shake out the mat after every 50–60 uses.
- **Kitchen sinks:** wipe daily.
- **Showers:** squeegee after each use; clean after 14 showers.
- **Stoves:** wipe off after every use; clean under stove elements after 20 uses.
- **Toilets:** clean after every 100 flushes.
- **Towels and face cloths:** wash after four uses.

**Spray a lint-free towel with window cleaner** and keep it handy for cupboards or tables with glass inlays.

**Collect pet hair from chairs and sofas** using rubber gloves and a circular motion—assuming you have pets that shed. Throw the rolled-up hair on the floor and vacuum it up later when you do the floor.

**Place any items from another level in a plastic bin near the stairs** and take them with you the next time you have to make a trip to that level. If you live in a multi-storey house, you'll save yourself time and energy in frequent trips if you do this whenever you spot something that is on the wrong level.

**Invest in a 7.5-metre extension cord for your vacuum.** This will save time as you won't have to plug it in again in every room.

**If it's truly not dirty, don't clean it.** There's no point in wasting time on a guest room or living room that's rarely used. Give it a light dusting and forget it.

# ASSEMBLE YOUR EQUIPMENT

**AN EFFECTIVE CLEANING** SYSTEM STARTS WITH GOOD TOOLS AND PRODUCTS. STOCK A PLASTIC OR RUBBER CLEANING CADDY WITH DIVIDERS WITH EVERYTHING YOU'LL NEED AS YOU MAKE YOUR ROUNDS. (ALTERNATIVES ARE A LARGE PLASTIC BUCKET, A SMALL TROLLEY OR AN APRON WITH LARGE POCKETS.) ARRANGE ITEMS IN THE CADDY SO THAT IT'S WELL BALANCED.

**Fill your caddy** with these:

- A glass cleaner.
- A general-purpose cleaner, such as Spray n' Wipe or Citro-Clean Multi-Purpose Cleaner (a concentrated orange-oil-based cleaner).
- A heavy-duty degreasing cleaner (Handy Andy, for example).
- A powdered scouring cleanser (such as Ajax).
- Wood polish.

**You'll also need a few extra tools.** Some of these items may not be mentioned in the weekly ZAP routine described next, but you will need them for some cleaning jobs you'll be doing:

- A lamb's wool duster.
- A nylon scrub pad.
- A stiff-bristled toothbrush for scrubbing around taps.
- A 4-centimetre, soft-bristled paintbrush for dusting lampshades and removing cobwebs.
- A toilet brush.
- Rubber gloves.
- Clean cotton rags.
- A large rubbish bag.
- A plastic squeegee for bathrooms.

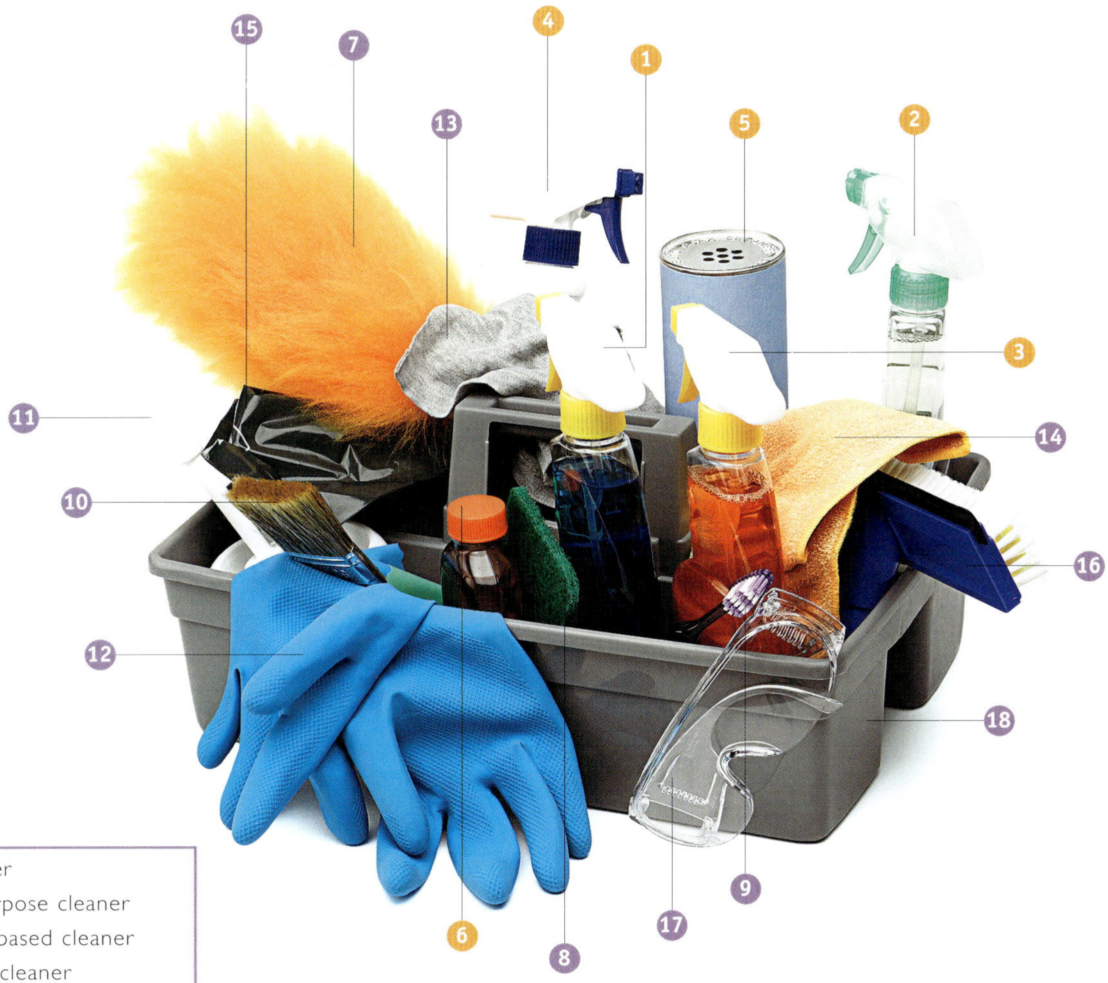


| | |
|---|---|
| 1 | glass cleaner |
| 2 | general-purpose cleaner |
| 3 | orange oil-based cleaner |
| 4 | degreasing cleaner |
| 5 | powdered scouring cleanser |
| 6 | wood polish |
| 7 | lamb's wool duster |
| 8 | nylon scrub pad |
| 9 | stiff-bristled toothbrush |
| 10 | 4-cm, soft-bristled paintbrush |
| 11 | toilet brush |
| 12 | rubber gloves |
| 13 | clean cotton rags |
| 14 | microfibre cloth |
| 15 | large rubbish bag |
| 16 | plastic squeegee |
| 17 | safety glasses |
| 18 | cleaning caddy |

- Safety glasses to protect your eyes from splattering cleaner or airborne dirt.
- A plastic bin for collecting items that belong on other levels or in other parts of the house.

**Check your tools** regularly to make sure they are up to the task. The tops of cleaners that don't squirt properly are frustrating. A crumbling sponge mop or worn-out broom causes you extra work. A vacuum cleaner with a broken guard will damage skirting boards and furniture.

**For a multi-level house,** keep a completely stocked cleaning caddy on each floor. Also keep basic tools, such as a dustpan, broom and mop, on every level. This will save you a lot of running up and down stairs to get the tools that you need and, truth be known, it will keep you from putting off certain cleaning tasks until another day.

## DIVIDE AND CONQUER

**DON'T KNOW WHERE** TO START? NO JOB SEEMS QUITE SO DAUNTING IF YOU BREAK IT DOWN INTO MANAGEABLE PARTS. THIS IS THE BASIS OF THE ZAP SYSTEM.

**ZAP is a systematic cleaning plan** for getting your home spotless, top to bottom, every week. It divides your home into four zones. Using easy-to-follow steps, you completely clean each zone before moving on to the next. ZAP is designed to eliminate duplication of effort, counterproductive moves like wiping dust onto a floor that you just vacuumed and provides extra trips for around the house. Your home is divided into the following four zones:

| | |
|---|---|
| ZONE ONE | bedrooms, bathrooms and hallways |
| ZONE TWO | kitchen, informal dining and family room |
| ZONE THREE | formal living room and formal dining room |
| ZONE FOUR | laundry and other miscellaneous spaces |

A lot of people have no idea how to clean. A step-by-step process will help those people realise what to do. The ZAP system doesn't leave any doubt in your mind. It's how the professionals work. Now you've got the whole process laid out for you here.

## ZONE ONE

## BEDROOMS, BATHROOMS AND HALLWAYS

**You're psyched up, fully equipped** and armed with the best speed-cleaning techniques. Now put it into action with the ultimate step-by-step plan for weekly house cleaning. We'll start where you will make the biggest impact, the high-traffic Zone 1 areas—bedrooms, bathrooms and hallways. This plan assumes you have a two-storey house. If you don't, you can adapt the plan to fit your home.

- Go into each bedroom, strip the sheets off the beds and throw them into the hallway. Go into each bathroom and throw the towels, hand towels, face cloths and bath mats into the hallway, too. Gather all of these washable items in a laundry basket and dump them in the laundry. Start a wash load with the bath mats and a couple of towels.
- Get the cleaning caddy you keep on the first floor. Go into the upstairs bathroom and start spreading around the cleaning chemicals. Spray toilet cleaner (stored under the basin) inside the toilet bowl. Spray all-purpose cleaner on the toilet rim, toilet seat, vanity top and basin. Sprinkle your bath cleaner in the bath.
- Empty the wastebasket into your plastic bag.
- Now use a little elbow grease. Spray a clean rag with

Vacuum after dusting each room to maximise dust pick-up.

window cleaner and clean the mirror. Scrub the inside of your toilet bowl with the toilet brush and wipe down the vanity, basin, toilet exterior and toilet rim. Scrub the bath with a nylon scrubber sponge. Rinse the bath. Spray all-purpose cleaner on the shower walls and wipe them down. (Note that this prevents mixing two cleaners in the bath—something you want to avoid.)

- Mop the floor, backing out of the room.
- Go into one of the upstairs bedrooms and empty the wastebasket into your plastic bag.
- Move any light furniture or other obstructions towards the centre of the room, away from the walls.
- Dust the entire room, starting at the door and moving from left to right (clockwise). Using your lamb's wool duster, take one wall at a time, working from top to bottom, including pelmets, window frames, curtains and furniture.
- Now vacuum around the entire perimeter of the bedroom—made easier with the furniture in the centre of the room. Return the furniture to its original position. Starting at the far corner of the room, vacuum the rest of the room, backing out the door.
- Go into the other upstairs bedrooms and repeat steps 6 through to 9.
- Give the upstairs hallway a quick dusting, moving left to right, top to bottom, one wall at a time.
- Put away the upstairs cleaning caddy. Vacuum the upstairs hallway, backing towards the stairs. Take the rubbish bag with you and back down the stairs, vacuuming the stairs as you go.
- For the ground-floor bathroom, repeat steps 2 through to 5 (except use your ground-floor cleaning caddy).
- For ground-floor bedrooms, repeat steps 6 through to 9.
- Dust and vacuum the downstairs hallway.
- Now it is time to concentrate on the laundry. Go to the laundry and unload the washing machine. Hang out the washing, or put everything but your rubber-backed bath mats into the dryer. Load the washing machine with dirty sheets and towels. Hang the rubber-backed mats on a clothes line or a clothes rack to drip-dry.

## ZONE TWO

## KITCHEN, INFORMAL DINING AND FAMILY ROOM

**Now you already have some of the biggest cleaning jobs behind you.** Next we tackle three other high-traffic spots: your kitchen, your informal dining area and the family room.

- Get your ground-floor cleaning caddy. Go into the kitchen and pull out a microwave-safe bowl. Pour in 2 cups of water, put the bowl of water in the microwave and cook on *High* for 3–5 minutes.
- While the microwave is running, go around the kitchen and dust all the surfaces, left to right, top to bottom. Then spray an all-purpose

cleaner on the stovetop (but make sure it's cool first), the oven door, the fridge and the benchtops.

- Take a clean cloth and move from left to right around the kitchen, wiping down the benches and appliances. While you're at the stove, wipe any food spills from the burner grates (gas stove) or coils (electric). Move any benchtop appliances and wipe under them as you go. When you get to the microwave, make sure the water has cooled for at least a minute. Dump the water out and wipe down the steamed interior of the microwave.

- Pick one section of cabinets to clean each time you clean the kitchen. Spray that section with all-purpose spray, then wipe.
- Throw out any old food in the fridge and pick one shelf or drawer to clean. Spray it with glass cleaner (for light cleaning) or get a disinfectant cleaner from under the kitchen sink (for heavier cleaning or disinfecting).
- Sprinkle the sink with scouring powder and scrub it with a nylon pad. Then rinse the cleaner off.
- Mop the floor.
- Go to your informal dining area. (If you have an eat-in kitchen, take care of the table and chairs in step 3.) Dust your way around the room, left to right, top to bottom. Dust the light fitting. Pull the chairs away from the table. Wipe up any spills or crumbs from the table and chairs. Mop or vacuum under the table and move the chairs back. Clean the rest of the floor.
- Go to your family room. Move any light furniture into the centre of the room. Move around the room dusting—from left to right, top to bottom, one section of wall at a time. Dust the pelmets, window frames, curtains, furniture and electronic devices.
- Now vacuum the perimeter of the family room. Return the furniture to its original position. Vacuum the rest of the room.
- Go to the laundry. Take the towels, face cloths and bath mats out of the dryer and put them on a bench. (You don't need to worry about folding.) Take the sheets and towels out of the washing machine and hang them out or put them in the dryer. Load any remaining sheets and towels into the washing machine.

## ZONE THREE

## FORMAL LIVING AND DINING ROOMS

**Take a deep breath,** you're almost done—and by using the ZAP system, you've left the easiest for last!

- Go into your formal living room. Move any light furniture (lamps, coffee tables and such) into the centre of the room.
- You know the drill by now. Dust the room, moving from left to right, one wall at a time. Dust from top to bottom, including pelmets, window frames, curtains and furniture.

- Vacuum the perimeter of the living room. Return the furniture to its original position.
- Lift the seat cushions out of the sofa and easy chairs, roll-up any rugs on the floor, and then vacuum underneath with the brush attachment. Vacuum the centre of the floor.
- Go to the dining room and repeat steps 1 through to 3.
- Dust the dining room table and the chairs around the table.
- Pull the chairs away from the table and vacuum under the table. Return the chairs to their original positions and then carry on vacuuming the rest of the room.

## ZONE FOUR

## LAUNDRY AND MISCELLANEOUS SPACES

**Time to polish off the last couple of rooms** of the house and then wrap up the loose ends.

- Go to the laundry, remove the sheets and towels from the dryer, and add them to the unfolded pile on the bench. Hang out the last of the laundry, or put it in the dryer.
- Empty the laundry's wastebasket into your plastic bag.
- Since this is not a high-traffic area, a quick dusting will do the trick. Move around the room left to right, top to bottom, dusting the shelves, appliance tops and sink. Wipe up any detergent spills on the appliances with a damp rag.
- Mop the floor.
- Continue the pattern of dusting and then vacuuming or mopping in the other miscellaneous spaces of your home—hallway, sunroom, enclosed porch, utility room, office.
- Put your vacuum cleaner and cleaning caddy away.
- Take your plastic bag full of rubbish out to the rubbish bin.
- While you're outside, take your doormats out onto the lawn and shake them out.
- Take your dirty cleaning cloths to the laundry and toss them in the washing machine.
- Once all of the sheets, towels and such are dry, spread out one of the sheets from an upstairs bedroom and put all of the other laundry on top of it, along with the rubber-backed mats that were drip-drying. Pull the corners of the sheet together to make a sack. Haul it all to the ground-floor bedrooms and put the sheets back on the beds. (This is why you didn't bother folding.) Return the towels, face cloths bath mat and rubber-backed mat to their places in the ground-floor bathroom. Then carry the remaining laundry upstairs and repeat. If, on the other hand, you prefer to rotate your sheets and towels, you will need to do a bit of folding. Don't leave it—do it now and put it away in sets for next time.

A regular light mop prevents serious dirt build-up and tougher cleaning jobs.

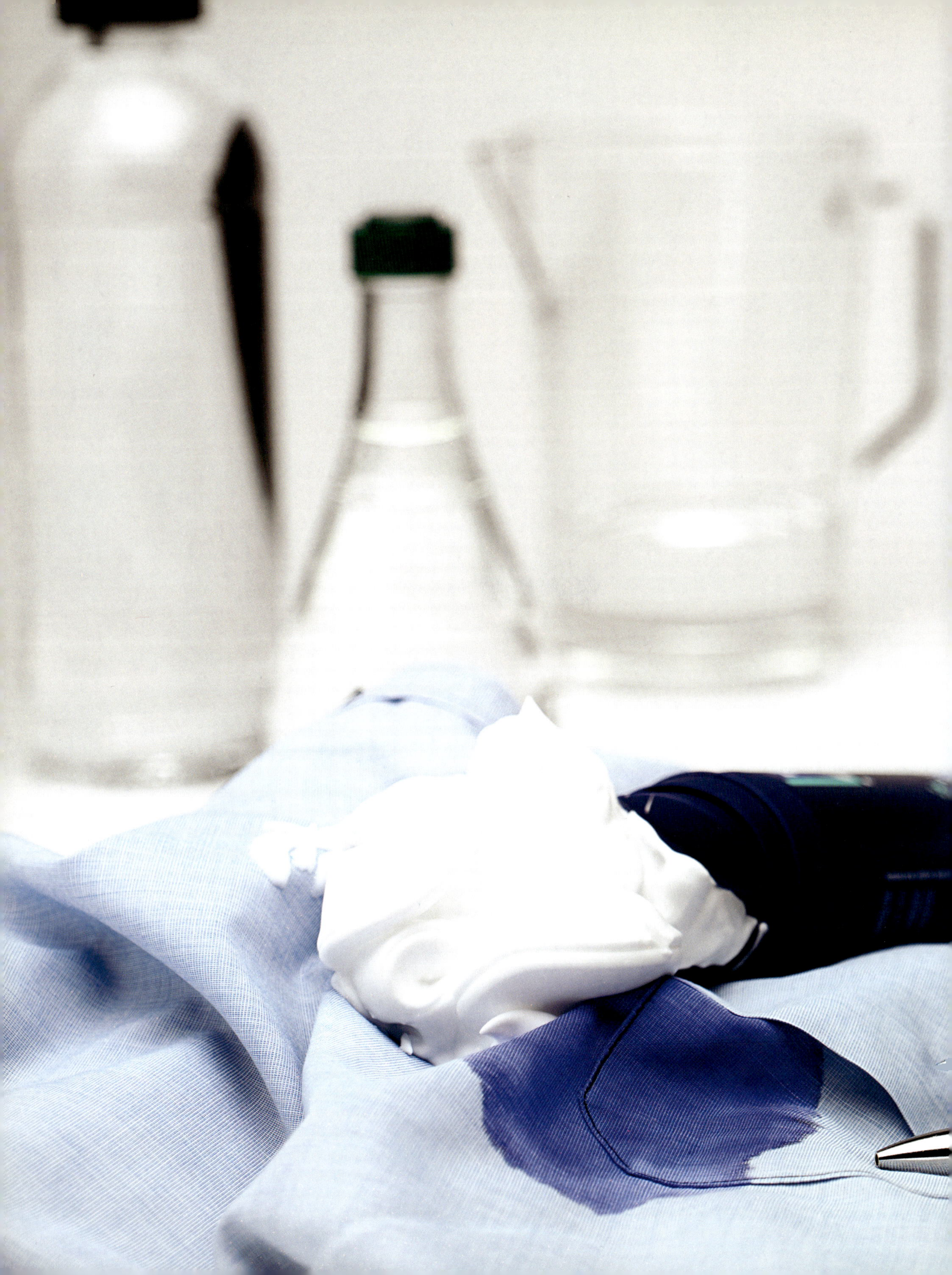

# 2

# a-z of everyday cleaning

# AIR

**WE USE AIR** EVERY MINUTE OF EVERY DAY—AND IT'S FREE. THE PROBLEM IS, HEAT AND AIRCONDITIONING DON'T COME FREE, SO WE SPEND MUCH OF THE YEAR WITH OUR HOMES HERMETICALLY SEALED TO SAVE MONEY. BUT TRAPPED IN THERE WITH US ARE DUST MITES, AIRBORNE CHEMICALS, COOKING FUMES AND, WITH SOME OF US, CIGARETTE SMOKE, CARBON MONOXIDE FROM FIREPLACES AND WOOD STOVES, PET ALLERGENS (HAIR AND SALIVA), AND OTHER POLLUTANTS AND IRRITANTS.

## For super sneeze control

For more serious allergen control, consider buying an air filter unit—especially if allergens are a medical problem and less expensive approaches haven't helped to solve the problem. There are several technologies to choose from, but for general removal of particles from the air, you'll probably have the most success with a HEPA filter (that's high efficiency particulate air filter, for you trivia buffs).

Most HEPA filters are small units, much like a dehumidifier, that sit in your room and trap microscopic particles by drawing air through fine disposable filters and returning the air to the room. The filters are so efficient that they're often used in hospitals and industrial 'clean rooms'. You can also get a HEPA filter for a central heating and cooling system, but that kind is very expensive.

**Some simple air-cleaning solutions cost nothing.**

- Good ventilation will do more than anything else to freshen the air in your home. When you get up in the morning, open a window in each room of the house for at least 5 minutes no matter what the temperature is outside.
- Smooth surfaces—tile or hardwood floors, for instance—will help to keep the air cleaner, too, because allergens love to collect in upholstery, curtains and carpets.
- Using bicarbonate of soda or vinegar to absorb odours may help to reduce unpleasant smells, but neither substance does much to clean the air. The same is true of aerosol spray air fresheners, which pump more chemicals into your environment.

**Clean filters and vents regularly.** Forced-air heating and cooling systems are major contributors to indoor air pollution. They blow air all around your house through a system of ducts, spreading dust, mites and mould. Change the air filter that stands between the motor unit and your home's ductwork at least a couple of times a year, and more often if the manufacturer recommends it. Also consider getting small vent filters that fit over the vents in each room. Avoid sleeping directly in the path of the vents, otherwise those blown particles will end up settling in your lungs rather than on your dresser, which could lead to health problems. If dust has built up inside the ducts, contact a professional duct-cleaning service to vacuum them out.

**Control the humidity in your home.** Heating systems can create extremely dry air, which can be corrected with a humidifier or by placing bowls of water near the heat source. Ideal humidity for your home is about 40 to 50 per cent. Let the air get much damper than that and you encourage mould growth. However, if you use a humidifier, remember to clean it frequently to prevent mould from growing in it. You might think house plants would do great things for your home's air, since they gobble up carbon dioxide and expel oxygen, but you might be better off flexing your green thumb outdoors—those moist pots of soil are also fantastic breeding grounds for mould.

**To control allergens in the air around you,** you'll have to go to the source of the problem. Try these solutions for common problems:

- To control pet allergens and mites, wash your pets frequently—every two weeks if someone in your home has allergies.
- To keep smoke to a minimum, limit the number of open fires you have in the fireplace and if you or another member of your household smoke cigarettes, go outside to do it.

See also:
• AIRCONDITIONERS
• FILTERS • FIREPLACES
• HUMIDIFIERS

• To keep dust mites under wraps, put a plastic mattress cover over that mattress where you spend a third of your life, and put a mattress pad over the plastic. (Otherwise, the plastic will collect your perspiration.) You can also buy special anti-mite mattress covers that are soft and microporous—more comfortable than plastic.

## AIRCONDITIONERS

**BEING COOL WILL** COST LESS IF YOU CLEAN YOUR AIRCONDITIONER PROPERLY. WHETHER YOU HAVE DUCTED AIRCONDITIONING (EVAPORATIVE OR REFRIGERATED), A SPLIT SYSTEM OR WINDOW UNITS, DIRT AND DEBRIS CAN RESTRICT AIRFLOW THROUGH THE FILTER AND AROUND THE COOLING ELEMENTS, FORCING THE UNIT TO WORK HARDER AND USE MORE ELECTRICITY THAN NECESSARY TO DO ITS JOB.

**Cleaning an airconditioner's filter** is the most important thing you can do to keep it functioning well. The air filter, which snatches dust and other gunk from the air that's being distributed around your house, is located behind the front grille in the indoor unit of your split system, or behind the ceiling grille of a ducted system. Every two weeks, open the front grille of the split system and pull the filter out for cleaning (see below left). Clean the filter with a vacuum cleaner or warm soapy water. Dry it upright in the shade, letting it dry thoroughly before sliding it back into place.

**To clean the filters of a ducted system,** use a screwdriver to remove the ceiling grille plates, remove the filter and wash as for a split system filter. The ducting of an evaporatively cooled central airconditioning system should be professionally cleaned every 18–24 months, as the humidity created by evaporative systems can encourage the growth of mildew.

**Some systems have optional plasma and deodorising filters.** After removing the air filter, remove the plasma filter and soak it in a solution of water and a pH-neutral detergent, such as Softly, for about 30 minutes. Allow it to dry completely, in the shade. It should be perfectly dry before re-installing.

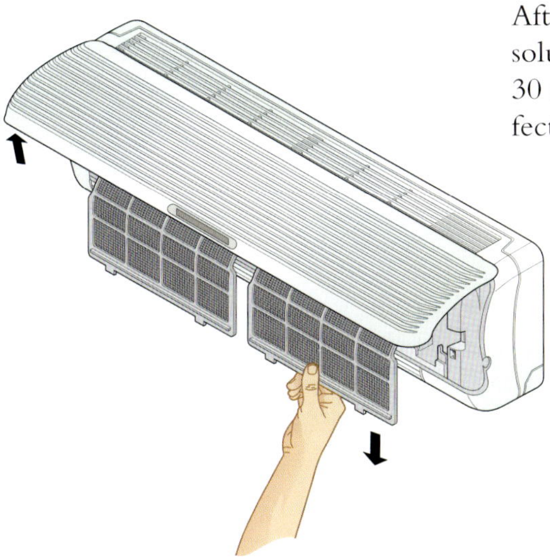

Open the front grille of the air-conditioner and very gently—don't yank—pull out the filter for cleaning.

**Do not wash a deodorising filter.** Instead, remove it from the unit and place it in the sun for 2–3 hours, before re-installing.

**If your system has an optional air purifying filter,** it should be removed and replaced every two years.

**Cleaning an airconditioner's outdoor unit** should be done once a year at the beginning of the peak use season. Have it done more often if you live near a dirt road or other source of dust and grime. Manufacturers do not recommend that you do this yourself. By all means, regularly check the exchanger coils and air intake and outlet vents, as dirty or clogged coils will reduce the operating efficiency of your system and cause higher operating costs. Use a brush or vacuum to clear dust, cobwebs and other debris from the vents. If they seem very dirty or clogged, call the manufacturer.

If possible, check your owner's manual to see which way the filter is removed, as every unit differs.

**Cleaning a window unit's filter** regularly during the cooling season is just as important as it is for a split or centrally ducted system. A window unit usually has a plastic filter that slides out of the front of the unit at the top, side or bottom. On some models, you have to open the front panel to lift out the filter. To clean the filter, wash it with warm soapy water in the sink or laundry tub, or spray it with a garden hose. Make sure it's absolutely dry before you replace it. The coils on the outdoor side of the airconditioning unit should be checked regularly, and if they are very dirty or clogged with grime, they should be professionally cleaned.

Do not be tempted to use a hose on any outdoor unit. Although the units are made to withstand outdoor conditions, they aren't meant to have probing jets of water flushed through their electrical parts.

## For a smooth-running airconditioner

- Before restarting an airconditioner in the spring or after a long shutdown, restore power to the unit for 24 hours. This produces the heat needed to separate the oil from the refrigerant so that the compressor can run more smoothly.
- Before restarting any airconditioner after a brief interruption, turn off the thermostat for at least 5 minutes to lessen strain on the compressor.
- To avoid damaging the compressor on an airconditioner, don't operate the unit when the air temperature is below 15 °C outside.
- Prune vegetation away from an outdoor unit by 60 centimetres on each side and above. When mowing, spray grass clippings away from the unit. And in the autumn, keep the fan grille free of leaves.
- Keep potential obstructions, such as curtains, furniture and house plants, at least 60 centimetres away from a window unit. Outside, trim back shrubs that block the unit's coils or the airflow to them.

# ALABASTER

**AS EARLY AS** THE FIFTH CENTURY BC, THIN SLICES OF TRANSLUCENT ALABASTER WERE USED AS WINDOWPANES IN THE MIDDLE EAST. BUT TODAY, YOU'RE MORE LIKELY TO FIND THIS DELICATE, POROUS STONE USED FOR VASES, URNS, BOWLS AND FIGURINES. TRANSLUCENT VARIETIES ARE USED TO DIFFUSE LIGHT IN LIGHT FIXTURES.

A pristine piece of alabaster, like this one, only requires a gentle wiping with a clean, dry cloth from time to time.

**EXPERT ADVICE**

**AH, THAT'S THE RUB**

After cleaning alabaster, you can give it a soft glow, remove surface scratches and provide a protective coating simply by rubbing it with petroleum jelly. Dip a soft cloth or chamois into the jelly, then gently rub it onto the alabaster with a circular motion.

**The safest way to clean an alabaster object** is just to wipe it clean with a dry, pure-cotton cloth, because alabaster is easy to damage. Don't soak an alabaster object in water or use any abrasive materials.

**If a piece needs more cleaning,** squirt some mild dishwashing liquid into water, dip a sponge into the soapy water, then squeeze. (You don't want the sponge dripping.) Sponge the water on and rub gently. Rinse the sponge with fresh water and gently wipe the object again. Dry with a cotton cloth. If the alabaster is from a light fixture, let it dry at room temperature for 2 hours before returning it to duty. Otherwise, the heat could cause the damp alabaster to expand and crack. Soiled or nicotine-stained alabaster can be wiped with a cotton wool ball moistened with mineral turpentine.

## ALUMINIUM

**MUCH OF THE** ALUMINIUM THAT ENTERS YOUR LIFE THESE DAYS IS EXTREMELY EASY TO CARE FOR.

Use an all-purpose household spray cleaner to keep your coated aluminium window and door frames clean, then wipe dry with a cloth.

**Cleaning coated aluminium window and door frames** is not a real problem. They are usually sold with a tough coating—white, primarily, but sometimes bronze or brown. An all-purpose household spray cleaner will bring them up nicely (see left). But why not take care of two cleaning jobs at once? Clean your windows with Windex Surface & Glass or another glass cleaner, or even methylated spirits, then wipe down the aluminium surface with the same stuff.

**Cleaning brushed or natural aluminium window frames** can be slightly more difficult if the metal has oxidised from exposure to the air, giving the surface a pitted, rough feel. Clean them with fine steel wool and an abrasive cream cleanser, such as Jif Cream (rubbing up and down, not in circles), or with a paste made from powdered whiting (available from hardware shops) and methylated spirits.

**Aluminium pots and pans** can be safely washed in a dishwasher, but coloured, anodised aluminium, such as saucepan lids and cake tins, should be washed by hand, as they quickly lose their colour in a dishwasher. Discolouration and stains on the inside of aluminium saucepans, such as those caused by boiling eggs, or using an aluminium pan as a pudding steamer, can be removed by boiling acidic fruit peelings—apple or citrus skins—or 2 teaspoons of cream of tartar, in water for 10–15 minutes. Never leave food standing in an aluminium saucepan after cooking, as it will pit the surface irrevocably.

# ANTIQUE CLOTHING

**CLEANING ANTIQUE CLOTHING** IS AN EXERCISE IN AVOIDING MODERN CONVENIENCES, WHICH ARE GENERALLY TOO HARSH FOR FRAGILE FABRICS. THIS IS EASY-DOES-IT HANDWORK.

**WATCH OUT** Don't take antique clothing to a regular drycleaner. The chemicals that drycleaners use are too harsh, and their pressing techniques may stress the fabric too much. If you really need professional help, find a drycleaner that specialises in old fabrics, or contact a textile conservator in a major city museum.

**The safest way to clean fragile garments** is to give them a sponge bath. But before you start, fix any tears in the fabric—otherwise the stress of cleaning will make matters worse. Then mix a squirt of mild detergent (such as Sunlight dishwashing liquid) in 4 litres of water and dab the solution on gently with a sponge. Rinse by sponging on clean water. Try not to get the garment sopping wet.

**To remove browning or stubborn stains** that don't respond to a sponge bath, treat them by soaking in a dilute solution of hydrogen peroxide until the stain disappears. You can also dissolve 2 teaspoons of borax in 1.5 litres of hot water, and soak the garment in the solution until clean. Then rinse with fresh water until the rinse water comes clean. If your tap water is hard, use distilled water for rinsing instead so that minerals won't discolour the fabric.

**Drying an antique garment** is a delicate operation: never wring antique fabric. Lay it flat to dry if at all possible. Be careful when moving a wet garment, especially lace or other fragile fabrics. Just the weight of the water can tear the fibres. To move the garment, lay it on a bedsheet and carry the sheet.

**Storing a fragile garment** also requires special care. Don't starch an antique garment before storing it. Starch attracts insects and stresses the fabric along folds. If possible, store the garment spread out flat. If space doesn't permit flat storage, roll it up. Rolling the garment around an object isn't necessary, but if you use wood or a cardboard tube, beware—they could brown the fabric. Protect the cloth from any such material (wood drawers and cardboard boxes, for example) with sheets of acid-free tissue paper (available from specialist paper shops, scrapbooking suppliers, bridal drycleaners and specialist suppliers of library or conservation materials). Don't store your garment in a plastic bag—it needs to breathe.

## rules of the game

WHEN CLEANING ANTIQUE CLOTHING

- Avoid regular drycleaners
- Mend any rips before you clean
- Don't use your washing machine or dryer
- Sponge clean
- Never wring dry: dry flat—not hung
- Don't store ironed or starched

# ANTIQUE FURNITURE

**WHEN IT COMES** TO CLEANING ANTIQUES, LESS IS BETTER. SOME OF THE CLEANING METHODS YOU'D READILY USE ON EVERYDAY FURNITURE CAN RUIN THE LOOK AND REDUCE THE VALUE OF AN ANTIQUE.

Keep antique furniture clean and protected by applying a thin coating of paste wax with a soft cloth. Then rub the wax off with another clean cloth until dry.

**The safest approach to cleaning antiques** is to limit it to simple dusting once every week or two. Wipe your antiques down with a soft, dry, non-abrasive cloth or chamois. Avoid furniture polishes—they will just leave a film that will attract more dirt, and polishing can sometimes damage the finish.

**A more aggressive cleaning method** might be considered if you're willing to risk it. But first make sure that the finish isn't too fragile (breaking down, separating or, in the case of veneer, lifting). If the finish is in good condition, wipe it down with a slightly damp cloth and follow up immediately with a dry cloth. (Never saturate an antique with water—that would ruin even a stable finish.) If you need stronger cleaning power, mix 1 tablespoon of mild dishwashing liquid in 4 litres of water. Dip your cloth in the solution, wring it out and wipe the furniture down quickly. Follow up right away with a dry cloth. (Test this method first on an inconspicuous spot to make sure the finish holds up OK.)

**Waxing antique furniture** is something you should only do once every three years—and, again, only if the finish is stable. A dark paste wax (available at hardware shops) is a good idea, because it won't leave a whitish residue in crevices, which lighter waxes tend to do. Apply a thin coating of the paste wax with a soft cloth. Follow up right away with a clean cloth, rubbing the wax off until it's dry (see left). (Normally, you would let the wax dry before buffing, but this technique allows you to apply a thinner coat and is friendlier to the finish, because it does not require such hard rubbing.)

**If an antique has a water stain**—and the item is not very valuable—you can try waxing the mark. Start by using a soft cloth to apply a paste furniture wax to the stain itself to see how much the surface darkens. Work your way outwards from the stain, attempting to create a match with the surrounding surface. If your antique is valuable, however, don't attempt to fix the stain yourself. Seek advice and help from a professional restorer.

Simple solutions

## Protect your antiques

- Don't store antiques in a dry room. A humidity level that's comfortable for your skin will be suitable for the furniture as well.
- Don't store antiques in a room with fluctuating humidity or temperatures. Both can result in cracking.
- Keep them out of direct sunlight.
- Don't place drinks or water-filled vases on antique furniture. Wipe up any water spills immediately with a clean, dry cloth.
- If an antique has gilding (gold leaf) anywhere, be extremely careful. A damp cleaning rag can wipe off water-based gilding. Use a dry rag and a delicate touch to clean gilding.

# APPLIANCES

**TO FIND OUT** HOW TO CLEAN MOST APPLIANCES, LOOK UNDER THE NAME OF THE APPLIANCE ITSELF. HERE WE OFFER SOME GENERAL INSTRUCTIONS ON KEEPING THOSE ENDLESSLY MULTIPLYING SMALL APPLIANCES SPICK-AND-SPAN.

**To clean a small electrical appliance,** first unplug it—and let it cool if it's been in use recently. Most small appliances can simply be wiped down with a damp cloth. If an appliance has food splatters on the outside, mix a solution of warm water and dishwashing liquid to dip your cleaning cloth into. Keep the water and suds away from the electronics. Never put an appliance in water unless its instructions say it's OK to clean it that way. Some appliances have washable parts that should be removed from the electronic base to make cleaning safer and easier (can-openers and slow cookers, for example).

*See also:*
• COFFEE GRINDERS • COFFEE MAKERS • ELECTRIC GRILLS • FOOD PROCESSORS • IRONS • MICROWAVE OVENS • OVENS • RANGE HOODS • REFRIGERATORS AND FREEZERS • STOVES • TOASTER OVENS • TOASTERS • WAFFLE IRONS • WASHING MACHINES AND DRYERS

# AQUARIUMS

**WITH AN AQUARIUM,** PROPER CLEANING IS A LIFE-OR-DEATH ISSUE FOR YOUR SMALL, FINNED FRIENDS, SO TAKE IT SERIOUSLY.

Simple solutions

## Nature's vacuum cleaners

Why not hire some live-in workers for your tank? The following species are happy to gobble up algae so you won't have to remove it for them. Just make sure they're compatible with the other species in your tank, and check with your local aquarium supplier for species that are appropriate and available in your area.

- **Freshwater**

Sucking catfish *(Gyrinocheilus aymonieri)*
Plecostomus species
Snails (assorted species)

- **Saltwater**

Turbo snails
Tangs
Certain hermit crabs (check with your supplier)

**For a new aquarium,** cleaning starts on Day One. Clean all your new gear—tank and accessories. Soap and detergent are definite no-noes, as the residue will damage the fish. For new equipment, just use plain old warm or cold water.

**Check your aquarium's water** once a week for its pH, nitrate, nitrite and ammonia levels. Read up on the chemical tolerances of your particular fish species, so you will know when it's time for a change of water. (The people who sold you all the gear may also be able to sell you a water chemical test kit.) A number of variables affect how often you will need to change the water: how many fish you have, how big they are, the species, the size of the tank, your lighting and the kind of filtration you're using. You don't really change all the water at once. Just change 10 to 25 per cent of the water in your aquarium, and expect to do it about every two weeks.

**To change the water,** round up enough buckets to handle 10 to 25 per cent of the water in your tank. (You can use the same bucket over and over, but you'll have to keep stopping the siphon while you empty it out.) Use a siphon hose to draw the water out. A clear hose is best, so you can see what you're sucking up.

Don't refill the aquarium with water straight from the tap. Nearly all tap water has chlorine added, which will hurt your fish. (Many aquarium suppliers will test a sample for you, or you can use a home water-chemical test kit.) To remove the chlorine, either use a chlorine neutraliser (available from aquarium suppliers), or let the water sit in a basin for 24 hours before pouring it in, giving the chlorine time to dissipate naturally. Make sure the new water is about the same temperature—within one or two degrees—as the water left in the aquarium.

**To remove algae,** use algae scrub pads (available from an aquarium supplier or pet shop) and clean the inside walls of your aquarium whenever the fuzzy little green stuff becomes visible. If you don't like having your hands sloshing in water, try a magnetic cleaning system. One magnet, attached to a scrub pad, goes on the inside of the glass, and another magnet goes on the outside for dragging the scrub pad around. Remember, algae thrive on light, so the more light your aquarium gets the more algae you're going to have to clean up.

**Clean the filter in your tank once a week**—or more often, depending on the feeding habits of your fish and how many fish you have. Most tanks have a mechanical filter, and models vary; follow the instructions that come with your tank for removing, cleaning and replacing the filter. A clean filter means better water, which means healthier fish.

Another filtering tool in your aquarium-cleaning arsenal is carbon. It gives your water that sparkling-clear look by removing the slightly yellowish cast caused by food and waste. Carbon may already be a part of your mechanical filter. If not, you can buy a carbon holder or even make your own. Put the carbon (available from your aquarium supplier or pet shop) into an old pair of pantihose, tie a tight knot to secure it, then cut away the excess fabric. Place your carbon filter where it will get good water flow in the tank.

**To thoroughly clean an old tank**—especially if some of your fish were diseased—remove any fish to another container and empty the tank. Then refill the tank with fresh water and add 2 teaspoons of

## An underwater dirt devil

That gravel at the bottom of your aquarium isn't just for looks. It's also a biological filter that traps gunk in the water. Give it a gentle vacuuming each time you change your aquarium's water. (If you're thinking of firing up your wet-and-dry vacuum, think again!)

You can buy special aquarium vacuums, but making your own is easy. Attach a clear plastic siphon hose to the top of a small plastic soft-drink bottle. (The hose needs to be large enough to fit tightly over the bottle.) Cut the bottom off the bottle, then place it on the bottom of the tank. When the siphon starts drawing water (don't forget to bring a bucket with you), it will suck up the dirt, waste and old food without disturbing the gravel. Move from one patch of gravel to the next, working your way across the aquarium floor.

Since you'll be using this technique at water-changing time, you'll have to stop when you've removed your target volume of water. It may take you two sessions to cover the entire aquarium floor. You can also install a special filter under the gravel, which will reduce the need for vacuuming.

Remove algae from the inside walls of your aquarium whenever it becomes visible. Ordinary scrub pads do the job quite nicely.

household bleach for every 4 litres of water. Let it sit for at least 30 minutes. Empty the tank, rinse it well and then refill. Now neutralise any bleach residue by using a chlorine neutraliser (see 'To change the water', on page 58), following the instructions for neutralising bleach. Empty the water once again and rinse. Now fill your aquarium with water that you have dechlorinated. Then your fishy friends can move back in and unpack their bags.

**Here are some preventive measures** that can cut down on the time you have to spend cleaning your tank:

- The location of your aquarium has cleaning ramifications. If you put it in direct sunlight, you'll have a constant algae battle on your hands, not to mention problems with overheating (the same problems you'll have if you leave your aquarium lights on too long).
- The cleaning considerations are not very different for freshwater and saltwater fish. But if you're a beginner, start with freshwater fish. They're less sensitive to variations in the chemical levels in the water. Besides, tracking the salinity of a saltwater tank is yet another management issue that could push a beginner over the edge.
- Don't give your water beasts too much food. Fish don't have refrigerators, so leftovers float around, driving up the levels of harmful chemicals. Watch your fish at feeding time. When they begin to slow down their rate of eating, dinner's over; don't add more food.
- Inspect your fish every day to see whether they have any injuries, infections or parasites. When you buy new fish, let them stay in a 'guest room' for a month—a separate quarantine tank—so you can monitor them for any diseases that could wipe out the rest of your fish.

## ARTWORK

**WHETHER THEY'RE VALUABLE** INVESTMENTS OR NOT, CLEANING AND PROTECTING YOUR ARTWORKS PROPERLY WILL ENSURE THEY STAY IN TOP CONDITION FOR A LONG TIME.

**With unframed paper-based artwork,** such as prints, etchings and drawings, it's best to approach cleaning with a healthy dose of forethought and prevention. Paper is easily damaged, and any medium applied to it has a much more tenuous bond than, say, oil on canvas. Prints, etchings, drawings, watercolours and pastels simply can't be cleaned. So do the sensible thing and preserve these pieces of art under glass and framing. That way, you clean the exterior casing, not the artwork itself. And the value and longevity of your artwork increase.

**To clean a framed work,** take it off the wall and lay it flat. Remove dust by wiping all surfaces—front and back—with a soft, dry cloth. Don't use a feather duster or a paper towel, which could scratch the glass or frame. To clean the glass, lightly moisten a soft cleaning cloth with glass cleaner and wipe the surface. Don't spray cleaner directly onto the glass. The cleaner could seep behind the glass and damage your artwork.

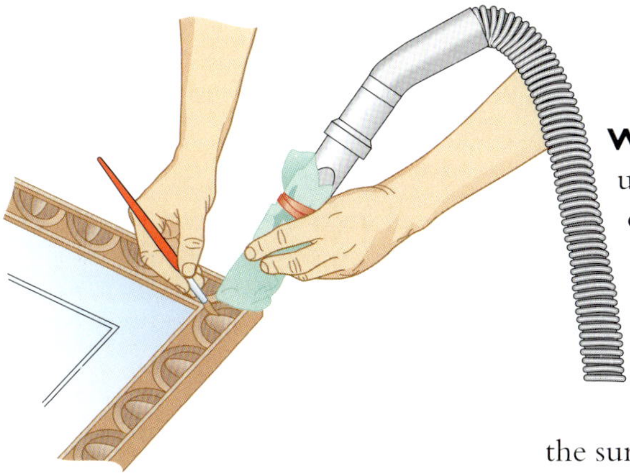

The only safe way to clean those tight little spaces on a delicate frame is with a watercolour brush. Use a vacuum with a soft flannel over its nozzle to suck up the bits of dust.

**When cleaning paintings,** there are more don'ts than dos, unfortunately. The good news is that dust doesn't tend to settle on paintings themselves, because they hang vertically. Don't attempt to dust a painting. Feathers from a feather duster or fibres from a cloth can snag on the paint surface and damage it. And leave that vacuum cleaner with its brush attachment in the cupboard as well. If you simply can't resist dusting a painting, wave a feather duster at it, making sure it doesn't actually touch the surface, and the resulting wind will do the job. Don't blow on your painting—there's inevitably some damaging saliva in human breath.

Dust will settle, of course, across the top of your painting's frame. But you still have limited options. The frames around valuable paintings often have delicate gilding—feather dusters and cloths are a no-no on an elaborate older frame. (If you have modern frames, they're OK.) But all is not lost. Remove any attachment from your vacuum hose and put a soft flannel cloth over the end, secured with a rubber band, to reduce the suction. Dislodge dust from the nooks and crannies of your delicate frame with a soft watercolour brush and use the covered hose to catch the airborne particles (see above left).

If there's a smoker in your family, protect your paintings by covering them with glass. (You can wipe the glass, of course, with a clean cloth that's been squirted with a glass cleaner, such as Windex or Mr Muscle.)

**Cleaning sculptures** is an exercise in the art of light-touch simplicity. Avoid the kind of harsh chemicals you get with commercial cleaners. And avoid soaps of any kind, since it's hard to know how they will affect various sculpting materials and finishes. Also resist the temptation to use feather dusters, as the feathers can get caught in crevices and break off a piece of the sculpture or damage veneer finishes. Clean plaster of Paris objects with a cloth lightly dampened in distilled water. For harder, more durable sculptures you can use plain tap water.

**To dust a wood sculpture,** sprinkle a few drops of paraffin oil, or eucalyptus oil, onto a soft rag (old T-shirts are great) and gently wipe the entire surface once a week, pulling dust out of crevices. You can use a very slightly damp rag on your wood sculpture, too, but take care that no moisture is left behind to damage the wood. This is not speed work. Proceed carefully, because some areas can be more delicate than others. Don't use silicone-based products and sprays which will soak into the wood and build up. If your sculpture is stained from long-time exposure to impurities from a fireplace or a heating system, take it to a professional conservator for advice.

You can also use the dusting method described for paintings: cover your vacuum hose with a piece of flannel cloth, secured with a rubber band. Use a soft watercolour brush to whisk up the dust, then suck it up with the vacuum cleaner.

**WATCH OUT** If in any doubt, do not attempt to clean a valuable piece of art yourself. Seek advice from the conservators at a big city museum, art gallery or library; they are the experts. By taking matters into your own hands, you could render your valuable artifact completely worthless.

**EXPERT ADVICE**

RESIST ALL TEMPTATION

There's an old wives' tale that claims you can clean a painting by rubbing it with a cut potato or a slice of bread. The theory is that mild enzymes or acid in the potato will clean the artwork and that the bread will absorb dirt particles. This is quite simply not true. Smearing food onto a painting will only do it damage, and restorers spend a good deal of their time fixing the cleaning mistakes of well-meaning amateurs. So resist all temptation and leave those jobs to the professionals!

**To wax a wood sculpture,** first remove any build-up from furniture polish or furniture cleaning soap. As a test, dip a cotton bud in white spirit or mineral turpentine and dab it on an inconspicuous spot to see whether it damages the finish. If not, apply the spirits to a soft cloth, such as an old T-shirt, and gently stroke the cloth over the sculpture. Be careful not to snag the cloth on any end grain of the wood, which could pull wood fibres free. Then apply your wax to another soft, clean cloth (again, a T-shirt) and gently rub it into the surface. Pure carnauba wax (available from hardware shops, antiques and restoration centres) works well and comes in a variety of colours (clear for a white sculpture). A mixture of beeswax and carnauba wax is good, too. Or, at a pinch, try brown shoe polish, which will match the colour of the wood and help cover any scratches. Talk to a conservator before waxing stone, marble, plaster of Paris or a painted surface.

*See also:*
• PHOTOGRAPHS

## ASPHALT

**WITHOUT A DOUBT,** ASPHALT IS TOUGH STUFF, BUT THERE ARE A SURPRISING NUMBER OF CLEANING CONSIDERATIONS WHERE THE RUBBER MEETS THE ROAD.

**To clean an asphalt driveway,** path or other asphalt surface, give it a good washing once a year. Sweep off leaves and dirt with a broom. Mix 1 scoop of laundry detergent in a bucket with 4 litres of water. Splash some onto the asphalt as needed for spot-cleaning and scrub with a stiff broom. Then, working as quickly as possible so as not to waste water unnecessarily, give it a good rinsing with a garden hose. (High-pressure hoses or steam washing could damage the asphalt.)

**Clean petrol and oil spills** as quickly as possible. Asphalt is a petroleum-based material. This means a puddle of petrol or oil could eat a hole in your path or driveway. Sop up a spill with paper towels (see below left), then spray away the remainder with a garden hose. For a little more muscle, mix laundry detergent in water as described above, and work at the spot with a stiff-bristled scrubbing brush. And next time, take preventive measures: lay down some cardboard, newspaper or plastic when you add oil or fuel to your lawnmower.

■ Blot up petrol and oil spills on an asphalt driveway with paper towels, then wash it clean with a garden hose.

**To remove asphalt stains on clothing,** pre-treat the stain with an enzyme stain-removal product from your laundry (anything with 'bio' in the name) and toss the article in the washing machine. You can also spray it with an orange-oil-based household cleaner, which will dissolve the stain, but you will have to rinse the cleaner out of the garment before putting it into the washing machine. If you get asphalt on your shoes, spray them with orange oil cleaner or WD-40, or wipe with eucalyptus oil, and scrape the asphalt off with a paint scraper or putty knife. (Make sure to rinse your shoes well before you go

stomping around the house.) If you do get it on the carpet, try rubbing the mark with eucalyptus oil, then sponge over it with warm soapy water. Repeat if necessary.

Tar- and asphalt-removal products, available from hardware and automotive shops, are great for removing tar stains on the body of a car.

**To remove asphalt stains on your tools,** again the orange oil cleaner, eucalyptus oil or WD-40 trick works. Spray or wipe it on, wait a few minutes and wipe it off. WD-40 lubricant will do the job, too (as will mineral turpentine, paint thinner, white spirit or kerosene, but they're not recommended because they're highly flammable). Don't forget the damage that these products can do to asphalt—it stands to reason that you should take precautions to avoid spilling any of these liquids onto an asphalt surface.

**To remove asphalt from your car,** drop by a hardware or automotive shop and pick up an asphalt- or tar-removal product designed for that purpose and follow the package instructions (see left).

**Here are some asphalt maintenance tips** that will help to keep your path or driveway looking better longer:

- Reseal your asphalt with a commercial sealant every two or three years to protect it from the weather and to maintain its looks. However, if you reseal an asphalt surface more often you'll get too much build-up of the material, which will start to crack.
- Fill cracks in asphalt a.s.a.p. Eventually, areas of heavy traffic will crack—that's just par for the course. Use an asphalt-patching product (available at hardware and home improvement shops). This is not just a cosmetic consideration. Filling cracks prevents weeds from growing in the holes, worsening the situation, and it deters erosion, which can undermine your driveway or path and cause more cracking.

## rules of the game

TO PAVE THE WAY FOR A WELL-KEPT PATH OR DRIVEWAY

- When your car is standing still, don't turn the steering wheel back and forth. (You may have to pass this information on to the kids.) It can damage the asphalt—and your tyres—especially on a hot day.
- Don't place heavy or pointed objects on fresh or hot asphalt. Examples of this include the kickstand of a bicycle or motorcycle, chairs or tables, ladders, or a car jack.
- Petrol and oil will damage asphalt, so wipe up spills quickly.
- Use a sealant on asphalt every two or three years to protect it from the elements and maintain that smooth black look.

# ATTICS

**NEGLECT YOUR ATTIC,** AND YOU COULD HAVE A DUST AND MOULD FACTORY HANGING OVER YOUR HEAD. GIVE IT A GOOD CLEANING ONCE A YEAR, AND YOU'LL NOT ONLY REMOVE A SOURCE OF THESE IRRITANTS FROM YOUR HOME, BUT YOU'LL ALSO HAVE A VALUABLE STORAGE SPACE THAT YOU WON'T DREAD GOING INTO OCCASIONALLY.

**Before you start**—especially if it's been several years since you even went into your attic—you should gear up to protect yourself. A disposable respirator is inexpensive and will protect your lungs from dust, spores, allergens and other nuisances. You may need an apron to protect your clothes, goggles to protect your eyes, and rubber gloves for your hands (latex gloves or something more heavy-duty, depending on the extent of the job).

**If your attic is already used for storage,** make sure everything's organised before you jump in and start cleaning. This means storing small items in labelled boxes, grouping together boxes that contain like items and opening up walkways so that you can get to any box in any part of the room. Think about storage solutions for keeping all those small, easy-to-lose bits and pieces together. Recycling plastic or glass jars is a common solution that works for many people.

**To actually clean the attic,** fire up the vacuum cleaner and start sucking up dust from the top down—ceiling, beams, walls and floor. (Wearing the disposable respirator is a good idea in any event, but if you're going the dust-pan-and-broom route, it's essential.) If your attic already has things stored in it, don't just clean around the boxes—clean under them, too. Once the major grime has been sorted out, you're ready to give the area a light once-over with a damp cleaning cloth dipped in a solution of water and mild dishwashing liquid.

**WATCH OUT** If you live in an old house in a city, and your attic is not sealed and floored, the chances are very high that the dirt in your roof space—perhaps the dirt of a century or so—is contaminated with lead. This is not something you should attempt to clean yourself. The dirt itself is nasty enough, but lead-laden dirt can be downright dangerous for you and your family. Seek professional help—your roof space can be industrially vacuumed before you use it as a storage area.

## Conquering attic mould

Mould in the attic is a sign that you have a moisture problem—maybe a leaky roof, maybe poor ventilation. To get rid of the mould, first cut off the source of moisture that's keeping it so happy. Get the leak fixed, or improve the airflow so that the attic stays dry. There should be soffit holes where the roof meets the floor and overhangs the walls of the house. Having a ridge vent system—a continuous vent along the peak of the roof—installed would make the airflow even better. This is something to consider when you reroof, but the less expensive option of installing rotating 'whirligig' roof vents can also be very effective.

When the leak or airflow problem has been fixed, it's time to clean up the mould. First, vacuum up what you can from the affected areas. Then, wearing a respirator (to avoid breathing in mould spores), use a stiff brush to loosen any mould that remains, then vacuum again. Finally, paint over the affected areas with a mould-inhibiting paint.

# AWNINGS AND CANOPIES

**A GRUNGY AWNING** OR CANOPY CAN MAR YOUR HOUSE'S STREET APPEAL, WHICH IS HOW REAL ESTATE AGENTS REFER TO THE IMPRESSION YOUR HOUSE MAKES ON PASSERSBY. EVEN IF YOUR AWNING IS NOT VISIBLE FROM THE ROAD, KEEPING IT CLEAN WILL HELP IT LAST LONGER.

**Cleaning acrylic awnings** is usually a breeze because most have a soil- and stain-resistant finish. Where necessary, use a stepladder to reach the awnings. Spot-clean by applying a solution of warm water and mild dishwashing liquid with a sponge. Rinse thoroughly with clean water and air-dry. For stubborn stains, use a fabric stain remover, following the instructions on the container. Again, rinse well and air-dry.

**Mildew on an acrylic awning** is usually found not on the fabric itself but on dirt, leaves and other materials that are not removed from the fabric. Acrylic awnings themselves don't promote the growth of mildew. To remove mildew, mix 1 cup of bleach with a squirt of mild dishwashing liquid in 4 litres of warm water. Apply to the entire area and allow it to soak in (but not to dry). Scrub with a sponge. Rinse thoroughly and air-dry. Avoid using bleach on logos or prints on the awning as it may damage or erase them.

Straight after applying a spray vinyl and fabric cleaner, give the awning a good scrub with a sponge or brush, then rinse thoroughly and allow to dry.

**Cleaning vinyl or fabric awnings** is usually done with commercial cleaners that work best if you don't wet the awning before cleaning it. On a stepladder, if necessary, apply a vinyl and fabric cleaner (such as PFC [Patio Furniture Cleaner] or Ripper Concentrated Cleaner) evenly in a saturating mist. Start from the bottom of the awning and work up. Before it dries, scrub the awning with a sponge or soft- to medium-bristled brush (see left). (Brushes work best on fabric awnings.) Never use abrasive cleaners or scrubbers. Rinse by spraying with a garden hose until the run-off water is clear. You'll want to remove all the cleaner, because leftover cleaner will leave a chalky film once it dries. Don't use a pressure washer to clean your awning. It's ineffective and can cause permanent damage.

**Mildew on a vinyl or fabric awning** can be removed using a solution of 1 cup of bleach per 4 litres of warm water. Before using the solution, however, test it by rubbing a solution-soaked cotton bud on a hidden section of awning to make sure it does not cause the colours to fade or run. Don't let the bleach solution dry on the awning. Rinse thoroughly with water, then air-dry.

*See also:* • UMBRELLAS

# BABY EQUIPMENT

**BABIES REQUIRE A** LOT OF EQUIPMENT, AND PROPERLY CLEANED EQUIPMENT PLACES FEWER DEMANDS ON THEIR FLEDGLING IMMUNE SYSTEMS. HOWEVER, IT'S IMPORTANT TO FIND THE RIGHT BALANCE BETWEEN CLEANLINESS AND GERM PHOBIA. ALTHOUGH CAREFUL CLEANING IS NECESSARY WHILE A BABY IS BUILDING IMMUNITY DURING ITS FIRST SIX MONTHS OF LIFE, IT'S NOT NECESSARY TO SCRUB DOWN AND STERILISE EVERYTHING IN SIGHT. THE MAIN AIM IS TO BE METICULOUS IN CLEANING ANY ITEM THAT ENDS UP IN A BABY'S MOUTH—BOTTLES, TEATS, DUMMIES AND ALL FEEDING UTENSILS.

To clean a high chair, just sprinkle bicarbonate of soda onto a damp paper towel, then give it a wipe.

**Cleaning baby bottles** is not as arduous as it used to be. Once upon a time, nervous new parents were told they had to sterilise their newborns' bottles by boiling them in water on the stove. That regimen has relaxed. As soon as the baby has finished their bottle, rinse it out under running water so that bacteria are less likely to develop and the bottle will come clean more readily. Wash the bottle and teat in hot water with dishwashing liquid, taking special care to remove any caked-on milk in the interior corners and the underside of the teat. (A bottle-brush will help with this.) Force soapy water through the hole in the teat and rinse thoroughly with running water. Position bottle and teat in a clean dish drainer or on paper towels to drain and air-dry.

An alternative is to put the separated bottles and teats in the dishwasher, positioning the bottles upside down and the teats pointing up so that water does not collect inside. Use high heat and the drying cycle.

You can store the clean bottles in a cupboard, but in most households with babies, the bottles don't sit still long enough to gather dust.

**In the absence of adequate cleaning facilities,** rinsed bottles, teats and caps should be sterilised in a commercial chlorine-based antibacterial solution, such as Milton.

**To keep a changing table clean,** place a couple of clean paper towels on it before each nappy change to protect the pad from germs. If the mess saturates the paper towels or extends beyond them, clean up with detergent or liquid soap and water. Rinse off the area with water, then pour a little methylated spirits on a clean cloth and wipe down the pad and table to finish off.

**To clean a nappy bucket,** use a freshly prepared solution of ¼ cup of bleach to 4 litres of water. Wear rubber gloves and rinse well with running water. A nappy bucket should have a tight-fitting lid. Line the bucket with a plastic bag, and when it's full tie the bag top tightly and then dispose of it in an outside rubbish bin.

**To clean strollers and high chairs,** sprinkle bicarbonate of soda on a damp paper towel or clean cloth and wipe down the item, then rinse with warm water (see left). (Bicarbonate of soda is a mild alkali that can make dirt dissolve in water. It acts as a mild abrasive when not totally dissolved.) A sponge is no good for washing the surfaces of baby equipment, because bacteria can become trapped in the sponge and spread to other surfaces the next time it's used.

**To clean a cot,** use bicarbonate of soda (as described above) and wipe the cot rails over. Wash baby bed linens in a washing machine, using hot water to kill bacteria.

**WATCH OUT** This news could save you from a serious meltdown. Baby bottles that are used and cleaned scrupulously day in and day out don't need to be boiled in a saucepan on the stove. And a good thing that is, too. New parents have more than enough to do without also making sure that babies' bottles haven't boiled dry on top of the stove. If you do boil them, don't do it when you're tired. You may wake up to find you've melted the lot!

## The hands that rock the cradle

When it comes to baby hygiene, the paediatrician's message is clear and simple: 'Wash your hands!'

A newborn baby's immune system starts working on its own at about six weeks of age. Before that, the sum of a baby's immunity consists of whatever the mother supplied during pregnancy and through breastfeeding. To fend off bacteria, encourage the entire family to wash their hands before holding the baby, and don't be afraid to ask guests to do the same. Frequent hand washing with soap and water will stop the spread of most common germs: no special antibacterial products are required. And don't forget that hand washing is equally important before preparing a meal as well as after changing the baby's nappy.

**When cleaning baby toys,** remember that a lot of plastic and rubber toys will stand up to the rigours of a dishwasher. Toss them into the dishwasher regularly to keep microbes or organic material on the toys to a minimum (see right). Give any grubby looking ones a quick scrub with an old toothbrush first. Wash stuffed animals in the washing machine, using hot water to kill dust mites that may be lurking.

Most plastic babies' toys are built to withstand a short cycle in the dishwasher every so often.

*See also:*
• STUFFED TOY ANIMALS

## rules of the game

KEEPING BABY EQUIPMENT CLEAN

- Clean, rinse and then sterilise bottles, teats and dummies during the first six months of a baby's life.
- Give a baby changing table a wipe down after each nappy change.
- Clean up food spills on high chairs and strollers as soon after they happen as possible. Use paper towels or disposable wipes for the job.
- Wash plastic toys in the dishwasher and soft toys in the washing machine.

## BACKPACKS

**A LITTLE BAG** OF TRICKS IS ALL YOU'LL NEED TO KEEP YOUR BACKPACK LOOKING GOOD AND STAYING STRONG.

Simple solutions

### Airing before storing

Whether a backpack is wet from rain or washing, mildew can destroy the fabric. Before you store it, put it out in the sun or in a dry room until it's dry inside and out.

**Cleaning a book bag** or keeping a nylon day-pack looking presentable is an uncomplicated task. Just toss it into the washing machine on the gentle cycle with your usual laundry detergent.

**Cleaning a hiking backpack** is simple, too. But with its stiff frame, a hiking backpack obviously won't fit into a washing machine. Instead, use a vacuum cleaner to remove dirt from the zippers and seams (see below). Applying water will work too, but it's messier. The important thing is not to let the grit build up, because it will damage the zippers and weaken the seams. Always clean up a backpack soon after a hike. Remove the items inside. If there is a food spill or crusted mud, wipe it off with a damp sponge dipped in a bowl of warm water with a squirt of dishwashing liquid. Remove stubborn stains with spot remover made for clothing. But there's no need to get carried away as most hikers view a well-worn backpack as a badge of honour, proving they've walked the walk.

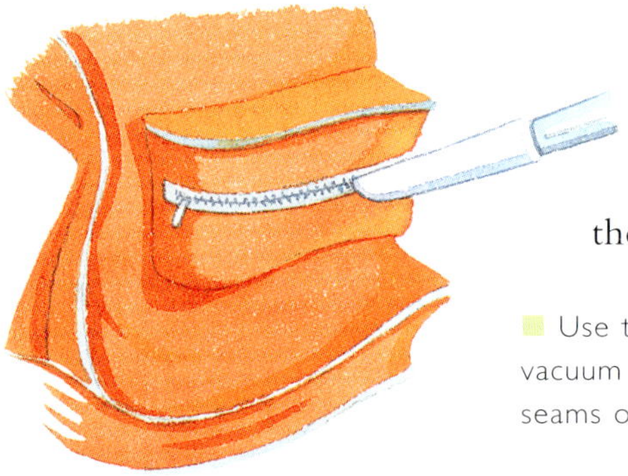

Use the crevice attachment on your vacuum cleaner to keep all the zippers and seams on a backpack free of dirt and dust.

## BANISTERS

**A BEAUTIFUL STAIRCASE** AND BANISTER CAN BE THE CENTREPIECE OF A HOME'S ENTRANCE, SO DON'T LET EVERYDAY GRIME DIMINISH ITS WOW FACTOR. IT'S WORTH THE EXTRA EFFORT TO KEEP IT SHINING.

**Dust a painted banister** with a soft, water-dampened cloth. If it's especially dirty, add a couple of drops of mild dishwashing liquid to warm water. Then wash and rinse a small section at a time, keeping the cloth well wrung out, then wipe with a dry cloth. Oil polish should be avoided on painted wood, since it can cause discolouration. Wax is rarely necessary when cleaning a banister, but if you use it, choose a light-coloured wax for light-coloured paint.

**Dust a wooden banister** with a soft cloth and furniture polish. That'll restore moisture to the wood and keep the dust collected on the cloth from floating back onto the balusters (the posts or spindles that support the banister). When dust collects in the intricacies of the balusters, use a cotton bud to clean out the really tight spaces.

**To make your own cleaner for banisters** or any other woodwork, mix equal parts of white vinegar, pure gum turpentine and boiled linseed oil in a jar. Shake the solution well (or it will separate) and wipe it onto the wood with a cloth. Rub the cleaner in and then make sure you wipe it off. (Otherwise, it will dry sticky.) Leave the cloth to dry outside to avoid the risk of spontaneous combustion.

# BARBECUES

**OUTDOOR COOKING HAS** NEVER BEEN BETTER, BUT BEFORE YOU FIRE UP THE BARBECUE, MAKE SURE IT'S PREPARED FOR OPTIMUM PERFORMANCE. A CLEAN MACHINE MAKES FOR TASTIER, HEALTHIER MEALS.

## Cleaning a barbecue

1 Use a stiff wire brush to remove most of the burnt-on food and grease.

2 Sponge both sides of the grate, as fat droplets often congeal underneath.

3 Re-season and protect the cleaned grate by spraying it with vegetable oil.

**To clean a barbecue,** remove the grill grates and clean it inside and out with 2 parts hot water to 1 part grease-cutting dishwashing liquid. (With gas barbecues, if the gas parts are not removable, you'll need to cover them with aluminium foil to prevent water from leaking inside.) Scrub with a nylon brush to prevent scratching, follow with a hot water rinse and towel dry. Finally, apply vegetable oil, using a clean cloth, to the barbecue's outside surface. That'll keep the barbecue shining and lubricated against the elements.

**To clean grates,** several methods work well. First scrub them with a wire brush and the hot water and dishwashing liquid combo described above. If they're too encrusted for elbow grease alone, spray them with a proprietary grill and hotplate cleaner, an oven cleaner or coat with a mixture of 2 parts ammonia and 1 part water. Place the treated grates in a garbage bag lined with paper towels, tie the top closed and stash the bag out of reach of pets and children for a couple of hours or even overnight—powerful, corrosive chemicals are at work. Take care not to let the chemical cleaner touch any aluminium or painted surface on the barbecue. When you reopen the bag to remove the grates, point the opening away from your face to avoid inhaling the potent fumes. Thoroughly hose off the grates, wipe them down with hot water and dishwashing liquid, then rinse.

If you have a self-cleaning oven, just put the barbecue grates in the oven and let the intense heat do all the hard work for you. After cleaning, put the grates back on the barbecue and re-season with vegetable oil.

### Thrills and spills

The wood-burning smoker is a favourite with serious barbecue fanatics and cleaning is simple. To clean the inside of a smoker, just build a hot fire in the cooker—hot enough to incinerate everything in there. But first, though, make sure you remove the smoker's thermometer, because when the inside heats to the required 150 °C to 200 °C, it can melt non-metal parts. The grates can be cleaned the same way you would a standard barbecue.

**When cleaning a gas barbecue,** it's a good idea to take these additional cleaning and maintenance steps—especially from the beginning of the barbecuing season:

- For starters, ensure the gas is turned off at the tank before cleaning.
- Inspect gas burners for cracks and corrosion and, if damaged, replace them. (Replacements are available from barbecue specialist shops.)
- Using a pipe cleaner or nonmetallic bottlebrush, clean the tubes, which carry gas to the burners. These tubes make an excellent hiding spot for spiders, whose nests can block the flow of gas and cause an explosion—not a great start to a barbecue dinner.

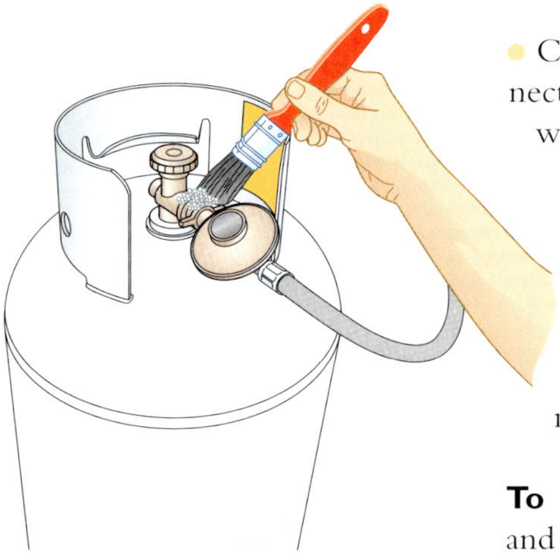

Brush soap suds over the connections between the gas bottle and hose, turn on the gas and watch for bubbles.

● Check for leaks in the gas bottle connectors. Brush around the connections between the gas bottle, the regulator and the hose with soapy water and turn on the gas (see left). If you smell gas or see bubbles, turn off the gas, tighten the connections and repeat the test. If the gas is still leaking, take the gas bottle and hose to a barbecue shop.

**To clean lava rocks,** use a stiff-bristled brush, or remove the rocks and clean them with a degreasing cleaner, available from barbecue specialist shops. As barbecues continue through the summer, turn the lava rocks periodically to burn off the dripped grease.

**To cut down on the clean-up,** burn off grease from the grates and rocks immediately after cooking. Leave the fire turned on for 10–15 minutes with the cover closed. Let the barbecue cool and then scrape away the residue with a wire brush. This job will be even easier if you lightly coat the grates with a non-stick cooking spray just before you throw on the food.

## BASKETS

**BASKETS ARE A** COMMON FIXTURE IN MOST HOMES, WHETHER THEY'RE STORED IN THE GARAGE UNTIL EASTER TIME OR DISPLAYED YEAR-ROUND. EITHER WAY, THEIR WOVEN CONSTRUCTION MAKES THEM VIRTUAL DUST MAGNETS. A FEW SIMPLE METHODS CAN HELP KEEP THEM IN TOP CONDITION.

**To clean an unfinished wicker basket,** a gentle vacuum is all that's required, since too much moisture will damage the basket. On fragile baskets, though, don't use a vacuum cleaner to remove dust and dirt—its suction may be too powerful. Instead, lightly dust in between the wickerwork with a damp cloth.

**To clean a varnished or painted basket,** start with a gentle vacuum, then use a spray bottle filled with water and a tablespoon of vinegar to apply a light mist. The spray allows you to penetrate the small areas between the wickerwork (see below). Wipe the basket dry with a very soft cloth, such as a baby washer, because it's less likely to get caught on rough edges. Use a cotton bud to get into any tight places. Air out the basket in the sun or a dry room, but keep it away from heat sources, which can result in warping.

**To clean most other baskets,** use a vacuum cleaner, followed by a mild solution of water and a bit of dishwashing liquid on a soft cloth. Apply

Keep your varnished or painted baskets clean by first vacuuming and then giving them a light misting with a water-and-vinegar solution. To finish off, dry with a very soft cloth.

a soft brush if needed for problem spots. Avoid using any cleaner with phosphates in it (read the fine print on the packet), which can eventually cause the basket to disintegrate.

**Simple solutions**

### New life for an old basket

To rescue a worn-looking basket, give it a coat of spray paint. First of all, check whether small pieces of broken wicker are sticking out. If they are, use wire cutters to trim them down. Then hang the basket on a metal clothes hanger, attach it to a tree and spray-paint it as evenly as possible. Let the basket hang there for a few hours to dry.

## BATHTUBS

**WHEN IT COMES** TO SOOTHING SENSATIONS, IT'S HARD TO BEAT A GOOD SOAK IN THE BATH. BUT BE PREPARED, KEEPING YOUR BATHTUB CLEAN TAKES REGULAR CARE.

**For everyday care,** wipe down the bathtub after each use with water and a cloth or sponge to keep stubborn soap scum under control (see below). Staying on top of the problem like this goes a long way, especially considering that most bathtubs today come with warnings about the danger of abrasive cleaners. And it's certainly true that if you scrub your way through the bathtub's protective finish, you'll soon have stains that are embedded in its material—whether it's made of fibreglass, porcelain or enamel.

Wiping down your bathtub after every use will help to avoid a bigger job later on. Just a sponge and water will do the trick—no need for cleansers.

**WATCH OUT** Avoid using abrasive cleansers on enamel bathtubs, as they wear down the surface finish. If you have a new bath, check what the manufacturer recommends you use. Gentle cleansers are usually OK for older bathtubs, but for badly worn enamel, avoid any kind of abrasive, even cream types.

**To clean a porcelain bathtub,** make your own simple rub-a-dub formula. Prepare a paste made of borax and water, dip a soft scrubber sponge in it and then start scrubbing away. To polish stainless steel parts of fixtures, gently rub with bicarbonate of soda on a damp sponge, then rinse well with water.

**To remove rust stains,** use one of the many available orange-oil-based, all-purpose cleaners. When the bathtub is dry, apply a small

amount of the cleaning substance to a soft scrubber sponge and rub in a circular motion. The rust stains should lift off without much trouble. Rinse with water and repeat if necessary.

**If the stain is old or really stubborn,** use a proprietary rust remover, such as CLR (Calcium Lime Rust Remover, which is available from hardware shops and supermarkets), but follow the manufacturer's instructions carefully, as this type of product is corrosive.

**To remove blue-green stains**—caused by water with a high copper content—make up a paste. Combine equal amounts of cream of tartar and bicarbonate of soda (usually a tablespoon of each is enough) and add some lemon juice drop by drop until you have a paste. Rub it into the stain with your fingertips or a soft cloth. Leave it for half an hour and rinse well with water. Repeat if necessary.

**Cleaning fibreglass bathtubs** can be difficult because mild cleaners have little impact on a seriously soiled unit and abrasive cleaners applied with too much scrubbing pressure will quickly dull the finish. For everyday cleaning, spray on a household cleaner or bath and tile cleaner, and wipe with a non-abrasive sponge. If it reaches the point that you have to bring out the big guns, use a powdered cleaner, such as Ajax, and a light-duty scrubbing sponge, such as Selleys Wash Up Wiz or one of the lighter Scotch-Brite pads. Always rinse well with water so that the chemicals won't stay on the surface of the bath.

**WATCH OUT** When using any new cleaning product that you're unsure about, always test it first on an inconspicuous area to make sure that it doesn't cause damage to the material you are cleaning. And don't mix bathroom cleaners, in case you create a toxic stew with noxious gases. Mixing chlorine bleach with ammonia is particularly dangerous. It's OK to use more than one type of cleaner as long as you rinse well between applications.

*See also:*
• SPAS AND JACUZZIS

## BEADWORK

**THE ANCIENT CRAFT** OF BEADING HAS TAKEN ON A NEW LIFE IN RECENT YEARS, AND THE BAUBLES ARE SHOWING UP ON EVERYTHING FROM VASES TO BLUE JEANS TO PICTURE FRAMES. SOME BEADS ARE REMARKABLY DURABLE, OTHERS QUITE FRAGILE. SO WHEN YOUR BEADS NEED A LITTLE BRIGHTENING, FOLLOW THE DOCTOR'S CREDO: FIRST, DO NO HARM.

**Beadwork on casual clothing** has become a fashion staple and can be cleaned at home more readily than the fine beading on formal clothing, which is best left to professionals. Beads used on jeans and casual clothing are typically made of plastic and can usually be put in the washing machine, with mild detergent, on the gentle cycle. Still, double-check the manufacturer's cleaning instructions on the label.

**Loose glass beads** are the easiest to deal with. Wash them in a bowl of warm water and mild dishwashing liquid. If the beads are textured, use a soft toothbrush to loosen grime in crevices. Then rinse thoroughly with water and towel dry.

**Strung beads** are more vulnerable than loose beads, because the thread that holds them all together needs special consideration. Wash a beaded necklace or bracelet in the same solution of warm water and mild dishwashing liquid in a bowl, but don't let the beads soak. Rinse them with water immediately after cleaning, pat dry with a towel and leave them lying flat—not hanging, which can stretch the thread—

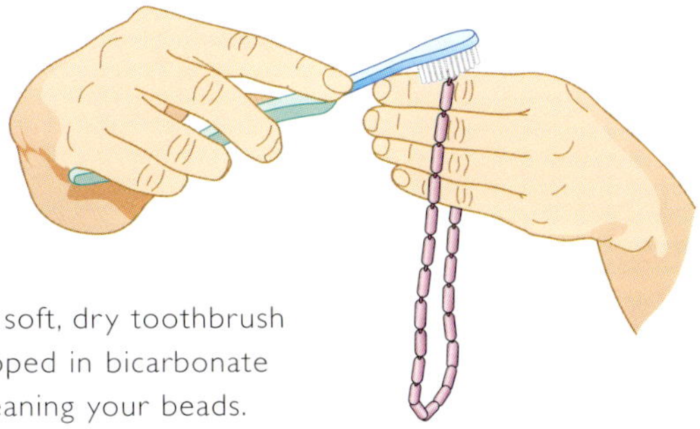

■ Use an old, soft, dry toothbrush that's been dipped in bicarbonate of soda for cleaning your beads.

Simple solutions

## Glued-on beads

Glass beads on a vase or picture frame or ornament can be cleaned with glass cleaner, but remember to spray the cleaner onto a cloth instead of directly on the item. And try not to soak the cloth with cleaning fluid so that it's wet, just dampen it. Then wipe the beads and leave to air-dry. Harsh solvents can loosen the glue that keeps the beads in place.

until the thread has had time to dry completely. Or use a soft toothbrush that has been dipped in a bowl of dry bicarbonate of soda and brush the beads gently (see above). Then rub them with a soft cloth.

**Vintage beads** require even more caution. Instead of submerging them in soapy water, wipe them gently with a damp cloth dipped in a solution of 1 part vinegar to 4 parts water, then air-dry.

## BEAMS

**EXPOSED BEAMS LOOK** GOOD AND LEND A SPACIOUS FEEL TO ANY ROOM—BUT IT'S BEAUTY AT A PRICE. MOSTLY FOUND IN CATHEDRAL CEILINGS, BEAMS TOWER ABOVE A CONVENTIONAL CEILING, AND REACHING THOSE LOFTY HEIGHTS IS USUALLY THE BIGGEST CHALLENGE.

**To dust beams,** get out your vacuum cleaner and its extension wand, snap on the brush attachment and then get ready for some serious neck stretches. Alternatively, you can attach a lint roller replacement tube to a paint roller and run it across the exposed surfaces to clean them. You may need a stepladder to reach the higher parts of a cathedral ceiling. It's a good idea to have another person on hand, just in case you need someone to steady the ladder or pass up equipment.

**If the beams are really dusty and dirty,** you'll need to wash them, which requires using an extension ladder. For wood covered with a urethane finish, mix a mild detergent with water, then wipe and rinse a small section at a time using disposable washcloths, such as Chux wipes, or, for harder-to-reach areas, a sponge mop. But go easy with the water solution—you want to wipe the beams, not drown them, because as wood absorbs water it expands and can become weakened. Being washed and wet regularly could result in warping and, in extreme cases, rotting. That's especially true of unfinished timber. For those beams, follow the same steps as for finished beams, but omit the detergent and clean only with water on a sponge that's been wrung out before wiping over the beams.

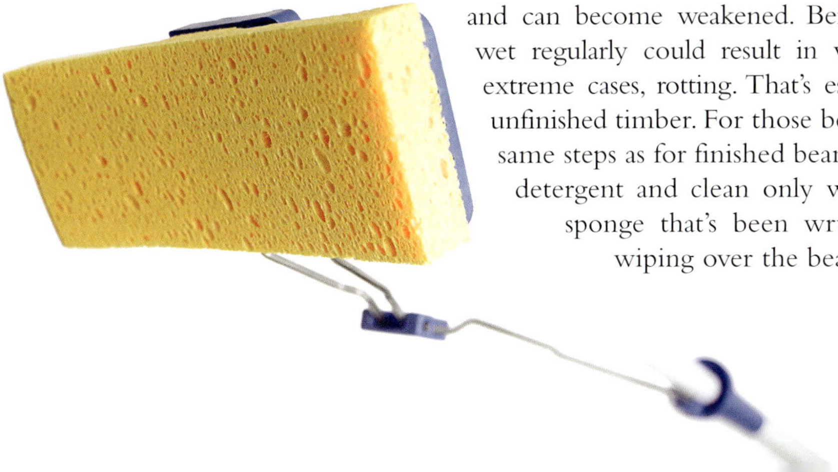

## BEDSPREADS

**THE TERM 'BEDSPREAD'** CAN MEAN A VARIETY OF THINGS, BUT WHETHER WE'RE TALKING BASIC CHENILLE, QUILTED OR FABRIC-COVERED BATTING, THEY'RE ALL CLEANED IN MUCH THE SAME WAY.

**Laundering a bedspread,** particularly if it's large or lofty with batting inside it, can be difficult to do at home. Most home washing machines and dryers just aren't big enough to accommodate them. So you might want to take your bedspread to a nearby self-service laundromat, where washing machines and dryers are bigger than most home varieties. Before washing a bedspread, check the care label to make sure it is washable. Pre-treat heavily soiled areas with a pre-wash product, such as Preen or Frend. Set the top-loading washing machine on the highest water level, delicate agitation and normal spin. Add a suitable detergent and then partially fill the washing machine's drum with warm water. Stop the machine, add the bedspread and push it down to submerge. Turn on the machine again, finish filling the drum with water and complete the washing cycle.

A couple of clean tennis balls thrown into the dryer will stop the bedspread from clumping.

**To dry a bedspread,** transfer it to the dryer and select the setting appropriate for its fabric type. Add a couple of clean, dry towels and then give it the Lleyton Hewitt treatment—toss in several clean tennis balls that will knock against the bedspread to prevent its filling from clumping (see left). Stop the dryer twice to make sure the bedspread isn't getting too hot. Shake it out once, too, to make sure the batting doesn't get jammed in one corner.

**To fluff up a chenille (candlewick) bedspread**—that durable, still-popular knotted or tufted kind your grandmother probably fancied—try this approach. Wash as described above, then hang it on an outside clothes line in a stiff wind, with the knotted sides facing. The knots will sit up as they rub against one another. Another way to fluff it up is to spread the dry chenille bedspread on a clean floor and then sweep it with a pristine broom.

### Practising prevention

Whenever you buy a new bedspread or have one custom-made, keep track of its fabric care instructions. Many bedspreads today are sewn from fabric coated with Teflon, Scotchgard or other stain repellents. These coatings wear off with repeated washings or dry-cleanings, but bedspreads can always be treated again to keep stains at bay. You'll need about three cans of Scotchgard to re-treat a double-bed bedspread. (Use the water-based formula.) Some drycleaners will also treat bedspreads for you.

If your bedspread is custom-made, information about the fabric's stain-resistant treatment, if any, is often printed on the fabric edge itself or on the paper bolt the fabric comes on. Check with the fabric retailer for details.

*See also:*
• BLANKETS • DOONAS
• EIDERDOWNS AND COMFORTERS

## BELTS

**DRY-CLEANING OR MACHINE** WASHING A BELT IS ALMOST ALWAYS A NO-NO. THIS IS BECAUSE FABRIC BELTS ARE USUALLY BACKED WITH VINYL, CARDBOARD OR PLASTIC, WHICH CAN STIFFEN, CRACK OR BLEED WHEN CLEANING SOLVENTS ARE USED. AN ALL-FABRIC BELT—ONE WITHOUT THESE BACKINGS—CAN USUALLY BE DRY-CLEANED AS LONG AS THE BUCKLE ISN'T METAL AND THE BELT IS SEWN AND NOT GLUED TOGETHER. PERSPIRATION-STAINED OR GRIMY FABRIC BELTS CAN BE SPRUCED UP AT HOME, AS CAN STRIPED WOVEN BELTS.

**To clean a fabric or woven belt,** cover your work area with a towel and spread out your belt. In a bucket, mix ½ cap of gentle fabric cleaner, such as Softly, with about 1 litre of cool water. Dampen a cleaning cloth with this solution and apply to a small part of the belt's edge to see whether it's colour-fast. If the colours don't bleed, carefully dab at the belt, without rubbing, one section at a time. As the cleaning cloth gets dirty, rinse and moisten again with the solution. Use another cloth, wrung out in water, to rinse and to blot. To dry, blot with a dry towel or use a hair dryer on the lowest setting. Another tactic is to spread the belt on a towel to air-dry. If a metal belt buckle gets wet in the cleaning process, buff it gently with a cloth.

**To protect a new leather belt** and prolong its life, apply a leather protector, one that contains no wax or silicone, according to the package instructions. (Look for these products at luggage and shoe shops.) If your belt gets dirty or stained, clean it with a damp sponge or cloth dabbed in saddle-soap. Wipe off the excess and buff it to a shine with a dry cloth.

## BENCHTOPS

**KEEPING BENCHTOPS PRISTINE** SERVES TWO PURPOSES: YOUR KITCHEN LOOKS NICELY KEPT AND THEY BECOME LESS OF A BREEDING GROUND FOR BACTERIA. BENCHTOPS HAVE COME A LONG WAY SINCE FORMICA. TODAY, THE MOST COMMON TYPE OF BENCHTOP IS A SOLID-SURFACE SYNTHETIC—CORIAN IS ONE POPULAR BRAND. OTHER TYPES INCLUDE MARBLE, GRANITE AND ENGINEERED OR SYNTHETIC STONE. ALWAYS READ THE MANUFACTURER'S INSTRUCTIONS FOR CLEANING BENCHTOP SURFACES.

**General benchtop maintenance** calls for removing the stuff on top first, then cleaning up surface dirt and crumbs with a soft-bristled brush or hand-held vacuum, such as a Dustbuster. Wet a nylon-backed sponge with soapy water (dishwashing liquid in warm water) and use the soft side of the sponge to wash the benchtop, backsplash included. Let the soapy water sit on the surface for a few minutes to soften any spots. Switch to the scrubbing side to remove any intransigent spots. Rinse with warm water and buff dry with a clean, lint-free towel. Or squirt with a window cleaner such as Windex, wipe clean with a sponge, rinse with water and dry so that it doesn't look dull or streaky.

**Plastic laminates,** such as Formica, don't take kindly to being cleaned with anything scratchy. Instead, sop up spills immediately with a sponge, then use a soapy sponge or all-purpose cleaner such as Ajax Spray n' Wipe to wipe the benchtop clean. For obstinate stains, try one of these two approaches:

- Sprinkle with bicarbonate of soda and rub with a soft, damp cloth. Then rinse and dry with paper towels or a soft cloth.
- Make a paste of lemon juice and cream of tartar, spread it on the stain and let it sit for 15 minutes. Then rinse and dry.

Remember, the older they get, the more laminates need a gentle touch. They can chip, scratch and lose their shine as they age.

**Solid-surface synthetics,** such as Corian, can withstand light abrasion. Wet a scrub sponge, such as a green Scotch-Brite pad, or squirt a mildly abrasive cleaner, such as Jif Cream (without bleach), on a damp sponge and apply with gentle pressure. Rinse with water on a sponge and dry with a soft cloth.

Regularly polishing solid surfaces is impractical for most people because benchtops are washed so often. But if you really lust after a high-gloss shine, use white polishing compound (TurtleWax makes one common brand).

**Stone benchtops,** usually made of marble or granite, are increasingly popular these days. Contrary to popular belief, stone-faced benchtops are rather delicate. Even mild acid etches marble, and anything greasy stains granite. To clean marble and granite, start with the don'ts: never use anything abrasive. Instead, wash with a few drops of plain or antibacterial dishwashing liquid on a damp sponge. Rinse the surface completely with clean water and dry with a soft cloth. Or buy a cleaner formulated for stone from your supplier.

**Engineered stone** usually resembles granite but requires no sealant and little extra care to keep it in good condition. Wash with soap and water, an all-purpose cleaner such as Ajax Spray n' Wipe, or a window cleaner such as Jif or Mr Muscle Glass Cleaner.

*See also:* • GRANITE • MARBLE

## Maintaining stone benchtops

There are a few key tips for taking care of stone benchtops, some of which may end up saving you the cost of repairing stained or damaged stone surfaces in your home.

- Blot up spills with paper towels as soon as they happen. And don't try to wipe them off, as that only makes matters worse. Flush the spot with warm water and a mild soap (do this by pouring water over it from a jug or drinking glass), rinsing several times before drying with a soft cloth.
- Use coasters, trivets or placemats under glassware and dishes to protect stone benchtops from scratching. Cork-backed coasters make a good choice. Heat damages marble, so never rest anything hot on it.
- Stone benchtops are sometimes sealed with a penetrating commercial sealant. Make sure that wherever you prepare food, the sealant is non-toxic. Vegetable oil is a cheap, effective, non-toxic, homemade coating for food preparation areas.

## BICYCLES

**WHETHER YOUR BICYCLE** IS A THREE-SPEED RELIC OR AN EXPENSIVE MOUNTAIN BIKE, KEEPING IT CLEAN MAKES FOR LONGER LIFE AND BETTER PERFORMANCE. WHEN YOU WASH YOUR BIKE, ALWAYS INSPECT THE TYRES FOR WEAR AND TEAR. BENT RIMS CAN CREATE SMALL PINCHES THAT GROW OVER TIME IF TYRES AREN'T INFLATED TO RECOMMENDED LEVELS.

**To make cleaning easier,** consider buying a bicycle work stand. It will stabilise the bike as you wash it and let you take off the wheels if you want. Work stands can be bought from bicycle shops. Another alternative is to suspend your bike with ropes from a strong, low-lying tree branch. If you're concerned about the mess that caked-on mud might make beneath you, work over a rubbish bin. Leaning the bike against a wall is OK, in a pinch, but makes your work more cumbersome and your bike more likely to topple over.

**Start cleaning a bike** by knocking off any visible dirt with a stiff-bristled brush (see below). Then use a garden hose on low pressure to rinse the bike. You want the water to trickle out, rather than spray with force, because water under pressure can force grime into the chain and other moving parts. For the same reason, never use a power washer or put your bike through a car wash.

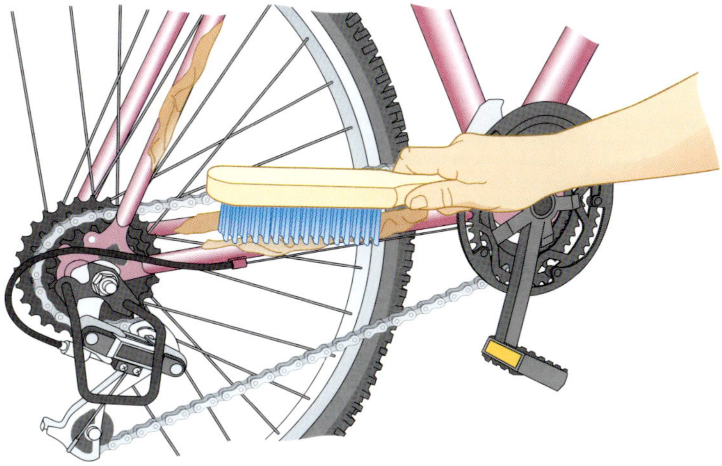

A stiff-bristled brush is all you need to knock obvious dirt off your bike frame. (Wire bristles will scratch the paint finish.)

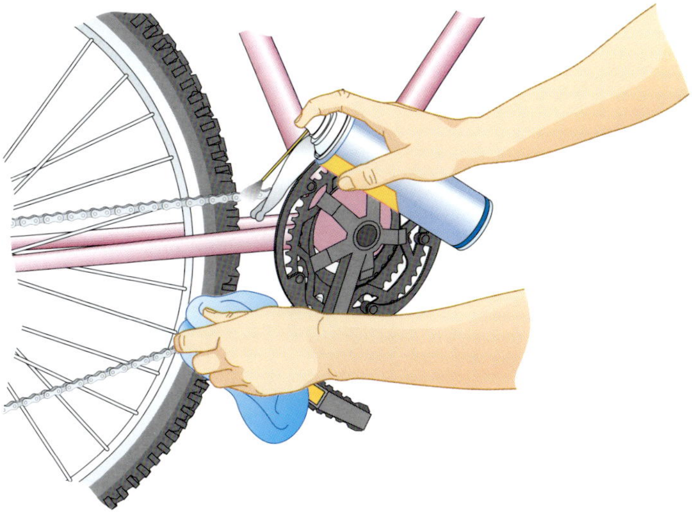

To clean the bike chain, spray on an aerosol degreaser, a few links at a time, then use a clean, soft cloth to give the links a wipe over to remove dirt.

**WATCH OUT** Cleaning a greasy bike drive chain can be a messy business. To avoid staining a concrete or asphalt driveway with grease and grime, park your bike over a grassy area to do the job. That way, any dripping oil will be quickly absorbed into the soil. And you can use the hose to give the bike a gentle rinse afterwards, before drying and re-lubricating.

**Degrease the drive train** next. The hardest parts to keep clean are the chain and the other parts of the drive train—the pedals, derailleur, rear hub and such—so tackle them first. If it looks as though it's going to be a really dirty job, wear a pair of gloves. Then apply a degreaser, such as Weldite Citrus Degreaser Spray or CRC Aeroclean, and clean the chain, a few links at a time, using a soft cloth. Move the pedals forward to work on a new section of chain. Once you've cleaned the chain, carefully remove it from the chain ring (also called the chain wheel)—the metal wheel whose pointed teeth keep the chain in place. Using a small screwdriver, carefully remove any caked-on gunk caught between the teeth. Then slip a cloth between them, rubbing it back and forth as if you were flossing your teeth.

**Now wash the entire bike.** Use a big sponge and ¼ cup of dishwashing liquid mixed in a bucket of warm water. Don't forget the seat and its underpinnings, handlebars and handgrips, and make sure you don't miss the brake levers and under the fork that connects the handlebars to the frame. Wash the wheel rims and tyres. Gently soap the drive train to remove any residue from the degreaser. Rinse the bike completely with a garden hose and then ride it in the work stand to slough off excess water. Towel off the bike and ride it a few blocks to shake off more water, then towel it off again completely.

**Lubricate the chain** with WD-40 or an aerosol lubricant, such as Weldite TF2 Lubricant Spray with Teflon or CRC 5-56, sold at most bicycle shops. Turn the crank backwards as you spray. Lubricant attracts dirt, so use it sparingly and wipe off the excess with a soft cloth.

**Wax a clean bicycle** for much the same reason that you polish a new pair of shoes. The wax protects the bike and deflects dirt, keeping your ride looking good. This applies whether you ride through puddles in your neighbourhood or down a mountain at breakneck speed.

Bike waxes, available in paste and liquid form, are sold at any bike shop. Following the instructions, apply wax with a soft cloth, being careful to hit the bike's various tubes, joints and other hard-to-reach spots. Or try an easier approach: spray your bike with a common aerosol furniture polish that contains wax (such as Clean 'N Shine Furniture Polish with Beeswax or Pledge).

**Store your bike** in a dry place to discourage rust. Never lay a bike on its right side; you could damage the freewheel, chain rings and derailleurs or throw them out of alignment. Use a rack to transport your bike by car, rather than laying it in the back luggage area. After every ride, brush mud and debris off the tyres. Wipe dirt and moisture off the frame, seat, handlebars, cranks and pedals with a soft cloth. If the chain is wet, dry it and lubricate it lightly.

# BINOCULARS AND TELESCOPES

**THERE'S NOTHING LIKE** A CLOSE-UP OF LENS DIRT AND DUST TO SPOIL A SKYWATCHING OUTING.

**To keep binocular lenses clean,** try blowing gently on each lens, without spitting, to remove loose debris and dust. Or use a lens-cleaning pen, which has a soft natural brush at one end and a cleaning tip at the other, to get into the crevices (see below left). (Most camera shops carry lens pens, lens tissue and cleaning fluid.)

Brush off the lens lightly with a sheet of lens tissue. With a clean sheet of lens tissue, sprayed lightly with lens-cleaning fluid, wipe the lens with a circular motion. Gentleness is the key here, since rubbing too hard can remove the protective coating. With a third sheet of lens tissue, remove the remaining fluid. Repeat with the other lens. Never use your shirt tail or facial tissue for this job because their fibres could scratch the coating. Also resist the temptation to use a commercial glass cleaner on your lenses. The ammonia in most glass-cleaning products will eat away the coating.

A lens-cleaning pen is the proper tool for removing dust particles from binocular lenses.

**To clean the exterior of binoculars,** dampen a soft cloth with water and wipe. Keep rubber eyecups and focus knobs lubricated with a vinyl or rubber preservative, such as Armor All.

**When cleaning a telescope,** less is always more. Telescope optics should be cleaned no more than twice a year because their reflective coatings are easily damaged. Carefully remove the mirror from the tube, then use a camel hair brush—sold at most camera shops—to remove surface dust and dirt. Dampen a sheet of lens tissue with lens cleaning fluid (or make your own cleaner using 3 parts isopropyl (surgical) alcohol to 2 parts distilled water). Wipe the mirror, eyepiece and lenses from the centre to the outer edge, using minimal pressure. (Telescope optics are even more delicate than binocular lenses and don't take kindly to being rubbed in circles.)

Should the optics collect dew outside, don't wipe them dry. Instead, let them air-dry, then clean with distilled water and lens tissue. (Distilled water leaves no spots.)

**WATCH OUT** Whatever you do, don't be tempted to use saliva to polish your camera or binocular lenses, or rub them dry with your shirt tail. Both actions could irreparably damage the delicate lenses. Take a bit of friendly advice and clean them as described at right.

**To protect your telescope,** always use the dust caps. And keep your telescope inside when not in use to prevent rusting. Most telescopes have an aluminium coating that can last for up to 10 years if it's kept spick-and-span. Before you store a telescope, wipe the outside dry with a soft cleaning cloth.

# BIRDBATHS, BIRD FEEDERS AND BIRD HOUSES

**JUST AS OUR** BATHTUBS, KITCHENS AND HOUSES NEED CONSTANT ATTENTION TO KEEP THEM CLEAN, SO DO THE IDENTICAL SPOTS WE SET UP FOR OUR FEATHERED FRIENDS. KEEP BIRDBATHS, FEEDERS AND HOUSES FREE OF FUNGI, ALGAE AND BACTERIA, AND THOSE BIRDS WILL KEEP RETURNING, TIME AND TIME AGAIN. ALL THAT'S REQUIRED HERE IS A BIT OF ELBOW GREASE, A SCRUBBING BRUSH AND AN OLD TOOTHBRUSH.

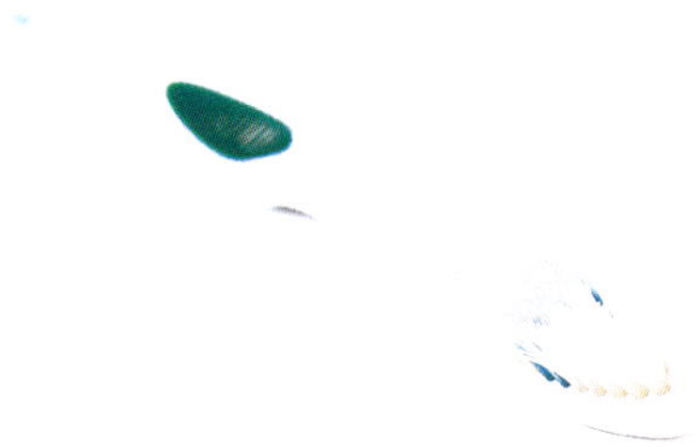

**Clean a birdbath** once a week during warmer weather—the busy season for birds of a feather to flock together in the sun-warmed bath you provide. Remember that birdbaths with stale standing water can turn into fertile breeding grounds for mosquito larvae, so dumping old water and cleaning out birdbaths is imperative.

First, use a scrubbing brush with stiff bristles and warm water to scrub out the birdbath. If the bath has a telltale ring from algae or other deposits or feels slimy to the touch, it's time to get aggressive. Mix a solution of 1 part bleach to 10 parts water in a clean bucket and use that to scrub the bath. Make sure you wear rubber gloves to protect your hands. (If you don't like the notion of using bleach, mix equal parts of white vinegar and water, then scrub.) Rinse well with fresh water and then allow to air-dry.

**Clean bird feeders** every two weeks year-round. This is because birdseed and other bird food get damp and mouldy in humid conditions, and the birds feeding at your trough could get sick. Take apart your wooden feeder, if you can. Dust off the pieces with a wire brush, then scrub with warm water and a stiff-bristled scrubbing brush. If the feeder is really dirty, wear rubber gloves and mix 1 part bleach to 10 parts water in a clean bucket. Vigorously scrub inside and out. Rinse thoroughly and then dry. For plastic or metal feeders, brush them out, then rinse with warm water and dry with a soft cloth. Or let them dry in the sun.

Let's not forget the feeders for birds that eat nectar. Flush out your bird feeder every few days during warm weather with hot water and then replace the stale sugar-water solution inside with fresh stuff. Nectar-feeding birds are susceptible to the diseases that can grow in mouldy sugar water.

## Ring around the bird house

Birds don't take kindly to the residue that soap can leave behind in a birdbath, feeder or house, so reach for the bleach instead. Using bleach to clean a bird house won't harm birds, as long as you use it in a weak concentration. Bleach also breaks down quickly in the environment, so there's no danger of causing long-term damage. The only risk is that it can sometimes whiten a wooden bird feeder or house. So don't soak them in a bleach solution. Instead, rinse thoroughly and swiftly, then dry.

And shy away from treating wooden bird houses and feeders with any sort of wood preservative that contains petroleum distillates. The strong fumes they emit could harm birds.

An old toothbrush is great for getting into tight spaces on a bird house—to clean them thoroughly and kill any germs that might be lurking.

**Clean a bird house** during cold weather, when birds aren't feathering their nests inside. If the bird house has a removable side or top panel, take it off and dip the pieces into a solution of 1 part bleach to 10 parts water. Using an old toothbrush, dig into the cracks and crevices—this is where feather mites, which feed on bird feathers, often lurk (see above). You don't want these pests infesting the next generation to take up residence in your bird house. To guard against mites, as well as fleas, flies, larvae and lice, use a 1 per cent rotenone powder or pyrethrin spray (available from hardware shops), or a proprietary aviary dusting powder or spray (available from pet shops).

## BLANKETS

**MOST BLANKETS, EVEN** SOME WOOLLEN ONES, CAN BE WASHED AT HOME. ALWAYS CHECK CARE LABEL INSTRUCTIONS BEFORE ATTEMPTING ANY AT-HOME WASHING, THOUGH. AND MAKE SURE THAT YOUR WASHING MACHINE AND DRYER WILL HOLD THE BLANKET COMFORTABLY. OTHERWISE, IT WON'T RINSE OR DRY PROPERLY. ALTERNATIVELY, TAKE YOUR BLANKET TO A LAUNDROMAT TO DO THE JOB.

**Before washing a woollen blanket,** check the label to make sure it is washable. If it isn't, have it dry-cleaned. If it is, measure the blanket and save the measurements for later. Pre-treat any spots or stains with stain remover, following the label instructions. If the binding (the narrow fabric along the edges) is looking really grungy, use a nylon-bristled nailbrush to gently scrub it with ½ cup of dishwashing liquid or make a paste of equal parts mild soap powder granules and water and apply it to the blanket carefully. Gentleness is critical here because the binding could shred if it's old and worn.

**To machine wash a woollen blanket,** fill a top-loading washing machine with cold water and a mild wool detergent (Softly or a eucalyptus wool wash), letting it agitate for a minute to dissolve the detergent. Add the blanket, distributing it around the agitator and wetting it thoroughly. Leave the blanket to soak for 15 minutes, then start the machine again and allow the washing cycle to complete. Spin

The bathtub provides a handy alternative when you're trying to wash blankets that won't fit into your washing machine.

the blanket for a minute, then push the timer forward to the deep rinse cycle. Allow the washing machine to finish its cycle.

**To hand wash a woollen blanket**—if your blanket won't fit into a washing machine, or you don't mind a slightly messier alternative—fill the bath with cold water and add ¼ cup of mild commercial wool wash or 1 teaspoon of dishwashing liquid. Put the blanket in and press down to wash (see above). To rinse thoroughly, refill the bathtub several times with fresh, cool water.

You can make your own gentle, no-rinse wool wash by combining 2 cups of Lux flakes, ½ cup of methylated spirits and 25 millilitres of eucalyptus oil in a lidded jar and shaking until thoroughly mixed. Use 2–4 tablespoons in a bathtub of lukewarm water and squeeze the blanket gently. There's no need to rinse (save water and your aching back), and the eucalyptus has the added advantage of smelling fresh while also helping to keep moths at bay.

Squeeze out—but don't wring—excess water by rolling up your sodden blanket in two or three large bath towels.

**To dry a woollen blanket,** you have several options:

- Use your dryer with the no-heat setting.
- Spread out a few dry towels on a shady outdoor table, flatten the blanket out on them and stretch it to its original shape, using the measurements you saved earlier on.
- Hang the blanket over two tightly strung clothes lines that won't droop under the blanket's weight.

If you chose the second or third approaches, plump up the blanket afterwards in the dryer on the no-heat setting.

**To clean a cotton or acrylic blanket,** it's OK to launder it. Wash the blanket in a washing machine with cold water as part of a normal load, being careful not to overload the drum. Dry a knitted cotton blanket in a dryer on *Low* so it won't pill. For other cotton blankets, the regular setting is OK. Or you can hang a cotton blanket from a taut clothes line to dry. Tumble dry an acrylic blanket on low heat.

*See also:*
• ELECTRIC BLANKETS

# BLINDS

**BLINDS OF ALL** TYPES ARE LIKE MINIATURE DUST-COLLECTING SHELVES. IGNORE THEM, AND YOU'LL HAVE AN ENTIRE DUST LIBRARY IN NO TIME. BUT DON'T WORRY, THERE ARE A FEW TRICKS THAT CAN MAKE THE CLEAN-UP EASY.

**To clean your venetian blinds,** use the brush attachment on your vacuum cleaner and adjust the blinds to expose the flat surface. Then, from top to bottom and left to right, vacuum the entire surface. Reverse the slats and repeat. Other options are to:

- Use a lamb's wool duster to clean the slats.
- Rub an old paintbrush along each slat.
- Saturate a cloth with methylated spirits and wrap it around a rubber spatula, which you then stick between the open slats to dust.
- Wear an old pair of thick, absorbent cloth gloves and wipe the slats one by one with your gloved hands (see below).
- Wood and bamboo blinds should not be immersed in water. Wipe them down with a damp rag soaked in a solution of dishwashing liquid and water. Then dry them quickly with a fresh rag.

An old pair of thick, absorbent gloves will do the trick when it comes to dusting your venetians.

**EXPERT ADVICE**

**CATCH THAT DUST**

A microfibre dusting cloth works wonders on blinds of all types. Once a week, lightly run the dusting cloth, which typically has more than 45,000 fibres per square centimetre, over the front and back of your blinds to keep all those dust particles from multiplying.

**Washing aluminium and vinyl venetian blinds** is fine, but don't use harsh cleaners or abrasives on them. And don't use any cleaner with ammonia on aluminium, because it will damage the finish. To clean aluminium or vinyl blinds, you have a couple of choices. You can wash them where they hang, or you can treat them to a quick stint in the shower or bathtub.

- To wash the blinds while they're on your windows, mix 60 millilitres of Tricleanium Ultra Concentrated Cleaner (available from hardware shops) in a bucket of hot water. Protect your eyes with goggles and put on rubber gloves and a long-sleeved shirt. Wipe down the blinds with a soft rag dipped in the mixture, then dry them with another soft cloth. You can also use sugar soap (according to packet instructions) for this job, but do not use it on aluminium.
- To give venetian blinds a bath, raise the blinds, unlock the brackets at the top, then remove them from the holder. Run enough warm water in the bathtub to cover the blinds and

Simple solutions

## Backyard spritzer

If your venetian blinds are washable, why not spray them off outside on a sunny day? Spread an old shower curtain or large piece of plastic on a level part of your front or backyard, open the blinds and then spray them with a garden hose. Then use either of the washing solutions mentioned here to clean the slats with gloved fingers. Rinse thoroughly. Dry with clean towels, or allow to air-dry.

add 1 to 2 cups of powdered dishwasher detergent, such as Finish. Protecting your hands with rubber gloves, place the blinds in the water and extend them. Dip the blinds several times to loosen grime. Then let them soak for 5 minutes. Use your gloved fingers to clean both sides of each slat. Drain the dirty water and either rinse the blinds in another tubful of water or give them a quick rinse in the shower. Spread out the blinds on a clean towel and blot dry with another towel. When the blinds are completely dry, wipe fabric softener sheets (the type sold for your tumble-dryer) on each slat. This acts as an antistatic and keeps them from attracting dust, hair, insects and other unappealing stuff.

**To keep other sorts of blinds** (roman, holland, austrian) from looking shady, dust them each week with one of those ticklish feather dusters or the soft brush attachment on your vacuum cleaner. If you have vinyl blinds, wash them twice a year with a sponge or soft cloth, using a solution of ¼ cup of white vinegar and 1 litre of warm water.

**Many fabric blinds can be washed**—carefully—and dried. Take a close look at the care instructions for your blind before attempting the following method:

- Take down the blind and immerse it for no more than a minute in a bathtub full of warm water to which you've added ¼ cup of mild dishwashing liquid.
- Use a soft brush to scrub both sides.
- Rinse with fresh water and hang to air-dry.

**If your blinds can't be washed,** scour them with polenta or flour, applied with a flannel rag. Or use an art gum or other soft pencil rubber to remove spots and stains. Alternatively, you could have them professionally dry-cleaned.

**Blinds made of natural materials** can be damaged by water.

- Parchment, paper or rice paper should not get wet at all. Clean them as you would non-washable wallpaper—with commercial cleaning putty or an art gum pencil rubber. Or find a spot remover that claims to work on the material at hand and test it on an inconspicuous area first.

**If you have parchment blinds,** keep them clean by applying a thin coat of paste wax (the same thing you'd use on wooden floors), buffing to a shine with a soft cloth.

- If a blind gets a small tear, seal it with clear nail polish. This also works with vinyl-backed blinds.

## BLOODSTAINS

**BLOODSTAINS ARE NOTORIOUSLY** DIFFICULT TO GET OUT, BUT DON'T DESPAIR, THERE ARE SEVERAL EFFECTIVE METHODS—SOME OF THEM QUITE SURPRISING—THAT WILL DO THE JOB EFFECTIVELY.

**Keep in mind these three points** when you come across a bloodstain that needs removing:

- Tackle a bloodstain as quickly as possible. The stain is much harder to remove as the blood dries.
- Always use cold water to flush a bloodstain, because any kind of warmth, be it from water or from a tumble-dryer, could set the stain.
- Refrain from scrubbing too vigorously. Otherwise, you'll leach the stain into the clean fabric that surrounds it.

**For blood spilled on clothing,** first blot the stain with cold water on a clean rag. Don't rub. If the stain persists, mix a few drops of dishwashing liquid with 1 cup of cold water in a bowl and dab it on the stain, allowing it to set for at least 10 minutes. Rinse by blotting again with a clean rag wrung out in cold water. Use a dry rag to blot it dry. If the stain won't come out, add a splash of ammonia to the detergent mixture and try, try again.

Here are some other tried-and-tested methods for attempting to remove bloodstains from garments:

- Hydrogen peroxide can work wonders on garment bloodstains, but only if the garment is white or otherwise colour-fast. (Test the fabric first by dabbing peroxide on a cotton bud, then on an inconspicuous area.) Spread out the stained area over a sink or laundry tub and pour full-strength hydrogen peroxide through the stain. Scrub gently with a scrubbing brush or an old toothbrush. Rinse with cold water.
- A tactic your grandmother probably used is to mix ½ teaspoon of table salt with ½ cup of water. Pour the water on the stain and allow it to dry. Rinse thoroughly with fresh water.
- Still another technique is to use an oxygen alkaline stain remover, such as Napisan OxyAction, on fabric that you know to be colour-fast. Make a paste of 1 scoop of OxyAction to 1 cup of water. Scrub this into the stain, let it dry for 2 hours and then rinse with cold water.
- In a pinch, and right after a bloodstain occurs, pour soda water through it or dab and blot carefully with a clean rag.

Treat fresh bloodstains on washable upholstery as soon as possible to avoid permanent staining.

**For bloodstains on washable upholstery,** cover a fresh spot as soon as possible with a paste made from equal parts cornflour and cold water (see left). Rub gently and dry in the sun, where the blood should leach into the cornflour. Brush lightly. If this doesn't work, try the technique a second time. Or make a similar paste with polenta and water or talcum powder and water and follow the same procedure.

**For dried bloodstains on carpeting,** cover the stain with a paste of equal parts borax and cold water. Let this dry, then vacuum up the dry powder. Or sprinkle a fresh carpet stain with table salt, then with cold water. Gently blot with a clean cloth and wipe with a sponge.

**For bloodstains on cotton bedding** as well as clothing, an unlikely but often effective method is to use shampoo. The key here, as always, is to attack the stain right away. Douse it with a capful of shampoo (any kind will do), making certain the shampoo covers every bit of the stain. Rub the area until the shampoo is completely absorbed, then wet with cold water. Once those telltale bubbles appear, scrub vigorously with a stiff-bristled nylon nailbrush. Rinse the stain in cold water. If a ring remains, repeat.

### Spit and polish

When nothing else is handy, you can use your own saliva to eradicate small bloodstains, a trick that every embroiderer or quilter knows. For small stains, thoroughly wet a piece of string or thread in your mouth and use it to blot at the stain. For larger spots, saturate a cotton wool ball or the edge of a clean rag with your saliva and blot. You can also try using full-strength toothpaste—the white kind, not a coloured gel—on bloodstains. Dab it on the stain and then wipe it up with cold water on a fresh rag.

## BOATS

**BUOY YOUR SPIRITS** BY WASHING THAT DIRTY BOAT UNTIL IT'S IN SHIPSHAPE CONDITION AGAIN.

**When washing a wooden boat,** you have to be careful. Most are painted, and solvents or abrasives can eat through the paint. Use a mild, biodegradable pH-neutral detergent, such as Gerni Wash, or one of the many specialist products for the task available at boat-supply shops. Dissolve 1 cup of detergent in a bucket of water and use a large sponge to clean your boat from stem to stern, preferably when it's out of the water. If dirt is particularly stubborn, use a cleaning pad with a bit of scratch to it, such as one of the gentler Scotch-Brite pads or Selleys Wash Up Wiz. To keep bare teak boats sparkling, mix 1 part ammonia to 10 parts water in a bucket and then scrub with a soft-bristled nylon brush.

**To wash a fibreglass boat,** the tools of choice are good old soapy water—mild, biodegradable detergent in a bucket of warm water—and a large sponge. When attacking stubborn crud or greasy stains, avoid using solvents such as lacquer thinner or

acetone, which could etch the tender fibreglass surface. Instead, use mineral turpentine on tough dirt, dabbed on a soft cloth. Thoroughly rinse the boat with water. Use marine wax, sold at boat-supply shops, as directed to rewax any spots where the wax has worn off. Always wax your boat with marine wax before you store it for cold weather.

**To wash a polyethylene vessel**—canoes, kayaks and other small boats today are sometimes made of this durable yet pliable plastic—give it the standard mild-detergent-and-water treatment described above. If you have obstinate stains, apply a touch of turpentine or acetone on a soft cloth. If these don't work, and only as a last resort, use a smidgen of lacquer thinner on a soft cloth to remove a stain.

**Wash your painted aluminium boat** as you would a painted wooden one (see 'When washing a wooden boat', on page 86). If your vessel is unpainted, consider it almost indestructible. That means that you can use a strong solvent, such as lacquer thinner or mineral turpentine, to remove any hardened grit and clean the surface thoroughly.

## BOOKS

**CHANCES ARE, THE** ONLY KIND OF DIRTY BOOKS YOU'LL EVER BE CONCERNED WITH ARE THE SORT THAT ARE GATHERING DUST ON A FORGOTTEN SHELF OR THAT GET SPLASHED WITH MUD ON THE WAY HOME FROM SCHOOL.

**To clean books,** it's best to just dust them, using a vacuum cleaner armed with its soft brush attachment (see below), or wielding a feather duster. Or dip a clean rag in water, wring it out, wipe the books and then dry with another rag. If the cover of a book is smudged with fingerprints or smeared with food, use a damp rag to remove spots. If you need more cleaning power, mix ½ cup of mild detergent, such as Softly or dissolved Lux flakes, in a bucket of cool water and test it on an inconspicuous spot. (Sometimes covers will come apart if you use

The simplest and easiest way to keep your books clean is to give them a quick going over with a vacuum while they're still on the bookshelf.

Simple solutions

### A book fan

Here's a simple technique for freshening a musty book: set up an oscillating fan nearby and open the book so that its pages rustle as the fan sweeps over it. Once the book is dry to the touch, sprinkle the pages liberally with medicated baby powder. Use a soft brush to remove any excess.

too much soap and water, so it's best to test first.) For a cover that appears safe, wipe with a rag slightly dampened with the detergent solution, then dry with a soft cloth.

Can't stand that grimy paperback cover? Use a soft pencil rubber to clean it up. But be careful, as too much pressure can rub off some coloured inks.

Grime and sticky label residue on covers can be removed by rubbing very gently with a dab of eucalyptus oil on a soft cloth until the residue has disappeared.

**When cleaning leather-bound volumes,** use restraint. Try wiping with a clean cloth first, or use the vacuum to remove visible dust. Fine booksellers sell leather cover cleaners, but be careful, as some conservationists no longer favour using products that contain neat's-foot oil, lanolin or other oils that can permanently darken or stain the cover and give it a greasy feel. Another consideration is that leather-bound books treated with oil tend to mould when they're jammed in close together in a bookcase.

## BOOTS

**MANY BOOTS COME** WITH A PROTECTIVE COATING THAT KEEPS THEM SHINY AND BRIGHT UNTIL THEY TAKE THAT FIRST STEP OUTDOORS. BUT IN MOST CASES THE COATING WILL WEAR OFF, SO THAT DIRT AND GRIME CAN WORK THEIR WAY IN, CLOGGING THE PORES THAT ALLOW THE BOOT TO BREATHE AND DRY, AND BREAKING DOWN SEAMS AS WELL AS THE LEATHER OR FABRIC ITSELF.

**To dislodge dirt,** first bang your boots together. Then wipe off surface grime and dust with a damp cloth, paying special attention to creases and wrinkles. Dive into those stubborn stitched areas with a dry, stiff nylon brush or an old toothbrush.

**To clean a boot,** close the zipper on the boot (if it has one). Wet the nylon brush and rub it on one side of a bar of soap. Then scrub down the zipper channel. Wipe it dry with a soft, clean cloth. Then undo the zipper and, using a dry corner of the soap bar, rub down each side of the zipper teeth to lubricate them for an easy slide. Wipe off the excess with a soft, dry cloth. If the zipper has a tendency to stick, you can lubricate it with a dry, non-oily lubricant, such as Selleys Ezi-Glide, instead of soap.

Simple solutions

## Scuffs aren't so tough

Here's how to give scuff marks the boot. They often come right off with a few swipes of a pencil rubber. For more stubborn scuffs, mix 2 tablespoons of ammonia with 1 cup of water and 1 cup of methylated spirits. Use a soft cloth to gently rub the solution into the scuff mark until it disappears.

For a smooth finish, get rid of the old wax or factory coating. Using either saddle-soap or a gentle fabric cleaner, such as Softly, and a dry cloth, rub the entire outside in small circles until stains disappear. Stuff the boots with crumpled newspaper and let them dry at room temperature. Then they're ready for polish.

**If you have white water stains** on your boots, they are probably mineral salt deposits left after the boots have been wet. Get rid of them fast—salt breaks down leather and fibre. Try rubbing the stained areas with vinegar or methylated spirits, then polish as usual. You can also rub the leather with milk (or a solution of 1 part methylated spirits and 2 parts milk), then rub in saddle-soap to restore the leather.

# BOTTLES

**CLEANING THE OUTSIDE** OF AN ORDINARY BOTTLE IS AS SIMPLE AS ANY OTHER GLASS-CLEANING TASK. THE REAL CHALLENGE IS REMOVING GUNK FROM THE INSIDE—UNLESS YOU HAPPEN TO HAVE A LILLIPUTIAN CLEANING CREW ON HAND.

**To scrub the outside of a bottle,** use warm water and dish-washing liquid. Mildly abrasive dishwashing pads are fine for use on modern glass. If the glass is pre-twentieth century, use copper-wool pads (not just copper-coloured pads).

**To remove hardened residue inside,** let the bottle stand full of soapy water (warm water and dishwashing liquid) for several hours, until the residue softens and can be loosened by shaking or by use of a bottlebrush. If dirt still remains inside the bottle, here are two ways to provide a little extra help:

- Pour a bit of uncooked rice or sand into the bottle (see below left), fill it again with warm, soapy water and shake.
- Fill the bottle with water and drop in a denture-cleaning tablet and allow it to completely dissolve to do its work.

Remove dirt from inside a bottle by shaking a mixture of uncooked rice and soapy water in it.

**A tough white crust** can build up inside a bottle that has held water for a long time. You may be able to remove this by filling the bottle with a cleaner designed for removing mineral deposits. CLR (Calcium Lime Rust Remover) is a good bet—but always follow the manufacturer's instructions.

Etching, caused by some elements of the glass leaching away after long-term exposure to liquid, is harder to deal with. A reliable and effective cure for etching is beyond the ability of the average person, unless you're prepared to spend hundreds of dollars on a tumbler machine. It's a job that's best left to the professionals.

*See also:*
- BABY EQUIPMENT (for baby bottles)
- DECANTERS

# BRASS

**THERE ARE TWO** KINDS OF BRASS TO CONSIDER—BRASS WITH A PROTECTIVE LACQUER COATING (MOST COMMON) AND RAW BRASS. RAW BRASS IS THE BIGGER CHALLENGE TO CARE FOR, SINCE THIS COPPER-AND-ZINC ALLOY OXIDISES WHEN IT IS EXPOSED TO AIR, RESULTING IN TARNISH.

**To remove dirt from lacquered brass,** mix mild dishwashing liquid, such as Down To Earth, with warm water and apply it with a non-abrasive sponge or cloth. Rinse with fresh water and dry thoroughly with a soft cloth. Buff with an extremely soft cloth or chamois. Avoid using terry towelling and paper towels, because they will scratch the surface of the brass.

**To remove tarnish from raw brass,** take a tip from antique dealers and the military: use a metal polish like Brasso, which contains cleaners to eliminate the tarnish, abrasives for polishing and oil to protect the brass from the air. Follow the instructions on the package. Only use a thin layer of metal polish—more is not better. To keep your unlacquered brass gleaming, polish it every few months.

**To spiff up soot-grimed brass fireplace equipment,** the cleaning techniques outlined above may not be sufficient. If they aren't, try rubbing the brass with extra-fine steel wool (000) or very fine emery cloth. But be careful because you're in abrasive territory now. Rub the metal in one direction only—not with a circular motion. Once the brass is clean, follow up with a commercial brass polish.

Simple solutions

## Getting a sticker off

To remove a sticker from brass, don't attempt to scrape it off—this could damage the finish. Apply methylated spirits or a citrus-oil based product such as Big Kev's Goo Remover, or De-Solv-It, to a soft cloth. Wipe the solvent onto the sticker and let it sit for a few seconds. Then wipe the sticker and its gummy adhesive away. Buff with a clean, soft cloth.

## When life hands you tarnish, use lemons

When a commercial brass cleaner isn't available for removing tarnish from raw brass, you can still get dazzling results with a lemon. Slice a lemon in half, sprinkle the cut surface with salt and then squeeze the lemon over the brass that needs cleaning. Wipe down the brass with one soft cloth and then buff it with a second soft cloth. The technique works equally well with lacquered and raw brass.

An alternative is to make a paste of bicarbonate of soda and water (or just use toothpaste, which is also a mild abrasive). Apply the paste to a soft cloth and then rub the brass. Wipe clean with a fresh cloth.

Once it's clean, rub unlacquered brass with a light coating of paraffin oil, olive oil or lemon oil to protect it from further tarnish. Lacquered brass doesn't need this sort of protection.

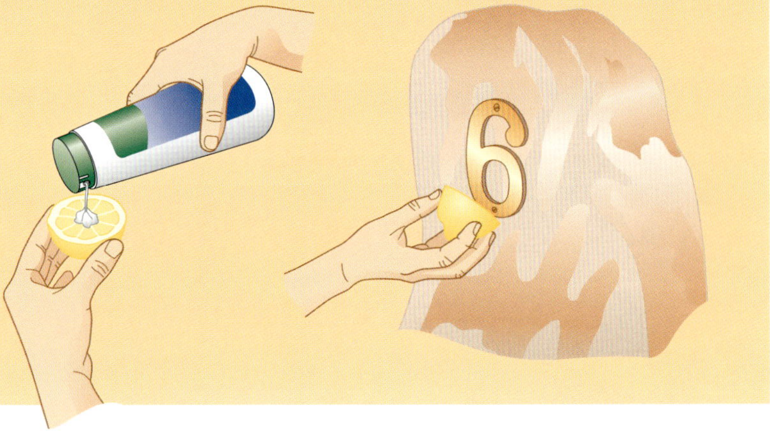

## BRICK

**EXPOSED INTERIOR BRICK** CAN BE CLEANED BY SIMPLY PUTTING THE BRUSH ATTACHMENT ON YOUR VACUUM CLEANER AND RUNNING IT OVER THE WALL. THE BRUSH WILL LOOSEN THE DUST AND DIRT, AND THE VACUUM WILL SUCK IT UP.

**On exterior brick that stays damp and shaded,** mould, mildew and algae are commonly a problem. To kill and remove the growth, mix 30 millilitres of bleach with 1 litre of water in a bucket. If you find you need more strength, increase the bleach. Wearing rubber gloves, dip a stiff-bristled brush (not metal) in the solution and scrub the brick. To rinse, hose the brick down with fresh water.

**For cleaning dingy brick,** some masonry professionals swear by lye, which is another name for caustic soda (sodium hydroxide). This is a chemical used in oven cleaners like Selleys Oven Kleen, or a drain opener like Drano Crystals. These are both extremely harsh substances, so wear rubber gloves, long sleeves and protective goggles. Oven cleaner, which comes in an aerosol container, is easiest to work with. To use, spray on full-strength oven cleaner. Caustic soda and drain opener come in crystallised form. To use, pour 3 tablespoons of crystals into a bucket and add 4 litres of water. (This way you don't have to do any mixing.) Apply the solution with an old rag. Whichever cleaner you are using, let it sit for 15 minutes and follow up with a scrubbing brush. Apply the cleaner again if necessary and scrub once more. Rinse with water.

All you need to clean soot-stained brick is ordinary cola, a general-purpose household cleaner, a bucket of water, and a brush and sponge.

**To brighten soot-stained brick,** try this old masonry trick. Mix 600 millilitres of a cola soft drink (its acid adds cleaning muscle), ½ cup of a household cleaner such as Handy Andy, and 4 litres of water in a bucket. Sponge the solution onto the sooty brick and let it sit for 15 minutes. Scrub with a stiff-bristled brush to loosen the soot. Rinse with a clean sponge and fresh water. (Outside, use a hose.) To make the solution more powerful, add more cola. An alternative is to buy a commercial soot remover from a store that sells fireplace gear, follow the product's instructions and save the cola to quench your thirst on a hot day.

**Simple solutions**

### Cleaning under pressure

A high-pressure hose can work magic in cleaning brick, but be careful—the pressure can damage both mortar and bricks, especially bricks with a sand finish. Use a low setting and keep the nozzle 60 cm from the wall. Aim for the brick, not the mortar.

## BRIEFCASES

**THERE'S NO POINT** CLEANING YOUR SUIT SO THAT YOU LOOK YOUR BEST WHEN THE BRIEFCASE YOU CARRY IS DIRTY. KEEP IT CLEAN INSIDE AND OUT SO THE ARTICLES STORED IN IT STAY CLEAN, TOO.

**To clean the inside,** empty the briefcase and shake it over a rubbish bin to get rid of broken pencil leads, scraps of paper and the grit and grime that accumulate in offices, airports and the boots of cars. Vacuum out everything else, using a hand vacuum cleaner, such as a Dustbuster, or the crevice attachment of a regular vacuum cleaner. Use a spray bottle of water to lightly spray the lining. Pour a little laundry or dishwashing liquid on a small towel and rub lightly on any persistent stains. Immediately wipe the lining with a dry cloth. Don't close the case—allow it to air-dry to prevent it from smelling musty.

**To clean the outside,** use a liquid saddle-soap or put a couple of drops of detergent in a small bowl of warm water. Swirl to create some bubbles. Dip a washer in the water and quickly wipe down the briefcase. If your briefcase has a zipper, take a dry bar of soap and rub it down the zipper. It will clean and lubricate the zipper at the same time. Remove excess soap by wiping with a dry washer.

## BROCADE

**BROCADE ISN'T JUST** A FABRIC. IT'S A COMBINATION OF FABRICS WOVEN INTO A RAISED DESIGN. SO WHEN ATTEMPTING TO CLEAN IT, YOU MUST TAKE INTO CONSIDERATION THE FABRIC CONTENTS OF THE WEAVE. BROCADE CAN BE MADE OF WOOL, COTTON, SILK, SYNTHETIC FIBRE OR ANY COMBINATION OF THESE. THE CLEANING DEPENDS ON THE FIBRE. BUT AN ON-THE-SPOT REMEDY OFTEN DOES THE TRICK.

**Removing a stain from brocade is an inside job.** The first thing to do is remove as much of the stain as possible by lifting it off with a dull-edged knife, such as a bread-and-butter knife (see below). Don't treat the remaining stain from the top, or you'll just work the stain into the fibres. Force the stain out from the back by placing the fabric, stain side down, on an absorbent towel. Soda water will help lift the stain, but if you don't have any, use lukewarm tap water. Pour a bit on a paper towel and dab it on the stain, forcing it onto the towel beneath. Dab a spot, then move to another spot and dab again. Keep dabbing until the stain disappears.

Before you attempt to clean a stain on brocade, first remove as much of the solid element as possible, using a dull-edged knife.

## BRONZE

**ARTISTS WITH SPECIALITY** PAINTS CAN RE-CREATE THE LOOK OF WEATHERED BRONZE IN A FAUX FINISH CALLED VERDIGRIS. BUT IF YOU'RE PATIENT, REAL BRONZE WILL DO THE JOB ALL BY ITSELF. WITH TIME, BRONZE CREATES ITS OWN PROTECTIVE PATINA—A PRETTY, EARTHY GREEN COLOUR. BUT WITH THE NO-COST NATURAL PROCESS, YOU STILL HAVE TO CLEAN IT AND YOU MUST BE CAREFUL TO REMOVE ALL RESIDUE OF WATER. LINGERING MOISTURE AND EVEN PLAIN OLD GRIME CAN DEGRADE BRONZE. IF YOU LOSE A LITTLE OF THE PATINA DURING THE CLEANING PROCESS, DON'T WORRY—IT WILL KEEP COMING BACK TIME AFTER TIME.

**To clean bronze,** remember that, in essence, you're cleaning two different metals at once. Bronze is an alloy that is a combination of copper and any other metal except zinc. Like any decorative surface that is exposed to the environment, bronze can accumulate a layer of film or dust (or dusty film) that needs removing. First, wipe away any loose or surface dirt with a soft cloth, then go at it again with a soft toothbrush to get into difficult crevices and ornamental work.

**For a more thorough cleaning,** carefully wash the bronze with a solution of 1 tablespoon of salt dissolved in 3 litres of water. For the toughest grime, dissolve 1 teaspoon of salt in 1 cup of white vinegar, then add enough flour to make a paste. Let it sit on the bronze for 15 minutes to an hour. Rinse with clean, warm water. Make sure you towel dry the piece thoroughly, because moisture and salt by themselves can degrade the bronze.

### Wipe lightly and carry a soft cloth

You can buy bronze with a factory-finish lacquer, which will protect it from changes in colour as well as corrosion. Never apply a chemical cleanser to lacquered bronze. A weekly swipe with a damp cloth will keep it in good shape. Better still, use a damp microfibre cloth. It removes dirt quickly and effectively and, best of all, you might not have to polish, because the microfibre cloth actually polishes as it cleans.

Lacquer, like lustre, doesn't last forever. If it begins to crack or peel, you will eventually need a fresh coat (a job for a professional metalworker). Otherwise, weather and dampness will creep in and corrode the bronze beneath. Regular dusting with a soft cloth is considered good maintenance. But don't rub too vigorously, especially if there are any decorative projections. Just wipe the bronze over thoroughly.

## BURNS

**IF YOUR CARPET** HAS A BURN MARK RIGHT IN THE MIDDLE OF THE ROOM, DON'T DESPAIR. A LIGHT BURN OR SCORCH MARK CAN SOMETIMES BE COMPLETELY REMOVED BY RUBBING THE AFFECTED AREA WITH PLAIN STEEL WOOL, WHICH WILL LIFT AWAY THE SCORCHED FIBRES.

**For deeper burns,** mix 1 teaspoon of laundry detergent powder in ½ cup of water and use an old toothbrush to rub this gently into the burn. Blot up any excess mixture and sponge again with a damp cloth. More of the stain can be removed by dabbing with a solution of equal parts hydrogen peroxide and water. After cleaning, carefully snip away any remaining charred material with a sharp pair of nail scissors and then allow the area to dry thoroughly.

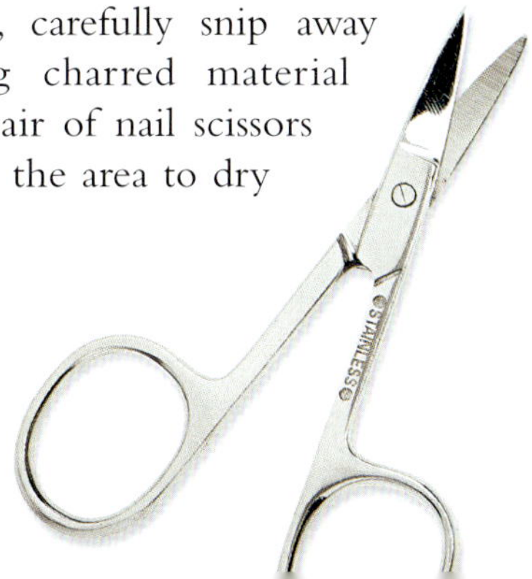

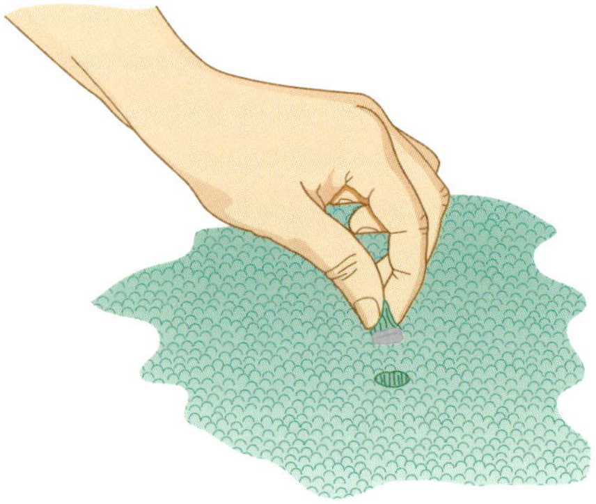

You can remedy a carpet burn, depending on its severity, by snipping off a few fibres elsewhere and then gluing them into the burn hole.

Snip some pile from an unobtrusive area of your carpet or from around the edges. Fill the burn hole with craft glue and stick the threads of carpet in place (see left). Trim to match the pile.

A very large burn area may need to be cut out with a sharp Stanley knife and replaced with a section of matching carpet—a good reason for keeping a few off-cuts when your carpet is laid.

**For burns on upholstery,** you'll have to cross your fingers. If the burn didn't completely penetrate the fabric, you might be able to disguise the scorch mark. Wet a paper towel with plain water and dab it on the burn. Be careful not to rub or you'll damage the fibres further. Blot with a dry paper towel. If that doesn't take most of the charred spot out, put a drop of mild liquid laundry detergent on a wet paper towel and blot the spot. Follow up by blotting with first a wet paper towel to remove the detergent and then with a dry paper towel to absorb the char stain itself.

For more serious charring or burn holes, there's not much you can do beyond patching the fabric, which probably won't look much good. The best advice is to take the furniture to a restorer to discuss whether it would be cost-effective to re-cover the piece.

If your upholstery is fake leather, you may be able to fix burns with a hole-patching kit, available at hardware and automotive shops. This repair will involve spreading a coloured paste over the hole and letting it dry. Follow the instructions on the package.

**With burns on wooden floors and furniture,** there's a little more hope. If the burn isn't all the way through the wood, you might be able to remove enough of the burn to make it less noticeable.

- If the burn is small, use a cotton bud to apply a little mineral turpentine to it. If char remains, rub lightly with some superfine steel wool (0000). If your handiwork leaves a small indentation in the surface, fill it in with clear nail polish. You might need to apply several layers of nail polish to build up the surface until it is level and smooth.
- If the burn is primarily a scorch mark, you might find that a little bit of methylated spirits works a lot of magic. Put a little on a soft cloth and dab it on the scorched area. It will dry quickly, but wipe away any residual moisture. Repeat the process until you are satisfied. If you don't have methylated spirits on hand, sprinkle lots of dry bicarbonate of soda on a wet sponge and then rub in small circular motions until the char disappears.
- If it's burned beyond a scorch but not too deeply into the surface, you might do a cosmetic fix using a thin paste of cigarette ash mixed with a little paraffin oil. With a soft cloth, gently rub in the direction of the grain. Do that twice, then follow up with coats of clear nail polish, as you would for a small burn or a scorch mark.

**WATCH OUT**

Attempting to fix a small burn on a wooden surface is probably within the realm of do-it-yourself jobs, but anything larger is not. Nail polish is OK for small, relatively inconspicuous burn marks, but it's not going to do the trick on a larger burn or on a surface that's in constant use. As always, if in doubt, contact a professional for advice.

# BUTTONS

**BEFORE BEGINNING, MAKE** SURE YOU KNOW WHAT YOUR BUTTONS ARE MADE OF. YOU DON'T WANT TO PUT STRONG METAL POLISH ON BUTTONS WITH A GOLD OR SILVER FINISH. AND YOU NEVER WANT TO USE SHOE POLISH ON BUTTONS—BODY HEAT COULD TRANSFER THE POLISH TO THE GARMENT. IF YOUR BUTTONS ARE COVERED WITH THE SAME FABRIC AS THE GARMENT, OR THEY'RE PLASTIC, CARE FOR THE BUTTONS THE SAME WAY YOU WOULD THE GARMENT.

**To clean leather buttons,** remove them from the garment. While a woollen jumper might make it through a machine wash, leather and some other natural button materials won't. Saddle-soap or a leather cleaning and conditioning solution with lanolin, such as mink oil, will clean leather or leather-covered buttons beautifully. But don't wash it off. Let it dry and then buff to a shine with a soft cloth (see below).

The safest way to clean leather buttons is to first remove them from the garment they're sewn on.

**To clean wooden buttons,** remove them from the garment and use a gentle wood oil cleanser, such as Howard Orange Oil Cleaner or Pledge with orange oil. Follow the instructions on the container. The buttons will absorb most of the wood oil. Remove any residue with a soft cloth.

**To clean bone or ivory buttons,** remove them from the garment. Mix a small amount of lemon juice with enough salt to make a paste. Lightly brush it on with a soft toothbrush and then wipe the buttons clean with a damp cloth.

**To clean buttons made of horn,** dampen a soft cloth with a small amount of mineral oil or baby oil. Rub to remove stains, then wipe with a dry cloth. Do not immerse horn buttons in water.

**To clean metal buttons,** you can try the age-old remedy of tooth-paste, but make sure it's natural, or one that doesn't have chemicals that wear down surfaces. (Avoid anything that boasts 'tartar control' or 'whitening'.) An alternative is to dissolve 1 teaspoon of non-iodised salt in a litre of water. (Iodised salt can cause discolouration.) Dampen a soft cloth in the salt solution and polish the surface. Rinse well with water. Then polish with a soft, dry cloth.



## How they button up at sea

Because boats have lots of rubber affixed to them, sailors know how to keep the stuff clean. A good thing to try on rubber buttons is glycerine. (You can buy a small bottle from a supermarket or pharmacy.) Just rub the glycerine into the buttons with a towel. They'll come clean, and they'll repel water and dirt for a long time to come.

## CALCULATORS

**MOST CALCULATORS SIT** ON THE DESKTOP WHERE THEY COLLECT DUST AND DIRT. ALL KEYBOARDS NEED TO BE CLEANED REGULARLY AND A CALCULATOR IS NO EXCEPTION. WHEN YOU CLEAN YOUR COMPUTER KEYBOARD, DO THE CALCULATOR AT THE SAME TIME.

**To clean a calculator,** first disconnect any electrical cord and move it out of the way. Then thoroughly dust both sides of the calculator with an eye-shadow brush, being careful to brush away lint and accumulated dust or dirt. If your calculator is completely fuzzy with lint, brush it off with a soft, dry toothbrush.

**Keeping the keys clean** can be difficult. Because fingers transfer all kinds of gunk, such as newspaper ink and sticky sugar, the keys are like magnets for lint and dirt. To get rid of anything that doesn't belong, dip a cotton bud into a small amount of methylated spirits and gently wipe it away (see below). Press the bud onto a paper towel to eliminate excess liquid. (Otherwise, who knows what kind of calculations you'll might come up with!) Swab each key lightly. For the bigger surfaces, such as the back of the calculator, you can use a cotton wool ball, dipped in methylated spirits, to get rid of unsightly dirt.

Clean the keypad on a calculator with a cotton bud dipped in methylated spirits.

## CAMCORDERS

**MOST CAMERA PROFESSIONALS** WILL TELL YOU NOT TO CLEAN YOUR OWN CAMCORDER. THERE ARE TOO MANY LITTLE PARTS THAT ARE EASILY DAMAGED. IF YOU DO AND SOMETHING GOES WRONG, THE CAMERA REPAIR SHOP MAY NOT TAKE RESPONSIBILITY FOR ANY SUBSEQUENT PROBLEMS. BUT THERE ARE TIMES WHEN IT MAKES GOOD SENSE TO CLEAN IT—WHEN A DRINK GETS SPILLED ON IT, FOR INSTANCE.

**Treat outdoor exposure** to salt, moisture or dirt as soon as you can. Reporters who cover extreme weather, such as cyclones, know how quickly exposure to the elements, especially to salt, erodes and rusts a camera and its workings. Although you don't want to go inside the camera to clean it, you can do what the reporters do: dampen a clean, soft cloth or towel with methylated spirits and wipe the surfaces thoroughly. You don't want the cloth to be saturated—just damp enough to remove that fresh coat of gunk or grime. Make sure that the dock where you load the cassette tape stays closed.

**When cleaning a lens,** it's best not to touch it or a viewfinder with anything other than lens tissue, which is inexpensive and available from anywhere that sells camera equipment. Household facial tissues frequently contain additives, such as lanolin, that you don't want on the lens. The only other acceptable alternative is to use a soft, natural-bristled brush (an artist's brush or a make-up brush). If you use the brush, make sure it's new. Even brushes that have been washed can contain residue that you don't want to transfer to your lens and viewfinder.

**To clean the heads in a camcorder,** go to the shop where you bought your camcorder and pick up a dry-cleaning tape that is compatible with your camera (see below left). All you have to do is load the tape, press *Play* and let it run for the recommended length of time.

Simple solutions

### Clean tapes equals a clean machine

As a precaution, keep your tapes dust free. Since it's better not to clean your camcorder at home, you can stretch the time between professional cleanings by storing your tapes in a box. When a tape sits out unsheathed, dust gets into the grooves. Then, when you load it into the camera, it introduces dust to the inside of the camera. A plastic case or a cardboard box will help to keep your tapes dust free.

## CAMEOS

**THE INTRICATE CARVINGS** AND GROOVES THAT MAKE CAMEOS SO CHARMING PROVIDE HANDY HIDING PLACES FOR GRIME THAT CAN DULL THEIR BEAUTY. CAMEOS ARE MADE OF CORAL, RESIN, CERTAIN STONES AND, MOST COMMONLY, CERTAIN SEASHELLS. DIFFERENT COLOURED LAYERS PROVIDE THE CHARACTERISTIC CONTRAST BETWEEN THE RELIEF CARVING AND ITS BACKGROUND. THESE MATERIALS ARE DELICATE, AND THEY NEED PROTECTION FROM DIRT AND DRYNESS.

**Cleaning a cameo** is straightforward, no matter how complex the design. A quick dusting periodically with a soft-bristled brush will help keep particles from settling into crevices. The brushing may be followed by rinsing with warm water and drying with a soft, lint-free cloth.

Give a cameo a soapy bath about twice a year, but never use a harsh cleaner. Put a few drops of mild dishwashing liquid or a gentle washing detergent, such as Softly, into a bowl with about 2 cups of warm water. Swish the cameo around, wet a soft toothbrush and scrub gently. Never let cameos soak, because soaking could damage the shell. After the soapy bath, rinse the cameo in warm water and dry it with a soft cloth.

**Moisturise a cameo** after it's been washed. A cameo that is too dry may become cracked or chipped. Use a fine oil, such as olive oil, paraffin oil or baby oil—or follow the old-fashioned practice of using oil of wintergreen, available in pharmacies and shops that sell essential oils, to give your cameo a fresh and surprising scent. Use a cotton bud to apply a tiny bit of oil to the surface of the cameo. Let it sit overnight, then wipe off any oil you can still see with a clean, soft cloth. Store cameos in a soft cloth or lined box away from heat and light. Wipe gently with a soft, dry cloth in between cleanings, to remove dust and keep the cameo looking its best.

# CAMERAS

**CAMERAS ARE COMPACT** BUNDLES OF EXTREMELY DELICATE PARTS AND CLEANING THEM WITHOUT DOING DAMAGE IN THE PROCESS CAN BE A DAUNTING TASK. WHAT YOU USE TO CLEAN THEM IS ALSO SOMEWHAT CONTROVERSIAL. IF YOU WANT ENDLESS DISCUSSIONS OF THE PROS AND CONS OF EVERY KNOWN CAMERA CLEANING PRODUCT, YOU CAN FIND THEM ON THE INTERNET. SEARCH UNDER THE NAME OF YOUR CAMERA AS WELL AS THE NAME OF THE PRODUCT YOU'RE INTERESTED IN.

A magnifying glass helps spot dust and dirt on your lens. Remove it by using a lens-cleaning pen, canned air or a lens-cleaning cloth.

**To clean a camera lens,** first examine it with a magnifying glass (see left). Any kind of foreign material, including stuff you can't see with the naked eye, will mar your photographs and may damage your lens.

To get rid of dust or dirt on the lens, start with air. Camera shops sell blower brushes, which, as the name suggests, combine a brush with a blower. The blower on most of these brushes, however, is actually ineffective. A bulb syringe, which you can get at any pharmacy, is a better alternative. Still more effective is a can of compressed air. Also known as 'canned air', it's an aerosol can containing air under pressure and a nozzle extension. Some people say canned air issues too big a blast, but it is widely used. Canned air is available from shops that sell photo supplies, computers or electronics.

If your lens is removable, check the back end occasionally and clean it in the same way as the front.

**To remove persistent specks** that don't respond to the air treatment, brush them away with a blower brush or soft watercolour paintbrush. You can also use a cleaning cloth. But you don't want to move specks around, as that will only damage the lens or its coatings. So take care in choosing a cloth. The best is a microfibre lens-cleaning cloth,

Simple solutions

## Keep it clicking

Some precautions will help to keep your camera clean and functioning at its optimum level:

- Protect the lens with an ultraviolet filter (even if you remove it for picture taking) and lens cap. With many new cameras, you can't lose the lens cap because it just slides aside. But you still have to close it after use.
- Don't store a camera where it will be exposed to direct sunlight, high humidity, rapid changes in temperature (which may cause condensation), or temperature extremes.
- Wipe off the batteries and the contact points in the battery chambers before inserting new batteries, to help prevent corrosion.
- Consult your owner's manual for hints about preventive maintenance and specific information about your particular brand and model.

## Keep it simple, and everything will click

The best advice for the amateur photographer is simple: don't clean it—keep it clean. That means don't do unnecessary things to the camera. Most experts agree that more lenses are destroyed by cleaning than anything else. Overpolishing a lens is a completely unnecessary thing to do. More cameras are thrown away because they're dirty than because they're broken.

Use special lens-cleaning fluids and cleaning cloths on the lens and treat the leather parts with neat's-foot oil and a rag dabbed with silicone spray.

If you look at the lens with a magnifying glass and see 'hairy things', it's mouldy. Wipe the lens with a rag dipped in a 50:50 mixture of ammonia and hydrogen peroxide or, better still, take it straight to a professional.

which can also be used on the body of the camera and can be washed and reused. These cloths trap particles among their fibres rather than on the surface, and are available from camera shops. If you can't lay your hands on a lens-cleaning cloth, go to plan B: lens tissues, also available at camera shops.

**To remove fingerprints** or really persistent specks, you may need to use lens-cleaning fluid. There are many types on the market. Check your owner's manual for recommendations. If your camera has a plastic lens, make sure the lens cleaner you buy is suitable for plastic as well as glass. Use a few drops of lens-cleaning fluid on a microfibre cloth—never directly on the lens—and clean the lens with a light, circular motion. Fingerprints should be cleaned off immediately in this way. If they are left for a long time, fingerprints can actually etch themselves into the glass.

Fingerprints are finger food for glass mould—a type that doesn't need as much moisture as most other moulds need. The mould will also feed on dust, and it can destroy the surface of a lens. Using your camera in the sunshine every so often will usually be enough to prevent glass mould. If you aren't going to be using your camera for a while, take it out of the case to prevent a build-up of moisture that could lead to mould.

**To clean inside the camera,** use compressed air and a soft watercolour brush to banish dirt from the film chamber, followed by a gentle wiping with a microfibre cloth. And don't forget the inside of the lens cap and the inside of your camera bag.

**When cleaning a digital camera,** unplug it before you start. One new product, a lens pen, combines a retractable brush on one end with a cleaning tip on the other. There are various models on the market at camera shops. They are especially recommended for digital cameras.

*See also:*
• CAMCORDERS

## CAN-OPENERS

**POISONED BY YOUR** CAN-OPENER? DON'T LAUGH, IT CAN HAPPEN. WHEN YOU CONSIDER THE MIXTURE OF CANNED SOUP, TUNA AND PET FOOD THAT COMES INTO CONTACT WITH A CAN-OPENER, ITS POTENTIAL TOXICITY ISN'T SURPRISING. THEY HAVE BEEN SHOWN TO CAUSE FOOD POISONING, SKIN INFECTIONS AND PNEUMONIA. MAKE IT A HABIT TO WASH THE BLADES ON YOUR CAN-OPENER AFTER EACH USE.

**Cleaning a hand-held can-opener** is easy. Just wash it with all the other dishes, either by hand or in a dishwasher.

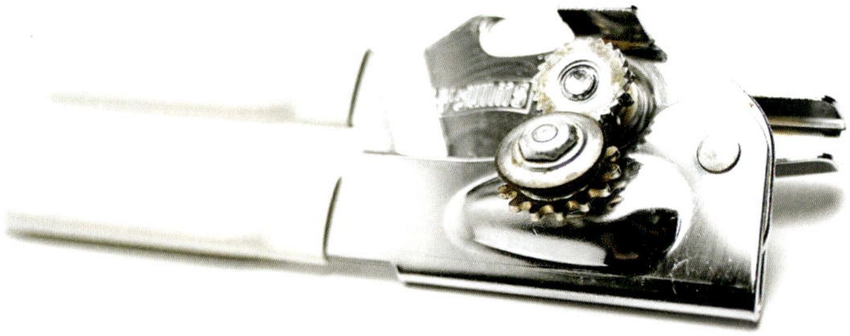

**Cleaning an electric can-opener** is also simple, because most have blades or cutting assemblies designed to be removed and washed with the dishes. Older models may not have detachable blades. In that case, clean the cutting parts, being careful not to cut yourself, with a cloth dampened with water and a little dishwashing liquid. If you're dealing with accumulated black gunk, scrub it with an old toothbrush. Regular cleaning thereafter will keep the machine clean. To clean the machine's body, wipe it with a damp cloth with the unit unplugged. Never immerse an electric can-opener in water.

## CANDLESTICKS AND CANDELABRA

**THE EASIEST WAY** TO CLEAN WAX FROM CANDLESTICKS IS TO WIPE THE WAX OFF WHILE THE DRIPS ARE STILL WARM AND SOFT, TAKING CARE NOT TO BURN YOURSELF IN THE PROCESS.

**To remove hardened wax,** try this general-purpose method. First, remove all you can with your fingers or with assistance from a soft wooden stick, such as a paddle-pop stick. You can also use a hair dryer or warm water to soften the wax as you work (see below). Never use a knife or other metal object. When you've removed all you can, clean the waxy residue with white spirits or mineral turpentine, available from

Use a hair dryer to soften wax while you work to remove it from a candle holder with a paddle-pop stick.

**WATCH OUT** When cleaning a candle holder, remember that white spirits or mineral turpentine aren't suitable for painted or gilded surfaces—they might remove the finish. They could also destroy the lacquer that covers some metals. Do a test patch first on an inconspicuous area, such as inside the candle holder itself.

*See also:*
• BRASS • COPPER • SILVERWARE

hardware and paint shops (see 'Watch out' box, at left). Dab it onto a soft cloth and rub the waxy spots until they're gone. Then polish the candlesticks with pantihose and finish according to the instructions for the material the candlesticks are made of.

**Don't put it in the fridge.** One recommendation that's been around for years is to remove hardened wax by first putting candlesticks in the freezer. The cold will make the wax brittle and easier to remove by breaking it off. However, experts usually advise against doing this because freezing could actually break your candlesticks. Some are made from two or more kinds of metal, which could expand and contract at different rates.

But the candles themselves are a different story. If you stash candles in cold storage for a couple of hours before using them, they'll burn more slowly and there'll be less dripping. That'll mean less mess for you to clean up and if you're using a tablecloth, it'll be spared.

## CANING

**USED ON ANTIQUE** AND CONTEMPORARY CHAIRS, FOOTSTOOLS AND OTHER SMALL FURNITURE PIECES, CANING IS MADE OF WOVEN BAMBOO OR REEDS. HISTORICALLY, IT WAS OFTEN INTENDED TO SUPPORT CUSHIONS, WHICH ALSO HELPED PROTECT IT. CUSHIONING IS STILL A GOOD IDEA.

**To clean caning,** use the brush attachment of a vacuum cleaner regularly to suck out loose dirt, or dust it with a small brush, such as a paintbrush. To wash dirtier caning, squirt some mild dishwashing liquid in water and then dip a sponge, cloth, or medium- or stiff-bristled brush in and apply it to the caning (see below). Rinse with clear water and dry thoroughly with a towel or soft cloth. Don't use harsh detergents or cleaners.

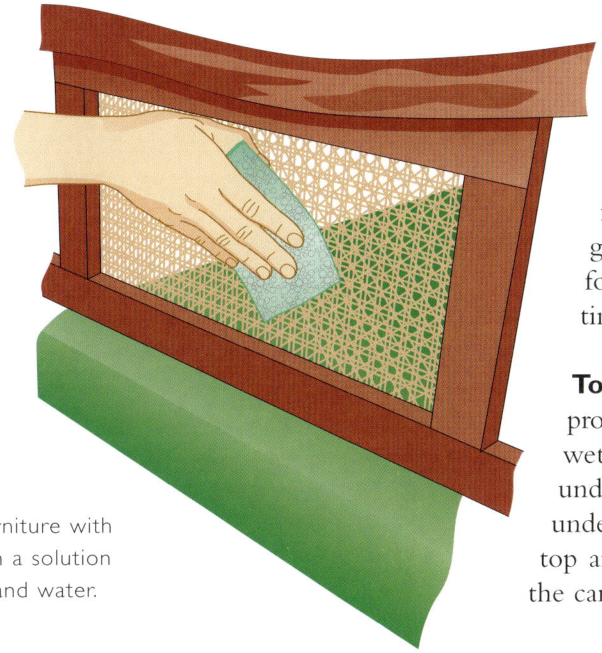

Clean caning on furniture with a sponge moistened in a solution of dishwashing liquid and water.

**To prevent stains on caning,** clean up any spills promptly with a wet cloth or soap and water. A stain may be impossible to remove. If you do get a stain, your best bet is to follow the lead of some old-timers and paint the cane.

**To fix a sagging cane seat,** provided the material isn't broken, wet the seat thoroughly from underneath with a sponge. The underside is more porous than the top and will absorb better. Then let the caning dry in the sun.

# CARPETS

**FOR ROUTINE CARPET** CLEANING, CARPET EXPERTS SAY THERE ARE THREE THINGS TO CONSIDER: VACUUM CLEANER, VACUUM CLEANER, VACUUM CLEANER. VACUUMING REMOVES ABOUT 85 PER CENT OF CARPET DIRT, SO TO GET DOWN TO THE DEEPER DIRT, YOU NEED TO PERIODICALLY GIVE YOUR CARPET A MORE THOROUGH CLEANING THAN A VACUUM CLEANER CAN PROVIDE. HOW OFTEN DEPENDS ON YOUR LIFESTYLE, BUT THE RECOMMENDED RANGE IS EVERY 6–18 MONTHS.

**Vacuuming your carpet** every day would be ideal, but we don't live like people did in 1950s TV commercials, where women seemed to spend most of their days doing housework—in high heels, no less. Let's face it, daily vacuuming is unrealistic for most households today. But it's worth making a point of vacuuming your carpet at least once a week, even if it doesn't look dirty on the surface. And heavily trafficked areas should be targeted more often than that. Make sure to vacuum up any obvious soiling straight away, before it gets ground in.

For vacuuming your carpet, the more powerful your machine is, the better. You can use either an upright vacuum, which was created with carpets in mind, or a canister vacuum with a power nozzle, which does almost as good a job as an upright. Both of these have a rotary brush, designed to loosen the dirt in carpets.

## EXPERT ADVICE

### GET WITH THE PROGRAM

Here are a few basic pointers for trouble-free vacuuming:

- Set your vacuum to the correct pile level of the carpet.
- Use slow, even strokes and go back and forth several times on each area, working against the grain. Finish with strokes in one direction.
- Vacuum under heavy furniture as best you can, and about twice a year move the furniture and give the area under it a good going over.
- Vacuum the underside of rugs occasionally.
- If you can't suck up pet hair, threads or other fine items, use a lint roller or a piece of doubled-over sticky tape to pick them up.
- New carpeting produces a lot of fluff, which is completely normal.

Vacuum the underside of rugs occasionally, too, to prevent a build-up of dust and other allergens.

**Professional steam cleaning** is the ideal way of removing deep down dirt from your carpet. There are several types of professional carpet-cleaning methods, but the Rolls Royce of them all is hot water extraction, or steam cleaning, done using a truck-mounted unit.

If you call in the pros, make sure that's really what you're getting. There is no shortage of glorified do-it-yourselfers pretending to be professionals. If you follow the suggestions in the 'How to choose a pro' box on the page opposite, you won't get any nasty surprises when they show up at the door. They'll swoop in with a truck, get the job done quickly and be out of your way. The truck's purpose isn't to impress you, but to hold powerful equipment. One piece is a heating unit that keeps the water very hot throughout the cleaning process. Another is a very powerful vacuum, which will suck up all the water that the cleaner puts down.

**If you steam clean carpeting yourself,** the results won't be as good as a professional job. But let's say you just don't want to fork out for the professional job. Maybe your carpet is old and you're going to replace it in a couple of years, but in the meantime you want to spruce it up with a do-it-yourself steam-cleaning job. In that case, the most economical solution is to rent the most powerful steam-cleaning machine you can find (see below left). At the same time, rent a shop vacuum that will suck up water as well as solids. Follow the instructions on the cleaning machine, and change the water often. At the end, go over the carpet with the shop vacuum and draw out as much additional water as you can. Get as much air circulation as possible in the room and don't walk on the carpet until it's completely dry.

If using a rental steam-cleaning unit persuades you that do-it-yourself cleaning is the way to go, and expense is no barrier, research owning your own deep-cleaning unit. Home machines are about the size and shape of upright vacuum cleaners. While they aren't as powerful as the professional or rental cleaners, some of the newest home machines do an adequate job.

Steam-cleaning units can be hired from a rental shop. Check listings in your local telephone directory.

## How to choose a pro

If you're prepared to go to the expense of hiring a professional to clean your carpets, make sure you get a good one. Here's how you can evaluate cleaning companies:

- Be sure the cleaner uses the water-extraction or steam-cleaning method supported by a truck-based unit.
- Ask what training the cleaner has had. Cleaning carpets does require some experience, believe it or not.
- Choose a cleaner with a professional certification, such as membership of the Australasian Carpet Cleaning Institute—all their members must carry photo ID. Another good sign is active membership in trade organisations.
- Expect the cleaner to inspect the job beforehand to make an adequate evaluation of the condition of your carpet and the type of fibre it is made of.
- Ask for a cost estimate in advance—in writing and itemised. (A good professional should provide it without being asked.) With a written estimate, you'll know what is covered, and you won't be surprised by extra charges. You can save money by doing a thorough vacuuming before the cleaner arrives and by moving the furniture yourself, but make sure the estimate reflects the tasks that you, rather than the professional, will be doing.
- Examine the guarantee carefully.
- Ask anyone you know that has had their carpets cleaned by that company if they were satisfied with the result.
- Check that the cleaner is insured.

**Three carpet-cleaning methods to avoid** at all costs are listed below. You may be tempted to save money by trying one of them—either doing it yourself or hiring a professional. But if you do, be prepared to be disappointed:

- Shampooing uses a machine with a very aggressive brush and a cleaner mixed with water applied to the carpet. The brush doesn't pick up any dirt. It swirls everything around to create a foam. The idea is to let that dry and vacuum up the crystals. It is not effective.
- Spin bonnet cleaning adapts floor-buffing techniques to carpets. A 'bonnet', or round absorbent pad, is dipped into the cleaning solution and wrung out, then attached to a machine that spins it around. The bonnet is supposed to be removed and cleaned or changed when it is visibly dirty. But it cleans only the top of the carpeting. It grinds in dirt, creates soil and detergent build-up and can damage the fibres and pile.
- Dry-cleaning is touted as an alternative method that won't cause overwatering of carpets. It uses an absorbent granular material, which is laced with a solvent. It is distributed over the carpet and brushed in, left to absorb soil, and then vacuumed up. The trouble is, it isn't very effective, and the solvent evaporates in the air, polluting your home.

**Removing spots on carpeting** is something you have to expect to do yourself, because onto every carpet a little wine must fall. Or barbecue sauce. Or animal poo. And chances are that you can't afford

## What's your carpet made of?

How carpet responds to dirt and your efforts to eradicate it depends on the material of the carpet and the dirt.

Unfortunately, most people have no clue about the materials their carpets are made of, unless the carpet is wool. Wool is the most expensive and it's usually chosen by people who specifically want wool carpet, so when people choose other fibres it's usually because of the look and price of the carpet, not because of what they want from the fibre.

If you're serious about owning high-quality carpet and keeping it clean, know your fibres and consider fibre when buying. There are two basic categories: natural and synthetic.

Synthetic fibres include nylon, olefin or polypropylene, acrylic, blends of those materials and also carpet made from recycled plastic soft-drink bottles (polyethylene terephthalate [PET], if you're interested in the full name).

- Nylon is the best of the synthetic materials. It is the toughest, and it resists soil and stains quite well. If the fibres get compressed by a heavy object sitting on them, they can be revived with steam.
- Polypropylene (Olefin) is cheaper and is also quite stain resistant. It is the only carpet material that can sometimes accept bleach. Its chief disadvantages are that the fibres crush easily and it will scar when exposed to flame.
- Acrylic is also relatively inexpensive and resembles nylon in some ways. But it is not as strong and is unsuitable for high-traffic areas. And it is susceptible to pilling and fuzzing.
- Blends have characteristics of their components, but since those components react differently to stains, removing stains may be more difficult.
- Recycled-bottle carpet resembles nylon and polypropylene and has similar stain-resistant properties.
- Wool is durable, flame resistant, antistatic, naturally resistant to stains and dirt, and more expensive than synthetics.
- Sisal, hemp, jute and seagrass are all natural fibres made from plants, and they come in a wide variety of weaves and prices. Plant-based materials are more likely to be found in rugs than in wall-to-wall carpeting. These carpets will not stand up to shampooing or steam cleaning. Use as little liquid as possible when treating stains on them.

## rules of the game

WHAT WOULD HIPPOCRATES DO?

When confronted with a spill on your carpet, remember Hippocrates' famous commandment to physicians: first, do no harm. If your first instinct is to grab a sponge and rub the spot, suppress the urge. Rubbing will only grind the spill more deeply into the carpet fibres. While treatment of spills will vary with the carpet material and the substance spilled, here are a few principles that apply to all:

- Scoop up any solids and use something absorbent to soak up any liquid that hasn't sunk in yet.
- After you've absorbed everything you can, blot the spot with white towels or rags. Work from the outside in so you won't spread the stain.
- When you've blotted up all you can, use water to dilute what remains, and then continue to blot the stain.
- If that doesn't complete the job, proceed to a low-tech cleaner. If that doesn't work, call in the professionals. Many amateurs do harm by using harsh, ineffective cleaners.

to call in the professional cleaners every time someone tips their gin and tonic on your carpet. So it pays to learn how to mop up the little messes in between deep cleanings.

The techniques for attacking stains are as varied as the stains themselves. The approach you use depends in part on how much you value your carpet. If your carpet is old and beaten up, you can afford to be daring. If it's brand-new, of high quality and carpeting you want to have for many years, be more cautious.

**Here's a pyramid** to help you decide which spot-removal technique to use. Choosing a spot-removing strategy is a bit like picking foods from the food pyramid. On the food pyramid, you're supposed to eat a lot of the foods depicted at the bottom (fruits, vegetables and grains) and eat the stuff at the top (fats, sugars and oils) sparingly. On the stain-removal pyramid the broad bottom part includes that most gentle and universal of cleaning substances—water. The higher you go on this pyramid, the more extreme the treatment and the less of it you should use.

Before we examine each step in the pyramid, there are a few basics to remember: stain removal usually requires tenacious blotting. (See the instructions in the 'Rules of the game' box, above.) Be sure to blot, not rub. Before moving on from one step in the pyramid to the next, test the next solution on an inconspicuous area of carpet. Put a little

Simple solutions

## Keep salt on the table

So you're celebrating your home renovation. Wouldn't you know it, someone has spilled wine on that brand new beige carpet. And it's red wine, too. Popular tradition suggests throwing salt on red wine, but professional carpet cleaners do not recommend this. Instead, blot the wine with paper towels or a dry cloth, then sprinkle the stain with (wait for it!) white wine. Blot again, then remove the remaining stain with a clean cloth and methylated spirits.

bit of the treatment on the carpet, let it sit for about 10 minutes, and then blot with a clean, white rag. Inspect the rag for any dye from the carpet, and inspect the carpet for any damage from the cleaner. If either occurs, the solution isn't really a solution; it's another problem. In the case of wool fibre, if it doesn't respond to water and the mild soap solution, you should call a professional.

**Everyday situations** require everyday solutions. Here are some techniques to try, in order, as you go up the stain-removal pyramid. Remember to blot, not rub. Use these techniques only one at a time, and rinse well between steps.

- After you've cleaned everything you can by blotting, dilute what remains with water and blot some more. You can also dilute spills with plain soda water (unflavoured). The fizziness and salts it contains will sometimes help it work better than water, and it's just about as safe.
- If after water and soda water treatment you still have a stain, here is a safe, simple, general-purpose spot-cleaner to try. Mix 1 teaspoon of a mild dishwashing liquid with 1 cup of warm water. Blot it on the spot. Be sure to rinse thoroughly, because getting cleaning chemicals out is important, too.
- Try a solution of 1 tablespoon of ammonia and ½ cup of water on old spots, blood and chocolate.
- Try a solution of ½ cup of white vinegar and 1 cup of water on mildew stains and spills with an odour, such as urine.
- Try full-strength 3 per cent hydrogen peroxide on tomato-based stains, red drinks, alcoholic drinks, fruit juice, grass stains, coffee and also chocolate stains.
- Use methylated spirits—full strength—on oily stains, ballpoint pen ink, candle-wax residue and grass stains.

**Special situations** may call for special removal techniques:

- For oily spills, such as mayonnaise, salad dressing and butter, try saturating the spot with cornflour, which is a good absorbent. Allow it to dry, then vacuum it up.
- For candle wax dripped onto your carpet, use a warm iron over a paper towel to take up as much wax as possible. Then dab methylated spirits on to the spot where the wax was. If there's still a stain, go to the general-purpose spot-cleaner (see under 'Everyday situations', above).
- Pet 'accidents' produce odours as well as stains, and the problem is compounded when urine is not detected immediately. The longer it stays, the worse it gets. First, flush the spot with water and blot with an old towel or rag. Then use the general-purpose spot treatment described above. Rinse that with the vinegar mixture (see under 'Everyday situations', above). Rinse again with water and blot. Finally,

apply a 1-centimetre-thick layer of dry, clean white rags, towels or paper towels, weight them with a heavy object, and allow them to sit for several hours. If they're still damp when you remove them, repeat with a fresh layer of absorbent materials until they come up dry. (This is also a good formula for treating beer spills.) The odour will not come out as long as any urine remains. Most commercial products sold to eliminate odour just mask the smell temporarily.

**WATCH OUT** Steam cleaning is an obvious choice for removing a stubborn carpet stain or giving your carpet a makeover, but it's not a suitable treatment for all carpet fibres. The steam removes dirt and grime, but it also removes the natural oils in wool. And woollen carpet undergoes shrinkage, just like all other woollen products, which means it can pull away from the wall after steam cleaning. Check with the manufacturer how often you can safely steam clean your carpet.

## For spills, pick up the phone

When you get a spill on your carpet and you're tempted to reach for one of those commercial spot-treatment products, try the phone instead. About 90 per cent of the time when a professional carpet cleaner is called in to treat really bad spots, such spot-cleaning products have made them worse.

Blot up what you can from a spill, dilute the residue with water and continue to blot. Beyond that, seek advice before using any kind of cleaner. If you know the kind of fibre your carpet is made of, so much the better.

Use your business phone directory to call a professional cleaner in your area. Professionals are usually happy to offer advice on spot-cleaning.

- If carpet has a musty smell, bicarbonate of soda will help. If you've been removing spots from the carpet, let the carpet dry out completely first. Then sprinkle bicarbonate of soda over the entire carpet, let it sit for 3–5 hours and then vacuum it up (see left).
- Not all substances can be removed from carpeting. Chlorine bleach, iodine, mustard, insecticides and plant fertilisers, just to name a few, are likely to create permanent stains. Many foods, beverages, medications and cosmetics contain dye, and their spots also may be permanent. Sometimes a professional restorer can fix a permanently damaged area by spot-dyeing, reweaving or retufting. Or a professional installer can replace a section of stained or damaged carpet using a scrap or a piece taken from an inconspicuous spot, such as your wardrobe floor.
- Loose sections of pile and small black dropping marks might indicate the presence of carpet beetle, which can do untold damage if left unchecked. If you suspect you have a carpet beetle infestation, you should call in a professional. If the damage is minimal, you can treat the infestation yourself by spraying or dusting an insecticide, such as permethrin, onto the affected areas.

A liberal sprinkling of bicarbonate of soda, followed by vacuuming, is an effective method for removing musty or unpleasant smells in carpeting.

# CARS

**FOR MOST OF** US, CARS ARE OUR SECOND MOST EXPENSIVE POSSESSION, AND REGULAR CLEANING HELPS TO MAINTAIN THE CAR'S VALUE. MODERN CAR FINISHES ARE PRETTY DELICATE: OVER THE PRIMER IS A SINGLE LAYER OF WATERBORNE ACRYLIC PAINT WITH PIGMENT AND THEN SEVERAL LAYERS OF PAINT WITH NO PIGMENT, CALLED CLEARCOAT, WHICH ADDS DEPTH AND BRIGHTNESS TO THE COLOUR.

**You need to maintain a clean surface** and a solid layer of wax to help protect the car metal from corrosive elements because the clearcoat's total coverage is no more than 5 millimetres thick. Interior surfaces need regular TLC, too. Ideally you should wash your car every 10 days and wax it every 6 months.

**Choosing a car washing site** is the first step. The weather has at last cleared and you're ready to give your car a much-needed clean. However, be careful not to wash your car in full sunlight. Sunshine is a car washer's enemy. You get water spots more readily on the clearcoat. The heated metal dries soap into a film before you can rinse it off, and your wax crusts into hard-to-wipe streaks.

So park it under a shady tree? Careful there, too, since debris falling from the tree can cause other headaches. (Imagine a fingernails-on-chalkboard squeak as you unwittingly scrub twig bits across the paint, or a rain of yellow pollen.) You may also experience two more enemies of car washing—bird droppings and tree sap. (Always wipe bird droppings off as soon as possible. However, it may take a specialised solvent to remove tree sap.) Better choices are a carport, a garage with good ventilation and drainage or, best of all, a shady grassed area not directly under a tree or too near a stormwater drain. Any run-off will soak into the soil and not end up as polluted stormwater in the local river, creek or stream. Another alternative is a coin-operated car wash bay.

Make sure you have a good 4 hours to devote to the process. Take off your watch and any belt buckle or jewellery that might scratch the car. It's now time to round up your tools and supplies.

**Selecting the right cleaner** is very important. All car experts are emphatic on this point: dishwashing liquid is only for dishes. Used on a car, it can do more harm than good. Its detergent can thin the vehicle's protective layer of wax or, if the finish is worn, it can even scratch or further break down the paint. So instead of the desired result of shiny-and-sparkly, you get dull-and-scratchy.

You'll find non-detergent car cleaners in supermarkets, and hardware and automotive shops. Avoid those that promise a shine, because they are more than likely to contain silicone, which can streak your paint finish and result in glare off shiny interior surfaces. Mix the cleaner according to label instructions for the exterior and in a diluted mix for interior surfaces (2–3 drops per litre). Look for established brand names or ask for advice before you buy.

**Selecting cleaning rags** is a matter of personal choice, but a universal favourite

## Go slow on the $H_2O$

These days, we all know that water is a valuable and scarce resource and that we all have a responsibility to conserve water. If you live in an area with water restrictions or you don't want to use a hose to wash your car, buy a watering can with a sprinkle head. It takes longer to wash your car but it's very effective, and economical with water. And if your car is only moderately dirty, consider using one of the new no-water alternatives, such as Meguiar's Quik Detailer, Microwipe Dust Magnet or a Kenco Shift-it microfibre, to remove light dirt and grime without scratching.

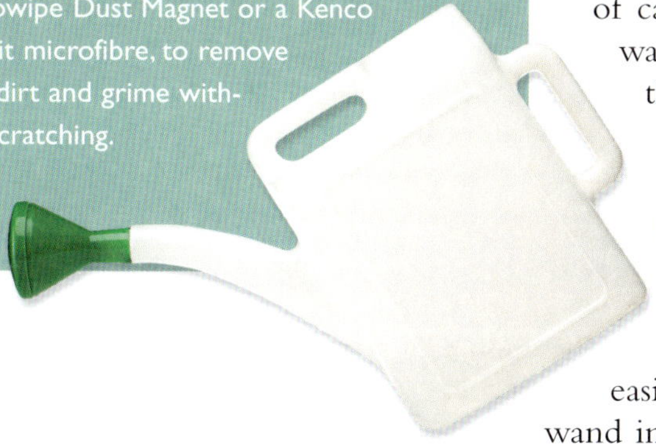

is a piece of 100 per cent cotton terry towelling. Towels are super-absorbent and grow softer with use and age. They're especially great for drying. Be sure to grab an old one—not one of the new fluffy monogrammed guest towels. When new, towels contain unstable dyes and silicone, so you'll have filthy guest towels as well as colour and silicone streaks on your car—something you'll want to avoid.

All-cotton shirts, T-shirts and shop rags are fine for the interior, but their weaves can be abrasive on your car's tender exterior. And be careful using sponges on the paint. Some, such as sea sponges, are notorious for hiding grit in their holes. Other options are disposable wash mitts filled with car soap, microfibre towels and mitts, and chamois cloths. A word of caution about chamois: it's clingy. Use it only to push water across the car, not to dry. Never drag it flat across the finish—it will drag away wax.

On the days you wash your dirty cleaning rags, skip the fabric softener and tumble-dryer sheets. These products contain silicone, which causes streaking.

**Where your local water restrictions** permit it, using a garden hose for rinsing makes life a lot easier. If you don't have a hose at home, you can use the wand in a coin-operated car wash. Spray in a steady, medium flow, not a high-pressure blast, which can grind dirt granules into the paint. With a continuous, moderate stream, the water flows across the car's outer surface in sheets, gently washing away sand, salt, pollen, dirt and other debris as well as soap. The wheels are the exception—there, a strong blast works well.

A rinsing rule of thumb is to spray in directions that water normally travels across or down the car, because that's the way the car is designed

## How to get away clean

There it is, in pale writing on the dirt-encrusted door of your boot: 'Wash me'. And you know it's time to obey. But before you grab the hose and begin, keep these rules in mind:

- Make it shady. During cleaning, the sun is not your car's friend. Park the car in shade—but not under a tree.
- Round up your supplies before you begin. You don't want to have to drive a soapy car to the automotive shop because you forgot something.
- Know your suds. Dishwashing liquid is only for dishes. Buy a non-detergent car cleaner.
- Get a good rag. With cotton rags, make it soft, 100 per cent cotton, clean and free of fabric softener or sizing. Old bath towels are a favourite.
- Rinse right. Resist the impulse to blast away dirt and grime, not least because it's a useless waste of water. Hosing with a moderate stream and constant flow of water creates a sheeting action that gently washes away debris and cleanser without scratching.
- Don't be a drip. Letting your car drip-dry leads to water spotting and soap film. Work in sections, washing, rinsing and drying as you go.

to slough off water. Otherwise, you may shoot water into the car vents and other design features where water isn't meant to go.

**Selecting a polish** should be done with care. Made with fine abrasives, polishes are designed to lift light oxidation so you can see the true colour of the paint better. As their name implies, they brighten the finish. Read labels. Find a polish that indicates that it's 'safe for modern car finishes' or 'safe on clearcoat'. And always apply polish on a clean car with a cool surface.

**Selecting a wax** is easy because a number of good brands are widely available. Liquid waxes are easiest to use. With a paste wax, it's easy to transfer grit into the original container—putting your finish at risk. Not only does wax give the paint its glossy sheen and sharpen the colour, but it also preserves the paint by helping it retain oils that reduce oxidation, the process that leads to the dreaded R-word, rust. It's also a layer between your paint and the world, a barrier to ultraviolet (UV) rays, pollutants, bird droppings, grime, insects, tar and tree sap. While waxing every six months is recommended to maintain a solid protective coat, you may need to do it more often if the season or the region you live in exposes the car to harsh conditions such as a heavy insect season, high dust and heat, or salt. And if your car is red, black or white, consider waxing more often, since these colours are more susceptible to acid rain and UV rays. However, a word of warning about spray-on, wipe-off detailer products that promise to help maintain that freshly waxed look between wax jobs: many of them are alcohol-based, so they actually strip wax.

**Use a bead test** to find out whether you're still getting protection from your wax, regardless of your timetable for waxing. Rinse the car with the hose and notice how the water droplets bead up around the car. If they are more than 1.5 centimetres across, or if the water stays on the surface in sheets, it's time to wax.

**Clear the drain holes** early in the car-washing process. These drain holes need occasional attention—the life of the car may be at stake! The drain holes are located under each bumper and quarter panel and at the bottom of each door panel. These rubber eyelets let out rainwater that leaks down the outside of the bumpers, panels and windows. If the holes are plugged with debris, the moisture gets trapped inside the body and can cause the vehicle to rust from the inside. Clear the holes by running a screwdriver or cotton bud into and across the opening (see above left). Later, when you rinse the car, any build-up will drain out.

Clear the drain holes to prevent water from being trapped inside the car body, which can cause the vehicle to rust.

**Start cleaning the car interior** by running a vacuum over the seats and seat crevices (a crevice attachment helps here), then the floor mats and floor carpeting. (Here's where you get to benefit from your habit of dropping change into tough-to-reach places.)

**Cleaning floor mats** is the next step after vacuuming. Take out the mats and hose them down. Fill a bucket with water and add 2–3 drops of non-detergent cleaner per litre. Dip in a stiff-bristled brush and scrub. After scrubbing, rinse the mats with the hose until the run-off is clear. Vacuum them with a wet-and-dry vac, if you have one, or just set them aside to air-dry—but not in full sun, which could fade them.

**Cleaning doorjambs** is definitely a smart first or second task. By starting with the parts of the door you don't see when the doors are closed, you don't risk getting cleaner and wax on surfaces you have already cleaned, such as your seats and carpet. Open the door wide and thoroughly clean around the door opening and the edges with a soapy rag. Once this has been done, take a dry exterior-use rag and wipe the inner door and sills dry. Dry all the painted surfaces, then polish and wax them. (See 'Wax', on page 379.)

**Cleaning carpets** is essential because the car floor is the interior surface that takes the biggest beating between washings. Scrub the carpets with a stiff-bristled brush and carpet and upholstery cleaner. (A household brand is OK.) If you're using a wet-and-dry vac, don't be afraid to wet the carpet with a little water to loosen tough deposits of grime and dirt before you scrub them. Then sweep up the water, loosened soil and debris.

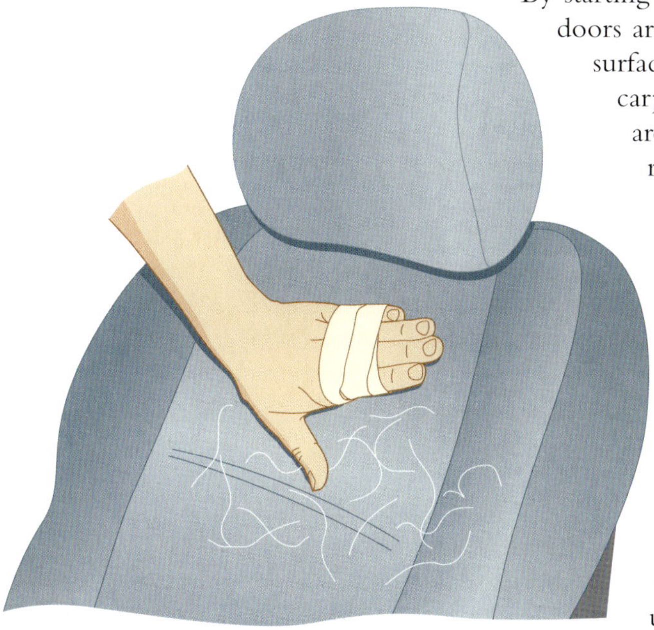

Pet hair can be quickly removed from car seats with masking tape wrapped around your hand.

**Cleaning seats** is simple because they usually need only a quick once-over. You have your choice of using upholstery cleaner and a soft-bristled brush, vinyl cleaner and a rag, or saddle-soap and a dampened sponge. To remove pet hair from upholstery, wrap wide masking tape around your hand (sticky side on the outside, of course) and wipe with the tape (see above left). For leather seats, make sure your rag or sponge is only damp, because too much water will damage them. After cleaning the leather, apply a thin layer of protective leather conditioner (available from luggage and shoe shops, or from specialist automotive shops). Don't over-condition. Leather needs to be able to absorb moisture from the air. Check out automotive shops for products that clean, moisturise and protect leather in one application; this will save on cleaning time.

**Cleaning door panels** is tricky because their surfaces have lots of crevices and, usually, electrical switches. After first wiping the panel with a soapy rag, dampen (don't get them sopping wet) an old toothbrush and a thin cloth and use the toothbrush to clean out crevices. Wrap the cloth around a plastic knife to clean the electrical switches, repositioning the cloth as needed to keep soft fabric over the knife edge. The trick here is that a damp cloth won't drip into switches and cause them to fail or short-circuit. (Use the same method for dials and switches on the dashboard.) Wipe dry.

EXPERT ADVICE

PUT UP WITH THE STATIC CLING

When you're washing your rags for car cleaning, don't use dryer sheets on them in the dryer. Dryer sheets contain silicone, which will leave streaks on your car.

**Cleaning window interiors** is important if you want to see out clearly, and avoid any potential accidents or frantic window cleaning while driving. Give the interior glass the treatment with a solution of 1 part white vinegar to 8 parts water, mixed in a spray bottle. Or use a non-ammonia glass cleaner. (Ammonia-based household glass cleaners and foam glass cleaners can dry out neighbouring plastic, rubber and vinyl.) You may hear hot water recommended for cleaning glass, but take care if you are working in icy conditions—the hot liquid could cause cracking.

Newspaper is an old favourite for cleaning glass windowpanes, as it is reputed to have a polishing effect. However, it is not as effective as it used to be, as modern ink formulations, used in printing today's newspapers, have changed. For streak-free drying, a better choice is a low-lint cloth. (Old pillowcases are a good choice.) Finally, roll the door windows down and clean the tops, where dirt and film tend to be thickest.

**Cleaning the dashboard,** steering column, centre console, and other vinyl and plastic surfaces is the finishing touch for the interior. If they are dusty, first wipe them down with a household dusting cloth. A convenient new alternative to a dusting cloth is a non-woven, disposable, protective dusting wipe such as the Armor All brand. Use a small, dry natural-bristle pastry brush to dust the hard-to-reach areas such as vents and dashboard corners.

Mix 1 part all-purpose, non-toxic, biodegradable household cleaner with 8 parts water in a spray bottle. Spray and wipe with a clean cloth. Use a damp cloth-covered plastic knife on dash dials and switches. (See 'Cleaning door panels', above.) If there are any scratches on the clear plastic lenses on your dashboard, mask them by rubbing on baby oil or a clear plastic treatment such as Meguiar's PLASTX Clear Plastic Cleaner & Polish, available from automotive shops.

Protect the dashboard and other non-upholstered, non-glass surfaces to prevent cracking and fading. Use a UV-blocking interior protectant, preferably one that's silicone-free.

**Start cleaning the car's exterior** by checking the finish and trim for any insects and tar, and then apply insect and tar remover to loosen them, following the manufacturer's instructions. Washing will remove the oily residue that the petroleum-based insect and tar remover leaves behind.

When water-blasting dirt and grime from the wheels and tyres, do it on the grass so the water soaks into the soil.

**Washing wheels and tyres** is one activity where it's OK to blast with water, since it takes force to dislodge stubborn road grime and send it packing. Use a pressure nozzle to hose out inside the wheel wells and give the tyres a cleaning blast (see left). Mix non-detergent car cleaner with water in a bucket according to the package instructions. Then scrub the wheels with the solution, using a stiff-bristled brush or a rag. A toothbrush will let you get at places where the brush won't fit.

A cardinal rule not to be broken is that once you've used rags, brushes and car-wash solution on the wheels and tyres, don't reuse these same dirty materials anywhere else on the car.

**Washing the car body** starts with using a hose to spray the car—working from the roof downwards. (Dirt, as they say, flows downhill.) With the first rinse, water will flow through those newly unplugged drain holes and wash away any residue from inside the doors and body. Mix non-detergent car cleaner with water in a bucket. Apply the solution with a car-wash mitt or a soft rag. Go for a mitt that's all wool or a wool–polyester blend. One hundred per cent polyester is just too rough on your paint. Never soap up the entire car and then rinse, because that gives the cleaner time to air-dry and leave a film. Work your way around, soaping, rinsing and drying the metal and trim in sections no larger than what you can reach without moving your feet (about 1 metre square). Work from the roof down, making sure your rag stays free of stones, tar and debris. Never continue to use a mitt or rag that's fallen on the ground.

An old detailer's trick that separates clean and dirty rags is to have two buckets of car cleaner solution, which can be used one of two ways. Either designate one for 'rough' or especially dirt-prone surfaces

Simple solutions

## A little bird flies by ...

When birds foul your car, you can't wait around till next Saturday's washing to deal with the problem. It'll only get worse, and the splat may etch into the paint finish. Mist-and-wipe detailing products, available at automotive shops, make the job easy. Spray the mist on the car and wipe it off with a clean cloth—before it has time to bond to the finish. An added benefit is that you won't have to wax as often. Disposable, pre-treated wipes that store easily in the glove box are also available in automotive shops and many discount retailers.

**EXPERT ADVICE**

### TRUE GRIT

A clever way to keep your wash mitt or rag out of the grit at the bottom of your bucket when you're washing the car is to place an old aluminium vegetable steamer or colander in the bottom of the bucket. The mitt rests on the steamer, and the grit settles to the bottom.

and the other for 'smooth', less debris-laden ones, or use one bucket for your first soap pass (the 'dirty' bucket) and the other for a second soap pass (the 'clean' bucket). Segregate your rags accordingly.

Wash and dry painted metal gently. There's no sense in thinning its protective wax layer or making it uneven by rubbing too hard. A detailer's secret for gentle drying is to hold a towel at both ends and drape it over the wet surface. Drag it across the surface towards you. That way, you don't apply any potentially wax-stripping pressure, as you might when rubbing with the rag in your hand. It is worth considering doing two rounds of drying as well, to make sure you've done a thorough job.

**Cleaning the trim** is the next step in the cleaning process. Spray vinyl and plastic parts with an all-purpose household cleaning solution (see 'Cleaning the dashboard', on page 112) or use a non-silicone vinyl cleaner (matte finish) according to label instructions. When cleaning chrome with chrome cleaner also follow the label instructions. Use fresh water to rinse completely under any mouldings—debris and dirt can collect there, creating a layer that can trap condensation. Trapped moisture eventually spells rust. Reverse the air direction on your vacuum cleaner and use it to blow-dry all the door handles, window mouldings and mirror cavities. Otherwise, when you drive they'll splash water that will unfortunately become water spots on your finish.

**Simple solutions**

### Car window winter wonder

If you live in a cold area, one of the things you hate most about winter is scraping that layer of ice off your windscreen when you're invariably late for work. To wake up to a frost-free car windshield, coat it the night before with a solution made up of 3 parts vinegar to 1 part water.

**Cleaning window exteriors** is no different from cleaning window interiors. Just squirt the glass and wipe it with a vinegar solution or non-ammonia cleaner. (See 'Cleaning window interiors', on page 112.) Make sure you use low-lint cloths for drying.

Once the car is clean, unless it's brand-new or you're sure the wax layer is holding up (see 'Use a bead test', on page 110), you may need to polish, wax and buff it.

**WATCH OUT** When washing your car use plenty of water on the surface and care in using your rag to avoid the risk of leaving small scratches from dragging a rag full of tiny particles. Some detailers lead with their free hand, feeling across the surface of the car before they drag their rag across it.

**Polishing** removes surface paint that has oxidised. Use a car polish if your paint finish appears bright, not hazy, and follow label instructions. A visible haze on the paint indicates more oxidation damage than a polish can mend and means your car needs a little professional help. Take the car to a detailer for the machine buffing and hand-rubbing, cleaning and polishing it will take to remove that level of oxidation. When you wash and wax your car regularly, you minimise the need to polish—or even eliminate it.

**Waxing** can be done with either a liquid or paste wax. Follow the label instructions to the letter. As noted earlier, it's easy to pick up grit with paste wax, so be careful how you handle the applicator. A favoured method for applying and removing wax is to use long, straight strokes that follow the same pattern that air takes as it moves around the car. The reason is that straight strokes don't leave behind the swirls in the finish that circular motions can. And if, by chance, you scratch the car, straight scratches are easier to remove. However, always read and follow label instructions for applying the product you're using. Again, work in sections. When your applicator or rag starts to drag as you pull it, flip it over or use a clean section. If the product instructions say to wait until the wax dries to a haze, do it—this gives the wax time to work and makes it easier to remove.

Make sure you keep wax away from plastic mouldings and rubber seals and trim pieces. If wax does get onto them it'll be next to impossible to remove it once it dries.

There's no need to scrub as you apply or buff wax. The idea is to leave a good coat of wax behind. Simply apply a steady, even pressure using the weight of your hand and arm.

**For buffing,** use your softest rags. Do it in the same straight motions you used to wax. When your rag moves smoothly across the surface and the residue is gone you're done.

# CASSETTE PLAYERS

**IF YOUR CASSETTE** PLAYER SOUND QUALITY IS DETERIORATING, IT'S TIME TO GIVE IT A CLEAN. THE AUDIO PROBLEM MAY VERY WELL BE CAUSED BY DUST AND GRIME COMBINED WITH THE OXIDE BUILD-UP THAT OCCURS WHEN AN AUDIOTAPE MOVES THROUGH THE PLAYER. YOU CAN IMPROVE THE SOUND BY CLEANING THE TAPE PATH. KEEP IN MIND THAT THE CHEAPER THE TAPE YOU'RE USING, THE MORE QUICKLY THE OXIDE WILL ACCUMULATE IN YOUR PLAYER. CLEAN THE PLAYER AFTER EVERY 75 HOURS OR SO OF USE AND AT LEAST TWICE THAT OFTEN IF YOU'RE USING POOR-QUALITY TAPES.

Wipe the insides of the cassette player with cotton buds soaked in surgical alcohol or methylated spirits.

**To clean the tape path,** you need to wipe over everything that the tape touches as it's played—the heads, tape guides, chrome pin and black rubber roller. Saturate three to four cotton buds with isopropyl (surgical) alcohol or methylated spirits, and thoroughly swab each area (see above). The chrome heads should be wiped both vertically and horizontally. Keep cleaning until the final cotton bud comes away with no brown residue. Don't worry about black residue from the roller—that's from the rubber.

You can also buy cassette cleaning tapes, which generally don't clean as thoroughly as the cotton bud method but are a good alternative for tape players whose insides are hard to reach, like those in car stereos. Most cleaning tapes contain a diluted alcohol-based fluid. You just pop the tape into the cassette player and let it rotate for 10–15 seconds.

**To extend the life of cassettes,** you need to store them properly. Keep them out of extreme heat (that includes the back seat of your car in midsummer) and away from direct sunlight. Also, it is important to store them in their cases away from magnetic fields created by computers, televisions and video equipment.

*See also:*
- CD PLAYERS AND CDS
- DVD PLAYERS

# CD PLAYERS AND CDS

**WHEN YOUR CDS** START SKIPPING OR THE DISC WON'T SPIN, THERE'S A GOOD CHANCE THE PLAYER'S LASER LENS NEEDS A QUICK CLEAN. A CLEAN CD PLAYER PRODUCES BETTER SOUND, AND A LITTLE REGULAR MAINTENANCE COULD MEAN YOU WON'T MISS A BEAT. A VARIETY OF MECHANICAL FAILURES CAN CAUSE PROBLEMS FOR YOUR PLAYER, BUT IT'S WORTH TAKING A FEW MINUTES TO SEE IF CLEANING WILL HELP—ESPECIALLY WHEN YOU FACTOR IN THE HIGH COST OF PROFESSIONAL REPAIR.

**Cleaning the laser lens** is inexpensive and simple on top-loading players and portable units. Front-loading players and carousel units require removing the player's cover and finding the lens. Often there are too many mechanisms in the way, and extensive disassembling should be left to the pros. In those cases, you can attempt to clean the lens with a cleaning disc, available in many shops that sell CDs. The disc looks like a CD, but its shiny side has tiny brushes on it, and as the disc spins it brushes the lens. However, the lens has to be able to 'see' before the disc can spin, so a really dusty laser lens often won't respond when a cleaning disc is inserted.

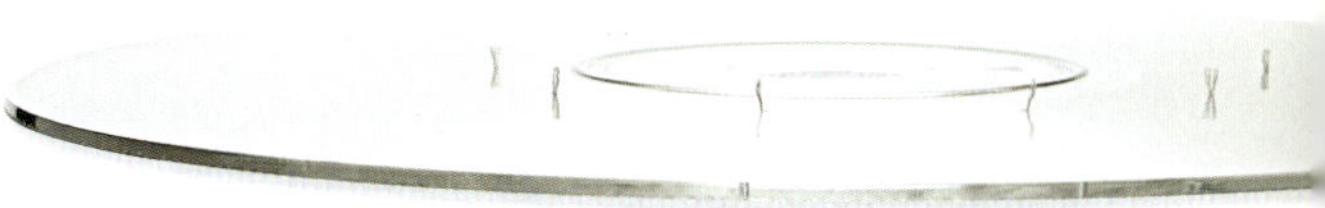

But if your player's laser is in plain view in a top-loading model, even the most inexperienced home mechanic can clean it. Before you begin, unplug the CD player. If it's battery-powered, make sure the unit is off. Then do the following:

- Locate the laser lens, which is a round glass bubble about 6 millimetres in diameter. The slightest bit of dust can prevent the laser from 'reading' the CD.
- Dip a cotton bud in methylated spirits and squeeze out the excess into a paper towel so it doesn't drip.
- Using a circular motion, gently rub the lens for 5–10 seconds. The lens will move a little, but that's OK.
- Let it dry. Depending on how much alcohol was left on the lens, it will take 10–20 minutes to dry. The CD player won't turn until it has sufficiently dried out.

**Cleaning your CDs** from time to time is also important, not only so that they play without distortion but also to prevent dust on the CDs from clogging up the player's works. Using a CD cleaning cloth or a soft cloth moistened with a little methylated spirits, hold the CD

Handle CDs very carefully while you clean and dust them, to avoid distorting the disc.

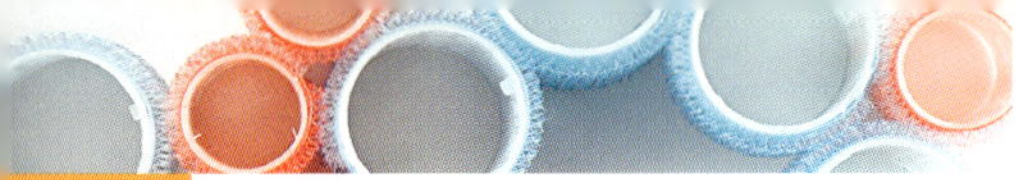



by its outer edges in one hand while cleaning with the other. Wipe the CD from the centre to the outer edge, as though you were wiping the spokes of a wheel from the hub to the rim.

**Proper storage of your CDs** will help extend their playing time. Store them in their cases, and inspect them periodically for dust and fingerprints, which can cause a tracking error. Keep your player and CDs out of direct sunlight.

*See also:*
• CASSETTE PLAYERS
• DVD PLAYERS

**One last tip:** if the player is brought directly from a cold location to a warm one, moisture may condense on the lens, which will prevent the unit from playing. If this happens, remove the CD and wait about an hour for the moisture to evaporate.

## CEILINGS

**IF YOU WANT** TO BRIGHTEN YOUR OVERHEAD VIEW, TAKE AIM AT THAT GRUBBY CEILING. CEILINGS ATTRACT AIRBORNE DIRT, CIGARETTE SMOKE AND GREASE. CLEANING THEM IS A PROJECT THAT'S TEMPTING TO PUT OFF, SINCE CEILINGS ARE HARD TO REACH AND AWKWARD TO CLEAN. BUT A FEW TRICKS OF THE TRADE CAN MINIMISE THE MISERY. WHENEVER POSSIBLE, USE LONG-HANDLED TOOLS INSTEAD OF BALANCING ON A LADDER OR STEPLADDER.

**Dusting the ceiling** is sometimes all that's required, and to do that, all you need, from a hardware or homeware shop, is a long, extension-handled duster that will capture and hold fine dust and dirt and also eliminate cobwebs without smearing. A long-handled lamb's wool duster or a vacuum with a brush attachment also works well.

**To clean a dirty ceiling,** you have to do the job by hand. First, you'll need to do a little preparation work. Put down drop cloths or newspapers to protect furniture, electronic equipment and floors. Wear safety goggles or other eye protection, because you're likely to dislodge small particles you can't really see coming at you (see above right). You may want to wear rubber gloves as well. You can use a sponge mop with an extender handle, but you'll have to be careful to apply even pressure and get an even distribution of the cleaning product so it won't streak. Or you can use a dry foam-rubber sponge, which means hauling out a stepladder. Take care to follow basic safety rules, such as placing the ladder securely on a level surface to prevent tipping, and never standing on the top step.

For painted ceilings, whether they're covered with oil-based or acrylic paint, a general-purpose cleaner, such as Handy Andy, or even liquid sugar soap, works well. Mix 60–90 millilitres

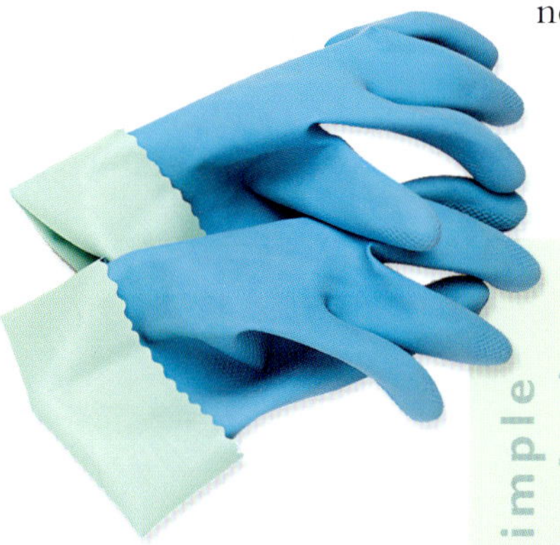

**Simple solutions**

### Face up to a drippy situation

If you use liquid cleaners to clean your ceiling, there's a better than even chance that some of that liquid will come dribbling down your arm onto your clothes or into your face. The solution is to wear rubber gloves and fold the ends up into cuffs, so anything that drips from your hands stays in the glove.

To prevent dirt from falling into your eyes, wear goggles when cleaning a ceiling.

of general-purpose cleaner in 4 litres of water (or follow product instructions), dip your sponge in the solution, wring out the excess and wipe the dirty area. Rinsing is necessary only if the ceiling is heavily soiled, but whether or not you rinse, you'll need to wipe away excess moisture with a dry towel to prevent bead marks.

**A spray-on acoustical finish** on a ceiling has a rough surface that is best cleaned using a vacuum cleaner with a soft brush attachment used for cleaning upholstery.

**An easy remedy for dirty acoustical ceiling tiles** can be found in your medicine cabinet: hydrogen peroxide, an environmentally friendly product that contains powerful oxidising agents.

**To clean vinyl-coated ceiling tiles,** buy 3 per cent hydrogen peroxide solution (rather than the special industrial-strength version), which is widely available in supermarkets and pharmacies. And wear goggles to keep debris and the peroxide mist out of your eyes. Mix about 30 millilitres of hydrogen peroxide in 1 litre of water and pour it into a spray bottle. Peroxide, a mild bleach, will whiten the tiles. Best of all, no rubbing is required—simply spray the mixture on the tiles, applying it evenly and let it air-dry.

**To clean non-coated ceiling tiles**—which generally aren't washable—use a dry sponge cleaner or a special microfibre mitt. Dry sponges are made from natural rubber and are sometimes treated with mild detergents. When using a dry sponge or mitt, wipe the ceiling tiles with an even, sweeping motion.

## CERAMICS

**WHEN POLISHING YOUR** MOST CHERISHED PIECE OF CLAY, EARTHENWARE OR PORCELAIN—USE CAUTION. HANDMADE CERAMICS THAT ARE FOR DISPLAY ONLY RUN THE GREATEST RISK OF BEING DAMAGED DURING HANDLING. SO USE BOTH HANDS WHEN LIFTING, AND SUPPORT THE ITEM FROM ITS BASE.

**Dusting a decorative ceramic item** is required only occasionally. And dusting mitts, available for a number of specialised jobs from your supermarket, work well because they contain no cleaning solutions to produce a residue that could discolour your pottery. The mitts are made of textured cloth and work by trapping dust and dirt in the fibres (see page 120). But if the object has a rough surface, like raku pottery does, use a dry, soft cloth for dusting. The tiny holes in textured mitts will snag on the ceramic's rough areas.

**Cleaning a ceramic item** depends on what kind of ceramic it is.

- Machine-made, functional ceramic bowls and other pieces that do regular kitchen duty can be cleaned in the dishwasher.
- Handmade ceramics should be cleaned by hand, using a soft cloth, mild dishwashing liquid and water. Don't soak the item, which can

lead to staining. Instead, dampen a cloth with soapy water, wipe away the dirt, rinse with a clean, damp cloth and let the piece air-dry in a drainer. Drying with a cloth increases the chance that the object will slip through your fingers.

Dusting mitts are ideal for gently dusting and cleaning the surface of smooth ceramic items.

**To protect decorative ceramics** on display in your home, place some Blu-Tack under your pottery to hold it firmly in place. If someone bumps into the table where it's displayed—or your cat brushes up against it—it won't go tumbling. The Blu-Tack can be easily removed, yet holds firmly enough that you have to twist the object to remove it.

## CHANDELIERS

**ANY HOME OWNER** WHO'S SPENT THOUSANDS OF DOLLARS ON AN ELEGANT CHANDELIER NEEDS TO KNOW ABOUT KEEPING CRYSTALS CLEAR. YOU CAN BUY THE FINEST CRYSTAL IN THE WORLD, BUT IF IT GETS DIRTY, IT'S INDISTINGUISHABLE FROM CHEAP CRYSTAL. A CHANDELIER SHOULD BE CLEANED WHEN IT LOOKS DUSTY, MILKY OR CLOUDY. THERE ARE SEVERAL METHODS TO RESTORE A CHANDELIER'S DAZZLE, BASED ON HOW DINGY IT HAS BECOME. BUT IF YOU MAINTAIN IT REGULARLY—A COUPLE OF TIMES A YEAR—YOU PROBABLY WON'T HAVE TO REMOVE ALL THE CRYSTALS TO WASH THEM BY HAND.

**If a chandelier is not too dirty,** set up a stepladder in one or two spots where you can easily reach the chandelier without stretching and use one of these two methods to clean the crystals:

- The simplest way is to lightly dampen a chamois cloth with water and wipe each crystal while it's still attached to the chandelier frame (see right). To clean the chandelier frame itself, just wipe it thoroughly with a dry cloth.
- Using two gloves is also popular. Buy a pair of white cotton gloves (available from home improvement shops or supermarkets), and slightly dampen one glove with a glass cleaner, such as Windex or Mr Muscle. Spray the cleaner onto the glove and never onto the chandelier,

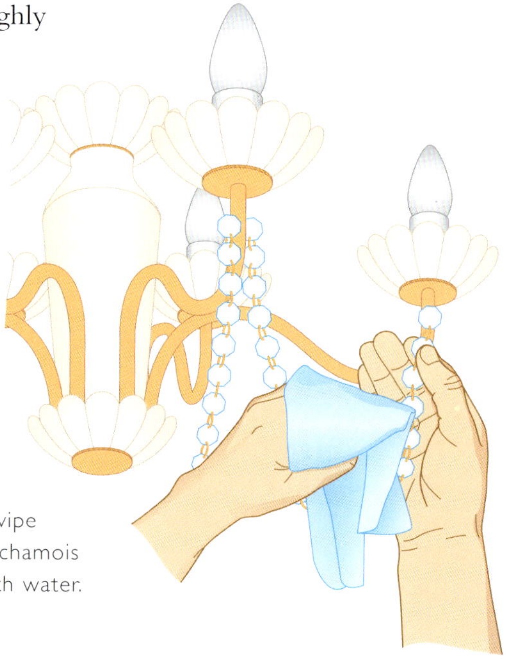

To remove dirt, wipe each crystal with a chamois cloth dampened with water.

**EXPERT ADVICE**

**A CRYSTAL JIGSAW**

Before you start removing any dusty chandelier crystals for hand washing, make absolutely sure you know how to put the chandelier back together again.

You can either clean a small section at a time or track down the diagram that came with the chandelier. If the diagram is long lost, take a photo of the intact chandelier or do a drawing before you start to disassemble.

since a spray cleaner will eventually work its way into any tiny nicks or scratches in the frame finish, which can cause corrosion and ruin the frame. Massage each crystal with the damp glove, then wipe it immediately with the dry glove.

**If a chandelier is really dirty**, you'll have to take down the crystals and wash them by hand—no dishwasher short cuts. Start by climbing your stepladder and removing the bulbs and setting them aside. Then carefully remove the crystals. Run warm water into a large pot or sink until it's about a quarter full. Add 1 capful of white vinegar and 1 drop of dishwashing liquid. The combination will remove any grease or residue on the glass but will minimise the suds created, which are hard to rinse off.

Place a folded towel in the bottom of the pot or sink. Wipe each crystal with your hands, then individually rinse each one under running water and dry with a soft cloth. If you don't dry them you'll have water spots,which will reduce the sparkle.

Finally, wipe the light bulbs with a damp sponge, dry them with a cloth, return them to their sockets—and enjoy the light show.

## CHEWING GUM

**WHEN CHEWED-UP** CHEWING GUM WINDS UP IN YOUR CARPET, CLOTHES OR HAIR, YOU'VE GOT A STICKY SITUATION THAT WILL ONLY GET WORSE. GUM HARDENS OVER TIME, MAKING IT INCREASINGLY DIFFICULT TO REMOVE. BUT PROMPT ACTION AND SOME TIME-HONOURED GUM CONTROL TECHNIQUES WILL GET YOU UNSTUCK.

**Using ice cubes to freeze gum** and make it easier to remove is a simple and popular trick for removing gum from carpets, upholstery and washable clothing. To begin, scrape off as much of the gum as possible with a dull non-serrated knife. Then put one or two ice cubes in a self-sealing sandwich bag and rub the bag over the spot until the gum freezes (see right). Once again, use the knife to scrape away more gum. Repeat as needed to remove all the gum.

Freezing chewing gum with ice makes it easier to scrape off.

**To remove gum from a carpet,** heat combined with a little chemical action is effective—but be sure to test this method first in an inconspicuous area to make sure the material is colour-fast. Start by heating the gum with a hair dryer for a minute or two. With a plastic sandwich bag on your hand, lift off as much of the heated gum as

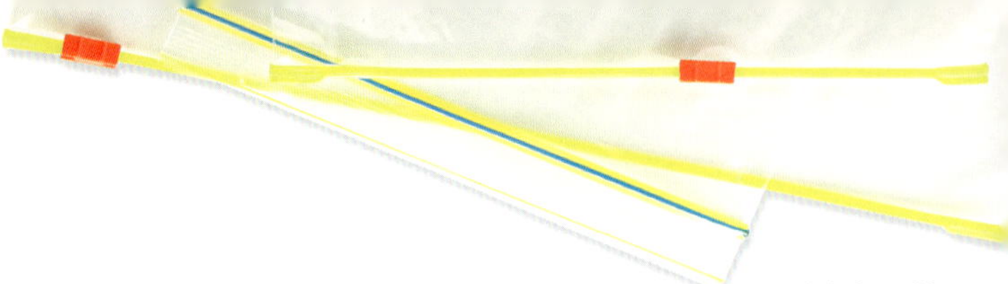





### Chew on this

Removing chewing gum from footpaths and streets is a huge and costly burden for cities throughout the world. For removing gum on a massive scale, chemical solvents are the premier cleaning method.

Although a jet nozzle attached to your hose is a non-toxic way of dealing with the wad of gum stuck on your own path, it's also a waste of water. Try wetting the gum with methylated spirits, eucalyptus oil, a citrus oil-based solvent (such as De-Solv-It) or mineral turpentine, then levering it off with a blunt knife—and save the much-needed water for the garden. The quicker you attack the gum, the more easily it will come off.

possible. If the gum starts to harden, heat it again and lift off more gum until you have removed as much as you can.

Then massage ½ teaspoon of deep-heating body rub into the spot. Use an extra-strength rub, if possible. Turn the hair dryer on *High* and heat the area for 30 seconds. Then use another plastic bag to lift off the remaining residue. Finally, add 1 teaspoon of mild dishwashing liquid to 1 cup of water and blot the spot with paper towels or a cloth rag to lift any stain. Stubborn stains can also be treated with spot remover or a dry-cleaning solvent, such as Murlex or Woolclean Spot Dry Remover No. 2.

**To remove gum from clothing,** follow the procedure described above for carpets, except apply the deep-heating rub to the opposite side of the cloth. After 30 seconds of blow-drying, the gum should peel off. Then wash the garment as usual, whether by hand or in a washing machine.

You can also try a variant of the ice-cube treatment. Seal the garment in a plastic bag and place it in the freezer. After it's frozen, just scrape the spot with a dull knife to remove the gum, then launder as usual.

**To get gum out of hair** try working peanut butter or cooking oil into the gummy spot for a minute to soften the gum. Gently pull out the gum with a paper towel, then shampoo and rinse the area. Eucalyptus oil is effective as well.

## CHIMNEYS

**WHERE THERE'S FIRE,** THERE'S SMOKE—AND WHEN IT'S IN YOUR FIREPLACE, YOU'LL EVENTUALLY HAVE A CHIMNEY THAT NEEDS A CLEAN SWEEP. CHIMNEY FIRES OCCUR WHEN CREOSOTE, A HIGHLY COMBUSTIBLE RESIDUE CREATED BY BURNING WOOD, IGNITES. THE RESULTING FLAMES ARE HOTTER THAN THE WOOD IN YOUR FIREPLACE AND THE RED-HOT SPARKS THAT BURST FROM THE CHIMNEY COULD SET YOUR HOME ON FIRE.

**To prevent chimney fires,** have your chimney cleaned regularly by a professional chimney sweep. Cleaning chimneys is difficult, dangerous work that requires special brushes and equipment tailored to fit the precise measurements of your fireplace flue. However, you can and should clean out the ashes in your fireplace when they start piling up. Shovel the ashes into a metal container with a tight-fitting lid—never a paper bag—and store it away from any combustible materials (including a wooden deck) before final disposal.

The frequency of chimney cleaning will depend on how much you use your fireplace. At the least, an annual inspection is needed.

**To inspect a chimney yourself,** you need to be in good shape and not mind climbing on the roof. Use a tall ladder to gain access to the roof and check that the tiles are not wet and slippery. With the aid of a powerful torchlight, check the chimney openings both from the hearth and from the roof. On the roof, you'll have to remove any spark arrester or weather cap before you start.

# rules of the game

WHERE THERE'S SMOKE, THERE'S FIRE

- Prevent chimney fires by having your chimney cleaned regularly by a professional chimney sweep who has business liability insurance. To find a chimney sweep look in the *Yellow Pages* or ask around.
- If you decide to go on the roof and inspect the chimney yourself, do so with caution and take a powerful torchlight. Look for obstructions, the extent of creosote build-up and indications of a chimney fire.
- To reduce creosote build-up, burn wood that's been dried for six months to a year, burn hardwoods instead of softwoods and never burn painted or chemically treated wood.

- Look for obvious obstructions like bird nests. This is important even if all you have is a gas-log fireplace. While gas burns more cleanly than wood, a gas fireplace must be inspected for proper venting to keep odourless, poisonous carbon monoxide out of your home.
- Check the extent of creosote build-up. The creosote will be black or brown and could vary from a dripping tar-like substance to a shiny hardened mass. The highest concentration of creosote usually occurs in the top one-third of the chimney.
- Look for indications that you've had a chimney fire. Chimney fires, which roar hot until the energy source is spent or extinguished, sometimes occur without anyone realising it. Such fires can weaken the mortar, crack the tile lining of the chimney or even cause the lining to collapse. Any of those factors mean that heat from subsequent fires could reach and ignite combustible parts of the house, such as the wooden framing. Signs of a chimney fire include puffy creosote with rainbow-coloured streaks, warped metal on the damper or metal smoke chamber, cracked or missing flue tiles, creosote flakes or chunks on the roof, and cracks in the exterior masonry.
- Inspect the outside of your chimney to make sure there are no cracks that could allow water to seep in. In very cold areas, changes in temperature will cause water that leaks in to freeze and thaw, which can cause mortar to crumble.

**To find a chimney sweep** in your area, check the *Yellow Pages*. Make sure that the company you choose carries business liability insurance in the event of accidents.

**To cut down on creosote build-up,** burn wood that's been dried for six months to a year. Freshly cut wood has a higher moisture content than seasoned wood, which results in a smokier fire. Hardwoods, such as eucalyptus, burn more slowly and with a steadier flame than softwoods, such as pine, which cause faster creosote build-up. Never burn painted or chemically treated wood.

*See also:*
• FIREPLACES • FIREPLACE SCREENS AND TOOLS

## CHINA

**THE TERM FINE** CHINA EVOKES IMAGES OF FRAGILE DELICACY, BUT MOST CHINA MANUFACTURED TODAY IS MADE TO BE FUNCTIONAL AS WELL AS ELEGANT. COMPANIES KNOW TODAY'S BUSY CONSUMER WANTS UTILITY AS WELL AS BEAUTY. SO MOST CHINA MADE IN THE LAST 25 YEARS IS DISHWASHER SAFE AND SAYS SO EXPLICITLY ON THE BOTTOM OF THE PIECE. A NOTABLE EXCEPTION TO THIS ARE DINNER SETS WITH BANDS MADE OF A PRECIOUS METAL SUCH AS PLATINUM OR GOLD. THE HIGH HEAT OF THE DISHWASHER'S DRYING CYCLE WILL CAUSE THE METAL TO SOFTEN. YOU SHOULD ALSO AVOID DETERGENTS THAT ARE LEMON-SCENTED, BECAUSE THEY CONTAIN CITRUS, WHICH CAN CORRODE THE METAL, WHETHER YOU'RE WASHING BY HAND OR MACHINE. HAND WASHING IS ALSO REQUIRED FOR ANTIQUE OR HAND-PAINTED CHINA. THE FORCE AND HEAT OF DISHWASHERS HAS PROVEN TOO MUCH FOR FRAGILE PIECES.

**Washing china in the dishwasher** does require a little extra attention. Load the pieces carefully so they won't bump into each other and chip. Make sure aluminium utensils and lightweight foil containers don't rub against dishes during the wash cycle, because that can create black or grey marks.

Line the sink with a tea towel or rubber mat and use a soft cloth when washing delicate china.

**To hand wash antique or hand-painted china,** start by lining the bottom of the sink with a rubber mat or tea towel. Half-fill the sink with warm water and a mild dishwashing liquid. To prevent chipping, take care not to overload the sink with dishes. Remove rings and jewellery to prevent scratching the china and, for the same reason, wash cutlery separately. Use a soft cloth or sponge for cleaning (see above). Here are some more tips:

- Wash or soak the items as soon after eating as possible, to prevent the problem of dried-on food and staining. Acidic foods such as eggs and mayonnaise can damage the glaze if left on for long periods.
- To remove dried food, soak the china in a grease-cutting dishwashing liquid, then scrub gently with a nylon scouring pad. Never use a metal pad, and avoid steel wool and gritty cleansers as well.
- Make sure you are careful when placing the dishes in the drainer to prevent scratches and chips.

**Wash china figurines** and sculptures by hand using the mildest soap—Sunlight, for instance. Hand dry with a soft cloth. If the piece has a wooden base, don't let the wood get wet.

*See also:* • DISHES

# CHOPPING BOARDS AND BLOCKS

**FIRST, THE BAD** NEWS. MEAT- AND POULTRY-BORNE MICRO-ORGANISMS THAT LINGER ON DIRTY CHOPPING BOARDS—SALMONELLA, E. COLI, CAMPYLOBACTER—CAN KILL YOU. BUT BEFORE YOU PANIC AND THROW AWAY ALL YOUR CHOPPING BOARDS, OR DECIDE NOT TO EAT STEAK AND CHICKEN, HERE'S THE GOOD NEWS. NOT ONLY IS DEATH BY MICRO-ORGANISM EXTREMELY RARE, BUT WHEN YOU PROPERLY CLEAN YOUR CHOPPING BOARD, WHICH IS A QUICK, SIMPLE TASK, YOU CAN KILL 99.9 PER CENT OF THE BAD STUFF AND CONTINUE EATING WHAT YOU LIKE WITHOUT FEAR.

**To wash a plastic chopping board,** just run it through a dishwasher, and the hot water and sanitising ingredients in dishwasher detergent will kill the harmful pathogens. Make sure you wash your chopping board as soon as possible after each use, especially after preparing meat or poultry products.

**To wash a wooden chopping board,** it's best not to use a dishwasher because the dishwashing process may warp or loosen the glue that holds together laminated wood. You're better off using a scrubbing brush to scrub the board by hand with dishwashing liquid in hot water each time you use it. The soap helps lift the meat debris that may harbour the pathogens, and the scrubbing action ruptures the cells of the micro-organisms. Done thoroughly, hand scrubbing is as effective as machine washing.

**To sanitise a chopping board,** a good thing to do occasionally is to mix 1 teaspoon of bleach in 1 litre of water and apply it directly to the chopping surface with a scrubbing brush. Do not rinse. Instead, let the board air-dry to give the bleach a chance to do its thing. If you need the board sooner than that, let it stand for at least 1 minute, and then pat it dry with a clean paper towel.

**The first step in keeping an unvarnished butcher block** like new is to season it when you first bring it home and regularly thereafter. To season a butcher block, warm a little medical-quality paraffin oil (from the pharmacy) in a double saucepan on the stove (or use a small bowl over a simmering pan). Don't let it get hot—warm will penetrate the wood nicely. Using a soft cloth dabbed into the oil, rub in the direction of the grain. Let the oil soak in for 4–5 hours, then wipe off any excess using a soft, dry cloth. Repeat the process. Seasoning your butcher block once a month sets the stage for a clean, sanitary work surface.

**To clean a butcher block,** don't ever use any household chemical cleaners. They could be harmful and, at the least, the residue will be distasteful on food. All you need to keep those prep surfaces sanitary is ½ tablespoon of chlorine household bleach mixed with 2 litres of water in a bucket. Dip a small scrubbing brush in the chlorine water and scrub in hand-sized circles, taking care not to saturate the wood. When wood absorbs water, it swells. Then, when it dries out, the wood

★★★ EXPERT ADVICE

### CHOPPING BOARD COMMONSENSE

If possible, have two chopping boards. Use one for meat and the other for raw foods, like fruit and vegetables. To recognise which one is which, use a non-toxic marker to label the handles or along the edge. And don't get too attached to any one board. If your chopping board has deep grooves from lots of cutting, you can't clean it as thoroughly. Throw it out and get a new one. It's a small price to pay for peace of mind.

cracks, making a convenient trap for everything you don't want—food, grime and germs. So brush the butcher block clean and quickly wipe away water with a tea towel.

**When you don't have any bleach,** here's another solution to getting the grime out of a butcher block without wetting the wood too much: mix just enough salt into lemon juice to make a paste. Rub it, with a sponge or cleaning cloth, hard enough onto the wood to free those stuck-on or wedged-in food particles. Then rinse out the cloth or sponge and wipe the butcher block clean. The result won't be as germ-free clean as cleaning with bleach, but it's a good alternative.

Clean butcher blocks by scrubbing them with a paste made from lemon juice and salt. Use a putty knife to scrape off any stubborn build-ups.

**If the surface is oily or sticky,** even after a brisk scrub, you might need to get out the toolbox. Scrape up any build-up with a putty knife (see left). Then gently attack the block with superfine sandpaper, beginning with a fairly coarse grain. Graduate to finer and finer grades of sandpaper until you're satisfied. Then wipe clean with a damp cloth or sponge.

Finally, don't forget to season the block again. Some say linseed oil will do the trick, but chefs prefer medical-quality paraffin oil, because it won't turn rancid.

## CHROME

**CHROME IS VERY** COMMON. OLDER CAR BUMPER BARS ARE PLATED WITH IT, AS ARE TOASTERS, ELECTRIC FRYING PANS, APPLIANCE HANDLES, SHOWER HEADS, METAL SHOWER FRAMES AND TAPS. SINCE CHROME IS USUALLY PLATED ONTO ANOTHER METAL, BE GENTLE WHEN YOU CLEAN IT, OR YOU CAN WEAR IT RIGHT OFF. AND DON'T GET ABRASIVE WITH CHROME. CLEANERS WITH 'SCRATCH' IN THEM CAN INDELIBLY MAR THE SURFACE.

**To clean chrome,** remember never to wash removable chrome items from your kitchen in greasy dishwater, because the next time the items get hot during cooking, that grease is likely to burn on. Trying to remove burned-on grease is a thankless task.

- To clean chrome, try dishwashing liquid in warm water first, using an old toothbrush to work into cracks and crevices. Then rinse with water and polish to a shine with a soft cloth.
- If that doesn't do the trick, use bicarbonate of soda sprinkled onto a damp sponge or cloth. Let the soda sit on the chrome for an hour, then rinse with warm water and dry with another cloth.
- Or rub down chrome with undiluted cider vinegar or white vinegar—no need to rinse. Ammonia can also be used—but rinse it off with water and dry completely.

**Here are some other tricks** for cleaning chrome:

- Chrome stove burner rings often get grimy and sticky. To shine them up, rub with a paste made from vinegar and cream of tartar.
- Did a plastic bread wrapper melt all over your chrome toaster or

sandwich toaster? Dab a little acetone or nail polish remover on the mess, then buff with a soft cloth. Keep the remover far from plastic parts, because it could eat them.

- Rub a chrome surface with half a lemon dipped lightly in salt. (If you have no lemons, use white vinegar and salt on a soft cloth.) Rinse well with water and buff to brilliance with a dry cloth or paper towel.
- For chrome trim on taps, kitchen appliances and cars, apply baby oil with a soft cloth and polish to restore lustre. If hard water has left deposits, a commercial cleaner should be used, such as CLR (Calcium Lime Rust Remover).
- Shine up chrome furniture bases using either cider vinegar or methylated spirits.
- To rid chrome of rust spots, especially on car trim and bumper bars, crumple aluminium foil into a wad and rub with gusto, shiny side exposed. This technique also works well on golf club shafts (see below).

Rub crumpled aluminium foil, shiny side exposed, to remove rust spots on chrome, including golf club shafts.

## CLADDING

**LIKE WINDOW SCREENS,** CLADDING ATTRACTS ALL SORTS OF GUNK—EVERYTHING FROM TREE SHEDDINGS, DUST AND MILDEW (ESPECIALLY IN SHADY SPOTS) TO POLLUTION, POLLEN AND RAIN. SOMETIMES TORRENTIAL RAIN CLEANS YOUR CLADDING. OTHER TIMES, IT JUST MAKES MATTERS WORSE. HERE'S HOW TO CLEAN ANY KIND OF CLADDING, WHETHER IT BE ALUMINIUM, VINYL OR WOOD.

**To remove dust and grime on your windows,** just dampen a cloth, sprinkle on a little bicarbonate of soda and wipe the dirt away.

**If your cladding needs only light cleaning,** try this once a year: squirt with the garden hose and scrub the cladding one section at a time, using a soft-bristled, long-handled brush. A long car-wash brush attachment on your hose is a good tool to use, letting you get to hard-to-reach areas (see page 128). Don't miss the underside of the cladding slats, where dirt loves to accumulate. Hose again to rinse.

**If your wooden cladding is really soiled,** use a deck cleaner, such as Dekswood Wood Cleaner or Cabot's Deck Clean. (If mildew and algae are a problem, choose a deck product that says it contains mould retardants.) Scrub the cleaner onto the cladding, and rinse. If water restrictions allow, a pressure washer hooked up to your garden hose is also an effective way to blast away the dirt on your cladding. You can also use sugar soap to remove grime from painted weatherboards.

## Pollution-stained cladding

If your aluminium cladding has dark streaks, they were probably caused by pollution, and there's a good chance they may not respond to Tricleanium, CRC Hydroforce or laundry detergent. In that case, you can try a liquid abrasive, such as Jif Cream. But it must be used carefully, because it's an abrasive, even though a mild one. Dampen a cleaning cloth with a little water, dab on some of the cream and rub it into the cloth. Then rub the cloth just on the streaks, very lightly. If water restrictions allow, rinse off immediately with a garden hose, or sponge off using a bucket of water.

**Clean aluminium cladding once a year.** Left to its own devices, your home's aluminium cladding will degrade over time, developing a chalky feel on the surface and eventually breaking out in tiny dark spots that can't be removed. To prevent this, clean the cladding with Tricleanium Ultra Concentrated Cleaner or CRC Hydroforce (available from hardware shops), or with an ordinary laundry detergent powder. Mix the concentrated cleaner with hot water, following the package instructions. Make sure you wear rubber gloves and protective goggles. If you're using laundry detergent, mix ¼ cup of bleach-free powdered laundry detergent with 9 litres of warm water in a bucket. Rub the cleaning solution on with a sponge and rinse it off with a garden hose, or sponge off using a bucket of water. Do not use sugar soap on aluminium.

A long car-wash brush attachment makes it easier to wash out-of-reach areas when you're cleaning cladding.

**Cleaning older bare aluminium,** the kind sold with a mill finish, presents more of a challenge. It may have started out shiny, but it tends to oxidise from years of exposure to the air, turning it a darker grey and giving it a rough feel. To clean this old-fashioned aluminium, apply some WD-40. (Spray it on or apply it with a cleaning rag.) Then go over the aluminium with fine steel wool (00). Move the steel wool back and forth (not in circles), and don't rub so hard that it scratches. When you're finished, wipe the oil off with a clean rag. Test this method on an inconspicuous area first. This technique will make your aluminium lighter and brighter, but the effects of oxidation can't be totally erased. If you're still not happy with the appearance of your aluminium, you may need to consider giving it new life with a coating of acrylic paint. (Oil-based paint won't stand up to the expansion and contraction that aluminium goes through outdoors.)

*See also:* • ALUMINIUM • VINYL

## CLOCKS

**WHEN CLEANING YOUR** CLOCK, WHAT YOU DON'T DO IS ALMOST AS IMPORTANT AS WHAT YOU DO. THE MOST IMPORTANT ASPECT OF CLEANING A MANTELPIECE, WALL, GRANDFATHER OR OTHER NICE MECHANICAL CLOCK IS TO MAINTAIN THE INTERNAL MECHANISM TO PREVENT WEAR AND TEAR.

**To take care of the inner workings,** it's best to entrust your clock to an expert to have it cleaned and oiled. Clocks are too easy to damage going the do-it-yourself route. Service the mechanism every two to three years. Remember that time may be your worst enemy, but dirt in any timepiece comes in a close second.

**Cleaning and oiling the inner workings** of a clock are possible if you're exacting. The first step is to wipe the inner workings with a dry, soft cloth to get rid of the worst of the dust and grime. Then apply special clock oil, which you can obtain at clock shops but not at hardware shops. It typically comes with a pen-like applicator. People often try using WD-40 first before they abandon the project and take the clock to a professional. Don't do it! WD-40 is not a proper lubricant for clocks—it can wear the mechanism out even faster by attracting dirt rather than repelling it.

**WATCH OUT**

One occupational hazard to note before you embark on cleaning the insides of a mechanical clock is if you don't tightly clamp down the springs and other movable parts, they can go flying every which way. If you don't really know what you're doing, let the experts clean your clock, especially on the inside.

**When you do clean and oil the inner workings yourself,** make sure you use a clamp to hold down springs and other movable parts. (See 'Watch out' box, above.) And don't put too much oil on the gears and the plate.

**Cleaning the wooden exterior of a clock** is done as you would do any other fine piece of wooden furniture. Use a furniture oil to feed the wood. (Orange oil works well and smells pleasant.) To dust a clock case, sprinkle a few drops of paraffin oil or orange oil wood cleaner on a soft cloth, not on the clock itself, and rub the case with the cloth.

**Cleaning the face covering**—be it glass, acrylic or another clear plastic—is simple. Wipe with a clean, soft cloth. If you know the cover is glass, it's OK to use a window cleaner, such as Windex or Mr Muscle, but never spray the cleaner directly on the clock. Always spray it on the cloth and wipe very gently.

## COFFEE GRINDERS

**WAKE UP AND** SMELL THE COFFEE! BE CAREFUL TO NEVER IMMERSE AN ELECTRIC COFFEE GRINDER IN WATER THOUGH WHEN CLEANING OUT—THIS CAN RUIN A PERFECTLY GOOD GRINDER.

**Clean a coffee grinder** after every use. Lest this become an electrifying experience, always begin by unplugging the unit. Brush out the grinder with a pastry brush (see right), old toothbrush or special coffee grounds brush, sold at gourmet kitchen shops and some coffee shops. This doesn't have to be a grind—simply make sure you leave the stainless steel inside the grinder shiny, so that tomorrow's batch of beans won't be sullied by stale grounds from yesterday. (The oils in coffee beans can go stale very fast.) Wash the plastic lid with a sponge in dishwashing liquid and warm water; rinse and dry with a soft cloth.

Use a pastry brush to clean out old coffee grounds from a grinder.

**Two more methods** you can try:

- Dampen a paper towel and swab the inside.
- Run a small handful of uncooked white rice through the coffee grinder (see left), especially if you use it for grinding anything other than coffee beans. Most coffee experts advise against using your machine for grinding dry spices since the smells from grinding ingredients, such as cinnamon sticks and dried basil, are nearly always impossible to get out.

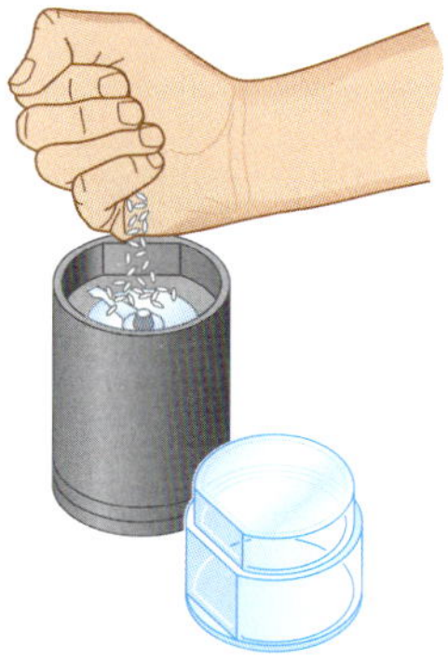

Grinding uncooked white rice gives the grinder a thorough clean.

## COFFEE MAKERS

**COFFEE MAKERS GET** CORRUPTED WITH MINERALS FROM THE WATER YOU USE. A DEPOSIT FORMS ON THE INSIDE AND AFFECTS HEATING AND BREWING TIME AND THEREFORE THE TASTE AND AROMA OF YOUR COFFEE. CLEAN THE MAKER ONCE A MONTH IF USED EVERY DAY, OR EVERY TWO MONTHS IF USED LESS OFTEN. CHECK THE FOLLOWING CLEANING METHODS IN YOUR OWNER'S MANUAL. IN GENERAL, NO ELECTRIC COFFEE MAKER IS TO BE IMMERSED IN WATER.

**To clean an electric drip coffee maker,** you have a choice of three tried-and-true methods:

- Fill the water reservoir, half with cold water and half with white vinegar. Place a clean paper filter in the basket—minus the coffee, of course. Run the coffee maker through its entire cycle. Repeat the brewing cycle two more times, using plain water each time to flush out the remaining crud.
- Fill the reservoir with water and add 2 tablespoons of decalcifier (such as CLR [Calcium Lime Rust Remover], available from supermarkets and hardware shops). Turn on the coffee maker and run it once through the complete cycle, then a second time with plain water.
- Fill the reservoir with hot water and add a denture tablet. Run the coffee machine through its complete brewing cycle, then run it once more using plain water.

Wash the coffee carafe in hot water with dishwashing liquid and rinse with water. Then remove any other removable parts and do the same. You can wash these pieces in the top rack of the dishwasher, but their colours may fade. If so, buff them with a soft, dry cloth.

**To clean an electric percolator**—the kind your mum and grandmother made famous—fill the pot with water and add ¼ cup of cream of tartar. Run through the complete percolating cycle, then wash it well with hot, soapy water, rinse with fresh water and let dry.

Keeping your espresso machine clean will extend its working life and you'll enjoy better tasing coffee.

**Cleaning a home espresso machine** is a little more complex than an electric percolator, and before you do anything, you should consult the manual for your particular model. Before starting, make sure that the machine is unplugged. The steam wand and froth head should be cleaned every time after frothing milk by removing the froth head and rinsing it under warm tap water. Wipe the steam wand with a damp cloth. Turn on the power and briefly set the selector control to the *Steam* position to clear any remaining milk from the steam wand.

**To clean the filters,** filter holder and brewing head, remove used coffee grounds directly after use and rinse the stainless steel filters and filter holder under running water. If the filter holes are blocked, use a nylon dishwashing brush to dislodge any fine particles. Wipe the brewing head with a damp cloth to remove any old coffee grounds. Every so often, you should run water through the unit with the filter in place, but without any coffee, to clean out any old grounds and remove oxidised coffee oil, which could give your coffee a stale taste.

**You will sometimes see backflushing** is recommended for espresso machine maintenance, but as none of the domestic espresso machine manufacturers recommends this, doing so could void your warranty. If you think your machine needs a more radical clean, consult the manufacturer.

EXPERT ADVICE

## BREW YOUR OWN CLEANING SOLUTION

Although commercial products are available to clean the water reservoirs of electric drip coffee makers, you can easily make your own inexpensive cleaning solution. Although you can use white vinegar or citric acid, you might prefer to use lemon juice because the smell is more pleasant.

Fill the reservoir half full with water, then to the top with pulp-free lemon juice. (You can use a ready-to-use lemon juice from the supermarket, such as Sunraysia Simply Lemon Juice, to save time and lemons.)

Run the coffee maker through its entire cycle. Discard the solution in the coffee pot, then run the brew cycle two or three more times with water until you don't smell lemon anymore. Wash all removable parts in hot, sudsy water, then rinse and dry.

## COINS

**TO COIN A** PHRASE, IF YOU'RE THINKING OF CLEANING A COIN YOU SUSPECT MIGHT BE VALUABLE: DON'T! CLEANING COINS AT HOME IS USUALLY A BAD IDEA IF YOU THINK THEY'RE WORTH SOMETHING. ON THE OTHER HAND, IF YOU DON'T LIKE THE IDEA OF GRUNGY SPARE CHANGE DIRTYING YOUR POCKET, THERE'S NO REASON WHY YOU SHOULDN'T WASH IT.

**To clean a valuable coin**—or just one that you think could be valuable—take it to a professional coin dealer or conservator for a careful facelift that will remove normal wear and tear. When a collectible coin is cleaned, its value can plummet unless the clean-up crew knows exactly what it's doing. A coin spruced up by an amateur develops an oddly dull, sometimes scoured look rather than bearing the blush of normal oxidation and handling.

**To clean ordinary coins,** wash them in warm water. Put the dirty coins in a lidded jar, add warm water and 1–2 drops of dishwashing liquid, put the lid on and gently shake. Then rinse with running water and pat dry with paper towels or a clean rag. Whatever you do, don't use lemon juice or anything else acidic. Never use abrasives either, as they'll scratch the surface.

### EXPERT ADVICE

HOT MONEY

Once you've cleaned your pocket change, bake coins in a low oven to dry them instead of allowing them to air-dry or hand drying each and every one. (Coins are made of metal, and they can corrode after exposure to water.) Instead, spread washed and rinsed coins on a baking tray, then dry them for 5–10 minutes in a 100 °C oven.

## COMBS

**COMBS COME IN** MANY SIZES AND SEVERAL MATERIALS THESE DAYS. MOST ARE FASHIONED FROM RUBBER, PLASTIC OR BONE; ALL DURABLE MATERIALS THAT TAKE KINDLY TO A SOUND THRASHING.

**To clean any comb,** first remove hair clinging to the teeth. Then try this nifty homemade version of the solution barbers and hairdressers use to sanitise their combs. (It also works for brushes; see 'Hairbrushes', on page 210.) Mix in a bowl or covered jar 500 millilitres of warm water, ¼ cup of household ammonia and ¼ teaspoon of dishwashing liquid or shampoo. Stir or shake to combine. Submerge the comb in the liquid and soak for 10 minutes (see below). Use a small, stiff-bristled nailbrush or old toothbrush to loosen up hair oils and grime clinging to the teeth. To sanitise the

Soaking your dirty comb in this sudsy homemade mix will help loosen grime and hair oil.

Simple solutions

### Wipe away that grime!

Here's how to add teeth to your comb-cleaning regimen: give that dingy comb a quick touch up by rubbing it with a disposable disinfecting wipe (available from supermarkets). Let the comb dry, then rinse and air-dry again.

comb even further, rub the teeth with a cotton wool ball saturated with methylated spirits or Dettol. Rinse the comb with warm water and allow it to air-dry.

**To clean a baby's comb,** swish it in a solution of 1 teaspoon of bicarbonate of soda dissolved in a basin of warm water. Rinse with fresh water and air-dry.

**To clean a fine-toothed metal comb** used to rid a child's hair of lice and their nits, or eggs, you need to take extra care. Here are three solutions:

- Soak the comb in a solution of 1 part chlorine bleach to 9 parts water for 15 minutes, rinse and air-dry. (If you don't dry it thoroughly, a metal comb will rust.)
- Soak the comb in hot water (at least 55 °C) for 5 minutes.
- Seal the comb in a plastic bag for two weeks. (Gasping for air, those nasty nits and lice eventually suffocate.)

## COMPUTERS

**COMPUTERS COLLECT** DUST, GRIMY FINGERPRINTS, CRUMBS, HAIR, FINGERNAIL CLIPPINGS AND OTHER UNIDENTIFIED MINIATURE OBJECTS. A COMPUTER CAN BE GIVEN A QUICK ONCE-OVER WITH A VACUUM OR DUST CLOTH AS PART OF YOUR REGULAR CLEANING PROCEDURE. BUT IT'S A GOOD IDEA TO GIVE IT A MORE THOROUGH CLEANING OCCASIONALLY. ONCE EVERY THREE MONTHS IS SUFFICIENT, ALTHOUGH YOU'LL WANT TO CLEAN THE SCREEN EVERY MONTH OR SO. IF YOU'RE UNSURE, TAKE IT TO A PROFESSIONAL. IF YOU OPT FOR THE AT-HOME TREATMENT, THE FIRST STEP IS TO MAKE SURE THE COMPUTER IS TURNED OFF AND UNPLUGGED.

**To clean the screen of a traditional tube monitor,** dust it with a clean cloth or a facial tissue. To remove fingerprints, wipe with a slightly damp cloth. Special towelettes, sold at office supply shops, may be used on the screen, but they can leave a soapy film. Try an all-purpose cleaner instead, such as Ajax Spray n' Wipe, sprayed on a cloth and then wiped on the screen (see right). Avoid ammonia-based cleaners, as they sometimes leave unsightly streaks.

Clean your screen with an all-purpose cleaner sprayed on a cloth.

**To clean a new flat screen monitor** or the screen on a laptop you need to use special care. First unplug the power supply, then lightly dampen a clean, soft, lint-free cloth with water and isopropyl (surgical) alcohol. Make sure it is not ethyl alcohol, or, another name for it, ethanol. (See 'Watch out' box, on page 135 for more information.) Wipe the screen gently with a back-and-forth-motion, never in a circle. Wipe the display case gently with a non-abrasive, soft, dry cloth to pick up dust. To prolong the life of your flat screen, never tap or touch the screen with your pen, finger or other object. And don't slap sticky notes on your screen.

**To clean the keyboard,** which is a magnet for all sorts of gunk, first turn it upside down over a wastebasket and give it a good shake. Most crumbs and dust will fall right out. Then vacuum it with your brush attachment. To clean the keys, rub them and the surrounding plastic with a cloth dampened with methylated spirits. Or purchase a special keyboard cleaner-degreaser, sold at electronics shops. Using a can of compressed air, available at hardware or electronics shops, blast away hair, crumbs and dust from between the keys. Rubbing keys with a fabric softener sheet will keep dust-attracting static at bay.

**To clean the mouse,** unscrew the mouse-ball cover on the bottom and take out the ball. Wipe it down with methylated spirits, using a soft cloth. Remove any dust or fluff inside the mouse-ball socket with your finger. Then, with a cotton bud dipped in metho, clean the three rollers the ball touches inside the socket (see left).

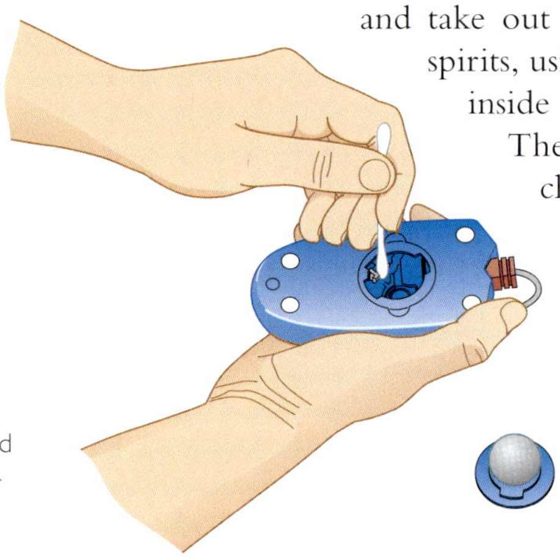

Cotton buds soaked in metho are ideal for cleaning the rollers inside the mouse.

**To clean inside the computer,** you can also use compressed air. To open an upright computer, unscrew one side of the case. One side is usually held by screws with knurled heads that you can turn by hand, but on some models you may need to use a screwdriver. Don't touch anything inside that you don't have to. Keep your fingers away from cards, cords and other parts. And make sure the compressed air extension nozzle is at least 10 centimetres from the machine. Blow air into the power supply box (that's where the power cord enters) and the fan at the back of the case. Then blast a bit of air into the CD and floppy disk drives. Before replacing the side, wipe it with a damp cloth. Let it dry before putting it back on.

**WATCH OUT** Don't use ordinary household spray cleaners on your computer keyboard. If the liquid should get under the keys, it can easily damage the keyboard by shorting the contacts under the keys.

## A mouse by any other name

People do all sorts of things near their computers. They eat over them, accidentally spill coffee and other drinks onto their keyboards, and sometimes jam four or five CDs at a time into the CD-ROM drive. And then, of course, there are those smaller children who love to pull cords out and are fascinated by little holes and shove big things into small places with their tiny hands. And, to top if off, beware of any odd smells emanating from your computer. It could be that a mouse—not the electronic kind, mind you—has set up shop inside. Mice are attracted to the heat exuded by computers.

**WATCH OUT** If you have a new flat LCD monitor—or a laptop—never use products containing acetone, ethyl alcohol (ethanol), toluene, ethyl acid, ammonia or methyl chloride to clean the screen. They can damage it.

**To clean computer equipment exteriors,** simply wipe the outside surfaces with an all-purpose cleaner, sprayed on a soft cloth. Dust can collect in ports where you attach cables. Use the compressed air with extension nozzle to blow the ports clean. Or give them a swipe with one end of a cotton bud dampened with methylated spirits. Use the other end of the cotton bud to dry them.

**To clean the glass bed of your scanner,** use mild soap or an ordinary glass cleaner without ammonia. (Ammonia cleaners, unless they're completely wiped off, leave a film that could make scanned documents look weirdly oily or speckled.) Spray the glass cleaner onto a soft cloth rather than squirting it on the glass itself. Methylated spirits is also good to use. And if there's a metal ruler scale along the edge of the glass, avoid getting it wet. That also goes for the glue holding it down. And never use paper towels to wipe your scanner. Even the more expensive types can make fine scratches on optical surfaces. Use soft, lint-free cloths instead. An old, clean T-shirt or microfibre cloth is perfect.

*See also:*
• PRINTERS

## CONCRETE

WHEN CLEANING CONCRETE THE ESSENTIAL FIRST STEP IS TO DETERMINE—IF YOU CAN—WHAT CAUSED THE GRIME OR STAIN, AND THEN ACT ACCORDINGLY—AND FAST. THE LONGER AN UNTREATED STAIN STAYS ON CONCRETE, THE MORE LIKELY IT IS TO SEEP IN TO BECOME PART OF THE WHOLE, AND INCREASINGLY MORE DIFFICULT TO REMOVE. METHODS VARY ON HOW TO CLEAN CONCRETE, BUT THE FACT IS THAT CLEANING UP THAT GARAGE FLOOR, PATIO, FOOTPATH, DRIVEWAY OR OTHER CONCRETE FEATURE IS AN ESSENTIAL PART OF REGULAR HOME MAINTENANCE.

**Clean concrete at least once a year.** Before you start, be sure to protect all adjacent glass, metal, wood, plants or other decorative materials with a tarpaulin or old shower curtain. Try one of the following methods that are listed in order of increasing wallop. To make sure it works, test the method in an obscure spot. Never use a metallic brush on concrete, as metallic fibres can get trapped in the concrete, where they'll eventually rust.

Only use non-metallic brushes to scrub stains off concrete.

- If the concrete is old and crumbly, brush it lightly with a soft brush. If that doesn't do the trick, try warm water and mild detergent, adding white vinegar to the water if the soil and stains persist.
- Wet the concrete with warm water and let it absorb the water. Then scrub with a soft, non-metallic brush (see above). Wash off the concrete with a garden hose fitted with a high-pressure nozzle and let it dry.
- If that doesn't remove it, add ¼ cup of mild dishwashing liquid to a bucket of warm water and scrub again.
- Failing that, use a liquid laundry detergent, mixed with water and ¼ cup of ammonia, applied with a stiff nylon brush.

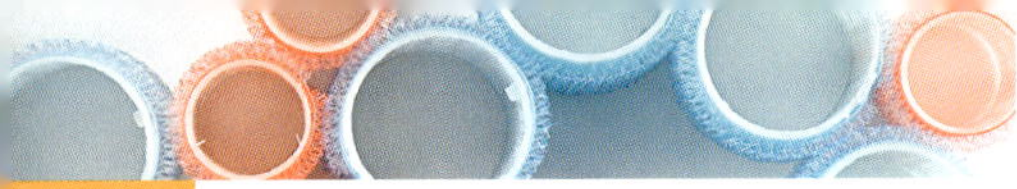

● For obstinate grime, mix a concentrated cleaner, such as Tricleanium Ultra Concentrated Cleaner or CRC Hydroforce (available from hardware shops), in a bucket with hot water, according to the package instructions for heavy cleaning jobs. Scrub with a rigid nylon brush, then rinse with a garden hose and allow to air-dry. You can also use sugar soap. Wear protective clothing when using both these products.

**To remove serious stains,** such as tyre marks, grease, oil and other stubborn materials, you're going to have to get aggressive. For fresh grease stains, first sprinkle dry cement, one of the clay-type kitty litters or sand on the spot, letting it sit for an hour to absorb the gunky mess. Then sweep it up with a dustpan and broom. For more irksome grease spots, use a commercial product that removes oil, grease and tar from cement, terrazzo and stone, such as Liquid Magnet or Selleys Heavy Duty Concrete Kleen. These can be bought from hardware shops, and make sure you follow the label instructions.

**If moss and mildew are proving to be a persistent problem,** you will probably need to scrub with a bleach-based product, such as 30 Seconds Outdoor Cleaner.

## CONTACT LENSES

DECIDING WHICH SOLUTIONS TO USE FOR YOUR CONTACT LENSES CAN BE TOUGH. PHARMACIES AND SUPERMARKETS ARE CHOCK-A-BLOCK WITH PRODUCTS. TO MAKE SENSE OF IT ALL, FIRST UNDERSTAND THAT THERE ARE TWO BASIC KINDS OF CONTACTS TODAY. SOFT LENSES, THE MOST COMMON, MAKE UP AROUND 85 PER CENT OF THE MARKET. GAS-PERMEABLE (GP) LENSES ARE RESPONSIBLE FOR MOST OF THE REMAINDER. (GP LENSES ARE NOT TO BE CONFUSED WITH THE OLD HARD LENSES, WHICH ACCOUNT FOR LESS THAN 1 PER CENT OF TOTAL CONTACT LENS SALES.)

**Here are a few basic guidelines** of sound contact lens care that you should follow routinely regardless of whether you wear soft or gas-permeable contact lenses:

● Clean and disinfect your lenses once a day. Always use fresh solution to clean and store your lenses.

● Always wash and rinse your hands thoroughly before handling the lenses. Don't use perfumed soaps or scented hand cream—let alone cook with fresh chillies or chilli powder—right before touching your lenses. And always dry your hands with a clean, lint-free towel.

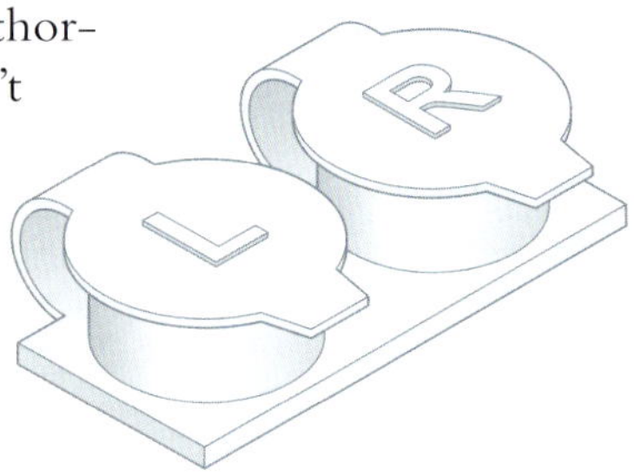


■ A lens holder is an ideal place to store and clean your lenses.

● Close the sink drain or at least cover it with a clean dishcloth.

● Never use tap or bottled water as a substitute for the shop-bought lens care system your eye care expert recommends. Water can bear a micro-organism (Acanthamoeba) that can cause serious eye infections.

● Always clean your accessories (lens case, cleaning and disinfecting containers, vials for enzymatic cleaners and the like) after each use exactly as the instructions advise. Typically, this also involves cleaning, rinsing and air-drying.

- Throw out your lenses once a month, or as often as it is recommended, to reduce the chance of infection.

**The cleaning program** for the two major types of contact lenses is basically the same: clean, rinse, disinfect. In times past, there were three different products for this. Today, cleaning, rinsing and disinfecting solutions are usually all-in-one. Get into the habit of always handling your right lens first to avoid confusion. Here's how to proceed:

- Remove the right lens and clean it by gently rubbing the lens in the palm of your hand with a few drops of rinsing and disinfecting cleaner. (Some newer solutions have a no-rub feature, useful for people who frequently rip their lenses while cleaning them.)
- Rinse the lens to remove any leftover contaminated cleaner, cosmetics and other substances. Be sure to rinse the lens for as long as package instructions direct.
- Place the lens in your lens holder (see below left) and fill it with your chosen disinfecting solution. This step kills micro-organisms that may have a mind to breed on your lens.

Repeat the cleaning and disinfecting process with the left lens. Disinfecting time varies from product to product, but most instructions will urge you to soak the lenses overnight.

**Two other important points** to keep in mind are these:

- Soft lenses pick up protein deposits more readily than GP types do. If your lenses start to feel grainy or your vision becomes clouded, chances are you need to use an enzymatic cleaner daily or weekly, according to package instructions.
- Some people have allergic reactions to some contact lens solutions. About 10 per cent of people, for instance, are allergic to thimerosal, a preservative sometimes used in saline lens solutions. Experiment to see what works for you.

*See also:*
• EYEGLASSES AND SUNGLASSES

Cleaning your contact lenses in a sterile lens solution before wearing them is essential.

# COPPER

**COPPER IS A** METAL AND, WHILE IT'S HARDER THAN SILVER, IT'S STILL SOFTER THAN EITHER BRASS OR BRONZE. IT COMES IN TWO TYPES: LACQUERED AND UNLACQUERED. LACQUERED COPPER, WHICH IS USUALLY ON DECORATIVE ITEMS, HAS A FINISH BAKED ON AT THE FACTORY. UNLACQUERED COPPER, FOUND MOSTLY ON COOKWARE, TARNISHES EASILY BUT WILL BRIGHTEN WITH ELBOW GREASE AND THE RIGHT TECHNIQUES. RARELY WILL YOU SEE LACQUERED COPPER COOKWARE OR UTENSILS. IF YOU DO, YOU SHOULD REMOVE THE FINISH BEFORE USING THEM FOR EATING OR COOKING.

**EXPERT ADVICE**

**DIFFERENT THOUGHTS**

You can scrub copper to a gleam with Gumption or Ajax, but another school of thought says that the duller the bottom of your copper pot, the better it is at transferring heat to the food inside.

**To clean a decorative copper item** with a lacquered finish, you only need to dust the piece with a dust cloth or vacuum as part of your regular cleaning process. If it's dirty, you might want to wipe it with a damp cloth. Lacquering on decorative pieces works OK until cracks start to appear in the finish. Then the piece must be stripped of its coating with acetone or lacquer thinner, applied full strength with a cloth. Or boil the item in 7 litres of water with 1 cup of washing soda crystals (available from supermarkets). The lacquer should peel right off. Then wash with dishwashing liquid, rinse with running water and dry with a soft cloth.

If you want to lacquer the piece again, employ the services of a professional metal finisher.

**To clean copper cookware,** you should first be aware of the don'ts. Never use any scratchy cleaning tool on copper. You run the risk of leaving marks. And bleach will seriously discolour copper if it is left soaking for a few hours or more. Don't use oven cleaners or glass cleaners like Windex or Mr Muscle, either—they'll make quick work of your copper because they will corrode it.

If copper cookware is really in bad shape, remove any corrosion before you polish. Several methods exist to do this:

- Salt mixed with a little white vinegar and applied with a soft cloth (see right).
- Cut a lemon in half, dip it in salt and rub.
- As long as the piece can stand the heat, boil it in a large kettle filled with water, 1 cup of white vinegar and ½ cup of salt.

A salt and white vinegar mix rubbed on copper cookware will remove corrosion.

Whatever method you use to clean your cookware, rinse with fresh water, dry well with a tea towel and buff with a soft cloth. If you want more shine, apply a commercial copper cleaner according to label instructions.

**Here are two more tips** to help you clean copper:

- Crevices—where the handle joins the pot, for instance—can be tough to clean. These spots can also be magnets for paste polish build-up. Use a cotton bud or horsehair brush and methylated spirits to get rid of the gunk.
- Swab small copper items with tomato or Worcestershire sauce applied to a cotton cosmetic pad or cotton bud. You'll be surprised by how quickly they gleam.

## CORK

**WHEN CLEANING A** CORK FLOOR BE SPARING WITH WHATEVER LIQUID YOU USE. MOST CORK FLOORS ARE SEALED WITH POLYURETHANE TO PREVENT THEM FROM LAPPING UP SPILLS AND OTHER STAINS. STILL, YOU DON'T WANT WATER OR OTHER LIQUIDS TO PENETRATE THE SEAMS AND CAUSE THE TILES TO LIFT.

**To clean a cork floor,** sweep up loose dirt with a dustpan and broom first. Then apply a cleaner suitable for cork, such as Pledge Wood Magic, with a damp mop. Dab a bit of cleaner on any sticky, persistent spots and then blot with a soft rag. Never use acids like white vinegar on your cork floor, whether it's sealed or not.

Heavily trafficked areas—the entrance, hallway and kitchen, for instance—should be coated with polyurethane every two to three years. Make sure a floor expert performs this task. Floors must first be scrubbed with a special pad to rough up old sealant.

**To clean cork walls**, which usually aren't sealed, rub them with a putty-style wallpaper cleaner or a dry foam-rubber sponge, available at hardware and paint shops. Any spots may be hand-sanded with superfine sandpaper to remove them. However, cork on walls is usually only 3 millimetres thick, so be careful not to turn your cork into an unsightly patchwork.

Sanding with pumice is the trick to cleaning a dirty cork item like a mat.

**To clean a cork or cork-backed item,** such as a coaster, a trivet or a mat, wet it with cold water and scrub with a pumice stone or pad (see left). Rinse with water and air-dry in a cool, dry place.

### Simple solutions

**Bread (and tape) to the rescue**

Ducks love stale bread, and you can make salad croutons and breadcrumbs with it, too. But there's yet another use: tear off a hunk of that dried-out bread and scrub gently on stained cork. It cleans the cork without damaging it. An alternative is to try patting the grungy spot with tape.

## CRAYON MARKS

**CRAYON-WIELDING CHILDREN** WILL ALWAYS BE MYSTERIOUSLY ATTRACTED TO THE WALLS OF YOUR HOME. THEY'RE ALSO KNOWN TO LEAVE THEIR MARK ON CLOTHING, FURNITURE AND CARPET. AND CRAYONS, WHEN LEFT IN A POCKET, CAN MELT AND MAKE A MESS OF THE DRYER AND STAIN CLOTHING.

**To remove crayon from most smooth surfaces,** including painted walls, glass, metal, tile, marble or porcelain, spray the marks with a penetrating lubricant (specifically, WD-40), then wipe with a soft cloth. The lubricant WD-40 is the weapon of choice when it comes to removing many crayon marks. It lifts off the stain by getting between the mark and the surface. Spray a little WD-40 first in an obscure spot to make sure it won't harm what you're cleaning. If that lubricant doesn't do the trick, dip a sponge into a solution of dishwashing liquid and warm water and wet the crayon mark, rubbing with a circular motion. Rinse with warm water, then air-dry.

**To remove crayon from clothing,** place the fabric on a layer of paper towels, then spray with WD-40 (see page 140). Spray more of the lubricant on a clean rag and apply it to both sides of the stain.

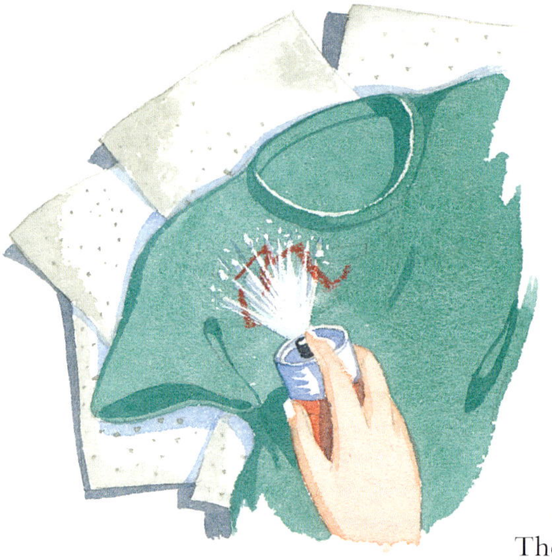

■ To remove crayon from clothing, the magic ingredient is WD-40.

Allow the lubricant to sit for 2 minutes. Then, using your fingers, rub 1–2 drops of dishwashing liquid into the stain on each side. Replace the paper towels as they absorb the crayon. Wash the clothing in the washing machine using the hottest water possible and the heavy soil setting.

**Other approaches** that you might try:

- Use a light touch on the stain with a dry, soap-filled steel wool pad.
- Or rub the stain gently with bicarbonate of soda sprinkled on top of a damp sponge.
- Pre-treat the stain with hair spray before washing.

**To remove crayon on upholstery and carpeting,** scrape up as much crayon as you can with a metal spoon or dull knife. Then wet the mark with WD-40 and let it stand 5 minutes. Apply elbow grease and a stiff-bristled brush, then wipe with paper towels. Spray again with WD-40. Dab 1–2 drops of dishwashing liquid onto the stain and work it in with the brush. Then wipe with a damp sponge. If the stain persists, repeat. Or use a dry-cleaning solvent (from pharmacies or hardware shops), according to instructions.

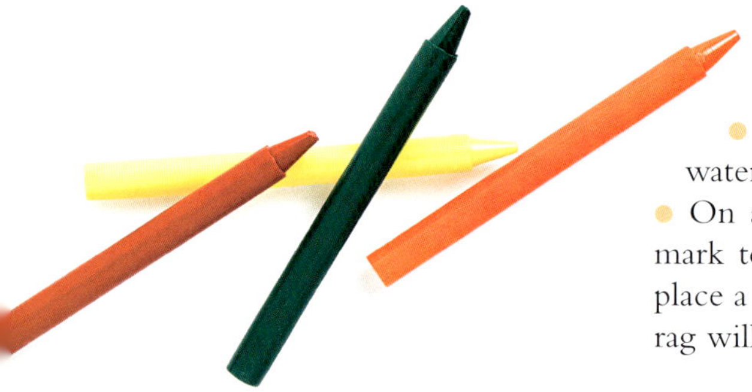

**To remove crayon on floors,** different methods are used depending on the type of floor.

- On vinyl no-wax flooring, use silver polish. Rinse well with water and dry with a paper towel.
- On a wooden floor, place an ice-filled plastic bag on the crayon mark to make it brittle, then scrape with a spoon or dull knife. Or place a clean rag on the mark and heat it with an iron (no steam). The rag will soak up the melted wax.

## CRYSTAL

**NEVER PUT CRYSTAL** IN THE DISHWASHER. IT IS TOO FRAGILE AND SOFT FOR THE DUAL ACTION OF DISHWASHER AND DETERGENT, WHICH CAN ETCH AND DULL ITS SURFACE. TO PRESERVE THE SPARKLE OF CRYSTAL, ALWAYS HAND WASH IT—UNLESS IT HAS SILVER OR GOLD GILT, IN WHICH CASE YOU SHOULD USE WARM WATER ONLY, NO SOAP.

**To wash crystal,** line the bottom of your sink with a doubled-up towel or rubber mat, fill the sink with warm water—not hot—and add 2–3 drops of dishwashing liquid. Wash one item at a time. Grasp glassware by the bowl, not the stem, and wash gently. A bartender's trick is to pump the glass up and down in warm water to rinse. Dry upside down on a lint-free cotton tea towel or vinyl-coated dish drainer. Better yet, put clean thick gloves or cotton socks over your hands and dry the crystal immediately with an old linen tea towel. This way, you'll leave no fingerprints or watermarks.

**To remove stains,** try this three-pronged approach:

- First, mix a paste of lemon juice and baking powder and rub gently on the crystal with a sponge, then wash and dry. (Baking powder is

about as abrasive as you can get with crystal without risking damage.)
- Tougher stains may be 'riced': put 2 teaspoons of uncooked rice into the crystal piece, add water and swirl. Repeat, if need be.
- For stubborn stains, fill the crystal receptacle with warm water and drop in a denture tablet.

**EXPERT ADVICE**

MAKE-YOUR-OWN BOTTLE BRUSH

For crystal with a thin neck too narrow for a bottle brush, straighten a wire coat hanger and wrap each end with terry towelling rags secured with rubber bands. Dampen one end and rub inside. Use the other to dry.

**Here are some more crystal-cleaning tricks** that are worth considering:
- Try the conservator's way of cleaning crystal. Mix equal parts methylated spirits and water and then add a few drops of ammonia. Apply the solution to the crystal with cotton cosmetic pads or those lint-free pads you use to clean a fax machine (available from office supply shops). Rinse and dry. (Don't try this on gilded crystal.)
- To dry a decanter or vase, use a hand-held hair dryer (Cool setting). Otherwise, it can take up to three or four days to air-dry a decanter without the stopper.
- For extra shine, add ¼ cup of borax, white vinegar or lemon juice to the rinse water.
- To wash the grooves of cut crystal, dip a frayed toothbrush into lemon juice, vinegar or soapy water, and scrub.

## CURLERS

**WHEN YOU CURL** YOUR HAIR, THE LAST THING YOU WANT TO SEE WHEN YOU GAZE IN THE MIRROR ARE TRACES OF GRIME IN YOUR HAIR LEFT OVER FROM DIRTY CURLERS. NOR DO YOU WANT TO RUIN YOUR HAIR WITH ANY HARSH CLEANING-CHEMICAL RESIDUE.

**To wash curlers** that are submersible in water, such as plain rollers, Velcro rollers and foam-coated wire sticks, fill your bathroom sink with warm water, mix in a couple of teaspoons of shampoo or facial cleanser to create suds, and let them soak. As a general rule, if a cleaner is gentle enough for your face or hair, it is fine for your curlers. Use a wide-toothed comb to gently pull out any hair stuck in the curlers (see below left). Then wipe with a rag to remove caked-on film. Rinse with fresh water and either dry with a clean towel or air-dry.

**For stubborn stains,** such as hardened setting lotions or gels, mix up a solution of ¼ cup of warm water and 1 tablespoon of liquid fabric softener in a cup. Gently scrub the solution in with a vegetable scrubber or nailbrush. Rinse with water and dry.

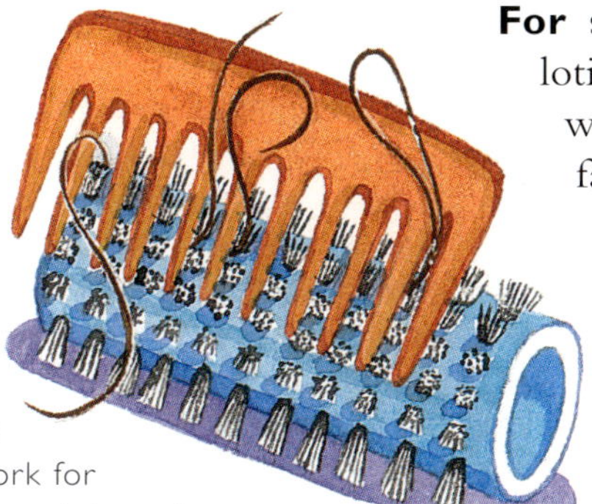

A wide-toothed comb makes easy work for removing hair stuck in curlers.

**To clean electric curlers,** which are not submersible, use a rag or nailbrush and the fabric softener solution. Rinse by wiping the curlers with a damp rag and then dry.

## CURLING TONGS

**CLEANING CURLING TONGS** CAN BE TRICKY. YOU MUST REMOVE THE SHELLAC-LIKE CRUST OF SINGED HAIR AND HAIR SPRAY THAT BUILDS UP OVER TIME. HOWEVER, BECAUSE THEY ARE ELECTRICAL APPLIANCES, YOU CAN'T SOAK THEM IN WATER. AND YOU DON'T WANT TO USE TOXIC CHEMICAL CLEANERS, SINCE THEY CAN LEAVE CHEMICAL RESIDUE IN YOUR HAIR. LUCKILY, WE HAVE A NON-TOXIC RECIPE THAT WORKS WONDERS. READ ON.

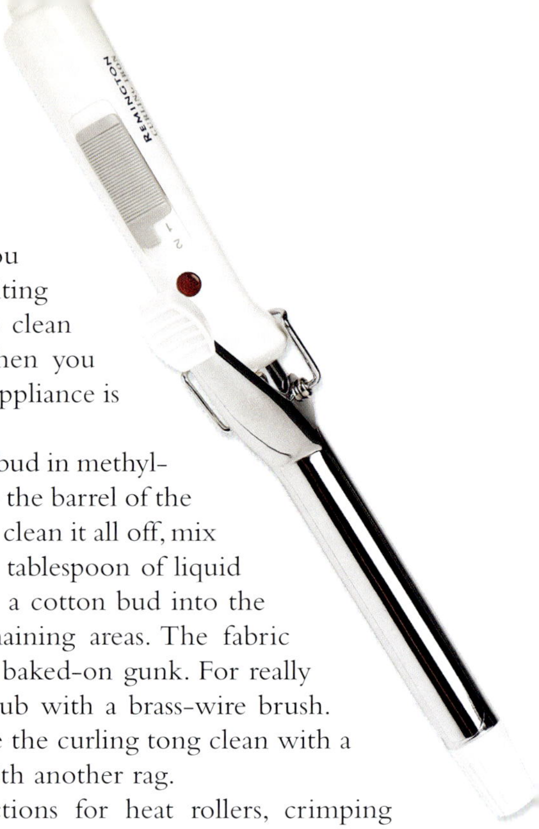


**Clean your curling tong** if it starts to smoke when you use it. But rather than waiting until it smokes, it's better to clean it about once a month. When you clean, always make sure the appliance is completely cool.

First, try dipping a cotton bud in methylated spirits and applying it to the barrel of the curling tong. If that does not clean it all off, mix ¼ cup of warm water and 1 tablespoon of liquid fabric softener in a cup. Dip a cotton bud into the solution and clean the remaining areas. The fabric softener should dissolve the baked-on gunk. For really stubborn patches, gently scrub with a brass-wire brush. When you are finished, wipe the curling tong clean with a damp rag and then dry it with another rag.

Follow the same instructions for heat rollers, crimping tongs and hair straighteners.

## CURTAINS

**CURTAINS ARE THE** UNSUNG HEROES OF THE HOME FURNISHINGS WORLD. DAY IN AND DAY OUT, THEY STAND SENTINEL AGAINST THE RAVAGES OF SUMMER SUN AND WINTER DRAUGHTS. AND—MOST PEOPLE DON'T KNOW THIS—THEY FORM AN INTEGRAL PART OF THE HOME'S AIRFLOW SYSTEM, FILTERING DUST OUT OF AIR THAT BLOWS IN AND OUT OF WINDOWS. YOU OWE IT TO YOUR CURTAINS—NOT TO MENTION YOUR LUNGS—TO KEEP THEM CLEAN AND DUST FREE.

**Dust your curtains** once a month or so as part of a regular household dusting. There's no need to take them down. (Who has the time to do that every month?) Instead, dust them where they hang using your vacuum cleaner with a dusting brush or an upholstery attachment (see below). Use an extension tube to reach the tops. If you don't have the right vacuum attachments, the tried-and-true cleaning implement, the feather duster, will suffice.

Dust your curtains using a vacuum cleaner and an extension tube to reach the tops.

# rules of the game

IT'S CURTAINS FOR DUST ON DRAPES

- Keeping your curtains free of dust is easy and good for your health.
- Always clean matching curtains at the same time.
- Vacuum them where they hang using a dusting brush or upholstery attachment. Start at the top and work down.
- Make sure you clean the places where dust tends to gather, which is usually on the tops and hems.
- To avoid sucking the fabric into the nozzle, either reduce the vacuum pressure or grasp the bottom and hold the curtains taut.

**Clean your curtains** about once a year. First, look for the manufacturer's cleaning recommendations, which should be on a tag sewn inside the hem. If there is no tag, try to decide what sort of treatment the fabric gets. Depending on the material, you will either machine wash, hand wash or dry-clean the curtains.

Upholstery brush attachments come in various shapes and sizes, and are a boon for removing dust from curtains.

**If curtains can be machine washed,** put them in the washing machine on the delicate cycle. They may look sturdy, but being continually exposed to the sun can weaken curtains by breaking down the fibres in the material. Consequently, the minute you wash them, they may begin to deteriorate. Likewise, be gentle when drying curtains in a machine. If you have one, use the permanent press setting on your dryer; it has a cool-down feature that will help prevent wrinkles. High heat from a dryer can set wrinkles in the fabric, especially when the cycle ends abruptly and leaves the curtains in a ball. An alternative to tumbling curtains until they are dry is to remove them from the dryer and hang them while they are still damp. This will reduce wrinkling and may even help you avoid having to iron them. If your curtains are not very dirty, skip the washing altogether and freshen them by tumbling them in a dryer using no heat.

**If curtains require dry-cleaning,** make sure that you find the best place for the job. Most neighbourhood dry-cleaners don't have the special knowledge or equipment to handle curtains. Find one that does. Some cleaners will even measure your curtains beforehand and guarantee that they will come back the same length, which is important.

# CUSHIONS

**KEEPING CUSHIONS CLEAN** IS MORE THAN JUST A MATTER OF APPEARANCE. MICRO-ORGANISMS CALLED DUST MITES, WHICH CAN TRIGGER ALLERGIES, OFTEN LURK WITHIN A DIRTY COUCH'S FOLDS AND FIBRES. FLOP DOWN AFTER A HARD DAY'S WORK, AND YOU MAY FIND YOURSELF IN A SNEEZING FIT. BY REMOVING THE DUST REGULARLY, YOU WILL NOT ONLY KEEP YOUR CUSHIONS LOOKING FRESH (AND KEEP THE DUST FROM STAINING THEM ONCE IT IS GROUND IN OR MOISTENED), BUT YOU ALSO IMPROVE THE QUALITY OF YOUR HOME'S AIR.

**To remove dust**—and the tiny insects inhabiting the dust—clean cushions about once a month using a vacuum cleaner with the appropriate attachments, such as an upholstery brush and a crevice tool. To avoid sucking out the feathers, don't vacuum down-filled cushions that are not lined with down-proof covering. No vacuum cleaner attachments? Use a soft-bristled brush to gently brush away the dust instead.

**To give a more thorough cleaning,** or to remove stains, wash your cushions. As a general rule, don't remove the cushions from the upholstery cover. First, check the upholstery manufacturer's suggestions, usually tagged to upholstery fabric sold after 1970. This tag will tell you whether you should use a dry-cleaning solvent, a water-based shampoo or neither of the two. Next, pick an inconspicuous spot on the cushion and pre-test whatever cleaning technique is suggested. If there is shrinking or bleeding or running of colours, contact a professional cleaner. If not, proceed.

Even if shampoo is allowable, use as little moisture as possible. You do not want to wet the cushions' stuffing, because it dries very slowly and can make conditions even rosier for moisture-loving dust mites. The trick is to clean using suds only.

- The easiest solution is to use a foaming commercial upholstery shampoo in an aerosol can. Follow the instructions on the can, which will typically tell you to allow the foam to stand until dry and then proceed to vacuum it off.
- To make your own shampoo, mix ½ teaspoon of dishwashing liquid per 1 litre of warm water. Make suds by squeezing a sponge in the solution. Scoop the suds off the top and apply them sparingly with the sponge to the cushion surface. Rub gently in the direction of the fabric's grain. Rather than letting the cushions dry as you would a commercial shampoo, work on a small area at a time, lightly rinsing each area as you go with a clean, damp sponge. Again, avoid soaking the fabric. Be sure to remove all the suds, or the residue will cause the fabric to soil faster.

**If the fabric calls for dry-cleaning only** and you want to just clean a stain, you can do it yourself, using a commercial dry-cleaning solvent such as Murlex or Woolclean Spot Dry Remover No. 2. Don't pour the solvent onto the stain. Instead, moisten a clean, white cloth with the solvent and use the cloth to draw the stain out. Blot repeatedly—never rub. Rubbing can stretch or damage the texture of the fabric. Always use solvents sparingly and in a well-ventilated area. And don't use solvents on cushions filled with latex foam rubber padding, because the solvent can dissolve the padding. However, if you need to clean the entire surface of a cushion, have it professionally cleaned.

# CUTLERY

**YOUR CUTLERY SHOULD** BE SO CLEAN AND SHINY THAT DINNER GUESTS COULD USE A KNIFE BLADE LIKE A MIRROR TO SEE THEMSELVES. THEY PROBABLY SHOULDN'T, BUT THEY SHOULD BE ABLE TO.

Simple solutions

## Silver lining

To get the most out of your good silver, take it out of hiding now and then. Frequent use and buffing will enhance the patina and will give pleasure to you and its other users. Store it in a clean, dry drawer. If you store your silver for long, use either flannel cutlery rolls or a wooden, felt-lined chest to deter tarnish. You can also prevent tarnish by storing silver pieces in plastic wrap, making sure to remove as much air as possible.

**Rinse your cutlery** under running water immediately after eating. You may not want to wash the dishes if, say, you're entertaining, but rinsing will remove food that might cause pitting or staining. Be especially diligent about eggs, fruit juices, tomato-based foods, lemon, vinegar, salty foods (including butter), mustard and salad dressings. Silver is most vulnerable, but stainless steel, despite its name, isn't completely immune to the threat of corrosion. You can also soak cutlery in warm water in a sink or washing-up bowl, but don't soak hollow-handled ware for long, lest it loosen the soldering.

**Wash stainless steel cutlery** in the dishwasher, along with your dishes, but don't spill detergent directly on the pieces, because it could pit or spot them. However, your cutlery will be shinier and more lustrous if you dry it by hand with a soft dishcloth.

If your stainless steel cutlery has dulled over the years, you can easily brighten it by soaking it in 4 litres of hot water mixed with 1 teaspoon of ammonia. Then rinse with clear hot water and dry well with a clean cloth.

**Wash silver cutlery,** both plate and sterling, by hand. Use dishwashing liquid in hot water. Rinse thoroughly with clear, hot water and dry immediately with a soft dishcloth. Don't use abrasive cleaners or scrubbers, such as steel wool, as they will dull the finish.

The sulfur in eggs and egg products (such as mayonnaise) will cause silver to tarnish—instantly. So do pollutants in the air, but they work more slowly. Tarnish is not removed by regular washing. You'll have to use a silver polish on that.

**Clean pewter cutlery** with methylated spirits on a soft cloth. Then follow up with the hot, soapy water treatment described above.

*For how to polish silver, see:*
• SILVER JEWELLERY • SILVERWARE
*See also:*
• PEWTER

# DECANTERS

**THE DIRTY DECANTER** IS THE CLEANING WORLD'S BRAIN TEASER. THE PUZZLE IS HOW TO REACH THE CAVERNOUS SPACE THAT LIES BEYOND A DECANTER'S NARROW NECK IN ORDER TO SCRUB AWAY STUBBORN STAINS SUCH AS LIME DEPOSITS AND RED WINE RINGS. AND AFTER YOU CLEAN IT, THERE'S THE CHALLENGE OF DRYING IT. BUT THE PUZZLE CAN BE SOLVED, SO READ ON.

Leave a towel-wrapped spoon or stick in a decanter to absorb moisture and prevent fogging up once the stopper is replaced.

**Begin with the outside,** washing your decanter by hand. Never put a decanter in a dishwasher, as the heat and vibration can easily break its delicate glass neck. If the decanter is an antique or made of fine crystal or cut glass, wash it in a plastic basin rather than in a hard sink to reduce the chances of breakage. Or you can line the bottom of your sink with a rubber mat or a doubled-over towel. Then just use a sponge or soft-bristled brush, warm water and mild dishwashing liquid to wash the outer surface.

**Cleaning the inside** depends on how dirty or stained the decanter is. There are several approaches. The simplest is to fill it halfway with soapy, warm water, hold your hand over the top and gently shake. Still stained? Swirl a mixture of rock salt and vinegar around inside the decanter. The salt will gently scour the surface while the vinegar helps remove stains, especially lime deposits. If rock salt and vinegar do not remove wine stains, try swishing a small amount of warm water, bicarbonate of soda and rock salt in the bottle.

Another approach is to put water in the decanter, drop in a denture cleaner tablet and let it stand overnight. No matter which method you use, rinse with clean, warm water.

**Dry your decanter** completely, so that it does not fog up after you replace the stopper. Worse than being unsightly, that moisture could harbour dangerous micro-organisms. Instead of drying your decanter by inverting it in your dish drainer, which increases the chance of breakage and takes forever, try this trick: drain most of the water out of the decanter by holding it upside down. To remove any final moisture, wrap a paper towel around the handle of a long-handled wooden spoon so that the towel extends slightly beyond the end. Stick the towel-wrapped spoon or stick into the decanter (see left) and let it rest on the bottom overnight to allow the towel to remove most of the condensation. If you can't wait until morning, gently blow warm air into the decanter with a hair dryer. Be careful, though: too much heat can crack delicate glass.

## DECKS

**THINK OF YOUR** DECK AS AN OUTDOOR ROOM, ONE EXPOSED TO SUN, WIND AND RAIN. TO KEEP YOUR DECK LOOKING ITS BEST, YOU NEED TO CLEAN IT—NOT AS REGULARLY OR METICULOUSLY AS YOU DO YOUR INDOOR ROOMS, BUT WELL ENOUGH TO MAINTAIN IT FOR THE LONG TERM. EVEN DECKS THAT ARE MADE OF WEATHER-RESISTANT OR PRESSURE-TREATED TIMBER WILL DETERIORATE UNLESS THEY ARE CARED FOR. AND, CONTRARY TO POPULAR BELIEF, THE PRESSURE WASHER IS NOT THE BEST WAY TO CLEAN A WOOD DECK.

**WATCH OUT** Don't be tempted to use a pressure washer to clean your deck. They are expensive, dangerous and harmful to the wood you are cleaning. Besides being a waste of water, the extreme water pressure will break up the wood fibres—what you're trying to prevent—leaving the surface fuzzy, more susceptible to the weather, and in poor condition for re-finishing with stains and sealers. And if the high-pressure jet can rip through wood, just imagine the damage it could do to the soft skin on an ungloved hand—so dress carefully.

**Sweep your deck regularly** to keep it free of leaves and twigs. This is the most basic step you can take. Otherwise, the tannins from tree fallout will stain the wood surface, and the piles of decomposing organic matter will hold moisture, leading to mildew and rot. Use a heavy-duty broom to sweep your deck regularly, taking care to keep the gaps between boards clean. If leaves or twigs get stuck in the gaps, scrape them out with a putty knife (see below). The more often you sweep, the easier it will be on you and the deck.

Leaves and twigs stuck between boards can be scraped out using a putty knife.

**To remove dirt and mildew** and brighten the colour of your deck, periodically (once a year or so) give it a more thorough cleaning, using a deck cleaner such as Dekswood Wood Cleaner or Cabot's Deck Clean, following the product instructions for use and safety. (Note: if you have a covered or partially covered deck that is not built to withstand rain, clean it as you would an indoor hardwood floor. Do not soak it with water.)

**To remove stains and stubborn mildew,** use this bleaching solution: 30–90 grams of oxygen bleach (any bleach that contains sodium percarbonate—it will have 'oxy' in its name) per 4 litres of warm water. Unlike chlorine bleach, which can break down the lignin that holds the wood together and harm plants, oxygen bleach is relatively gentle and non-toxic. Simply apply it with a mop or brush. Don't scrub. Wait 15–20 minutes for it to soak in and then hose down the deck to remove the solution.

**If you use a decking oil** or other timber sealer on your deck, you will need to reapply it after washing the deck with oxygen bleach or a deck cleaner. Both of these cleaners strip away any sealers that have been used along with dirt and mildew. A timber oil, such as Cabot's Natural Decking Oil, will nourish the scoured wood and help to preserve it against the ravages of the weather.

## DECORATIONS

**CHRISTMAS DECORATIONS DO** MORE THAN MAKE YOUR HOUSE LOOK FESTIVE; THEY EVOKE FAMILY TRADITIONS, MEMORIES AND SENTIMENT. THE LOWLIEST DECORATION MAY OCCUPY THE MOST EXALTED POSITION ON YOUR TREE, MANTLE OR CENTREPIECE. TO ENSURE MANY HAPPY CHRISTMASES TO COME, PROPER CLEANING AND STORAGE OF YOUR DECORATIONS ARE ESSENTIAL. NEW DECORATIONS OFTEN COME WITH INSTRUCTIONS. MAKE SURE YOU READ THEM BEFORE CLEANING.

**To clean painted ornaments,** separate them so you can pick them up one at a time by the hanger. Lightly dust each ornament with a feather duster (see below). Try not to handle the ornaments, since the oils in your hands can damage the paint; if you need to, wear latex or cotton gloves (particularly if your ornament is old and fragile).

Hold painted baubles by their string, then dust, one at a time, using a feather duster.

**To clean glass ornaments,** spray regular glass cleaner onto a soft cloth and wipe gently. (Do not use glass cleaner on acrylic or perspex, wipe with a solution of dishwashing liquid and water instead. For more serious grime, wipe with a little citrus-oil based cleaner.)

**To clean porcelain or crystal ornaments,** use a feather duster, brushing across the surface in a downward motion. Don't handle crystal decorations unless you wear gloves. A buffing jewellery cloth is also great to use on crystal. Simply wipe over the surface with the cloth. To clean resin and wood ornaments, a soft cotton cloth works well. Again, just wipe across the surface.

## A holiday recipe

You can whip up an inexpensive solution for cleaning ornaments in seconds. The solution works wonders on glass, perspex, plastic and wood decorations.

Mix 2 teaspoons of vinegar in a cup of water and apply it to the decorations with a 100 per cent cotton rag. Dip a corner of the rag in the solution and then squeeze the rag. Put the rag over your index finger and gently wipe your finger over the ornament surface. By using only one finger, you'll have much better control and can pay attention to cleaning the fine details on the ornament.

Always test a small, inconspicuous area first. Be very careful with hand-painted or old, painted decorations, because the dyes may not hold up as well. Lead or acid-based older paints will come off if cleaned with anything, so test, let the surface dry and check for any discolouration.

**Sterling silver and gold-plated ornaments** come clean when wiped with a polishing jewellery cloth. Apply the cloth in circular motions to remove dust and fingerprints.

**Cleaning glittered ornaments** is a tricky business. Try using a feather duster on one area. If a lot of glitter comes off, it may be best to leave the decoration alone.

**Storing your clean ornaments properly** will ensure they will be sparkling, dust free and ready to hang the next year. Here are some simple tips to follow:

- Store ornaments in a large box with a lid, a plastic storage container or, if you still have it, in their original box.
- Place a thick layer of scrunched-up tissue paper (use only non-acidic paper) in the bottom of the container.
- Lay a full layer of ornaments on top of the scrunched-up tissue paper on the bottom of the container.
- Put the more sturdy ornaments on the bottom and the delicate ones on top. Don't use more than two layers. Try to offset the upper layer so that the ornaments don't sit directly on top of the ornaments below. Don't pack the ornaments tightly, because they might break and the older ones, in particular, may be difficult to replace.
- Wrap each ornament individually using just one layer of tissue paper for the ornament.
- Gently lay one or two layers of flat tissue paper on top of the first layer of ornaments.
- Place the second layer of wrapped ornaments on top of the tissue paper over the previous layer of ornaments.
- Store your ornaments in a cool, dry, out-of-the-way place.

■ Cellulose packaging or polystyrene beads can also be used to protect delicate baubles when you're packing them away.

# DEHUMIDIFIERS

**DEHUMIDIFIERS ARE PART** OF A HOME'S AIRFLOW SYSTEM. THEY CUT DOWN ON MOISTURE AS WELL AS THE MOULD AND MICRO-ORGANISMS THAT THRIVE IN MOIST ENVIRONMENTS. IF YOU DON'T CLEAN YOUR DEHUMIDIFIER, YOU MAY CANCEL OUT ITS BENEFICIAL HEALTH EFFECTS. AND AS WITH ANY OTHER ELECTRICAL APPLIANCE, KEEPING YOUR DEHUMIDIFIER CLEAN IS IMPORTANT FOR ITS OPERATING EFFICIENCY AND LONGEVITY.

*See also:*
• AIRCONDITIONERS

**Cleaning a dehumidifier is easy,** but you do need to be diligent with its care. Periodically dust the outer cabinet with a damp, oil-free cloth, and clean the front grille and the coils under the grille using the upholstery attachment on a vacuum cleaner (see below). Once a month—or more often, depending on use—scrub the drip pan and the inside of the water reservoir with a sponge or soft cloth and mild dishwashing liquid to discourage the growth of mould or mildew. At least once a season, remove the dust and lint from the cold coils inside the unit with a soft-bristled brush. Most dehumidifiers have an air filter in the front grille area. Replace or clean it at least once a season. The procedure is the same as it is for a window airconditioner.

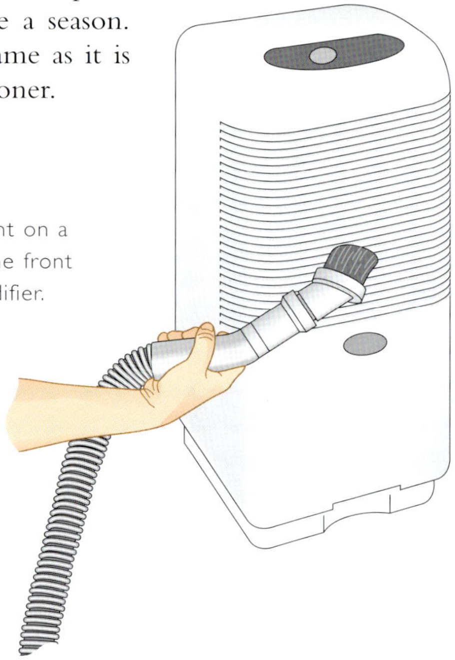

The upholstery attachment on a vacuum cleaner will clean the front grille and coils of a dehumidifier.

# DENTURES

**THE MESSAGE BEHIND** DENTURE ADS IS: BUY OUR DENTURE CLEANER AND EAT WORRY-FREE. LIKE MANY ADS, THEY CAN BE MISLEADING—BUT ONLY SLIGHTLY IN THIS CASE. WHILE NOT AS SIMPLE AS DROPPING YOUR DENTURES INTO A GLASS OF CLEANING SOLUTION, DENTURE CLEANING SHOULD REQUIRE LITTLE MORE EFFORT THAN BRUSHING YOUR ORIGINAL SET OF TEETH.

**As with real teeth,** your dentures should be kept free of food particles, plaque and stains so that your mouth can remain healthy and attractive. And removing plaque—that germ-harbouring dentists' nemesis—from dentures requires the same regular brushing that real teeth need. The difference, of course, is that with dentures, you take them out to brush them.

**Brush your dentures twice a day.** Dentures are surprisingly delicate and—we hardly need mention—expensive. They may break even if dropped a few centimetres. For that reason, always brush them over a folded towel or a bowl of water. Go over them lightly with a recommended denture brush or a soft nylon toothbrush, using a cleanser your dentist recommends. For an economical alternative, mild hand soap or dishwashing liquid can be used instead. And

## Protect those dentures

Here are some precautions you should take to protect your dentures:

- Never use a brush with stiff, coarse bristles, which can damage the materials that make up dentures.
- Don't use gritty powdered cleansers or toothpastes, which can also cause damage.
- Don't clean dentures with bleach. It can whiten the pink part of the dentures and corrode the metal framework on partial dentures.
- Never use hot water to rinse your dentures. The heat could warp them.
- Never let your dentures dry out, which could also warp them or make them brittle.

remember, you can keep your dentures cleaner by also lightly brushing your gums, tongue and the roof of your mouth. (But not with hand soap!)

**Soak your dentures** for at least 30 minutes a day in a dentist-approved denture cleanser (like the ones you see advertised on TV). Soaking will remove stains and kill germs, which will reduce mouth infections and odour. For convenience and privacy while you're without your teeth, soak your dentures overnight or while you're showering. Then rinse off the cleanser by lightly brushing the dentures with the soft-bristled brush under cold running water.

# DISH DRAINERS

**SINCE YOUR DISH** DRAINER IS MEANT TO HOLD CLEAN DISHES, A DIRTY DISH DRAINER DEFEATS THE PURPOSE. IT IS IMPORTANT TO KEEP YOUR DRAINER CLEAN AND FREE OF MOULD AND BACTERIA.

**Wash your dish drainer** periodically in warm water with dish-washing liquid, using a clean sponge. Do it separately, not while you're washing other dishes, since harmful bacteria can taint the dishes you are trying to clean. Use a scrubbing brush to remove stuck-on food and mould. Air-dry the drainer upside down on a clean tea towel.

Sanitise the dish drainer every few weeks by soaking it in a solution of ¼ cup of bleach per 4 litres of warm water (see below).

Sanitise your dish drainer every few weeks to prevent harmful bacteria contaminating your clean dishes.

# DISHES

**THESE DAYS, THE** OLD FAMILY RITUAL OF STANDING AROUND THE KITCHEN, DOING THE WASHING UP TOGETHER AFTER A HOME-COOKED DINNER IS MORE OF A MEMORY THAN A REALITY, THANKS TO DISH-WASHERS. BUT DISHWASHERS BLAST JETS OF HOT WATER THAT CAN CAUSE ANY ORNAMENTATION TO FADE. ANYTHING WITH A METAL DECORATIVE BORDER IS DOOMED. SO IF YOU REALLY WANT TO TAKE THE BEST CARE OF YOUR HEIRLOOM CHINA, DON'T TAKE ANY CHANCES, AND DO IT THE WAY YOUR GRAND-MOTHER DID—BY HAND.

**To hand wash delicate china**—any china that's fragile, antique or gold plated—get out the rubber gloves and the dishwashing liquid. And don't even think of using steel wool or anything else with texture. A sponge or a dishcloth will do everything you need. Before you even turn on the tap, place a tea towel in the bottom of the sink. Then remove your rings or at least turn any jewels on them inwards, towards the palm of your hand. This will cut down on any chipping caused by jewellery while you wash. Also turn the tap to the side to avoid clashes with delicate objects, such as your grandmother's gravy boat.

**The first step is to fill the sink** with moderately hot water and a healthy squirt of mild dishwashing liquid. And it never hurts to add 2 tablespoons of white vinegar to the water. (This boosts the power of inexpensive dishwashing liquid and makes even the best detergent work better.) Then slowly slide the dishes in edgewise, which allows the temperature of the dish to equalise gradually. If very hot water hits a fragile dish too quickly, it could crack the china (something you are trying to avoid!). Once the dishes are stacked carefully in the sink, pour a little extra dishwashing liquid on a sponge or dishcloth. Then resist the urge to scrub. Instead, wash in small circular motions. It might take longer than a vigorous scrubbing, but it will protect your china. Put 1 tablespoon of white vinegar in the final rinse, and you'll be able to see your smile in the reflection.

## Getting the most from your dishwasher

Here are some dishwasher-use tips that will help you get your dishes (and pots and pans) cleaner and help conserve energy and water:

- Load dishes so that they are separated and face the centre of the dishwashing machine. Put glasses and cups between prongs, not over them.
- Don't position large dishes (or pots or pans) so that they block the spray arm, the spray tower or the flow of water to the detergent dispenser.
- Use only dishwasher detergent in your machine—never soap, laundry detergent or dishwashing liquid. Follow the label instructions for the amount. Less is needed if your water is soft (or artificially softened), more if it's hard.
- Use a rinse agent to speed drying if your water is hard, but don't bother with if you have soft water.
- Run hot water into the kitchen sink and wait until it feels hot before turning on the dishwasher.
- Don't bother to pre-rinse moderately soiled dishes. Just scrape off any food.
- Run the machine only when it's fully loaded and do it at night or during off-peak utility hours. During hot weather, running the machine at night will also save on cooling costs.
- Use the hold-and-rinse cycle only when you need to leave dishes overnight but want to avoid odours.
- If your dishes aren't very dirty, use the lightest washing cycle.
- Air-dry dishes when you don't need rapid drying. And don't warm plates in a dishwasher; use the oven instead.
- Keep your dishwasher scrupulously clean. Empty the filter basket after every wash and periodically remove the filter screen at the bottom and give it a good wash with a nylon brush and detergent. Every two to three months, unscrew the spray arms and flush with water to make sure there is nothing blocking the spray holes. Wipe any built-up gunk and mildew from the rubber seals.
- There are many commercial products available for freshening and de-scaling the inside of your dishwasher, but for an effective and inexpensive alternative, put 4–5 tablespoons of bicarbonate of soda or 2 cups of white vinegar into the machine and run through the rinse cycle—with no dishes of course.

## Give your china a facelift

No matter how careful you are, delicate china is going to get its dings and smudges. But it's easy to rejuvenate china that's showing its age.

- To get rid of those hairline cracks that seem to come from nowhere, soak the china overnight in a large bowl of warm milk (no warmer than what you would feed a baby). Then gently hand wash as usual. Those lines will disappear.
- Where did those mysterious black marks come from? Did you eat dirty food? Scuff a shoe on a plate? Probably neither. Black marks can be the result of a couple of things, such as cutlery in the hands of a zealous eater or contact with aluminium in the dishwasher. To get rid of the black marks, sprinkle a little bicarbonate of soda on a damp cloth and rub the spot. Or try a bit of non-gel toothpaste on a plastic scouring pad.
- To lift tea stains from cups, mix 2 tablespoons of chlorine bleach in a litre of water. Soak the cup in the solution for no more than 2 minutes and rinse immediately. An alternative cleaning technique is rubbing gently with dry bicarbonate of soda.
- Hard water sometimes causes a film to develop on china. To remove it, fill a bowl with 1½ cups of chlorine bleach and place it in the lower rack of the dishwasher. Load your china into the washer and run it up to the dry cycle, then shut it off. Empty the bowl, rinse it out, pour in 1½ cups of white vinegar, and return it to the dishwasher. Turn the dishwasher back on and let it run through the rest of the drying cycle.

**Brushes, cloths and sponges** that are used for washing dishes can quickly become smelly and dirty. Soak them overnight in the sink with a handful of Epsom salts, and rinse well. Nylon brushes will benefit from a cycle in the dishwasher with the cutlery.

**Before doing good china in a dishwasher,** it's best to run a test. Buy the most inexpensive piece that's made in your pattern. Put it in the back of the dishwasher and forget about it for a month while you use the machine normally. At the end of the month, take a look. If there's no change in its appearance, you'll know it's safe to use the dishwasher for your good china. If it's faded, well, you'll be buying more rubber gloves.

**When storing good china,** it's important to be gentle, too. Try to store your china so that it doesn't touch. A layer of pliable paper—paper towel, paper plate or serviette—will keep pieces from scraping. Hang cups, if possible. And when dealing with tops—to tureens, sugar bowls and teapots—turn the top upside down, so that the handle or other protruding part is protected inside the bottom piece.

# DOG KENNELS

**TRUE ENOUGH, YOU** DON'T HAVE TO CHANGE YOUR PET'S BEDDING AS OFTEN AS YOU CHANGE YOUR SHEETS. BUT MOST OF US WAIT WAY TOO LONG TO FRESHEN OUR PET'S COSY CORNER. ONCE A MONTH ISN'T TOO OFTEN.

*See also:*
• PET EQUIPMENT

Simple solutions

## Put those fleas to rest

There are all sorts of commercial flea powders that you can use to dust your pet's bedding, but the herb pennyroyal also works very effectively. Combine 30 drops of pennyroyal oil, 2 teaspoons of methylated spirits and 2 cups of water in a trigger spray bottle and use this mix to mist your pet's mattress and blankets while they're drying in the sun.

**Start cleaning a dog kennel** by tossing it like you would a teenager's bedroom. Get everything out. If you use straw, throw it away. If your dog likes to curl up in blankets, pull them out and toss them in the washing machine, just as you would your own blankets. Hose down the house or kennel, inside and out. You might need to lift one end to drain all the water. Then get ready to scrub.

**When washing a doghouse or kennel,** don't use anything that you wouldn't want your pet to lap up. Chemical household cleaners will make a home sparkle. But dogs aren't as particular about the way their home looks as they are about the way it smells. A pine-scented habitat might smell clean to you, but your dog might disagree. Instead, use a plastic-bristled brush to apply an organic cleaner, such as Down to Earth, or try one of these homemade solutions:

- Mix 4 tablespoons of lemon extract (available from supermarkets) or lemon juice with 4 litres of water.
- Mix 1 cup of vinegar to 3 cups of water.

Either of these environmentally friendly alternatives will get rid of all the must and dirt and will leave your dog's habitat clean and smelling good without a hint of chemicals.

**Replacing the bedding** is the last step. If your dog likes straw, put in some fresh straw and sprinkle it with bicarbonate of soda to make the freshness last longer. If your pet prefers blankets, let the washed blankets dry in the sun for extra freshness; then sprinkle some bicarbonate of soda on them (see below).

A sprinkle of bicarbonate of soda on your pet's clean blankets will absorb odours and keep them fresher for longer.

# DOLLS

**A COLLECTOR'S DOLL** MAY BEAR A HEFTY PRICE TAG, BUT A CHILD'S BELOVED BABY DOLL—NO MATTER HOW BEDRAGGLED—IS PRICELESS FOR THE MEMORIES IT CARRIES. AND JUST THE AMOUNT OF HANDLING A CHILD'S FAVOURITE DOLL GETS MAKES IT A MAGNET FOR DIRT. CAREFUL CLEANING AND MAINTENANCE ARE EQUALLY CRITICAL FOR SAVING A PRIZED BABY DOLL FOR FUTURE OFFSPRING OR FOR MAINTAINING THE VALUE OF AN EXPENSIVE COLLECTOR'S ITEM.

**To wash a doll's clothing,** begin by stripping the doll. Then make sure its clothes can be washed—do a test on an inconspicuous spot on the clothing. Using an eye-dropper, put a drop of liquid laundry detergent where it won't easily be seen, such as on a seam or a hem. If you can't see the detergent after it dries, you're in the clear. Place the doll's clothing in a lingerie bag and put it in the washing machine with the laundry detergent in cold water on the delicate setting. Don't dry the clothes in the dryer, however. If the clothes shrink, you can't expect your doll to diet. If the weather is good, hang them to dry on an outside clothes line for a fresh smell. If the weather is bad, lay the pieces on a towel to dry.

**To clean the doll itself,** remember that a damp cloth will remove a lot of the grime a doll picks up in the garden, in the sandpit or just from being loved. If the doll needs a bath, fill a sink with warm water and mix in 2 tablespoons of lemon extract (available from supermarkets). If the doll's body is all plastic or rubber, dunk the doll, much as you would a real baby. You might even invite your child to give the doll a scrub with a cloth made soapy with a little dishwashing liquid. Saliva mixed with anything—dirt, rolled oats, sugar—can set like cement, so to remove that extra-tough dirt a gentle scrub with a soft toothbrush does the trick. If you need a little extra cleaning power, dip the toothbrush in a solution of 1 tablespoon of hydrogen peroxide and 2 cups of water. Just make sure you rinse everything well before handing the doll back to the child.

**To clean a collector's doll,** also begin by stripping the doll. Never use a damp cloth on a porcelain collector's doll, because it might etch the paint. Instead, use a dry, soft cloth to remove surface dirt from the 'flesh' surfaces. For detailed areas—around the eyes or fingers, for instance—use a natural bristle artist's paintbrush to remove trapped dirt and dust. This should be all you need to do, because, luckily, collectors' dolls don't tend to pick up serious stains. If the clothing is old or delicate, you can remove the musty smell that comes with age by simply hanging the clothes out in fresh air. If the clothing is not fragile, you might want to consider washing it using the method described for regular doll clothes—but be sure to do the eye-dropper test first. For clothing stains that you don't want to wash, a household spot remover might get them out. Check the label for the best application procedure. Or you might try a solution of 2 teaspoons of lemon juice mixed with 2 cups of water. Dip an absorbent cloth or a paper towel into the solution and dab—don't rub—at the stain. It should lighten up right away.

## DOONAS

**THE MOST DIFFICULT** THING ABOUT WASHING YOUR DOONA IS ITS SIZE—ANYTHING BIGGER THAN A SINGLE DOONA WILL PROBABLY NOT FIT IN YOUR WASHING MACHINE OR DRYER. A TRIP MAY BE NEEDED TO THE LAUNDROMAT TO USE THE COMMERCIAL-SIZED MACHINES. BUT BEFORE YOU SET OFF, CHECK THE CARE LABEL ON THE DOONA: MOST CAN BE WASHED, BUT SOME CAN'T. IF THE LABEL SAYS 'DRY-CLEAN', YOU CAN PROBABLY STILL WASH IT; IF IT SAYS 'DRY-CLEAN ONLY', YOU SHOULD SET OFF FOR THE DRYCLEANERS, NOT THE LAUNDROMAT.

*See also:*
• DOWN

**A 50:50 feather-and-down or 100 per cent polyester quilt** can be washed using a gentle warm machine wash or by hand. Follow with a warm rinse and reduced or gentle spin. Do not bleach, soak or wring. Line dry over several lines (to take the weight), pulling to shape and shaking frequently. When almost dry, the Doona may be tumble dried on the warm setting. Two or three clean tennis balls added to the dryer drum will help to keep the Doona fluffy. The feather-and-down quilt can also be dry-cleaned (air thoroughly afterwards to allow the chemicals to dissipate), but polyester should not be dry-cleaned.

**Lamb's wool Doonas**—pure or blended—should be gently hand washed in an approved wool detergent, such as Softly. Squeeze the quilt gently to release dirt. Do not spin. Line dry, as before, but don't tumble dry. Pure lamb's wool Doonas may be dry-cleaned, but it is not recommended for wool blends.

## DOORMATS

**YES, DOORMATS ARE** SUPPOSED TO GET DIRTY—IT'S THEIR JOB. BUT AT SOME POINT, YOUR DOORMAT WILL HAVE ABSORBED ALL THE DIRT IT CAN TAKE. THEN IT SIMPLY BECOMES THE BRIDGE OVER WHICH DIRT TRAVELS INTO YOUR HOUSE.

**Knock out the dirt to start;** don't be timid. Grab two adjacent corners of the doormat and shake hard. The loosest dirt will leave willingly. Then drape the mat over a post or a clothes line and use a bat or stout piece of wood to beat it (see below). After you've beaten out all the loose dirt, take a wire brush and dislodge the stubborn stuff. If there's any gooey gunk like wax or chewing gum still clinging to the mat, press an ice cube against the offending lump until it's brittle enough to scrape off with a spoon.

Watch the dirt fly out when you give a grubby doormat a good beating.

**To remove serious stains** on a doormat made of rubber or rope, use a spot remover, such as Murlex or Woolclean Spot Dry Remover No. 2. If it needs a more thorough cleaning, hose it down and scrub with a detergent solution. For wooden doormats—or for troublesome doormat stains generally—mix 4 tablespoons of lemon extract (available from supermarkets) or lemon juice with 4 litres of water. Use a stiff plastic brush to scrub with the solution until the stain goes away.

## DOORS

**DOORS COLLECT DUST** AND DIRT JUST AS WALLS DO. SO WHATEVER CLEANER YOU USE ON THE WALLS IS PROBABLY JUST RIGHT FOR DOORS AS WELL. HOWEVER, VERY FEW DOORS ARE AS FLAT AS WALLS, SO YOU HAVE TO BE WELL-EQUIPPED TO ATTACK THOSE CREVICES TO GET THEM REALLY CLEAN.

**To remove surface dirt,** dust down the door with a dry towel. Then tie a soft, old towel over the bristle end of a broom and brush into the angles and crevices where dust mounts up. If there's a lot of detail work on the door, use a soft toothbrush to get into the corners.

**Wash the door** once you've cleaned off all the surface dust and dirt. If you have a stained wooden door, use wood soap (such as Howard Clean-A-Finish Wood Soap or Briwax Furniture Cleaner) according to the instructions on the label. Follow with Howard Orange Oil or Pledge to re-nourish the wood. For painted doors, a couple of home brews will do the job effectively:

- Mix 4 litres of warm water with ½ cup of ammonia, ¼ cup of white vinegar and ¼ cup of washing soda crystals. (Washing soda can be found in the laundry section of supermarkets.)
- Mix 1 cup of ammonia and 1 teaspoon of mild dishwashing liquid in 4 litres of warm water.

**Soak a natural sponge** until it's completely pliable. Then squeeze out as much water as possible. You should wash from the bottom upwards to avoid run marks. So beginning at the bottom of the door, scrub with the sponge in small circular motions. Rinse the sponge often and thoroughly to avoid putting dirt back on the door. If you keep a clean solution, you won't have to rinse.

**To clean door hardware,** the good news is that you don't have to remove it off the door to clean it. Leave the screwdriver in the toolbox and grab a box of plastic wrap. Place a layer on the door surface around the hardware you want to clean, securing the plastic with masking tape. If you're dealing with metal, such as a doorknocker or kick plate or even a doorknob, a metal cleaner, such as Brasso, will polish up all types of metal, including brass, copper, chrome, aluminium, stainless steel and enamel. It has jeweller's rouge in it, so it's very gentle but does an excellent job. With glass or ceramic doorknobs, you don't need the plastic wrap. Just take a few swipes with a rag dampened with methylated spirits, which won't hurt the great cleaning job you've just done on the door.

# DOWN

**WASHING DOWN ITEMS** ISN'T DIFFICULT. IN FACT, YOU USE ONLY WHAT YOU NORMALLY USE TO DO LAUNDRY: YOUR WASHING MACHINE AND SOME DETERGENT. IT'S ALL IN THE TECHNIQUE. IF YOUR WASHING MACHINE IS LARGE ENOUGH, PUT IN AS MANY DOWN ITEMS AS IT WILL HOLD: JACKETS, VESTS, PILLOWS, EVEN SLEEPING BAGS.

**Do a test first**—if you want to be sure the down item will come out looking at least as good as it went in. Mix ¼ cup of water with 2 tablespoons of powdered laundry detergent. Put a few drops on an inconspicuous spot of the fabric, such as on the lining, the hem or an inside seam. Don't rinse. Wait until it's dry. Then you can see whether the dyes have been affected. It's the colour of the item that you need to worry about; the down itself will be fine.

**To wash a down item,** check that there are no holes in it before you even turn on the water—that little place where you nicked your jacket with your ski pole can flood your washing machine with tiny feathers. When you're sure items are secure, add to an empty washing machine the amount of detergent instructed on the box; then fill the drum halfway with water. (Cold water is best. Try warm water if the outside of the garment really requires more cleaning muscle. However, never use hot.) Add and submerge the down items. They'll soak up the water. Place towels on top of the down items to keep them submerged and then finish filling with water. Run the washer through a cycle, using regular agitation. Stop the washer at least once during the cycle to press air out of the down, as this will keep the items submerged. And use only the regular spin cycle. A high-speed spin will unfortunately send all the feathers down to one end of the garment, unless it's quilted or baffled.

### EXPERT ADVICE

**DOWN AND DIRTY**

Your down garment will no doubt have a tag that says you have to dry-clean it. But if the tag just says 'Dry-clean', you can get away with gentle machine washing. If the tag gets wordier—'Dry-clean only'—pay heed. Whichever you decide, stick with one method of cleaning or the other. Don't alternate dry-cleaning with washing. Dry-cleaning will remove all the natural oils from the down, which makes the feathers brittle. If you then decide to wash the garment, the feathers will break.

**To dry a down item,** it's fine to use a dryer, but be sure to do it at the low temperature setting to avoid any problems. Some people prefer to toss in their sneakers or tennis balls to keep things fluffed. (If you do, make sure they're perfectly clean.) But you don't have to use anything at all. Instead, part way through the drying cycle, remove the down item from the dryer and fluff it by hand. Then return it to the dryer. If your machine has an automatic sensor that tells you when drying is done, ignore it. Down can fool the sensor. The cover may be dry, but the feathers inside may still contain moisture and extra drying time is required.

## DRAINS

**STRIKE QUICKLY WHEN** A DRAIN BECOMES SLOW MOVING. IT WILL MAKE LIFE SO MUCH EASIER AND CHEAPER THAN USING A PLUMBER FOR A FULLY-FLEDGED CLOG. THE SOLUTION IS SIMPLE AND YOU ONLY NEED COMMON HOUSEHOLD ITEMS.

**If you have a slow-moving drain,** it means sludge is building up in the pipe. When that happens, pour 1 cup of salt into the drain, followed by 1 cup of bicarbonate of soda. Then pour a full kettle of boiling water down the drain. The abrasive salt and bicarbonate of soda mixture will break down the clog. If the problem is congealed grease, the clog will be loosened immediately. Don't turn on the tap for several hours, if at all possible. The longer that you can go without diluting your work, the better.

**If hair is the problem,** you'll need a stronger solution. This one will definitely work: place 2 cups of washing soda crystals (available from the laundry section of supermarkets) over the plug hole, then slowly pour through a kettle of boiling water.

**Each of these methods** can be made more effective by following them with a rubber plunger (available from hardware shops). Place the rubber cup tightly over the plug hole and push the handle down and up rapidly, creating a vacuum which might just help shift the blockage.

### Whip up a twister

You can help prevent a drain from blocking by using a sink strainer (see right). However, to avoid any potential clogging, treat your drain to a little maintenance. A monthly dose of the following homemade cleaner will ensure smooth sailing down the drain. Pour 1 cup of bicarbonate of soda right down the drain. Don't turn on the water. Instead, immediately follow the soda with 1 cup of white vinegar (see far right). It will fizz and form a little white tornado. Wait 30 minutes, then flush with cool water.

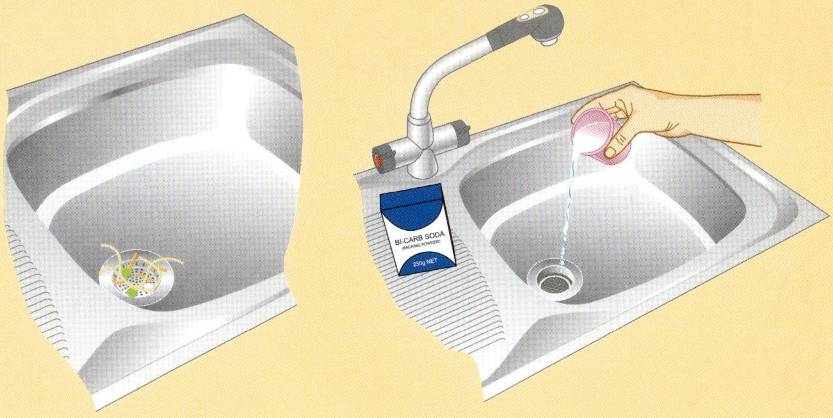


**Once you have a clear drain,** keep it that way. Invest in an inexpensive plastic or metal sink strainer (see above left)—and use it. You'll be amazed at the gunk you collect that would otherwise be going into your drains. Make the commitment (and tell the rest of the family) that nothing other than water will be going down your drain from now on—no fat, oil, coffee grounds, tea leaves or leftovers. Once a month, or more frequently, tip boiling water, or one of the natural cleaners as mentioned, down your drain and blockages will be a thing of the past, as will the angst that goes with them.

## DRAWERS

**WE ALL HAVE** JUNK DRAWERS, FULL OF THINGS THAT HAVE NO OBVIOUS HOME. CLEANING IS STILL A MUST, HOWEVER, IF JUST TO MAKE SURE NOTHING LIVING HAS TAKEN UP RESIDENCE WITHIN.

**Sort through the contents** of the drawer you want to clean first. Empty the drawer. Dump it. Everything, no matter how much it makes you cringe. Lay down some old newspapers before you start, and you'll save yourself the chore of vacuuming up all the grit, paper scraps and bits of plastic that have broken off one gadget or another.

Separate the dumped contents into as many piles as you think necessary, beginning with 'keep' and 'toss' piles. You can sub-categorise, if you want. If you're like most people, you'll find a year's supply of pens. (Transfer the ones that still have ink to the mug or desk drawer where you store spare writing implements.) Eliminate everything else you're not sure you'll need.

**To clean the drawer,** you first need to check to see what your drawer is made of.

- For wood, spray with a wood cleaner, such as Howard Orange Oil Cleaner or Pledge, or mix 1 litre of warm water with 2 tablespoons of dishwashing liquid in a large bowl.
- For laminated plastic, use 2 tablespoons of white vinegar mixed with 1 litre of warm water.
- For metal drawers, put some bicarbonate of soda in a small bowl and add just enough water to make a paste.

Thoroughly soak a sponge and squeeze well, then wipe away at the drawer, inside and out. You can let the drawer air-dry, but if you're in a hurry to fill the drawer again, with only the must-keep stuff, dry it with a paper towel.

## DUST

**THE AVERAGE HOUSE** WILL ACCUMULATE 18 KILOS OF DUST A YEAR. DUST VARIES FROM HOUSE TO HOUSE AND FROM LOCATION TO LOCATION AROUND THE COUNTRY.

**The dust film** that your children love to write their names in is made up of particles of more than 5000 different materials, including skin flakes; human hair; pet hair, skin and saliva; food bits; pollen grains; mould spores; insect parts; sawdust and fibre. So it is important to be diligent and effective when it comes to dusting.

**Just pushing dust around** is what many methods of dusting do. Feather dusters are great, for instance, for cleaning blinds—as long as you make sure to shake the duster outside frequently. A dry dust cloth just moves the dust or suspends it. Even a vacuum cleaner—unless it uses a HEPA (high-efficiency particulate air) filter—redistributes a certain amount of the dust it's supposed to be removing, but it's still the major weapon in the dust war.

**Why do we dust?** Aesthetics are a big reason, of course. But there are some important health concerns related to dust. Dust can be a reservoir for contaminants. Lead and pesticides, for instance, are known to accumulate in household dust. In addition, there are a lot of

## Dust busters

Here are some tricks to try when you are keen to do some dusting:

- To clean stained or natural-finish woodwork, put a tea bag in hot water and let it cool down. Then dampen your cleaning rag or sponge with the cooled tea and run it over the woodwork (see below).

- To clean blinds, which can get filmy with dust, wipe the slats with a cloth dampened with vinegar, which sanitises as it cleans. This is also a good trick for those dirty chandeliers.
- To remove dust, lint or hair from furniture or an item of clothing, wrap masking tape around your hand and then press your hand over the surface of the item. Unwanted dust or fluff will stick to the masking tape.
- To get rid of all the dust trapped in a pleated lampshade, use a small, medium-bristled paint-brush. This method also works well for delicate figurines that need dusting.
- To give freshly dusted furniture a good sheen, mix ½ teaspoon of light olive oil (not dark) in 1 litre of water. Apply with a clean rag.

elements in dust, such as mites, that can cause allergic reactions related to asthma and sometimes to eczema.

**To dust a room** and cut down on the time dusting takes, vacuum everything first—furniture, windowsills, walls, upholstery, the coffee table, it doesn't matter. Vacuuming is the key to dust removal, because it removes a lot of dust without creating a dust storm in the process. Follow up with a damp cloth, and your room should be dust-free for a while.

Naturally, you want to truly remove the dust, rather than kicking it up into the air. Electrostatic cloths, dusters and cleaning mitts, for example, hold the dust. A damp washcloth or microfibre cloth will also hang on to the dust. And so will a simple cloth duster impregnated with a few drops of paraffin oil, or an oil-impregnated disposable dust cloth, such as Chux Yellow (available from cleaning suppliers). But if you use a washcloth instead of disposables, make sure you wash it after every use. If the damp cloth doesn't seem to be quite enough, mix 1 tablespoon of lemon extract (or 2 tablespoons of vinegar) in 1 litre of water. Use the solution to re-dampen the cloth, and you'll cut through the film.

## DUVETS *SEE* DOONAS

# DVD PLAYERS

**THE MORE MECHANICAL** PARTS YOUR DVD PLAYER HAS, THE MORE SUSCEPTIBLE IT IS TO COLLECTING DIRT AND DUST. PORTABLE MODELS ARE EVEN MORE SUSCEPTIBLE, BECAUSE THEY ARE MOVED FROM ONE PLACE TO ANOTHER. DIRTY LENSES OR DISCS LEAD TO MIS-TRACKING, SKIPPING, IRREGULAR SPEED AND BAD REPRODUCTION QUALITY. WHEN YOUR PLAYER DISPLAYS ANY OF THESE SYMPTOMS REGULARLY, IT MIGHT BE TIME TO GIVE IT A CAREFUL GOING-OVER.

**Cleaning the player's lens** is the most important part of keeping the player running smoothly. But don't open anything that requires a screwdriver. Most warranties become void if you open the casing. You're better off sending it away for a service. Instead, just press the button to open the mechanical drawer where the DVD sits. Spray a gentle blast of compressed air inside the opening to force out any dust or lint. It's not a bad idea to spray the disc tray, too, but be careful to hold the can perfectly level, as you might get a shot of the propellant in its liquid form, and you don't want to have anything liquid near a DVD player. Hold the can at the recommended distance from the player. The intensity of the blast is controlled by adjusting the distance between the can and the player. If too close you may damage the laser reader mounted on an arm inside, and it's that arm that reads discs, the same way an old-fashioned record player needle reads vinyl.

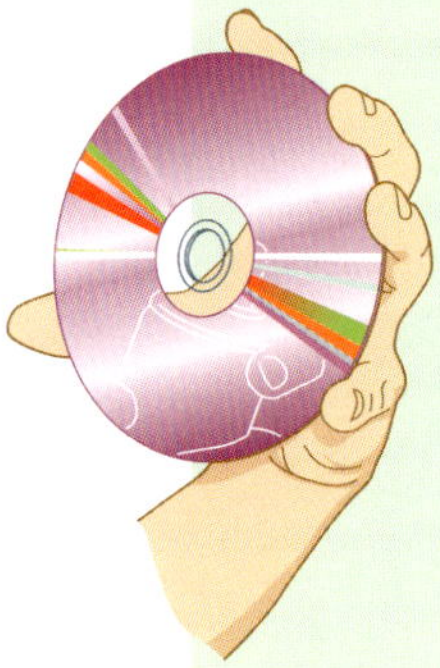

Simple solutions

## Cleaning DVD discs

Keeping your discs clean is the first step in maintaining a DVD player, because discs can carry dirt into the player's interior. Always hold them by the edges. A shot of compressed air is the quickest way to rid discs of dust (see left). If a disc needs more attention, wipe it with a soft, dry cloth, starting at the centre of the disc and moving straight out to the edge like the spokes on a wheel. Don't use solvents or household cleaners on a disc. Always store a disc in its case to keep it dirt free. Keep it out of direct sunlight and away from heat sources.

**WATCH OUT** Never put a damaged or warped disc into the player. It can hit the laser arm, which requires perfect alignment to work properly. It's these small preventive steps that count.

Some manufacturers make special lens-cleaning discs that will keep the laser lens as good as new. Just open the drawer that holds the DVDs and place the cleaning disc in the tray. When you close the disc tray and hit *Play*, the cleaning action begins. Some cleaning discs use an angular brush made of ultra-fine synthetic fibres containing copper. These sorts of discs not only clean the DVD player's lens, but also dissipate static that will attract dust.

**To clean a player's exterior,** a simple wipe down with a soft, dry cloth is usually all that's needed. If the cabinet is extremely dirty, mix some dishwashing liquid in water and get your cleaning cloth just barely damp before wiping it down. Avoid cleaning solvents (for example, alcohol), since they could damage the casing.

# EIDERDOWNS AND COMFORTERS

**TYPICALLY, AN EIDERDOWN** OR COMFORTER IS QUILTED AND REVERSIBLE, COVERS THE TOP OF THE BED, AND DROPS 40 CENTIMETRES OVER THE EDGE AT THE FOOT AND SIDES. MODERN COMFORTERS AND EIDERDOWNS ARE COMMONLY FILLED WITH BONDED POLYESTER FILL, BUT ANTIQUE OR TRADITIONAL ONES USUALLY HAVE DOWN INSIDE THEM.

*See also:*
• BEDSPREADS • DOONAS
• DOWN • QUILTS

**Check the fabric care label first** to make sure that the eiderdown or comforter is washable. If it is, check that it fits into your washing machine and dryer without being crammed in. They can be troublesome to launder at home because most home washing machines and dryers simply aren't big enough to swallow them. If the eiderdown or comforter is crowded in the washing machine, it won't be cleaned properly. (And when jammed into a dryer that's too small, it could scorch in some areas while remaining wet in others.) If your home equipment is too small, take it to a self-service laundromat, where the equipment is bigger. Or, if the care label dictates, have it dry-cleaned.

**To wash an eiderdown or comforter,** first make sure the fabric is colour-fast by rubbing a bit of pre-wash stain remover, such as Preen or Sard Wonder Spray, in an inconspicuous spot. Pre-treat stains and heavily soiled areas, working the stain remover into the fabric gently with a soft, nylon-bristled nailbrush. Then wash your eiderdown or comforter on its own in your washing machine, with warm water and a suitable laundry detergent, on the gentle cycle.

**To dry an eiderdown or comforter,** select the right heat setting on your tumble-dryer for the fabric type. Add two clean, dry bath towels, a clean tennis shoe or several pristine tennis balls to the drum to knock against the filling and keep it from clumping together. Stop the dryer at least once to make sure the eiderdown or comforter doesn't scorch inside. And also shake it out once during the drying process, to make sure the filling doesn't clump in one corner.

**To clean a down-filled eiderdown,** you need to check the care label instructions. If it can be washed at home, follow the instructions under 'Down', on page 158.

## Give it a quick vacuum

Before washing an eiderdown or comforter, use an upholstery brush attachment to vacuum it, to get rid of excess dust. Be careful not to suck up any loose threads. (If your comforter has lots of loose ends, put nylon netting, available from fabric or bridal shops, over the brush end of your vacuum and secure it with a strong rubber band. An old pair of pantihose also does the trick.)

## ELASTIC

**WHETHER IT'S UNDERWEAR** OR SOCKS, EXERCISE GEAR OR CASUAL CLOTHES, ALMOST EVERYTHING THESE DAYS HAS AT LEAST A HINT OF ELASTIC OR AN ELASTIC DERIVATIVE, SUCH AS SPANDEX, IN IT.

Simple solutions

### Give your costume an extra dip

Wash your swimming costume after every wear. Rinse first to remove chlorine, salt, body oils, sweat and sunscreen. And before you toss it into the washing machine, buckle buckles, tie ties and zip zippers so it will retain its original shape after washing.

**To keep your elastic clean** and in good shape, launder frequently in a washing machine, using warm water (37 °C is ideal). Whatever the item, if it touches your body, body oils will get on it. Body oils can damage elastic, and cold water will never rinse out the body oils completely, meaning your elastic will break down over time. Regular laundry detergent is all you need if the water you use is nice and warm. If you must bleach, use only non-chlorine bleach. And if there's a particular stain you're worried about, let it sit for 15 minutes in an enzyme pre-soak, such as Sard Wonder Soaker.

**To maintain the life of elastic,** dry it on a low setting and don't overdry. You don't want your stretchy stuff to become crunchy.

## ELECTRIC BLANKETS

**THE NEW GENERATION** OF ELECTRIC BLANKETS IS SIMPLE TO KEEP CLEAN BECAUSE MANUFACTURERS HAVE MANAGED TO CIRCUMVENT THE WATER AND WIRING PROBLEM BY PRODUCING REMOVABLE CONTROLS AND WATERPROOF HEATING ELEMENTS. HOWEVER, YOU SHOULD FOLLOW THE LABEL INSTRUCTIONS ON YOUR BLANKET TO THE LETTER, AND IF IN DOUBT, SEEK ADVICE BEFORE CLEANING IT.

*See also:*
• BLANKETS

**To clean a washable electric blanket,** first make sure that the heat-setting controls are unplugged from the blanket. Then, depending on the manufacturer's instructions, it may be hand or machine washed. Whichever method you choose, use an approved wool detergent and gentle warm washing and rinsing, or a wool cycle. Do not wring the blanket or spin it at full speed. Dry it as flat as possible by laying it over several clothes lines and do not use pegs on the wired areas of the blanket. The blanket can also be tumble dried on a low setting for a maximum of 15 minutes. Make sure it is thoroughly dry before putting it back on the bed.

**You can also spot-clean a non-washable blanket.** Use a solution of mild wool detergent and water to sponge the affected area, then sponge with clean water. Do not allow the area to become completely sopping wet. Press the blanket between two large bath towels to remove any excess water and then allow it to dry thoroughly before replacing it on the bed. Do not use harsh solvents on electric blankets as the chemicals could damage the wiring.

**If you want to store the blanket** rather than returning it to the bed, roll or fold it loosely—tight folding could result in the wires kinking or weakening, which is potentially dangerous.

## ELECTRIC GRILLS

**THERE ARE SEVERAL** MAKES OF ELECTRIC BENCHTOP GRILLS, SUCH AS THE GEORGE FORMAN RANGE AND BREVILLE'S HEALTH GRILLS, BUT WHEN ATTEMPTING TO CLEAN ANYTHING THAT HAS A CORD OR THAT BEGINS WITH THE WORD ELECTRIC, MAKE SURE THE UNIT IS UNPLUGGED BEFORE YOU EVEN TURN ON THE WATER. THE GRILLING SURFACE REQUIRES THE MOST THOROUGH CLEANING AND IF YOU'RE CLEANING IT STRAIGHT AFTER COOKING, MAKE SURE THE SURFACES HAVE COOLED A LITTLE FIRST.

**If the grilling surface is not removable,** don't immerse the unit in water. (Some electric grills have parts that can be safely cleaned in the dishwasher.) Most electric grills are one-piece models that typically come with a non-stick finish and are meant for benchtop use. Many have a long plastic drip tray for catching grease, as well as a plastic cleaning spatula contoured to fit over the ribbed grilling surface. But any rubber spatula or tool will do the job, as rubber won't scratch the non-stick surface. Do not use abrasive cleaners, scouring pads or caustic oven cleaners on the grilling plates as they may damage the non-stick surface. Once you have scraped off the larger bits of food, wipe the ribbed grilling surface with a damp sponge or cloth—not a wet one. To tackle especially sticky stuff, put a bit of dishwashing liquid on the sponge. Rinse the sponge frequently, since it will get grimy quickly. Follow the sponging step with a few swipes of a damp cloth—not a wet one—to get rid of as much moisture as possible.

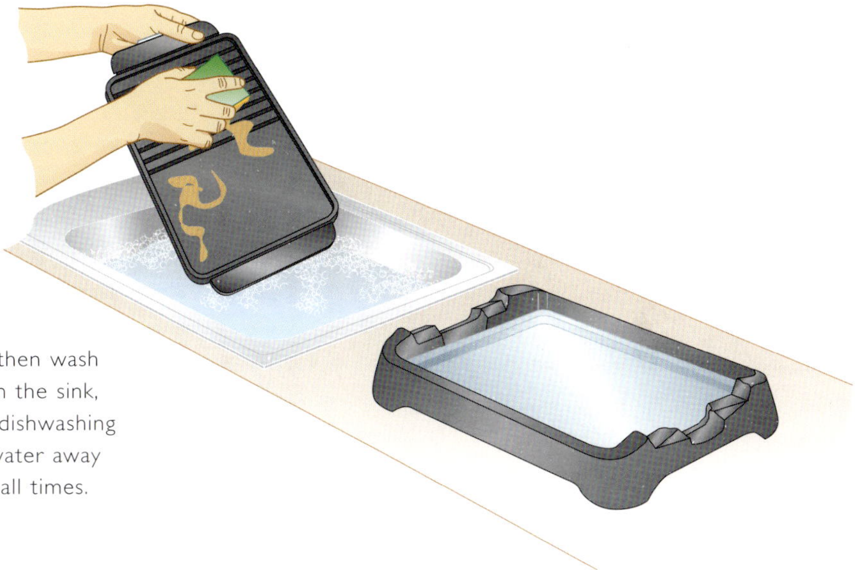

Scrape off excess food, then wash a removable grilling plate in the sink, in a solution of water and dishwashing liquid. Be careful to keep water away from the electrical inlet at all times.

**WATCH OUT** After washing a removable grilling plate in the sink (with the electrical inlet away from the water, of course), rinse and then allow it to air-dry thoroughly before replacing it on its base or using it again. And always unplug the electrical cord for storage, to remove the possibility of moisture seeping into any part of the unit.

**To make cleaning the drip tray easier,** some manufacturers recommend lining it, before cooking, with aluminium foil or absorbent paper towel. To clean the drip tray, remove and dispose of any paper towel or aluminium foil used to line the tray during cooking.

After disposing of the collected grease, wash the drip tray with dishwashing liquid and a wet sponge. If the spatula has collected a thick layer of greasy, charred food, soak it for a few minutes in warm water with a squirt of dishwashing liquid, and then wipe it clean with a scrubber sponge. Rinse the drip tray and spatula thoroughly with running water and allow them to air-dry.

**To clean the outside of an electric grill,** first remove the grilling surface (if it's removable) and leave it out while you attack the other surfaces. A quick wipe of the exterior with a damp sponge will take care of most grease splatters. If it needs something a little stronger, spray an all-purpose, citrus-oil-based cleaner onto a cloth and wipe over the greasy surface with that.

Let the cleaned grill air-dry or, if you need to accelerate the drying process, use a hair dryer on a low setting. Make sure the grill is perfectly dry before you plug it in again.

Whether you're cooking meat, vegetables or flatbread, electric grills need to be cleaned thoroughly after use.

**To clean a hibachi-style electric grill**—one that has a grilling rack like a conventional charcoal grill—unplug it, let it cool and dismantle it according to your owner's manual. With the electrical elements set aside, wash the grilling rack, the lid and the metal or ceramic basin in warm water with a squirt of dishwashing liquid. Scrub as needed with a nylon cleaning pad. Wipe over any plastic parts with a soft cloth dipped in the water-and-detergent solution, then rinse thoroughly with fresh water.

Never immerse the electronic parts of the grill in water. If it's necessary, wipe the heating element with a soft cloth or soft brush, taking care not to scratch the surface.

## ELECTRIC SHAVERS

**IT'S HUMAN NATURE.** YOU HAVEN'T SEEN THAT TINY LITTLE BRUSH THAT CAME WITH YOUR ELECTRIC SHAVER SINCE YOU OPENED THE PACKET ON YOUR BIRTHDAY TWO YEARS AGO. NOW YOUR SHAVER IS RUNNING IN LESS THAN OPTIMAL CONDITION.

**To keep your shaver in proper working order,** brush it after each use to dislodge dust, dead skin and other stuff that's clogging the works and damaging the blades. Many shavers have a removable head cover. Pop it off and brush the underside (see below), avoiding the delicate screen. If you've lost the tiny brush that came with your shaver, use a small toothbrush (one that's no longer used, obviously). Then remove the shaving head and gently brush the cutting mechanism itself. A blast from a can of compressed air will also dislodge any embedded material that stands in the way of a smooth shave.

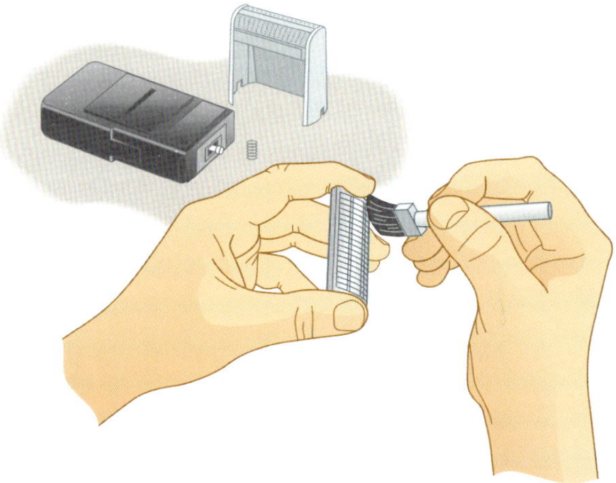

Brush underneath the head cover of your electric shaver regularly, to remove whisker dust and skin flakes.

If you use a shave stick—a compressed powder product that dries up perspiration and facial oils to create a smoother shave—the powder can block up your electric shaver blades. To fix this problem, dip a cotton bud in methylated spirits and wipe the blades.

**If your shaver requires more cleaning,** it's time to go commercial. Some manufacturers of shaving goods, such as Remington, sell an aerosol spray cleaner for their electric shavers. In general, you spray the cleaner on and run the shaver for several seconds. Follow the instructions on the shaver package.

**To clean the exterior,** unplug your shaver and wipe the surfaces with a damp washer. If anything insists on clinging to the outside, use a bit of methylated spirits to wipe it off.

## ENAMEL

**IMAGINE THAT INSTEAD** OF THE GLOSSY APPLIANCES AND BOWLS YOU USE EVERY DAY YOU HAD TO MAKE DO WITH RUSTY SURFACES ON YOUR REFRIGERATOR, WASHING MACHINE, STOVE, OVEN, BATHTUB AND SINK. THAT'S WHAT YOU'D HAVE IN A WORLD WITHOUT ENAMEL. ENAMEL IS A BAKED-ON COATING FOR METALS THAT DOESN'T RUST OR REACT WITH ACIDS OR CHEMICALS AND IS USUALLY EASY TO CLEAN. ENAMELLED STEEL OR ENAMELLED CAST-IRON COOKWARE CAN BE MORE OF A CHALLENGE TO CLEAN BECAUSE OF THE HEAT-MEETS-FOOD FACTOR.

*See also:*
• STOVES

**To clean enamelled surfaces,** such as appliance surfaces, dissolve 2 tablespoons of bicarbonate of soda in 1 litre of warm water. Wipe the surfaces with a cloth or sponge dipped in the solution and rinse with fresh water on a clean cloth or sponge.

**To clean enamelled cookware,** let the pot or saucepan cool first. Never begin your clean-up by putting cold water into a hot pot (or vice versa). Wash the cooled enamelled cookware in hot water with dishwashing liquid, rinse in running water and then dry. Pots with metal or plastic handles can usually be washed in the dishwasher safely, but pots with wooden handles should not be as it damages the wood finish. Never use an abrasive cleaner or metal scouring pad; a plastic or nylon scourer is fine.

**To care for enamelled cookware,** remember:

- Keep the cooking heat on low or medium except when boiling water.
- Never subject an empty pot to high heat.
- Use non-scratch wooden or plastic cooking tools.

**Simple solutions**

### Burned-on food

Even experienced chefs face this problem. Cover the baked-on food with bicarbonate of soda and let the pot sit for several minutes while the bicarb absorbs the acids and oils. Then wash the pot or saucepan as usual. If the food still won't budge, add 1 litre of water and 2 teaspoons of bicarbonate of soda to the pot, simmer for 15 minutes and then give it a good wash again.

## ERASERS

**OLD-FASHIONED SLATE** BLACKBOARDS ARE A RARITY THESE DAYS, BUT FELT ERASERS STILL WORK OK ON MOST NEWER BOARDS—WHITE BOARDS, GREEN BOARDS AND DRY-ERASE BOARDS—DEPENDING ON WHAT TYPE OF MARKER IS USED.

Wash dry-erase board erasers with plain soap and water, then allow to air-dry thoroughly.

**The simplest method for cleaning felt erasers** works as well now as it did in times past. Go outside, hold an eraser in each hand, and clap them together, trying to keep the chalk dust from invading your clothes and lungs. If the job can't be assigned to a school student, enlist a vacuum cleaner, which also works quite well.

**Erasers made for dry-erase boards** should be cleaned with bar soap or dishwashing liquid under running water (see below left). Allow them to air-dry before using again.

**To clean a pencil rubber,** rub an emery board or piece of sand-paper over it until the black part that makes those annoying smudges is gone. This method will also help rejuvenate a rubber that has become hard and brittle. The newly exposed surface will be clean and soft.

Simple solutions

### Contained cleaning

To keep school kids from beating blackboard erasers on the footpath or the side of a building, give them a piece of plywood about 30 x 60 cm. Let them take the board outside the classroom, lean it against the building and then clap the erasers against that.

## EXERCISE EQUIPMENT

**FOR MANY PEOPLE,** CLEANING GYM EQUIPMENT IS NOT A BIG DEAL, BUT YOU DO NEED TO KEEP THE EQUIPMENT CLUTTER FREE. IT SHOULD BE BOTH CLEAN AND OPERATING SMOOTHLY.

**Wipe the perspiration off** the equipment after you've finished using it, because the salt in your sweat is corrosive. This goes for all machines, especially those with metal parts. You should also wipe down control panels to keep moisture from seeping into them and ruining the sensitive electronics. To make it easier, keep a roll of paper towels handy in your work-out room.

Every once in a while, wipe down the equipment with a sponge or cloth moistened with a bleach solution: 30–60 millilitres of bleach in 1 litre of water. This will kill any lingering germs.

**To clean a treadmill** and keep it running properly, use your vacuum cleaner to clean under the machine every second week. Every three months, vacuum around the motor casing. Most people don't realise it, but dirt is the biggest killer of treadmill motors. Along those lines, here are two tips from a personal trainer:

- Firstly, don't wear the same shoes on your treadmill that you wear outside. Instead, keep an indoors-only pair for treadmill training.
- Secondly, consider putting your treadmill on a rubber mat instead of directly on the floor or carpet. All that friction causes a build-up of static electricity, which attracts motor-clogging dust and carpet lint.

Follow both of these tips and you'll soon find that you have to clean less and you'll have a longer lasting treadmill.

**WATCH OUT** Do not use a rubber and vinyl protectant, such as Armor All, on the belt of your treadmill. It might look shinier than when it was new, but Armor All has one major drawback: it's slippery, and you could easily go flying off the machine as a result.

**To clean an elliptical machine**—the machine that combines the exercise of climbing stairs with that of riding a bicycle—simply wipe it down with a moist rag. To keep an elliptical machine from squeaking and skipping, clean and lubricate the machine's rails and wheels regularly. Follow the manufacturer's recommendations or wipe it with a cloth that has been moistened with silicone spray.

**To clean a weight machine,** treat it like a car. (It probably cost as much.) The painted metal parts are similar to your car's painted metal body. Once a year, use a car cleaner (available at automotive shops), diluted according to the package instructions, to clean the grime off the paint. Rinse with a clean, wet towel and dry with a bone-dry towel. Wax the machine with your preferred car wax, again following the package instructions. This prevents scratches, reduces grime build-up and also brings out a warm shine.

Periodically, clean and lubricate the weight machine's guide rods to keep the weight stack from sticking. Clean the rods with a dry paper towel and then wipe them over with a cloth moistened with silicone spray. However, don't overdo it, because too much lubrication can also result in them sticking together.

**To maintain a stationary bike,** the most important thing to do is clean and lubricate the chain every three months or so. Clean the chain by carefully holding a dry rag on it and slowly turning the pedals to run the chain through the rag a few times. Next, lubricate the chain with a Teflon or silicone spray lubricant, available at bike shops. To avoid splattering, don't jump on and pedal straight away; allow the lubricant to dry, which should only take a few minutes.

**Have your equipment** professionally serviced every year or so if you use it regularly. It's a good idea to ask the people you bought the gear from to recommend a service technician.

**EXPERT ADVICE**

READ THE INSTRUCTIONS FIRST

You might think you don't need instructions for an exercise bike—get on it and pedal, right?—but the instruction booklet that came with the bike contains valuable tips for cleaning and maintaining your equipment in optimum order. More importantly, you can hurt yourself on equipment that is not working properly.

# EXHAUST FANS

**HERE'S A TEST:** HOLD A TISSUE UP TO THE GRILLE WHERE THE AIR ENTERS THE EXHAUST FAN IN YOUR BATHROOM, KITCHEN OR ATTIC. TURN ON THE SWITCH. IF THE TISSUE STAYS TIGHT AGAINST THE GRILLE, THAT'S GOOD. IF THE TISSUE FLUTTERS, THAT'S BAD—YOUR EXHAUST FAN HAS BECOME AN EXHAUSTED FAN; DIRT MAY BE THE PROBLEM. ATTIC AND BELOW-GROUND ROOM FANS SHOULD BE CLEANED ONCE A YEAR; BATHROOM AND KITCHEN FANS, EVERY SIX MONTHS.

**To clean an exhaust fan:**

- Turn the switch off. Unplug the fan or disengage the circuit breaker.
- Remove the fan grille and wash it thoroughly in warm water and dishwashing liquid, then rinse and dry. A kitchen exhaust fan will also have a filter that needs washing.
- On many models, you can remove the fan and motor by unscrewing the mounting bracket and unplugging the cord (see below).
- Whether you remove them or not, vacuum the fan blades using the crevice attachment, then wipe them off with a damp cloth. You also need to vacuum and wipe the inside of the housing.
- Clean the motor and other dusty parts with a stiff paintbrush.
- If you notice dodgy wiring or if the fan doesn't work, call an electrician—don't attempt to fix it yourself.

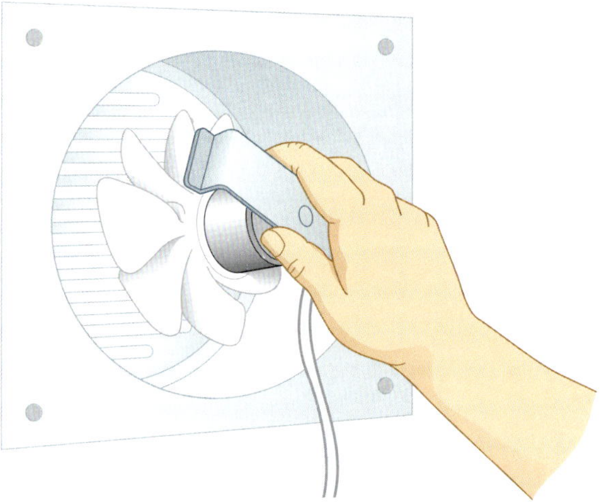

To clean fan blades, first unplug the electrical cord, then remove the fan and motor.

**Wash the filter** in a range hood exhaust fan every month or two. This filter, usually aluminium, is for catching cooking grease. Remove it and wash it in the dishwasher or in a solution of hot water and dishwashing liquid. Don't use ammonia, which will darken the metal. Rinse, dry and re-install the filter.

Range-hood fans that recirculate the air, rather than venting it outside, have a charcoal filter that must be replaced every six months.

*See also:*
• RANGE HOODS

**EXPERT ADVICE**

DON'T TAKE A CHANCE

It's not just a matter of not working efficiently—very dirty exhaust fans have been known to start fires. Take extra care if you're renting, because tenants come and go, and no one thinks about cleaning those dirty fans, which could leave you at risk.

# EYEGLASSES AND SUNGLASSES

**IN THIS AGE** OF STYLISH EYEWEAR, DIRTY GLASSES ARE A REAL NO-NO. THEY COMPLETELY DETRACT FROM WHAT YOU ARE LOOKING AT, AND THE WAY PEOPLE LOOK AT YOU!

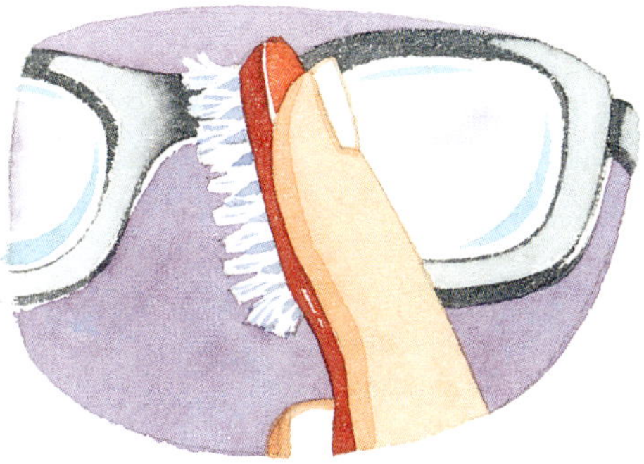

Use a soft toothbrush to give your grubby frames a gentle scrubbing.

*See also:*
• CONTACT LENSES

**For general cleaning of eyeglasses,** wet cleaning is better than dry cleaning. Most of us have grabbed a tissue or pulled a handkerchief out of a pocket to wipe our glasses, but that can smear dirt around and scratch the lenses. Dirt particles are hard, whereas lenses are soft and getting softer. Almost all lenses today are plastic, and plastic lenses are especially susceptible to scratching.

For an everyday clean, move the glasses around under running water and then dry them with a tissue or a clean microfibre cleaning cloth made especially for glasses. Microfibre cleaning cloths are washable and can be bought at some supermarkets or from an optometrist. Packaged, single-use towelettes made for glasses are also effective cleaners and are more convenient when you're on the move.

**To remove oily smears from your glasses,** pick up a specially formulated lens cleaner at a pharmacy or from an optometrist and follow the package instructions. These cleaners are ideal for all cleanings, so use them at least periodically if not every time you clean. Using water alone will not remove oils. Even mild dishwashing liquid can damage coatings over time, and harsher cleaners (including anything with ammonia) can damage them immediately. Lens cleaners may seem like an unnecessary expense, but they will help to prevent your lenses getting cloudy and scratched, which will prolong the life of your glasses. Even the best lens cleaners leave behind a thin film, a kind of instant coating, which further brightens the lenses.

A wide variety of special lens coatings, including polarising, tinted, transitions, mirror, ultraviolet protective and anti-reflective, are available for glasses. Regular lens cleaners are OK for all but the last two in this list of coatings; they require a special anti-reflective cleaner.

**To clean the frames of your glasses,** mix a few drops of mild dishwashing liquid in 2 cups of water. Dip a clean, soft toothbrush into the solution and gently scrub around the frame, the nosepiece and the earpieces, avoiding the lenses as much as possible (see above left). Rinse under running water and dry with a clean cloth.

Simple solutions

## Got a screw loose?

Next to dirty lenses, the most common and annoying problem is having a screw loose in one or both arm hinges of your glasses.

If a screw comes loose repeatedly, you need something more than a screwdriver. A thread sealant will solve the problem—you will need to visit a hardware or automotive shop to buy one of these. Put a drop on the tiny screw before screwing it into the hinge, and it will hold. A very small drop of clear nail polish will also do the trick, although it may not last as long.

# FANS

**DUST BUILD-UP ON** CEILING FANS LOOKS AWFUL AND IT WREAKS HAVOC ON THEIR EFFICIENCY. GIVE THEM A REGULAR CLEANING AND DON'T FORGET THAT TABLE FANS, FLOOR FANS AND WINDOW FANS ALSO NEED A REGULAR GOING OVER.

*See also:*
• AIRCONDITIONERS

**For day-to-day cleaning,** take out a lamb's wool duster and a stepladder or a stool that is high enough to let you reach the ceiling fan, and give the blades a quick dusting. Other types of fans have grilles that protect the blades. Clean the grilles and other housing regularly using a vacuum cleaner with an upholstery brush attachment.

**Do a more thorough cleaning** every month or two during times of heavy use. First, disengage the circuit breaker for a ceiling fan and unplug others. Remove the grilles and then mix up a solution of water with a squirt of dishwashing detergent added to it and use a sponge to clean the blades. Dampen the sponge and wipe the blades. Rinse the sponge in clear water and wipe again, then dry with a clean cloth. Be careful not to bend the blades, because that could upset their balance and make the fan wobble.

If the grilles have accumulated a lot of grime, it might be simplest to take them outside and wash them under a hose. Use a stiff brush to clean off any stubborn dirt and dust.

**Portable evaporative coolers** should be maintained like any other airconditioner, to promote maximum efficiency. Removal of blockages will ensure greater saturation of the filter pads, which means more efficient cooling. You should check your evaporative cooler regularly, and remove any dust that might have collected on the fan or the condenser coils at the back. If water has been sitting idle in the unit for any length of time, it might have collected dust and mould spores—it should be drained and replaced before starting up the cooler again.

EXPERT ADVICE

FOR OLD-FAN FANCIERS

If you buy a vintage table fan, gently clean off built-up grease and oil with a citrus-based cleanser. Use a lacquer thinner to remove lacquer on brass blades and cages, then polish with a metal polish, such as Brasso. Fan parts made of early plastics can be cleaned and shined with a specialist plastic-and-vinyl cleaner, sold at boat-supply and automotive shops, or try using a plastic-and-vinyl cleaner and protectant, such as Armor All, made for car interiors.

## FIBREGLASS

**FIBREGLASS IS COMMONLY** FOUND AROUND THE HOME IN BATHTUBS, SHOWER RECESSES, SINKS, FIXTURES, OUTDOOR FURNITURE AND WINDOW PARTS. ITS SMOOTH SURFACE LAYER IS EASILY MARRED, SO LEARN HOW TO CARE FOR FIBREGLASS WHILE IT'S STILL BRIGHT. SPARKLING FIBREGLASS IS EASY TO CLEAN. DULL FIBREGLASS IS MUCH HARDER TO BRING A SHINE TO.

**To clean fibreglass,** always use non-abrasive cleansers and scrubbers. After each shower, rinse the shower walls with water and wipe them down with a squeegee or chamois cloth to avoid a build-up of water residue and soap scum. Once a week, wash with a few drops of dish-washing liquid and warm water, applied with a sponge. Always rinse cleansers off with clear water.

**To attack mould and mildew,** mix bicarbonate of soda with enough water to make a paste. Wet the fibreglass with water, dip a sponge into the paste and rub gently. Rinse with clear water. This also works for general cleaning. If something a bit stronger is needed, apply kerosene on a soft, wet cloth.

**To remove soap scum on your fibreglass,** mix a solution of 1 part ammonia to 4 parts water. Rub on with a sponge or clean rag and rinse immediately and thoroughly with clear water.

If you live in a hard-water area, hard-water deposits can also be removed using boat hull cleaners. Look for such cleaners at hardware or boat-supply shops and follow the instructions on the package.

**To remove glue,** tar or oil-based paint stains, put a little acetone nail polish remover or paint thinner on a clean cloth and lightly rub the glue until the spot disappears. Then wash with dishwashing liquid and water. Finally, rinse with clear water.

Simple solutions

### How to preserve the finish of fibreglass

A couple of times a year, use an automotive white polishing compound on any dull or scratchy areas. Then apply a light coat of automotive white paste wax. Buff with a clean cloth. The surface will be slippery, so use on walls only, not on floors. This treatment will also help protect your outdoor furniture.

## FILTERS

**ANYTHING DESIGNED TO** CATCH DIRT SHOULD BE CLEANED OFTEN. MOTORISED FILTERS WILL END UP COSTING YOU MORE MONEY TO RUN IF THEY'RE LEFT DIRTY, BECAUSE MORE ENERGY IS USED TO PASS AIR OR WATER THROUGH THE FILTER.

**Cleaning air filters** is usually pretty easy. Airconditioner filters, which may be disposable or washable, need monthly attention. If the filter is washable, remove it and vacuum up as much dust as you can. Then rinse it under warm running water or swirl it around in a solution of 1 tablespoon of bicarbonate of soda and 1 litre of water. (Don't use soap.) Rinse and then dry thoroughly.

Air cleaners can be tabletop, room or whole-house models. The disposable fibreglass or washable, metal mesh filters on whole-house systems should be changed or cleaned with warm water monthly when they're in use. Filters in which the air passes through a medium, such as charcoal, should be changed annually.

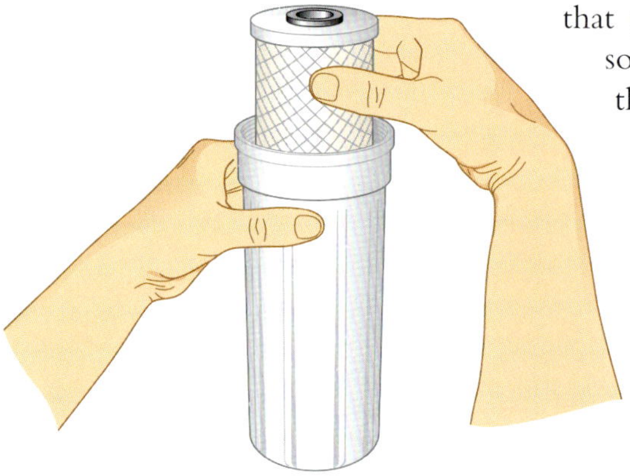

Your drinking water is only as fresh as the filter that cleans it. Make sure you check it and change it frequently.

Room or tabletop models of air cleaners may use filters that need to be changed every few months. Others use ionising technology that gives dust particles a negative charge so they will stick to something with a positive charge. The best advice is to follow the filter-cleaning instructions that come with your unit.

**Home water-filtering systems** often use activated carbon filters that tend to collect gunk. The activated carbon usually comes in cartridges that need to be replaced when they no longer work. The tricky part is figuring out when they've stopped doing their job. Sometimes you can tell by the taste of the water, if the filter is designed to remove chlorine, for example. Some filters come with lights or other indicators telling when it's time to change them. Others provide an estimate of how long they last on the packet.

You might want to make sure your filtering system conforms to national standards (it will tell you this on the packaging). Then you'll know that the manufacturer's instructions for changing the filter have been tested and found adequate.

## rules of the game

WHEN CLEANING A FILTER

- Keep your owner's manuals. Use them to set up a schedule for cleaning or changing filters on machines or appliances that use them.
- Check the manuals for instructions about how to get at the filters (sometimes that's the hardest part), whether to replace or clean them, and how often you need to do so.
- If you don't have a manual, do an Internet search for the company that made the appliance and either download the appropriate manual from the company's web site, order a manual online or call the customer service number.

## FIREPLACES

**IRONICALLY, CLEANING YOUR** FIREPLACE IS SIMPLER WHEN IT'S BEING USED MORE FREQUENTLY.

**During the fire-burning season,** cleaning will usually consist merely of removing some of the ashes periodically. (The fireplace will actually work better with about 5 centimetres of ash remaining—this is especially true of the Jetmaster fireplaces, where the ashes are collected at the bottom of a metal firebox.) Many fireplaces have an ash pit, which is a receptacle underneath the area where you build a fire. If yours does, open it and push excess ashes into it. Or use an ash shovel to deposit the ashes into a metal bucket with a tight-fitting lid. Store the ashes outside in the tightly covered bucket for at least two days before you finally dispose of them—an important precaution because 'dead' ashes containing live embers have been the cause of

Use an ash shovel to remove ashes, then tip them into a metal bucket with a tight-fitting lid. Leave the ashes in the bucket for a few days before final disposal.

many accidental fires in the past. (Make sure that the bucket isn't leaning against anything.)

**During the off-season,** do a more thorough fireplace cleaning. Use a clean pencil rubber on any smoke streaks that have crept up the exterior of the fireplace. If your fireplace has warm-air circulators, clean the ducts with a vacuum cleaner.

The off-season is also the time to have the chimney cleaned. This is a job for a professional chimney sweep—not a job you should take on yourself—who will check the flue for leaves, bird nests, cracks and soot build-up.

**To clean up the black build-up of creosote,** a highly combustible residue created by burning wood, on the inside of the firebox, you'll need to employ a bit of elbow grease. (The firebox is the place where you build your fire. Some people like to use the firebox for displays of candles or flowers when their fireplace is not in use during the warmer months.) Remove the screen, andirons and grate, and sweep up all the ashes with a dustpan and broom. Use a wire-bristled brush for the first attack on the creosote. If you want your brick or stone firebox to be cleaner, use ¼ cup of washing soda (available from the detergent section of supermarkets) in 4 litres of water and apply it with a sponge. Brush with a stiff-bristled brush and rinse with clear water. Wear rubber gloves to protect the skin on your hands, since washing soda is caustic. Do not wash a metal firebox.

*See also:*
• BRICK • CHIMNEYS
• FIREPLACE SCREENS AND TOOLS

## The ashless answer

A cosy fire is appreciated by most people, but the mess that goes with burning wood in a fireplace is much loathed. Many people have solved that paradox with a gas fireplace that simulates a burning log or coal fire—either open or within a glass-fronted firebox.

- Gas is a clean fuel, and a properly working gas fireplace basically needs no cleaning on the part of the home owner. It should, however, get an annual cleaning and inspection by a professional to ensure that the venting, controls and valves are working properly. The retailer who sold you the gas fireplace may do such servicing or else direct you to someone who does.
- Don't ever burn anything except gas in the fireplace, and learn how your particular model operates. (There are four types.)
- Read the owner's manual—don't start the fire with it. If the fireplace is working properly, don't tempt fate by tampering with the log or its internal workings. However, if you smell gas or if excessive volumes of soot suddenly show up on the log or the glass, that's definitely a sign to call the professionals in for servicing.

# FIREPLACE SCREENS AND TOOLS

YOUR FIREPLACE ARRANGEMENT MAY DAZZLE YOU IN THE EVENING, BUT IN THE HARSH LIGHT OF THE NEXT DAY, YOUR EQUIPMENT IS PROBABLY LOOKING A BIT BATTLE WEARY. MAKE CLEANING IT A PROJECT FOR THE WARMER MONTHS.

**Clean a fireplace screen** with a vacuum as part of your regular cleaning routine in the room. A screen catches more than the sparks that want to go flying into the room. It also catches a lot of dust. Periodically, give it a more substantial cleaning with soap and water. If you pick a sunny day and work outside, the job can be almost pleasant. Make a sudsy solution of warm water and a few squirts of dishwashing liquid and scrub the screen with a stiff-bristled brush dipped in the solution. Then rinse it off with a garden hose. If you're working inside, rinse with a sponge dipped in clean water. Allow the screen to dry thoroughly. If it has brass parts, clean them with a brass polish.

Clean fireplace tools (shovels, pokers and tongs), as well as andirons and grates, with the same brush and soapy solution. Use extra-fine (000) steel wool to remove rust or stubborn dirt. Dry the tools with a soft cloth, then give them a light coat of paraffin oil using a clean cloth. Wipe them dry with another cloth.

**If rust is a problem** on your fireplace screen or tools, you can renew the finish with a quick coat of high-temperature, black spray paint, available from most hardware shops (see below).

After removing rust, a coat of high-temperature, black spray paint will bring up your fireplace tools nicely.

**Clean glass fireplace doors** with a touch of caution. (See 'Watch out' box, above left.) Doors should be cleaned only when they're cool, never when they're hot. Common glass cleaners, such as Windex or Mr Muscle, don't work very well on black creosote deposits. A solution of ammonia and water will clean them up, but the solution may also strip your doors of their heatproof coating. Instead, try this:

- Dip a damp rag in ashes from the fireplace and rub the glass with that. Then wipe dry with a clean cloth. Or dip a cloth in white vinegar and wash. Dry with crumpled-up newspaper.
- If you want perfection, rub them with automotive white polishing compound (available from hardware shops or automotive shops).

**WATCH OUT** Cleaning fireplace doors is a subject that's rife with conflicting advice. Your best bet is to check your owner's manual for its recommendations. Fireplace doors are usually made of safety glass, which makes them harder to break, but some also have heatproof coatings that may be damaged by some harsh cleaning materials.

*See also:*
• BRASS

## FISHING RODS

**IF YOU'VE BOUGHT** SOME NICE FISHING GEAR YOU'LL WANT TO KEEP IT IN TOP CONDITION FOR YEARS TO COME. THE BIGGEST ENEMIES OF FISHING GEAR ARE SAND AND—ESPECIALLY—SALT, WHICH ARE ABUNDANT AT MOST FAVOURITE FISHING SPOTS (UNLESS YOU FISH IN FRESH WATER). THE TRICK IS TO CONSISTENTLY CLEAN UP AFTER EVERY OUTING YOU MAKE. IF YOU PUT EQUIPMENT AWAY WHILE IT IS WET, SLIMY AND SALTY, ITS PERFORMANCE WILL SUFFER.

**To clean your rod,** mix 1 teaspoon of dishwashing liquid in 1 litre of water. Dip a cleaning cloth in the solution and wipe the rod. Rinse the soap off with running water, then wipe it dry with a clean cloth.

If mud or other stuff has built up around the line guides, scrub them with an old toothbrush dipped in the soapy solution. Use the same treatment on dirt around the reel seat that can't be wiped off.

Don't shine your fishing rod with oil, as it can destroy the protective coating and eventually loosen the line guides and reel seat. Bamboo rods are an exception—you can safely polish them with a cream-type furniture polish.

**To lubricate the joints** of the ferrules (those metal connector sleeves) and keep them clean and smooth, dab a little petroleum jelly on one joint and slide the two pieces together and apart several times. Use a cotton bud to wipe off the petroleum jelly and dirt. If the ferrules have become rusty, you may be able to clean them with fine steel wool (00) or sandpaper, but you don't want to spoil the fit and wind up with a rod that flies apart when you're casting. It may be best to send the rod to a repair specialist.

**To clean the rod grips,** use the same cloth and soapy solution. Cork demands careful handling, because rough treatment could cause chunks of it to break off. A very dirty or damaged cork grip is yet another candidate for a professional repair job. Allow cork grips to air-dry before storage, to avoid mildew.

### Not reel simple

Reels are loaded with springs, screws, nuts, washers, bearings, gizmos, sprockets, shims and shafts, most of them tiny. It is a huge challenge to take a reel apart for cleaning and get it back in working order with nothing left over. You can avoid the job, or at least postpone it, by careful routine care, which simply means washing the reel after every outing. Use water or a teaspoon of dishwashing liquid in a litre of water. Scrub gently with a soft-bristled toothbrush. Also wash your tackle, including any lures that you used. Rinse everything well and dry with a clean cloth.

After every couple of outings, partially disassemble your rod's reel. Strip out the main drive gears and the pinion gear and soak them in a degreaser, available at hardware shops and wherever fishing supplies are sold. Then wash them with warm water and dry well.

Periodically, a reel will need to be completely taken apart, cleaned and then oiled. If you are determined to do the job yourself, first make sure you have the internal diagram of the reel and a list of parts that came with the reel, and follow the instructions to the letter. However, cleaning reels is a job best done by the professionals. Check with your nearest fishing tackle and bait shop or send the reel away to a repair specialist.

# FISH PONDS

**FISH PONDS NEED** TO BE CLEANED REGULARLY, BECAUSE FISH URINE, LIKE THAT OF OTHER ANIMALS, CONTAINS TOXIC AMMONIA. THE BEST APPROACH IS TO WORK WITH NATURE RATHER THAN AGAINST HER. EVEN A SMALL POND IS A COMPLEX ECOLOGICAL SYSTEM, AND THE RIGHT MIX OF TWO PLANT GROUPS—SUBMERGED PLANTS TO OXYGENATE THE WATER AND FLOATING PLANTS TO PROVIDE SHADE—WILL HELP CONTROL ALGAE. THE MIX MUST BE IN THE RIGHT PROPORTIONS TO WORK EFFECTIVELY. A GOOD BOOK ON CREATING PONDS WILL TELL YOU HOW TO DO IT.

**Routine pond maintenance** consists mostly of removing debris such as dead leaves from the water. Use a long-handled swimming pool skimmer net. Don't expect your pond to be absolutely clear; the water should be more of a pale green. Environmental balance takes a long time to establish, so don't be too quick to upset it by emptying and refilling the pond.

**A major pond cleaning** is called for when there is a lot of muck or too many fish in the water. The pond may have been overstocked, or the fish may have multiplied. In either case, you may have to find new homes for some of your scaly friends. A rule of thumb is that each fish in a pond should have about a barrel of water. The best time—and many experts say the only time—to clean a pond is in very early spring, when cool temperatures provide a less stressful environment for the fish and plants. Even so, always keep the fish and plants that you remove from the pond in the shade to avoid stressing them. Here's what to do to begin cleaning your fish pond:

- Start by removing the edge plants and then the floating ones, pot and all. Put them in the shade.
- Use a bucket to draw water off the top (the cleanest part) of the pond. Place a children's wading pool in a shady spot and fill it with the water, which will be the right pH and temperature to hold the fish. Save as much of the rest of the pond water as you can in extra containers, unless it is really disgusting.
- Start removing the remaining water with a pump or siphon (a length of garden hose will do). As the water level drops, remove the submerged plants and put them in the wading pool, too.

## Cleaning a fish pond

1 Carefully remove the fish from your pond and store them in a wading pool.

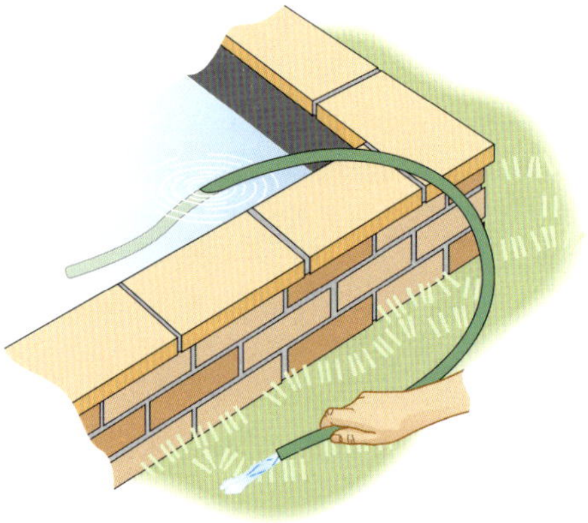

2 After the fish have been removed, syphon all the water from the pond.

3 When the pond is completely empty, give it a thorough scrub.

solutions

### A cleaner home for your fish

To keep your fish pond cleaner, an aerator of some kind (any device, such as a fountain, that mixes air into the water) will help, as will freshwater snails. And don't forget that some birds do this too.

- When the pond has been half drained, remove the fish with a net and transfer them to the wading pool. Cover it with a mesh screen, in case you have any fish that are likely to jump and flop out.
- While there is still water at the bottom of the pond, clean the sides with a soft-bristled scrubbing brush. Continue to drain until the bottom layer of crud is in sight. Then stop pumping and remove the remaining debris with a dustpan.
- Rinse the sides of the pool with a hose and then remove the pump and rinse that. Gently scrub the bottom.
- Replace the plants before you begin refilling. Use a water conditioner, available from pet shops or aquarium suppliers, to neutralise chlorine in the new water. Return the water you saved in the extra containers to the pond, and allow the clean fish pond to warm up a bit before putting the fish and the water from the wading pool back in.

## FLAGS AND BANNERS

**MOST FLAGS AND** SPORTING BANNERS HAVE COLOURS THAT, IF EACH WERE THE COLOUR OF AN INDIVIDUAL ITEM IN YOUR LAUNDRY BASKET, YOU'D SEPARATE AND WASH IN DIFFERENT LOADS. BANNERS, OFTEN WITH APPLIQUÉD DESIGNS AND DEPICTING SEASONAL OR WHIMSICAL THEMES, ALSO OFTEN USE CONTRASTING COLOURS.

**To keep the colours pure,** first check the box or bag that your flag or banner came in—if you still have it—to see whether it has instructions for cleaning. If instructions aren't available, try to determine what kind of fabric the flag or banner is made of. Those of recent vintage are usually cotton, nylon or polyester.

**Washing a nylon or polyester flag** or banner is usually safe. Put it in the washing machine on a gentle cycle in warm water with a mild laundry detergent. You can hang it out to dry on a clothes line or dry it on a low setting in the tumble-dryer.

**Dry-cleaning a cotton flag** or banner is usually necessary—especially if you value it highly—because it is likely to bleed if washed. An old wool flag or banner should always be dry-cleaned. If you're willing to take a chance on washing it yourself, go ahead and launder a cotton flag or banner. If the colours run, you may be able to undo the damage with Dylon Run Away, a dye remover whose name is self-explanatory. Look for it at supermarkets, mass merchandisers, fabric shops, and arts and crafts supply shops.

Simple solutions

### Keep it flying proudly

To extend a flag's life, take it down when it rains, hails or is very windy. If a flag does become wet, let it dry thoroughly before you fold or roll it. Otherwise, you're inviting mildew to take up residence. Old flags with historical value should be treated with great care. Get professional advice on how to clean them from a museum conservator.

# FLOORS

**THERE ARE VAST** DIFFERENCES BETWEEN SPECIFIC FLOORINGS, EVEN AMONG GENERAL CATEGORIES SUCH AS WOOD, STONE OR TILE. MAPLE ISN'T PINE, MARBLE ISN'T GRANITE AND QUARRY TILE ISN'T GLAZED. STILL, ALL FLOORS ARE SUBJECTED TO DIRT AND WEAR, AND SOME BASIC CLEANING TECHNIQUES APPLY UNIVERSALLY. CHECK THE 'FLOOR-CLEANING PYRAMID' BOX ON PAGE 181 FOR GENERAL FLOOR CLEANING METHODS, AND WHEN YOU'VE EXHAUSTED THOSE, TRY OUR RECOMMENDATIONS FOR SPECIFIC FLOOR TYPES.

**WATCH OUT** Acids (such as vinegar) will etch marble, and strong alkaline solutions (such as washing soda or ammonia) will break down the smooth marble surface and leave it rough.

**To clean wooden floors,** the bad news is that you really should get down on your hands and knees. And you can't swab water all over the floor—it must be used sparingly.

When damp mopping isn't going to do the trick, try making one of these general-purpose cleaners:

- Mix ½ cup of cider vinegar in 4 litres of warm water.
- Brew some tea using 2 tea bags per 1 litre of water.

Dip a soft cloth or sponge in the solution, wring it out and wipe the floor. Buff with a soft, dry cloth.

**The object of caring diligently for wooden floors**—aside from keeping them looking good—is to avoid having to do a sanding job. It's a lot of work if you do it yourself and it's a lot of money if you have it done professionally. It's also messy and it removes not just the old finish but also a layer of wood from your floor. Each time you sand, you're working your way towards the foundations.

**Determining a wooden floor's finish** will help you determine how to care for it. If the floor was installed or last refinished before the mid-1960s, the finish is probably varnish or shellac. These finishes rest on top of the wood, are often waxed and require a whole-floor sanding before a new finish can be applied. More recent floor finishes might be polyurethane, which penetrates the wood, should not be waxed and can be touched up by new urethane applied to just those places that have become worn.

You can tell one from the other by scratching the surface with a coin in an inconspicuous place. If the finish flakes, it is more likely to be shellac or varnish. If the finish does not flake when scratched, it is probably a polyurethane finish.

To check if your floor has been waxed, put a couple of drops of water on the floor. Wait for 10 minutes and then check to see whether white spots have appeared under the water. White spots mean the floor has been waxed. If there are no white spots, it hasn't.

## The lowdown on wax build-up

High-traffic areas on wooden floors wear out their wax sooner than low-traffic areas. This means the road less travelled can get a build-up of wax. A telltale sign is a yellowed or discoloured floor. Removing all the wax requires harsher cleaning than usual and should only be done when necessary and no more often than once a year.

Here are two easy and effective recipes for a wax stripper:

- ½ cup of ammonia and 1 cup of laundry detergent in 4 litres of warm water.
- ½ cup of washing soda (available from the laundry section in supermarkets) in 4 litres of warm water.

In either case, apply some solution and scrub with a stiff brush, electric scrubber or extra-fine steel-wool (000) pads to loosen the old wax. Work on a small area at a time and mop up the solution after the wax has been softened. Repeat the process in other areas until the entire floor is stripped of wax. Rinse thoroughly with a solution of 4 litres of water and a cup of vinegar. After drying completely, apply new wax to the floor.

## The floor-cleaning pyramid

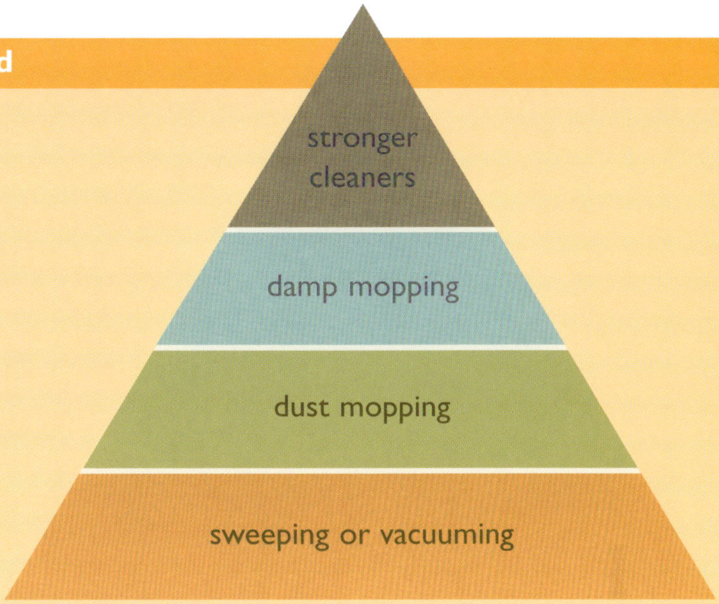


Remember the famous food pyramid? You're supposed to choose a lot of the foods depicted at the bottom of the pyramid (fruits, vegetables and grains) and eat what's at the top sparingly (fats, sugars and oils). On the floor-cleaning pyramid, the broad bottom includes the cleaning methods that apply to all types of floors and that are suitable for using most frequently. Frequency of use declines as you go up the pyramid, and the top is reserved for more specialised cleaners for specific flooring materials.

Here are some other general guidelines for floor cleaning:

- Vacuum or sweep up loose dirt, dust and pet hair frequently.
- Dust floorings with a dust mop.
- Wipe up any spills immediately to make bigger cleaning jobs easier.
- Clean floorings with a damp mop or cloth (using plain water) once a week or more often if necessary. Change the water as soon as it gets cloudy.
- Go to stronger cleaners only when a damp mop doesn't do the job properly.
- Rinse the floor thoroughly after using any kind of cleaning product.

Floor polishers can be rented from equipment rental shops. Check your local telephone directory for listings.

**On varnished or shellacked floors,** a solvent-based liquid wax for wood works well. It removes dirt and most of the old wax (preventing wax build-up) and leaves a thin coating of new wax. You can apply the cleaner with a soft, dry cloth attached to a long-handled wax applicator, but you would do a better job on your hands and knees. You can also use an electric polisher (see left), changing pads frequently. In any case, you need to buff afterwards with a clean cloth. Never use water-based, self-polishing wax on wood floors.

**On urethane-finished floors,** rub with a cloth containing a little furniture oil to give them more shine. (Read the label to make sure it doesn't contain any wax.) Only use a little bit; too much oil will attract dirt—and make the floor very slippery.

**To clean stone flooring,** sprinkle damp sawdust over the floor (available from hardware shops or a timber yard), scrub with a stiff brush and sweep up the sawdust with a dustpan and broom, then vacuum.

Many kinds of stone flooring, especially marble, need a neutral-pH cleaner (sold by businesses that sell and install stone flooring). A mild dishwashing liquid mixed with water will also work nicely. Consult the dealer who sold you the stone for recommendations for specific cleaners if more power is needed. There are also professionals whose specialty is refinishing stone floors.

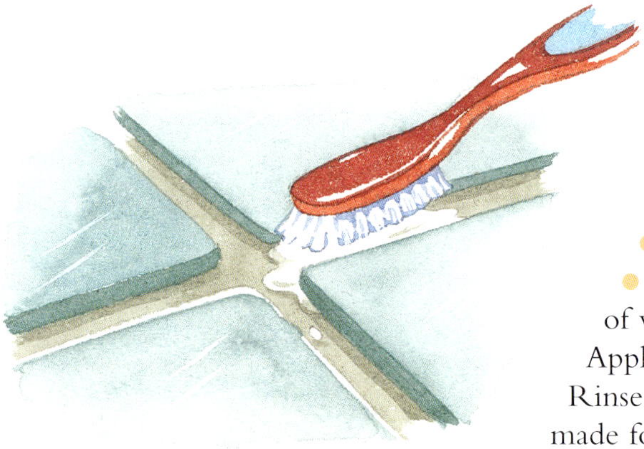

You can clean up grout nicely by scrubbing it with a toothbrush dipped in a vinegar-and-water solution.

**To clean ceramic tile floors,** a quick going over with a damp mop is often all that is needed. Actually, cleaning ceramic tile would be a breeze if tile were all you had to clean. It's the grout between the tiles that's a problem.

When damp mopping alone isn't going to do the job properly, mix one of these cleaning solutions:

- 1 capful of methylated spirits in 4 litres of water.
- 1 tablespoon of borax and 2 tablespoons of ammonia in 4 litres of water. (Wear gloves, as borax is a toxic substance.)

Apply the solution with a mop or an electric cleaner–polisher. Rinse well with clear water on your mop. A commercial cleaner made for tile floors (read the label) will also do the job.

If the grout needs special attention, mix ¼ cup of vinegar with 4 litres of water and scrub the grout with a toothbrush or nylon scrub pad (see above left). For heavy-duty treatment, scrub with a mixture of 1 cup of chlorine bleach in 2 litres of water (wear rubber gloves). Let the solution stand for 20 minutes, mop the floor twice with clean water to rinse thoroughly and wipe dry. To make future cleaning easier, seal the grout with a silicone sealer, which is available from hardware shops or shops that specialise in tile.

**To clean vinyl flooring** that just needs touching up, use a damp mop. If the stain requires something stronger than water, mix 1 cup of white vinegar with 4 litres of water and apply with a mop. If that doesn't do the job, try 2 tablespoons of borax in 4 litres of warm water. In either case, apply a small amount with your mop, then rinse thoroughly by mopping with plain water.

For more shine, apply a thin coat of wax to a clean, dry floor. The one-step, wax-and-clean products don't work as well as a regular wax. A self-polishing wax (such as Pledge One Go) is easy to apply, but it will build up over time. A solvent-based paste wax is more work and must be buffed but it does provides superior results.

Wax-free vinyl has a polyurethane finish intended to keep a shine without waxing. It will stay shiny for a long time if it is kept clean, but eventually the finish will dull. Follow the manufacturer's instructions for a polish or sealer to renew the shine. Waxing it would make it slippery.

If hair spray has built up on the wax-free floor in your bathroom, use shampoo to wash it off. (It works on hair, after all.) Mix a squirt of shampoo in 4 litres of warm water, mop and rinse.

**To clean laminate flooring,** keep in mind that, like wood, it should not be mopped by slopping lots of water around on the floor. (Laminate is the manmade flooring that comes in tongue-and-groove planks that often simulate wood.) Don't use ammonia, solvents, abrasives, general-purpose cleaners, polishes or waxes on laminate. Despite these restrictions, laminate is really easy to clean.

Simple solutions

### How to handle scuffs

The heels of shoes often end up leaving stubborn black scuff marks on your floors. Try rubbing off heel marks with a pencil rubber first and if that doesn't work, rub a hardwood floor with a rag dabbed in a bit of mineral turpentine. On vinyl flooring, smear a drop of baby oil or eucalyptus oil over the mark, wait a few minutes, then wipe the mark away with a rag.

Some manufacturers recommend their own special cleaner, which is usually fairly expensive. Here is a less expensive version that works just as well: 1 cup of white vinegar, 1 cup of methylated spirits (to make it dry faster), 1 cup of water and 3 drops of dishwashing liquid. Mix the ingredients together in a spray bottle, shake, spray it on the floor and then spread it with a mop. No rinsing is needed.

If your laminate gets scratched, you may be able to buy a touch-up stick from the manufacturer. In the event of severe damage, a professional installer may be able to replace a plank or two.

*See also:* • CORK

## FLOWERPOTS

**A BEAUTIFUL FLOWER** IN A DIRTY POT IS LIKE A BEAUTIFUL CAKE ON A FOOD-ENCRUSTED PLATE. YOU DON'T CLEAN FLOWERPOTS JUST FOR AESTHETIC REASONS, THOUGH. PLANTS AND THEIR SOIL MAY CONTAIN VIRUSES, BACTERIA, FUNGI OR INSECT PESTS, WHICH CAN BE PASSED ALONG TO THE NEXT PLANT THAT'S PUT IN THE POT.

**Clean your flowerpots** using the same method, whether they're made of plastic, glazed or unglazed clay, ceramic, or other materials. Wash with dishwashing liquid and water, as you would dishes. Scour with a stiff brush to remove algae and mineral deposits, then wash again with a solution of 10 parts water to 1 part chlorine bleach. Rinse with fresh water and dry in the sunshine, which is a great steriliser.

**Here are some more tips** for cleaning flowerpots:

- If you'd prefer to avoid scrubbing, soak the pots for about an hour in a solution of 2 parts water to 1 part white vinegar. The minerals and algae should wash completely off.
- To avoid a crusty, white build-up of mineral deposits around the top inner edge of the pot, rub an old candle around the rim (see below). The wax will seal the surface, making mineral build-up less likely.

Discourage the build up of crusty, white deposits on the inside rim of pots by rubbing them with an old candle.

- You might also take note that the white scaly stuff is a sign that you're giving your plants too much fertiliser. Many keen gardeners do that, so consider taking a more minimalist approach and also get a good book on caring for house plants to check advice on fertilising.
- To keep dirt from spattering out of the flowerpot when it rains or when you water the plant, put a layer of pebbles on top of the dirt.

# FLOWERS

**FRESH FLOWERS ARE** A GREAT WAY TO ENJOY THE COLOUR AND SMELLS OF SPRING INSIDE AND THEY DON'T NEED MUCH LOOKING AFTER, BUT ARTIFICIAL AND DRIED FLOWERS DO NEED REGULAR ATTENTION TO KEEP THEM CLEAN.

**Dusting artificial or dried flowers** is something you need to do occasionally. The first line of defence is to blow off the dust. Use a feather duster or a hair dryer on its lowest, coolest setting for sturdy blooms (see below). Or you could try using a turkey baster to squirt air on more fragile artificial or dried flowers.

The term 'silk' flowers is usually a misnomer today. Most fabric flowers are made of polyester or other blends.

A quick and easy way to dust artificial flowers is to give them a blast of air with a hair dryer.

**For a more thorough cleaning,** try this method, which is safe for both plastic and fabric flowers. (Some people say they've used it successfully on dried natural flowers, too, but proceed at your own risk.) Draw enough water into the sink (or bathtub, if necessary) so that the flowers can be submerged. Add a squirt of mild dishwashing liquid and slosh it around to make suds. Then put the flowers in the water, holding them down to cover. Gently raise and lower them a couple of times. Drain the water and rinse the flowers gently under the shower. Allow them to air-dry thoroughly.

## Making flowers last longer

Here are some ways to slow the passage of blooms to has-blooms:

- Cut off any leaves below water level.
- Wash the vase and change the water frequently; daily if necessary.
- Use a simple preservative in the water, such as 2 tablespoons of white vinegar and 2 teaspoons of sugar to a litre of water. (Sugar feeds the flowers while the vinegar inhibits the growth of unwanted mould or fungus.) Or use 1 part tonic water to 2 parts water.
- Keep the flowers cool and out of direct sunlight to avoid wilting.
- Cut off stray ends periodically to keep the arrangement looking neat.

**Here are some more** flower-enhancing tricks that you might want to try for artificial or dried flowers:

- Use a steam iron, set on the lowest setting, to liven up those tired paper flowers that are looking a bit crumpled and sad.
- Dried natural flowers will last longer if they've been given a few light coats of sealer from an aerosol spray can. You can use hair spray or a clear lacquer or acrylic sealer (available from hardware and craft shops). The flowers can be resealed after cleaning.
- For a more ambitious finish, you might want to consider revamping flowers that are passed cleaning. Spray artificial or dried flowers with gold or silver spray paint and use them for Christmas or other decorations.

## FOAM RUBBER

**THE NICE THING** ABOUT FOAM—WHETHER IT'S THE OLD RUBBER USED FROM THE 1940S TO THE 1960S OR POLYURETHANE, THE PREFERRED MATERIAL SINCE THE 1970S—IS THAT IT'S POROUS. THAT MEANS ALL YOU HAVE TO DO TO KEEP THE FOAM IN YOUR CUSHIONS, PILLOWS OR MATTRESSES FRESH IS TO VACUUM IT. HOWEVER, SPILLS REQUIRE A BIT MORE ELBOW GREASE.

**To clean spills or marks** on the foam's surface, first remove any covering (clean it separately), then use a rag dampened with dish-washing liquid and water and rub the surface. Never put soap and water directly on the foam, because it will absorb the liquid. Let the foam air-dry thoroughly before you put the cushion cover, sheet or pillowcase back on, to avoid the growth of micro-organisms.

Heavy spills that have seeped into the interior of the foam require special attention. Run water—only water—through the foam, then squeeze out as much excess as you can. If you use soap or other cleaning agents, you'll just have to rinse those out, too, or you run the risk of creating a breeding ground for bacteria.

**To clean a deep stain** from a small cushion or pillow, place the foam in the bathtub or sink and run water over it. For larger cushions, use a shower nozzle or garden hose. However, don't try this on a mattress, which can only be surface cleaned.

Even when you're dealing with a very difficult stain, keep water use to a minimum, because it will take 24–48 hours for the foam to dry completely. And there's nothing you can do to speed the drying process, either. Above all, don't ever rest foam near a heater or heat source to try to dry it faster or put small pieces in a tumble-dryer—foam is highly flammable.

No matter how good a job you do on cleaning your foam objects, some odours and stains—such as pet urine and saliva—may not come out if they seep into the interior of the foam rubber. You might just have to bite the bullet and replace it.

### Dirty pillow? Bag it

To quickly and thoroughly clean a foam rubber pillow or cushion, all you need is a plastic bag and a vacuum cleaner. Remove any attachment from the end of the vacuum cleaner's hose. Put the pillow in a plastic bag and stick the end of the vacuum hose in the bag, twist the top of the bag closed and hold it in place, then turn on the vacuum. The foam will become condensed as the vacuum sucks the air and dirt out of the foam. When you turn the vacuum off, the foam will return to its original shape. This nifty technique cleans both sides of the pillow at the same time.

# FOOD

**CLEAN FOOD STARTS** WITH A CLEAN YOU. THE MOST IMPORTANT THING YOU CAN DO TO KEEP YOURSELF HEALTHY AND PREVENT THE SPREAD OF ILLNESS IS TO WASH YOUR HANDS FREQUENTLY WITH SOAP AND WATER. AND TRAVELLING IS NO EXCUSE FOR LETTING UP ON CLEANLINESS: PACK DISPOSABLE WIPES TO USE WHENEVER YOU NEED THEM.

**To clean fruit and vegetables,** you don't need anything special. Washing with plain water will do. Just make sure you don't skip any fruit and vegetables—even the organic ones. They all need to be washed. While organic items may not have residual chemicals on them, they can have the same amount of dirt, dust and mould spores.

**Here are cleaning specifics for certain foods:**

- For fruit and vegetables with a firm surface that doesn't require peeling, such as potatoes, celery and apples, just use a vegetable brush to scrub the skin clean under running water (see below).

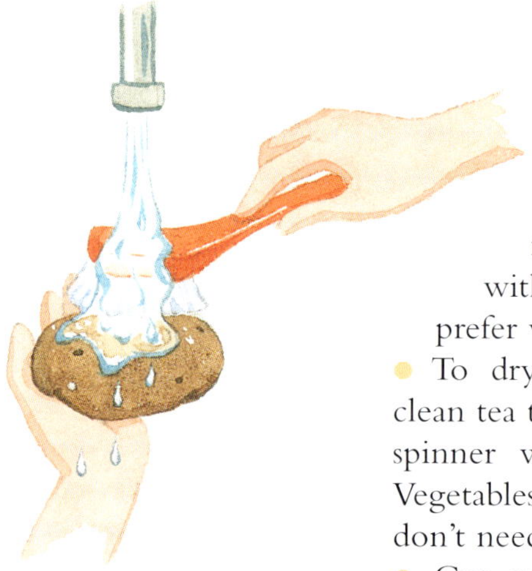

Give tough-skinned fruit and vegetables a scrub with a vegetable brush before cooking.

- For leafy vegetables and fruit with a soft skin, such as peaches, strawberries and raspberries, rinse under running water only.
- It's not necessary to wash mushrooms; simply wipe them with a damp paper towel. If you prefer washing, use running water.
- To dry vegetables and fruit, use a clean tea towel or paper towel. A lettuce spinner works well for most greens. Vegetables that are going to be cooked don't need to be dried first.
- Cut away any bruised or damaged areas from fruit and vegetables with a sharp knife. Immediately refrigerate any freshly cut fruit or vegetables.
- Rinse fish quickly in cold water to remove ice, slime and any loose small scales you can't see.

**And here are some don'ts:**

- Don't use a brush on soft-skinned vegetables or fruit. You'll only damage them by breaking the skin open.
- Don't use detergents or soap on fresh foods. The produce could absorb the residues, which you could ingest.
- Don't wash raw poultry, beef, pork, lamb or veal before using. You may think you're helping to make the meat safer, but you're not. Cooking destroys surface bacteria at 70 °C.
- Keep raw meat, fish and poultry in containers. Never place them directly on benchtops or refrigerator shelves. Never let the juices of raw meat drip onto other foods, and never use the same utensils on cooked foods that you have used for handling raw meat.
- Don't wash eggs before storing or using them. They have already been washed during commercial egg processing. You'll just remove more of the 'bloom'—the natural coating on just-laid eggs that helps prevent bacteria from permeating the shell.

### EXPERT ADVICE

#### HOW TO GET THE GRIT

Rinsing is not enough to get the grit out of lettuce or spinach leaves; the greens need a bath. Fill a clean kitchen sink with enough cold water to cover the greens and submerge them for 30–45 seconds. Swish the leaves around with your hand and then empty the water in the sink. Clean the sink to remove the sand and grit, then repeat the process. Keep washing, draining and washing until there is no more sand and grit visible in the sink when you let the water out.

## FOOD COOLERS

**IDEALLY, YOU SHOULD** CLEAN YOUR COOLER AFTER EACH USE. THE METHOD FOR CLEANING DEPENDS A LOT ON WHAT YOU'VE HAD IN IT. IF IT'S ONLY BEEN STORING SOFT DRINK, JUST RINSE IT WITH WATER.

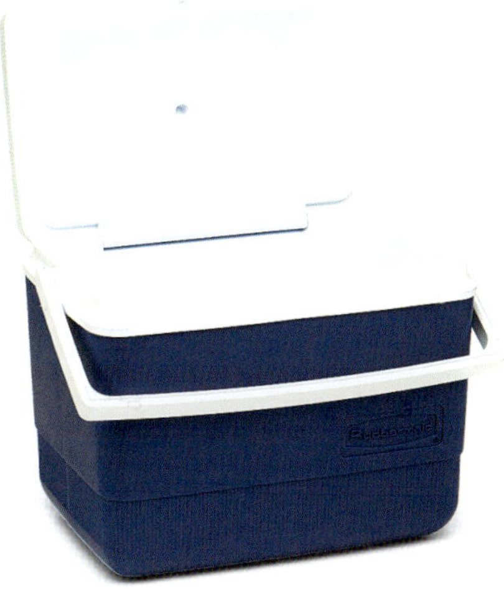

**To clean a large, rigid cooler** (such as an Esky or polystyrene cooler) more thoroughly, haul it into the backyard and give it a hose down. Pour a couple of drops of dishwashing liquid onto the wet cooler and scrub it, using a clean rag, sponge or a nylon dishwashing brush. Then turn the cooler on its side, so water will drain out, and rinse with a garden hose. (You can do this just as easily in the bathtub, where the hot water would help with tougher cleaning jobs. Just wash very small food coolers in the kitchen sink.)

**To sanitise a cooler**—if you've been carrying raw meat in it, for example—mix 1 teaspoon of bleach in 1 litre of water. Apply the solution to the cooler with a sponge or rag, or pour it into a spray bottle, squirt it on and wipe. Then rinse with fresh water. Once your cooler is clean, leave it to air-dry with the lid open before you store it. To keep it smelling fresh for next time, wipe it down with a damp sponge that's been sprinkled with vanilla essence, or place a small open container of bicarbonate of soda inside, before replacing the lid.

**To remove stubborn food stains,** make a paste by mixing bicarbonate of soda and water in a bowl. Dip a clean rag or sponge into the paste, rub the spot and then rinse. If that doesn't work, apply a non-abrasive household cleaner, such as Ajax Spray n' Wipe or Earth Choice Multi-Purpose Spray, with a rag. Using an abrasive cleaner could scratch the interior of your cooler, giving dirt and bacteria a place to hide—and making your cleaning job harder.

**To clean a soft-structure cooler,** mix mild dishwashing liquid in water and wipe the cooler down inside and out with a clean rag or sponge. Rinse (with a little vanilla in the water, if you like) and air-dry. Don't machine wash, and don't use bleach on this type of cooler.

## FOOD GRATERS

**IF YOU'RE A** COOK WHO LIKES THE FRESHNESS OF HOME-GRATED CHEESE, CITRUS RIND AND HARD SPICES, SUCH AS CARDAMOM, NUTMEG AND CINNAMON, A GRATER IS ESSENTIAL. BUT THEY'RE TRICKY TO CLEAN BECAUSE SOME FOODS GET TRAPPED IN THE GRATES OR LEAVE A RESIDUE BEHIND.

**To keep a grater cleaner** when you're grating citrus rind on the finest grate, wrap the grater in plastic. The plastic wrap adheres tightly to the form and shape of the grater, keeping the rind out of those nooks and crannies and allowing for easier collection of all the zest.

Simple solutions

### Grate stuff!

Keep a clean pastry brush handy for removing every last skerrick of grated food left behind in the tiny grates—it works like a charm on both sides of the grater.

**To clean the grater,** soak it in warm to hot, soapy water. Use a dishwashing brush with short bristles or even an old toothbrush for the smaller grates. To protect the brush bristles, hold the grater upside down and brush with a bottom-to-top stroke (the opposite of the grating motion). You can put a grater in a dishwasher, as long as the grater isn't made of tin, which can quickly oxidise when it's not dried thoroughly. To dry, place the grater on a dish drainer or a lint-free towel.

## FOOD MINCERS

**SAFETY COMES FIRST** HERE BECAUSE A FOOD MINCER IS OFTEN USED TO PROCESS RAW MEAT, POULTRY AND SEAFOOD, SO PROPER CLEANING IS CRITICAL TO AVOID THE TRANSMISSION OF HARMFUL BACTERIA, SUCH AS SALMONELLA. THE BEST MINCERS COME APART COMPLETELY, ALLOWING YOU TO CLEAN EACH PIECE THOROUGHLY.

**To clean the grinding plates,** first soak the parts in a soapy solution of hot water and dishwashing liquid to dislodge most of the food. You can finish the job in a dishwasher (always consult the manufacturer's instructions first), set on a heavy cycle.

If you're cleaning the parts by hand, soak with some salt (1 tablespoon of salt to 2 litres of cold water) for about 10 minutes to dislodge the food. Then you're ready to scrub the plates and blade with a brush in hot, soapy water to any kill bacteria that may be lurking. To help get meat or other remnants out of the holes in the plates, poke wooden kebab skewers through the holes.

Lay the parts on a tea towel and allow them to air-dry fully. Or you can place the parts in an oven at a temperature of 70 °C for 10–15 minutes. If you put aluminium alloy blades in the dishwasher, they'll quickly start to rust when they sit and dry. Once the blades are dry, lightly rub vegetable oil over them to protect them from rusting.

**To clean a food grinder's motor unit,** wipe it with an antibacterial, all-purpose cleanser, or a solution of 30 millilitres of bleach to 4 litres of warm water. Fill a spray bottle with the solution, spray it on the housing unit (the outside only), and then wipe it off.

**Non-electrical food mincers,** such as a Mouli, should be taken apart and washed in warm soapy water, then dried.

**EXPERT ADVICE**

BEFORE THE OLD GRIND, CHILL OUT

Some of the natural sweetness of meat can be lost in the mincing process—unless you happen to know this professional secret: chill your food mincer in the freezer first. This way, the machine remains cool for the mincing process and the sweetness of the meat is maintained before cooking.

## FOOD PROCESSORS

**SOMEWHERE AMONG THE** JUNGLE OF GADGETS ON YOUR KITCHEN BENCHTOP THERE IS PROBABLY A FOOD PROCESSOR. THEY PUREE, MINCE, MIX, KNEAD, BLEND AND MORE. BUT MUCH LIKE A FOOD MINCER, FOOD PROCESSORS NEED TO BE CLEANED PART BY PART.

**For general cleaning,** rinse off most of the gunk and wash in hot, soapy water with a nylon brush for dislodging stuck food. If you clean it as soon as you've used the processor, it shouldn't be a long or difficult process. Another time saver is to cover the bowl with a strong piece of plastic wrap before locking on the lid (only if your recipe doesn't require the use of the feed tube on top of the processor). This will prevent splattering on the lid and minimise cleaning.

**To clean the power unit** of your food processor, turn it off and unplug the unit. Wipe it with a damp cloth and wipe off the safety motor drive cover, then reinstall it on the unit, if necessary. Never use coarse or caustic cleaning products on the power unit or immerse it in water.

**To clean the attachments,** put them in the dishwasher—all except the blades. Since items can shift in the dishwasher, the blades could bend, be dulled or be burned if they touch a heating element. Wash the blades in hot, soapy water, dry with a cloth and store for future use. Some experts prefer to hand wash the plastic bowl of a food processor in hot, soapy water. This protects the bowl from the harsher dishwasher detergent, which can make the plastic brittle and prone to breakage. On some models, the plastic bowl has a safety spring located where the bowl attaches to the food processor. It's difficult to get this spring thoroughly dry, so after you've given the bowl a quick wipe, let it air-dry before reassembling the processor. Otherwise, the spring may rust.

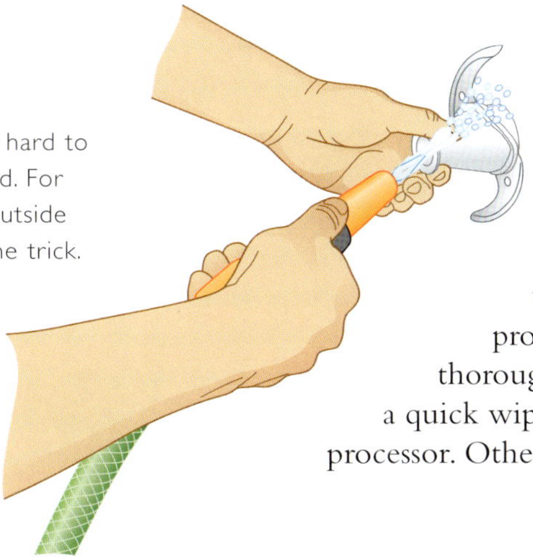

Some food can be particularly hard to clean off, especially when it's dried. For really tough jobs, a quick squirt outside with the garden hose might do the trick.

## FOUNTAIN PENS

**ALL FOUNTAIN PENS,** WHETHER THEY HAVE A METAL OR GOLD NIB, SHOULD BE CLEANED AFTER FOUR OR FIVE FILLINGS, OR AFTER USING FOUR OR FIVE INK CARTRIDGES.

**To clean your fountain pen,** flush the nib section by running it under plain tap water at room temperature. For ink deposits that may have stood in the pen for a long time, make one of the following four solutions. They'll help the water penetrate areas in the pen more quickly and thoroughly to clean it out:

- 1 drop of dishwashing liquid in 1 cup of water at room temperature.
- A couple of squirts of household cleaner, such as Ajax Spray n' Wipe, in 1 cup of water.
- A few squirts (about a teaspoon) of a bleach cleaner, such as White King Bleach Spray, in 175 millilitres of water.
- 1 cap of non-sudsy household ammonia in 1 cup of water.

**To clean self-filling pens,** the kind you dip into the ink, place your cleaning solution (see 'To clean your fountain pen', on page 189) in a glass and draw it into the pen, just as you would to fill the pen with ink. Then place the nib in the water and let it all soak for 2 hours to 2 days, depending on how long the ink has been in the pen. To rinse, draw fresh water into the pen and empty it.

To clean a pen that's not heavily caked with ink, fill the pen with solution and empty it two or three times.

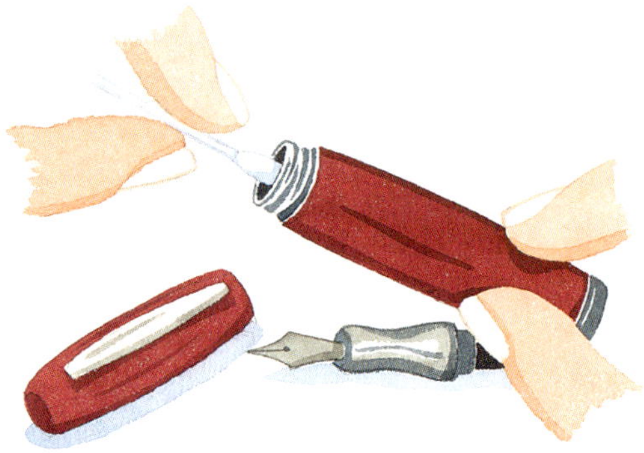

Use a cotton bud to clean inside the narrow barrel of your fountain pen.

**Cleaning ink-cartridge pens** is a little trickier because there's no device on the pen to force the cleaning solution through the very fine internal channels of the nib. Squeeze an empty ink cartridge to force the air out, dip it into one of the cleaning solutions mentioned on page 189, then release it, drawing the solution into the cartridge. Attach the cartridge to the nib section as if it were full of ink and squeeze the cleaning solution out of the cartridge and through the nib. Repeat the procedure a couple of times.

More tips for cleaning fountain pens include:

- India ink or waterproof inks aren't recommended for fountain pens. These sort of inks should be used only with the type of pens that are dipped into an inkwell repeatedly, such as a quill.
- Avoid letting hot water, alcohol or acetone come in contact with your fountain pen because they could damage certain parts of it.
- The barrel (the shaft that holds the ink) and cap of your pen can be washed in cold water. Use a cotton bud to clean the interior of these long, narrow cylinders (see above left).
- Dry each section of your fountain pen before putting it back together again. A cotton bud is useful for this particular task, because it can get to all the hard-to-reach parts.

## FURNITURE

YOUR WOODEN FURNITURE NEEDS REGULAR MAINTENANCE. AN EVERYDAY DINING ROOM TABLE COULD BE TOMORROW'S ANTIQUE TREASURE.

**Figuring out what type of finish** your furniture has is the first order of business. If your furniture has an oil finish, you should only dust and re-oil it. If it has the more common hard finish—such as varnish or lacquer—you have more options.

**Oil finish or a hard finish?** Here's how you tell the difference: put a few drops of boiled linseed oil on the wood and rub it in with your finger. If the wood absorbs the oil, you have an oil finish. If the boiled linseed oil beads up, you have a hard varnished or lacquered finish.

**To clean oiled furniture,** dust with a dry cloth. Don't use a dust-attracting product on the cloth, and make sure the cloth is soft and free of buttons, zippers and anything else that might scratch the wood.

## Protecting oiled furniture

Rule number one is never put cloth items or water on oiled furniture. Cloth items absorb moisture from the oil and dry out your furniture. Ironically, oil offers the least protection from any finish—get any water on it and it's wrecked yet it requires the highest maintenance of the various furniture finishes.

Then apply oil to the wood (boiled linseed oil, tung oil or an oil recommended by the furniture's manufacturer, such as Howard Orange Oil or Pledge). Rub the oil in with a clean cloth. Do this an average of once a month. If it's been a while since you oiled a particular piece of furniture, do it every two weeks for a couple of months to allow it to catch up on missing oil, then resume a once-a-month routine.

**To clean varnished or lacquered furniture,** dust first with a soft rag or feather duster. It's OK to add a bit of dust-attracting product, such as a few drops of paraffin oil, to the rag or duster but not straight onto the furniture. Let it dry before you dust. If necessary, you can clean hard-finished furniture with a damp cloth and mild detergent, such as Dawn (although a specialist wood product, such as Howard Orange Oil or Pledge, will clean and polish at the same time). Then you can polish.

**To polish a hard finish,** apply a furniture polish, such as Clean 'N Shine or Pledge, in an aerosol can. First, mist the surface of the furniture and use one area of a rag to spread the polish, wiping in a circular motion. Turn the rag over and wipe off the excess polish. Avoid polishes that consist mostly of silicone and paraffin wax, because both of these ingredients tend to build up and eventually soften or ruin a finish.

**To clean varnished or lacquered kitchen furniture,** take a different approach, because it is exposed to grease and cooking oils. Use a cloth that has been barely dampened with dishwashing liquid and water to remove the oily substances. Follow up with a cloth dampened with plain water and then polish. For more cleaning power, use a wood soap, such as Howard Clean-A-Finish or Briwax, according to the package instructions. (Test an inconspicuous spot first.) Polish your kitchen table at least three times a week. Every three months, clean it using the mineral spirits method described below.

**To give a hard finish** a thorough cleaning and remove built-up wax, you'll need a few very soft rags. Old nappies that have been washed many times are perfect for this job. Soak one rag with mineral turpentine. Wipe your furniture thoroughly, flipping the rag frequently. Thoroughly go over all areas several times with the rag, and don't be afraid to apply more mineral turpentine frequently. Now dry the surface completely with a soft, dry rag. Repeat this wiping and drying process at least three times using a fresh rag each time. For seriously dirty or damaged surfaces, you might need a professional wood product, such as Howard Restor-A-Finish or Briwax Furniture Reviver, which should be used in conjunction with superfine (0000) steel wool.

Once the furniture is clean, you can polish or wax to re-nourish and protect the surface. Spray the polish on the wood and rub it in with a rag, going in a circular motion. Now use another clean, soft rag—or flip the polishing rag to a dry spot—and wipe with the grain of the wood to remove excess polish. Carved wood should be cleaned in the same way, regularly with polish and once a year with mineral turpentine. The only difference is that you'll need a soft toothbrush to get into the intricately carved details.

**If a finish has become sticky,** this usually means it has failed—the result of too much polish build-up, exposure to oils over the years or the finish's having degraded over time. Use mineral turpentine, Howard Restor-A-Finish or Briwax Furniture Reviver, and superfine steel wool (0000) to remove the old finish, rubbing with the grain of the wood. Wipe three or four times with a rag and fresh mineral turpentine. When you're done, the furniture will have to be refinished. Talk to a professional or follow the package instructions on the finishing product you choose. Don't do this to a valuable antique, take it to a professional.

**To clean painted wooden furniture,** dust it with a water-dampened cloth. If necessary, use a mild, non-abrasive detergent (such as dishwashing liquid) and warm water. Dip a rag into the cleaning solution and wring it nearly dry. Work on a small section of wood at a time. Rinse with clear water. Dry the surface with a clean cloth quickly before continuing.

Waxes and polishes are usually not needed on painted furniture, but if you do use a wax on a light-coloured painted piece, use a white, creamy type polish to avoid discolouration. Never use oil, oil polishes or oil-treated cloths on painted furniture.

Usually, a very old piece with its original finish should not be repainted or refinished because you risk ruining its value.

**To make your own furniture cleaner** for removing old polish and dirt, put 1 litre of water in a pot on the stove, add 2 tea bags and bring to the boil. Cool the solution to room temperature and then dip a soft cloth in the brewed tea and wring the cloth until it's damp. Wipe the furniture, buff it dry with a soft cloth and decide whether you should then polish it to finish off.

To make your own furniture polish, follow either of these formulas:

- Mix together ⅓ cup of white vinegar and 1 cup of olive oil.

**EXPERT ADVICE**

### DITCH THE PLASTIC

Modern furniture finishes and plastic don't mix. Actually, they mix too well—so keep the two apart. Finishes applied to furniture within the last 10 years or so have chemical properties that can mix with the chemicals in plastic or rubber (a plastic tablecloth, for instance). This 'plasticiser migration' damages the furniture's finished surface, so make sure you put a material such as felt between your furniture's surface and any plastic or rubber covering.

## A nutty cure for watermarks

Peanut butter can sometimes remedy white water spots on furniture. Rub some smooth peanut butter into the finish with a soft rag, over and over in a circular motion. If scratches appear, reapply, following the grain. The oils and abrasion from the peanuts will have a renewing effect on the finish. Next, take a dry cloth and wipe well. If the area now appears shinier than the rest of the surface, apply a car wax with a mild cleaner in it, such as TurtleWax or Meguiar's, then polish your furniture.

Peanut butter can work miracles, particularly with recent, hazy, white water spots. However, solid white water spots and the more severe black water spots that appear on furniture require a more specialised approach. Apply Howard Restor-A-Finish or Briwax Furniture Reviver along the grain, using superfine (0000) steel wool and elbow grease. When the mark has disappeared, wipe off any excess, then polish with orange oil or a wax-based wood preserver, such as Howard Feed-N-Wax or Briwax.

- Mix 3 drops of lemon extract in 1 cup of fine paraffin oil. (You can substitute baby oil for the olive or paraffin oil.) Rub the polish into the surface with a clean rag, using circular motions.

Here are some more tips for dealing with special situations involving stains and spills on your wooden furniture:

- Removing candle wax from furniture is risky because you can cause further damage. Use ice directly on the wax to get it as cold as possible and immediately wipe up excess water. Once the wax is very cold, try carefully inserting a butter knife under the wax to see whether it will pop off. If this method doesn't work, don't attempt anything else. Avoid damage by consulting a professional.
- If you have a fresh paint stain on your furniture, remove acrylic paint with water; remove enamel (oil-based) paint with mineral turpentine. To remove a dry stain, saturate the spot in boiled linseed oil. After the paint softens, lift it off carefully with a putty knife. An alternative is to wipe with a cloth dampened in the boiled linseed oil. Remove residue by making a paste of boiled linseed oil and rottenstone, a polishing powder sold where you buy refinishing supplies. Rub the paste along the grain and then wipe it dry and wax or polish it.
- If paper is stuck to your wooden furniture, dampen the paper thoroughly with vegetable oil, wait 5 minutes and then rub along the grain with superfine (0000) steel wool. Wipe the surface dry.

*See also:*
• ANTIQUES • BRONZE • CHROME • FIBREGLASS • GLASS • MARBLE • OUTDOOR FURNITURE • UPHOLSTERY • WICKER, RATTAN AND BAMBOO

# FURS

**EXQUISITE TO LOOK** AT AND SOFT TO THE TOUCH, FUR CLEANING JOBS BELONG IN THE REALM OF PROFESSIONAL FURRIERS. IF YOU TRY TO CLEAN—OR EVEN BRUSH—ITEMS OF FUR YOURSELF, YOU COULD EASILY CAUSE DAMAGE. THE ADVICE HERE APPLIES WHETHER YOUR FUR IS THE REAL THING OR FAKE.

**Have your fur cleaned regularly** by a fur specialist—known as a furrier—not a drycleaner. Fur should be cleaned or serviced once a year, unless it has hardly been worn. In that case, have it cleaned at least every second year. The only cleaning you can do yourself includes giving your coat a light dusting, putting the coat on a clothes hanger and holding the neck of the hanger while you shake the coat.

**When you put away your coat** between uses, it needs to breathe. Never keep a fur coat in a suit bag or covered with a plastic garbage-bin liner. It will eventually dry out. If you insist on some kind of covering, use a cotton bag, which allows for some breathing.

**If your fur coat gets wet,** let it dry on its own. Don't place it near a heater or attempt to blow-dry it. The skin will burn, and it will get hard and stiff because the oils in the skin will be drying out too. Fur will easily stand up to snow or light rain, but if your fur gets totally soaked, take it to a professional furrier straight away.

**To store any type of fur coat,** it should ideally be placed in a cold storage (7 °C) unit with constant humidity (50 per cent). Once the first frost appears, fur coats can be taken out of storage. Check with a fur retailer about whether they can provide storage.

### EXPERT ADVICE

A WEARER'S GUIDE TO FUR

- Don't pin jewellery on your fur garment, and avoid sharp necklaces or bracelets. Use shoulder bags sparingly.
- Wear a scarf around your neck to protect the collar of your fur, especially if you wear make-up.
- Avoid insecticides, mothproofing and other chemicals around your fur, including perfume and hair spray.
- Get into your car carefully. Don't sit on fur, or at least don't sit on the same spot consistently. When you get out of a car, shake out any crushed places.
- On a plane, leave it on your lap or fold it loosely, lining out, and place it in an overhead locker on top of luggage.

## GAMES

**MOST GAME MAKERS** THESE DAYS ARE SAVVY ENOUGH TO KNOW WHO THEIR MAIN CUSTOMERS ARE—CHILDREN—AND TO MAKE THEIR GAMES AS INDESTRUCTIBLE AS POSSIBLE. PLASTIC PARTS AND PIECES ARE EASILY CLEANED, BUT WHEN GAME BOARDS ARE MADE OUT OF PAPER THE CLEANING GETS TRICKY.

Sprinkle clean, dry cards with talcum powder every so often, to keep them smooth and grease free.

**To clean plastic or rubber game parts,** wipe them off with a sponge or cloth dampened with a solution of mild dishwashing liquid and warm water. Rinse by wiping them over with a clean, damp sponge or cloth. Air-dry completely in a benchtop dish drainer or on a tea towel folded on your kitchen bench.

**To clean paper-coated game boards,** first try rubbing gently with a pencil rubber to remove any marks that are likely to come off that way. You can also rub marks with one of the new foam hard-surface erasers, such as Chux Magic Eraser. For general cleaning, wipe with a cloth or sponge dampened only with water (wrung out as much as possible beforehand). You want to avoid soaking the paper, which could damage the board or cause it to buckle. If the game board's colours begin to bleed, stop. If you need more cleaning power, try wiping with the soapy solution mentioned above for plastic parts. Pat the board dry with a clean, white cloth.

**To clean non-plasticised playing cards,** rub each one on both sides with spirits of camphor (available from pharmacies). When they're dry, sprinkle the pack generously with talcum powder and shuffle thoroughly (see left). Repeat the powder treatment every so often to keep the cards smooth and grease free.

**Simple solutions**

### Protect your games

- To remove dirt and leave your paper game board stiff and glossy, lightly spray it with laundry starch. Wipe it up quickly with a damp cloth, then pat it dry with a dry cloth.
- Mist your clean game boards with a spray furniture polish, such as Mr Sheen, then quickly wipe it off with a clean cloth. This will make wiping off sticky fingerprints easy.

## GARAGES

**A DIRTY, UNTIDY** GARAGE IS, AT THE LEAST, AN INEFFICIENT USE OF SPACE, AND AT THE WORST, CAN BE DOWNRIGHT DANGEROUS. IF YOU'VE GOT NO IDEA WHAT'S IN THOSE HALF-EMPTY BOTTLES OF GARDEN CHEMICALS AND PAINT TINS, IT'S TIME FOR A MAJOR CLEAN-UP.

**First, put the car in the street.** Start by chucking out anything in a bottle, jar or tin that looks dodgy. (But don't just throw them in the bin—contact your local Poisons Information Centre and ask where you can take the products for safe disposal.) You should also get rid of any other junk—broken things, rusty tools and so on. Now roll up your sleeves, strap on a dust mask and get ready to give those rubber gloves a work-out. Knock down cobwebs with a long-handled broom, then thoroughly sweep the floor and brush away debris from the walls. In a bucket, mix hot water and an alkaline-based household detergent, such as Handy Andy, according to label instructions. If the walls need cleaning, wash them first, using a strong-bristled floor brush

with a long handle. Always start at the bottom and work up to prevent streaking. While standing in one spot, wash as much as you can reach, then rinse with warm water. Continue until the walls are finished.

Next, scrub the floors, again using hot water and household detergent. Because concrete is porous, strong odours, such as animal waste, can be hard to eradicate. If a strong scrubbing doesn't do the trick, or if the floor is grimy with grease and tar from the car, you can use a commercial concrete cleaner, such as Liquid Magnet or Selleys Heavy Duty Concrete Kleen. When it's clean and dry, you can seal the floor with a concrete sealer, which is stronger than wax. Follow the label instructions and spread it on with a mop. Repeat the application for a really tough surface. After cleaning, open any doors or windows to air out the room and help the drying process.

**If mould or mildew is a problem,** (as it often is in garages below ground level), take an extra step after cleaning. Mop the walls and floors with a solution of ½ cup of chlorine bleach to 9 litres of water, then rinse well. Keep in mind that the bleach will kill existing mildew, but the mildew will keep on coming back unless the source of the moisture problem is found and dealt with properly.

**Now go to a specialist storage shop,** or a large chain, such as Ikea, and invest in a series of hooks, clips and inexpensive shelving to hold, hang and store your tools, bicycles and garden chemicals (a locked cabinet is best for these if there are children around), so that your newly cleaned garage remains clutter free.

## GARBAGE BINS

**NO MATTER HOW** TOUGH, MOST BRANDS OF GARBAGE BAGS LEAK AT ONE TIME OR ANOTHER. WHEN THEY LEAK, REVOLTING LIQUIDS ALWAYS MANAGE TO FIND THEIR WAY INTO YOUR BIN, ATTRACTING FLIES AND MAKING YOUR STOMACH TURN EVERY TIME YOU OPEN THE LID.

**Clean your garbage bin outside,** where you can do the job properly. Use a garden hose to flush out any residue and then fill the bottom of the bin with a bleach solution (125–250 millilitres of chlorine bleach for every 4 litres of water). If you can use warm water, even better. Add a squirt or two of dishwashing liquid. Using a toilet

■ Sprinkle a bit of borax into the bottom of a completely dry garbage bin, to discourage insect pests.

brush (a clean one that's reserved just for this job), clean the bottom and sides, sloshing the bleach-and-soap solution up the sides as you do. Empty and rinse thoroughly with your hose. Air-dry outside.

**To repel flies, ants and other insect pests,** sprinkle borax on the bottom of the bin once it is dry. (Borax is widely available from pharmacies and supermarkets.)

## GARDEN ORNAMENTS

**TO CLEAN OR** NOT TO CLEAN: THAT IS THE QUESTION. JUST AS ONE SCHOOL OF THOUGHT IN THE ANTIQUES WORLD SUPPORTS LEAVING ORIGINAL FINISHES INTACT, SOME PEOPLE FEEL THAT A LITTLE ALGAE, PLUS A BIRD DROPPING OR TWO, GIVE AN IVY-COVERED CONCRETE CHERUB A MORE NATURAL LOOK. IF YOU DECIDE TO GO WITH CLEANING, FOLLOW THESE TIPS.

**To clean garden ornaments,** realise that much of what you'll be cleaning is actually alive. Organic matter, such as algae, moss, mould and mildew, all thrive on statuary, birdbaths and the like—anywhere there is moisture and warmth. Add to that dust and dirt, dead organic matter and those bird droppings, and you end up with quite a mess (or just what you're looking for, depending). You can kill the organic stuff and remove the rest with a simple, inexpensive solution of 125–250 millilitres of bleach to 4 litres of water, with a squirt or two of dishwashing liquid thrown in and worked into suds. Apply it with a long-handled brush and gently scrub until clean. Rinse with a garden hose. This works for nearly all of the popular lawn ornament materials, including concrete, stone and polyester resins.

Because bleach can damage garden plants, move the ornaments to the driveway for cleaning. Or use the cleaning agent sparingly and rinse with a sponge and bucket of clean water instead of the hose. Don't use chlorine to clean a pond that contains fish. And if you clean a birdbath, be sure to flush out the cleaning solution completely.

### Cleaning a garden ornament

1 Use a suitable sized, long-handled brush to help clean those hard-to-get-at spots.

2 Dirt that's been loosened with the brush can be rinsed off with a garden hose.

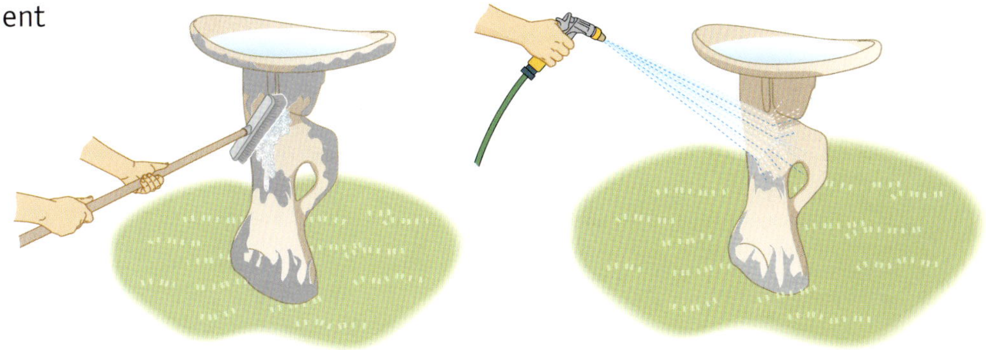

**To clean gazing globes** (aka mirror balls), use a window-cleaning solution. Mix 1 cup of white vinegar in 4 litres of warm water and add a squirt of dishwashing liquid. Apply it with a spray bottle or a clean cloth. Gently scrub until clean and either rinse with a hose or dry with a dry towel or newspaper. If the ball is stainless steel, wax it with car wax once a year to renew its shine and give it a protective coating. And wipe out scratches with an automobile scratch remover.

*See also:*
• BIRDBATHS, BIRD FEEDERS AND BIRD HOUSES

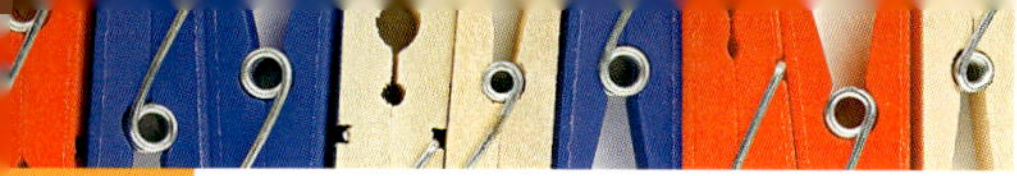



# GARDEN TOOLS

**THE TOOLS WE** USE IN OUR GARDENS RANGE FROM BASIC IMPLEMENTS TO HIGH-TECH MOTORISED DEVICES WITH COMPUTER-CONTROLLED INNARDS. IN THE FORMER CATEGORY ARE AXES, SHOVELS, FORKS, SPADES, RAKES, MANUAL EDGERS, HAND CLIPPERS, PRUNING SAWS AND WHEELBARROWS, TO NAME JUST A FEW. THE MORE MODERN PETROL-POWERED OR ELECTRIC TOOLS INCLUDE TRIMMERS, CLIPPERS, LEAF BLOWERS, POWER EDGERS AND CHAINSAWS.

**To help your garden tools last longer** and work better, follow these general cleaning guidelines:

- To ensure safe, effective operation, especially of power tools, read and keep your owner's manuals. Refer to them often.
- To keep dirt from becoming caked-on, clean tools after each use. Remove grass, leaves and dirt with a brush of appropriate size and stiffness, and wipe the tools with a dry or damp cloth.
- To keep tools from rusting, don't leave them outdoors. Put them away after each use and store them under cover. Organise a special place to hang them so they're easy to find and easy to put away.
- To stay on the cutting edge, sharpen cutting tools regularly. Sharp tools not only work better but are also safer. Dull tools are more likely to miss the mark, break or kick back, not to mention frustrate the user. Most hand tools can be sharpened safely and effectively with a file, which you can buy from a hardware shop.
- For power tools such as chainsaws and hedge trimmers, consult your owner's manual for sharpening instructions or take them to service centres that do the job.
- Pay special attention to handles, especially of power tools. Make sure they are dry and free of oils and grease, which can build up over time. A slip of your grip could result in a serious accident.
- Inspect screws and nuts periodically to make sure they're tight.

**Before putting tools away for the season,** follow a thorough cleaning and maintenance routine to ensure long life and trouble-free operation. Here are some tips for doing just that:

- To care for hand tools, wipe wooden handles with a mixture of equal parts vinegar, boiled linseed oil and mineral turpentine. The latter two items are available from hardware and paint shops. This treatment will help keep the handles from becoming brittle and breaking off. Wipe the metal parts with a rag dampened with kerosene or old motor oil. To make tools such as shovels and saws really glide, polish their metal working surfaces with car wax.
- To prepare petrol-powered tools for storage, empty the fuel from the tank and run the tool until it stops. That will use up the fuel in the carburettor. Take the fuel to a recycling centre—don't save it for future use. Wipe all metal parts with a damp cloth followed by an oil-dampened cloth. Follow any other instructions in your owner's manual, such as for cleaning air filters, spark plugs and mufflers.
- To prepare electrical tools for storage, first unplug. In fact, unplug them whenever they're not in use, but especially when you're working on a tool. Follow any other instructions in your owner's manual.
- To clean plastic parts, wipe them with a damp cloth or use one dipped in a solution of a few squirts of dishwashing liquid and water. Do not use strong detergents, household cleaners or solvents, such as kerosene or mineral turpentine.

solutions

## More than a drop in the bucket

Here's a good, abrasive way to scrub some hand tools. Fill a bucket with sand and saturate it with old motor oil. Push the business ends of shovels, spades and hand-weeding tools into the sand-and-oil mixture and then move them in and out several times. Wipe them with a dry cloth after cleaning. Put a lid on the bucket so that you can use the mix again and again.

● To remove rust from your garden tools, scrub them with a steel-wool pad that's been dipped in kerosene or mineral turpentine.

**To care for your wheelbarrows,** wash them regularly during the gardening season with a garden hose. Before putting them away at the end of the season, scrub with a stiff-bristled brush if they need it and wipe all the metal surfaces with oil on a rag to protect them. Repaint only as necessary. Lubricate the wheels with a few drops of general-purpose oil.

# GLASS

**COMMERCIAL GLASS CLEANERS** ARE FINE FOR CLEANING YOUR WINDOWS, THOUGH THEY USUALLY CONTAIN AMMONIA, WHICH CAN DAMAGE THE FINISH ON PAINTED WOOD AND TENDS TO LEAVE STREAKS. HERE'S HOW TO MAKE YOUR OWN MILD BUT EFFECTIVE WINDOW-CLEANING SOLUTION.

**To make your own non-toxic glass cleaner,** mix 1 cup of white vinegar in 4 litres of warm water and add a squirt of dishwashing liquid. Apply it with a plastic spray bottle. (A funnel will make filling the bottle easier.) Scrub the windows clean with a clean sponge or cloth. For caked-on grime, scrub with a soft, long-bristled brush.

**To avoid leaving lint traces,** wipe larger windowpanes with a squeegee and polish smaller panes with newspaper (see below). If you choose the latter method, select paper that is black and white print only; no coloured stock or glossy pages. Try to avoid washing windows when the sun is shining, because they will dry too quickly and streak. When cleaning glass tables or any other glass that lies flat, use newspaper or a microfibre glass cloth instead of a squeegee.

## Body rub

The earliest squeegees, dating to around 500 BC, were cleaning tools, but they were not used for glass. Often fashioned out of gold or bronze, the spoonlike strigils, as the instruments were called, were used to scrape the oils and sweat from the skin of Greek athletes after exercising or competitions. The word 'squeegee', which wasn't coined until the mid-nineteenth century, possibly derives from the Middle English word 'squelen', which is the root of the word squeal—the high-pitched, squeaky sound a rubber squeegee makes when it is drawn across a smooth surface.

Sheets of crumpled-up newspaper are perfect for polishing smaller windowpanes in your home.

Here are some more tips for cleaning glass:

- To remove hard-water mineral spots, use straight vinegar.
- For scratches in glass, rub a bit of white toothpaste (not the coloured gel type) into the scratch and polish with a soft cloth.
- To peel off paint and stuck-on adhesives, scrape them off with a razor blade. Don't use a putty knife, however, because it has a duller edge, which can damage the glass.

See also: • WINDOWS

## rules of the game

WHEN YOU CLEAN YOUR WINDOWS

- Start at the top and clean down.
- Apply the solution with a spray bottle.
- Lightly scrub with a sponge or cloth.
- Wipe clean with a squeegee or polish with newspaper.
- If you're cleaning with a squeegee, keep a rag in each pocket—one for wiping the squeegee itself, and the other for cleaning the corners of the glass to avoid a build-up of dirt and grime.
- If you're cleaning inside windows, lay a towel on the windowsill to catch any stray drips that may stain your carpet or flooring.

## GLASSWARE

**ANYONE CAN CLEAN** A DRINKING GLASS, BUT TO GET RID OF STREAKS, SPOTS AND UNAPPETISING RIM STAINS, THE TRICK IS KNOWING HOW TO DRY THEM PROPERLY.

**Clean glassware first** when you're washing dishes by hand, since glasses are usually less dirty than pots, pans, plates and utensils. (If you don't clean the glasses first, then change the washing-up water before you get to them. Otherwise, the glasses will end up being dirtier than they were when you started.)

Use dishwashing liquid mixed with hot water and wash with a soft, clean sponge or dishcloth. Don't reach for the abrasive pot scrubber—that can scratch glass. Rinse with even hotter water—as hot as you can safely stand. Hot water not only helps cut grease, but it also beads up and steams off (the first step towards good drying). Avoid excessive suds, which make glasses harder to rinse and slippery to handle, increasing the chance of their breaking or chipping.

No matter how well you've cleaned glassware, if there is slow-drying water left on your glasses, chances are it will leave streaks or spots. Fogging causes some of the worst spotting. To avoid the 'greenhouse effect'—when glasses placed upside down on their rims fog up inside—dry glasses upside down on a dish drainer. If you don't have a drainer, put them upright on a tea towel and make sure air can circulate inside the glass for rapid drying.

**To remove the lime build-up** on glassware that can occur when you wash it in the dishwasher, use a commercial rinse agent (such as Finish Supershine Rinse Aid) during the washing cycles. This helps

water sheet off while the glass is drying inside the foggy washer. Or fill a large plastic bowl with white vinegar and give each glass a 15-minute bath. Then rinse with running water and air-dry.

**To remove food-colouring stains** left in glassware by the dyes in powdered soft drink mixes and other beverages, fill the glass with a solution of 2 tablespoons of household ammonia in 1 litre of hot water. Let it stand for about 30 minutes and then rinse thoroughly with clean, cool water before drying.

**Hand washing is best for fine glassware** (even if you'd prefer to use your dishwasher). To avoid scratching the glasses, remove your rings, watches and bracelets, especially those with diamonds. Swing the tap head out of the way, so there's no chance you'll accidentally smack your great-grandmother's goblet against it. Using both hands, clean one piece at a time in hot, soapy water. Gently wash with a soft cotton cloth or clean sponge. For stubborn dirt, scrub gently with a soft toothbrush. Rinse twice, first in a sink or plastic tub full of tepid water with a capful of vinegar mixed in, and next under a gentle shower of tepid water from the tap.

**To clean really fine glassware,** try using a conservator's formula that will clean your fine glassware without damaging it. Mix equal parts ethanol (ethyl alcohol, or methylated spirits) and water and then add a few drops of ammonia. The water and ammonia are all that's required to do the cleaning, while the ethanol aids evaporation so that the glassware dries quickly. Apply the solution with make-up remover cotton pads or the lint-free pads used for cleaning fax machines. Don't use this technique on glass with decorative gilt.

## rules of the game

GLASSWARE
HAND CARE

- Put a rubber pad or heavy, folded tea towel in your sink (or use a plastic tub). In a divided sink, also put a tea towel over the ridge.
- Wash in hot water with a few drops of mild dishwashing liquid added. Avoid too many suds. Rub stuck-on food gently with bicarbonate of soda but never anything more abrasive.
- Handle stemware by the bowl, not the stem.
- Rinse glasses in the sink or plastic bowl filled with hot water.
- Air-dry upside down on a dish drainer. Or arrange the glasses upright on a tea towel. Never stand them upside down on a flat surface. This leads to fogging and spotting.
- For that special dinner party, buff your dried glasses with a soft, white, lint-free cloth.

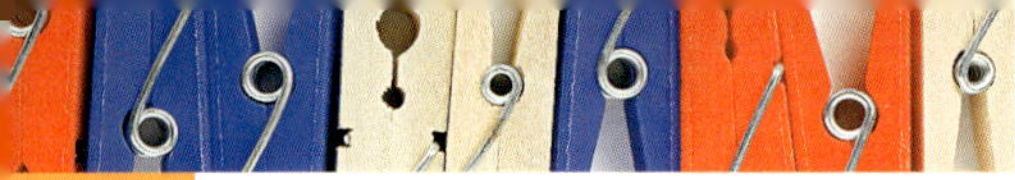



# GLOVES

**CLEANING GLOVES CAN** BE TRICKY FOR A COUPLE OF REASONS. FIRSTLY, IN ADDITION TO STAINS AND SOIL ON THE OUTSIDE OF GLOVES, YOU HAVE TO REMOVE THE DIRT AND OILS LEFT BY YOUR OWN SKIN ON THE INSIDE OF GLOVES. SECONDLY, GLOVES ARE COMPLICATED, FULL OF CRACKS AND CREVICES DESIGNED TO CONFORM TO THE SHAPE OF OUR HANDS. THERE IS A TRICK, THOUGH, THAT ALMOST MAKES CLEANING GLOVES FUN, ASSUMING THAT THEY ARE WASHABLE.

**To clean washable gloves,** wash them while they are on your hands (see below), instead of awkwardly trying to flatten them out to scrub the palms and then clean in between each flaccid finger. This way you can position each glove exactly as you'd like it, while scrubbing with the other hand. Mix up a mild, sudsy solution of warm water and a drop or two of dishwashing liquid or a mild laundry liquid such as Softly. When you're finished washing, remove the gloves and rinse them in a sink full of clean water, emptying the sink and repeating until there is no more soap residue.

An easy and very effective way to wash your gloves is to wear them while you wash them.

*See also:*
- LEATHER OR SUEDE if your gloves are made from either of these materials
- SPORTS EQUIPMENT to clean a softball glove

**To dry gloves,** roll them up in a dry towel. After unrolling them, blow them back into shape and lay them out flat on the towel at room temperature. Never squeeze or wring gloves and don't dry them using a heat source, such as a radiator or hair dryer. If you have to iron the gloves, lay them between the folds of a clean towel and move the hot iron over the top layer of the towel.

# GOLD JEWELLERY

**THE WHOLE POINT** OF GOLD IS ITS SHINE. WHILE IT DOES NOT TARNISH LIKE SILVER, GOLD WILL OVER TIME DEVELOP A DINGY, OILY FILM FROM LOTIONS, POWDERS, SOAPS AND THE OILS FROM YOUR SKIN. AND GOLD THAT HAS BEEN ALLOYED WITH OTHER METALS, SUCH AS COPPER, SILVER OR NICKEL, CAN TARNISH AND SMUDGE. TO REVIVE YOUR GOLD JEWELLERY'S LUSTRE, CLEAN IT REGULARLY.

**The mildest method of cleaning gold**—and it's also the easiest and most economical—is to mix a bowl of warm water and a little dishwashing liquid into a sudsy solution. Soak the gold jewellery briefly and then gently scrub crevices and design details using a soft toothbrush or eyebrow brush. Place the jewellery in a wire strainer and rinse under warm running water (see below). Pat it dry with a chamois cloth. (Otherwise any clean, white, soft cotton cloth will do.)

Place your jewellery in a wire strainer and rinse under warm running water.

**For a stronger cleaning solution,** mix equal parts cold water and ammonia (and save the money you would have spent on a commercial jewellery cleaner). Soak the jewellery in the solution for around 30 minutes. Again, gently scrub with the toothbrush or eyebrow brush. Rinse with water. Let the jewellery dry on a soft towel.

**Having your gold jewellery professionally cleaned** is the safest and most effective—if also the most expensive—method. Take your jewellery to a jeweller and have it cleaned with an ultrasonic cleaning machine. They dip your jewellery in a container of liquid, send high-frequency vibrations through the liquid and, almost instantly, the dirt and grime drop off. Have several things cleaned at once, and you will save money on each piece. Or, if it's the same jeweller you bought the piece from, they might do it free of charge.

**WATCH OUT**

- Avoid getting chlorine on gold at all costs. It will cause the gold to deteriorate over time. Remove any gold jewellery when cleaning with chlorine bleach and even before entering chlorinated pools and spas.
- Don't clean gold with toothpaste, even though some jewellers recommend it. Some toothpastes contain abrasives, such as silica (found in quartz), which can dull a glossy gold finish.

### White gold's shiny little secret

If your white gold is beginning to yellow, that probably means it was rhodium-plated. Most white gold is. Contrary to popular belief, there is no such metal as white gold. Rather, white gold is gold (naturally yellowish in colour) alloyed with silvery metals, such as palladium, and usually plated with rhodium to increase its brightness even more. You normally won't see any worn plating on earrings and necklaces, but on white gold jewellery that gets physical abuse, such as rings and bracelets, you might notice yellow blotches on the surface. (Our gold-cleaning techniques will not remove the plating.) If so, simply have your jeweller re-plate the jewellery with rhodium.

## GORE-TEX FABRIC

**GORE-TEX IS THE** BRAND-NAME OF A MEMBRANE, FOUND IN WATERPROOF JACKETS AND OTHER OUTER GARMENTS. IT HAS THE AMAZING ABILITY TO BE SIMULTANEOUSLY WATERPROOF AND BREATHABLE. THESE FUNCTIONS WILL BE IMPROVED BY KEEPING YOUR GORE-TEX FABRIC CLEAN. GORE-TEX IS BOTH WASHABLE AND DRY-CLEANABLE, WHICH MAKES IT PARTICULARLY EASY TO CARE FOR.

**To clean a Gore-Tex garment,** follow the cleaning instructions on the label in that garment. Typically, the instructions will be to put the garment in a washing machine with warm water and a standard laundry detergent, but no fabric softener or bleach, and then tumble in a dryer. If the garment calls for dry-cleaning, tell the cleaner you want a clear, distilled solvent rinse.

**To preserve a Gore-Tex's water-resistant shell,** you need to reapply a water-resistant coating every so often, because multiple washings (or a single trip to the drycleaner) will remove the shell's fine water-resistant layer. (When water no longer beads up on your garment's outer shell, that's a sign that you've lost it.) The actual Gore-Tex layer will be OK, but the outer shell will need a new application of its coating, called durable water repellent (DWR). Gore-Tex sells an easy-to-use, spray-on, durable water repellent called Revivex. Look for it at camping and outdoor shops, or high-performance bicycle shops.

## GRAFFITI

**THE TRICK TO** REMOVING GRAFFITI IS TO DO IT AS SOON AS POSSIBLE. MOST GRAFFITI IS DONE WITH PAINT, WHICH IS APPLIED WET AND SOLIDIFIES AS THE PAINT SOLVENTS EVAPORATE. THE SOLUBILITY OF PAINT, THEREFORE, IS REDUCED THE LONGER IT HAS A CHANCE TO HARDEN. IF YOU REMOVE THE PAINT RIGHT AWAY, YOU WILL HAVE A GOOD CHANCE OF SUCCEEDING.

**To remove some markings,** try a simple solution of warm water and dishwashing liquid. If the paint or marker used was water-soluble and you've caught it early enough, this might just work. Carefully scrub the graffiti with a nylon- or natural-bristled brush. Rinse with the spray nozzle on your garden hose, if possible. The low pressure might lift the stain without damaging the surface it's on.

**To remove stubborn graffiti,** which won't wash off with water and dishwashing liquid, you will need to try a chemical paint remover. (Keep in mind, however, that if the graffiti is on a painted surface, these paint removers won't discriminate between paints, and you may end up having to repaint your entire wall.) Gels and pastes typically work well because they are easy to apply and don't drip. However, avoid aerosol graffiti removers, which can dissolve paint and then run down the wall, staining a previously clean area.

An alkaline paste that contains a caustic substance—sodium hydroxide or potassium hydroxide—(such as Selleys Heavy Duty Concrete Kleen) works well. These are harsh chemicals, though, and you should follow the manufacturer's safety and use recommendations carefully. With such a paste, you typically wipe it on, let it stand and loosen the paint for a few minutes, and then wipe it off. Then you rinse with water and neutralise with a separate acid-based neutralising agent (such as vinegar, or a mild acid wash). The neutralising agent keeps the caustics from staining stone and other surfaces.

**If all else fails,** consider blasting the graffiti off. You've got three options—pressure washing, steam cleaning or sandblasting. All can be

extremely harmful to wood, old brick and stone. And all but the finest-grade sandblasters will damage metal. You can rent a pressure washer at an equipment rental shop. Follow all safety instructions and use extreme caution, since these machines can be dangerous and harmful to your house. One way to reduce your chances of damaging the surface is to begin with a low-water pressure and gradually increase it as necessary. If you live in an area of water restrictions or would prefer to get professional help, look in the *Yellow Pages* under 'Cleaning Contractors'. And you should definitely leave sandblasting up to the pros, so also look in the *Yellow Pages* under 'Sandblasting'.

**If you can't beat them, join them.** If it's a painted surface, you can paint over the graffiti with a fresh coat or two of your original wall paint. Or you may decide now is the time to change colour.

**To remove graffiti from glass,** it's best to use a single-edge razor blade. Put it in a flat scraper (available from hardware shops), hold the scraper at a 30-degree angle to the glass and patiently scrape the paint. Avoid paint strippers. They aren't as effective on glass, as they tend to smear the paint and make it harder to remove the vestiges. And also once you apply the paint stripper, the razor blade is not as effective, because the paint is now thinner.

## GRANITE

**WHAT YOU THINK** IS GRANITE MAY NOT BE GRANITE—IT MAY HAVE ONLY THE APPEARANCE OF GRANITE. WHEN IT COMES TO CLEANING, KNOWING WHETHER THE MATERIAL IS GENUINE GRANITE IS IMPORTANT, BECAUSE SOME CLEANERS THAT ARE SAFE FOR GRANITE MAY REACT NEGATIVELY WITH YOUR STONE. THE ACID IN VINEGAR, FOR INSTANCE, EATS AWAY AT CALCIUM, WHICH IS NOT USUALLY PRESENT IN GRANITE BUT MAY BE IN YOUR STONE.

**To aid cleaning granite,** you need to know the different types of surface finishes to your granite. They vary from raw stone to highly polished stone to chemically sealed stone. This helps decide what cleaning approach to take and, once known, cleaning the stone is easy. The best approach is always the simplest.

**To care for granite,** keep it clean from sand and dirt, especially on flat surfaces, where it can be ground down by the soles of shoes. The grit can scratch the stone. For walls, floors and other such surfaces, use either a vacuum cleaner or a dry dust mop. For benchtops and tables, dust with a clean, dry rag. Wipe up spills immediately to avoid any staining. With due care, cleaning granite doesn't become an effort.

**To clean granite benchtops in kitchens and bathrooms,** first try using only warm water, wiping with a soft cloth or sponge. Let caked-on food soak a bit before wiping. You should be able to remove spills, crumbs, sauces and other things this way. If not, then add a little dishwashing liquid to the water. Rinse well with lots of clean water. Too much soap can leave a film or cause streaking. Avoid stronger cleaning products, such as bath and tile cleaners or scouring powders, as these can stain or scratch your stone.

Before you attempt to clean any granite surface, find out what sort of surface finish it has to avoid problems.

**To remove difficult stains,** keep it simple and be patient. Most stains are solid residue jammed in between the crystals of the stone after the liquid that carried it has evaporated. The trick is to put the solid back into liquid form so it can be removed. First, determine whether your stain is water-based (for example, from spilled orange juice) or oil-based (salad dressing).

- If the stain is water-based, pour hot water (from the tap, not the kettle) on the stain and let it stand for a few minutes. Wipe away the excess water. Then stack around 5 millimetres of paper towels on the stain and saturate with hot water. Cover with a piece of plastic (plastic wrap will do) and a flat, heavy weight, such as a cast-iron frying pan or a book (be careful not to ruin the book). Let it stand for about 10 hours. (Do it overnight, and you won't have to worry about anyone moving it.) Next, throw away the paper towels, and the stain should go with them. Let the spot dry and then observe. If some of the stain is still present, repeat the treatment.
- If the stain is oil-based, follow the same procedure, only instead of water, use acetone (but do not heat). After the 10 hours is up, throw away the paper towels and rinse the spot with clean water. If necessary, repeat. Acetone can be found in the paint thinner section of most hardware and homeware shops, and in supermarkets.

## GREASE STAINS

**GREASE STAINS WILL** GET WORSE OVER TIME, AS DUST AND DIRT ATTACH THEMSELVES TO THE STICKY SURFACE. THE LONGER YOU WAIT TO CLEAN A GREASE STAIN, THE HARDER IT WILL BE TO DO IT PROPERLY. HOW YOU CLEAN DEPENDS ON WHAT YOU'RE CLEANING.

**To remove grease from fabric,** first remove excess grease with a paper towel, a plastic spatula or the dull edge of a knife. If possible, have the fabric professionally dry-cleaned, but if you can't, follow these steps:

- Lay the stain face down on a soft, white, absorbent cloth.
- Apply a dry-cleaning solvent, such as Murlex or Woolclean Spot Remover No. 2, to another cloth.
- Blot from the inside of the garment, forcing the stain out and into the other cloth as the solvent dissolves it.

**Always closely follow the instructions** on the solvent product label. Before using a dry-cleaning solvent on a fabric, always test it in an inconspicuous corner of the stained item.

**To remove grease from carpets,** follow the same steps as for stains in fabrics. When it comes to applying the dry-cleaning solvent, make sure to moisten a cloth with the solvent and blot the stain. Don't pour the solvent onto the carpet, because it may soak into the padding beneath and trigger new stains.

As a good substitute for a dry-cleaning solvent, use an acetone-based nail polish remover. But don't use it on anything made of acetate, because the acetone will dissolve the fabric. It's always safest to test in an out-of-sight corner of the material first.

Remove a grease stain on concrete by sprinkling dry cement over it. Once it has absorbed the grease, sweep it up.

**To remove grease from a concrete floor,** sprinkle dry cement over the grease (see left). Once it has absorbed the grease, sweep it up with a dustpan and broom. If you don't have dry cement handy, then try salt. If that fails, wet the stained area of concrete with water and sprinkle it with powdered dishwasher detergent. Wait a few minutes and then pour boiling water on the area. Wearing rubber gloves to protect your hands, scrub with a stiff-bristled brush and rinse with water. For really tough or old stains, you might need a proprietary product, such as Liquid Magnet or Selleys Heavy Duty Concrete Kleen—but take care to follow the instructions.

*See also:* • CONCRETE

## GREENHOUSES

**THINK OF YOUR** GREENHOUSE AS A HOSPITAL—THE CLEANER IT IS, THE HEALTHIER THE PLANTS WILL BE. DUST, DEBRIS AND CLUTTER ARE MAGNETS FOR INSECTS, DISEASES AND HARMFUL MICRO-ORGANISMS. DIRTY WINDOWS BLOCK THE SUN'S REJUVENATING LIGHT. FOLLOWING A FEW SIMPLE GUIDELINES WILL ENSURE A HEALTHY ENVIRONMENT FOR YOUR PLANTS TO THRIVE IN.

**Dust your plants** to remove fungal spores (such as grey mould and powdery mildews) and mites (such as the omnivorous spider mite). Most people hose off their plants, which is fine but tends to unsettle and spread the dust. An easier—and more effective—method is to vacuum them. Use a hand-held vacuum (such as a Dustbuster) with a dusting attachment. This works best on sturdy leaves that you can hold in your hand while you quickly whisk the brush over the surface. Doing this once a year is enough to halt the growth of the plant predators mentioned above.

**Cut down on clutter in your greenhouse.** Piles of dead plants, stacks of dirty pots and sacks spilling over with potting mix can all be places for insects and micro-organisms to grow in. Remove all of these things—and any other clutter—regularly. Try not to pile them right next to the greenhouse. Either get rid of them or store them in a shed, garage or under the house. Dead plant material is the worst offender. Purge dead plants and routinely pick up dead leaves.

**Keep your greenhouse weed-free** to get rid of yet another source of food for insects and bacteria. Weeds also boost a greenhouse's humidity level, which will make conditions even riper for disease and pestilence. Keep a sack of hydrated lime on hand (but don't clutter up the greenhouse with it). Sprinkle it under benches and in corners to deter weed growth. It lasts for a long time and is non-toxic to humans. You can buy hydrated lime at your hardware shop or local garden centre. However, never use herbicides in your greenhouse. (See the 'Watch out' box on page 208.)

**Wash the greenhouse windows** at least once a year. Do it when you have the least amount of living plant material in your greenhouse—or before you bring in those new seeds or seedlings to get growing for spring transplanting. For most people, window-washing time is during the autumn. Your goal is to keep the glass or polyurethane as clear as possible, as well as to kill any harmful microbial growth on the inner surface. Use a mild dishwashing liquid, as it not only loosens dirt but also has ingredients that break up proteins and fats—and subsequently rupture the membranes of bacteria and fungi. Depending on the size of your greenhouse, either put the dishwashing liquid in a hose-attachment sprayer or mix it with water in a clean spray bottle. Rinse by spraying with the garden hose or wiping down with clean water and a sponge.

**WATCH OUT** Don't get so hell-bent on killing weeds that you nearly kill yourself—care does need to be taken. If you spray herbicides, or worse, a petroleum-based product, such as petrol or kerosene, on weeds inside the greenhouse, you can come back 3 hours later, and it will look like Armageddon has hit. The chemicals are so powerful and volatile that on a hot day, the fumes will not only kill the weeds, they'll also kill every plant in the greenhouse. And with all those toxic fumes, you unfortunately won't be able to go back into the greenhouse for weeks.

## GUTTERING AND DOWNPIPES

**WATER IS YOUR** HOME'S WORST ENEMY, AND ALONG WITH YOUR ROOF, YOUR GUTTERING SYSTEM IS YOUR BEST LINE OF DEFENCE. BUT GUTTERS AND DOWNPIPES MUST BE CLEAN TO WORK PROPERLY.

**Beware of blocked guttering,** it is worse than no guttering at all. It forces water down along the side of your house; sagging, water-and-rubbish-heavy guttering can damage the fascia boards under your roof; and in winter, if you live in a cold area, collected water can freeze and crack downpipes and gutterings. And if you live in a bushfire area, twigs and leaf debris represent a fire hazard and should be removed before the start of summer.

**Clean out your gutterings** any time they are backed-up. Usually this is in the autumn, after the leaves have fallen; in the spring, after the heaviest pollen, flower heads and seeds have dropped; or after a very heavy downpour. Wear heavy work gloves (as thorns and roofing nails end up in gutterings). Use a ladder tall enough to reach the gutterings safely. Have someone on hand to hold the ladder, and to help move it each time you need to reach a new section of guttering. Begin at the downpipe and work your way to the other end, scooping the leaves and twigs that have collected there.

**To make your own guttering scoop,** cut the bottom off an empty plastic bottle that has a rectangular shape—the kind that motor oil and some fruit juices come in, for instance (see above right). Or just use your gloved hand to remove the gunk. Don't scrape the inside of the gutterings with any sharp tools—spades, putty knives or the like—because you might damage the metal. If you need to scrape, try scrubbing instead with a nylon-bristled brush.

**Flush the gutterings** with a garden hose once you've removed all the debris. (Flushing before scooping is a no-no, because you'll

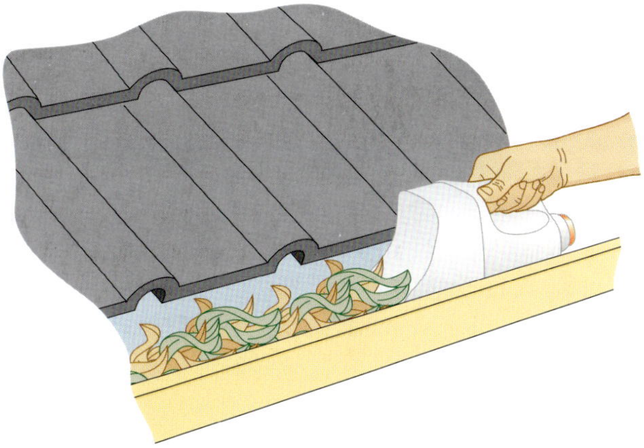

It's easy to scoop up leaves in your gutters using a plastic bottle with the bottom cut out of it.

probably clog the downpipe.) If the downpipe is clogged, push the hose down into it to clear the pile-up. If that does not work, try to push the hose into the pipe from the bottom end. Dismantle the pipe if you have to. As a last resort, you may need to drop a plumber's eel down the pipe. You can rent one at an equipment rental shop.

**Make a guttering bucket, too.** A guttering bucket is a handy tool to help with cleaning gutterings, and it's easy to make. Take a plastic bucket with an all-metal handle. Using wire cutters, make a cut in the middle of the handle. Bend each end of the handle into a hook shape, turn the hooks towards the same side of the bucket, and hang the bucket from the guttering. Dump all the debris from your guttering into the bucket, rather than dropping the mess into the shrubbery below or onto your unfortunate helper's head. When the bucket's full, climb down and empty it on your compost heap. Soggy, old leaves make a great garden additive.

**Clean the outside of the gutterings** with a cleaning solution. This is not important for the functioning of the gutterings, but it will make them look crisp and new and help keep them in good shape.

- For removing dirt, mix ⅓ cup of laundry detergent, ½ cup of liquid sugar soap and 4 litres of warm water.
- For mildew and algae, mix ⅓ cup of detergent, ½ cup of liquid sugar soap and 1 litre of bleach with 3 litres of water.

In either case, put on your rubber gloves, wipe the solution on with a rag and then rinse with a garden hose.

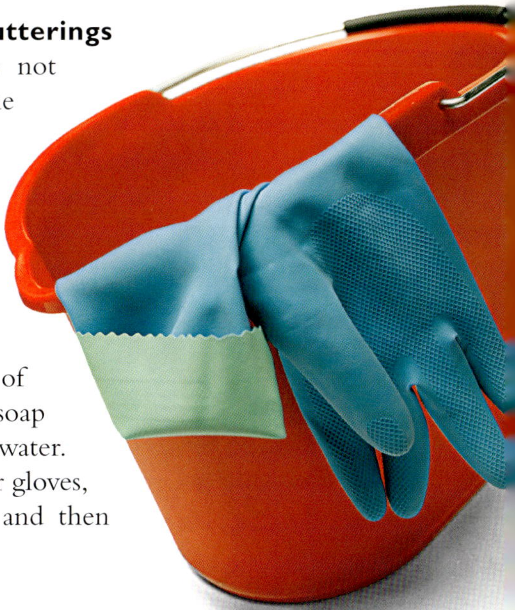

# HAIRBRUSHES

**MOST OF US** DON'T CLEAN OUR HAIRBRUSHES OFTEN ENOUGH. WHEN WE FINALLY GET AROUND TO IT, WE SPEND MORE TIME UNTANGLING THAT HAIR BALL MESS THAN WE DO ON THE CLEANING JOB ITSELF. CLEAN MORE OFTEN BY USING THE FOLLOWING TIPS, AND YOU'LL SAVE TIME IN THE LONG RUN.

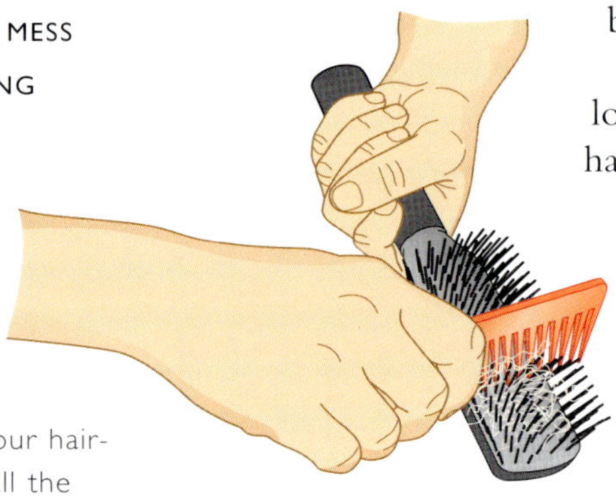

Before cleaning your hairbrush, first remove all the loose hair using a comb.

**WATCH OUT** Don't submerge natural hair make-up brushes (such as squirrel hair) in dishwashing liquid. The detergent will dry the hair out and the moisture will dissolve the glue that holds the hair to the handle.

**To clean a hairbrush,** first pull out any loose hair from the bristles. Using a comb is often the easiest way (see below). Then make your own economical and effective cleaning solution by mixing 2 teaspoons of shampoo and ¼ cup of vinegar in a sink filled with warm water. Soak the brush in the solution for several minutes, then pull a clean, wide-toothed comb down each row of bristles to remove any remaining hair.

By now, the solution should have loosened any build-up of oil, dirt, gel and hair spray on the brush. Scrub the brush clean with a nailbrush (hold it down in the bathtub to contain the splatter) and rinse with warm running water. Let the brush air-dry.

**To clean a make-up brush,** avoid using commercial make-up brush cleaners, which often contain harsh chemicals. The chemicals aren't good for the sensitive skin of your face and can dry out a make-up brush, which can be quite expensive—especially the ones made of real animal hair (mink, yak or squirrel). For a safe, non-drying alternative, mix 2 parts water with 1 part gentle fabric wash, such as Softly. Dip the brush (tip only) into the solution. Don't dip the wooden or metal handle, because water can cause the bristles to fall out. Rinse in clean water. Repeat until the brush is clean (no more make-up colour) and free of the wash solution. Dry the brush gently with a towel, being sure to move the towel 'with the grain', or direction of the hair.

# HAIR DRYERS

**MODERN DRYERS ARE** FAIRLY HARDY AND REQUIRE MINIMAL UPKEEP. BUT THAT LITTLE BIT OF MAINTENANCE IS ESSENTIAL. A DRYER WITH A DEBRIS-CHOKED FILTER CAN OVERHEAT. IT WILL PERFORM POORLY AND POSSIBLY EVEN DAMAGE YOUR HAIR. TO KEEP IT BLOWING PROPERLY, PLAN TO CLEAR ITS FILTER EVERY THREE MONTHS IF YOU USE IT DAILY.

**Cleaning a hair dryer is all about it's airflow.** Dryers work by fanning the surrounding air, directing it through the appliance's heating mechanism and blowing it out through the nozzle as a stream of hot air. But the dryer also pulls in dust and lint along with the air, and those particles can lodge in a screen that filters the air before it hits the heating coils. Over time, enough debris can accumulate in the filter and block air from flowing through. That's when things start to overheat. Don't be surprised if you detect a warning odour like that (not surprisingly) of burning hair.

When a dryer overheats, its thermostat attempts to cool things down by turning the heating coils off and on. You feel alternating hot and cold air blowing out, which won't provide the styling effects of consistently warm air. Extreme blockage may trigger the dryer's non-resettable shutdown device. However, this dryer demise is something you can avoid by cleaning your dryer's filter.

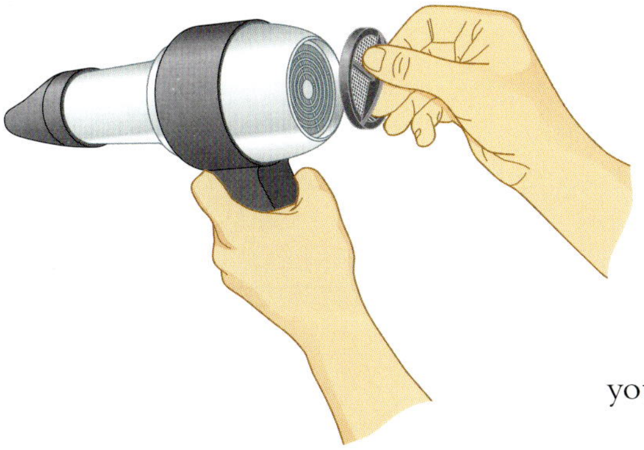

A dryer's filter needs to be cleaned regularly to prevent overheating and possible damage.

**To clean your dryer filter,** first unplug the dryer. Premium dryers have a filter cover that lifts off (see left), giving easy access for cleaning. Scrub the filter with a dry, soft-bristled brush or toothbrush to get out the lint, dust and hair. Or use a vacuum cleaner with a crevice attachment. Pull out any stubborn bits with tweezers. If your dryer doesn't have a filter cover, you'll need to brush, vacuum or tweeze the filter from the outside.

**To clean the dryer body and accessories,** just wipe with a damp rag (not a wet one, which could drip water into the heating element). Even the stickiest, slipperiest hair products are generally water soluble, so a damp cloth should remove them.

## HAMMOCKS

**HAMMOCKS ARE ALL** ABOUT RELAXING—WHICH YOU WOULDN'T BE ABLE TO DO IF YOU THOUGHT YOU WERE RECLINING IN GRIME AND MILDEW. MOULD AND MILDEW, THE BACKYARD SPOILSPORTS, THRIVE IN MOISTURE. ANOTHER THREAT TO YOUR HAMMOCK IS ROT, CAUSED BY STRONG SUNLIGHT AND DETERGENTS THAT WEAR AWAY AT A HAMMOCK'S NATURAL-ROPE FIBRES.

**To make your hammock last longer,** you need to keep it not only dirt free but as dry as possible. So, to enjoy the good life, a good dose of prevention is also called for.

- After unpacking and before its maiden swing, spray your hammock with fabric guard, following the label instructions. Renew the treatment every three to five months.
- Don't hang the hammock in full sun as the rays will fade synthetics and weaken cotton fabric.
- Find a dry indoor spot to store the hammock in bad weather or whenever you won't be hanging it out for a while.

**A successful, universal hammock-cleaning approach** is to mix 30 millilitres of mild dishwashing liquid with 9 litres of water. Spread the hammock out on a large, debris-free, hard surface, such as a deck. Keeping the wooden spreader bars dry, scrub one side of the hammock with a soft cloth or sponge, then flip it and clean the other side. A soft-bristled brush will let you gently scrub dirty areas. Rinse well with clear water and hang the hammock to air-dry, preferably in a low-humidity breeze but not in direct sunlight. Quick drying keeps the fibres strong and discourages mould and mildew. The hammock should be fully dry in two days. Other cleaning approaches depend on the fabric and construction of your hammock.

**To clean white cotton or cotton-polyester rope,** just spot-clean dirt using 1 part gentle fabric wash, such as Softly, to 8 parts water. If you see mould or mildew, put the hammock in the bathtub and soak it in a mild bleach solution (1 capful of chlorine bleach per 4 litres of water) for 30 minutes.

**To clean synthetic fabrics** such as polyester and acrylic, bind the hammock so that it won't tangle—if it is a simple model that has no spreader bars, such as a Mayan-style hamaca. Fold the hammock in half, bringing the two end rings together. Bind it with twine just below the rings, then at the fold and finally in the middle of your bundle. This keeps the hardware out of the strings and saves the strings from becoming a tangled puzzle. Drop the bundle into a pillowcase and tie it closed. Put it in the washing machine on the gentle cycle and add 60 millilitres of gentle fabric wash. After washing, unbind and spread the hammock out to dry. Give it two days to dry, and you'll be back in the swing of things!

If you would prefer, you can also hand wash it in a solution of 1 part gentle fabric wash to 4 parts water.

If the yarn is solution-dyed, meaning the dye was added when the synthetic was still liquid, you can rid it of mildew and stains by hand washing it in a bleach-and-water solution. Don't go any stronger than a 50:50 mix. Use rubber gloves and test for colour fastness on an inconspicuous corner.

**EXPERT ADVICE**

**A LARGE BATH!**

Want a quick way to clean your cotton- or cotton-polyester rope hammock? Take it for a swim! Holding the spreader bars, take the bed of the hammock for a few laps through the chlorinated water of your swimming pool. The pool's mild chlorine will help bleach it clean. Rinse it thoroughly with water and hang it up to dry.

**To clean a coloured rope,** fabric or quilted fabric hammock, scrub it using ¼ cup of laundry detergent in 20 litres of warm water. Test to see if it is colour-fast first. Hit mildewy areas with the mild bleach solution suggested above for cotton–rope hammocks. Spot-wash hammock pillows using your mild dishwashing liquid solution and a soft-bristled brush. Avoid soaking the filling inside.

**If your hammock has wooden spreader bars,** they will come covered with a protective coating such as marine varnish, which you can replenish every six months. You'll find marine varnish at hardware shops and boat-supply shops. Follow the instructions on the label. If your hammock is suspended on a wooden frame, touch up the frame with linseed oil every three to six months.

## HANDBAGS

**THROUGH THE AEONS,** POUCHES FOR FIRE-STRIKING FLINT AND TRADING SHELLS EVOLVED INTO HANDBAGS FOR CAR KEYS AND ATM CARDS. THESE DAYS, A BAG IS AN ESSENTIAL ACCESSORY ITEM FOR MANY WOMEN AND A FEW MEN. SO HOW DO YOU KEEP YOUR HANDBAG FROM LOOKING LIKE THAT ORIGINAL CAVE DWELLER'S POUCH?

**The general approach** to cleaning a handbag is to first empty the bag of its contents—which in itself may be a big job. Then brush away loose dirt—inside and outside the bag—with a soft, white cloth, or vacuum it using an upholstery attachment. Next up (with the exception of suede) is to wet a soft cloth in a cleaning solution appropriate for your bag's material. (See opposite page for the different materials.) Wring the cloth nearly dry and rub the bag inside and out, taking care to avoid dampening it any more than it takes to clean it.

Beyond the visible dirt, you'll wipe away skin oils, hand lotion, make-up and perspiration. On the exterior, a bag's handle, clasp and straps are areas where a lot of grime collects. And when cleaning, don't forget the inside—wipe the liner, especially the bottom, and interior hardware, such as zippers.

**To clean a leather bag,** it's best to use a cream leather cleaner and conditioner or saddle-soap, both of which are available from shoe repair shops. Follow the label instructions. Always follow saddle-soap with a solvent-free leather conditioner, such as Waproo Zorbel, to avoid drying out the leather. Then buff with a soft cloth.

■ How you clean a handbag depends entirely on what it's made of, so check before you buy any products.

**To clean a fabric bag,** use ½ teaspoon of a gentle fabric wash, such as softly, in ½ cup of lukewarm water for all-over cleaning of strong, sturdy fabrics. Use it full strength for spots. For more delicate fabrics, use barely damp baby wipes. To help keep your fabric bag protected, spray it with a fabric protector, such as Scotchgard, after it's been cleaned.

**To clean patent leather,** use a cream cleaner and conditioner (such as waproo patent) if it's real patent leather. Be gentle—patent leather scratches easily. If it is imitation patent leather, use mild dishwashing liquid or a car interior vinyl and plastic cleaner, such as Meguiar's, available from automotive shops.

**To clean plastic, polyurethane or vinyl,** try a specialist plastic cleaner (sold at boat-supply and automotive shops, as well as by suppliers of restoration products), if the handbag is made of a hard plastic. Wipe softer synthetics with a solution of dishwashing liquid or a gentle fabric wash and water. Alternatives are baby wipes or a car interior vinyl and plastic cleaner. To restore the shine to shiny plastics, squirt them with silicone wax spray after cleaning, then buff. There are also specialist products available from shoe shops that clean and silicone polish in the one operation, such as Waproo Shu-Glo.

**To clean a straw bag,** wipe with a cloth dipped in 1 part liquid hand soap to 3 parts water. Rinse with a cloth wrung out in clean water. Do not get a straw hat too wet or it may shrink.

**WATCH OUT** Never stack a leather handbag on top of or directly under a plastic one. The dye from the leather bag can leach and be absorbed by the plastic. Then you'll be holding a bag of a different colour!

**To clean a suede bag,** brush the nap with a natural-bristle shoe brush, which will remove surface dirt. If it needs a bit more cleaning, visit your shoe shop to investigate products made especially for suede and nubuck. Otherwise, have it professionally dry-cleaned. Once it is clean, remember that prevention is better than cure—give it a light spray with water and stain protector, but use protectant sprays sparingly on suede, since some attract dirt.

# HARD-WATER DEPOSITS

**IF YOU'RE IN** A HARD-WATER AREA, YOU'LL KNOW IT: SURFACES THAT GET WET FREQUENTLY WILL HAVE COLOURFUL STAINS, WHITISH SPOTS OR CRUSTY DEPOSITS. THE DREADED BLIGHTER LIME SCALE MAY BUILD UP ENOUGH TO INTERFERE WITH THE FUNCTION OF FIXTURES LIKE SHOWER HEADS AND TAPS. SOAPS WILL SEEM TO LEAVE A RESIDUE, AND IT WILL TAKE A LOT OF DETERGENT TO GET THINGS CLEAN. THE EFFECTS OF HARD WATER INCLUDE DULL, STICKY HAIR; DINGY, SCRATCHY CLOTHES; AND SPOTTED DISHES. THE CULPRITS ARE THE MINERALS IN YOUR WATER—CALCIUM AND MAGNESIUM. MODERATELY HARD WATER HAS CONCENTRATIONS OF AT LEAST 61 MILLIGRAMS OF THESE MINERALS PER LITRE, AND REALLY HARD WATER HAS DOUBLE THAT AMOUNT.

**To prevent mineral deposits,** you need to keep hard water away from the surfaces that it typically damages. Hard water does its mischief by evaporating and leaving behind mineral deposits. So to beat it, keep wet surfaces from air-drying in the following ways:

- Dab taps dry.
- Keep lawn sprinklers away from windows.
- Fix leaks and drips.
- Rinse sinks, bathtubs and shower recesses after use and then wipe or squeegee them dry.

It also helps to have on hand a spray solution containing a non-precipitating water conditioner, such as Calgon, which is available from hardware shops. Mix ½ teaspoon of water conditioner in 1 litre of water in a spray bottle and spray it on wet surfaces to capture the mineral particles along with the water as you wipe things dry.

**To remove mineral deposits,** a number of cleaners attack hard-water deposits with special chemicals. These compounds include:

- sequestrants, which capture (or sequester) minerals so they don't leave a deposit (the phosphates used in automatic dishwasher detergent are sequestrants);
- surfactants (short for surface acting agents), which loosen soil by reducing surface tension, allowing the water to wet things faster (the main ingredient in laundry detergent is a surfactant);
- acids, which help break down mineral deposits;
- alkalis (present in some cleaners), which help suspend soil so it can be rinsed away.

See the 'Navigating hard water' box, on the opposite page, to select the best cleaner for curing your hard-water problems.

**To get rid of hard water completely,** you should consider installing a water-softening filter system. These systems typically treat the water with sodium, which trades places with the calcium and magnesium particles in the water. But to properly address all of the minerals in the water—including manganese (brown-black stains) and iron (reddish-brown stains)—your water-softening system has to be customised to fit the water in your area.

Simple solutions

## Give your shower head a bath

Is your shower head clogged with lime scale? If possible, unscrew the shower head and soak it overnight in a bowl of white vinegar. In the morning, remove the deposits with a brush with moderately stiff bristles.

If you can't unscrew the shower head, don't worry. Just pour the vinegar into a plastic bag and pull the bag up around the shower head. To see how this is done, see 'Showers', on page 302.

## Navigating hard water

Those pesky hard-water deposits can collect on a bewildering array of surfaces in your home. Here is a simple guide on which cleaners to use where. Read product labels to make sure you've got the right kind of cleaner, and test surfaces before doing an all-out clean-up. And be careful to never mix chlorine bleach with ammonia-based or acidic products.

**Brass (unlacquered)**

- Mildly abrasive brass cleaner, such as Brasso.

**Ceramic tile**

- Kitchen–bathroom cleaner formulated for mineral deposits and soap scum, such as Orange Power Shower and a bath & tile cleaner. Avoid bleach.
- Non-abrasive, all-purpose cleaner, such as Ajax Spray n' Wipe.
- 1 part white vinegar to 4 parts water.
- Lime-scale remover, such as CLR (Calcium Lime Rust Remover).

**Chrome**

- Non-abrasive ammonia-based chrome cleaner, such as Windex or Mr Muscle.
- Kitchen–bathroom cleaner labelled suitable for chrome, such as CLR Bathroom & Kitchen Cleaner.

**Dishwashers**

- Lime-scale remover, such as Dylon Oust Dishwasher & Washing Machine Cleaner & Freshener.
- 1 part white vinegar to 4 parts water.
- Non-abrasive, all-purpose cleaner, such as Ajax Spray n' Wipe.
- Kitchen–bathroom cleaner labelled safe for fibreglass.
- Spray solution of ½ teaspoon of non-precipitating water conditioner, such as Calgon, per 1 litre of water.

**Glass** *(windows and shower doors)*

- Extra dishwasher detergent. Use up to double for tough hard-water film.
- Kitchen–bathroom cleaner formulated for mineral deposits and soap scum, such as CLR Bathroom & Kitchen Cleaner.

**Glassware** *(permanent etching or iridescent discolouration is not removable)*

- Undiluted white vinegar. Soak for 15 minutes, rinse and dry.
- Add dishwashing rinsing agent, such as Finish Supershine Rinse Aid to dishwasher.

**Plastic laminate** *(such as Formica)*

- Bicarbonate of soda. Dip rag into bowl of warm water, then into bowl of bicarbonate of soda, and rub. Wipe clean with a dry cloth.

**Porcelain enamel**

- Kitchen–bathroom cleaner formulated for mineral deposits and soap scum, such as CLR Bathroom & Kitchen Cleaner. Some toilet-bowl cleaners contain stronger acids—don't leave on surface for long.
- Non-abrasive, all-purpose cleaner, such as Ajax Spray n' Wipe.
- Lime-scale remover, such as CLR (Calcium Lime Rust Remover).
- Rust remover, such as CLR (Calcium Lime Rust Remover).

**Stainless steel**

- Non-abrasive, all-purpose cleaner; such as Ajax Spray n' Wipe.
- Spray solution of ½ teaspoon non-precipitating water conditioner, such as Calgon, per 1 litre of water.
- Lime-scale remover labelled suitable for stainless steel, such as CLR Bathroom & Kitchen Cleaner. Rinse well.

**Tap bases**

- Paste of non-precipitating water conditioner, such as Calgon, and water on a damp sponge.

**Vitreous china fixtures**

- Lime-scale remover, such as CLR (Calcium Lime Rust Remover).

# HATS

**HATS AREN'T JUST** PIECES OF CLOTHING THAT SIT ON YOUR HEAD. THEY'RE MADE FROM A WIDE VARIETY OF MATERIALS, AND, BECAUSE OF THIS, REQUIRE SPECIAL METHODS TO CLEAN THEM.

**To keep a fur, felt or velour hat clean,** regularly brush the dust and dirt from the surface with a nylon or horsehair brush. It's important for a hat to be dust free because if the hat gets wet, the dust will be harder to eliminate. With fur and felt hats, always brush with the nap (in the direction of the material) and use separate brushes for light and dark hats. You can often refresh a tired felt hat by holding it over steaming water for a second or two and brushing with the nap (see page 216). For light soiling, an Akubra hat can be rubbed with a little dry-cleaning fluid once it has been brushed to remove dust. A car upholstery cleaner, such as Kitten Interior Cleaner, can also be used. Take great care not to use too much cleaner. To deal with more extensive stains or soiling, take your hat to a professional for cleaning and shaping. It's a job specific to the hat and is based on fabric and soil,

New life can be given to a felt hat by simply brushing it over the steam of a boiling kettle.

variables only a professional is equipped to handle. Avoid the temptation to use stain-removal products. There's a good chance you'll damage your hat further and create stain rings.

**If you spill something on your hat,** blot it immediately with a soft, absorbent cloth to prevent it from seeping into the hat. If your hat gets spotted with mud, let it dry first. Then lightly brush it off with a nylon or horsehair brush.

**To clean a baseball cap,** there is a new school of thought that suggests you can give it a single cycle on the top shelf of your dishwasher, held in place with a couple of plastic pegs or stretched over a plastic bowl. Remove the cap before the drying cycle and let it air-dry. It's certainly worth a try, as long as the cap isn't a family heirloom. Most modern baseball caps are made from polyester or cotton and will survive a cycle in the washing machine. (Brims these days are made of rigid plastic, rather than cardboard, so they will not disintegrate in water.) Do not tumble dry. If you are concerned about the fragility of your cap, or if it is made from wool, wash it gently by hand using an approved wool wash.

**To clean a straw hat,** brush it with a brush or dry cloth to remove dust and loose dirt. Other than that, these hats are not really cleanable, even by a professional. However, if you've nothing to lose, try this old-fashioned remedy for cleaning a natural-coloured straw hat. Beat an eggwhite until stiff, then beat in the juice of a lemon and 1 teaspoon of Epsom salts. Brush this paste over the hat with a toothbrush, wipe with a damp cloth and leave in the sun to dry. With time, straw hats naturally turn yellow, and there's nothing you can do about it.

**To clean a wool hat,** use a sticky fabric roller designed to remove hairs and lint from clothing, or use a whisk broom. Brushes that are firmer are too rough to use on wool hats.

**If a hat has faded in spots** and you're ready to hang it up for good, here's how to get a little more life out of it:

- For a white hat, apply talcum powder using a dry sponge. (A make-up sponge works well.)
- For coloured hats, grind down a crayon that matches the colour, mix with the talcum powder and apply.

EXPERT ADVICE

TAKE THE INSIDE OUT

If the satin lining of your hat is removable, you can wash it. Fill a sink with cold water and add a couple of drops of dishwashing liquid. Place the satin lining in the water and rub it with a stiff scrubbing brush. To rinse, hold it under cold running water. Let it air-dry. If you want to remove wrinkles, expose it to the steam from your steam iron—without actually touching the iron to the lining.

## HEARING AIDS

**HEARING AIDS OPEN** A NEW WORLD TO SOME PEOPLE. HOWEVER, THEY MUST GET DAILY ATTENTION TO REMAIN IN TOP WORKING ORDER. WAX AND MOISTURE ARE COMMON CAUSES OF HEARING AID MALFUNCTION—WAX ACCUMULATES ON HEARING AIDS THAT FIT INSIDE THE EAR, AND MOISTURE COMES FROM PERSPIRATION ON HEARING AIDS WORN OUTSIDE THE EAR.

**WATCH OUT**

• If you wear a behind-the-ear hearing aid, apply hair spray before you put on your hearing aid. The spray could damage the microphone.

• Don't wear your hearing aid when you're doing heavy work in the garden. Perspiration, hose water, dirt and grass clippings could damage it.

**To clean an in-the-ear hearing aid,** start by washing your hands to avoid contaminating the device. Then, using a brush (either one that your hearing care provider gave you or a clean toothbrush), remove any wax on the exterior of the hearing aid. Do this daily if you get a lot of wax, or every other day if you don't. Another option is to wipe the surface with a dry, cotton cloth (an old T-shirt works well) or a cloth lightly dampened with methylated spirits. If you're using methylated spirits, wipe only the shell of the unit, not over the microphone or receiver, which can be damaged by moisture.

**Cleaning a behind-the-ear hearing aid** is a two-part operation. To clean the ear mould that fits inside the ear, use water and mild soap (Sunlight, for instance) or an antibacterial liquid hand wash soap. Put the soap on a cotton cloth dampened with lukewarm water. Wipe the ear mould clean, giving it a good rub. Rinse the mould with lukewarm water and dry with a towel. To clean the hearing aid itself, use just a brush—a toothbrush is fine.

Every three months, take the hearing aid to your hearing care specialist for a thorough cleaning. They should have the appropriate tools for cleaning more deeply into the interior of your hearing aid.

**The special tools and accessories** that you use in combination with your hearing aid need cleaning, too. In-the-ear hearing aids have wax guards that protect the receiver from getting clogged with wax. Clean them with a brush. Behind-the-ear hearing aids can be fitted with a sleeve jacket that covers the component behind the ear and protects it from moisture. Wipe the sleeve clean with a cloth.

Like a computer, a hearing aid has an electronic chip in it. Water is its enemy, so watch the amount of liquid you use when cleaning. It's also a good idea to keep your hearing aid in a dry place when you're not using it—for example, in the bedroom while you're taking a shower, instead of in the bathroom.

**Simple solutions**

### Put it in dry dock

Keep your hearing aid working longer by storing it at night in a dry aid kit that absorbs moisture, also called a dehumidifier kit. You can purchase one from a hearing aid dealer.

To make your own, get a jar that has a good seal and a desiccant bag. Put the bag and your hearing aid in the jar and close it up. A desiccant bag will last for six months. Desiccant bags can be bought wherever you buy hearing aid equipment.

# HEATERS

**WHETHER IT'S A** SINGLE BAR RADIATOR OR A GAS-LOG FIRE THAT LOOKS LIKE THE REAL THING, ALL HEATERS SHOULD BE KEPT DUST FREE. A DUSTY HEATER CAN BE COSTLY. LAYERS OF DUST CAN ACTUALLY COMPROMISE THE ABILITY OF YOUR HEATER TO DO ITS JOB. SO DON'T LET DUST BUILD UP—A WEEKLY DUSTING WITH A FEATHER DUSTER OR A DUST CLOTH WILL KEEP ACCUMULATION DOWN, BUT BEFORE ANY CLEANING, ALWAYS TURN THE HEATER OFF, UNPLUG IT AND LET IT COOL DOWN.

Rust spots can be removed by rubbing gently with fine steel wool moistened with a little oil.

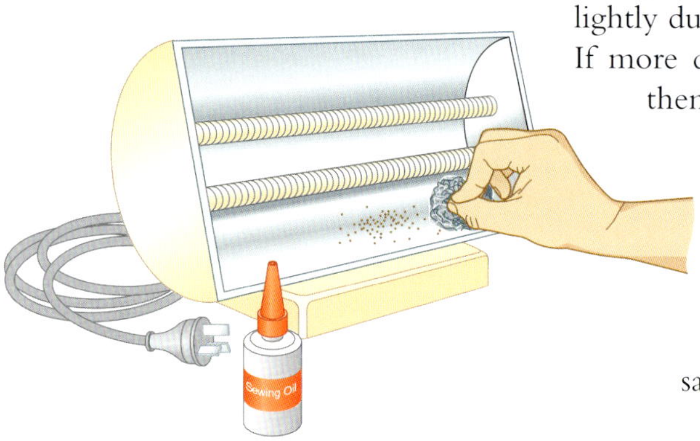


**To keep dust accumulation down** put your portable heater, electric or gas, away for the summer, stored in a plastic rubbish bag.

**Any heater with a vent or grille** should be vacuumed regularly with a brush attachment to keep airflow areas as clear as possible. This is especially important for heaters with fans, as these tend to attract dust through the air-inflow vents. To remove any other grime, food spills or sticky fingerprints from the outside of your heater, use a damp cloth wrung out in a little water and dishwashing liquid. Do not pour the liquid directly onto the casing and do not let things get too wet. Wipe the casing dry after cleaning.

**If your heater came with an instruction manual,** consult it. Some of the more modern gas-space heaters have filters which need to be regularly cleaned, and some even have a little light that blinks when you need to do this.

**To clean a portable electric oil-filled column heater,** make sure you unplug it before you begin. Remove as much of the surface dirt as possible using a hand vacuum or the brush attachment of your vacuum cleaner. The brush can actually go some way towards getting in between the tubes. But the crevice attachment goes further. You won't get everything out with a vacuum, and you'll find that there are more effective ways to clean inside the crevices between the tubes.

**To reach the dust between the tubes,** use a couple of common kitchen items. Wrap a paper towel around the broad end of a kitchen spatula or wooden spoon and secure it with a rubber band. Then slide the spatula up and down both sides of each tube of the radiator. For resistant substances, like sticky spills, spray some all-purpose cleaner, such as Citro-Clean Multi-Purpose Cleaner or Mr Muscle Orange Energy, on the paper-swathed spatula and have another go at it.

**Radiant heaters**, the ones with a shiny plate that reflects heat, need to remain shiny in order to be efficient. To clean the reflector plate, unclip or unscrew the protector grille at the front of the heater then lightly dust the plate, taking care not to damage the heating elements. If more cleaning is necessary, wipe with a well-wrung soapy cloth, then wipe again with a cloth dampened with methylated spirits.

**If rust spots** have already begun to form on a reflector plate (this is what happens if you don't dust regularly), you can rub the spots gently with fine steel wool moistened with a little sewing machine oil or vegetable oil (see left), then wipe over with methylated spirits. Always replace the safety grille before turning the heater on again.

See also:
• CHIMNEYS
• FIREPLACES • WOOD STOVES

**Flued or flueless gas-log fires** should be serviced annually by a qualified technician to keep them operating efficiently. In between servicing, you should only need to wipe the exterior down with a well-wrung soapy cloth and keep the air vents dusted. If the exterior of the glass needs cleaning, you can use a little glass cleaner, such as Windex or Mr Muscle, but never attempt to clean the glass while it is still warm. Cleaning the inside of the glass is a job for the technician.

## HOSES

**THANKFULLY, HOSES ARE** ALMOST, BUT NOT TOTALLY, MAINTENANCE FREE.

**Always start cleaning garden hoses** with the least abrasive method and work your way up. They probably require little cleaning other than removing dirt by spraying water from the hose onto the hose. If you need some extra cleaning muscle, dampen a rag in warm water and add to it some biodegradable soap. Rub it over the hose and use clean water from the hose to rinse. If you still have some dirt stuck on the hose, use a vinyl cleaner on vinyl hoses or rubber hoses coated with vinyl. Follow the manufacturer's instructions.

**If your hose has stopped running** and you have no kinks in it, you could have a build-up of calcium deposits from minerals in the water, if you happen to live in a hard-water area. Bend the hose back and forth along the entire length of the hose to break up the build-up. If there's a nozzle on the end of the hose, remove it and then turn on the water to flush out the loosened deposits.

Store a hose on a reel. It prevents kinks and knots and keeps the hose out of sight.

### Give your garden hose a long and happy life

To increase the life expectancy of your hose, here are some more things you can do:

- Even though hoses have UV retardants in them, remove your hose from adverse conditions, such as sunlight and freezing temperatures. Over time, sunlight can break down the material so that it becomes brittle and the hose will become less flexible.
- While your hose isn't in use, store it on a reel to prevent it from forming kinks or knots (see above). Place the reel out of sight (they're not that attractive, anyway) and out of the sun or on the east side of the house (so it only gets the morning sun).
- If you live in a very cold area, drain the hose and store it indoors for winter. To drain it, first detach the hose from the tap. Starting at the end of the hose, pick it up so that the water runs through the hose ahead of you. Make large loops with the hose over your shoulder as you go. When you reach the end of the hose, all the water will have run out. If you have a long hose that's too heavy to loop over your shoulder, make loops around a bench or make your loops on a raised patch of ground.
- Place the hose out in the sun for up to two days to thoroughly dry it.
- Store the hose flat in large relaxed loops. If you hang your hose outside, you'll get bends that may freeze and damage the material.
- Never walk on or drive over a hose. Hoses aren't designed to withstand that much external pressure.

# HOT-WATER SYSTEMS

**UNLESS YOU LIVE** IN A HARD-WATER AREA, THE CLEANING AND MAINTENANCE OF YOUR HOT-WATER SYSTEM IS STRAIGHTFORWARD. MOST HOT-WATER TANKS ARE POWDER-COATED STEEL AND THE EXTERIOR MODELS ARE BUILT TO WITHSTAND HARSH CONDITIONS—THE OUTSIDE CASING OF THE TANK SHOULD NOT NEED MORE THAN A WIPE DOWN TO REMOVE DIRT AND GRIME, AND THE OCCASIONAL VACUUM IF COBWEBS ARE A PROBLEM. CHECK THAT SPIDERS, LEAVES OR DIRT HAVE NOT BLOCKED THE DRAINPIPE. APART FROM THAT, ALL YOU NEED TO DO IS REMEMBER TO EASE THE PRESSURE RELIEF VALVE (LOCATED NEAR THE TOP OF THE HEATER) FOR AROUND 10 SECONDS EVERY 6 MONTHS, TO ENSURE CORRECT AND SAFE OPERATION OF YOUR HEATER.

**All water has some sediment in it,** and one of its purposes in life is to create problems for water heaters if you live in a hard-water area. You're probably already familiar with the floating stuff you see in the bottom of a glass in which ice has melted, or with minerals in the kettle. The cause, in both cases, is calcium and magnesium salts, which precipitate out of water when it is frozen or heated.

**To counteract mineral build-up,** you have several choices:
- Make sure that you install a hot-water system that is appropriate to your area. In hard-water areas, manufacturers make modifications to standard systems to allow for the higher saturation index of the water. If you are unsure of the quality of your water, seek advice from your local water supply authority.
- Have a plumber flush the heater or install a water softener.
- Buy a 'self-cleaning' water heater.
- Buy a 'tankless' water heater. It's more expensive, but it's also more energy efficient.
- Flush the heater yourself.

**If you decide to do the job,** here's how:
- Turn off the heater and the cold water that runs into it.
- Hook a garden hose to the drain valve (the one near the bottom of the tank). Make sure there are no kinks in the hose. Put the other end of it where you want the hot water from the tank to go.
- Open the drain valve.
- Disconnect the cold water inlet pipe on the top of the water heater to let air into the water heater so it will drain. After all the water has drained, close the drain valve.
- Pour 4 litres of a food-grade de-limer (available from plumbing supply shops and some hardware shops) into the cold water inlet pipe. Pour only one cup at a time and pause between cups. Leave the de-limer for several hours to let it do its work.
- Drain the cleaner.

Simple solutions

## Check for the hard stuff

To determine whether your water is hard, look in the kettle. If there's white, scaly stuff inside, that's just a little of what you have in your water heater. The precipitate will:
- Cut the efficiency of the heater.
- Cost you more money in electricity or gas bills.
- Reduce the water-holding capacity of the tank.
- Cause the heating element in an electric heater to eventually burn out.
- Cause an alarming rumbling sound in a gas heater, which means your heater is inefficient but doesn't mean it's about to blow up.

- Reconnect the cold water inlet pipe, open the valve and let water run through the heater for several minutes, flushing out the cleaner and dissolved sediment.
- Close the drain valve and open the hot water tap nearest to the water heater. Let the water heater fill up.
- When water comes out of the open tap, reopen the drain valve and let the water heater rinse until the water running out appears clear.
- Close the drain valve and open all the hot-water taps to remove the air from the heater and pipes.
- Turn the water heater back on and remove the garden hose from the drain valve.

## HOUSE PLANTS

**YOUR PLANTS NEED** MORE THAN REGULAR WATERING. TO MAINTAIN YOUR PLANTS' ABILITY TO GROW, YOU NEED TO CLEAN THEM.

**Remove dust and dirt from your house plants** the same way that you remove dust and dirt from yourself—with a shower. This is important to do, because grime is the enemy of photosynthesis, the process in which leaves absorb sunlight and carbon dioxide to make food for the plant. The shower will also help remove any insects.

First, prepare the plant's pot. Put the pot in a plastic bag and tie the bag tightly around the base of the plant without injuring it. You want to be sure the plant doesn't get over-watered in the shower. If your plant has multiple stems, lay extra plastic bags between the stems. Put the plant in the shower and sprinkle tepid water, which is neither hot nor cold, over the plant for a few minutes (see left).

Sometimes minerals found in the shower water will build up on the plant's leaves, making them look dull. To clean the minerals off hard-surfaced (not hairy) leaves, wipe with a dry, clean rag. Support each leaf with your free hand as you wipe. Another method to use is to gently scrape the minerals off with your thumb.

Cleaning plants with hairy leaves is a little trickier. First give them a gentle dusting with a feather duster and then hit the shower, as mentioned above.

Just like humans, house plants are re-invigorated after a shower to remove dust and dirt.

Keep your cactus clean to allow it to reach its maximum potential.

**After the plants have had their shower,** allow them to dry thoroughly in the shower recess, or set them on paper towels or old newspapers until they're not dripping any more. If you return them to direct sunlight too quickly and they're still wet, the light could unfortunately burn the leaves.

Now check each plant's surroundings. Make sure the window you set your plant in is clean so that the plant will get optimal sunlight. White mineral deposits can be toxic to your plants, so gently scrape them from the soil surface and the inner rim of the pot. If you have an extreme case of mineral build-up, put the pot in a sink, where it can drain freely and run a lot of water through the soil to remove the minerals. (Don't do this during times of low light or dormancy. Plants should be actively growing; otherwise they may develop root rot.)

**Cleaning a cactus** requires a gentle touch—not only to prevent skewering yourself, but also to protect the waxy coating that helps the plant conserve moisture in desert climates. Stick to misting your cactus with a spray bottle filled with water, and even then only clean the areas of the plant that are showing dirt or dust. Make the cleaning quick and gentle, and let the cactus dry before putting it back into direct sunlight. As an alternative, you can use long tweezers to carefully pick off any dust particles.

To clean succulents with fuzzy leaves, use a feather duster or a soft paintbrush to remove dust. The fuzziness protects the plant in arid conditions, and washing can be hazardous to the leaves.

## HUMIDIFIERS

**A HUMIDIFIER PREVENTS** DRYNESS OF YOUR NOSE, THROAT, LIPS AND SKIN. THE AIR IT DAMPENS WILL ALSO ALLEVIATE STATIC ELECTRICITY, PEELING WALLPAPER, AND CRACKS IN PAINT AND FURNITURE. HOWEVER, HUMIDIFIERS CAN ENCOURAGE THE GROWTH OF ORGANISMS SUCH AS DUST MITES AND MOULD, SO PROPER CARE AND CLEANING ARE ESSENTIAL. TO REDUCE SPORE GROWTH, PLAN A DAILY CLEAN, WITH A MORE THOROUGH CLEAN EVERY THREE DAYS, AND A REGULAR DISINFECT.

**To clean a portable humidifier,** first turn it off. Empty the reservoir (the tank where the water sits) every day and wash it out with hot, soapy water, using a brush or other scrubber to remove mineral deposits or film. Rinse well under running water, taking care that no water gets into the motor. Wipe all surfaces dry with a clean cloth, and fill the reservoir. The use of distilled water is preferable because you'll avoid the build up of mineral deposits, but tap water will suffice.

**Every three days,** you need to clean your humidifier more thoroughly. Begin as you would the daily cleaning. After rinsing, wipe the reservoir with white vinegar (diluted with water, if you wish) to break up mineral deposits. Wipe off the mineral deposits, rinse again, wipe dry and refill the reservoir.

**Disinfecting your humidifier** will reduce spore growth. Mix a solution of ½ cup of household bleach with 4 litres of water and add it to the humidifier's reservoir. Run the humidifier until it starts to mist or steam. (Make sure you do this outside or in a well-ventilated area and don't stand near the steamed bleach—it can injure your lungs.) Turn off the humidifier and let the bleach sit for a couple of minutes. Empty the reservoir into a sink and rinse the reservoir with running water. Fill it again with fresh water, run the system for 2–3 minutes, and then turn it off. Empty the reservoir and rinse again. Repeat the cycle until you no longer smell the bleach.

If the manufacturer's instructions don't recommend bleach, don't use it. They may recommend instead a 3 per cent solution of hydrogen peroxide, which is fine but does not work as well as bleach.

**If your humidifier has a filter,** check it every third day. If it's grey, replace it. The filter can't be cleaned.

**At the end of the humidifying season,** clean the humidifier following the bleach method described previously. Make sure all parts are dry, and store the unit in a dry location. When it's time to use the humidifier again, clean the unit again and wipe up any dust on the outside with a damp cloth.

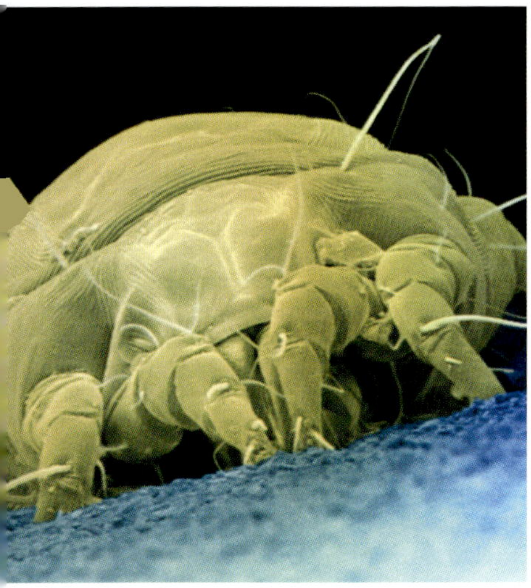

Dust mites (one seen here close-up) in humidifiers can cause allergic reactions such as asthma.

**Humidifiers that are part of a central heating system** need to be cleaned regularly. Otherwise, they may become breeding grounds for mould. The designs of such units vary widely, but typically a tube carries water from the water heater to a rectangular box mounted on the air-supply duct that goes from the heating unit to the rest of the house. The water flows across a disposable water panel or, in the case of older models, a rotating drum. The water evaporates into the air being fed throughout the house, thus raising the humidity. A drain removes the excess water.

**If you have a newer system** (no older than mid-1990s), replace the water panel every year. Do it more often if you have hard water, which builds up on the panel and makes it less effective. Clean the water distribution tray at the same time. To do this, open the access panel on the box and unsnap and discard the water panel. Unsnap the water distribution tray, take it to a sink, and give it a quick cleaning in warm water and dishwashing liquid. Wipe the drain (it's not removable) with a soapy rag and rinse with a wet rag. Reassemble the unit with a new water panel.

**Cleaning the inner workings of an older system** is not very different. Once a year, open the unit and replace the filter that wraps around the rotating drum. Remove the water tray and wash it in the sink. Two or three times a year, check the filter for mould or mineral deposits. If it needs cleaning, soak it for several hours in a solution of 1 part vinegar to 2 parts water. Rinse the filter thoroughly with fresh water and return it to the drum.

# INK STAINS

**IF THE SIGHT** OF INK ON YOUR CARPET OR CLOTHING THROWS YOU INTO A PANIC, STOP, TAKE A DEEP BREATH AND REACH FOR THE ALCOHOL—METHYLATED SPIRITS, THAT IS. IT'S DEFINITELY THE BEST REMEDY FOR REMOVING ANY KIND OF INK FROM LEATHER, CARPET, UPHOLSTERY AND CLOTHING (AS LONG AS THE STAIN ISN'T PERMANENT INK, MADE BY FELT-TIP PENS, SUCH AS MAGIC MARKER, INDIA INK OR PAINTING INK). CLEAN AN INK STAIN IMMEDIATELY, AND ALWAYS USE COOL WATER WHEN YOU DO IT, AS HEAT WILL SET THE STAIN. BEFORE USING A CLEANER ON ANY FABRIC OR SURFACE, TEST AN INCONSPICUOUS SPOT TO CHECK ITS COLOUR-FASTNESS.

**To remove ink from leather, vinyl and most fabrics,** moisten a section of clean, white terry towelling with methylated spirits and dab the metho on the ink stain. Let the metho sit for 30 minutes to give it time to dissolve the ink. Then use a fresh white cloth to blot up the stain. Move to a new spot on the cleaning cloth each time you blot, to avoid spreading the stain. Reapply the methylated spirits if necessary. Finally, rinse with a solution of ¼ cup of white vinegar per 1 litre of water and then rinse again with plain water. (Methylated spirits, being alcohol, usually evaporates, but the rinsing ensures that the material won't be damaged by any lingering traces.)

**If the ink resists removal with methylated spirits,** try foam shaving cream (see below). Shaving cream contains two or three kinds of alcohol that can remove ink and many stubborn food stains. Apply the foam, wait 10–15 minutes and then rinse as above. And there is no point in using gel shaving cream, as it doesn't work.

Try foaming shaving cream to remove an ink stain if methylated spirits doesn't do the trick.

**When removing ink from fabrics,** here are some other simple tips to keep in mind:

- Blot—never rub—the alcohol on. Rubbing the fabric will break down the fibres and weaken the material.
- To prevent large stains from spreading, work from the outside of the stain towards the centre.
- Remember to protect your working surface when removing a stain from clothing. Place a piece of plastic on the work surface, with a clean, white towel on top of that. Do the same between layers of clothing.
- Wash clothing or washable fabric after removing the stain and air-dry. Professionally dry-clean silk, wool and linen that specifies dry-cleaning. If the garment is hand washable, allow the alcohol to set only 5 minutes and rinse with cool water. Reapply if needed.
- Polyester reacts differently to ink stains than cotton and other fabrics do. If alcohol and shaving foam don't completely remove the ink, rinse the fabric with cool water, apply 3 per cent hydrogen peroxide, then rinse again. The hydrogen peroxide will bleach what is

left of the ink so that it won't be noticeable. Peroxide is safe for coloured clothing, but test an inconspicuous area first. Don't use peroxide on a wool, silk or Persian carpet.

**To treat ink stains** with hydrogen peroxide instead of alcohol (methylated spirits), mix equal parts 20 per cent hydrogen peroxide and water and proceed as mentioned above.

**To remove ink from carpet,** moisten a section of clean, white terry towelling with methylated spirits and gently blot the spot. Wait 30 minutes for the alcohol to dissolve the ink, then press the knuckle of your index finger into the barely damp rag. Work your knuckle forwards and backwards over the stain. Change to a clean spot on the towel and repeat, this time working your knuckle left to right. Replenish alcohol if needed. To finish removing the stain, again press your knuckle into the damp towel, but this time twist your wrist in a clockwise direction. Carpet fibres are twisted clockwise. This motion will help remove stains from between the fibres without causing the carpet to fuzz. Rinse with a solution of ¼ cup of white vinegar per 1 litre of water and then rinse again with plain water, applied using a fresh towel and the same knuckle technique.

**To remove a surface ink mark on wood,** apply a small amount of methylated spirits to the mark with a cotton bud and then wait 5 minutes. Then blot the stain with a clean, white towel. If ink remains, apply alcohol again. Wait 24 hours for the wood to completely dry and then polish it. If ink remains after two alcohol applications, use an orange-based cleaner to remove the mark.

**The ink from felt-tipped pens and markers** is almost impossible to remove—they are called 'permanent' markers, after all. For washable fabrics, mix equal parts talcum powder and borax with enough methylated spirits to make a paste. Spread this over the stain and leave for an hour or so, then wash out with your usual laundry powder. This might lighten the stain if it doesn't remove it entirely.

## rules of the game

OUT, DAMNED SPOT

- Always treat an ink stain immediately.
- When water is called for in the cleaning process, make sure it's cool.
- Methylated spirits (alcohol) is the most effective ink remover, but give it time to work—generally 30 minutes.
- Apply methylated spirits to the stain with a clean, white towel. Later, blot the stain.

# IRON

**WROUGHT IRON, AS** DEFINED METALLURGICALLY AND BY THE PROCESS USED IN WORKING THE METAL, IS NOT PRODUCED ANY MORE EXCEPT FOR RESTORATIONS. (REAL WROUGHT IRON IS WORKED WHITE HOT, THEN HAMMERED AND TWISTED INTO SHAPE.) TODAY THE TERM IS OFTEN USED, INCORRECTLY, TO INCLUDE DECORATIVE IRON, 'MILD STEEL' OR CAST IRON.

**Indoor iron pieces**—such as bed frames, lamps and chandeliers—are dust magnets. If your piece has a black-satin finish, you might as well be shining a spotlight on the dust—everyone will see it. The easiest and quickest way to clean indoor pieces is with compressed air. It just blows the dust away and is especially good for all the edges, corners and crevices of detailed iron, which defy the reach of a conventional cleaning rag. You can also dust that intricate ornamentation with an unused, soft-bristled paintbrush.

To clean a smooth piece of wrought iron, wipe first with a soft cotton rag, to remove dust, and then wipe with any furniture polish sprayed onto a clean section of the rag. If there's dirt stuck to the wrought iron, the furniture polish may help lubricate and remove it. Water isn't recommended. It will collect in areas that can't be reached by a drying cloth, leading to rust. Furniture polish, on the other hand, provides a protective coating that repels water and resists dust.

**To clean outdoor furniture** that has a rust look or patina, let your item reach the desired rusty brown before you clean. Wipe off loose rust, dust or dirt with a rag. Then coat the piece with a clear lacquer paint (available from hardware shops) to protect it from the elements and to prevent further rusting.

Outdoor furniture that isn't supposed to rust needs to be cleaned only when it looks dirty or has mud or grime caked on it. Remove dirt by spraying with a garden hose. Periodically check the piece for rust, which may start around areas such as bolts. If you do see minor oxidation, gently apply a dry wire brush to remove the rust (see left). Wipe off any dust particles you create. Before applying touch-up paint to the surface, wipe the area clean with acetone or paint thinner on a cotton cloth. This will make the paint adhere better by removing oils that got on the iron from your hands. It will also dissolve any remaining paint in the rusty area. Let the paint thinner dry before painting. Wear gloves and goggles, as acetone and paint thinner can be quite harsh to the skin and eyes.

If your wrought iron has a lot of rust on it, you may have to take it to a professional for sandblasting.

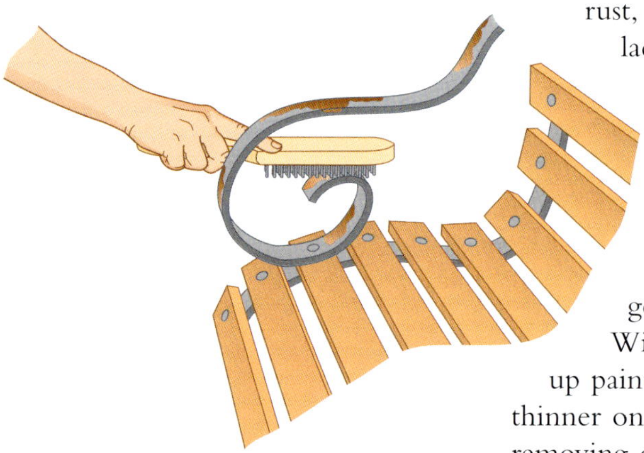

■ Use a dry wire brush to scrub off rust before applying touch-up paint.

**To clean cast iron**—the stuff poured into a mould at a foundry—use the same cleaning methods used on wrought iron. Cast-iron items typically include doorknobs, mailboxes, railings and fences. Hose down such an item and then inspect it for rust. If you find rust, clean it with a wire brush. Then wipe away any dust your cleaning produced. A rust-preventive paint (check out the range at your hardware or paint shop) comes in many colours and is great for small touch ups—indoors and outdoors—to protect the object from further rusting. Spray- and paint-on versions are available.

## The seasoning process

When you buy a new piece of cast-iron cookware, you always need to season it before you use it. Seasoning is a process that will protect your new pot from rust and give it a natural non-stick surface.

There are a number of methods for seasoning a new iron pot, but here's a tried-and-true technique:

First, you need to clean the new pot with dishwashing liquid and warm water to remove oils and debris from the manufacturing process. Fill the pot about two-thirds full with water. Add ⅓ cup of white vinegar per 4 litres of water and boil the mixture for 1 hour. Let it cool and then remove the vinegar water. If the pot is rough, scour the inside with fine-grit, wet-and-dry sandpaper or steel wool.

Wash the pot inside and out with plain water. Apply a light coating of vegetable oil on the inside and outside surfaces. (Using a spray cooking oil is fine.) Heat the pot in an oven at 130 °C to 180 °C for an hour and then turn off the oven and let the cookware cool with the oven door closed. When the item has cooled, wipe off any excess oil. The seasoning is complete. (Once seasoned, dishwashing liquid should not be used inside the cast-iron pot. If it is, you'll have to re-season the pot.)

Store the cast-iron pot dry, with a very light coating of oil. Too much oil will leave a sticky mess.

The more you cook, the better the seasoning gets. With proper care, your pot should not rust. But if it does, repeat the seasoning process.

**WATCH OUT** There are some things cast-iron cookware doesn't like, including soap, detergent and the dishwasher. And never be tempted to pour cold water into hot cast iron—that could break it. Extensive cleaning with soaps or detergents will remove the seasoning, and you'll have to repeat the seasoning process.

**Cleaning well-seasoned iron cookware** requires very little effort. Generally, all that's required is a little boiling water, some light scraping with a wooden spoon and a quick wipe with a clean cloth. Dry thoroughly and lightly oil again. For badly burned-on food, use a copper-wool scouring pad. For extreme cases of burned-on food and grease, use any common oven cleaner according to the package instructions. Rinse well. Then re-season the item as if it were a new piece. (See 'The seasoning process' box, above.)

Store pots with the lids off to prevent condensation. Keep your cookware clean, dry and oiled. Soak badly rusted pots overnight in kerosene, then scour. A wire brush is the best tool for removing rust. Avoid letting your pot get to the stage where bad cases of rust require sandpaper or commercial rust removers.

## IRONS

**A CLASSIC IRONING** CLEAN-UP JOB IS WHEN SYNTHETIC FIBRES GET STUCK TO THE SOLE PLATE—YOUR IRON'S FLAT UNDERSURFACE.

**To remove fibres such as nylon and polyester,** heat the iron until the fibres liquefy. Now iron over an old cotton rag, removing as much of the synthetic material as possible. Then, on non-stick and aluminium or chrome sole plates, use a wooden spatula or flat stick (for instance, a paddle-pop stick) to scrape off the fibres. Never scrape with plastic, metal or anything abrasive. Instead, the better option is to run the iron over a terry towelling cloth or some other rough material that the remaining fibres can stick to.

If you don't know what's stuck on your sole plate and the mark doesn't liquefy when you heat the iron, use any hot iron cleaner, available from supermarkets, and fabric and hardware shops.

If the stain still remains on an aluminium or chrome sole plate, your next option is to make a paste of bicarbonate of soda and water in the consistency of toothpaste. Rub it on a cool iron with a soft cloth, then wipe it off with another damp cloth. Don't use this method on non-stick sole plates, such as Teflon or Silverstone.

**On Teflon or metallic coating non-stick surfaces,** a damp cloth should wipe off any water marks, and a wooden spatula should remove any fibre stains. Should any marks still remain, rub a nylon scouring pad gently on the iron's sole plate when it's cool.

**Here's how to clean specific substances** from your iron:

- To clean sticky, oil-based residue from an aluminium or chrome sole plate, use an all-purpose cleaner on a cold iron. Spray the cleaner onto the sole plate and rub with a soft cloth. To remove the cleaner, rub with a wet cloth. (Never rinse the electrical appliance in water.) Before using the iron again, heat it and rub the sole plate on a terry towelling cloth to remove any traces of the cleaner and residue.
- To clean acetate or nylon that has melted and hardened on the sole plate, use acetone on a cloth and rub the affected area until the melted residue is gone. Don't get the acetone on the plastic shell of the iron, because the acetone will melt it.
- To clean a waxy stain (from a crayon, for instance), heat your iron as hot as possible and iron newspaper until the wax is gone (see left). Don't worry—the print won't come off on your iron.
- To remove small bits of burned lint, use your iron's 'burst of steam' feature as instructed.
- To prevent stains from forming on the sole plate (so you can avoid having to clean as above), use a press cloth, a lightweight pure-cotton cloth, which will act as a barrier between the iron and your clothing. A press cloth will prevent synthetic fibres or starch from attaching to the iron.

Iron over a newspaper to get rid of the waxy stain on the sole plate of your iron—the newspaper will absorb the hot wax.

**To clean the iron's steam chamber,** check the manufacturer's guidelines about the type of water to use—distilled or tap water. Generally, newer models use tap water—the minerals actually help in the steaming process. With the cord unplugged, fill the iron with water. Then plug in the iron and, depending on your model, either turn the iron to its cleaning mode function (most manufacturers recommend using the self-cleaning feature once a year) or to the steaming feature. Hold the steaming iron over a sink, the sole plate face down, until the steam stops. Unplug the iron and leave it in the empty sink for another half an hour to fully dry. An alternative is to place the iron face down on a heat-proof cooking rack while it steams. The steam will remove lint, dirt, dust and mineral deposits that have built up in the steam vents. Finish by wiping with a dry cloth.

If you haven't cleaned the steam chamber for a while, you may find that the water or steam looks rusty. This is actually burned lint, which

can stain your clothes. So it's important to clean your steam chamber and vents every couple of months.

**Another way to clean the steam chamber,** if the technique described above doesn't remove the mineral deposits, is to try using vinegar if your manufacturer's instructions allow it. Pour white vinegar into the steam chamber and steam it through the vents. Rinse out the vinegar and refill the chamber with water. Let the water steam through the iron to remove all the vinegar. If you're not careful about removing the vinegar, it may stain your clothes the next time you use the iron. The acidic nature of the vinegar may also etch and damage the interior of the iron if left inside the steam chamber, and you also don't want your clothes to smell of vinegar.

In case the steam vents on the sole plate become clogged, unbend a paperclip and push it into the holes to reopen the vents before steaming the iron (see left).

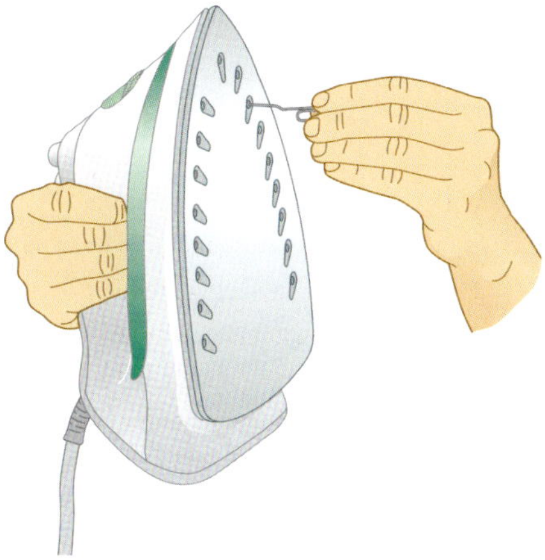

Unbend a paperclip and use it to unclog and clean the vents on the sole plate of your iron.

**Cleaning the iron's outer shell** is a very simple job. Just wipe it regularly with a damp rag.

**Always dry and cool your iron** before putting it away, and store it in an upright position on the heel rest.

## IVORY AND BONE

**IVORY AND BONE** NEED TO BE TREATED WITH CARE. WHETHER YOU'RE CLEANING A FIGURINE OR A BEADED NECKLACE, YOU MUST ALSO ASSESS THE CONDITION OF THE ITEM, BECAUSE THAT WILL DETERMINE YOUR APPROACH.

**Whether it's ivory or bone depends** on the animal your ivory piece came from. If it came from the tusk of an elephant or mammoth you have true ivory. Today, however, the tusks of other mammals, such as those of walruses and certain whales, and some synthetics are considered ivory as well. Ivory is chemically similar to bone and antler, but there are differences. Ivory has no blood vessels, whereas bone does. Bone is fragile and porous, whereas ivory is dense. Ivory and bone are similar in this respect: they're sensitive to heat, light and moisture.

**If your ivory item is fragile,** take it to a conservator to be cleaned. Because ivory readily absorbs oils and stains, wear white cotton gloves while working with ivory, or, at the very least, wash your hands with soap and water to remove oils and dirt.

**If your ivory or bone is sturdy and stable,** clean off the surface dirt with a barely damp cotton cloth or cotton buds. To dampen, use a solution of mild dishwashing liquid and water or use just water. If you use too much moisture, surface fractures may appear on the ivory. Now wipe the surface of your item with a dry cloth and apply a second cloth or cotton bud dampened with mineral turpentine to remove any soap residue. Wipe with a dry cloth.

**WATCH OUT** All of these factors could damage your ivory or bone:

- Display areas exposed to sunlight or a spotlight.
- A closed display case with light bulbs inside, heating the interior.
- Nearby ventilation or heating ducts, the tops of appliances or other sources of heat or cold.
- Sulfur in rubber-based paint, storage materials and adhesives (because sulfur in rubber can discolour ivory).

Never rub the surface of ivory and bone. You don't want to remove the original surface coats, pigments or patinas.

**To remove wax or oil from ivory,** use a cloth or cotton bud that has been barely dampened with mineral turpentine. If your ivory or bone has scrimshaw (engravings or decorations) on it, test an inconspicuous part of the scrimshaw to see whether it will withstand the cleaning technique. If it doesn't react well to the test, don't clean the scrimshaw yourself, take it to a conservator.

**If your ivory or bone is stained** (a yellowing stain is typical), you'll also have to take it to a conservator. These stains are usually due to oxidation that comes with age or may be caused by the oils on your hands. Sometimes, placing the ivory or bone in sunlight bleaches it and helps it regain its warm white colour. Keeping ivory or bone in the dark accelerates the yellowing associated with ageing. But do not expose ivory or bone to long periods of intense sunlight or heat, because that will dry it out and cause it to crack.

**Store your ivory and bone** in a carefully controlled environment, ideally 45 per cent to 55 per cent relative humidity and about 21 °C, in low light. Conditions should be kept constant, as the most severe damage to ivory and bone is caused by fluctuations in humidity and temperature. Low humidity will dry ivory out, causing shrinkage and cracking. High humidity and changes in temperature can cause your ivory to expand and contract.

*See also:* • PIANOS

## JOGGERS AND SNEAKERS

**MOST SHOE MANUFACTURERS** DISCOURAGE MACHINE WASHING OF JOGGERS AND SNEAKERS. BUT SOME SIMPLE CANVAS OR ALL-SYNTHETIC SHOES CAN SAFELY TAKE A SPIN IN THE WASHER. BEFORE CLEANING ANY TYPE OF JOGGER OR SNEAKER, CHECK THE LABEL INSTRUCTIONS. YOU MAY WANT TO PURCHASE A SNEAKER CARE KIT DESIGNED FOR ATHLETIC SHOES, PARTICULARLY IF YOU HAVE LEATHER SHOES.

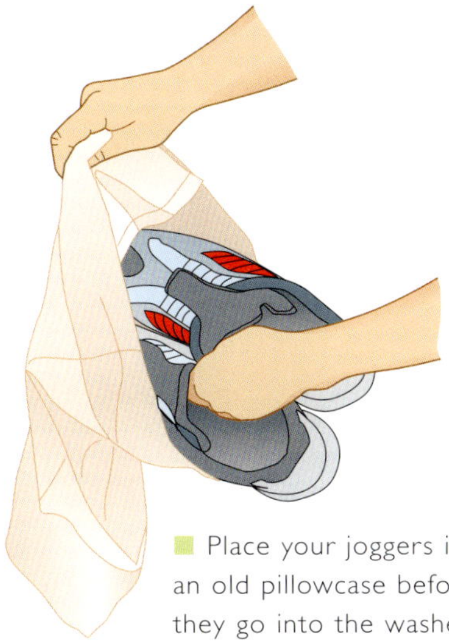

Place your joggers in an old pillowcase before they go into the washer.

**For leather joggers or sneakers,** it's best to use a regular leather cleaner and conditioner. Just don't use saddle-soap. It may be great for saddles, but it can damage other kinds of leather.

**To clean canvas or synthetic joggers or sneakers in the washing machine,** spray them first with a stain-removal spray, especially if the sneakers are grass-stained. Wipe the spray around the shoe, let it sit for a couple of minutes and then put the shoes in the wash. Include light-coloured towels in the wash. The rubbing action of the towels will not only help clean the sneakers, but will also keep them from bouncing around. If you have items in the same wash load that you want to protect, put the sneakers in an old pillowcase (see below left).

**To clean canvas and synthetic joggers or sneakers by hand,** rinse the shoes in clear water. Use a soft brush to scrub the shoes with a pH-neutral laundry liquid, such as Softly or a eucalyptus wool wash, which leaves a nice fresh smell. For scuff marks, scour with a white, nylon-backed scrub pad. Rinse to remove all traces of detergent and then air-dry. Stuff the shoes with white paper to retain their shape.

An alternative for canvas sneakers is to squirt on foam shaving cream, let it sit for half an hour and brush off what remains. Then wipe your sneakers with a clean, damp cloth.

**To dry your cleaned sneakers faster,** place them below the refrigerator door so the warm air blowing out hits them. Don't dry your sneakers in direct sunlight, as it might fade them. And don't stuff your shoes with newspaper—the ink might transfer to the fabric. Make sure your shoes are completely dry before you wear them.

**To give joggers or sneakers a fresh smell,** place a sheet of fabric softener in them overnight. Or make a bicarbonate of soda sachet: a couple of teaspoons of bicarbonate of soda in the centre of a cotton cloth, close the cloth with a string or rubber band and put one sachet in each shoe overnight. The sachets can be reused in any kind of shoe.

**If you want to waterproof non-leather joggers or sneakers,** use a waterproofing product specifically designed for sneakers.

## rules of the game

TO MACHINE WASH SNEAKERS OR JOGGERS

- Brush the exterior free of soil.
- Give them a cold machine wash with regular laundry detergent.
- Leave the laces in, but untied.
- After washing, tie the laces to help maintain the shoe's shape.
- Air-dry on a rack.

# KITCHEN CUPBOARDS

**MOST KITCHENS OPERATE** AS POWERHOUSES OF STORAGE, CONTAINING MANY HOUSEHOLD ESSENTIALS. KEEP KITCHEN CUPBOARDS CLEAN AND TIDY SO THAT THINGS KEPT IN THERE ARE EASY TO FIND AND READY TO USE.

**To routinely clean the cupboard exteriors,** dust with a clean cloth regularly and wipe with a damp cloth from time to time. (In terms of frequency, the meaning of 'regularly' and 'from time to time' will depend on your specific cupboards and their frequency of use.) Never use abrasive cleaners or scourers on kitchen cupboards. Also avoid using a tea towel that's been used for other purposes, because it may contain grease or detergents that can add streaks and smears.

**To wipe away the stains** around handles on cupboard doors and drawers, bring on the heavy artillery, because those stains will probably be the most difficult, being a mixture of skin oils, food smears and softened finish. On cupboards made of plastic laminate, metal or glass, try a strong all-purpose household cleaner, such as those you find in supermarkets. Spray it onto a cloth or sponge and apply to the dirty areas. Let the cleaner sit for a few minutes and then wipe it off with a rinsed-out cloth or sponge. Wipe with a dry cloth.

**To clean wooden cupboards,** first try a bit of dishwashing liquid applied directly to a cloth or sponge. Rub into the dirty areas around the hardware. For serious grease and grime, wash the entire cupboard with a wood-soap solution. Mix up the wood soap (such as Howard Clean-A-Finish Wood Soap or Briwax Furniture Cleaner) according to instructions. Apply with a cloth dipped in the solution and wrung out. Then go over the cupboards with a cloth dampened in plain water, followed by a dry cloth.

**To protect the surface** of the wooden cupboards after cleaning, apply a polish or wax, such as Howard Orange Oil, Feed-N-Wax or Briwax. Apply thinly to a clean surface with a clean cloth and then buff.

**To clean cupboards** that have windows, wash the glass with a cloth or paper towel sprayed with a little glass cleaner, such as Windex or Mr Muscle. Don't spray cleaner, or even plain water, directly onto the glass—it can drip down and damage the surrounding wood.

**To clean the shelves,** use the same methods as for the exterior surfaces. Shelves need cleaning only once or twice a year—assuming you clean up any spills as soon as they happen. To remove an old spill, sprinkle with bicarbonate of soda and wipe with a damp cloth.

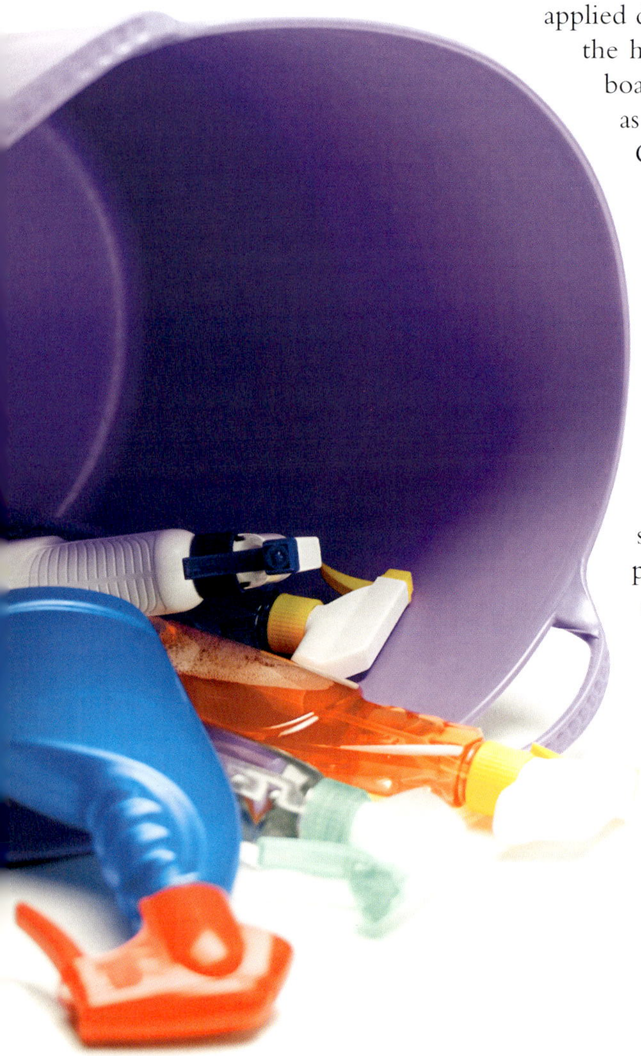

# KNICK-KNACKS

**DUST MORE, WASH** LESS. OR DUST LESS, WASH MORE. TAKE YOUR PICK. IF YOU CLEAN AWAY THE DUST FROM YOUR GLASS COLLECTION OR KNICK-KNACKS OFTEN, IT WON'T HAVE A CHANCE TO TURN TO STICKY GRIME THAT WILL REQUIRE A MORE INTRUSIVE CLEANING JOB.

**WATCH OUT** Don't use soap and water—and especially not the dishwasher—to clean hand-painted or antique knick-knacks. If a prized piece needs cleaning, as opposed to just dusting, wipe it lightly with a damp cloth. The same gentle touch applies for wooden knick-knacks, which can be gently wiped over with a dusting cloth that has been impregnated with a few drops of wood oil, to nourish the wood.

**To dust a whole rack of knick-knacks,** use a hair dryer or feather duster (real or microfibre) every couple of days—if you're in the habit of using those sorts of tools for dusting. Alternatively, wipe them, one at a time, with a clean microfibre cloth once a week. Either way, you'll probably rarely need to wash them.

**To wash your knick-knacks,** mix a few drops of dishwashing liquid in warm water in a plastic bowl and immerse the knick-knacks, as long as they're made of china, glass, plastic or metal. Use a clean, thick cotton sock, over your hand, as a cleaning mitt. That will get into most crevices. Use an old toothbrush on places that your hand can't get to. Rinse the items well with fresh water and dry with a clean cloth.

For an even speedier wash, run your knick-knacks through the dishwasher on the gentlest setting, but only do this for things that you know are robust enough to stand it. If in doubt—don't.

**To clean cloth items,** try the vacuum cleaner first, using the brush or crevice attachment. If that isn't enough, put the articles in a paper bag, add a couple of tablespoons of bicarbonate of soda, shake and then shake some more. Remove the items from the bag and brush or gently vacuum off the bicarbonate of soda (see below).

Bicarbonate of soda is useful for cleaning fabric-covered boxes and things that can't be washed in water.

# KNIVES

**STAINLESS STEEL KNIVES** STAY BRIGHT AND SHINY ALL THE TIME. THE DOWNSIDE IS THAT WHEN STAINLESS STEEL LOSES ITS EDGE, IT DOESN'T TAKE WELL TO SHARPENING. IF YOU PREFER A REALLY SHARP KNIFE, LOOK FOR CARBON STEEL. THE DOWNSIDE THERE IS THAT IT'S DIFFICULT TO KEEP SHINY. HOWEVER, BOTH ARE EASY TO KEEP CLEAN.

**To clean stainless steel or carbon steel knives,** wash immediately after use in a little dishwashing liquid and hot water with a cloth or sponge. Rinse with hot water and wipe with a dry cloth.

**To remove stains from a carbon steel blade,** try a paste made of salt and vinegar. Rub it on the blade with a cloth. Or dip a slice of lemon into salt and rub that on the blade. Some stains will respond to a nylon scrubber or steel wool.

**To shine the blade,** use silver polish, or even better, Simichrome, a German all-metal polish available from some automotive shops, or Staintune Liquid Mirror Polish (available online). To protect the edges of knives, store them in a rack or, if in a drawer, cover the blades with cardboard sleeves. You can make a sleeve by cutting a piece of cardboard (from a cereal box, for example) the length of the blade and twice as wide. Fold the cardboard in half lengthwise. Use tape to seal the side and one end. Insert the knife in the open end.

**To clean a pocketknife,** open all the blades—and in a Swiss Army-type knife, all those other bits and pieces, too. Wash them in hot, soapy water. Remove dirt from the little slots with an old toothbrush. Rinse in hot water, dry with a clean cloth and leave the knife open for a while to allow the slots to dry thoroughly. Lubricate the hinges periodically with a drop of sewing machine oil, available from fabric shops.

**To clean a hunting knife,** use the same method as for a pocketknife. After using your knife in the field, rinse it off in a creek, if possible, or wipe it clean with leaves or grass.

## Life on the edge

A sharp carbon steel knife edge has lots of virtually invisible 'teeth', which get bent out of line during use. Keep them as straight as possible by using a honing steel before each use.

- Hold the steel in your left hand (if you're right-handed).
- Place the knife against the steel at a 20- to 25-degree angle.
- Draw the knife across, heel to tip, so that the entire blade passes over the top of the steel.
- Repeat with the other side of the knife on the bottom of the steel so that you are honing both edges of the knife blade. Continue for about a dozen or so strokes.

After a while, the knife blade will get so dull that honing will no longer be effective. Then it's time for sharpening, a process that removes some metal and leaves a new edge. Some hardware shops and department stores offer a knife-sharpening service.

# LACE

**FUNNILY ENOUGH, BOTH** PRIZE-WINNING SHEEP AND LACE ARE BEST WASHED WITH THE SAME SOAP, AS THEY COME UNDER THE HEADING OF DELICATE TEXTILE MATERIALS. USE THE UTMOST CARE WHEN CLEANING LACE.

**Some precautions first.** Lace is a delicate material, so you shouldn't be surprised that there's a list of don'ts when it comes to cleaning it:

- Don't use the washing machine, dryer, your usual detergents or soaps, chlorine bleach, lemon juice or salt.
- Don't rub lace or lift it by itself while it's wet.
- Don't send it to a drycleaner, except for recently made lace that specifies dry-cleaning on the care label.
- Don't clean fragile, old or valuable lace yourself. Turn the job over to a professional. You should only wash sturdy lace—a tablecloth of no great value, for example.

**To clean lace,** place a clean, white towel in the bottom of the sink or bathtub where you're planning to do the cleaning. Lay the lace cloth on the towel. Mix 1 teaspoon of Orvus WA Paste for every 4 litres of warm water. (Orvus, the animal-cleaning soap mentioned in the introduction, is a synthetic, anionic, pH-neutral detergent that will remove most dirt and stains, and is safe for all textiles except silk. It is available from the heritage preservation company, Zetta Florence, who distribute their conservation products to fine arts suppliers, art galleries and museums. Check their web site for your nearest supplier.) Make enough of the solution to cover the cloth. Soak for 15 minutes and then agitate by gently lifting and lowering the towel.

**To rinse lace,** use room-temperature distilled water as it's much gentler and has no additives. Keep changing the water until it's totally clear, then drain. Use the towel as a sling to lift the lace.

**To dry lace,** first blot up as much water as possible with dry towels and then lay the lace flat on a clean, dry towel to dry completely.

**To restore the shape of lace** that has to fit a dress collar, for example, trace its shape on a piece of paper before washing it. Place the tracing on a cork pin board and put a sheet of clear plastic over it. After washing the lace, place it over the plastic and gently shape it to fit the tracing under the plastic. Then use stainless pins to hold the lace in place while it dries (see left).

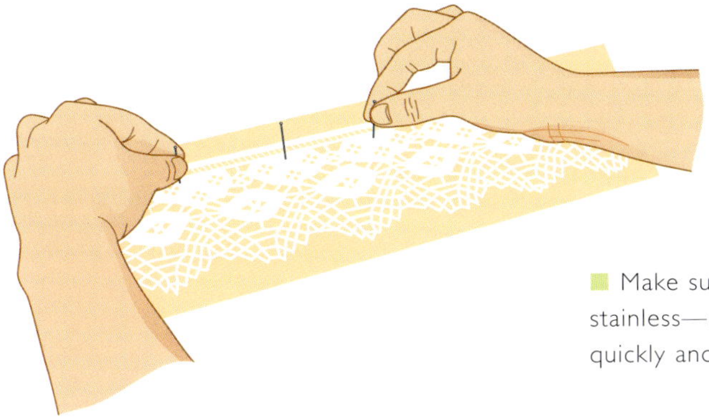

Make sure the pins you use are stainless—rust marks can appear very quickly and spoil all your hard work.

## LACQUER

**LACQUER IS EYE-CATCHING** BECAUSE OF ITS MIRRORLIKE FINISH AND ALSO BECAUSE THE FINISH IS OFTEN FOUND ON FURNITURE, SUCH AS A PIANO, THAT IS THE FOCAL POINT OF A ROOM.

**To dust a lacquered surface,** use a large, folded piece of cheesecloth slightly moistened with water. Don't wipe in a circular motion—that could leave 'whirlpools' on the finish. Wipe in one direction only, preferably the one in which the piece was originally polished, if it is possible to determine that.

**To clean, when dusting isn't enough,** mix a few drops of dishwashing liquid in tepid water, dip in a soft cloth and then wring it out. Wipe the surface down. Wipe again with a rinsed-out damp cloth, then again with a dry cloth.

**WATCH OUT**

• Don't use solvents, waxes, polishes or harsh cleaners on old lacquer-finished surfaces. On modern finishes test any cleaner or polish first on an inconspicuous area.

• To avoid scratching a lacquer finish, don't place objects on the bare surface. Protect a dining table with a tablecloth or place mats and coasters. And don't let the piano player rest their drink on top!

**To polish a dulled lacquered surface,** choose a non-silicone paste wax. (Silicone tends to cause problems later on if a piece ever needs to be refinished.) Apply the polishing wax with a soft cloth in one direction and buff the same way. Don't overdo the buffing, because rubbing creates static electricity, which will attract dust particles and create more work for you.

## LAMPS

**CLEANING YOUR LAMPS** WON'T LEAD TO FAME AND FORTUNE AS IT DID FOR ALADDIN, BUT IT WILL SAVE YOU MONEY, AND IT'S GUARANTEED TO BRIGHTEN YOUR SURROUNDINGS.

**To remove dust from a lamp,** use a microfibre cloth regularly. The vacuum cleaner with its brush attachment may work better on some materials, such as unglazed pottery or wood. The more often you dust, the less often you'll have to do more intensive cleaning of your lamp.

Include the light bulb in your routine—that's where the money-saving comes in. Dust build-up reduces bulb efficiency, wastes energy and hikes up your electricity bill.

**To remove dirt,** first unplug the lamp and remove the shade and the bulb. Start with a clean cloth or sponge dampened with plain water. Wipe all parts of the lamp, starting with the base and working up. Be very careful not to wet the socket or the plug.

To avoid dulling the finish, buff the lamp immediately with a clean, dry cloth. To attack more stubborn dirt, try cleaning it with a solution of about ½ teaspoon of dishwashing liquid applied directly to a cloth or sponge. Wipe the dirty areas, scrubbing gently if necessary. Rinse the cloth or sponge in clear water and go over the surface to remove the detergent. Follow with the dry cloth. Polish the lamp base occasionally with a suitable polish.

**EXPERT ADVICE**

### RESTORING A RELIC

Bringing an antique lamp back to life involves more than spit and polish. Start by removing old wiring and taking the lamp apart. Then strip off lacquer and accumulated grime with paint remover. Hand polishing follows, with a metal polish, such as Simichrome (see 'Knives', on page 234) or Rubbedin Metal Magic metal cleaner (check the web site for availability: www.rubbedin.com.au). You can relacquer the lamp, using a satin finish, or leave it unlacquered. Then have the restored lamp rewired.

**To wash glass globes or chimneys,** clean them with a cloth or sponge and a solution of hot water and dishwashing liquid. It's OK to immerse those parts as long as they don't have electrical connectors. Rinse with a solution of hot water and a dash of ammonia and wipe dry with a clean cloth.

## LAMPSHADES

**LAMPSHADES CAN** BE WEIRD AND WONDERFUL TO LOOK AT, BUT MORE IMPORTANTLY THEY SET THE MOOD IN A ROOM BY DIRECTING AND SOFTENING LIGHT. THEY DO THIS BEST WHEN THEY'RE CLEAN.

**To remove dust,** go over the surface of the lampshade with:

- the brush attachment of a vacuum cleaner for sturdy cloth shades.
- a microfibre cloth for glass, plastic, paper or metal shades.
- a narrow-head, soft-bristled horsehair paintbrush for silk, acetate and pleated shades (see below left).

Regular dusting will help you avoid higher-impact cleaning, which can be messy for you and dangerous for your lampshade. Water can dissolve glue, for example, and this can cause the shade to fall apart.

**To remove serious dirt,** the safest cleaning method after dusting is to use a special sponge that's intended to be used dry, such as Chux Magic Eraser. Use it like a pencil rubber to rub away dirt. Try it on any shade, but be sure to use it instead of water on paper shades and any other shade that is held together by glue.

A soft brush is perfect for dusting as it can be gently worked in between the pleats on a fabric lampshade.

**To clean fabric shades** that are stitched rather than glued together, wash them in the bath. And while you're going to the trouble of doing one, you might as well do all the lampshades that need to be cleaned. Metal and plastic shades can also be cleaned in the bath at the same time. To wash the shades, begin by running about 5 centimetres of tepid water into the bath. Add 1 tablespoon of dishwashing liquid and swish it around. Lay the shade on its side in the bath and gently roll it in the water. Metal and plastic shades can stand a little more vigorous cleaning with a cloth or sponge. Change the water when it becomes dirty and wash the shade again.

To rinse, drain the wash water and run clear water. Again, roll the lampshade in the water and change the water when it has turned grey. Metal and plastic lampshades can be rinsed under running water and wiped dry with a clean cloth.

**To dry a cloth shade,** use a towel to press out as much water as you can. Finish with a hair dryer, tipping the shade upside down frequently so that no water settles in the bottom of the shade, where it could leave a water stain. Drying quickly is important, because the metal parts of the shade can rust and stain the fabric.

**To clean a glass shade,** fill a sink with warm water and add 1 or 2 teaspoons of ammonia. Immerse the shade in the water and wash it with a cloth. Use an old toothbrush to get into crevices or difficult-to-reach spots. Rinse and dry with a clean cloth.

## LATTICE

**LATTICE MAKES AN** ATTRACTIVE SCREEN ON A PATIO OR IN THE GARDEN, BUT THOSE CRACKS AND CREVICES CREATE LOTS OF PLACES FOR DIRT AND GRIME TO HIDE.

**To clean lattice with no plants attached to it,** use a hose with a nozzle that sends the water out in a tightly focused stream. Use a stiff-bristled nylon or fibre brush to scrub dirty spots. If the lattice is wood, use the brush sparingly; you can use a freer hand on lattice of plastic, fibreglass or metal. You may also use a power washer, available wherever tools can be rented, if your local water restrictions allow it.

To attack that green mouldy or mossy stuff that grows in shady spots, mix a solution of 4 litres of water and 1½ cups of chlorine bleach in a bucket. Scrub the solution on with a stiff-bristled brush, then rinse with plain water.

Simple solutions

### Plants in your way?

To clean lattice that is supporting plants, wash it in the early spring. Prune the plants back to about 15 cm—most vines can easily take it—and remove the rest of the plant material from the lattice so that you can get to all of the crevices.

## LAWNMOWERS

**TAKE GOOD CARE** OF YOUR LAWNMOWER, AND IT WILL TAKE GOOD CARE OF YOUR LAWN. GOOD CARE MEANS KEEPING THE MOWER CLEAN AND MAINTAINING IT IN GOOD WORKING ORDER.

**To clean the underside,** make sure the engine is off and can't accidentally start. Remove the spark plug wire (or in the case of an electric mower, make sure it is unplugged). Turn the mower on its side or prop one side on blocks if that's easier, but don't turn it completely over (see below). Use a garden hose to wash off loose grass and dirt. Then remove the remainder with a putty knife, followed by a stiff-bristled brush. If you do this every time you use the mower, you'll never get that caked, cruddy grass build-up.

Turn the lawnmower on its side or chock it using wooden blocks, but don't let it tip upside down.

solutions

### A kitchen solution to a garden problem

To prevent grass and dirt build-up under the deck of your lawnmower, use spray-on vegetable cooking oil. Clean the underside and then apply the oil on the metal after it dries. This will make it easy to clean the mower after each use.

**On the mower's exterior,** keep the engine free of dead grass, leaves and grease, which presents a fire hazard. To keep the mower running well, brush off the air-intake screen and the cooling fins on the engine with a stiff brush to keep them free of debris.

**Attend to the mower's air filter** after every 25 hours of use. Replace a disposable paper filter (available where lawnmowers are sold). A foam-type filter has a removable sponge that should be soaked in warm water and then dried. Follow up by putting a few drops of clean engine oil into the sponge and squeezing it to distribute the oil. Then reinstall the sponge.

**An annual professional tune-up** for your lawnmower will save you a lot of trouble. It should include a carburettor adjustment and a cleaning of belts, cables and switches. It can also include sharpening the blade and changing the oil, spark plug and air filter if you prefer not to do those things yourself.

## LEATHER

**LEATHER MEANS ANY** SKIN OR HIDE THAT HAS BEEN TANNED, BUT AFTER THAT THE SIMILARITIES END AND THE DIFFERENCES BEGIN. TWO MAIN CATEGORIES OF LEATHER—NATURAL AND COATED—REQUIRE DIFFERENT CLEANING TECHNIQUES.

**Natural leather** has little surface protection and is highly susceptible to staining. It is not dyed with pigments, has no finish coat of polyurethane and is recognisable by its rustic, natural appearance. Even water or treatments suitable for other kinds of leather, such as saddle-soap, may ruin its surface.

**Coated leather** has a pigment-dyed surface treated with a polyurethane coating. Most—but not all—leather garments, upholstery, purses and shoes are made of coated leather.

A few guidelines apply to both kinds:

- If you have instructions from the manufacturer, follow them.
- Test any cleaning product on an inconspicuous area before using it.
- For any valuable leather article or serious cleaning problem, consult a professional, such as a drycleaner who specialises in cleaning leather.
- Avoid harsh cleaners and even excessive water, which can leave stains and remove dye and lubricants.
- Never dry wet leather near a heat source.

**To clean natural leather,** rely on frequent dusting with a soft cloth. You could try removing dirt with an art gum eraser, available from newsagents and art supply shops, but even that might leave a smudge. There is little more you can do without making a problem worse.

**To clean coated leathers,** dust regularly with a cloth, occasionally with a dampened cloth. Wash every six months or so with saddle-soap,

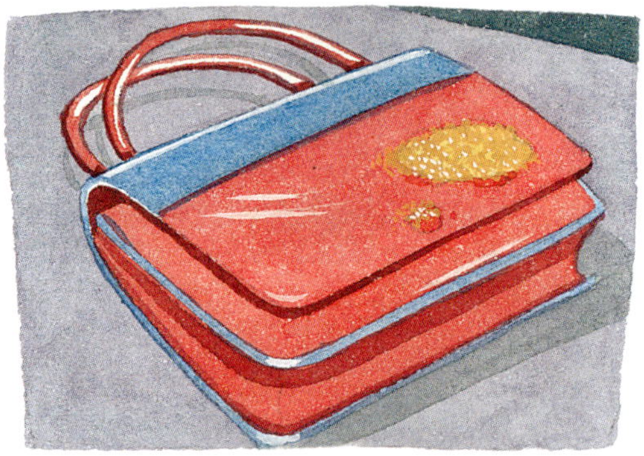

Putting a small pile of cornflour or talcum powder on greasy spots will sometimes work to absorb a stain.

which is available from saddleries, sporting goods shops, some shoe shops and hardware shops. Here's how:

- Remove loose dirt with a stiff brush or damp cloth.
- Rub a damp cloth on saddle-soap and work up a lather.
- Rub the soapy cloth on the leather article using a circular motion. Wipe away the excess soap and moisture with another damp cloth. Then allow to air-dry.
- Buff with a clean, soft cloth.
- Finish off the cleaning with a coat of protective leather cream recommended by the manufacturer or a general-purpose one sold by leather retailers and shoe shops.

**To treat spots on coated leathers,** try these methods—but don't forget to test on an inconspicuous area first:

- Apply cornflour to greasy spots and let it absorb the grease. Wipe off the excess with a dry cloth (see above left).
- Rub with a cotton bud dipped in methylated spirits.
- Make a paste of equal parts lemon juice and cream of tartar, work it into the spot (including scuff marks) with a cloth, let it sit for an hour or so and then wipe clean.
- Treat those ugly white stains on shoes and boots caused by the mineral salts in water with a 50:50 mixture of water and white vinegar. Dip a cloth into the solution and blot.
- On mildew, use a 50:50 solution of methylated spirits and water on a cloth. Saddle-soap also may work.

*See also:*
• SHOES • SUEDE

## LIGHT FITTINGS

**INSECTS ALWAYS MANAGE** TO SNEAK INTO A CEILING LIGHT FITTING THAT HAS NO VISIBLE GAPS. WHATEVER THEIR SECRET, NOW AND THEN YOU WILL WANT TO REMOVE THEIR DRIED-OUT LITTLE BODIES—AND CLEAN THE FITTING TOO.

**To clean a wall or ceiling fitting,** first turn off the switch and plant a sturdy stepladder nearby. Remove any grilles, shades, shields, globes, light bulbs or light tubes. This is one time when you could use an extra hand, as you may have to hold on to a globe while you remove screws and balance yourself at the same time, to keep from falling.

**To wash the removable parts,** fill the sink with hot water and add a few drops of dishwashing liquid. Lay a towel or rubber mat on the bottom of the sink to prevent damage. Immerse the pieces—except for the light bulbs or tubes—and clean with a soft cloth or sponge. Rinse and dry well with a soft cloth. Wipe the light bulbs or light tubes with a damp cloth, avoiding the ends that go into the sockets.

**To wash the fixed parts,** use a cloth or sponge dipped into the same cleaning solution and squeezed until it's barely damp. Wipe the fitting, being careful not to get any moisture in the socket or on the wiring. Rinse the sponge or cloth in clean water and wipe the fitting with it again. Wipe with a dry cloth and reassemble the fitting.

## LITTER TRAYS

**HOW, AND HOW** OFTEN, YOU CLEAN YOUR CAT'S LITTER TRAY DEPENDS ON THE LITTER AND THE TRAY—AND ALSO THE CAT ITSELF.

Here are the basics for keeping your cat litter tray sorted:

- To clean a litter tray, remove solids daily—and don't slack off, or your cat may find another spot to use.
- For a clumping litter, remove the poo and the urine clumps with a slotted scoop, available from pet shops and supermarkets (see below). Clumping litter should be dumped and the tray washed about every two weeks—sooner if your nose or eyes say it's time.
- For non-clumping litter, remove the solids daily with a scoop, and change the litter and wash the tray once a week or more if needed.

**To wash the tray,** use few drops of dishwashing liquid and water and scrub with a stiff-bristled brush. Avoid using any cleaner with a strong smell, such as scented detergents or ammonia, which could turn up a sensitive feline nose. But you should disinfect with a solution of 1 part chlorine bleach to 10 parts water to kill the germs that hang around. Rinse thoroughly with plain water and, if possible, dry in the sunshine, which is a natural disinfectant. Otherwise, wipe dry with a clean cloth before adding fresh litter.

**To stop the footprints** emanating from the litter tray area, put a piece of carpet or a rubber mat where your cat walks out of the tray. This will collect some of the kitty litter granules.

**WATCH OUT** You might have the best intentions in the world when buying scented litter, thinking your cat will appreciate the scent as much as you do. But alas, cats' noses are extremely sensitive—and unpredictable. Some cats take offence at even such a mild, inoffensive substance as bicarbonate of soda.

If your cat suddenly stops using its litter tray and has substituted something else—such as the dining room carpet—this may be the problem. Switch to an unscented litter and see if that helps. If not, buy a new litter tray. A lingering, if faint, urine smell embedded in the plastic could also be the cause of your cat's litter tray issues.

Use a slotted litter spoon to remove solids from cat litter daily, to keep odours to a minimum.

## LOCKS

**YOU MAY NEVER** HAVE GIVEN A THOUGHT TO CLEANING A LOCK. BUT WHEN TURNING THE KEY BECOMES DIFFICULT OR IMPOSSIBLE, DIRT MAY BE THE PROBLEM.

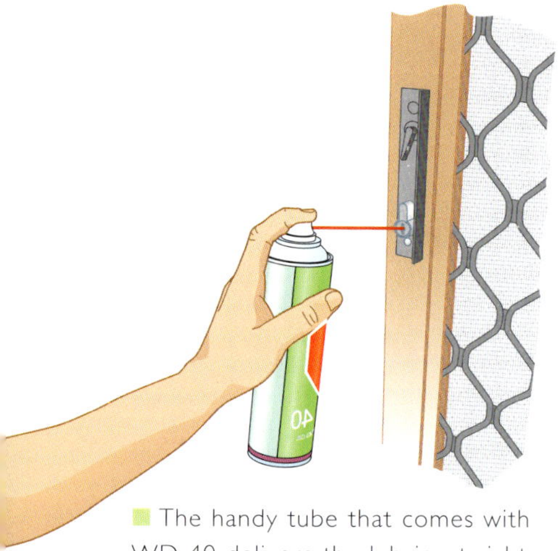


The handy tube that comes with WD-40 delivers the lubricant right into the lock with minimum mess.

**To clean the exterior of a door lock,** wipe with a damp cloth or sponge. For more power, use a few drops of dishwashing liquid applied to the cloth. Rinse the cloth before rinsing the lock parts. Wipe dry with a clean cloth and then buff.

To achieve more shine, apply a polish appropriate to the lock's metal, or use an all-metal polish, such as Rubbedin Metal Magic (available from many supermarkets or online at www.rubbedin.com.au).

**To clean the inside of a door lock,** give it a good dousing with a penetrating lubricant such as WD-40. Take the tiny tube that comes with the lubricant and fit it over the spray nozzle. Poke the other end of the tube into the keyhole and spray for 10 seconds (see left). You can hold a rag underneath to catch excess lubricant. This will flush out any grime and will not attract dirt. Don't use conventional oil inside a lock, as dust will stick to it and cause havoc with the mechanism.

**To clean a lock that no longer works,** first take it apart. Wash the inside parts with a degreaser, following the label instructions. Then lubricate the parts with a multipurpose lubricant. Both are available from hardware and automotive shops.

Simple solutions

### The hard-to-turn lock

To loosen a dead bolt that resists turning, insert graphite shavings into the keyhole. Graphite comes in a tube and is available from hardware shops.

## LOOSE COVERS

**HOW OFTEN YOU** CLEAN LOOSE COVERS WILL DEPEND ON HOW OFTEN YOU USE THE FURNITURE WITH LOOSE COVERS ON, HOW MANY CHILDREN YOU HAVE AND WHETHER YOU HAVE PETS. ON AVERAGE, LOOSE COVERS SHOULD BE CLEANED THREE OR FOUR TIMES A YEAR—MORE OFTEN IF THEY LOOK OR GET GRUBBY SOONER.

**To remove dust and debris,** give the loose covers a going-over with your vacuum cleaner while they're still on the furniture, using the upholstery attachment. On cushion covers, use the vacuum nozzle without any attachments.

**To clean loose covers,** remove them and give them a good shake outside. You'll either be able to wash the loose covers (follow the fabric care instructions), or you'll need to take them to the drycleaner. Most loose covers can be washed, with the exception of rayon, which often requires dry-cleaning. Either way, clean all matching loose covers at the same time so that the colour stays even, since they may fade with washing. For example, on a couch, wash all the loose covers and cushion covers at the same time, using exactly the same amount of detergent and the same water temperature. Wash the curtains, too, if they're made of the same fabric.

EXPERT ADVICE

ON THE RACK

Here's a trick for getting the best fit for your loose covers. Put the covers on the frame or cushions before they're completely dry—somewhere in between being damp and almost dry. This way they'll stretch around the object nicely (especially true of fitted loose covers). This method will help iron the wrinkles out, too. You can speed the drying process by using nature—open the window in good weather—or use an electric fan strategically placed. If you use this technique, don't use the furniture until the covers are completely dry.

*See also:*
• STAINS

**Pre-treat any stains** after removing the loose covers and before washing. Use a method appropriate to the stain. Place the loose covers in the washing machine on a soak cycle to remove extra soil before the wash cycle begins. Don't leave the covers in the wash cycle for long, as this could loosen their stitching. Wash in warm water with any laundry detergent and use a cold rinse. Loose covers will sometimes shrink the first time they're washed, but it shouldn't be very much. While your loose covers are washing, vacuum the upholstery of the furniture while it's uncovered.

**Before drying the loose covers,** check to see whether the stains have been removed. If the stains are still there, drying will set them. You'll need to treat the stains once more and rinse or wash again. And if you do that, you should wash every other item a second time, too, to keep the colour even.

**To dry your loose covers,** check the care label and either hang the covers over a drying rack or put them in a tumble-dryer. Some people feel that tumble drying is too harsh and recommend laying the loose covers flat. If you use a tumble-dryer, dry on *Low* and avoid over-drying. If you air-dry, don't dry on a clothes line, because the weight of the cover might pull the fabric out of shape.

Once the loose covers are dry, put them back on the furniture, smooth them and pull all the seams and piping into place. Pinch any pleats into sharp creases and smooth any ruffles. If you like, iron the pleats before refitting to the furniture.

## LOUVRES

**MANY PEOPLE LIKE** THE LOOK AND THE BREEZINESS OF LOUVRES, BUT THEY DREAD THE CLEANING. HOWEVER, FREQUENT DUSTING WILL POSTPONE THE DAY YOU HAVE TO TACKLE ANY HEAVY DIRT BUILD-UP.

**To clean glass louvre windows:**

- Mix a solution of 1 cup of vinegar in 4 litres of water.
- Open the window to its fullest extent so the slats are running perpendicular to the window frame.
- Take an old, thick, white cotton sock and dip it into the solution; wring it out thoroughly.
- Put the sock over your hand like a mitten and clean the slats on both sides, one at a time, starting at the top.
- Use another clean, dry sock to dry the slats in the same manner.

**To dust louvres,** you have several options. Use these tools, either separately or in combination:

- The brush attachment of a vacuum cleaner
- A soft paintbrush
- A clean, white cloth wrapped around a ruler or putty knife or another longish, flat object
- A lamb's wool duster

A soft paintbrush is all you need to dust between the slats on louvres. Flick the bristles to clean off dust.

Dust from top to bottom, using a gentle wiping action, not a flicking one that will send dust back into the air. Give the duster a good shake outside, not in the house.

**To clean dirt from painted louvres**—or louvres that have been coated with varnish or polyurethane—wipe with a damp cloth. For any grime you can't remove that way, rub with a little dishwashing liquid applied directly to the cloth. Rinse the cloth in plain water and wipe again. Some alternatives include:

- Scrubbing with a clean paint pad that has a handle (available from hardware and specialist paint shops), which should fit between all but the most tightly spaced louvres.
- Dampening a cotton glove in water, squirting some dishwashing liquid on it, putting the glove on and then sliding each finger between a different slat. With this method, you can clean several louvres at the same time. Rinse with another damp glove or a damp cloth.

**To clean wood that has an oil finish,** wipe with a cloth dampened with boiled linseed oil, mineral turpentine or a citrus-oil wood cleaner, all available from hardware and paint shops.

## LUGGAGE

**SPACE-AGE TECHNOLOGY** HAS IMPROVED THE MATERIALS USED IN TODAY'S LUGGAGE, MAKING EVERYTHING FROM FLIGHT BAGS TO BRIEFCASES LONGER LASTING AND EASY TO CLEAN.

**To clean soft-sided luggage,** use a mild, all-purpose cleaner mixed with water, such as Earth Choice or Simple Green multi-purpose spray (available from supermarkets). Mix 1 part all-purpose cleaner to 7 parts water and use a brush, cleaning cloth or sponge to scrub dirt or spots with a circular motion, working your way outwards. Most soft-sided luggage is made of tough nylon materials backed with plastic to repel water, and is easily cleaned.

**To clean hard-sided luggage,** use a few drops of dishwashing liquid in warm water. Wipe with a sponge or cloth that's been dipped into the solution and wrung out. Then rinse and dry. You can brighten the piece by waxing with a silicone-based auto or furniture polish, available from hardware shops. Follow the instructions on the package. Don't use a combination cleaner–polish.

**To clean leather luggage and briefcases,** determine whether the leather has a natural or coated finish and follow the instructions in the 'Leather' entry on page 239.

**To clean aluminium pieces,** wash with a cloth dipped in the dishwashing liquid solution mentioned on the opposite page. Never use ammonia-based cleaners, as they will darken the metal. For a nice shine and protection, polish with an all-metal cleaner, such as Rubbedin Metal Magic (available from supermarkets or online at www.rubbedin.com.au). Do not use it on anodised aluminium.

Simple solutions

### For the infrequent flyer

To eliminate a musty, mildewy smell from luggage, wipe it with a solution of 1 cup of white vinegar in 5 cups of water. Then wipe with a cloth dampened in plain water. Leave the luggage open to air-dry for a few days. Store luggage where it won't be subject to extremes of temperature or humidity, and air it out periodically.

## LUNCH BOXES

WITH ALL THE FOOD-BORNE ILLNESSES FLOATING AROUND, DON'T LET ANY FLOAT INTO YOUR ENVIRONMENT VIA A LUNCH BOX.

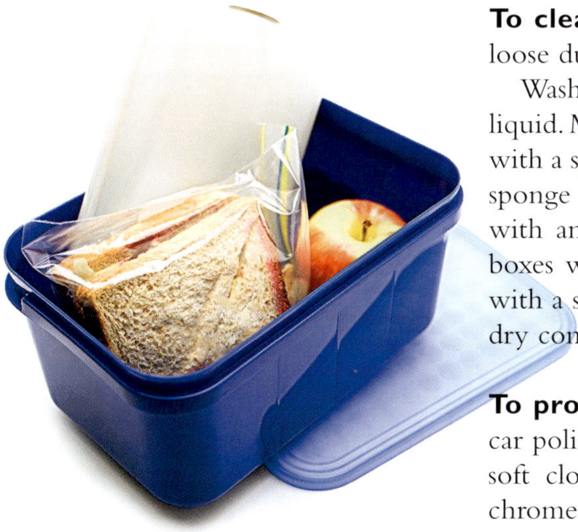

**To clean metal or hard plastic lunch boxes,** wash with a sponge or cloth in hot water and a few drops of dishwashing liquid. Rinse and dry. Do this after each day's use.

**To clean soft-sided lunch boxes and bags,** wipe the inside with a damp sponge or cloth. For spills, use a sponge dampened in hot, soapy water. Allow to air-dry.

**To clean a grimy old metal lunch box,** begin by removing any loose dust or dirt with the upholstery brush on your vacuum cleaner.

Wash the lunch box using hot water with a bit of dishwashing liquid. Mix it in a separate container—not in the lunch box itself. Wash with a sponge or soft cloth, never with anything abrasive, and rinse the sponge under running water frequently. Scrub tough grime gently with an an old toothbrush, which is also useful for cleaning lunch boxes with handles. Rinse in clear, warm water and dry thoroughly with a soft cloth. Leave the lunch box open for an hour or so to let it dry completely. Any wet areas are susceptible to rust.

**To protect and polish the metal surface,** apply a non-abrasive car polish with a soft cloth, followed by a buffing with another clean, soft cloth. Use a chrome polish on the metal hardware. Car and chrome polishes are available from hardware and automotive shops.

## MARBLE

**HERE'S A STONE-COLD** FACT TO KEEP IN MIND WHEN CLEANING MARBLE: IT MAY SEEM INDESTRUCTIBLE, BUT IT'S ACTUALLY POROUS, STAINS VERY EASILY AND IS NOT IMPERVIOUS TO HARSH TREATMENT.

**In general, clean marble** with a gentle, pH-neutral liquid soap (not detergent), and take it easy. Mix about 2 tablespoons of mild liquid soap (such as Softly, or a special marble cleaner) in 2 litres of water. Using a soft sponge, or a sponge mop if you're cleaning a marble floor, wipe the marble clean. Follow with two to three water rinses, depending on how soapy the cleaning mixture is. Then dry with a soft cloth. Light grime can also be removed by wiping with a cloth dampened with mineral turpentine, then washing with soapy water. Rinse even more thoroughly if using this method on a benchtop.

**Clean marble floors regularly,** before dirt and grit have a chance to scratch the surface, and wipe up spills immediately. As with a wood surface, avoid putting drinking glasses directly on marble, which can leave water rings. Marble will also quickly be etched by the acids in foods such as tomatoes, citrus, vinegar, wine and fruit juice. Water should bead on the marble. If the marble appears to be absorbing liquid, it's not sealed properly and is susceptible to staining and etching.

Marble floors should be resealed annually to keep them stain resistant.

**Reseal your marble floor annually**—it's as easy as waxing a floor (see above). Buy a stone or marble sealer from a home-improvement shop, builders' merchant, specialist cleaning supplies shop or from a supplier of stone floors and benchtops. (You can also find specialist products on the Internet under 'marble cleaning'.) Take a sponge, sponge

mop or rag and cover the entire marble surface, including corners and the splashback. There's no need to strip the floor before you seal.

**Marble benchtops or vanities** should also be protected against everyday wear and tear. One of the best ways to do this is to impregnate the stone with a protective stain repellent, such as Lithofin Stainstop, which will make the marble water and oil repellent. The surface should be cleaned thoroughly first with a marble cleaner such as Lithofin MN Power-Clean, to remove grease, oil and any other stains.

**WATCH OUT** Never use lemon, vinegar or any other acidic ingredient on marble. Acids will eat through the protective finish and damage the stone. Avoid ammonia as well. Abrasive cleaners, such as Ajax or Jif, should not be used either, since the grit can scratch and dull the shiny marble finish.

**To clean surface stains on marble,** it is best to use a specialist marble-care product. You will sometimes find tips that suggest toothpaste, poultices of ammonia and hydrogen peroxide, and various abrasives. But marble is very easy to damage and you may end up with a bigger mess than you started with. If the marble surface you're cleaning is stained but not of great value, you can try removing stains with a thick paste made of bicarbonate of soda and water. Apply the paste to the stain. Cover the paste with a sheet of plastic to keep the paste damp, and let it sit for 10–15 minutes before wiping it off. Rinse with warm water and dry. Repeat the procedure if the first application doesn't fully remove the stain. If stains still remain, it's time to look for specific marble-care products or call a professional marble restorer.

## MATTRESSES AND MATTRESS BASES

**IF YOU NEVER** GIVE A THOUGHT TO CLEANING YOUR MATTRESS, HERE'S A WAKE-UP CALL: DUST MITES ARE ALMOST CERTAINLY PRESENT IN YOUR NEGLECTED BED, AND MOULD SPORES MAY ALSO BE MULTIPLYING.

**Dust mites**—tiny organisms that feed on the microscopic flakes of dead skin we all shed—can cause allergic reactions in some people, particularly those with asthma. Just washing your sheets with hot water instead of cold and occasionally vacuuming the mattress will help keep dust mites under control.

**Periodic care and cleaning of a mattress** will prolong its life even if you don't have allergies. Here's how:

- Every six months, rotate your mattress end to end and vacuum the exposed surface. Run the upholstery brush attachment over the entire

**Simple solutions**

### Accidents will happen

If bed-wetting is a problem in your house, invest in a waterproof mattress cover. But don't totally enclose your mattress in plastic. It needs to breathe. Get a cover with cloth sides and an open bottom.

Urine smells and stains are difficult to remove from a mattress. Sprinkle dry borax on the wet spot. Rub it in, let it dry and then vacuum. Or try sponging the stain with white vinegar or cloudy ammonia on a dampened cloth. Sponge away the residue and dry as quickly as possible.

Use the frothy suds rather than the liquid beneath to clean your mattress.

mattress, including the sides. This will remove not only dust mites, but also mould spores. Empty the vacuum cleaner bag outdoors after cleaning or, if the bag is disposable, throw it away.

- Once a year, flip the mattress over and vacuum it again. Remove the mattress and vacuum the mattress base with the upholstery attachment as well. If you have the type of mattress base with exposed springs, use a bottlebrush to reach in there and lift away dust.

**Removing stains from your mattress** can be tricky, because moisture is a mattress's enemy. Clean with upholstery shampoo, following the package instructions. Or you can lift the stains out using dry suds, which are made by whipping a grease-cutting dishwashing liquid or clothes detergent in water. Keep mixing until you have lots of frothy suds to use as the cleaning agent.

Using a clean cloth, soft brush or sponge dampened with warm water, apply the suds in a circular motion to the stain (see above). Then draw out the moisture with a clean, dry towel. Repeat the procedure

## rules of the game

BASIC MATTRESS MAINTENANCE

- Every six months, rotate your mattress end to end and vacuum to remove dust mites and mould spores.
- Once a year, flip the mattress over and vacuum it again.
- Remove stains as they happen, but do not let the mattress get too wet, and remember to dry cleaned areas as quickly as possible.
- Keep exposed springs dust-free with regular vacuuming.

if necessary, then wipe the area with a clean cloth dampened with clear water. Again, press a dry towel against the spot to draw out the moisture. The key is to leave as little water on the mattress as possible, because moisture in the mattress filling can lead to mould growth.

To speed drying, blow an electric fan towards the mattress, or haul the mattress outside and let the sun do the job. If you've cleaned the entire mattress (one small section at a time), you may want to use a dehumidifier in the bedroom to draw out even more moisture.

*See also:*
• WATER BEDS

**Working on the assumption** that prevention is better than cure, invest in a mattress protector. It will prevent the build-up of perspiration and will also help to prevent staining of the actual mattress. Remember to launder the mattress protector regularly.

## MEDICINE CABINETS

**FAMILY SAFETY IS** THE WATCHWORD WHEN IT COMES TO KEEPING YOUR MEDICINE CABINET CLEAN. REVIEW THE CONTENTS OF YOUR MEDICINE CABINET ANNUALLY AND THROW OUT EXPIRED MEDICATIONS, LEFTOVER ANTIBIOTICS AND STERILE GAUZE IN BROKEN PACKAGING.

**Begin your review of medicines** by examining the expiry date on each bottle or packet and inspecting the contents for signs of deterioration. Ask at your local pharmacy about safe disposal—they will either take the medications from you, or tell you where you can safely dispose of them. Do not pour expired liquids down the drain or flush expired tablets down the toilet or put them in the garbage where they will end up as landfill. If you can't find an expiry date, it probably means the product was manufactured before expiry dates became mandatory. That means it's old enough to retire. At the very least, expired medications are ineffective. At worst, formulations that have degraded over time can create new problems when they're taken. So when in doubt, throw it out, and don't feel that you're being wasteful.

Developing an annual clean-out habit works best if it's tied to some other event, such as spring cleaning.

*See also:*
• MIRRORS

**Cleaning the medicine cabinet** itself is simple. Use a sponge and mixture of mild dishwashing liquid in warm water to clean the interior and shelves. Or remove the shelves and put them in the top rack of your dishwasher.

### EXPERT ADVICE

**KEEP MEDICINES HIGH AND DRY**

The bathroom is actually not the best place to store your medicines. Keep all medicines in a cool, dry place, since heat and humidity can affect their potency. Store them in a sealed container on a high shelf in a wardrobe, out of the sight and reach of children, rather than in bathroom medicine cabinets.

## MICROWAVE OVENS

**MICROWAVE OVENS HAVE** REVOLUTIONISED EVERYDAY COOKING, AND FAST PREPARATION ISN'T THEIR ONLY VIRTUE. COMPARED TO CONVENTIONAL OVENS, MICROWAVES ARE REMARKABLY EASY TO CLEAN.

Heating a container of lemon juice and water on *High* is a very effective way to rid a microwave of odours.

**To clean fresh food splatters** before they have had time to dry, simply wipe down the microwave's interior with a sponge or paper towel dipped in a mixture of dishwashing liquid and water. Follow with a clean water rinse. Use the same method for washing removable trays or turntables in the sink.

**To remove dried-on food,** heat a bowl of water inside the microwave before cleaning. Heat 2 cups of water for 3–5 minutes on high power. The resulting steam will soften the dried food. Then wipe down the interior with a sponge or soft cloth.

**To get rid of odours in your microwave,** wipe the interior with a solution made from 1 cup of warm water and 1 tablespoon of bicarbonate of soda. Rinse with warm water. Or combine 1 cup of water with ½ cup of lemon juice in a measuring cup or bowl and heat it on *High* for 3–5 minutes (see left). Let it stand in the microwave for 5–10 minutes before removing.

**To remove stains from the microwave's ceramic floor or turntable,** make a paste of bicarbonate of soda and water and apply it to the stain. Let it sit until the stain disappears, then wipe it off and rinse with a wet sponge or cloth.

**Clean the microwave door** with paper towels and glass cleaner.

## MILDEW

**MILDEW IS LIKE** AN INVASION—AN INTRUDER THAT CAN DESTROY FABRIC AND UPHOLSTERY, EAT THROUGH PLASTERBOARD, DISINTEGRATE WALLPAPER AND TRIGGER ALLERGIES. BUT WITH SOME SIMPLE TOOLS AND KNOW-HOW, YOU CAN DEFEND YOUR HOME AGAINST THIS COMMON MICRO-MENACE ATTACK.

**Mildew occurs whenever moisture combines with mould,** which is always present in the air. Mildew flourishes in damp, warm, dark places. Moisture can come from almost anywhere—dripping pipes, a leaky roof or simply high humidity. When conditions are right, mildew begins to grow within 24–48 hours and will continue unabated until you address the problem.

**To prevent mildew,** dry out water-damaged areas as soon as you notice them. By keeping your house clean, dry and well-ventilated you will prevent most mildew problems. Cleaning with soap and water will often take care of mildew stains, but actually killing mildew requires the power of bleach. Don't use straight bleach, though, as it's too powerful and can create toxic fumes.

**To remove mildew from the bathroom,** mix 1 part bleach with 11 parts water. Wear rubber gloves and use a sponge, cloth or soft-bristled brush to apply the solution. Rinse with a damp sponge and then wipe down the area with a squeegee. Turning on a vent fan before showering cuts down on moisture retention in the bathroom.

## Your clout with grout

To remove mildew from tile grout, pour 30 ml of bleach into a 1 litre spray bottle and fill it the rest of the way with water. Spray the tile walls, and the mildew will fade away. For severe cases of mildew, make the mixture stronger by adding a tad more bleach.

**To remove musty odours in below-ground rooms and basements**, which are prime mildew breeding areas, spray with a bleach solution (see 'Odours', on page 257). For a more serious problem, you can sprinkle chlorinated lime (also known as calcium hypochlorite and available from pool shops) over the floor. Let it soak up the odour for a day and then sweep or vacuum it up. If you use a vacuum, dispose of the bag afterwards. If you sweep with a broom, collect the residue in a dustpan and dispose of it in a rubbish bin. But take care—chlorine is corrosive and dangerous if inhaled, so always ensure adequate ventilation, and wear protective clothing.

**To remove mildew stains from fabric or upholstery,** take the item outside. Begin by knocking off the surface mildew with a stiff brush and then air out the piece in the sun. If spots remain, wash the item according to the manufacturer's instructions. Use hot water and laundry bleach if the fabric can tolerate it.

**To remove mildew from leather,** use a solution of alcohol and water. Combine 1 cup of methylated spirits with 1 cup of water. Dip a clean cloth in the solution, wring it out and wipe the affected area. Follow with a cloth dampened only with water and then dry the leather item in an airy place.

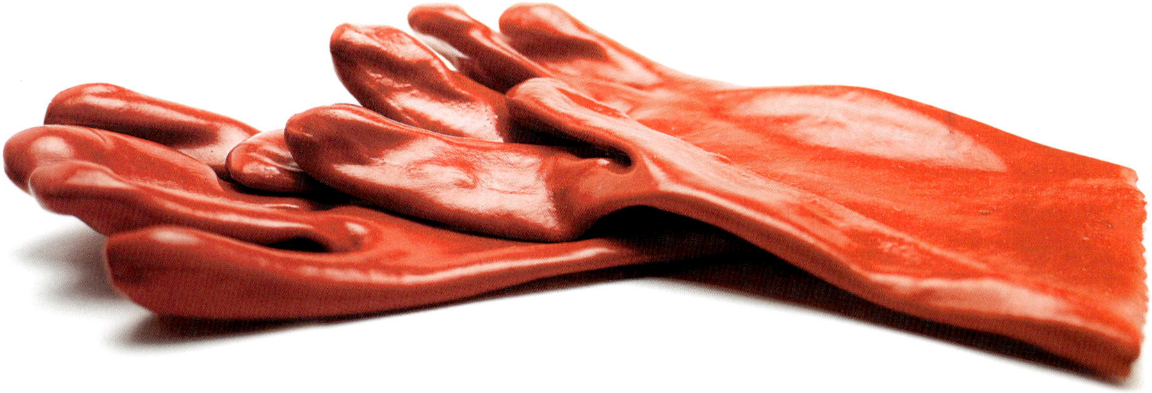

## MIRRORS

**THERE ARE MANY** LOW-COST CLEANING METHODS TO PRODUCE SPARKLING MIRRORS THAT REFLECT A STREAK-FREE IMAGE.

**To shine up a mirror with glass cleaner,** make sure you spray the glass cleaner on a lint-free cotton cloth or rag rather than directly on the mirror's surface. Not only do you use less cleaner, but you also prevent excess cleaner from running down the mirror's edges, where it can cause the mirror's silver backing to oxidise, turn black and brittle, and eventually flake.

**Once upon a time, our old newspapers** did an excellent job of cleaning glass. But this is no longer the case, as the composition of modern printer's ink has changed. You will get far better results by using methylated spirits, or equal amounts of vinegar and water, and a microfibre glass cloth. Rub the glass with either solution, then finish with a dry microfibre cloth to eliminate streaking.

A little glycerine will keep a bathroom mirror mist-free after cleaning.

**For an extra shine** after the mirror is dry, a good trick is to wipe it with a clean blackboard eraser.

**To remove any caked-on hair spray,** wipe it off with a little methylated spirits that has been dabbed on a soft cloth.

**To keep a mirror** from misting up in a steamy bathroom (which can be very annoying), wipe it over with a little glycerine, applied with a soft cloth.

**WATCH OUT** Never clean mirrors using abrasive or acidic cleaners. Mirrors are composed of reflective layers of tin, silver and copper, which are backed by a layer of paint. Abrasive cleaners can easily scratch the glass. And acidic solvents can damage and corrode the reflective layers.

# MOTORCYCLES AND MOTOR SCOOTERS

**MOTORCYCLE MANIA ISN'T** JUST FOR HARLEY-RIDING BAD BOYS ANY MORE. AND IF YOU HAVE ONE, A GLEAMING BIKE IS THE WAY TO GO. IF WATER USAGE RESTRICTIONS IN YOUR AREA PERMIT IT, USE YOUR HOSE. TRY TO WASH YOUR BIKE ON A GRASSED AREA IN THE SHADE AND NOT IN THE IMMEDIATE VICINITY OF A STORMWATER DRAIN. AND IF WATER IS LIMITED, YOU'LL GET PERFECTLY GOOD RESULTS WITH A BUCKET AND WATERING CAN.

**To keep water out of cables and controls,** cover the handlebars with plastic before washing the bike. The plastic sleeves that newspapers are delivered in cover handlebars well. Put a piece of plastic tape over the ignition keyhole, too, to keep water out of the lock.

**Before washing, spray the bike with a garden hose.** If the bike is badly caked with mud and road grease, you might want to use high-pressure water. But take care to not let the pressurised water hit the instruments, ignition keyhole, carburettor or brakes. They could be damaged if water were to get inside. Motorcycle shops sell a variety of wash sprays that remove oil and road grime. Use such a spray on the engine and wheels, wipe with a clean cloth and immediately rinse.

**Next, wash the bike's painted areas.** You'll find that car wash solutions work well, and a terry towelling cotton mitt will allow you to get into tight spots without cutting your fingers. Don't use laundry or dishwashing detergents—they're much too harsh and can take off the wax and leave streaks. Rinse the bike well with fresh hose water before any solution-coated areas have time to dry.

**WATCH OUT** When washing a motorcycle:

- Remove all rings and bracelets that could scratch the bike.
- Wait about an hour after riding before cleaning it. Never clean a hot engine, as the exhaust pipes can burn through skin if they haven't had time to cool.
- Always clean the bike on level ground; otherwise the side stand could slip and cause the bike to fall on you.

**Dry the bike to prevent water spots.** Cotton towels will work, but a synthetic chamois is best because it sheds less. It's a good idea to ride the bike within an hour of washing it, to get rid of any water drops that have collected in the engine, handlebars and controls. Taking your bike for a spin also completely dries the brakes, which can be damaged by corrosion if water builds up.

**When your bike's finish starts to look dull,** give the painted surfaces a coat of wax, which you apply with a dampened sponge. Cleaner waxes and polishes are fine for older bikes. But on newer bikes, use carnauba wax, a natural wax that doesn't contain cleaners. You need to be careful, as cleaners can literally take off the top layer of paint on a bike that is less than six months old.

## MUSICAL INSTRUMENTS

**A CLEAN INSTRUMENT** PRODUCES A CLEARER SOUND, AND PERIODIC CLEANING EXTENDS AN INSTRUMENT'S LIFE. YOU CAN REDUCE THE NEED FOR CLEAN-UP WITH A LITTLE PREVENTIVE MAINTENANCE: HABITS AS SIMPLE AS WASHING YOUR HANDS BEFORE PLAYING AND RETURNING THE INSTRUMENT TO ITS CASE WHENEVER IT'S NOT BEING USED GO A LONG WAY. HERE ARE SOME TIPS FOR KEEPING THE MOST COMMON MUSICAL INSTRUMENTS IN TOP SHAPE.

**Clean a brass instrument regularly after using it.** If you don't, the sound quality will gradually deteriorate. All that blowing pushes saliva down into the horn's bore, where it reacts with zinc in the metal to produce lime deposits. The gradual build up of lime will cause the bore of the horn to get smaller and smaller, which in time will affect the quality of the sound. To avoid this, you'll need to do routine maintenance after each use.

Empty water from the horn. Then open each water key and blow through the instrument. Work the valves at the same time so excess water will be blown out. Wipe the outside with a clean, soft cloth, paying special attention to the area your hands have touched. Use a mouthpiece brush to clean the rim of the mouthpiece. When clean, always store the instrument in its case, but make sure it's always completely dry before putting it away.

**Clean a brass instrument thoroughly every month or so,** depending on how frequently you play your instrument. The process takes about an hour. Start by taking the instrument apart. If the valve caps or slides are stuck, don't try to force them. Instead, forget the home cleaning and take the instrument to a repair person. (To find the name of a good repair person, consult your music shop or ask an instructor who plays your instrument.)

But if you're able to disassemble the instrument easily, put the valves, caps and slides aside, and keeping the valves in their proper order. (Each valve is numbered, with number 1 corresponding to your index finger.) Fill a sink or bathtub—depending on whether you're cleaning a trumpet or a tuba—with lukewarm water (hot water can damage the finish) mixed with a squirt of dishwashing liquid. Submerge the body of the instrument and the slides and swish the water around. If you have a cleaning snake, run it through each part.

EXPERT ADVICE

**OF TEMPERATURE AND TEMPO**

Extreme temperature shifts in a short time pose a hazard to drum shells and their finishes. As temperature and humidity change, the changing moisture content can cause the shells to expand, contract, warp or even crack. Drums are safest when stored in a temperate climate—the same kind that feels comfortable to you.

Rinse all the pieces in clean, warm water and dry them with a cotton towel. Place the parts on a clean, dry towel so the insides can dry. Clean the valves and caps by rinsing them with warm water, being careful not to get the felt at the top of each valve wet. Wipe them dry and let them air with the other parts.

When all the parts are dry, lightly lubricate each slide with slide grease and reinsert it. Use valve oil to lubricate the valves and then re-install them and the valve caps in their proper order.

**To clean your drums,** use a soft, damp cloth to remove any dust that has collected. Wipe off the head and outside of the drum.

You'll need to do a thorough cleaning of your drums once a year. Remove the heads and hardware. Mix 1 teaspoon of mild dishwashing liquid in a couple of cups of water. Dampen a soft cloth in the solution and wipe down the drums, heads and hardware—taking special care to keep the springs from getting wet. The tension rods may need additional attention. If they're black and coated with old grease and grime, give them a quick bath using grease-cutting dishwashing liquid. Use old rags to wash and dry the rods, because the stains left behind on the cloth are tough to remove. Rinse by wiping all the drum parts with a cloth dampened only with water. Then dry each piece individually with a clean cloth.

**As for cymbals,** it's best to simply dust them with a dry cloth and leave more rigorous cleaning to the pros. Cymbals are usually coated with a lacquer designed to prevent tarnishing. Cleaning solvents can eat through the coating.

**Clean a stringed instrument** after each time you play. Wipe the fingerboard and strings with a clean, dry cloth or chamois.

Every month or so, clean the instrument's body, which will increase the life span of the finish. Use a soft cloth dampened with a suitable cleaner—which will vary depending on whether you're cleaning a guitar, violin or cello—and apply evenly, following the grain of the wood. It's very important not to flood the instrument or allow cleaner to soak into seams or peg holes. After a good rub-down, go over it again with a dry cloth.

When you replace strings, clean the fret board. Usually, the built-up gunk—perspiration from fingers or rosin from a bow—can be removed with a soft cloth (see left). If necessary, give it a light brushing using steel wool (000 or 0000).

The metal tuning mechanisms will corrode over time and should be polished when they start looking dirty. But first consult with the repair department in a music shop for product

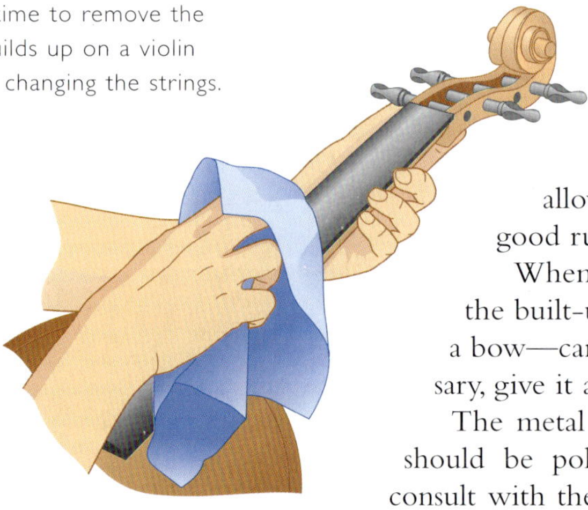

An ideal time to remove the gunk that builds up on a violin fret is when changing the strings.

recommendations. As a preventive measure, you can occasionally lubricate the gears on the tuning keys with a little penetrating lubricant such as WD-40.

Older or more valuable instruments should be professionally cleaned once a year, since the varnishes are tricky and can be ruined by inexperienced hands.

**Maintaining a woodwind instrument is important,** although a thorough cleaning should be left to a professional, as an amateur could damage it. For serious players, have your instrument cleaned professionally every year. Every other year will suffice for casual players.

For regular maintenance, take these steps every time you play:

- Remove the reed (unless you have a flute or piccolo, of course), which will warp if left on the instrument. Dry the reed with a soft cloth and return it to its reed case.
- Swab inside each section of the instrument with a cotton handkerchief after each use. For flutes, you'll need to buy a cleaning rod, which is available from music shops (or you may still have the one that came with the instrument when it was new). To use a cleaning rod, thread a corner of a cotton cloth through the eye of the rod, wrap the cloth around the rod and insert it in the flute body, rotating it to soak up moisture. Then withdraw the rod.
- Take special care with the pads that cover the tone holes on a flute and other woodwind instruments. They're usually made of a felt covered with a very thin, treated animal skin. When wet, they're easily torn. You can maintain the life of the pads by drying them after each use. Fold a clean, absorbent paper towel, place it between the keys and the body, close the keys, and let the paper absorb the moisture. Don't pull the paper towel out while the key is closed, as this can tear the skin. Instead, open the key and remove the paper.
- Wipe the body of the instrument with a soft, clean cloth to remove all fingerprint impressions.
- Clean the mouthpiece weekly, either with a mouthpiece brush or, particularly on larger instruments, by pulling a handkerchief through the mouthpiece.
- Every month or so, take an artist's sable brush and brush out any dirt that's built up in the ribs (the body of the instrument where the keys are attached). You want to prevent dirt and grease from getting into the pads and mechanisms. Stay away from polishes, which can remove the top layer of metal on an instrument.
- Always make sure a woodwind instrument is completely dry before putting it back in its case.

solutions

### Face the music

Guitar strings are easy to clean with pre-moistened face wipes. The pads contain alcohol, which helps with the cleaning, and they're just the right size to wrap around the string and slide up and down.

*See also:*
• PIANOS

# NEEDLEWORK

CLEANING NEEDLEWORK ISN'T AS SIMPLE AS IT MAY SOUND. TECHNIQUES VARY ACCORDING TO THE AGE OF THE PIECE AND THE FABRIC ON WHICH IT'S EMBROIDERED. IF YOU ARE UNSURE OF AN ITEM'S AGE OR FABRIC, CONSULT A PRO WITH PROVEN EXPERIENCE, PARTICULARLY IF IT IS A FAMILY HEIRLOOM THAT HAS SENTIMENTAL VALUE.

**WATCH OUT** Dry-cleaning isn't the best choice for cleaning needlework, as dry-cleaning fluids contain chemicals that could damage the piece. This is especially true if you're unsure of the type of fabric you're cleaning. In addition, the steam machines used by drycleaners will take the sizing out of the piece, making it extremely difficult for you to block again. When in doubt, or when dealing with an antique piece, ask for advice from your local needlework shop or from a textile conservator at a museum.

**To clean needlework less than 15 years old** that's embroidered on cotton or wool, follow these steps:

- Use care in taking the item apart, whether it's cross-stitch in a frame or needlepoint on a pillow. Zigzag any cut edges that might unravel, on a sewing machine, before cleaning. Measure the piece so you'll be able to return it to its original size.
- Fill a clean sink with slightly warm water and a squirt of gentle wool wash, such as Softly. (If you're unsure whether the threads are colour-fast, use cold water. Red threads, in particular, are notorious for running colour when warm water is used.) If the piece seems fragile, you can also use the pH-neutral Orvus WA Paste favoured by textile conservators. Distributed by Zetta Florence (www.zettaflorence.com), the paste is available from museums and fine art suppliers.
- Gently work the soapy water through the fabric, squeezing and agitating the piece. For stains, use a spot remover made for cotton or wool, or alternatively pre-soak the piece for at least 30 minutes in the soap and water solution.
- Rinse the item several times in clear, cold water, making sure you get all the soap out so that it doesn't turn the whites yellow.
- After you've thoroughly rinsed the piece, place it on a cotton towel, roll up the towel to remove excess water and unroll.
- Using a blocking board, pin the piece face down at its original measurements (see below) so that it will return to square as it dries. (Check your work with a T-square.) Blocking boards are scarce, but you can make your own by using a cork board or the kind of foam core board used for matting artwork. Cover it with muslin, and secure the muslin with staples.

Treat your needlework with care. After a gentle wash, pin it face down onto a blocking board so it will dry to its original shape.

# ODOURS

**SOME ODOURS, LIKE** AMMONIA, CAN CAUSE PHYSICAL PAIN. BUT THE MAJORITY OF SMELLS, SUCH AS PET URINE, REFRIGERATOR ODOURS AND THE LINGERING STENCH OF COOKED FISH, SIMPLY CAUSE MENTAL ANGUISH, WHICH IN SOME WAYS IS WORSE. BUT TRYING TO REMOVE ODOURS CAN BE DIFFICULT, AS YOU'RE TRYING TO CLEAN SOMETHING YOU CAN'T SEE. MASKING THE SMELL WITH AIR FRESHENERS AND OTHER PERFUMES IS ONLY A TEMPORARY SOLUTION. TO TRULY QUELL A SMELL, YOU MUST REMOVE WHAT CAUSES THE SMELL—AND DO IT PROMPTLY AND COMPLETELY.

An open box of bicarbonate of soda in the fridge will absorb odours.

**If you have a culinary disaster in the oven** and the kitchen fills with smoke, exchange the sooty, smelly air with fresh air. Turn off the oven. If the stove has an exhaust fan, turn it on *High*. Open windows to create cross-ventilation. (Windows on opposite sides of the room are ideal.) If possible, close doors leading to other parts of the house to confine the smoke to one room.

**To remove lingering cooking smells in your kitchen,** be they from culinary catastrophes or masterpieces, use a clean sponge or cloth to wipe down kitchen surfaces (other than those that come into contact with your food) with a grease-cutting, all-purpose spray cleaner. As you're trying to remove the particles and grease carried by smoke, steam and splatter, clean the walls and other surfaces that are close to the stove. And because heat rises and is drawn to cool areas, you need to wipe down windows and window trim, light fixtures and upper cabinets. You will also need to wash kitchen curtains and exposed tea towels in your washing machine.

**Reduce rubbish bin smells** by regularly cleaning your rubbish bin. Take it outside and hose it out, if weather permits. Scrub the inside with a nylon-bristled brush and a solution of water and bleach (125–250 millilitres of bleach per 4 litres of warm water) plus a couple of squirts of dishwashing liquid. Air-dry completely. Once the bin is dry, sprinkle borax in the bottom of it to prevent the growth of odour-causing moulds and bacteria. A wipe-over with eucalyptus or tea-tree oil also helps to keep it smelling fresh.

**To cut down on refrigerator odours,** maintain a constant vigil against spoiled foods. Periodically remove from your fridge old luncheon meats, rotting vegies, sour milk and mouldy leftovers. Wipe the inside surfaces with a sponge and plain water. A few drops of vanilla essence in the water also adds a sweet, fresh smell. Be sure to clean the rubber gasket that seals the door, because it's likely to hold odours. Once clean, keep an open box of bicarbonate of soda on a shelf (and have another in the freezer) to absorb odours (see left). Replace the boxes several times a year.

**To absorb stronger refrigerator odours,** spread several grams of fine, activated charcoal, available from shops that sell aquarium supplies, in a shallow pan and put the pan on a refrigerator or freezer shelf. (The pan of charcoal will not harm food.) After about 8 hours, put the pan in a 180 °C oven for 20 minutes to reactivate the charcoal. By reactivating the charcoal, you can reuse it many times. Put the charcoal back into the fridge until the smell is gone. At a pinch, clay-type kitty litter can be used in a pan to absorb smells. (No need to put it in the oven.) Ground coffee (unused) will do the same.

**To remove musty smells in your downstairs rooms** or other parts of the house, first ventilate. The musty smell comes from mould and mildew, which thrive in dank, dark environments where the air is stale. Open windows and doors, use fans to circulate the air and run a dehumidifier to reduce the air's humidity. Then proceed to kill the odour-producing growth, using one of these methods:

- Mix up a solution of 30–60 millilitres of bleach per 1 litre of water. Pour it into a spray bottle. Spray any surfaces that won't be harmed by the bleach, such as concrete-block walls and concrete floors. (Test any coloured materials first by applying the solution to an inconspicuous corner.) Scrub with a nylon-bristled brush.
- Sprinkle chlorinated lime (calcium hypochlorite) on the concrete floor. (See 'Mildew', on page 250.)
- Wash any washable fabrics that may have mildew growing on them in the washing machine.

**To remove pet accident odours,** quickly remove the urine or poo using newspapers, paper towels or a heavy-duty vacuum cleaner. For a full discussion, see 'Pet clean-up', on page 270.

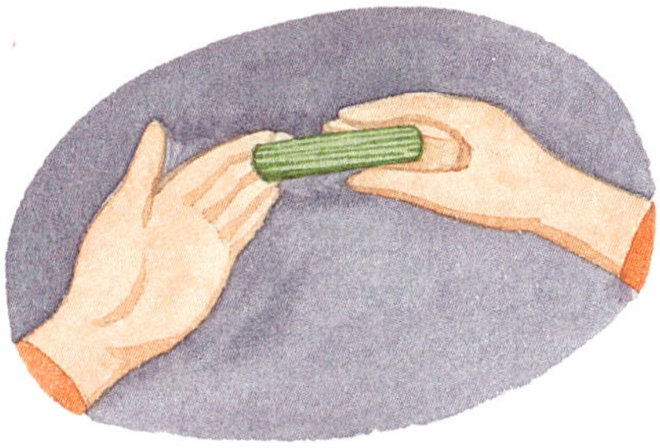

Simple solutions

### Three odour-conquering strategies

- A quick fix for cutting cooking odours is to boil ¼ cup of vinegar per 1 litre of water. The rising heat will carry the odour-neutralising vinegar particles to the same surfaces on which the smoke and grease landed.
- To reduce an onion smell on your hands, rub them before and after you cut onions with the sliced end of a celery stalk (see left). Vinegar rubbed on your hands before or after cutting onions has the same neutralising effect.
- A short-term solution to a smelly below ground-level room is to cut an onion in half and leave it on a plate in the room. The onion absorbs musty odours. This also works for a freshly painted room.

## OUTDOOR FURNITURE

**USE THE HOSE** TO CLEAN OUTDOOR FURNITURE THAT IS MADE OF ALUMINIUM, PAINTED METAL, VINYL OR PLASTIC. CLEANING ONCE IN THE SPRING AND ONCE IN THE AUTUMN SHOULD BE ENOUGH.

**Pick a warm day,** and dress appropriately. Begin by brushing off any large matter, such as leaves, sticks and bird droppings. You can put on a glove and use your hand or use a nylon-bristled brush. Doing this while the furniture is dry is easier and leaves less chance for staining. Now you can use the hose.

**To remove dirt, pollen, tree sap and other grime,** use a hose to spray down your outdoor furniture and then scrub it with a nylon-bristled brush dipped in a bucket of warm water with a squirt or three of dishwashing liquid. Use an old toothbrush for cleaning out small crevices. Rinse by spraying with the hose.

**WATCH OUT** To avoid stripping away the protective coatings often found on vinyl and other materials used in outdoor furniture, don't scrub with abrasive brushes or pads. And also don't clean with bleach, bleach-based cleaning products or solvents.

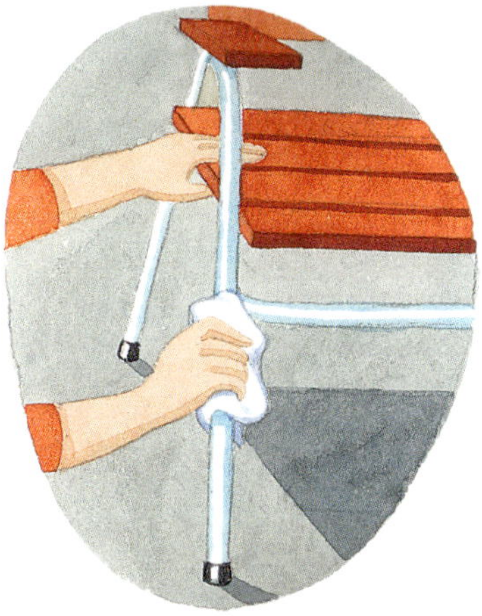

Protect outdoor furniture frames with a coat or two of car wax.

**What about mildew?** Mildew grows only on organic material, which means that if you have mildew-covered vinyl seat cushions, the mildew has probably sprouted on pollen and other organic droppings that have accumulated. It also means that you don't need to use bleach to kill it. Just scrub off the organic matter, and the mildew will be gone too. However, if mildew is a recurring problem, your hardware shop will sell you a cleaner that is specifically made for outdoor furniture, such as PFC (Patio Furniture Cleaner) This cleaner not only inhibits mildew but also cleans and protects a variety of materials, such as plastics, resin, vinyl, PVC, canvas, wrought iron, wicker and rattan, from fading and discolouration.

**To protect your patio furniture's frames,** polish them with a car wax. Following the manufacturer's instructions, lightly wax the frames' arms, legs and other exposed areas (see left). Two thin coats are better than one thick coat. Use it on painted metal, aluminium and plastic. Car wax gives the furniture a nice shine and protects it from rain, dust, tree droppings and other harmful substances. Be careful, however, not to get the wax on the vinyl. It can stain vinyl and get gunked in the vinyl mesh that commonly covers patio seat cushions. And since vinyl, like leather, needs to breathe to stay pliant and strong, the wax is bad for it because it clogs its pores.

**To restore aluminium furniture's shine,** wipe it down with a cloth soaked in a one-to-one solution of vinegar and water. Aluminium does not rust, but it can tarnish when exposed to airborne pollutants. The vinegar solution helps, as does coating the frame with car wax. Don't clean aluminium with alkaline cleaners, such as ammonia, bicarbonate of soda or sugar soap, which will discolour it.

**Wooden outdoor furniture requires slightly different care.** This furniture is usually made of teak, western red cedar or other hardwood and although it is designed to withstand the weather, a little care and cleaning will keep it looking good for much longer. Grey or mildewed hardwood tables, chairs, benches and barbecue trolleys can be restored to their former natural wood colour by scrubbing with a deck cleaner, such as Dekswood or Cabot's Deck Clean. Once completely dry, the clean timber should be protected with a wood oil, such as Cabot's Garden Furniture Oil. This should be applied annually, to protect and preserve the wood's natural finish.

Renew the colour of outdoor wooden furniture with deck cleaner.

★★★ EXPERT ADVICE

**THE VINYL COLOUR CODE**

Some vinyl colours stain more easily than others. When they took the lead out of vinyl, browns and beiges began to stain worse. Other easy stainers are peach, rose, red, burgundy, orange and mauve. Yellows, greens, blues and whites don't stain as easily.

**Canvas director's chairs** can be kept in good condition by treating spills and stains as soon as possible. Scrub dirt with a nylon brush dipped in soapy water and rinse. Treat stubborn stains with a paste of bicarbonate of soda (or with PFC [Patio Furniture Cleaner]), leave for 5 minutes, then rinse off. Allow the canvas to dry thoroughly in the sun before folding the chair for storage.

*See also:* • UMBRELLAS

## OVENS

**OVEN SPATTERS AND** SPILLS ARE A REAL CLEANING CHALLENGE. FIRST, THERE'S THE GREASE. EVEN WORSE, THOUGH, ARE THE MELTED CHEESES, THE OVER-FLOWING CASSEROLE'S JUICES AND OTHER FOODS THAT GET FIRED TO THE HARDNESS OF POTTERY GLAZE ON AN OVEN'S WALLS AND BASE.

Simple solutions

**Oven grease guard**

No matter what kind of oven you have, you can easily retard grease build-up by periodically wiping the interior of the oven with a cloth soaked in vinegar.

**Proper cleaning improves your oven's efficiency,** extends its life and, most importantly, reduces the risk of fire. Cleaning an oven properly doesn't involve jackhammers or hours of backbreaking scrubbing. Even if you have a self-cleaning or continuous-cleaning oven, neither of which is entirely self-sufficient, some of the tips that follow will help you to get rid of those messy oven deposits.

**Wipe the exterior surfaces of your oven** to remove food spills every time you wipe down your benchtops. All you need is a moist sponge. Make it a habit, and you'll save time in the end, because even the exterior surfaces get warm enough to bake food on fast. Besides, this is the part of your oven people do see.

**To clean the interior,** start by removing all oven racks and grill pans. Wash them by hand in a sink, regardless of the type of oven you have. Use a solution of warm water and dishwashing liquid. Scrub with a nylon-bristled brush or other gentle, non-metal scrubber. Anything abrasive, such as steel wool, will scratch the metal's finish, which can lead to rusting and will make food stick even more the next time.

**To loosen baked-on deposits in a conventional oven,** fill a glass bowl with ½ cup of full-strength ammonia. After making sure the oven has cooled, put the bowl of ammonia in the oven, close the door and let it stand overnight. The fumes will release the bond between the crusty food and the oven interior. The next day, open the door and let the fumes dissipate. Then remove the bowl and wipe away the loosened food with a cloth or sponge.

**To remove stubborn food** that did not come off completely after the ammonia treatment in your conventional oven, try scouring with a non-abrasive scrubber dipped in a solution of warm water and dishwashing liquid. As with the racks and grill pans, avoid scratching the

Plastic spatulas and ice scrapers make handy, non-scratch oven tools.

oven's finish. On a flat surface, such as the door glass or the oven bottom, try scraping with a plastic ice scraper—the kind you use on your car windscreen (see left).

**As a last-ditch effort when cleaning a conventional oven,** try a commercial oven cleaner. Follow the instructions carefully and wear protective rubber gloves when applying. These products are strong and harmful to humans. Never spray a commercial oven cleaner on a hot oven, electric elements or oven lights. Heat can make the cleaner even more caustic.

**Help your self-cleaning oven** by doing a little prep work. Self-cleaning simply means disintegrating food spills with temperatures as high as 480 °C. However, the high heat doesn't reach all parts of the oven, and in areas such as the frame around the oven opening and the edge of the door outside the gasket, the self-cleaning cycle can actually bake food on even more. So clean those parts first with a non-abrasive scrubber dipped in a soapy solution of hot water and dishwashing liquid. Rinse well using a sponge and a bucket of clean water.

Once the self-cleaning cycle is complete and the oven has cooled down, wipe out the ashy residue with a damp sponge.

**Give your continuous-cleaning oven** that human touch. The interior of this type of oven is coated with a chemical mixture that lowers the temperature at which heat will dissolve foods. So whenever you bake or roast at a temperature above 180 °C, you're disintegrating food that has splattered on the walls or bottom. However, major spills, especially those involving sugar, can cancel out the effect. Therefore, clean up major spills as soon as possible. Occasionally wipe out the entire oven using a non-abrasive scrubbing pad and warm water. Then run the oven empty for an hour or two at 240 °C to disintegrate any grease or food that the oven's normal cooking and cleaning cycle didn't take care of. Never use abrasive cleaners or cleaning tools in a continuous-cleaning oven.

**WATCH OUT**

- Never use commercial oven cleaners in a self-cleaning oven. When heated to those high temperatures, the chemical residue in commercial cleaners grows dangerously caustic.
- Never use commercial oven cleaners, cleaning powders or metal scrubbers to clean a continuous-cleaning oven. These products may ruin the chemical mixture that allows the oven to clean itself.

## PAINTED SURFACES

**PAINT IS NOT** ONLY DECORATIVE—IT'S ALSO A PROTECTIVE COATING. BUT EVEN THOUGH PAINT IS MADE TO STAND UP TO CONSIDERABLE WEAR AND TEAR, YOU NEED TO TAKE CARE WHEN CLEANING IT. STRONG CHEMICAL CLEANERS OR TOO MUCH SCRUBBING TO REMOVE GREASY FINGERPRINTS CAN DULL THE PAINT'S FINISH IN SPOTS OR, WORSE, REMOVE IT ALTOGETHER. SINCE TOUCH-UP PAINTING, EVEN WITH A COLOUR MATCH, TENDS TO LOOK SPLOTCHY, CLEANING MISTAKES CAN LEAD TO COMPLETE REPAINTING.

**Dust painted surfaces regularly,** when possible, to keep dirt and grime from staining the surface when smeared or moistened. For painted furniture, shelves, door and window trim, or knick-knacks that are coated in a semi-gloss or glossy paint, use a clean dusting cloth, either dry or slightly dampened with water. Dusting—especially wet dusting—entire walls is not feasible, since many walls are covered with flat, water-based paint, which wet dusting could actually remove.

**To remove stubborn stains from semi-gloss or glossy paint,** first try wiping gently with a cloth dampened with a sudsy solution of warm water and dishwashing liquid. If that doesn't work, try an all-purpose cleaner, such as Handy Andy, but only after testing the cleaner on an inconspicuous corner of your painted surface first. Clean from the bottom up so that your cleaning solution won't drip down, pick up grime and leave dirty streaks.

Rinse with a clean, moist cloth or sponge. Dry well with clean towels to prevent water from damaging the paint or what's beneath it.

**To remove marks from surfaces,** such as walls, that are coated with flat paint, first try rubbing the area with a white vinyl pencil rubber, the kind you find at newsagents, for erasing pencil marks (see right). If that doesn't do the trick, try gently wiping the marks with a water-moistened cloth. Blot dry soon afterwards with a clean towel. But watch out, water can stain or even remove flat paint.

## PAINTING EQUIPMENT

**THE BEST PAINTERS** WILL TELL YOU THAT A GOOD CLEAN-UP AT THE END OF THE DAY IS ESSENTIAL. NOT ONLY DOES IT KEEP YOUR TOOLS IN TOP SHAPE, WHICH MEANS EASIER APPLICATION AND CLEANER LINES, BUT IT ALSO PROLONGS THE LIFE OF YOUR PAINT ROLLERS, TRAYS AND BRUSHES.

**Start by putting the excess paint** back into the paint container. Squeeze as much paint as you can from your brushes (wrap them in newspaper and press them between your hands as firmly as you can), empty your roller trays and also scrape paint off your rollers with the curved scraper on a five-in-one painter's tool, which is available from specialist paint and hardware shops. Then wipe off as much of the remaining paint as possible using something disposable, such as an old rag, newspaper or piece of cardboard. Let the rag or paper dry and then dispose of it in an outside garbage bin.

**Use a two-bucket system to keep things tidy.** Whether you're using water-based or oil-based paint, use two large buckets (plastic 18-litre buckets work well) to contain your mess: one for washing and one for rinsing. The system is economical (because you can re-use solvents), it's friendly to the environment (you reserve rather than throw out paint or used solvent), and it's neat.

solutions

### The painter's secret

To renew an old, stiff paintbrush, place it in hot vinegar (acetic acid) for about 15 minutes, wash the brush in dishwashing liquid and warm water, rinse, then air-dry.

**Use one bucket for washing.** If you're cleaning up after using water-based paint, mix warm water with a squirt of dishwashing liquid in the bucket. If you've been using oil-based paint, put a small amount of paint thinner or mineral turpentine into the bucket; 5–8 centimetres in the bottom should be enough. Immerse the brushes and use your fingers to gently work the paint out of them. Use a brush, comb or an old fork to clean between the bristles. To remove paint from the metal band on the handle, scrub gently with a wire brush. Use a roller spinner, available from most paint shops, to remove paint from the rollers, either spinning it in the wash bucket or, better yet, in a third, empty bucket. (The paint really flies.) Wash the roller pans over the washing bucket using a soft-bristled brush. Leave the dirty water or solvent in the bucket, cover the bucket with cardboard or newspaper to prevent evaporation, and let it stand.

**Use the second bucket for rinsing,** after you've removed the bulk of the paint from your brushes or rollers. For a water-based paint clean-up, use clean water; for an oil-based paint clean-up, use fresh thinner. When the water or solvent squeezed from the brushes or rollers comes out clear, you'll know you're finished. As with the wash bucket, cover the rinse bucket containing water or solvent with cardboard or newspaper and let it stand.

**Let the paint solids settle** to the bottom of the washing and rinsing buckets overnight. The next day, carefully pour the water off the top of the paint solids. Using a putty knife or paint stirrer, carefully scrape the paint off the bottom of the buckets onto newspaper and discard it according to the method determined by your local council. (Methods of disposal vary between councils, so ring first to make sure you do the right thing.) As for paint thinner or turpentine, you can reuse it. Carefully pour the relatively pure liquid on top back into its original container. (Never store solvents in plastic, because solvents will damage plastic containers.) Again, scrape the solids up and discard.

### The professional painter's clean-up: four easy steps

**1** Squeeze, pour and scrape excess paint from brushes, roller trays and paint rollers back into the paint tin. Wipe off what's left on an old rag, newspaper or a piece of cardboard and then dispose of it.

**2** Use an 18-litre bucket for washing. For water-based paint, use warm water with a squirt of dishwashing liquid. For oil-based paint, put 5–8 cm of paint thinner or mineral turpentine into the bucket. Leave the dirty water or solvent in the bucket, cover the bucket and let it stand.

**3** Use another 18-litre bucket for rinsing. Again, for water-based paint, use clean water to rinse equipment. For oil-based paint, use fresh paint thinner. As with the wash bucket, leave the water or solvent in the bucket and cover it.

**4** Allow the paint solids to settle on the bottom of the buckets overnight. The next day, pour the water off the top of the paint solids. Or pour the clean solvent off the top into the solvent's original container for re-use later on. Scrape the paint from the bottom of the buckets, using a putty knife or paint scraper, onto newspaper and discard.

**If you'll be using oil paint again the next day,** you don't need to thoroughly clean your brushes and rollers. Just give your oil brushes and rollers a cursory cleaning (squeeze and scrape off the excess paint), and then wrap them tightly in aluminium foil or plastic wrap (see left). This will keep them from drying out—and will save you the hassle of cleaning up twice. You can save the thorough, two-bucket clean-up routine for the end of the painting project.

For short stops during painting, or overnight, wrap your brush tightly in plastic wrap to prevent it drying out.

**If a water-based brush or roller just won't come clean,** it may be because many of today's water-based paints contain resins, similar to those used in oil-based paints, to improve adhesion, gloss and durability. After cleaning and rinsing the brush or roller in water, try a second rinse in paint thinner or mineral turpentine to completely clean it. Afterwards, wash with clean, soapy water to remove the thinner.

**Simple solutions**

### For supple bristles

To keep the bristles on a clean oil brush soft, rub a bit of petroleum jelly (Vaseline) into them. Before using the brush, rinse it in paint thinner or mineral turpentine. Never rinse out an oil brush in water, as it tends to make bristles become dry and brittle.

## PANELLING

**PANELLING COMES IN** TWO MAIN VARIETIES: REAL WOOD AND SIMULATED WOOD, ALSO KNOWN AS HARDBOARD. REAL WOOD PANELLING, MADE OF WALNUT, OAK, MAPLE OR OTHER WOODS, IS HARDLY DIFFERENT IN QUALITY FROM FINE WOODEN FURNITURE. IT IS USUALLY SEALED WITH EITHER VARNISH OR POLYURETHANE, OR IT CONTAINS A PENETRATING STAIN OR OIL FINISH. HARDBOARD IS MADE TO LOOK LIKE REAL WOOD, AND IT IS OFTEN COATED IN PLASTIC. THESE DIFFERENCES ARE CRUCIAL WHEN IT COMES TO CLEANING PANELLING.

**To remove dust from raised moulding,** carving or other features on either real wood or hardboard panelling, vacuum regularly using your vacuum cleaner's upholstery brush attachment, or wipe with a cloth. For hardboard, you can use a moistened dust cloth, but avoid using water on real wood, as moisture can cause damage.

**To clean real wood panelling with a surface coat,** such as polyurethane, you may have to use water, but begin by trying a spray-on furniture polish, such as Clean 'N Shine or Kiwi Marveer. These products remove dirt and dust while adding a hard wax finish. For heavier cleaning, try a cloth lightly dampened with a neutral cleaner, such as Howard Clean-A-Finish Wood Soap or Briwax Furniture Cleaner.

**To clean real wood panelling with a penetrating finish,** such as oil, use a cloth dampened with a mineral spirit, such as mineral turpentine, which is a type of solvent. Wipe gently back and forth in the direction of the wood grain. Mineral spirits will lift dirt and grime but they will also remove the oil finish from wood surfaces, so when you've finished cleaning, you may need to touch up—or reapply—the panelling's oil or stain finish.

**Clean simulated wood panelling** the same way you would a glossy painted surface. Its plastic coating, while not impermeable, means you can wipe it down with a cloth using a solution of warm water and a squirt of dishwashing liquid. If you need something stronger, try an all-purpose cleaner, but only after testing the cleaner on an inconspicuous corner. Clean from the bottom up, so your cleaning solution doesn't drip down, pick up grime or leave dirty streaks.

Rinse the hardboard panelling with a clean, moist cloth or sponge. Once the surface is clean, dry well with clean towels so that the water won't damage the glue in the compressed wood beneath the coating.

## PATIOS

**THE PROBLEM WITH** BEING OUTSIDE IS THAT PATIOS WIND UP BEING STAINED BY GREASE DRIPPINGS FROM THE BARBECUE, RUSTY METAL FURNITURE AND LEAF TANNINS. THE ADVANTAGE, THOUGH, IS THAT YOU CAN HAVE A GO AT THOSE STAINS WITH HEAVY-DUTY CLEANERS—AND, IF WORST COMES TO WORST, A HIGH-PRESSURE POWER WASHER.

**To reduce staining,** sweep the leaves and other debris off your patio regularly. Use an outdoor-quality millet broom or a push broom.

**Give your patio a more thorough cleaning** at least once a year using a solution of 9 litres of warm water and ½ cup of Tricleanium Ultra Concentrated Cleaner or CRC Hydroforce, available from hardware shops. Use a stiff-bristled brush (a long-handled one will be easier on your back and knees) to scrub the patio. Rinse with a hose. Use the Tricleanium solution to spot-clean grill grease, tannins and other stains. You can also use sugar soap, according to packet instructions, for this job.

**To deep-clean a really dirty stone, brick or concrete patio,** you can use a pressure washer. Take care not to etch your patio material or injure yourself. Never use pressure greater than recommended by the manufacturer; never use a pinpoint nozzle (instead, use a 15- or 25-degree fan nozzle, or better still, a covered powerhead to reduce overspray); and never hold the jet too close to the patio surface. If you rent a power washer, make sure you ask for detailed safety instructions.

A covered powerhead on a pressure washer helps to reduce overspray.

## PEARLS

**UNLIKE HARD, CRYSTALLINE** GEMSTONES, PEARLS ARE AS SENSITIVE AS THEY ARE BEAUTIFUL. PERFUME, COSMETICS AND HAIR SPRAY CAN STAIN THEM; THE ACIDS IN YOUR PERSPIRATION CAN EAT AWAY AT THEIR FINE COATING, CALLED THE NACRE; AND SINCE A PEARL'S VALUE IS LARGELY DETERMINED BY ITS COLOUR, LUSTRE AND THICKNESS OF NACRE, CLEANING IS ESSENTIAL FOR MAINTAINING VALUE.

**Wipe off your pearls after each wearing.** Use a barely damp, very soft cloth. (Chamois is best.) This removes harmful substances such as perspiration, perfume and make-up, that can penetrate the pearls' porous surface. As a preventive measure, always apply perfume, make-up and hair spray before you put on your pearls.

**Occasionally clean your pearls more thoroughly** to restore their natural finish and lustre. Use a mild bar soap, such as Sunlight or Preservene, and lukewarm water to create light suds. Dip a soft cloth into the suds and gently wipe the pearls. Rinse with clean water and then dry with another soft cloth. Never soak your pearls because that will get the string too wet and weaken it.

**When drying pearls,** here are some things to keep in mind:

- To make sure the pearls and string are dry, lay them on a slightly damp cloth. When the cloth is dry, the pearls will be too.
- If you wear pearls when their string is wet, the string might stretch and attract hard-to-remove dirt.
- Never hang pearls to dry, since that might also stretch the string.

**To remove stubborn lumps of dirt,** use your fingernail, which has a hardness of 2.5 or less on the Mohs' scale (a scale of mineral hardness on which 1 represents the hardness of talc and 10 represents diamond). Pearls have a hardness of 2.5 to 4.5, which means your fingernail probably won't scratch them, but proceed with caution anyway. Just keep in mind that, as mentioned earlier, pearls are quite sensitive, so treat them accordingly and they'll look good for years.

**WATCH OUT** Pearls can be harmed by many common cleaning substances and methods, including ammonia, commercial jewellery cleaners with ammonia, ultrasonic cleaners, steam cleaners, detergents, bleaches, powdered cleansers, bicarbonate of soda, vinegar, lemon juice and most dishwashing liquids.

## PENCIL MARKS

**IF YOU HAVE** CHILDREN, IT IS INEVITABLE THAT PENCIL MARKS WILL FIND THEIR WAY ONTO CLOTHES AND POSSIBLY YOUR WALLS, TOO. PENCIL MARKS ARE TRICKY TO CLEAN, BUT THEY'RE NOT AS DIFFICULT AS SOME INKS.

**If it's pencil,** reach for a pencil rubber. Try removing pencil from walls and fabric using a soft pencil rubber, preferably a white vinyl one (available from newsagents) that will not leave marks of its own.

**To remove pencil marks from washable fabrics** (if the vinyl pencil rubber does not work), put a few drops of ammonia on the mark, then rinse with water. Put a little bit of laundry detergent on the stain, then rinse. Repeat until the stain is gone.

**To remove pencil marks from walls** (again, if the pencil rubber didn't work), try rubbing the stain with a slice of fresh rye bread.

## PERSPEX

**WHEN IT COMES** TO CLEANING SHEET PLASTIC OR PERSPEX, SOMETIMES KNOWN BY THE BRAND NAME PLEXIGLAS, BE CAREFUL: DON'T USE COMMERCIAL WINDOW CLEANERS. IT MAY SEEM LOGICAL TO REACH FOR THE WINDEX, BUT MOST WINDOW CLEANERS CONTAIN AMMONIA, WHICH WILL EAT INTO ACRYLIC. SO WHETHER YOU'RE CLEANING PERSPEX STORM WINDOWS, WINDSHIELDS, FURNITURE OR SERVIETTE HOLDERS, FOLLOW OUR ADVICE.

**To clean acrylic plastic,** use a solution of dishwashing liquid and lukewarm water and apply it with a soft cloth. Avoid dry dusting, which can grind dirt into the acrylic's surface. If the surface is extremely dirty, let the soapy solution loosen the dirt and then rub gently with the cloth, turning it and rinsing it often. Remove oil or tar by dabbing with kerosene and then washing immediately with the soapy solution. Don't use solvents (such as acetone, petrol or thinners) or scouring powders on sheet plastic. If the mild soap solution isn't enough and you need a plastic cleaner or polish, check out the autocare section of your hardware shop, or a specialist automotive shop.

## PESTS

**REMOVING PESTS IS** NOT AS SIMPLE AS BLASTING THEM WITH SOME PESTICIDE. FOR ONE THING, THE CHEMICALS MAY HAVE HARMFUL SIDE EFFECTS FOR HUMANS. ALSO, THIS SINGLE-MINDED APPROACH DOES NOT NECESSARILY WORK. TO GET RID OF PESTS, YOU NEED A PLAN THAT INCLUDES KILLING AND PREVENTION—REMOVING PESTS AND BLOCKING THEIR ENTRY.

**For general pest prevention,** it's a good idea to tighten up the house. Fill gaps in below-ground floors and walls with caulk (gap filler) and grout. Make sure skirting board moulding forms a tight fit between the wall and floor. (If you have gaps, fill them with a paintable gap filler—check hardware shops for the most appropriate product—or cover with quarter-round trim.) Inspect things like boxes and firewood for hitchhikers—cockroaches, ants and spiders, for instance—before bringing them into your house. Cockroaches, for one, will eat nearly anything that is organic, including cardboard.

Next, cut off the pests' food and water supplies. Use gap fillers and sealants around sinks and tubs to stop water from leaking behind fixtures. Repair leaky pipes, and don't let water stand in appliance drip pans (such as a coffee machine drip tray) or house-plant dishes. Keep food in tightly sealed containers. Wipe down benchtops. Remove food that spills on the sides of and behind the stove.

Also attack pest breeding and living areas by filling holes in walls and floors, removing piles of cardboard and paper bags inside or around the house, and eliminating general clutter.

**When ants decide to move indoors,** they can drive you mad with their persistence. Sealing up their entry point is the first approach. If this is impossible, try creating a barrier: they won't walk over a thick smear of petroleum jelly (Vaseline) or a line of salt, borax, chilli powder or even talcum powder. If they find a way through

Powdered borax is effective in killing cockroaches, but sprinkle it out of reach of pets and small children.

Simple solutions

### A deadly pool for fleas

If you think you have fleas but aren't sure, turn on a gooseneck or folding-arm lamp about 15 cm above a shallow dish of water containing a squirt of dishwashing liquid. If you do have a flea infestation, at night they will spring up for the light and then drop down into the soapy water and drown.

your defences, a quick spray with a mixture of water and dishwashing liquid should do the trick nicely.

**As a last resort,** you can bait them using a mixture of equal parts borax (powdered boric acid, available from supermarkets and hardware shops) and icing sugar, but don't let animals or children near this mixture, as borax is poisonous if ingested.

**Rid your home of cockroaches.** Kill existing cockroaches with borax, available from supermarkets and hardware shops. Wearing gloves and a dust mask, sprinkle it along skirtings (see left), behind kitchen cupboards and appliances, and in below-ground rooms, garages, bathrooms and anywhere else they might live.

**You can also use the ant deterrents,** described at the bottom of page 267, but place borax and chilli powder in out-of-the-way places. They will kill cockroaches but again, remember they will also be attractive to pets and small children, so don't use them if traps are likely to be investigated. A less toxic solution is to place a bit of stale beer or wine in the bottom of a greasy margarine container. Cockroaches are attracted to the liquid, crawl into the container and are then unable to get out, and drown. Remember to empty the trap daily.

**To keep your home flea-free,** here are some tips for controlling fleas (besides the light set-up suggested in the 'Simple solutions' box at left, which makes a decent trap). Even though your pet probably attracted the fleas, it's vital to keep your home clean, because 90 per cent of a flea's life cycle is spent off the pet and in the bedding or rugs in its egg, larva and pupa stages. Designate a pet sleeping area, such as a tiled laundry, that is easy to clean, and clean it regularly—more often than the rest of the house if necessary. Cover your pet's bed with a washable blanket. Then all you have to wash is the blanket, not the bed. When you pick the blanket up, carefully lift all four corners, so flea eggs won't roll off. Wipe the pet's basket or bed frame with a bit of pennyroyal oil before replacing the laundered bedding (which can also be lightly sprayed with a pennyroyal solution—see 'Dog kennels', on page 154.) If you have fleas, vacuum rugs and upholstered furniture, then seal the flea-contaminated vacuum bags in plastic bags and discard them immediately. Steam cleaning carpets is even more effective.

**To kill adult fleas and their eggs,** bathe pets with a pyrethrin flea shampoo. (Take care, as pyrethrin is toxic for some cats, so checking with your vet first is a good idea.) If fleas present a continual problem for your pet, talk to your vet—a combined approach using both topical and oral treatments is often needed to reduce flea infestation and keep recurrence under control. For serious flea infestation in your

home, you may need to treat infected areas with an insect growth regulator (IGR), such as methoprene, which is found in so-called 'flea bombs'. IGRs have not been found to be harmful to pets and humans, although flea bombs contain other pesticides which can be toxic, so use them strictly according to the manufacturer's instructions.

**Like death and taxes,** it seems that flies are always with us. Basically, in summer, you need to screen doors and windows to keep them out of the house. You can also grow a pot of mint or basil on a kitchen windowsill or at the back door, as it seems to deter them. Wiping door and window frames with pennyroyal, eucalyptus or lavender oil has the same effect.

Add a basic paper funnel to a jar of yeast-sprinkled bananas for a cheap and simple fruit-fly trap that works.

**Keep the things that attract flies to a minimum.** That means don't leave uncovered food out of the fridge, or dirty plates by the sink. Keep your garbage and compost bins tightly lidded, remove your kitchen garbage daily, and remove any dog poo from your courtyard or garden in a plastic bag, then dispose of it in an outside garbage bin.

**Trap fruit flies.** Fruit flies are still a major annoyance, hovering over benchtop fruit bowls like vultures over fresh road kill, eating away and spoiling your beautiful summer stone fruit. Before you waste any more energy trying to swat them away, try this trick: put banana slices in a glass jar and sprinkle them with yeast (see left). Make a paper funnel and slip it into the top of the jar. When the jar fills up with flies—along with their larvae—fill it with very hot tap water and slap the lid on it to kill both. Empty and then insert a new funnel and fresh bait.

**Mosquitoes can make life miserable,** not to mention downright dangerous if you live in an area infected by Murray Valley encephalitis, Ross River fever or even malaria—all mosquito-borne diseases.

**Stop mosquitoes from breeding near your home** by eliminating any source of stagnant water from around the house. This could be anything in which the smallest amount of water can collect—the base of flowerpots, a neglected watering can, the dog's water bowl, a flat spot on the roof, clogged guttering or an ornamental pond.

**Screen your doors and windows** and sleep under mosquito nets. When you're outside, the least toxic repellents are good old mozzie coils and citronella. You may also want to consider using a personal repellent, such as Rid or Aerogard, to keep the mosquitoes off.

**Eliminate clothing moths.** Thoroughly clean clothes before storing them in cupboards or drawers. These moths are attracted to the food, perspiration and urine on soiled fabrics rather than to the wool

or cotton itself. Once clean, seasonal clothes (except leather, which needs to breathe) should be stored in airtight bags or plastic containers. Commercial moth repellents usually contain paradichlorobenzene or naphthalene, which are harmful to humans, according to the Australian Environmental Protection Agency. Instead of using toxic chemicals, kill and deter moths with essential oils—cedar, eucalyptus, pennyroyal, lavender and tansy—available from most health-food shops.

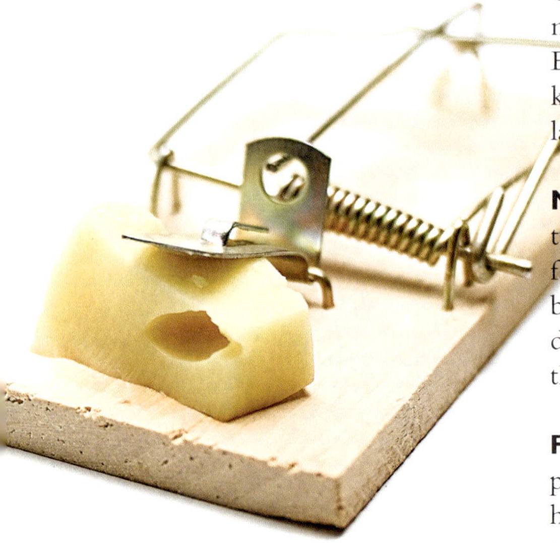

**Make mice vanish for good.** Did you know that in six months, two mice can eat 2 kilograms of food and leave behind about 18,000 faecal pellets? While plenty of people have tried, it's hard to invent a better mousetrap than the standard snap-back trap. Poisons can be dangerous to your pets and can leave dead mice out of reach—where they can become a food source for other household pests.

**For acute rodent problems,** use lots of the traps, baited with peanut butter, oats or cheese, and spread them strategically around the house. Put them perpendicular to walls that mice scamper along. Mice are renowned for their powerful noses, so wear gloves when baiting the traps to avoid leaving your scent behind. If you don't like the mess of baiting traps with food, use cotton wool balls, which greedy mice will try to grab when building nests.

## PET CLEAN-UP

**PETS, EVEN THE** BEST-TRAINED ONES, MAKE A MESS. AND UNTIL WE CAN TEACH THEM TO CLEAN UP AFTER THEMSELVES, WE'LL HAVE TO PICK UP POO, WIPE UP URINE AND PET VOMIT, AND REMOVE PET HAIR FROM CARPETS AND FURNITURE. IN ANY CASE, ADEQUATE PET HYGIENE KEEPS THE HOUSE LOOKING GOOD AND REDUCES ODOURS, BOTH OF WHICH MAKE OWNING A PET MORE PLEASURABLE.

**To remove pet hair from sofa cushions,** start with the vacuum cleaner. Buy a lint-brush attachment for your vacuum if you don't already have one. This gadget first lifts up and then sucks up short, wiry hairs that have imbedded themselves in the upholstery. If you can't get your hands on a lint-brush attachment, wear a damp rubber glove and rub your hand across the sofa cushion. The hair will clump together for easy removal.

**Vacuum your pet.** If your pet sheds, try giving them the once-over with a vacuum every week using a dusting or brush attachment. As long as you are careful—and as long as your pet does not mind the sucking action and noise—this is a good way to catch hair that is bound to fall out. You might find that your dog, or even your cat, loves the attention. It's like a pet massage. Then again, if the mere sound of the vacuum cleaner sends your pet scrambling under the bed, combing or brushing is a much kinder alternative.

**To clean up pet vomit,** start with the solids. Remove them with a paper towel or spatula. If the vomit is on a hard surface, such as a vinyl or wood floor, simply wipe up the liquid with moist paper towels and then mop the spot to clean it and remove any odours.

Simple solutions

## Be a pet detective

To locate old pet urine stains in a room, you need to think like a crime scene investigator. Turn off the lights and scan the room with a black-light bulb (ultraviolet light), which makes otherwise invisible stains visible. It's important to clean up these old stains because these are what keep a cat or dog, with its keen sense of smell, coming back. Outline the spots with pieces of string or by lightly tracing with chalk. Then follow our directions for removing urine stains.

Simple solutions

## Is it ... alive?

When you see the word enzymes on packaging, just what does that mean? That you have a box of microscopic insects on your hands?

No. All organisms—plant and animal—make enzymes, but enzymes themselves are not alive. They are complex chemicals, each one targeted to a specific purpose. You have about 1300 different enzymes making themselves at home in your body right now, for instance, breaking down nutrients, rebuilding cells and otherwise helping the body function.

The enzymes found in cleaning products are made by bacteria, and their targeted purpose, you won't be surprised to learn, is to break down soil.

If the vomit is on fabric, a carpet or rug, or upholstered furniture, blot up as much of the liquid as possible using paper towels. Next, apply an enzymatic cleaner, such as Exelpet Enz Stain & Odour. The enzymes in these special cleaning products, available from pet shops and in the pet section of larger supermarkets, actually digest the proteins found in the vomit. But they usually take a while. Let the cleaner stand for as long as the product's instructions suggest. Then, for clothing, wash and rinse or dry-clean according to label instructions. For carpeting or furniture, blot with clean, cool water to rinse (but avoid using too much water, especially if there is a pad under the carpet or stuffing in the upholstered furniture). Then remove excess liquids by either repeatedly blotting with fresh, dry paper towels or using a wet vac or extraction machine, available from equipment rental shops. As with any pet accident, the key is to clean up the vomit immediately.

**To clean up pet faeces,** begin by removing any solids with tissue paper, then flush down the toilet. If there is little or no residue (as with firm faeces on a hard floor), clean with soapy water and paper towels. Then rinse with clean water and paper towels. If there is residue (as with loose faeces on a carpet), follow the steps listed for cleaning up vomit. Blot up as much of the liquid as possible using paper towels and apply an enzymatic cleaner. Wash and rinse according to the material.

**To remove a fresh urine puddle,** wipe it up using paper towels or newspaper. Another efficient way to remove pet urine is with a heavy-duty vacuum cleaner capable of picking up liquid, or a wet vac. The sooner you clean up your pet's indiscretion, the more likely it'll be that you'll stop the odour and keep your pet from revisiting the spot for a reprise. Urine is by far the worst pet odour in a home. Once it has soaked in and dried, it can be tough to remove.

**If the urine is in a carpet,** soak up as much of it as possible with paper towels. Then cover the spot with a thick layer of dry paper towels, with newspaper on top of that. (Watch out for newsprint rubbing off on the carpet.) Stand on it for a minute, then remove the soaked padding and take it to your pet's toilet area—the cat's litter tray or the dog's designated outdoor area—to lure your pet there the next time. Repeat the process. Apply an enzymatic cleaner, available from pet shops, to digest proteins, which will help to remove the urine smell. Then rinse the accident zone by blotting with a cloth soaked in clean water. Remove excess water by blotting with paper towels (as described above) or with a wet vac or an extractor. (As noted earlier, an extractor can also be rented from an equipment rental shop.) Avoid using fragrant chemical cleaners, vinegar or ammonia on a urine spot. As with the urine smell, these odours could draw the pet back to the scene of the crime and result in repeat offending.

# PET EQUIPMENT

**KEEP YOUR PET'S** THINGS CLEAN: THEIR BEDDING, BOWLS AND TOYS. CLEANING PROLONGS THE LIFE OF THE EQUIPMENT, KEEPS YOUR PET HEALTHY AND REDUCES THE INCIDENCE OF UNPLEASANT ODOURS.

**Wash food and water bowls** daily to avoid the growth of bacteria. Put them in the dishwasher, if they are dishwasher safe. You can include them with your own dishes—the high dishwasher temperatures will sanitise everything. Or hand wash using hot, soapy water. (Do this separately.) Keep two sets of dishes for your pet, and rotate them. Stainless steel bowls are the easiest to keep clean.

**Clean leashes periodically** to remove dirt and salt, which can corrode the metal parts. Soak non-leather leashes in a sink full of warm water with a squirt of dishwashing liquid and a dash of liquid fabric softener, to keep the leash soft, not stiff (see below). Rub clean with a sponge. Rinse in clean, warm water. Don't wash leashes in the washing machine, because they could get tangled and the metal clasps could dent your machine. Hang to dry. (See 'Leather', on page 239.)

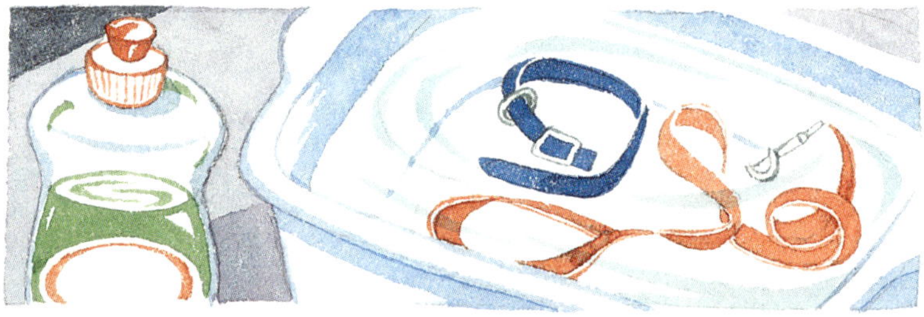

Non-leather dog collars and leashes can be washed.

**WATCH OUT** If you decide to spoil your dog with an expensive hand-knitted, 100 per cent wool dog jumper from one of those posh, pampered pet shops, treat it as though it were one of your own luxury garments. That means don't put the jumper through a washing machine cycle or in a tumble-dryer. Read the care label and follow the instructions. It might belong to your dog, but you should wash it as though you were going to wear it yourself.

**Hand wash dog jumpers** using the same care you'd use on your own woollens—unless the care instructions say otherwise. Most dog jumpers are made from the same materials as people jumpers—wool or acrylic. Fill a basin with lukewarm water and add a gentle fabric wash, such as Softly or a eucalyptus wool wash, or a squirt of mild dishwashing liquid (the eucalyptus wash has the added bonus of repelling fleas). Soak and then gently rub out any stains. Rinse thoroughly in clear, lukewarm water. Gently wring the jumper out. Wrap it in a clean towel to remove moisture. Lay the towel out on a flat surface and work the jumper into shape with your hands. Let it dry. Alternatively, have the jumper dry-cleaned.

**Wash pet toys regularly** to keep them clean and bacteria free. Wash rubber and plastic toys in a sink full of hot, soapy water with a dash of bleach thrown in. Scrub with a nylon-bristled brush. Stuffed toys and rope toys can go in the washing machine and the dryer. When they fray, or the stuffing starts to escape, toss them and get a new toy.

**To wipe slobber off a Frisbee** (or rubber ball) you've been throwing for your dog, use a wet wipe. Take along a portable travel pack of wipes when you play in the park with your dog—or any other time you're away from your garden hose. All those fellow dog owners you meet and greet (with a handshake) will thank you.

*See also:*
• DOG KENNELS • PESTS

## PEWTER

**PEWTER IS THE** FOURTH MOST PRECIOUS METAL, BEHIND PLATINUM, GOLD AND SILVER. A TIN ALLOY, PEWTER HAS LONG BEEN PRIZED FOR ITS LASTING VALUE. IT DOES NOT RUST AND TARNISHES ONLY SLIGHTLY OR NOT AT ALL (DEPENDING ON THE ALLOY'S METAL CONTENT). ANTIQUE PEWTER, WHICH IS USUALLY HIGH IN LEAD, CAN LOOK DARK AND DULL, BUT THAT PATINA IS PART OF ITS APPEAL AND VALUE. BEFORE CLEANING, DETERMINE WHETHER YOUR PEWTER PIECE IS AN ANTIQUE OR A MORE MODERN EXAMPLE.

**To remove dirt and grime from antique or newer pewter,** wash it in a sudsy solution of warm water and dishwashing liquid. Gently wipe the surface with a sponge or soft cloth. Rinse with clean water and then drip-dry in a dish drainer or on a folded tea towel. Never put pewter in the dishwasher. If your piece is an antique, stop here. Because of its metal content, polishing it won't necessarily make it shine—but it may decrease its value.

**To make bright, modern pewter shine,** use a silver or brass polish or a mildly abrasive scouring powder, such as Ajax, and a soft cloth. For severe corrosion, try applying the metal polish with ultra-fine steel wool (see right). Use grade 00000 only. Any coarser steel wool will scratch the finish. Buff with a soft cloth after using the steel wool.

Use ultra-fine steel wool on pewter to avoid scratching.

## PHOTOGRAPHS, SLIDES AND NEGATIVES

**PHOTOGRAPHS, SLIDES AND** NEGATIVES ARE EASILY DAMAGED, AND YOUR OPTIONS FOR CLEANING THEM ARE QUITE LIMITED. SO KEEPING THEM OUT OF HARM'S WAY IS THE MOST IMPORTANT THING. HOW MUCH YOU'RE WILLING TO DO FOR A PHOTOGRAPH PROBABLY DEPENDS ON WHETHER IT'S A FAMILY HEIRLOOM OR JUST ONE OF MANY SNAPSHOTS FROM LAST YEAR'S HOLIDAY.

**The ultimate protection for a photograph** is a glass covering and a frame. This way, the only thing that gets dirty is a hard surface that's easy to wipe clean. A frame will enhance the photograph's value and help it last longer. But don't put the photograph directly against the glass—use acid-free matting between the photo and the glass. And don't hang the photo in the path of direct sunlight.

**To clean the framed photo,** take it off the wall and lay it flat. Spray some glass cleaner onto a soft, clean cloth and wipe off the dust. Never spray directly onto the glass—the cleaner could drip behind the frame and damage the photograph.

**For valuable unframed photos,** acid-free paper, plastic envelopes and acid-free storage boxes offer good protection. Another good storage option is an album made of high-quality materials.

Remember that high temperatures, high humidity and direct sunlight will damage photographic materials.

**Handle photographic materials very carefully.** The salts and oils from your skin can damage them easily, so never touch the image area directly. Ideally, you should handle photographic material while wearing white cotton gloves. If you must use bare hands, handle your photos, slides and negatives by the edges only.

Try to use white cotton gloves to handle your negatives; it will prevent them being ruined by fingerprints.

**If your photograph has dirt on the surface,** see if it will come off with the gentle swipe of a soft brush. If not, don't do anything more—take it to a professional photo lab to be washed.

**If your photo has fingermarks around the edges** or on an unimportant part of the image, you may be able to wipe it away. Dip a cotton bud in distilled water and wipe at the mark very gently. Don't go over the mark again and again, because you'll soften the emulsion and damage it. Let the photo dry before you store it.

**To clean dust from slides and negatives,** pick up a can of compressed air at a camera, computer or electronics shop. Test the can by spraying your skin first. If the can has been exposed to high temperatures or has been shaken, you might get some water spraying out with the compressed air, which you don't want to get on photographic materials. Wearing white cotton gloves, hold your slide or negative by the edges and position the nozzle to the side, 10 centimetres from the film surface. Spray in several quick bursts to remove any dust.

## rules of the game

TO PROTECT PHOTOS

- Handle photos, slides and negatives only by the edges, preferably using white cotton gloves. Never touch the image area.
- Frame important photos under glass, using acid-free matting.
- For removal of serious dirt, take your photographic materials to a professional photo lab.
- Limit exposure to heat, humidity and sunlight.
- Use acid-free storage materials (envelopes, sheathes, album pages, boxes and anything of that nature).

**An antistatic cloth** can remove dust from slides and negatives—provided you use a light touch. Buy an antistatic cloth at a camera shop. Hold the slide or negative by the edges in one hand. With the other hand, fold the cloth around the film so that it touches both sides. With as little pressure as possible, draw the cloth down the surface, moving in one direction only. The more pressure you apply, the more likely that you'll drag the dust across the surface and scratch it.

**To protect your negatives from dirt and dust,** slip them into the sleeves of 22 × 28 centimetre clear plastic sheets that are sold in camera shops and photo labs. Do this the moment you get the negatives home from the photo lab. These sheets fit into ring binders and are an excellent way to mark and catalogue your negatives.

## PIANOS

**RESTRAINT IS THE** NAME OF THE GAME WHEN IT COMES TO CLEANING A PIANO. IT'S NO SMALL TASK, AND MOST PROFESSIONALS RECOMMEND THAT HOME CLEANING IS KEPT TO THE BASICS. A THOROUGH CLEANING IS NEEDED EVERY THREE TO FIVE YEARS, AND A PROFESSIONAL WILL COME TO YOUR HOUSE TO DO THIS. THE SMALLER JOBS YOU CAN TACKLE YOURSELF INCLUDE POLISHING THE PIANO EXTERIOR, VACUUMING THE KEYBOARD, CLEANING THE KEYS AND ALSO DUSTING THE SOUNDBOARD.

**If your piano's casework** is covered with a high-gloss, black lacquer finish, it needs only dusting with a soft, dry cloth. Give it some extra elbow grease if you're buffing away fingerprints. (See 'Lacquer', on page 236, for more details on caring for this finish.) To brighten mahogany pianos, wipe with non-silicone, oil-based furniture polish. Put the polish on a soft cloth sparingly—just enough to remove that last bit of dust clinging to the wood. Avoid wax-based polishes as they can build up and cloud the finish of the wood.

**To clean the piano's keyboard,** go over it with a vacuum, using the upholstery attachment. To clean plastic or ivory key tops, mix a solution of mild dishwashing liquid and water. Dip a cleaning cloth into the solution and wring it out thoroughly. Clean each key individually and then dry it immediately. As you clean, make sure that no liquid drips down the sides of keys. Both plastic and ivory key tops can warp and pop off when wet, and moisture can severely damage the working mechanism of the instrument. Rinse with a barely damp cloth and dry off with a clean towel.

Use a barely damp cloth when cleaning the keys of your piano.

**WATCH OUT** Never polish the top of a piano bench—the polish will combine with skin oil and perspiration and soak deep into the wood, making it virtually impossible to get out.

Ivory keys, which yellow with age, can be cleaned with a cloth dampened with methylated spirits—but remember the yellowing of ivory is natural, and it can't be completely whitened. An alternative is to dab some ordinary, white (non-gel) toothpaste on a damp cloth and rub the keys. Wipe the toothpaste off and then buff with a dry cloth. Sunlight also helps whiten real ivory keys, so try to position a piano so that it gets some sun (but not direct sunlight) and leave the cover open. (Sunlight has the reverse effect on plastic keys—it yellows them—so for plastic, leave the cover closed.) To protect the tuning, don't place a piano against a poorly insulated outside wall.

**Cleaning the soundboard** is the trickiest task. Grand pianos, with their open lids, collect a lot of dust. Use the bare hose of your vacuum cleaner, held just above the soundboard but not actually touching it, to suck away dust and dirt. You can cut down on dust by shutting the lid when the piano isn't being used or by placing decorator felt (available from piano shops) over the soundboard.

**On an upright piano,** cleaning the soundboard requires removing the bottom panel, which is heavy and therefore requires extra care. A spring that releases the panel is usually found beneath the key bed. Before vacuuming, look for small parts that may have fallen out of the piano or into the piano cabinet—a broken hammer, for instance. Again, the vacuum hose (with no attachments on it) should hover above the soundboard and strings, but never come into direct contact with them.

## PILLOWS

**FOR ALLERGY SUFFERERS,** PILLOWS CAN BE A SOURCE OF PROBLEMS. DUST, BODY OIL, PERSPIRATION AND DEAD SKIN PARTICLES GATHER ON (AND INSIDE) PILLOWS. PILLOWS ALSO HARBOUR DUST MITES—MICROSCOPIC ORGANISMS THAT MANY PEOPLE ARE ALLERGIC TO. IF YOU HAVE GOOSE DOWN, DUST AND DIRT ACT AS ABRASIVES AND SHORTEN THE LIFE OF THE DOWN. SO AT LEAST TWICE A YEAR, GIVE YOUR PILLOWS A GOOD CLEAN.

**Most fibre-filled pillows** can just be thrown into the washing machine. While you should always follow the instructions on the pillow's care label, generally you can use the cold-water cycle for fibre-filled pillows and tumble dry them on low heat. Or you can dry them on a clothes line. Simply hang the pillow in the sun by one corner. Make sure the pillow is completely dry before using.

**Down and feather pillows** should be machine washed or dry-cleaned depending on the manufacturer's instructions. Some people

**Simple solutions**

### For fluffy pillows

A quick way to freshen up pillows is to tumble dry them on low heat for about 10 minutes. It's much easier than a complete washing, and it's an effective way to remove at least some dust and dried skin particles. Do it twice a year, in between washings, to keep your pillows clean and non-allergenic.

recommend dry-cleaning only, claiming that machine washing down and feathers reduces their natural resilience. If you do decide to dry-clean your pillows, take them to a drycleaner with experience in cleaning down filling. If there are any lingering dry-cleaning solvent fumes, air the pillows until they are all gone.

**If you machine wash down pillows,** use a gentle cleanser, such as Softly, making sure that it is completely dissolved before immersing the pillow into the wash. Don't wash more than two pillows at a time. Tumble dry your down pillows on low to medium heat. And if you toss in a couple of clean tennis balls it will help fluff the feathers. Be prepared to wait—it might take four or more hours to completely dry them. To line dry, hang the pillow in the shade by one corner (not in the sun, as you would fibre-filled pillows, discussed above). Direct sun can make the feathers sweat, which creates an odour. Follow up a line drying by fluffing in a tumble-dryer on low heat.

*See also:*
• DOONAS • DOWN

## PLASTIC CONTAINERS

**PLASTIC IS TOUGH,** RESILIENT AND EASY TO CLEAN. HOWEVER, SOME FOODS, MOST NOTABLY TOMATO-BASED SAUCES, ETCH THEIR WAY INTO ITS PORES AND CAUSE WHAT SEEM TO BE PERMANENT STAINS. BUT DON'T GIVE UP HOPE. THERE IS A WAY TO CLEAN THEM OFF.

**Nearly all plastic food containers are dishwasher safe.** This includes the Tupperware and Decor brands, to name two of the most popular. You can also hand wash them in hot, soapy water, using a sponge or nylon-bristled dishwashing brush to scrub off stuck-on food.

**There is very little you can do** to completely remove stubborn stains, such as the ones left by tomato sauce, although you might have some success by soaking the plastic container in a solution for sterilising baby bottles, such as Milton. (This product contains bleach. If you use it, or even a solution of household bleach, make sure you wash and rinse the containers thoroughly before re-use.) This technique will also help to remove stale smells from plastic containers. So will wiping them out with vinegar, then rinsing.

**To remove other stains,** mix a paste of bicarbonate of soda and warm water and scrub with a nylon-bristled brush if the stain is light. For heavier stains, try one of the following techniques:

- Scrub with a solution of ¼ cup of dishwasher detergent mixed with 1 cup of warm water, then rinse well.
- Soak in a solution of ¼ cup of bleach mixed with 1 litre of warm water. (Wash in soapy water afterwards and then rinse well.)
- Let the container stand in direct sunlight for a day or two.

**To clean large, plastic storage containers** not meant for food, wipe out with a moist cloth. For stubborn stains, try scrubbing with a sponge or nylon-bristled dishwashing brush in a solution of warm water with a squirt of mild dishwashing liquid.

# PLAYGROUND EQUIPMENT

**BECAUSE IT WAS** BUILT TO BE OUTSIDE, IN THE ELEMENTS, PLAYGROUND EQUIPMENT IS DURABLE AND EASY TO CLEAN. ALL YOU NEED TO DO IS KEEP IT SAFE—FREE FROM SLIPPERY MUD AND MILDEW—AND RESPECTABLE LOOKING.

**Spray down playground equipment** with a garden hose once every couple of weeks, inside and out. This will remove sticks and leaves and muddy footprints. Depending on traffic, every so often scrub down parts with a solution of dishwashing liquid and warm water. Scrub swing seats, slides, platforms, vinyl tarps and other areas with a soft-bristled brush to loosen stubborn bird poo and other grime. Rinse by spraying everything down with a hose. Don't use bleach or cleaning products containing chlorine on playground equipment. These chemicals can eat away at rubber material and destroy glue. Soapy water and a garden hose should be sufficient.

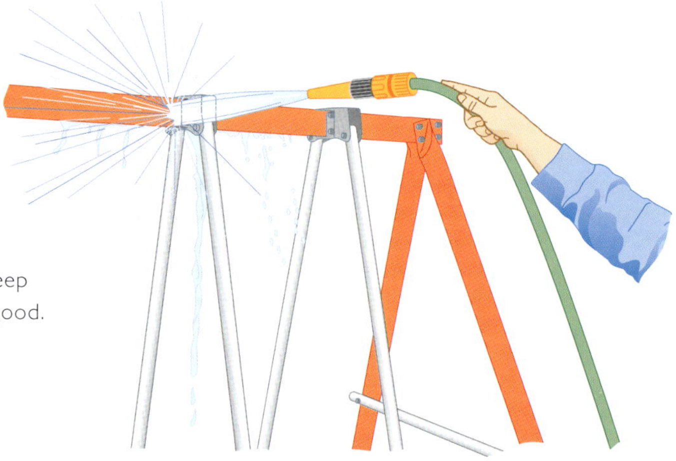

A quick rinse with a hose will keep children's play equipment looking good.

**To clean plastic bubbles and windows,** use the same soapy solution and a soft cloth. Don't scrub with a brush, since you may scratch these surfaces. If the surface is extremely dirty, let the soapy solution loosen the dirt, or loosen it with a jet from the garden hose, and then rub gently with the cloth, turning and rinsing the cloth often. Remove oil or tar by dabbing with kerosene, and then washing immediately with the soapy solution. Don't use solvents (such as acetone, petroleum or thinners) or scouring powders on clear plastic.

# POOL TABLES

**DESPITE THEIR BULKY** SIZE, POOL TABLES ARE PRECISION INSTRUMENTS, WITH FINELY BALANCED SLATE TOPS AND VERY SMOOTH FELT COVERINGS. LUCKILY, THERE'S NOT MUCH YOU NEED TO DO TO KEEP THEM CLEAN.

**Dust the wooden legs and rails** as you would any fine furniture (see 'Furniture', on pages 190–193). Follow the pool table manufacturer's instructions for the type of finish that's on the wood. When in doubt, use a dry dusting cloth or a feather duster.

**Brush the felt top after each use.** Use a soft horsehair- or nylon-bristled brush specifically designed for table felt (available from billiard supply shops). Brush in one direction only—the direction in which you usually break. This keeps the nap of the felt in good condition.

Use a specially designed brush to keep your pool table felt in condition.

**Gently dust the felt top periodically** using your vacuum cleaner and a soft upholstery attachment. This picks up chalk and other dust from under the cloth, which can abrade the felt fibres over time. Be careful not to use a nozzle that will pull the cloth away from the bed.

Simple solutions

### Take your cue

Here are two handy hints that will help to keep your pool table in top game-playing condition:

- Keep a lint roller nearby for picking up loose particles from the felt top of the table while you're using it.
- Keep your table covered when not in use. This will keep dust off and reduce the amount of cleaning you must do. Use a plastic or vinyl covering. Ready-made ones are available wherever pool and billiard supplies are sold.

## PORCELAIN

**PORCELAIN IS ONE** OF THE MOST FRAGILE OF ALL CERAMICS. FIRED AT VERY HIGH TEMPERATURES, IT IS GLASSLIKE, SO CLEAN WITH CARE. HOW YOU CLEAN DEPENDS ON WHICH FINISH YOUR PORCELAIN HAS—A BISQUE, OR UNGLAZED, FINISH OR A GLOSSY GLAZED FINISH.

**To wash porcelain,** use a plastic basin or a sink lined with a tea towel or rubber mat to protect against breakage.

**To remove dirt and grime** from either glazed or unglazed porcelain, first try using a mild solution of warm water and dishwashing liquid. Wipe with a washcloth or scrub gently with a soft, nylon-bristled dishwashing brush. An old, soft toothbrush is great for getting into all the nooks and crannies. Rinse well using clean water.

If that doesn't remove all the stains, try something stronger; an all-purpose cleaner, such as Down To Earth, is a good bet. And always rinse porcelain well, immediately after cleaning. These cleaning compounds can stain or etch the delicate surface. Air-dry in a dish drainer or on a folded tea towel on the benchtop.

**To remove coffee or tea stains** from the inside of porcelain cups or a porcelain teapot, scrub gently with a cloth or soft-bristled brush and a paste made from bicarbonate of soda and water.

**WATCH OUT** When cleaning porcelain, don't go straight for the bleach. Use all your other cleaning steps first and only use bleach as a last resort—and even then, with caution. Sometimes the chemical reaction of bleach and whatever stain you're dealing with can fix the stain permanently.

**To remove dirt from hard-to-reach crannies,** such as inside porcelain flowers or in the folded hands of a figurine, use a spray-on, bleach-based product, such as White King Bleach Spray. (You should have to do this only on bisque porcelain. On glazed porcelain, scrubbing the same crannies with a toothbrush and soapy water should be sufficient.) Spray the product on, wait a few minutes and then rinse it well with fresh water. Always clean before trying the bleach spray. Otherwise the bleach may set the stain. (See 'Watch out' box, left.)

**For really stubborn stains on bisque porcelain,** soak the piece (or the stained part of the piece) in a container filled with hydrogen peroxide. Leave it until the stain is gone, which could take anything from 15 minutes to 72 hours. To rinse the piece, soak it in clean water (distilled water is best for really fine pieces of porcelain) for as long as you soaked it in the hydrogen peroxide.

## POTS AND PANS

**THE GOOD NEWS** IS THAT IT'S OK TO PUT SOME COOKWARE IN THE DISHWASHER. THIS GOES FOR STAINLESS STEEL AND ALUMINIUM (AS LONG AS THEY HAVE ALL-METAL HANDLES), AS WELL AS GLASS COOKWARE. BUT TO BE SAFE, CHECK THE MANUFACTURER'S INSTRUCTIONS.

**Cast iron and copper** should not go in the dishwasher, and manufacturers of non-stick cookware often advise against putting any of those pots or pans in the dishwasher as well. The environment in a dishwasher—with hot water spouts and spray rinses—is much harsher than soapy water and gentle care in the sink. Besides all that, dishwasher detergents generally rely on alkaline-heavy cleaners to cut through grease, and extremely alkaline cleaners can damage cookware just as badly as acidic cleaners can.

**Hand wash pots and pans** that can't be put in the dishwasher much as you would dishes. Scrape out any food residue with a wooden spoon or rubber spatula. Fill the sink with moderately hot water and add a squirt of dishwashing liquid. As soon as the pot has cooled sufficiently, slide it into the soapy water and let it sit for a minute. Then gently scrub the pot with a circular motion, using a sponge, nylon-bristled dishwashing brush or a dishcloth. Many non-stick surfaces—especially older ones—are easily scratched, so pay attention to the manufacturer's instructions for cleaning. Clean the pot inside and out, sides and bottom. You'll know it's come clean when it's smooth to the touch. Rinse in clean, hot water and dry with a tea towel.

**Removing burned-on food** from your pots and pans can be done without working up a sweat or potentially damaging the surface of your expensive cookware—but you do need lots of patience, lots of hot water and a bit of dishwashing liquid. Squirt some dishwashing liquid into the pot or pan, fill it with hot water and then leave the kitchen. Nothing removes burned-on food like a good 2-hour soak in hot, soapy water. (Try to avoid burning food in the same pot twice.)

## When germs float in uninvited

When the dirty pots and pans pile up, you probably fantasise about a massive flood swooshing through the kitchen and cleaning it all in seconds. Unfortunately, it doesn't work that way. As any home owner who's been in a real flood knows, a lot of silt and mud get left behind. Germs, too. If your kitchen—and cookware—has been through a flood, all you can do is mix hot water with soap and start scrubbing. If you're concerned that elbow grease won't get all of the germs, bake the offending cookware in a 130 °C oven for an hour. This is even OK for cookware with plastic handles. Most plastic handles won't stand over 180 °C, but they'll be fine for an hour at 130 °C.

**If your grill tray is covered in greasy, burned-on gunk,** scrape off as much as you can with a spatula, sprinkle the tray with washing soda (available from supermarkets) then pour over boiling water. Leave it to soak for 10 minutes or so, then wash as usual.

**If you have built-up layers of baked-on food** on cookware that is neither aluminium nor non-stick, mix ½ cup of ammonia with 2 litres of hot water in your pot and let it sit for a couple of hours. (Don't mix ammonia or even vinegar with household cleaners, or you'll wind up sniffing noxious fumes.)

*See also:* • ALUMINIUM • COPPER • DISHES • IRON

# POTTERY

**THERE'S POTTERY, SUCH** AS JUGS, PLATES, FLOWER VASES AND GARDEN CONTAINERS, AND THEN THERE'S POTTERY THAT BELONGS IN AN ART GALLERY OR MUSEUM. IN THE FORMER CATEGORY, THERE ARE TWO TYPES OF POTTERY: GLAZED AND UNGLAZED. THE RULE OF THUMB IS THAT THE THICKER THE GLAZE, THE EASIER TO CLEAN. YOU CAN GET TOUGHER ON GLAZED POTTERY.

**To clean glazed pottery**—such household items as plates, mugs, serving trays and flower vases—proceed much as you would with your dishes. This stuff has been fired at 1100 °C, meaning it can stand up to any heat your dishwasher can hand out. Hand wash fragile or expensive pieces in the sink with warm water and dishwashing liquid, so they won't run the risk of getting chipped in the dishwasher. A scrubber sponge will do nicely for most hand washing, but the glaze will even stand up to the abrasion of a steel-wool pad.

To remove heavy dirt and grease, first dampen a cloth in methylated spirits, wipe it over the glazed pottery and then wash as usual in the dishwasher or sink.

**To clean unglazed pottery**—such as terracotta flowerpots—just wash them in the sink with warm water and a squirt of dishwashing liquid. Unglazed

Most glazed pottery will stand up to quite a robust cleaning.

pottery is porous, meaning it will soak up water. It may take a day or two for the pot to dry out completely, but the water won't hurt it.

**WATCH OUT** Some pottery is painted with acrylic, followed by a spray-on glaze that is not kiln-fired. This kind of glaze will not stand up to washing in water. To clean it, wipe with a damp cloth.

**Fine antique or museum-quality pottery** should be cleaned delicately if at all. If nothing is flaking loose on the surface, you can safely dust it with a soft paintbrush. If more cleaning is required, just wipe gently with a damp cloth or a damp cloth with a bit of dishwashing liquid squirted on it. However, always inspect the piece first, and if the pottery has been repaired in the past, even cleaning it like this could result in damage to the repair job. For more extensive cleaning, consult a professional conservator in a museum.

## POWER TOOLS

**IF YOU DON'T** CLEAN YOUR POWER TOOLS PERIODICALLY, THEY'LL GET YOU BACK—BY GOING INTO PERMANENT RETIREMENT. DUST, SAWDUST AND RUST CAN SEEP INTO THE MOTOR AND ACCUMULATE, EVENTUALLY BRINGING THE TOOL TO A STANDSTILL.

**How frequently you clean your power tools** depends on how often you use them and how carefully you store them. In general, give them a good cleaning any time you notice a build-up of residue such as sawdust, oil or grease. To keep everything running smoothly, don't store your tools where weather can affect them. And remember, if you don't clean them often enough, simple dust clogs can render built-in safety features useless.

**To clean your power tools,** first disconnect the power source. Unplug them or, if they run on batteries, remove the batteries and wipe out the battery compartment with a soft, dry cloth.

Do not, under any circumstances, spray anything liquid into the motor of any tool you're cleaning. Instead, get out the professional gadgeteer's favourite cleaner—a can of compressed air (available from camera shops, and computer and electrical supply shops). Make sure you hold the can level before you point the extension nozzle and hit the spray button. If you don't hold the can perfectly level, you might wind up spraying liquid into the motor, and that would be disastrous. Spray a blast of air into the air vents. If you see a cloud of dust puff out of the motor, you know you've waited too long to clean your tools.

If you're particular about your tools' appearance, avoid using abrasive cleaners on them. Just squirt some glass cleaner, such as Windex or Mr Muscle, onto a paper towel and wipe away any grimy stuff.

**EXPERT ADVICE**

FOR STICKY SITUATIONS

Glue this here, drill that there ... and before you know it, your power tools are smeared with adhesive. No problem. Just apply a dab of petroleum jelly (Vaseline) and rub the glue spot with a dry cloth until the mark has completely gone.

# PRESSURE COOKERS

**PRESSURE COOKERS ARE** TRICKY. FOOD PARTICLES CAN GET TRAPPED IN THE PRESSURE GAUGE (THE THING THAT RATTLES WHEN THE COOKER IS DOING ITS JOB), AND SO THE GAUGE SHOULD BE CLEANED AFTER EVERY USE TO KEEP FOOD PARTICLES FROM TURNING INTO BACTERIAL DEBRIS.

**For cleaning out the pressure gauge,** the best tool is a large safety pin. (Even though a toothpick would do quite nicely, it could break off in the little hole and then there would be no more pressure cooking at all.) Go at the little hole from both sides. You'll be amazed at the gunk you can force out.

**Also give regular attention to the gasket,** that rubber ring sealing the whole thing, located between the cooker and the lid. If you don't keep it clean, food build-up can result in bacterial build-up, and that's not good news in terms of hygiene. Remove the gasket, pour a bit of dishwashing liquid into your hands, hold them under the tap until you have suds and then massage the gasket until you're confident you've removed anything that might breed bacteria. Be careful not to stretch the gasket unnecessarily.

solutions

## Cleaning for canning

If you use your pressure cooker for canning, be sure to add ¼ teaspoon of cream of tartar or ¼ cup of white vinegar to the water before heating. This will prevent a ring from forming at the water level, and clean-up will be a breeze.

Keep the rubber gasket on your pressure cooker clean and supple.

With repeated washing, the gasket can stretch and lose its shape. And a gasket that doesn't fit properly is as good as no gasket at all. It can also get crunchy with wear, so after you wash and dry it, rub the gasket with some oil—olive, canola or vegetable are all suitable choices.

It's a good idea to keep an extra gasket on hand. (If you have trouble finding one for your pressure cooker, order one from the shop where you bought it or call the manufacturer for a list of places that sell the kind that fits your model.)

**To clean the inside of the pot,** nothing works better than good old garden-variety dishwashing liquid, hot water, a plastic scrubbing sponge and a bit of muscle power.

# PRINTERS

**FIRST, REMOVE ANY** PAPER FROM THE PAPER TRAY AND, IF THE TRAY COMES OFF, REMOVE IT. USING A DRY CLOTH, WIPE OFF THE TRAY. YOU DON'T WANT WATER ANYWHERE NEAR THE PRINTER INNARDS.

**Clean the paper rollers** to prevent paper from sticking to them. Clean plastic rollers with cotton buds dipped in methylated spirits. For rubber rollers, use a citrus-based sticky goo remover, such as De-Solv-It. It will do wonders to clean and revive rubber rollers. Take care never to touch the printing mechanism.

Clean paper rollers very gently, avoiding the printing mechanism.

**Cleaning the printer's insides** shouldn't be necessary, unless you have the bad habit of leaving the top of the printer open. If it looks terribly dirty or dusty, talk to your nearest computer shop about the problem, or search the Internet for specialist computer or printer cleaners. Whatever you do, don't put your fingers inside, except to change the ink cartridges. This is a situation where zapping an electronic machine with compressed air isn't a good idea.

**If you spot a toner spill in a laser printer,** wipe it up carefully with paper towels. Toner can be toxic; don't inhale it. Avoid getting toner on your hands or clothes—it's hard to remove.

**Cleaning the outer casing is a simpler matter.** You can get rid of any mysterious blob that won't budge with a bit of methylated spirits on a gauze pad. Or, if you have them, you can rip open one of those little alcohol prep pads the doctor wipes your arm with before you get an injection. A brisk swipe or two, and the offending substance goes away. Remember, though, this is only for the exterior.

*See also:* • COMPUTERS

# QUILTS

**IF YOU BUY** A QUILT IN A SHOP THESE DAYS, IT'S ALMOST ALWAYS WASHABLE. JUST CHECK THE CARE LABEL AND FOLLOW INSTRUCTIONS. BUT SOME QUILTS ARE OLD AND HANDMADE, REQUIRING SPECIAL CARE. THOSE THAT HAVE BEEN HANDED DOWN OR FOUND IN FLEA MARKETS OR ANTIQUE SHOPS HAVE CHARACTER THAT COMES FROM HAVING BEEN CHERISHED. UNFORTUNATELY, THAT CHARACTER OFTEN APPEARS IN THE FORM OF WATER RINGS, DYE BLEEDS, STAINS OF UNKNOWN ORIGIN AND TEARS—ALL OF WHICH WILL DICTATE HOW YOU WASH A QUILT.

**Even with meticulous care,** you shouldn't expect your hand-me-down or heirloom quilt to look like new. Instead, embrace the flaws, the water rings, the colour bleeds, the rips and the mystery stains.

And remember, if you're in any doubt about whether your old quilt will stand up to cleaning, do nothing until you have consulted an expert, such as a textiles conservator at a large, city museum.

**After you've tested for bleeds and deterioration** (see the 'Test first, wash later' box, on page 286), it's time to wash. The more colour-fast your quilt is, the warmer the water you can use, but don't go much warmer than tepid. If the quilt has weak spots in the seams or fabric, put it in a mesh laundry bag or a cotton quilt bag (see below) and keep the washing machine on the lowest agitation level.

A laundry bag can help to protect a worn quilt during washing.

**If you're wary of a machine wash,** fill your bathtub with enough water to cover the quilt with 7–10 centimetres to spare. (Don't put the quilt in yet.) Add laundry detergent, 30 millilitres of detergent per 4 litres of water. To get rid of general soil and yellow rings, you can add 1 or 2 tablespoons of colour-safe oxygen bleach (non-chlorine). Swirl the water to mix, then lay the quilt in the water, spreading it as much as possible. Stay near the bathtub for about 10 minutes, swishing, smoothing and squeezing as you go to release the soil on the quilt. If you detect a colour bleed, drain the bathtub immediately and rinse the quilt thoroughly with cold water. But if all goes well, you can leave the quilt soaking in the bath for up to an hour.

When it's time to rinse, drain the tub and push the quilt to the end away from the drain. Bunch it up in the end until all the water has drained from the bath. Then squeeze the quilt to force out the excess

## Test first, wash later

When you're dealing with a vintage or heirloom quilt, there are many uncertainties. How was it stored? Was it ever dry-cleaned? Are the fabrics colour-fast? Depending on the quilt's history, there may be stains, tears and deterioration that require special care. To avoid a disaster, follow these steps before washing:

- Test the fabric strength. Some fabrics are so fragile that they tear like tissue paper. Depending on the quilt's age and how much it was cherished or neglected, some pieces of the fabric can deteriorate by being touched. If you have such a weak patch, baste the area with needle and thread or consider replacing the patch altogether.
- Test dyes. You could have cotton, velvet, acetate or silk, all in one patchwork quilt. Each piece of fabric and each dye need to be tested for colour-fastness.
- To test, mix 1 tablespoon each of ammonia and liquid laundry detergent per 3 tablespoons of water. You might have to fiddle with the proportions, depending on how hard or soft your water is. You'll want just enough soap to eliminate friction and not enough to generate lots of suds.
- Dampen a white towel or cloth nappy with the solution. Make sure you don't wet the testing cloth too much, or you could do exactly the damage to the quilt that you're seeking to avoid. Touch—don't press—the damp cloth or towel to an obscure corner of the quilt. Leave it on for 30 seconds, then lightly blot the spot with a dry part of the cloth. Did any of the fabric colour bleed onto the cloth? If not, go for stage two, which is a slightly more aggressive version of what you just did.
- Go to another part of the quilt, a colourful one that you suspect might bleed. Find a dry spot on the white cloth and dampen it in the solution. This time, press harder on the damp cloth and wait a whole minute before blotting.

Be patient. On the second go around, you might see some dye or staining or soiling come off on the blot cloth. If you see any hint of dye, you'll know there will be a little bit of bleeding when you wash the quilt. But if you just see dirt, your quilt is probably colour-fast. To make absolutely sure, take a third run at it. Go to another part of the quilt, press harder with the damp cloth so that the quilt actually absorbs a bit of the cleaning solution, then lightly rub. If your white cloth is still white or has picked up no more than a trace of the colour from the test spot, you're safe to wash.

water. Pick up the wet quilt and cradle it as best you can, until you've refilled the bath with tepid water. Rinse by agitating the quilt just as you did in the washing step. If the rinse water becomes discoloured, repeat the drain-and-rinse process. If you used bleach, rinse it twice. Squeeze the quilt again.

**To dry the quilt,** try tumbling it in the dryer with cool air, if you think the quilt can stand it. If not, hang it on a clothes line to dry.

# RANGE HOODS

**BECAUSE THEY'RE SET** OVER THE STOVE, RANGE HOODS COLLECT A LOT OF FAT RESIDUE. THE SPATTERS FROM WHATEVER YOU'RE COOKING GO UP WITH THE STEAM, AND TINY FILAMENTS OF DUST ATTACH TO THE FAT, FURTHER CLOGGING UP THE RANGE HOOD, INSIDE AND OUT.

**To clean the outside of the hood,** mix 1 teaspoon of dishwashing liquid with 4 cups of warm water to cut the grease. Soak a sponge in the solution and, to keep it from dripping, squeeze it thoroughly before attacking the hood. If your hood isn't painted, wipe the sponge with the grain of the stainless steel so you won't leave swirly marks.

If a food splatter is stuck to the hood, use a nylon dishwashing brush or your fingernail to dislodge it. If that doesn't work, squirt the spot with an all-purpose cleaner such as Ajax Spray 'n Wipe (see below), let it sit for 5 minutes and then scrub with a sponge. Don't use anything abrasive because it will scratch the surface and take some paint off.

Allow sprayed solution to work on grease before wiping.

**To clean the underside of the hood,** lay a towel on top of the stove to catch falling dirt. (Firstly, check that the burners are off and are cool.) If you have a gas stove, lay a couple of pans across the stovetop first to create some separation between the towel and the pilot lights. In a trigger spray bottle, mix a solution of 1 part dishwashing soap to 2 parts warm water. Spray underneath the hood and let the solution sit for 15 minutes. While the solution breaks down the accumulation of grease, you can remove the fan filter. Some newer range-hood filters can go into the dishwasher. But if your model doesn't allow for dishwasher cleaning, soak the filter in a solution of ½ cup of warm white vinegar, 1 teaspoon of dishwashing liquid, and warm water until you see the greasy debris loosening. Rinse the filter first with warm water to get rid of any remaining sticky stuff and then with cool water. Once the underside of the hood has been soaking for 15 minutes, wipe up the grease with paper towels. (You'll ruin cloths.) If grease remains, give it another spray and wipe over.

**EXPERT ADVICE**

THE ONLY WAY TO FRY

When you fry foods, use only canola oil or peanut oil. Although corn oil is a popular ingredient in a lot of Asian food, it tends to leave a much filmier, stickier residue that's harder to clean off appliances than other cooking oils.

# RECORDS

**SOME PEOPLE STILL** PREFER TO COLLECT AND LISTEN TO RECORDS. MOST OF US NEGLECT THE ALBUMS, BUT A BIT OF REGULAR CLEANING WILL MAKE THEM LAST LONGER AND SOUND BETTER.

**Velvet record brushes** are the favourite of many who do clean their records. They have a handle for gripping and a velvet-grained fabric on the bottom. They come with a liquid, which is mostly water with a dash of mild soap. Harsher chemicals will damage record vinyl.

Put a few drops of the liquid on the brush. Place the record on the turntable (if you're too young to know what a turntable is, you're reading the wrong entry) and turn it on. Hold the brush lightly on the surface of the record as it spins. This will get rid of any dust that might interrupt a pleasurable listening experience with skips.

Wipe gently with a barely damp cloth as the record spins around.

**Antistatic carbon-fibre brushes** are also available from specialist retailers. The brush cleans dust from vinyl records but also makes the records antistatic, so they don't go on attracting dust. If you want to use specialist cleaning products for your records, but can't find them, search the Internet under 'record cleaning'—you'll find lots of information, and most companies will sell by mail order.

**If you don't have a velvet record brush,** you can just as easily use a very soft cloth with a fine weave to clean your records. The main thing is that you don't use anything that creates lint—that's what you're trying to get rid of. Make a mixture of 99 per cent water and 1 per cent baby shampoo. Barely dampen the cloth—make sure it isn't wet—and hold it lightly on the record as it spins (see left). Be careful not to touch the record with a fingernail.

**If you have heavier, sticky grime on a record,** have another go at it again with the baby shampoo mixture mentioned above, but use a bit more pressure on the cloth this time. If that doesn't get rid of the grimy stuff, take the record off the turntable, holding it only by its edges. Carefully rest an edge against your body and hold the other edge of the record in one hand. With your free hand, wipe the record over with the cloth that's been dampened in the baby shampoo and water mixture, moving back and forth in the direction of the grooves.

# REFRIGERATORS AND FREEZERS

KEEPING YOUR REFRIGERATOR AND FREEZER CLEAN IS NOT ONLY IMPORTANT TO THE APPEARANCE (AND SMELL) OF YOUR HOME, IT'S ALSO CRUCIAL FROM A SANITATION POINT OF VIEW. THERE ARE THREE ASPECTS OF KEEPING FRIDGES AND FREEZERS CLEAN: REMOVING DIRT, KILLING GERMS AND THEN DEODORISING THE INTERIOR.

**Cleaning the fridge is just a half-an-hour job,** so there's no need to haul out the Esky to keep your refrigerated goods cold, unless it's a particularly hot day. Instead, empty one shelf at a time, so food on the other shelves can stay chilled. Remove the first shelf and spray it liberally with a disinfecting, all-purpose cleaner, such as Pine O Cleen spray or McLintocks Vanilla Fridge Wipe, to vanquish the inevitable sticky spills. (Glass cleaner probably isn't going to do the job.) Or sanitise it with a squirt of good old white vinegar in a spray bottle. Wipe the shelf dry with a paper towel and reinsert it in the refrigerator. Repeat the procedure with each shelf.

**To clean refrigerator drawers,** pull them out of the fridge one at a time, place them in the sink and then fill them with warm water and a healthy squirt of dishwashing liquid. Let the water sit in them for about 10 minutes. Then pour the water out, rinse with fresh water and wipe them dry with a clean tea towel.

**Keeping your fridge germ-free is a priority.** Meat and poultry juices dripping on refrigerator surfaces are not only unsightly, they are potentially harmful vehicles for the spread of salmonella and *E. coli*.

Simple solutions

## A sweet-smelling fridge

To deodorise your refrigerator or freezer, open a box of bicarbonate of soda, leave it inside and change it every few months. This tried-and-true method will absorb most of the odours you don't want emanating from your fridge, but it may not go far enough to suit you. For a clean, fresh smell, find a spray disinfectant with a scent that you find appealing. When you have your food items removed for cleaning, spray and wipe all the shelves, drawers and interior walls with it. This will ensure a uniformly fresh smell. And don't forget that a few drops of vanilla essence on your damp sponge will also give a fresh, sweet smell.

Even though a refrigerator's temperature is low, it isn't low enough to stop the growth of all bacteria. Some bacteria can grow even in refrigerated temperatures. And, while some are harmless, some can make you very sick. For instance, when you're thawing meat or poultry in the fridge, if those juices drip down or contaminate a shelf, it could lead to serious health problems. So as you remove each shelf, spray the inside of the refrigerator with a disinfecting, all-purpose cleaner. Remember, just because it looks clean doesn't mean that it is clean.

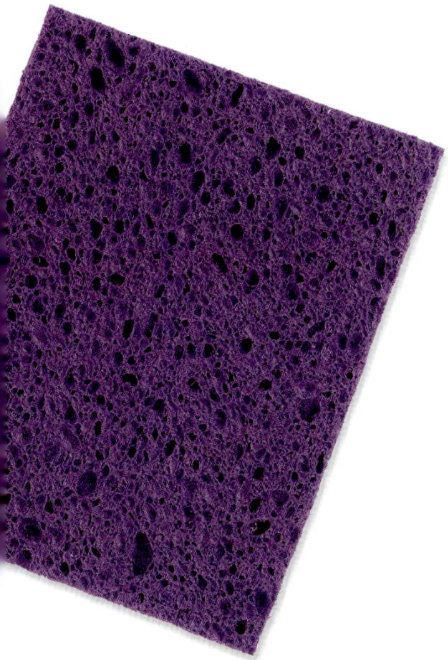

**Cleaning the freezer** isn't quite the ordeal that cleaning the refrigerator often is. Most freezers aren't so big that they take more than 20 minutes to clean, and it takes frozen food hours to thaw, so you probably won't need to enlist a friend's freezer or even your trusty Esky. Just put the food in the sink. If you pile frozen items on top of each other, they'll keep each other cold.

Soak a sponge in warm water and squeeze out enough water that you won't create trickles that will add to your work. Wipe each rack in the freezer, top and bottom. If you have a thick, frozen spill, scrape it first with a stiff plastic spatula that has a thin edge (no metal), and then spot-clean it with a soapy sponge.

**Regularly sanitising the door handles** is perhaps the most important aspect of fridge cleaning. When you're preparing food it's best to wash your hands each and every time you handle raw meat. That's easy to forget in the midst of creating an elegant entrée, however, and when you transfer that contamination to the door handles, another family member who uses the refrigerator could pick up the germs. The solution is to keep a box or tube of all-purpose wipes near the refrigerator and make it a habit to wipe off the handle frequently.

## A crack cleaning technique

Those egg cups in the door of your refrigerator are a bane and a blessing. They're good at keeping eggs from bumping into each other. But somehow, the odd egg cracks, despite the efficient design, and then you've got trouble.

Eggs are a popular breeding place for salmonella, so that egg ooze drying right under your nose could be quite a hazard. Take these steps to remedy the situation:

- Firstly, remove as much of the substance as you can with a paper towel.
- If it has begun to harden, try scraping it out with a spoon.
- If the broken egg has had a while to harden, there may be some stubborn residue left. An all-purpose, disinfecting degreaser is just about the only thing that will cut that sort of residue. Spray the cleaner on and let it sit for several minutes while you clean the rest of the fridge. By then, you should be able to lift the rest of the egg spill out with a paper towel. Rinse thoroughly afterwards.

Vacuum regularly to keep your refrigerator coils dust-free.

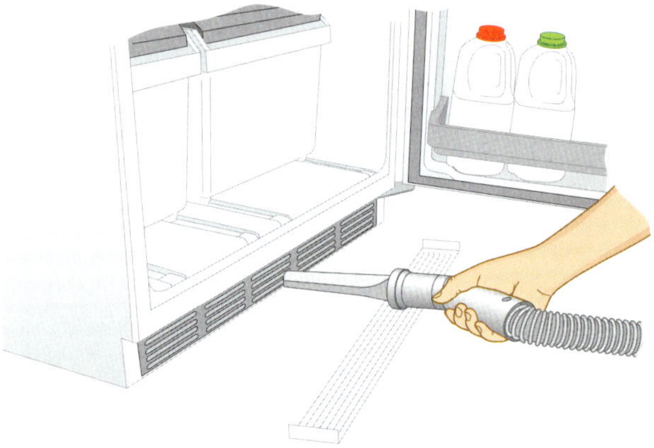

**Vacuuming the coils under a frost-free fridge** (or on the back of a cycle defrost unit) should be a part of your regular kitchen clean-up about once a month—especially if you have a shedding pet. Unplug the refrigerator and push the crevice tool as far under the unit as you can (see above). Be careful not to bend the tubing or the fins.

## RESINS AND PLANT SAP

**RESIN IS THE** STICKY STUFF, SOMETIMES KNOWN AS PINE SAP, THAT CAN MAKE A GOOEY MESS ON CLOTHING, CARPETING AND SKIN. A HOT-WATER WASH WON'T DO THE TRICK—RESIN NEEDS A MORE AGGRESSIVE APPROACH. WHEN REMOVING TREE OR PLANT SAP FROM CLOTHING AND CARPETING, TRY OUT THESE METHODS.

**If you're confronted with lumps of resin or sap,** first scrape off what you can with a dull knife or clean paddle-pop stick. Then apply eucalyptus oil, turpentine, methylated spirits, cleaning solvent or a pre-wash stain remover, such as Preen or Frend, testing a hidden part of the garment or carpet beforehand to make sure it's colour-fast.

**To treat a garment,** place it face down on a clean, absorbent rag. Sponge or spray solvent (see list above) full strength on the front and back of the sticky stuff to saturate it. Allow it to dry. (If you use methylated spirits, dilute it, using 1 part alcohol to 2 parts water, just to be safe.) The resin or sap should dissolve and seep into the rag underneath. If it doesn't, repeat the process.

Simple solutions

### There's the rub

Gardeners often find that the milky sap from pruned plants, such as Chinese jasmine (*Trachelospermum*) dries on the hands to a sticky, dark residue that won't come off with soap and water. Pour a heaped spoonful of ordinary white sugar into the palm of your hand, add enough eucalyptus oil to moisten the sugar and rub your hands together until the stains disappear. Then wash with soap and water.

**For small resin spots,** saturate a cotton wool ball or bud in eucalyptus oil or full-strength methylated spirits and dab on the spot, blotting all the time. Then launder the garment separately, using liquid laundry detergent and the hottest water the fabric can take. If the stain persists, mix equal parts liquid laundry detergent and ammonia and soak. Then launder again as before.

**For carpets,** always apply the solvent of your choice to a clean rag and then apply the rag to the sappy mess and blot.

**To remove resin from skin,** dab eucalyptus oil or full-strength methylated spirits on the stain with a cotton wool ball or bud. Wash with soap and the hottest water you can stand.

## ROOFING

**MOSS, ALGAE AND** MILDEW ADORE YOUR ROOF. THEY ESPECIALLY FEAST ON WOODEN SHINGLES AND BURROW BELOW, CAUSING SHINGLES TO BLACKEN AND LOSE LAYERS. EMBARK CAUTIOUSLY ON DO-IT-YOURSELF ROOF CLEANING. WHEN YOU COMBINE A STEEP PITCH WITH THE USE OF LADDERS AND CLEANERS THAT MAKE THE ROOF SLIPPERY, YOU HAVE A RECIPE FOR POTENTIAL DISASTER.

**To clean asphalt roofs** as well as cedar and other shake-shingled roofs, first go to a home improvement shop and pick up a cleaner for treated-wood decks—one that contains oxygen bleach. (Don't use chlorine bleach.) On a cloudy day, when the roof is cool, mix the cleaner according to the package instructions and squirt it on the roof with a garden sprayer. (High-pressure sprayers will damage the roof.) Let the cleaner sit for half an hour. Then give it a scrubbing with a broom or brush. Rinse thoroughly with a garden hose.

**Tile roofs** can attract moss and other growth, too, but cleaning them yourself is not recommended because wet tiles are delicate and extremely slippery. Let a professional do the job.

**To create an inhospitable environment for growth on your roof,** apply zinc strips close to the top (or ridge) of the roof. Rainwater reacts with the zinc and drips down the roof, discouraging growth. To get the strips, contact a roofing supply company.

### ★★★ EXPERT ADVICE

#### PAINT ON A COOL TIN ROOF

Although modern roofing metal usually has a permanent finish, the biggest problem with maintaining an old tin roof is keeping it painted. Paint often sheds from tin roofs in sheets. Then you've got big problems, mostly with rust.

Choose a sunny but cool day to paint a tin roof. Wash it first, using a soapy solution in your garden sprayer, then rinse well. Allow it to dry. Then paint with a rustproof, oil-based paint. If you are going to collect rainwater from your newly painted roof, talk to a paint consultant about which paint to use.

**Several kinds of metal roofing,** including powder-coated steel and copper, need little maintenance. Costly to install, these roofs nonetheless last many years.

# RUGS

**THE BEST WAY** TO KEEP A RUG LOOKING FRESH IS TO KEEP IT FROM GETTING DIRTY IN THE FIRST PLACE. REMOVE YOUR OUTDOOR SHOES WHEN ENTERING THE HOUSE AND YOU'LL CUT DOWN ON 80 PER CENT OF THE DIRT TRACKED IN. DURING WET WEATHER, GIVE RUGS A GOOD, REGULAR SHAKE OUTSIDE. VACUUM THEM OFTEN, FRONT AND BACK, AGAINST THE NAP TO PICK UP GROUND-IN DIRT. RUGS IN HIGH-TRAFFIC AREAS NEED A MORE THOROUGH CLEANING AT LEAST ONCE A YEAR; THOSE IN OUT-OF-THE-WAY PLACES, LESS OFTEN.

**To shampoo a small rug,** follow these steps:

- Vacuum the rug.
- Mix ½ cup of mild dishwashing liquid or rug shampoo with 2 litres of cool water in a clean bucket. (Don't use harsh detergents, sudsy ammonia or regular ammonia on your rugs.) Aerosol carpet and rug sprays also work well on smaller rugs or small areas of carpet. Test the cleaner you're using on a hidden spot to make sure the rug is colour-fast—many Persian rugs, especially old ones, are not.
- With a long-bristled, soft brush or a firm, non-shedding sponge, brush the solution on the pile in the direction of the nap, but don't scrub. Wet the rug thoroughly.
- Wash the rug's fringe, if it has one. If the floor is wood or otherwise easily damaged by water, place a plastic or rubber drop sheet under the fringe. Then put a clean, white towel on top of that (still beneath the fringe). Using a brush or sponge moistened (not sopping) with the cleaning solution, brush the fringe from the knots out to the end. To rinse, replace the first towel under the fringe with a dry towel and blot the fringe with yet another towel dampened with warm water. Allow the fringe to dry on a third dry towel.
- To rinse the main part of the rug, wet clean rags with warm water and press them against the rug.
- Squeeze out excess. (A window squeegee works well.) Squeegee the pile in the direction of the nap until no more water comes out. Use more towels to mop up any excess.
- If you have plastic underneath the rug and it's now wet, replace it with dry plastic. Lay down dry towels and lay the rug flat on the towels to dry thoroughly on one side. Then flip it over to dry the other, replacing the towels again if need be. Another technique is to dry the rug on top of an outdoor or picnic table in the shade outside.
- If the pile feels stiff, vacuum or brush it gently.

## Cleaning a rug

**1** Work cleaning solution into the rug in the direction of the rug's nap.

**2** A squeegee works well to remove excess moisture after cleaning.

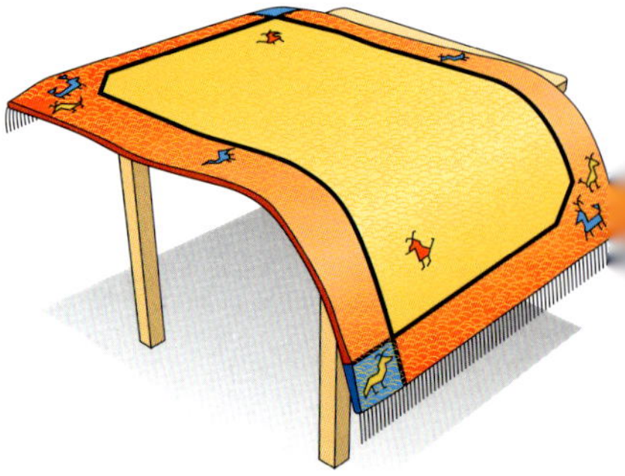

**3** Dry the cleaned rug over a table outside in the shade, to avoid fading.

**To remove a rug stain,** several rules of thumb apply. You should attempt to attack problems in this order:

- Blot stains, using clean rags or absorbent white towels.
- Scrape up whatever solids you can, using a kitchen knife, spatula or putty knife (the idea is that it's a blunt knife).
- Work from the stain's outer edges to its centre, rather than from the inside out, which could spread the stain.
- If the stain has penetrated the entire rug, place a clean rag underneath the rug to absorb whatever seeped through.
- Dilute the stain by blotting with a cloth dampened with water or plain soda water (not flavoured or coloured soda water).
- Try a dab of rug and carpet cleaner, according to package instructions. (Test first on an inconspicuous area.)
- If this doesn't work, mix 1 teaspoon of mild dishwashing liquid with 1 cup of warm water. Blot with a white towel dampened with clear water, but be careful not to saturate.
- Shaving cream can also work wonders. Moisten the spot with water, work in the shaving cream and then rinse the stained area with a clean rag dampened with cool water.
- Mix 1 tablespoon of household ammonia with ½ cup of water. Dab the solution on with a clean rag. Then mix ½ cup of vinegar and 1 cup of water. Blot this mixture on to curb the ammonia action. Rinse with a clean rag dampened with cool water.
- Mix enough powdered enzyme laundry detergent with water to make a paste. Make sure the detergent has no bluing or whitening agents. Let the paste sit for 10 minutes and then remove any residue with a wooden spoon. Blot with a clean towel and rinse with another towel wrung out in warm water.

*See also:*
• CARPETS

# RUST

**RUST IS UNSIGHTLY** AND DESTRUCTIVE. WHEN METAL REACTS WITH AIR, RUST PROLIFERATES—AFFECTING IRON, STEEL, CHROME, BATHTUBS, TOILETS, SINKS, CONCRETE, GARDEN TOOLS, METAL OUTDOOR FURNITURE, CARPETS AND FABRIC, AMONG OTHER THINGS.

**Tips for cleaning rust off iron and steel** include:
Banish rust from iron and steel by first removing the rust and then repainting. Use fine sandpaper or steel wool for the removal job. If more drastic measures are needed, dip your abrasive in kerosene.

A dousing with cola soft-drink will dissolve mild rust on a baking dish.

**Remove rust from metal baking dishes** and other cookware by sprinkling powdered dishwasher or laundry detergent onto the spot and scouring with the cut edge of a raw potato half. Another

## Beware the water

Very occasionally, municipalities or water companies (depending on where you live) flush the lines of their water systems. Or sometimes, your own water pipes can be old and rusty. Rust from inside those pipes can wind up in your water, causing all sorts of problems with your clothes. If you unwittingly wash clothes during 'the flush', your laundry could easily become rust-stained or yellowed. (Often, local councils or water companies warn residents in a particular area that they're about to do pipe maintenance or a 'flush', so take heed of those warnings and refrain from washing your clothes until the pipe maintenance work is well and truly finished.) Should your clothes get stained in this manner, don't ever dry them in a tumble-dryer—this only sets the stains. Don't use bleach either; chlorine makes a temporary rust stain permanent.

Here are your choices:

- Wash the clothes immediately in clear water using heavy-duty detergent.
- Wash the clothes with 1 cup of non-precipitating water conditioner (such as Calgon)—no detergent! (Sometimes water conditioner can set a rust stain.)
- For white clothing, fill a large pot with water and boil with 1 cup of cream of tartar. Dip the garment for a few minutes, then rinse thoroughly.

method is to pour cola on the rust and let it work its magic overnight (see bottom of page 293). Then wash off the cookware in the morning.

**For rust on bathtubs, toilets and sinks,** rub with automotive rubbing compound on a clean rag. If the rust is really thick, use a pumice stone to penetrate the rust, along with more rubbing compound. Rubbing compound and pumice are readily available from most hardware and home improvement shops.

**If your stainless steel sink** gets rusty, rub it with lighter fluid. Be careful though, because this stuff is highly flammable.

Simple solutions

### Rust-free scourers

If rusty steel wool drives you crazy, simply store it in a zip-seal plastic bag or container in the freezer after each use. That way it won't rust and will last much longer.

**To tackle rust stains on concrete,** sprinkle dry cement powder on the rust and use a small piece of flagstone (what patios are often made of) to rub out the stain. The combination of powder and stone acts like pumice and will often eradicate the rust.

**To remove rust stains from patio stones,** here's a technique you wouldn't expect. Wet the area with a hose and cover it with powdered lemonade mix (from the drinks and cordials section of supermarkets). Cover that with a piece of plastic (to prevent the moisture from evaporating) and hold it down with something heavy. Let it stand for 10 minutes or so. Scrub with a stiff-bristled brush and rinse with the hose. Repeat if necessary.

If the lemonade mix does not work, or you'd rather drink the lemonade, use CLR (Calcium Lime Rust), available from large supermarkets and hardware shops. This product is corrosive, so wear rubber gloves and follow the manufacturer's instructions.

**You can also first rinse the area with water** and then apply a solution of 1 part muriatic acid (from pool shops) to no fewer than

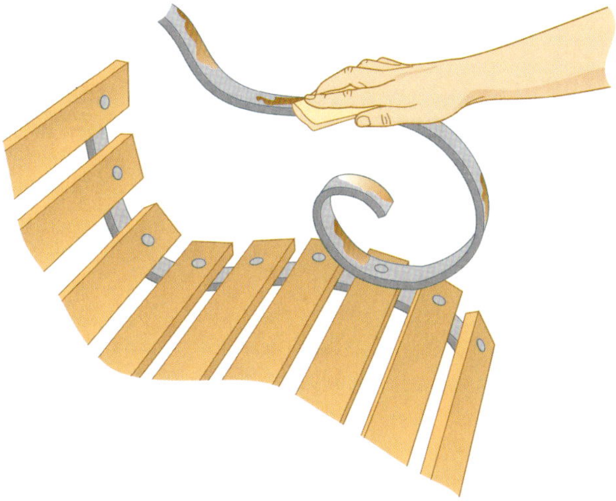

Sand rust from metal furniture after softening it first with kerosene.

5 parts water. Let the solution stand for a few minutes and then rinse with water. Again, wear rubber gloves and eye protection when using muriatic acid, and do not breathe in the fumes.

**When metal deck and porch furniture is badly rusted,** wrap the rusted part in a kerosene-soaked cloth for a few days. Then sand with medium-grit sandpaper (see above). Wash, rinse and dry thoroughly and then paint the furniture with a rustproof paint.

**If your carpet or rug has rust stains,** try mixing water with bicarbonate of soda into a paste. Apply the paste to the stain, allow it to sit 3–4 hours, and then use a commercial carpet shampoo according to the instructions on the package.

**For rust stains on clothing,** apply a paste of lemon juice and bicarbonate of soda to a hidden spot to make sure the colour holds. If all is well, apply the paste to the rust stains. Let it sit an hour before hanging the clothing outside to dry, then launder the garment as usual.

**For rust on white clothes,** try this alternative remedy: mix cream of tartar with lemon juice and apply it to the stain. Allow the garment to dry and then rinse thoroughly before washing as usual.

**If these gentle methods for fabric don't work** and you're desperate, you can try diluting 1 part CLR (Calcium Lime Rust) in 20 parts water and dabbing on the rust mark with a cotton bud, holding an old, white towel behind. The stain should disappear. Rinse immediately, as the solution will continue to react with the fabric and the product is not manufactured for use on fabrics. Always check for colour-fastness in an inconspicuous spot before trying this method.

# SADDLES AND TACK

HOW OFTEN YOU CLEAN SADDLES AND TACK DEPENDS ON HOW OFTEN YOU USE THEM. AT A MINIMUM, PLAN TO CLEAN AND CONDITION THEM AT LEAST TWICE A YEAR—MORE OFTEN, IF YOU'RE CAUGHT IN THE RAIN OR LIVE IN A COLD CLIMATE, WHICH CAN LEACH NATURAL OILS FROM LEATHER AND CAUSE DRY ROT TO TAKE OVER.

**WATCH OUT** If your saddle seat is suede, don't use soap and water on it. Instead, clean it with a stiff-bristled suede brush (available from shoe shops).

**EXPERT ADVICE**

### HOW TO HANDLE MILDEW AND FUNGUS ON LEATHER

For saddles and tack in humid climates, where leather can get mouldy and mildewy, a saddle oil boosted with a fungicide is sometimes recommended. But most saddlers recommend waterproofing of the saddle after conditioning to overcome this problem. If it's a problem in your area, clean the saddle then finish with a product containing wax to help keep the leather water-repellent, which will in turn keep mould and mildew away.

**To clean a saddle,** use saddle-soap, a sponge and warm water to work up a foamy lather. Stirrups, stirrup leathers and fenders attract the most dirt, so pay particular attention to those, wiping them on both sides. If dirt is really ingrained, let the foamy saddle-soap sit to soften it. Rinse off the soap—and be sure to do it thoroughly. (If you leave soap residue on the leather, it will attract rather than repel dirt.) Use toothpicks to lift out dirt on deeply tooled leather (see below).

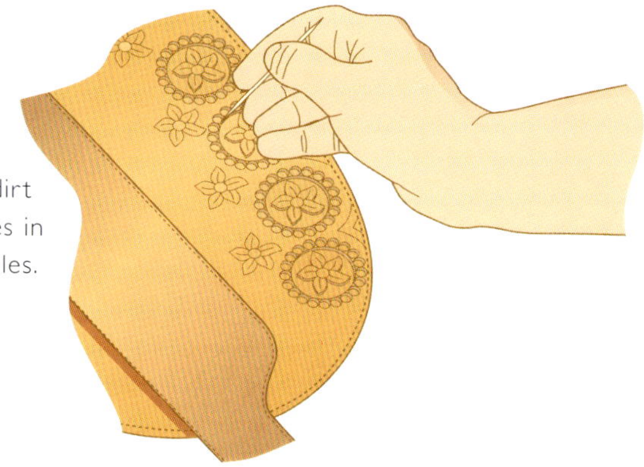

Use a toothpick to lift dirt out of all those tight spaces in deeply tooled leather saddles.

Allow the saddle to air-dry for 8–10 hours, but not in the sun, where it could dry out too much, then condition the leather lightly. On Western saddles, use either pure neat's-foot oil (a light yellow oil made from cattle shinbones and feet) or a leather conditioner, such as Joseph Lyddy Zorbel. Remember that neat's-foot (or any other oil, for that matter) will darken the leather. On English saddles, use a leather dressing, such as RM's Own Leather Dressing, applied with a soft cloth. Don't miss the underside of the seat, fenders and (on Western saddles) jockeys, the pieces of leather underneath the seat of the saddle. Then buff with a clean, soft cloth to bring out the leather's natural shine.

**To clean your tack,** use the same general technique as with saddles, but always take it apart first. Bits must be taken off the headstall and reins, for instance. Brush off any loose dirt with a rag or soft brush. Storing your saddle and tack is also important.

- Store a saddle on a rack with air circulating around it freely.
- To preserve that characteristic twist in the leather strap that connects Western-style stirrups to the saddle, turn the stirrups in the correct direction and then insert a wooden dowel through one stirrup, under the saddle and through the other stirrup.
- Hang bridles and halters on a rack shaped like a horse's head. (Nails or hooks can cause leather to bend and weaken.)
- Finally, keep your saddle free of dust and the dirt that accompanies dust, by shrouding it with a dust cover.

## SATIN

**CLEANING SATIN IS** TRICKY BECAUSE THIS SHINY FABRIC PICKS UP AND SHOWS GREASE AND OTHER STAINS MORE EASILY THAN MOST.

**WATCH OUT**

• Shield sheets made of silk and nylon from the sun. Never line dry nylon satin sheets, because the sun is nylon's public enemy No. 1. If your bedroom is sunny, choose acetate or polyester satin instead.

• Never dry woven acetate sheets in a tumble-dryer.

• Be especially careful when wringing silk satin sheets—silk is usually thin and tears easily.

**If you get a greasy stain on satin of any kind**—be it on blanket binding, satin sheets, pillows, Christmas decorations or other items—try blotting, but don't rub, the stain first with a clean, white rag. Then cover the stain with flour or polenta. Let it sit for an hour. The milled grain should absorb most of the stain. Gently brush the fabric with a soft-bristled brush and launder a washable item according to the instructions on the fabric care label. If a blanket is washable, its binding is too. Treat stains first with a pre-wash stain remover. If an item is not washable, take it to a drycleaner.

**Satin sheets** are a little trickier to care for because there are several types available on the market.

- If you have woven acetate sheets or silk satin sheets, dry-clean them, or hand wash them in a laundry tub or bathtub in room-temperature water and a gentle fabric wash, such as Softly. Hand wring gently, wrapping up the sheet in an absorbent white towel, then hang to dry.
- Polyester and nylon satin sheets are more durable. You can machine wash them, but hand washing will keep pilling to a minimum. If you are putting them in a washing machine, use warm or cool water and very little detergent. Never use bleach. Put them in the dryer on the lowest setting. Never line dry nylon sheets in the sun.

**To clean satin pillows and Christmas decorations,** vacuum them using the soft upholstery brush attachment. Give greasy stains the flour or polenta treatment described above. If stains persist, launder a satin pillow only if its cover comes off. It's best to dry-clean satin Christmas decorations (such as stockings), as well as satin curtains, bedspreads and comforters. Differences in their linings may cause the fabrics to dry differently.

## SCISSORS

**TO KEEP SCISSORS** CUTTING WELL, IT'S IMPORTANT TO CLEAN THEM. BUY DIFFERENT KINDS OF SCISSORS FOR DIFFERENT TASKS: A PAIR FOR CUTTING PAPER AND FOR CRAFT PROJECTS, ANOTHER PAIR FOR WORKING WITH FABRIC, SCISSORS FOR SNIPPING HAIR, AND SO ON.

**To keep your scissors cutting smoothly,** wipe the blades after each use with a soft rag. This prevents lint and other stuff from getting caught in the blade pivot area, where it can interfere with the performance of your scissors.

Oil scissors occasionally at the pivot area (around the screw head and between the blades) using a penetrating lubricant, such as WD-40. Never use vegetable oil or any other oil that attracts dirt and gets gummy. Gently work the blades a few times to force the lubricant into the joint. Wipe off any excess with a clean, dry rag, to avoid staining the item you're cutting next time you use them

**If your scissors get dirty,** wash them in dishwashing liquid and water, removing any sticky stuff with lighter fluid. Dry scissors thoroughly with a soft cloth before storing them.

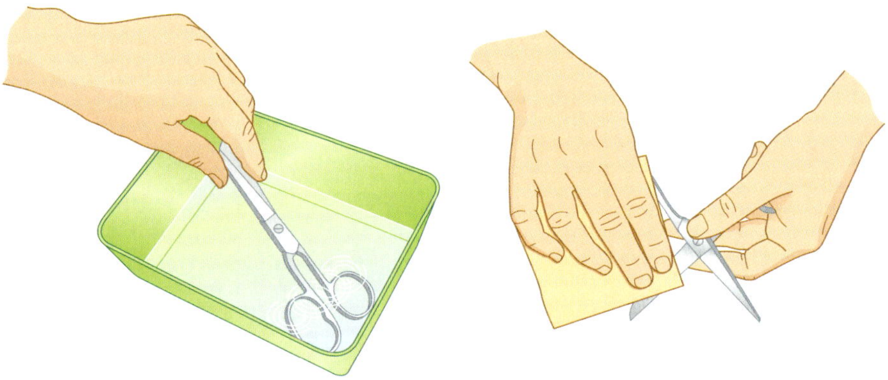

Soak rusty scissors in white vinegar, then sand them gently until they are smooth again.

Simple solutions

### Watch how you use pinking shears

Prolong the life of pinking shears by making sure there is always fabric between the blades when you cut. Never open or close the blades without fabric in between.

**If your scissors get rusty,** soak them first in white vinegar. Then use fine sandpaper on the handles and blades, being careful to avoid the cutting edges (see above). Store scissors in a dry, cool, clean place.

**To keep those blades sharp,** some scissors makers recommend using sharpeners. Most experts, however, suggest that you take them to a professional. In the meantime, if you cut across a piece of sandpaper a couple of times, it will temporarily sharpen the blades.

**To clean haircutting scissors,** try these steps:

- Wipe the blades clean after each use with a clean, soft cloth.
- Spray scissors occasionally with an antibacterial solution (Dettol, for instance, or see 'Combs', on page 132, for a recipe). Dry completely.
- Oil the pivot with light shear oil or clipper oil, available from beauty salons or barber shops. When you're not using your scissors, close the blades and store them somewhere dry.

## SCREENS

**WINDOW SCREENS CAN** GET ABSOLUTELY FILTHY, WHICH IS NOT SURPRISING WHEN YOU CONSIDER THAT THEIR JOB IS TO KEEP DUST, POLLEN, INSECTS AND OTHER AIRBORNE DETRITUS OUTSIDE. CLEAN YOUR SCREENS AT LEAST ONCE A YEAR, PREFERABLY WHEN THE WEATHER BECOMES WARMER AND THEY'RE BEING USED A LOT.

**To clean window screens,** move them to a flat surface, being careful not to place them where underlying objects can damage them. If you lay them in your garden, remove rocks or other sharp objects underneath. Placing them on top of a large drop sheet or old shower curtain is a good idea, or just lay them on a paved driveway.

In a large bucket, mix 3 parts warm water with 1 part ammonia and 2 tablespoons each of dishwashing liquid and borax. (Or purchase an all-purpose cleaner from a hardware shop.) Wearing rubber gloves, pour the mixture into a trigger spray bottle. Wet the screens thoroughly with a garden hose. Spray the cleaner onto the screens, front and back, being careful not to miss those grimy corners. Allow the cleaning solution to sit on the screens for at least 5 minutes, to better penetrate the mesh and do the dirty work for you. The less scrubbing you do on screens the better, as they get brittle and often loosen with age.

**EXPERT ADVICE**

### GETTING SCREENS IN THE RIGHT WINDOWS

Number your screens, so that you can tell which one goes where. Or put a number on each window frame, in a hidden spot, and then write or scratch the corresponding number on its screen frame.

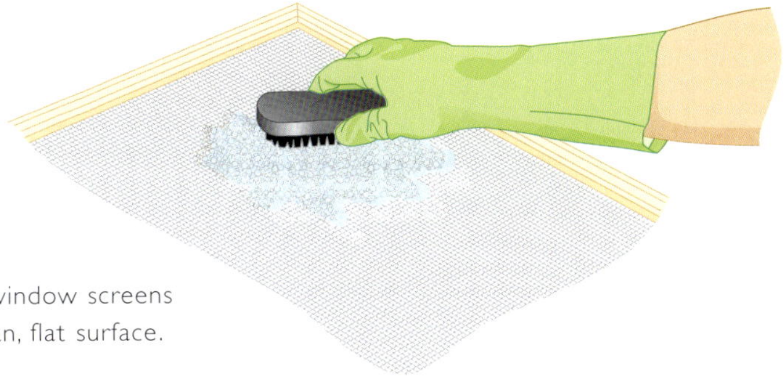

Scrub your window screens gently on a clean, flat surface.

Scrub both sides—gently—with a soft-bristled brush (see above), using an old toothbrush to get into grimy corners. Rinse the brushes as you work so that you don't end up smearing around more grime than you remove. Rinse the screens thoroughly with a hose and then air-dry them in the sun, propped up against the house or bushes.

## SEWING MACHINES

**IF YOU TAKE** CARE OF YOUR SEWING MACHINE IT WILL LAST LONGER AND SEW BETTER. THE INSTRUCTIONS IN THIS ENTRY APPLY PRIMARILY TO TRADITIONAL MECHANICAL SEWING MACHINES OPERATED BY AN ELECTRIC MOTOR. TO CLEAN THE MORE FRAGILE COMPUTERISED MACHINES, FOLLOW THE INSTRUCTIONS IN YOUR OWNER'S MANUAL.

**For a mechanical sewing machine,** always use the right oil to keep it humming. Use sewing machine oil (available from fabric shops and sewing machine shops). Other common lubricants, such as WD-40, dry too fast and will eventually cause the machine to seize and stop. Put no more than one or two drops of sewing machine oil in each of the 30-odd holes that pockmark your machine.

**Floss your machine** to banish the fuzzies and keep it running smoothly. Slide the edges of a thin piece of calico between the tension disks (those metal pieces the thread passes through). Make sure the presser foot is up to slacken the tension springs. (If you don't have calico, gently slide a credit card between the disks to loosen dust and dirt caught between them.) Remove the machine's cover. Using a can of compressed air or a hair dryer, hit movable parts with a stream of air, from back to front, to remove any loose threads, lint and fuzzy stuff.

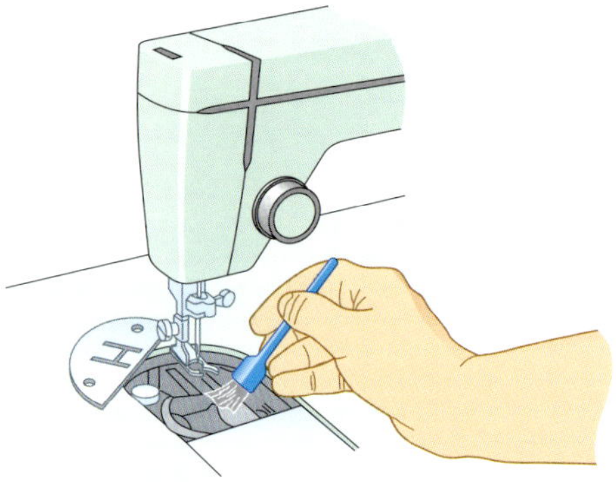


Clean out dust and lint regularly from your machine.

**Take off the throat plate** (sometimes called the needle plate), paying close attention to how it is removed and replaced. On some models, it screws in. On others, it's spring-loaded. Same thing goes for the bobbin, bobbin case (also called the shuttle) and hook race—watch what you're taking apart, or you may not get it together again. Use compressed air, a hair dryer or a small, stiff-bristled nylon brush to clean these parts (see left). At a pinch, a pipe-cleaner will extract small fibres from moving parts. But don't use toothpicks—they're too flimsy and could break off inside and wreak havoc with the mechanism.

**Dust the outside with a clean cloth.** (Microfibre cloth works well.) A mild household cleaner, such as Spray n' Wipe or Windex, does the job on grimy fingerprints. Spray first on a cloth and then wipe. If the case is metal, sewing-machine oil or WD-40, sprayed first on a rag, will shine it up nicely.

**WATCH OUT** Never oil a computerised sewing machine (unless the manual specifically instructs you to do so) or use any kind of liquid anywhere near it. Oil and liquids can irreparably damage the computer circuit boards. Use a hair dryer to blow away lint. If you're unsure about cleaning your computerised sewing machine, take it to a sewing machine repair shop.

**Keep your machine clean** by covering it when you're not using it. Ready-made plastic covers are sold at fabric and sewing machine shops. Or make one yourself from an old pillowcase. Keep the machine away from heat, light and open windows.

## SHELLS

**SEASHELLS COME IN** A MYRIAD OF SIZES, COLOURS AND VARIETIES, BUT THEY'RE MAINLY CHARACTERISED AS EITHER DEAD OR ALIVE. NEVER REMOVE A LIVING SHELL FROM NATIONAL PARKS OR WILDLIFE MARINE RESERVES.

**To clean empty seashells,** soak them in a 50:50 solution of bleach and water. How long you do this depends on the shells you're cleaning, as well as how many you do at once. Soak first for 30 minutes, longer if you want shells bleached white or if they feel really grimy. Before removing them from the solution, make sure that the periostracum—the leatherlike, flaky covering on some shells—is gone. Rinse thoroughly with fresh, warm water.

- If barnacles and other clingy stuff stay stuck onto the seashell, use a pointy toothpick or scalpel to remove them.
- If the lip of a seashell gets chipped, use a rotary grinder or file to smooth out the rough edges.
- If you like your shells to shine, coat them with a light layer of paraffin oil or baby oil.

**To clean seashells still containing residual decayed matter,** you have a choice of cleaning methods:

- Bury the shells 45 centimetres deep in your garden for a month or two. Insects, bacteria, worms, larvae and other tiny organisms will eat everything you want to get out of the shell.
- Give them the deep-freeze treatment. Place the shells in a waterproof bag, add enough water to the bag to cover the shells and stick

them in the freezer for a few days. Then allow them to thaw to room temperature. You should be able to grab the remaining dead tissue inside and pull it out without too much difficulty.

- Boil water in a pot and submerge the shells for 5 minutes. Using tongs and being careful not to burn yourself, remove one shell at a time and, grasping it with gloves or a towel, pull out the tissue inside.
- A smelly but no less effective way to clean shells is to 'cook' them in the microwave. (Time will vary depending on the oven's power and the strength of the shell.) Start with 30 seconds and increase the time in 10-second increments. Use tongs and special care as you remove the shells and grab whatever decayed animal tissue remains.

Should tiny pieces of animal tissue remain, put the shell outdoors and allow flies, insects and ants to eat away what's left. Once all the flesh is gone, treat the shells as described above, then give them a bleach bath and rinse completely.

## SHOES

**MUCH OF THE** FOOTWEAR MEN, WOMEN AND CHILDREN WEAR TODAY IS NOT LEATHER. STILL, TAKING CARE OF YOUR SHOES, WHATEVER THEY'RE MADE OF, MEANS YOU'LL EXTEND THEIR USEFULNESS AND THEIR ATTRACTIVENESS.

**To protect new leather shoes,** spray or rub them with a water and stain repellent such as Waproo Water Proofer before wearing them. Make sure you use a repellent made especially for leather. Then polish them before stepping out. Leather shoes are usually malnourished and dry when they come out of the box, and the extra layer of polish will give them that extra bit of protection.

**To give leather shoes and boots a shine**—without the spit and polish—follow these steps:

- Remove laces
- Brush off loose dirt with a stiff brush or cloth
- If the shoes are especially dirty, clean them with saddle-soap, following the package instructions
- Rub a clean, cotton cloth in polish and then onto the shoes. Let the polish dry for 10 minutes
- Buff with a clean cloth or old pantihose.

**To clean patent leather shoes,** first remove any scuff marks with a pencil rubber. Then shine them with baby oil, furniture polish, petroleum jelly (see left) or cream leather cleaner and conditioner (available from shoe repair shops). Buff with a paper towel or clean cloth. Be gentle—patent leather scratches easily. In a pinch, rub leather or patent shoes with hand cream and then buff. On imitation patent leather, use mild dishwashing liquid or a car interior vinyl and plastic cleaner, such as Meguiar's (available from automotive shops).

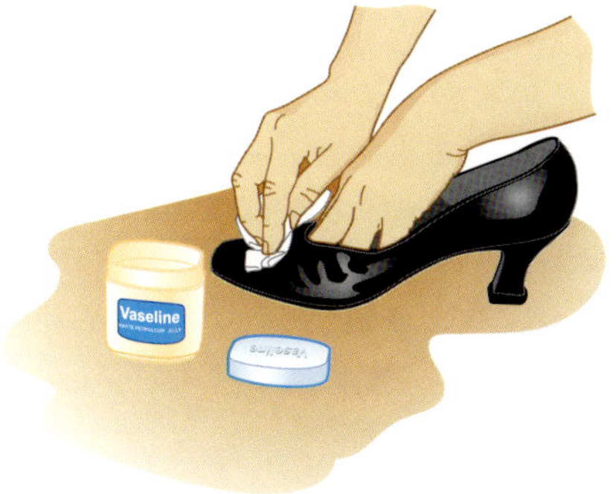


Petroleum jelly will help keep your patent leather shoes shiny longer.

**To remove mineral salt stains** from leather shoes that have been wet, rub with equal parts of water and vinegar, using a cotton pad.

Simple solutions

## When you don't have time to polish

For an instant shine for your shoes, use baby wipes. This technique will dry out the leather over time, so follow up with polish later on.

*See also:*
• JOGGERS AND SNEAKERS

**To clean white shoes,** give them a swipe with a cloth dabbed in ammonia. (This works well on canvas, too.) Remove scuff marks with a dab of white toothpaste, then buff.

**To protect suede shoes,** apply a stain repellent designed for suede or nubuck. Use a rubber-tipped or plastic brush to brush the nap and remove dirt. If you get a stain, remove it straight away with a solvent made for either material. Or you can dab an oily stain with a bit of dry-cleaning fluid, then cover the stain with baby powder or chalk dust (which you can pulverise in a zip-lock plastic bag using a small hammer or rolling pin). Allow the powder to sit overnight until completely dry again, then brush it off.

**To remove scuff marks on smooth leather shoes,** rub the marks with the cut edge of a raw potato and then buff.

# SHOWERS

**HOW CAN THE** SHOWER—THE PLACE WHERE YOU CLEAN YOURSELF—GET SO DIRTY? NOWHERE, SAVE FOR THE KITCHEN SINK, DOES A HOME SHOW GRIME MORE THAN IN THE SHOWER. SOAP, SHAMPOO AND DIRT FROM THE SHOWER'S TEMPORARY OCCUPANTS COMBINE TO MAKE AN UNSIGHTLY MESS.

**To keep your shower sparkling,** try these tips:

- Next time you shower, clean the shower, too. The steam from your shower will help loosen any grime and make the job easier.
- For tiled shower walls and floor, use dishwasher detergent (either powder or liquid will do). Mix ¼ cup of dishwasher detergent with warm water in a small pump spray bottle and shake to dissolve the detergent. Spray liberally on walls, let it sit for 2–3 hours and then scrub with a sponge. Use a sponge mop to scrub high spots and the floor.
- To clean tile grout, make a paste of bicarbonate of soda and bleach (add bleach to the powder until it's a thick paste). Smear the paste on with a spatula. Air-dry for an hour and then scrub with a toothbrush and water (see below). (Never use ammonia nearby, since ammonia and bleach don't mix.)
- To prevent water spots, rub the shower walls and doors with a squeegee straight after you have had a shower. If you don't have a

## Cleaning tile grout

**1** Liberally smear bicarbonate of soda paste onto the grout with a spatula.

**2** After about an hour, scrub the tiles clean using an old, soft toothbrush.

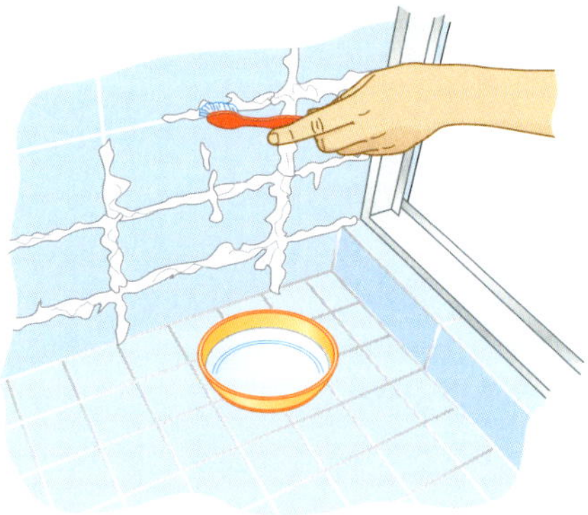

### Easy come, easy go

Frustrated by stubborn grout grunge? If you've tried other methods to no avail, put on some rubber gloves for protection and spray on some oven cleaner. Wipe the cleaner off with a sponge within 5 seconds, then rinse thoroughly with water. Make sure the bathroom is well ventilated when you do this.

Soak your shower head overnight in a plastic bag filled with white vinegar.

squeegee, an old wiper blade will do. Or try a daily shower cleaner (available from supermarkets). Spray surfaces straight after you shower, while the walls are still warm and wet. The shower cleaner will prevent deposits from forming on shower walls and will wash down the drain the next time you take a shower.

**If your shower sprouts mould,** try this trick. Wipe down the walls with a solution of 1 teaspoon of water softener (washing soda crystals will do), 1 tablespoon of ammonia and 1 tablespoon of vinegar in ¾ cup of warm water. Rinse with fresh water and buff dry.

**To clean your shower doors,** follow these pointers:

- Wash them with white vinegar to remove soap scum.
- Alternatively, use leftover white wine that's rapidly turning to vinegar, empty it into a trigger spray bottle and squirt it on your shower doors. Rinse well with water and dry with a soft cloth.
- Wipe down the doors with a solution of washing soda and water on a damp cloth. Buff with a clean, dry cloth.
- Another way to keep soap scum away is to wipe down the shower doors with lemon oil. Baby oil works too, as does furniture polish, buffed with a soft cloth. (This also works on tiled showers, but don't put these slippery substances on a shower floor.)
- Scrub shower door runners with white toothpaste and an old toothbrush. Brush with vinegar to rinse. Or dip a stiff-bristled paintbrush in vinegar and scrub the runners thoroughly.
- To keep runners from growing a bumper crop of mildew, run the head of a small sponge paintbrush along the bottom runner channels after you've finished showering.

**To remove soap film on a plastic shower curtain,** place it in the washing machine with two or three large bath towels. Add ½ cup of vinegar and wash, removing it before the spin cycle. Hang it up straight afterwards to dry. If mildew is out of control, use ¾ cup of chlorine bleach instead. To avoid that soapy build-up on the bottom of the shower curtain, rub it with baby oil. Always keep a shower curtain unfurled to give the fuzzy stuff a less inviting place to grow.

**Mould on a nylon shower curtain** can be removed by soaking the curtain overnight in a bleach solution—oxygen or chlorine—then washing in the washing machine.

**To clean the shower head,** remove it and soak it in a container with a 50:50 mix of hot water and white vinegar.

If you don't want to take the shower head off, pour 8 centimetres of vinegar into a plastic sandwich bag and then pull the bag up over the entire head. Secure the bag and leave it overnight (see above left).

*See also:*
• BATHTUBS • TILES

# SHUTTERS

**IT'S ONE OF** THOSE CURIOUS LITTLE IRONIES OF LIFE THAT SHUTTERS OFTEN BECOME MORE UNSIGHTLY THAN DECORATIVE AS THE DUST AND GRIME ACCUMULATE.

**Regular maintenance** will keep your indoor shutter-cleaning jobs to a minimum. Dust every month on both sides with the soft brush attachment of your vacuum. In between sessions with your vacuum, touch up the shutters with a microfibre cloth or feather duster.

**To clean indoor shutters,** remove the shutters from their hinges and put them somewhere level—a workbench topped with a white towel, for instance. Spray the shutters with a gentle, all-purpose cleaner, such as Earth Choice or Ajax Spray n' Wipe, taking special care to penetrate the cracks and crevices. Allow the cleaner to sit on the shutters for 5 minutes before rolling up your sleeves. Pull on some rubber gloves and start cleaning at the top of shutters and work towards the bottom. Clean the slats with a terry towelling cloth, your rubber-gloved fingers, or a small, soft-bristled brush for nooks and crannies. Use a trigger spray bottle filled with warm water to spray away dirt and other grime from the slats. Using a dry cloth, dry the slats one at a time. You can reach hard-to-dry areas with a rag wrapped around the handle of a wooden spoon or stick (see below).

To dust shutters, after they've been taken off their hinges, wrap a rag around a wooden stick or spoon and get into the awkward crevices between slats.

**Cleaning outdoor shutters** is basically the same operation—with a few refinements. Remove the shutters from the outside walls and lay them flat or prop them against a sawhorse or other secure support. Wet down the shutters with an all-purpose cleaner or a spray bottle of water with a squirt of dishwashing liquid added. Leave the cleaner on for a few minutes. Then use a screwdriver, wrapped in a towel, to attack hard-to-reach spots. Rinse with a garden hose, using as much water pressure as your hose can muster. Dry the slats with a towel. Leave them to finish drying in the sun.

*See also:*
• LOUVRES

# SILK

**WHEN CLEANING SILK,** YOU DON'T WANT TO TURN A SILK PURSE INTO A SOW'S EAR BY USING THE WRONG TECHNIQUE. MANY SILK GARMENTS ARE WASHABLE IF YOU ARE CAREFUL. CHECK THE FABRIC CARE LABEL INSTRUCTIONS.

**Treat stains from spills** and similar accidents before you wash silk clothing. (See 'Perspiration and deodorant stains', below.) On a hidden spot, apply a paste of powdered laundry starch and cold water to make sure the silk is colour-fast. If it is, apply the paste to the stain, let it dry and then brush it away.

**To wash a silk garment,** you can either do it by hand or use the delicate cycle and cool or warm water in your washing machine. A mild detergent, such as Softly, works best. Carefully roll the garment in an absorbent white towel to blot up excess moisture (see below). Then either lay it flat to dry or hang it on a padded coathanger.

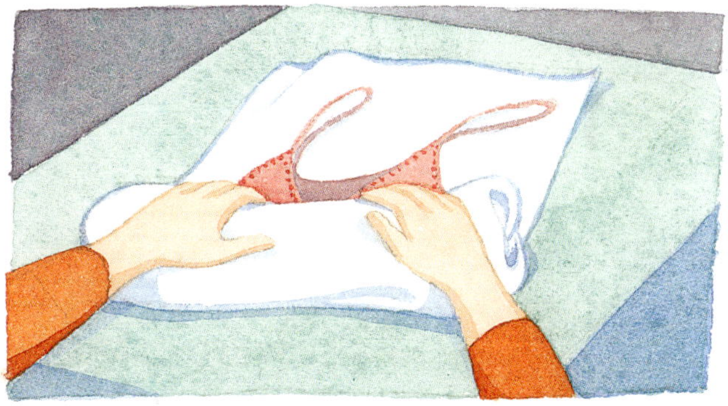

Roll delicate silk garments in a white towel to remove excess moisture.

**WATCH OUT** When cleaning silk, always keep these precautions in mind:
- Never use chlorine bleach; it can irreparably damage the fabric.
- Never dry silk garments in sunlight; it will fade and weaken the fabric.
- Never wash silk ties; both the silk and its lining are prone to shrinkage. (The lining will usually shrivel first.) Instead, take them to a drycleaner.
- When you're dressing, apply hair spray, make-up and other beauty products before putting on anything made of silk. The alcohol in them could cause dyes to bleed into the fabric.

*See also:*
• SATIN

**To iron silk,** use a low-heat setting and iron gently, on the inside of the garment only.

**Perspiration and deodorant stains** can discolour and weaken silk. (The salt in perspiration, and aluminium chloride and other chemicals in deodorants and antiperspirants, can stain silk.) Dry-clean or wash perspiration-stained garments as soon as possible.

To treat perspiration or deodorant stains on washable silk garments, try one of these remedies, but first test it on a hidden spot to see whether the fabric dye holds:
- Soak the perspiration stain in warm water and a paste of table salt and white vinegar.
- Make a paste of cream of tartar and warm water and apply it to the stain. Allow the paste to dry, brush it off and launder.
- Apply a mixture of warm water and water softener to the stained area and then rub with a bar of laundry soap. Brush it off and then wash as usual.
- Dissolve two aspirin tablets in ½ cup of warm water and apply it to the stain. Let it dry for a few hours, brush it off and launder.

To avoid perspiration stains in the first place, apply deodorant and then use your hair dryer to dry your underarms before you dress.

# SILVER JEWELLERY

**AIR AND LIGHT** ARE THE TWO BIGGEST FOES OF SILVER JEWELLERY. SO HOW YOU STORE YOUR SILVER JEWELLERY MAKES A BIG DIFFERENCE TO HOW MUCH IT TARNISHES.

**WATCH OUT**

- When cleaning silver pieces with precious stones, don't use abrasives near the stones.
- Don't soak pieces with stones for longer than a few seconds; water can dissolve the glue that holds them.
- Silver hates chlorine, so take it off before jumping into the pool.

**Always store clean silver jewellery** in a cool, dry place, wrapped separately in a soft cloth and then enclosed in a resealable plastic bag to prevent it from getting jostled about and scratched.

**Clean your silver jewellery once a month** if you wear it a lot. The best cleaner is still a good old-fashioned silver paste or liquid polish. Apply with a soft cloth as instructed and then buff with another cloth. Rinse gently in warm water if needed.

**Another method** is to rub with a soft cloth dipped in bicarbonate of soda, using a frayed toothbrush for hard-to-reach areas. Rinse well in warm water and buff dry with another cloth.

**Still another trick** is to line a small bowl with aluminium foil, shiny side towards you. Fill the bowl with hot water and mix in 1 tablespoon of bleach-free powdered laundry detergent (not liquid), such as Omo. Put the jewellery in the solution and let it soak for a minute. Then rinse completely and air-dry.

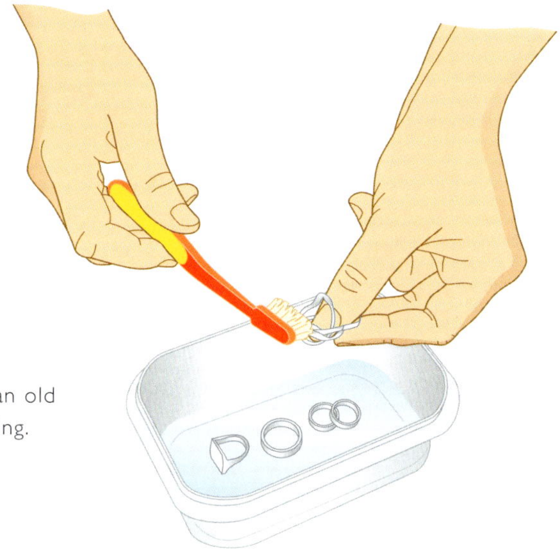

Scrub stubborn tarnish with an old toothbrush after overnight soaking.

**To clean badly tarnished or dirty silver jewellery,** fill a small plastic bowl with warm water and add a few drops of dishwashing liquid. Soak the jewellery in the solution overnight. Should the dirt persist after the overnight soak, clean the piece with an old toothbrush (see above). Then rinse and dry carefully with a soft cloth.

**Specially treated anti-tarnish cloths,** available from most supermarkets, may also be used to touch up silver jewellery.

## SILVERWARE

**SILVERWARE, WHETHER PLATED** OR STERLING, BENEFITS FROM FREQUENT USE. ROTATE YOUR PIECES SO THAT THEY WILL AGE UNIFORMLY.

A quick rub with a silver cloth will restore silver's shine between cleanings.

**EXPERT ADVICE**

CHECK THE MENU

Silver reacts badly to mustard, salt and tomato sauce, so clean it straight away if it touches any of these foods. And don't serve eggs or mayonnaise on silver surfaces, either. The sulphur in these foods will tarnish the silver.

**Clean your silver twice a year** following this tried-and-true method. Use a high-quality silver polish with anti-tarnish ability (Goddard's Silver Foam is one), a soft cloth to apply the polish in a circular motion, and warm water to rinse.

**If you have candle wax on your silver,** don't scrape it off—you could scratch the surface. Instead, soften the wax in a warm oven or with a hair dryer on low, then peel it off or gently prise it off using a paddle-pop stick. Or dribble on a bit of mineral turpentine or methylated spirits to dislodge the wax. Do not put a silver candlestick in the freezer to harden wax for removal, as it may damage the silver.

**To clean ornate silver pieces,** sprinkle on a bit of bicarbonate of soda and then rub gently with a soft cloth.

**To wash silver,** do it by hand in mild dishwashing liquid and warm water and dry immediately with a soft cloth. Water left on silver can pit and corrode it. Be especially careful with silver candlesticks, candelabra and knife handles filled with paste or wax, because if you rub too hard or rinse in hot water they could soften and bend.

As a general rule, don't wash silver in the dishwasher; it's too soft to withstand the jostling and abrasion. If you do, keep it away from metals such as copper and stainless steel. They will mark if they touch.

**To restore silver's shine between cleanings,** use polishing gloves and impregnated cloths or a jeweller's rouge cloth—flannel treated with a red polishing powder (see above left). These items are available from hardware shops and many department stores.

**To store a silver serving piece,** slip it into an anti-tarnish bag or cloth. Non-buffered tissue paper, an acid-free product sold at craft shops, also works. Then place that in a plastic bag. (Don't use newspaper, as the carbon in the printing ink can eat into silver.) Silica gel packets placed inside will help to inhibit moisture. Don't use rubber bands to close the bag—they contain sulphur, which damages silver. Store silver servers away from sunlight.

## SINKS

**ALL THE SOAPY** DEPOSITS, FOOD STAINS, RUST AND WATER SPOTS ACCUMULATING ON SINKS ARE A SIGN THAT REGULAR CLEANING SHOULD BE A ROUTINE THING.

**For general cleaning of any sink,** regardless of the material it's made of, get out the dishwashing liquid, liquid laundry detergent or all-purpose cleaners, such as Earth Choice or Spray n' Wipe. Using a small amount of detergent and a couple of drops of water, scrub the sink with a soft sponge. Rinse away residue. Don't use an abrasive cleaning agent or applicator. A gentle cream cleanser, such as Jif, is good for very bad stains.

Rub a freshly cut lemon around a porcelain sink to remove stains.

**For a lightly stained porcelain sink,** try one of these treatments:

- Rub a freshly cut lemon around the sink to cut through the grease (see left). Rinse with running water.
- Use bicarbonate of soda in warm water. Sprinkle a little bicarbonate of soda around the sink and then rub it with a damp sponge. Rinse with vinegar or lemon juice to help neutralise the alkaline cleaner and then rinse with running water.
- Make a paste the consistency of toothpaste with bicarbonate of soda and water and gently rub the sink with a sponge or soft nylon brush. Polish with a paper towel or soft cloth.

Never use scouring powders or steel wool on porcelain sinks, because they will scratch.

**To remove heavy stains,** even rust, rub the sink with a paste consisting of 250 grams of powdered borax (available from supermarkets) and 60 millilitres of lemon juice. Dab a cloth or sponge in the paste, rub around the sink and then rinse with running water.

**To remove rust from stainless steel or iron sinks,** wipe WD-40 on the rust mark with a cloth and rinse thoroughly.

**To remove water spots from any sink,** use a cloth dampened with methylated spirits or vinegar.

Simple solutions

## Neutralise that acid

You can cut down on the time you spend cleaning by not leaving acidic foods—citrus fruits, berries, vinegar, salad dressings, tea or coffee—on your sink's surface for a long time. Either wash the dishes straight away or put them in a dishwasher. Dry the sink immediately after use to prevent water spotting.

**For a sparkling white sink,** place paper towels across the bottom and saturate them with household bleach. Let them sit for 30 minutes, then rinse with running water. Do not use bleach in coloured porcelain sinks, because it will fade the colour. Clean these sinks with mild dishwashing liquid, vinegar or bicarbonate of soda.

**To maintain your sink's lustre,** apply a car wash and wax, with a soft, cotton towel. Wipe the cleaner on, let it dry for 5–10 minutes and then wipe it off. Do this every three months or so.

**Stains in Corian-type sinks** can be removed with toothpaste or a paste of bicarbonate of soda and water. Gently scrub the paste on with a non-scouring scrubbing pad, available from home improvement shops. Your last resort is scrubbing very gently with 800 grit wet-or-dry sandpaper. Scrubbing too hard could wear a groove in the material. Polish the cleaned spot with a special polish made for Corian surfaces sold at home improvement shops or from Corian benchtop suppliers.

**Water spots** that are etched into a sink's porcelain are difficult to remove. Buff them out with a polishing compound as soon as you notice the spots. Use jeweller's rouge (from jewellery making suppliers), or rub gently with a pink-coloured silver polish, such as Goddard's.

**EXPERT ADVICE**

### THE TROUBLE WITH TAPS

The white mineral deposits that settle on tap spouts and handles succumb to white wine vinegar. Soak a paper towel in the vinegar, squeeze out the excess and wrap the towel around the chrome fixture. After 10 minutes, take off the wet towel and buff the chrome with a dry one. Voilà—clean chrome! Do not use this method on brass or coloured fixtures, as these finishes might react or discolour. While you have the vinegar out, it also works to unclog sink drains blocked up with soap residue and all the other things that go down the sink. And it's safer than chemical drain cleaners.

**To cover a chip or scratch on a white porcelain surface**—including sinks, tubs and appliances—pick up a container of white enamel paint at your hardware or paint shop. Following the package instructions, paint over the trouble spot with a small artist's brush, let it dry, rub with fine sandpaper, then paint again. Repeat the process until the painted area is even with the surrounding surface. If you want to get fancier, buy a porcelain repair kit, which will include filler, hardener, cleaning spray, sandpaper and more.

## SKIRTING BOARDS AND KICKBOARDS

**SKIRTINGS AND KICKBOARDS** TAKE QUITE A BIT OF PUNISHMENT IN THE AVERAGE HOUSEHOLD, AND BLACK SCUFF MARKS ARE JUST THE BEGINNING. ADD TO THEM FOOD SPILLS THAT DRIBBLE DOWNWARDS AND GREASE AND GRIME ON THE FLOOR THAT SOMEHOW MAKES ITS WAY UPWARDS, AND YOU'VE GOT YOUR WORK CUT OUT FOR YOU.

**To clean wooden skirting boards** and kickboards covered with polyurethane or oil-based (gloss or semi-gloss) paint, remove scuff marks and dirt with a sponge and a grease-cutting, all-purpose dishwashing liquid. You can also use a household spray cleaner, such as Spray n' Wipe, but remember to spray the cleaner on a cloth rather than on the skirting board, to prevent streaking. For really tough stains, test an inconspicuous corner with scouring powder and a plastic scrubbing pad. If it doesn't affect the finish, you can apply the method to the entire skirting board. A general cleaning rule of thumb comes into play here: use the least aggressive cleaner initially, then resort to more aggressive tactics as the scuffs dictate. Skirting boards and kickboards covered with satin or flat paint require the gentlest cleaning method (water, dishwashing liquid and a washcloth).

**To clean vinyl or rubber skirting boards and kickboards**—more properly called cove moulding—spray on a wax stripper and let it soak in for a few minutes to loosen old wax and grime. Scrub with a nylon brush and rinse. Then, to make the job easier next time, apply a coat of floor finish, such as Pledge One Go.

**An ounce of prevention** can save you a lot of work. Skirting boards and kickboards take a beating in most homes, especially while you're vacuuming carpets or mopping floors. So make sure the rubber bumper guard on your vacuum is fully attached and doing its job. If you use a squeegee mop, check for sharp metal edges that could leave a nasty scrape along skirting boards and kickboards. And if you use a strong cleaner on floors, quickly wipe away spills and splashes that could discolour skirting boards and kickboards. Always wear gloves when cleaning around the skirting boards, as they can harbour a variety of micro-organisms.

# SKYLIGHTS

**WHAT BETTER WAY** TO LET NATURAL LIGHT INTO YOUR HOME—WHILE MAINTAINING YOUR PRIVACY—THAN WITH SKYLIGHTS. TO KEEP FROM LOOKING INTO A DIRTY SKY, DO SOME SIMPLE MAINTENANCE TO PRESERVE YOUR VIEW. THE MATERIALS DEPEND ON WHETHER YOU HAVE GLASS OR ACRYLIC SKYLIGHTS.

Remove dust and cobwebs from a skylight easily and effectively using a cobweb brush or a barely damp mop.

**To clean the exterior of your glass skylights,** either climb onto the roof and clean them while you're standing securely on a ladder (preferably with someone holding the ladder steady for you), or reach the skylight with a telescopic pole and attachments—a squeegee and a sponge mop end. (If you feel safer, climb onto the roof and squat next to the window.) You can use a detergent-and-water solution (30 millilitres of dishwashing liquid to 600 millilitres of water), any alcohol-based cleaner, such as Jif Glass Plus, or a 50:50 solution of vinegar and water. (Alcohol-based cleaners give a streak-free finish.)

To remove loose and caked-on dirt, wet the window with a hose, dip the sponge mop into your cleaning solution (or spray it onto the mop head until it's damp), and wipe over the window. Rinse out the mop and wipe again with water, then dry it with the squeegee. Clean the frames around your skylights at the same time that you clean the glass, watching for any sharp edges. A twice-a-year cleaning of your skylights and frames is sufficient because you don't want to wear down the silicone seal around the skylight and cause leaks.

**The interior of your glass skylights** is cleaned much the same way. Remove loose dirt and dust with a round-headed cobweb brush, or a barely dampened mop (see left), rinse out the mop or change it, and then clean with one of the solutions mentioned above. (Don't forget to protect your carpet or floor.) Do this monthly—or perhaps just twice a year if the skylight is difficult to reach. Wooden frames can be cleaned with a furniture polish if reachable. They'll also need to be finished, painted or stained every three years to protect the wood against damage from ultraviolet rays.

**If your skylight is made of acrylic,** strong cleaning solvents can easily scratch and damage the acrylic. Even using glass cleaner on acrylic can be a problem. To clean the inside and outside of your acrylic window, mix 1 tablespoon of dishwashing liquid in 4 litres of warm water. Dip a soft cloth into the solution, wipe over the window and rinse well. If stubborn stains remain, use any specialist plastic cleaner, available from the auto-care section of supermarkets. Spray the cleaner on a cloth and wipe over the acrylic pane. Also use the plastic cleaner to remove marks on vinyl frames.

If you find that roof tar has stuck to the exterior of the acrylic window, use a citrus-based cleaner, such as Citro Clean Multi-Purpose Cleaner. If it doesn't work, try kerosene dabbed on a cloth and wiped over the marks. (Don't forget to wear gloves.) Rinse thoroughly with a hose or a bucket of clear water. Don't use a power washer; it could damage the insulation around the window, cause leaks and loosen tiles.

**If your skylight has a screen,** you'll need to remove it to clean the inside of the window. If this is too difficult, open the window and clean the inside at the same time that you clean the outside. To clean the screen, vacuum it using the upholstery brush attachment. If the screen is particularly dirty and you can easily remove it, give it a wash with a soft brush dipped in a solution of dishwashing liquid and warm water. Then rinse it thoroughly and allow to air-dry.

## SLATE

**WHETHER YOU HAVE** SLATE FLOORING, A SLATE MANTEL OR A SLATE KITCHEN BENCHTOP, LIGHT CLEANING IS SIMPLE.

Ordinary cornflour will help absorb an oil stain on a slate benchtop.

**To remove dust on slate,** simply vacuum or wipe the slate surface with a damp cloth or a damp mop.

**To remove floor dirt,** mix ½ cup of ammonia in ½ bucket of water (5 litres). Apply the cleaning solution with a sponge mop. (You can use other cleaners, such as multipurpose or cream cleansers, or warm water with a squirt of dishwashing liquid added to it. However, the advantage of using ammonia is that it requires no rinsing.) If you dust weekly, you can do a thorough cleaning with ammonia once a month or every other month.

**To protect slate floors from staining,** apply a stone sealer—either gloss or satin—after it's installed. Slate is especially susceptible to oil stains (from salad oils, for instance). So sealing a slate floor in a kitchen or eating area may be a good idea. If you choose to, follow the coat of sealer with a wax finish that can protect the sealer and make it last longer. The sealer and the wax work together to make slate easier to clean on a regular basis.

**To clean a slate benchtop,** scour the surface using a cream cleanser, such as Jif, and a damp sponge. Do not use abrasive pads because they might remove some of the stone and change its appearance.

**To clean up oil stains on a slate benchtop,** sprinkle a liberal amount of cornflour on the surface and let it sit for 10 minutes (see above left). Then scrub the surface with a grease-cutting cleaner, such as Spray n' Wipe, or use warm water with a squirt of dishwashing liquid.

**To protect a slate kitchen benchtop,** oil it with a 50:50 mixture of boiled linseed oil and turpentine. Wipe the solution on the slate with a cloth and then buff the slate with a clean, soft cloth, terry towelling rag or old bath towel until it's dry (old nappies are good for this, too). Oil will darken the slate and give it a satin finish while creating a protective barrier. Oil your kitchen benchtop once or twice a year. Oil other non-floor surfaces—mantels or hearths, for instance—every couple of years.

# SLEEPING BAGS

**SLEEPING BAGS COME** WITH ONE OF THREE TYPES OF INSULATION: NATURAL (DOWN OR DOWN AND FEATHER), SYNTHETIC FIBRES OR FIBRE-PILE (FLEECE). BUT WHATEVER TYPE OF SLEEPING BAG YOU HAVE, IF YOU USE IT ONLY A COUPLE OF TIMES A YEAR AND TREAT IT WELL, YOU MAY BE ABLE TO GO 10 YEARS WITHOUT HAVING TO GIVE IT A THOROUGH CLEANING.

**To keep a sleeping bag in good shape,** here are some guidelines:

- To avoid getting the inside dirty, use a liner or wear pants and a T-shirt when you're using the sleeping bag.
- Spot-clean it after a trip with a sponge and soapy water.
- After a camping trip, air your sleeping bag for a couple of hours or place it in the dryer for 10–15 minutes to get rid of any moisture.
- Store your bag in a large breathable storage sack, not in its own stuff sack (if it's impermeable) nor in a plastic bag.

**To hand wash a sleeping bag**—the most careful way to do it—fill a bathtub with warm water and just a little soap. For down bags, you can safely use a mild laundry detergent, such as Softly or a no-rinse eucalyptus wool wash. Don't use any detergent containing bleach on a down bag (but it's OK for synthetic-fibre bags). Check the package instructions to determine the amount of detergent to use. Remember that using too much will mean more rinsing later on. Gently knead the bag to help the soapy water penetrate the material (see below).

If your sleeping bag has a waterproof outer shell, you will need to turn the entire bag inside out before you immerse it so the soapy water will be able to penetrate the sleeping bag.

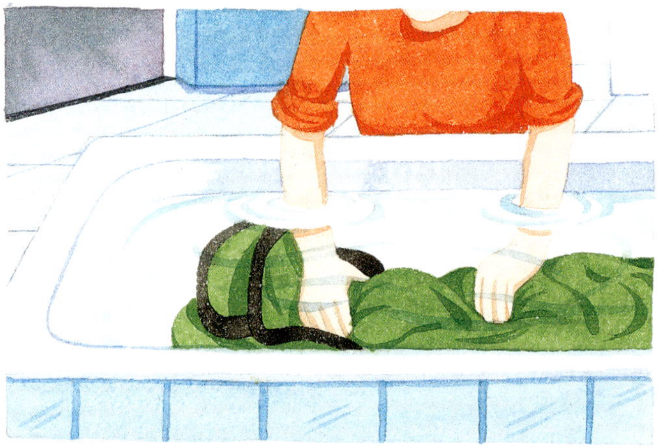

Gently knead the sleeping bag in the soapy water to loosen dirt and grime.

**Rinse your bag twice**—several times if necessary—with clear water (unless you're using no-rinse wool wash). Don't cut corners on this step, particularly if you're working with a down bag. It's very important to remove all the soap before the down has dried. Do not wring water from your sleeping bag. Instead, squeeze out the water by rolling up the bag tightly and carefully.

**WATCH OUT** Dry-cleaning is not recommended for down or synthetic sleeping bags. It can strip the natural oils in the down and take the silicone coating off the synthetic-filled bags. But you probably can dry-clean a fibre-pile sleeping bag, but always check the manufacturer's recommendations first.

**To machine wash a sleeping bag,** your best bet is to visit a self-service laundry. Using a front-loading commercial machine to wash down or synthetic-fibre sleeping bags is a good idea, as top-loading agitator machines can damage them. You can machine wash just about any sleeping bag if you use warm water and a gentle cycle, but it's

### Washing made easy

When hand washing a sleeping bag, try this simple trick to prevent the compartments formed by baffles (those stitched partitions that keep the fill evenly distributed) from inflating and floating to the surface. Keep the bag in its own stuff sack and immerse both bag and sack in the tub of water. You've already forced the air out of the bag when you put it in the stuff sack. Once both are immersed, you can remove the sleeping bag from the sack and work the soapy water into the bag.

always best to check the manufacturer's label. The last spin cycle should remove a lot of the water, but make sure the bag is evenly distributed in the machine. This will save dryer time.

**Dry your sleeping bag well to preserve it.** If your bag is not dried thoroughly before you store it away, the matted lumps that formed when it was wet will stay that way. The bag will lose its loft, will no longer offer optimum insulation and may be susceptible to mildew. For these reasons, it's better to dry your bag at a self-service laundry, where you can use a large dryer. In a home dryer, the sleeping bag will take up so much room that it won't tumble well. Consequently, the clumps of down or synthetic fibres will not be broken up during drying.

If you decide to wash your sleeping bag at home and then dry it at a self-service laundry, put it in a plastic bag for the trip to the laundry. Use the largest dryer and set it to high heat. Melting the nylon shell is not a danger because the bag has room to tumble, but if you're in doubt, use a lower setting. Once the nylon shell is dry, set the dryer on medium heat so that the interior feathers can dry. Throw in a couple of clean tennis balls to help break up clumps of down. Remove the bag as soon as it's finished tumbling.

Check that your bag is definitely dry. Even if your bag feels dry, the down insulation may not be. Look for lumps—a sign the down is still wet. After drying a sleeping bag with fibre-pile insulation, gently fluff up the fleece with a comb or brush.

*See also:*
• DOWN

## SLIDE PROJECTORS AND SCREENS

TO CLEAN ELECTRONIC GADGETRY IS NOT ROCKET SCIENCE. IT MERELY REQUIRES KNOW-HOW (SUPPLIED BY THIS BOOK) AND PATIENCE (SUPPLIED BY YOU). IF YOU GET INTO A RUSH, YOU MAY DAMAGE YOUR PROJECTOR.

**To clean a slide projector,** start with the outside of the unit (but only if it is completely cool). Separate and set aside the optical assemblies—the lens, which is easily removable from its track, and the lamp, which slides out the back of the projector. Use an aerosol can of deionised compressed air (from computer or camera shops) to blow any dust or loose dirt off the projector casing (see page 314). (If it's really dirty, walk outside to spray it, so that you won't have another mess to clean up inside.) Spray any openings inside the casing to loosen dust. With a clean, 3-centimetre bristle paintbrush (preferably new), dust all the nooks and crannies, making sure to clean around the gate area, which catches the dropping slides, and the exhaust grill, where dirt tends to collect. Once again, blow compressed air on the case to remove any remaining dust. Spray a surface cleaner (either a product such as Windex, Mr Muscle or a lens cleaner from a camera shop) on a clean, lint-free cloth and wipe the exterior surfaces of the projector to remove fingerprints and grime.

**To clean the projector's optics**—which you removed and set aside—be extra careful not to scratch the lenses. Use the compressed air to first dust the projection lens. Place a couple of drops of surface cleaner on both the front and rear of the lens and, with the lens tissue, gently rub in a circular motion to remove dust or water condensation marks. No matter how tempted you may be—and this goes for audiovisual geeks as well as the rest of us—don't try to clean the internal lens. The optics are very sensitive parts. Among other things, unskilled fingers can disturb the finely calibrated focusing mechanism. (Every five years or so, have the slide projector serviced by a professional, who can clean and lubricate the internal systems.)

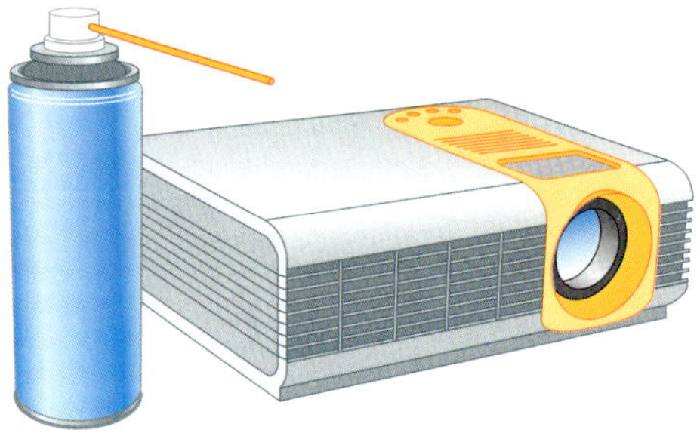

Use compressed air to dust the projector case, the lens and the lamp.

**To clean the projector's lamp,** set the cleaned projection lens aside and locate the lamp, which is typically next to the exhaust fan and tends to get really dirty. Again, remove dust with the compressed air, loosen dirt with the paintbrush and give the lamp a final blow with the compressed air. Using the lens tissue and surface cleaner, gently wipe the mirror that accompanies the lamp. There should be a clear condenser lens bracketed in front of the lamp. Unscrew the bracket, gently remove the lens (holding it on the edges only) and clean it as you did the other lenses. Reattach it to the lamp assembly. If the condenser lens is tinted green (as it often is on models made more than a decade ago), take even more care when handling it. Don't touch the lens with bare fingers (handle it with a clean cloth or tissue), and if you must set it down, do so on a cloth. This time, don't use the cleaning solution; wipe it very gently with the lens tissue.

**After reassembling the projector,** turn it on. You may smell a strange odour, generated by the dust disturbed during the cleaning. The smell will stop after the dust has settled. If the unit still smells after 30 minutes, something is probably wrong. Call a service centre for advice—or a friend who knows what they are talking about when it comes to audiovisual equipment.

**Cleaning the projection screen is the easy part.** Although there are different screen materials, the cleaning techniques are the same for nearly all. Make a solution of mild dishwashing liquid and warm water. Gently wipe away dust and dirt with a sponge dipped in the solution. Rinse by wiping with a clean, wet sponge. Blot dry using a clean cloth. That's it. Never use solvents, such as acetone or paint thinner, and never use abrasive cleaners.

**If you have a glass bead screen** or a screen with a delicate surface, don't clean it with water and soap. Instead, simply brush away dust using a soft-bristled brush or a clean, lint-free cloth.

## SLIDING DOORS

**THAT SLIDING GLASS** DOOR TO OUTSIDE PROVIDES A NICE VIEW BUT ALSO COLLECTS A LOT OF SAND, DUST AND DEBRIS IN ITS TRACKS. HOW YOU CLEAN THE DOOR DEPENDS ON ITS FRAME—WOOD, ALUMINIUM OR, MORE COMMON IN NEWER CONSTRUCTION, VINYL.

**Vacuuming the sill tracks** is the first step in cleaning any sliding door. Run the vacuum over the tracks (see below) at least once in the spring and autumn—or weekly if you use the door frequently (at a beach house, for instance). A timesaving tip is to regularly sweep or vacuum the area just outside the sliding door to help reduce the amount of dirt that gets dragged into the tracks.

Vacuum the sill tracks regularly to keep them free of grit and dirt.

**To keep your door sliding smoothly,** spray Selleys Ezi Glide lubricant or a similar product on a soft, dry cloth and wipe it onto the track. The Ezi Glide will not harm wood surfaces or the weather strip. Lubricate rollers with a light machine oil, such as sewing machine oil.

**To clean the outside of a vinyl frame,** use a mild dishwashing liquid. Add a couple of squirts of detergent to 4 litres of hot or warm water and apply the soapy solution with a soft sponge or cloth. Rinse with clear water. Make sure you clean the frame before you wash the window so that you won't get your clean window wet and smeary again. Start at the top of the frame and work down.

**WATCH OUT** Don't clean aluminium frames in direct sunlight or very hot or cold temperatures, because the cleaning solution may dry too quickly and streak the surface. If that happens, it could be very difficult to restore the aluminium to its original appearance.

**To clean the inside of a vinyl frame,** wipe with a damp cloth at the time that you clean the window. Don't use abrasive cleaners, abrasive scouring pads or sandpaper in an attempt to buff or shine the vinyl frame or to remove marks.

**To clean wood-framed sliding doors,** fill a misting bottle with warm water and a squirt of mild dishwashing liquid. Spray the sliding door frames and wipe off any dirt with a soft cloth. Finish by gently drying with another soft cloth. Never use a hose or any high-pressure washer on the door. Likewise, if your wooden door frame is painted, never use abrasive cleaners, as they can soften acrylic paint. A few will even soften oil-based paint. If the residue won't come off with water or a mild detergent, consider lightly sanding it and then re-finishing.

It's important to make a thorough inspection of your wooden door frame at least once a year—monthly in coastal or harsh climates. That's

because wood is highly susceptible to attacks by fungi and other deterioration. Prevent this from happening by careful monitoring.

**To clean aluminium-framed sliding doors,** once again your best bet is mild dishwashing liquid and water applied with a sponge or soft brush from top to bottom. Rinse the frames immediately. Air-dry or wipe with a soft, dry cloth. For a protective coating, apply a fine car wax to the aluminium. You should plan an annual cleaning for all your exterior aluminium frames.

**Next, clean the glass, inside and out.** (See 'Windows' for cleaning solutions and techniques, on page 383.) Any window cleaner will be fine, but avoid getting the cleaner on the window frames, because ingredients in some glass cleaners will damage the frame materials.

**Finally, clean the screen door**—if you have one—by gently vacuuming it with a brush attachment, as this will not harm the mesh. Remember to vacuum both sides.

## SMOKE

'SMOKE GETS IN YOUR EYES' SOUNDS ALMOST BENIGN, EVEN ROMANTIC, IN THIS FAMOUS SONG. BUT IN REALITY, THERE'S NOTHING AT ALL APPEALING ABOUT THE STALE SMELL OF SMOKE IN YOUR HOUSE OR ON YOUR CLOTHES.

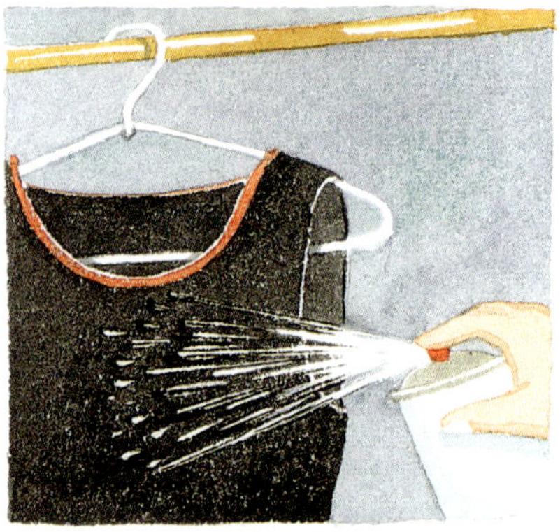

Fabric deodorisers will neutralise any residual smoke odour.

**To remove smoke odour from clothing,** whether it's from a fire or cigarettes, hang the clothes outside in the sun. Sunlight will break down the smoke molecules, and fresh air is great for the fabric. You may want to attach a fan to an extension cord and allow the fan to force air across the clothes. Check the clothing every 2 hours and leave it outside until the smell dissipates. You'll have more effective results in the wash—your next step.

**To wash smoky clothes,** first pre-soak the garment in a sink filled with ¾ cup of bicarbonate of soda and 20 litres of water. Then place the garment directly into the washing machine, using a laundry detergent with oxygen bleach, such as Omomatic. These detergents remove the odour, not merely mask it with a perfume. Wash contaminated clothing separately from your general family laundry.

After washing, hang the clothes to dry. Avoid using a dryer—the heat can set the smoke odour into any fabric from which it hasn't been completely removed. Neutralise any residual smoke odour with a deodoriser such as Febreze (see left).

If the clothing label says 'Dry-clean only', that's what you should do, and make sure the drycleaner specialises in smoke removal. Your drycleaner will appreciate you airing the clothing first.

**Removing protein-generated smoke**—from cooking ham or chicken, for instance—can be more difficult because these items produce heavy, greasy smoke that fabric readily absorbs. (Wood smoke

★★★
EXPERT ADVICE

CLEARING THE AIR

Nothing clears the smoky smell from rooms as well as an ozone machine. So if you have bought a house and the previous owners smoked for years, these devices are your best shot at freshening the air. They work by oxidising smoke-odour particles, eliminating them from cracks and other hard-to-get-to places. You can rent or buy an ozone machine (sometimes called an ozone generator) although they can be a little difficult to track down (check the Internet under 'ozone machine' or contact www.appliedclimate.com.au). You'll need to vacate any room the machine is working in. And open all doors and cupboards in the area, because the machine doesn't penetrate objects.

*See also:*
• SOOT

tends to be flaky and easier to clean.) Air clothing affected by protein smoke on a hanger outside, maybe for a day or two if necessary. Then, before you wash the garment, soak it in an oxygen-based, pre-wash soaker, such as Napisan Oxyaction.

**To remove just a little smoke** from a small area in your home, such as a chest of drawers, is an easy task. Either use bicarbonate of soda, cedar blocks or even a bowl of sliced apples to absorb the odour. Close up or seal off the area first.

**If smoke has penetrated a large part of your home,** you will have an extensive clean-up job on your hands involving a variety of materials that require different cleaning techniques. Your safest bet, to ensure a successful clean, is to contact your insurance company and get some professional cleaners in to do the job.

**To clean smoke from walls and ceilings,** first vacuum up any visible smoke residue. Then dilute a special heavy-duty cleaner and degreaser recommended for smoke removal, such as Research Crossfire (available online from www.tensens.com.au), according to the package instructions. Fill a spray bottle with the cleaner. Spray and wipe one section of the wall or ceiling at a time, using a clean cloth. For walls, start from the bottom and work your way up to avoid streaking. You may have to repeat the process several times. Oil-based paint will hold up well to washing. However, acrylic paint can wear off if you scrub aggressively or wash too many times. You can also try a sugar soap solution.

## SMOKE ALARMS

**YOU PROBABLY ALREADY** KNOW TO CHANGE THE BATTERIES IN YOUR SMOKE ALARMS YEARLY. BUT DID YOU KNOW THAT YOU SHOULD ALSO CLEAN THEM EVERY OTHER MONTH? COBWEBS, DUST AND EVEN SPIDERS CAN CAUSE YOUR SMOKE ALARM TO MISBEHAVE.

**Clean the outside and inside of the alarm** using a vacuum cleaner and a brush attachment (see below). Flip open or unscrew the casing to get inside. If you can't reach the alarm with your vacuum's extension tubes, stand on a ladder. A can of compressed air can also be sprayed on the casing and inside the alarm to clean it.

Vacuum your smoke alarm every couple of months to ensure it functions properly.

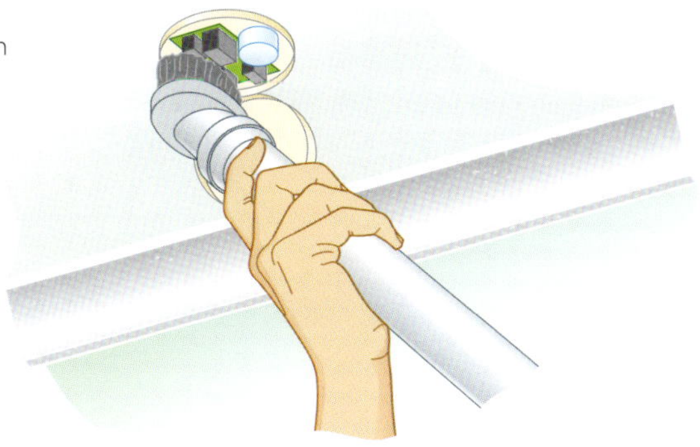

EXPERT ADVICE

**BUGGED BY FALSE ALARMS?**

A smoke alarm is an ideal place for spiders to build nests. The nests or the spiders can block the alarm and make it go off. So vacuum your smoke alarms frequently.

**Test your alarm,** once you've cleaned it, to see that it's working properly. Stand by the alarm, light a candle and then blow it out. The smoke should activate the alarm. Or, if your system's activated by light (it should say so on the box), shine a torch into the alarm to set it off. Simply pressing the button on the alarm casing is not a test. That only indicates the horn is working, not the detection mechanism.

**Cover the alarm** any time you're doing work in the house that could send dust into the air. Don't forget to remove this covering promptly after you've finished. You should also protect the alarm if you're painting around it—never paint the alarm casing.

## SOOT

**THE OILY BLACK** FILM KNOWN AS SOOT IS NASTY TO CLEAN. A BY-PRODUCT OF SMOKE, THIS COMBINATION OF OIL, CARBON AND TAR CAN SETTLE INTO MICROSCOPIC CRACKS IN MANY AREAS OF YOUR HOME. RUN YOUR FINGER ACROSS A WALL WITH SOOT ON IT, AND THE OILS IN YOUR FINGER, COMBINED WITH THE SOOT, WILL PERMANENTLY MARK THE SURFACE. EVEN AFTER YOU CLEAN THE WALL, THAT SOOT MARK WILL REMAIN. SO WHAT SHOULD YOU DO?

**Before you start,** assess how widespread the soot contamination is to see whether you need to call a professional. Test in two or three rooms in an inconspicuous, high area. Take a paper towel folded into a pad, dampen it with water and wipe across the surface. If the paper towel turns grey, you've got dust. If it turns black, you've got soot. If there's a lot of black on wiping and in several areas, call a pro.

In general, you can treat light surface soot if it isn't widespread. Widespread surface soot may need professional attention, because if soot isn't totally cleaned, it can recirculate in the house through the heating system. Call a professional any time you have greasy soot.

**To eradicate soot,** systematically plan your cleaning. The general rule is to work from the top to the bottom of an area—except when using the wet method described on the opposite page. Then you'll need to work from the bottom up. First remove as much soot as you can through a dry method. Wear old clothes, rubber gloves, a baseball cap, a disposable paper dust mask and safety goggles, especially when you are removing loose particles.

**To use the dry method of cleaning soot,** follow these steps:

- Vacuum, sweep or feather dust the surfaces involved. Use a quick, flicking motion with a broom or duster (see above right) or keep the vacuum head about 6 millimetres from the surface to avoid scratching. Don't rub—unless you want a huge smear to clean! Place newspapers under affected surfaces to catch soot for easy removal.
- Vacuum upholstery. If this doesn't work, call a professional fire and smoke restorer or even a drycleaner specialising in soot removal (ask at your local fire station if there is anyone they would recommend).

For light soot, a quick flick with a duster should solve the problem.

- On lampshades and on sturdy but small objects, try compressed air to blow the soot off the object. Take it outside to do this.
- Use a heavy-duty cleaner and degreaser specifically recommended for smoke removal, such as Research Crossfire (available online from at www.tensens.com.au), on walls and ceilings or on unfinished wood. Saturate a sponge with the cleaner, wring it out thoroughly and apply the sponge to the surface in methodical lines so you can keep track of where you have cleaned. To apply to ceilings or walls, attach the soot sponge to a pole. When the sponge is filthy on all sides, wash it out and begin the process again.

**Next, use the wet-cleaning method,** following these steps:

- The wet method is the last resort after you've removed as much of the soot as possible by vacuuming (or dusting or brushing) and using the soot sponge (the dry method). Put down a plastic drop cloth and wash the surfaces with a solution of warm water and a couple of drops of degreaser (such as Research Crossfire). Apply liberally to the surface with a sponge, rag or hard-bristled scrubbing brush (see below left). Rinse with water and wipe dry. If necessary, repeat this procedure.
- If a small stain remains after repeated washing, apply mineral turpentine carefully with cotton buds made by tightly rolling cotton balls around the end of a wooden skewer. These are preferable to commercially available cotton buds, because solvents can dissolve the plastic stalks. Lightly moisten the bud with the turps and gently roll it across the object. Don't rub or wipe, since this might ingrain the soot and carbon in the surface of the object. Never fully immerse an object in solvent. Work slowly and methodically. Test this method on an inconspicuous part of the object first.

Use a degreaser and a scrubbing brush for bad soot stains. Rinse with water and wipe dry.

**Some tips for specific soot-removal jobs:**

- On objects with a glossy finish, such as coffee tables, vacuum first. Dampen a cloth with cleaner such as Spray n' Wipe, Windex or Mr Muscle and wipe over the surface after testing on an inconspicuous area.
- For vinyl surfaces, including wallpaper, vacuum and then use the wet method straight away. A soot sponge (the dry method) will not absorb the soot on glossy surfaces, and it will leave smeary marks.
- To clean ceilings, try vacuuming and then using the soot sponge for a flat, painted ceiling. Then follow up using the wet method.
- To use the wet method on walls, you clean from the bottom up. Start in small sections, wipe the wet sponge onto the wall in a circular motion and then wipe dry with an old towel or rag. It's very important to wipe any soot drips immediately.

- Clean floors first and last. Before attacking any other part of the room, vacuum thoroughly to get up any loose material so it won't be ground into the flooring. Then protect the floor with drop cloths while you clean the rest of the room. Return to the floors again for a thorough cleaning at the end. Try water and a degreaser first on wood and tile, and for carpeting use a regular carpet shampoo applied either with a carpet-cleaning machine or a wet vac. If a wooden floor won't come clean, you'll have to re-finish it. If small soot stains remain on the carpet, apply turpentine or dry-cleaning fluid, scrub and then shampoo the carpet again. Seek professional help if this doesn't work.
- If sooty marks remain on walls, ceilings or cabinets despite your best efforts, painting is the last option. First, seal the mark using a special stain-resistant primer-sealer, available from paint shops, and then paint with the colour of your choice.

*See also:*
• SMOKE

## SPAS AND JACUZZIS

**TO GET THE** MOST OUT OF YOUR SPA OR JACUZZI YOU NEED TO BE ON TOP OF THE CLEANING. GREASE FROM BODY OILS, BLOCKOUT CREAM OR SOAP CAN CLOG THE FILTER, WHICH WILL ENCOURAGE BACTERIA TO GROW. AND EAR, EYE OR SKIN INFECTIONS MAY OCCUR.

**How often should you clean your spa or jacuzzi?**

- If two people use it three nights a week, clean it thoroughly and drain it every three months.
- If you have a lot of kids, and the family uses it up to six nights a week, step up your cleaning to every two months.
- If your spa is more for decoration than relaxation, clean it as required. You'll still have to test the chemical levels weekly.
- If you aren't keeping track of your use, a good rule of thumb is to drain the water every three to six months. You won't need a calendar to know when you've waited too long. The water will be cloudy or foamy, or it'll smell like a science experiment.

**Cleaning your spa or jacuzzi's filter** is important because a dirty, worn-out filter will fail to trap spa contaminants and will put undue strain on your spa's pump motor and heater. Remove your filter (see left) and rinse it weekly with water to get rid of coarse dirt and debris. Take a garden hose, apply the stream at a 45-degree angle and give it a pressure washing inside and out. Allow the filter to dry. Next, remove any fine particles of dirt carefully with a brush or by applying a stream of compressed air (from an air compressor or from an aerosol can, available from supermarkets as well as camera, computer and discount shops) to the filter's outer surface.

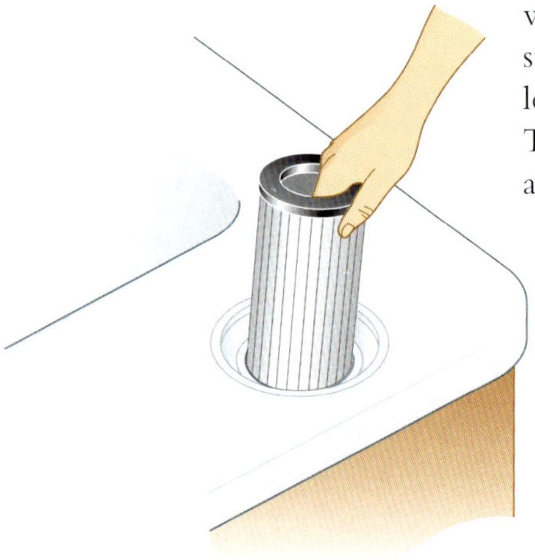

Each week, rinse your filter with water to get rid of dirt and debris.

**If algae, suntan oil or body oils** still leave a coating, you can soak the filter overnight in a degreaser cleaning solution (available from your spa and swimming pool shop). Some experts recommend soaking the filter monthly in a degreaser. If clogging persists, check your water chemistry and adjust, drain and clean the spa, or buy a new filter cartridge. Replace the filter annually.

**Every three months,** drain the water and clean the acrylic shell inside and out with a non-soap-based cleaner from your pool shop. Spray it on the spa, let it sit for a minute and then wipe off any scum or stains, or rub with a sponge. Make sure you don't spray the cleaner into the jets. You can also wipe the spa surface with bicarbonate of soda and water, then rinse well with water. Refill the spa right away. If you plan to leave it empty, talk to your pool and spa shop about products to protect the surface.

**If you're still getting cloudy water,** or your jets aren't working properly, or gunk is appearing on the water, you may have clogged pipes, and you'll have to use a spa-cleaning agent. You really can't afford to mess about when bacteria might be involved.

**To clean spa or jacuzzi covers,** use a vinyl cleaner, such as White Knight Vinyl Guard (from hardware shops). Applying an automotive paste wax to your cover is a good idea—it creates a barrier between the cover and the sun, slowing down the sun's fading action.

**When the cleaning is done,** you're ready to refill the spa with cold water. It will take about an hour. Once full, do your water tests and add the amount of chemicals and sanitisers recommended by your spa's manufacturer. Start the spa. It will take 6–12 hours for the water to reheat. Until the next water change and cleaning, your chemicals and filtering will keep the 39 °C water clear and fresh.

**Indoor spa baths have two areas that require cleaning:** the spa surfaces and the circulation system.

To clean the spa surfaces, wipe with a cloth after each use. Clean periodically with a solution of hot water and dishwashing liquid, followed by a rinse. Don't use abrasive scrubbers or cleaners, which will harm the glossy finish.

To clean the circulation system, follow the instructions that came with your unit. Or do this:

- Adjust the jets so they are not drawing air.
- Leave the water in the spa bath after using.
- Add 7 litres of white vinegar. Or add 2 teaspoons of powdered dishwasher detergent and 2 cups of chlorine bleach.
- Run the spa-bath system, following the operating instructions, for 5–10 minutes.
- Drain and refill with cold water. Circulate for 5 minutes.
- Drain and wipe dry with a clean cloth.

How often you clean the circulation system really depends on the recommendation of the manufacturer and how often you use the spa. Recommendations can vary from once every three months to as often as twice a month or more.

## SPILLS

**AS LONG AS** THERE IS GRAVITY, THERE WILL BE SPILLS—SO PREPARE YOURSELF FOR THE NEXT CUP OF SPILT FRUIT JUICE OR PUDDLE OF RED WINE. TO PREVENT SPILLS FROM CAUSING PERMANENT DAMAGE, YOU HAVE TO KEEP YOUR COOL, WORK FAST AND, ABOVE ALL, KNOW WHAT YOU'RE DOING SO THAT YOU WON'T MAKE MATTERS WORSE.

**To tackle spills on hard surfaces,** such as vinyl or wooden floors, simply soak up the excess liquid as soon as possible with paper towels, a cloth or some other clean, absorbent material. Once the liquid is wiped up, rinse by wiping with paper towels or a cloth moistened with clear water. Dry with paper towels or a cloth.

For the best results, tackle spills as soon as they happen.

**For spills on textiles,** such as carpet, upholstery or clothing, begin by blotting up as much of the excess liquid as possible. For washable fabrics, soak in cold water (hot water can set some stains, such as those that are protein-based). Don't rub or brush, because you might damage the textile's texture. For big spills, work from the outer edge of the spill to the centre to contain it. Your next step depends on what spilled. Follow the specific guidelines in 'Stains', starting on page 328.

## SPORTS EQUIPMENT

**MOST SPORTS EQUIPMENT** IS MADE OF TOUGH MATERIALS AND CAN STAND GETTING DIRTY AND SCUFFED. IN FACT, OVER-CLEANING CAN BE AS MUCH OF A PROBLEM AS UNDER-CLEANING, SINCE RACQUETS, BALLS, SKIS AND OTHER SPORTING GOODS OFTEN CONTAIN FINELY CALIBRATED, HIGH-TECH MATERIALS. THE TRICK IS IN KNOWING NOT JUST HOW TO CLEAN YOUR SPORTS GEAR, BUT ALSO HOW OFTEN.

**To keep your archery gear clean,** wipe off your bow and the shafts of arrows after each use with a clean, moist cloth. To remove stubborn dirt, wipe them with a mild solution of dishwashing liquid and warm water. Rinse with a water-soaked cloth. Dry with a clean towel. Don't use solvents on your bow or bowstring.

To keep your string from drying out and breaking, wax it monthly using string wax. These days, most compound bow pulley systems are self-lubricating, so there is no need to lubricate wheels and cams. Wipe off the metal limb bolts (which hold the compound parts together) with a silicone-soaked rag, available from shops that sell fishing gear. Periodically spray arrow feathers with an arrow waterproofing spray.

**To clean a baseball glove,** first brush away dirt with a stiff-bristled leather-care brush, available from shoe shops. If the glove gets muddy, let the mud dry and then brush it off. Don't use water on your leather glove. If your glove gets rained on, let it dry naturally in a warm, well-ventilated place. Don't put it on or near a heater or fireplace. After all, you've probably spent a lot of time getting the leather soft and supple, and heat does just the opposite—it causes leather to stiffen and crack. After the glove has dried, use lanolin or a lanolin-based shaving cream to soften the leather.

**To clean an outdoor basketball,** which is typically made of rubber, use a cloth and a solution of water and dishwashing liquid. When clean, rinse the basketball with plain water and air-dry. Indoor basketballs are made of either leather (the really high-end balls) or synthetic leather. When cared for properly and kept indoors, neither should need much cleaning.

**To clean cricket gloves,** mix 3 tablespoons of water, 2 tablespoons of methylated spirits and 1 tablespoon of cloudy ammonia, and scrub the gloves with this solution. Don't saturate them. Cricket bats should be allowed to dry naturally if they are damp—never expose them to heat, or leave them in the boot of a hot car. Brush away loose dirt and debris, but don't try to clean away the ball marks—they're part of the game! Warm, dry conditions can dry out the willow wood and cause splits and cracks. Keep your bat conditioned by oiling it lightly with raw linseed oil every two to three weeks, but do not over-oil.

**To keep darts clean,** there's not much you have to do. Keep the points free of burrs by turning them gently in the concave part of a round sharpening stone (available wherever darts are sold). And every so often, remove the number ring from your dart board and rotate it, so that the wear is distributed evenly.

**To care for a football,** which is usually made of synthetic leather, keep it dry. When your football gets dirty, wipe it with a moist rag. When it gets wet, air-dry it. Don't use a heat source such as a hair dryer or a heater to dry a football.

Every so often, vacuum out the bottom and pockets of your golf bag.

**To keep golf clubs clean,** wipe the dirt and mud off them after each day of golfing. Use a cloth and plain water or a mild solution of dishwashing liquid and water. Rinse by wiping with a wet cloth. Dry well with a dry cloth. Try not to get the leather grips wet. Large deposits of dirt on your clubs can affect your game, so keep a moist cloth handy while playing to spot-clean after digging up divots.

**To clean a synthetic golf bag,** wipe it with plain water or the same mild, soapy solution recommended for golf clubs. Remember to vacuum out the bottom and the pockets occasionally (see left). To clean a leather golf bag, follow the instructions for coated leather in the 'Leather' entry, on page 239.

**To keep hockey gear in good working order,** the most important thing is to allow it to dry properly—which means letting gear dry naturally, not with the help of an additional heat source. Proper care also means taking gear out of the car boot and stick bag a.s.a.p. After each game, dry and store pads (hanging them, if possible) in an upright

position. The same goes for the stick. If it's ice hockey you play, dry ice hockey skates and blades with a cloth after each use to avoid rusting. Wipe visors clean with a moist cloth after each use.

**To get the most out of your rollerblades** (in-line skates), rotate the wheels as soon as you notice that they are wearing down. Switch the most worn with the least worn. Switch from one skate to the other. Since wheels wear faster on the inside edge, turn the less worn side inwards. If the bearings get wet, remove them from the wheels and wipe them dry as soon as possible, using a clean, lint-free cloth. Don't lubricate the outside of the bearings—that will attract dirt.

Clean bearings that have removable outer shields. You'll know they need cleaning when they spin slowly or make a noise while spinning (the sound of dirt inside). After following the manufacturer's instructions for removing the shields, clean the bearings by inserting a stick, pen or pencil through their doughnut-shaped casing. Dip them in a container of mineral turpentine or kerosene and spin them in the liquid until the dirt is gone (see left). Lay the bearings on a paper towel to dry, or blow them dry with a can of compressed air. Then lubricate them with bearing lubricant, available from skate supply shops.

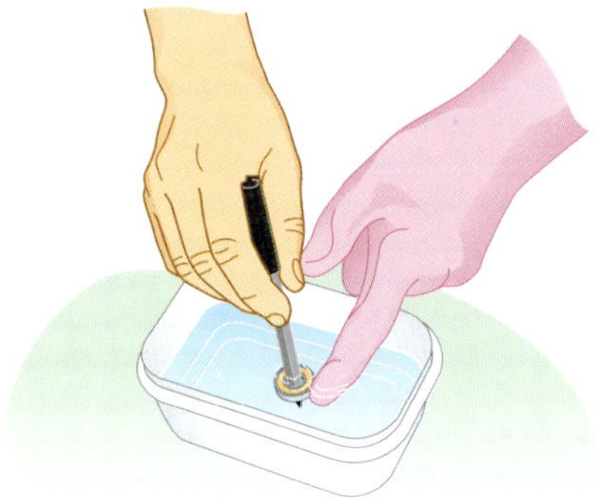

To clean the bearings, spin them in a solution of mineral turpentine or kerosene until the dirt is gone.

**To maintain a skateboard,** keep in mind that most skateboards are made of laminated wood and shouldn't get wet. Dry them if they do. To clean dirty decks, scrub the grip tape with a soft-bristled brush dipped in clean water. Rinse by wiping with a wet cloth or sponge. Dry well with a clean cloth as soon as you've finished rinsing.

As with rollerblade wheels, skateboard wheels should be rotated when you notice they are wearing down. Switch the most worn with the least worn. If the bearings get wet, remove them from the wheels and wipe them dry as soon as possible using a clean, lint-free cloth. Don't lubricate the outside of the bearing, because that will attract dirt and create unnecessary cleaning.

If your bearings have removable outer shields, you can clean and lubricate them. Follow the instructions described above for cleaning and lubricating in-line skate bearings.

**To clean skis and poles,** wipe them down with a moist rag and then dry with a dry rag, or use a soapy solution of warm water and dishwashing liquid. Rinse and dry them well. Wax your skis every few times you use them. When you wax them, clean the bases either by using a spray-on and wipe-off base cleaner (available from ski shops) or by putting on hot wax with an old iron and scraping it off with a plastic scraper before it has dried. (Scrapers are available from ski shops, or at a pinch you can use a plastic windscreen scraper. Once you've used an iron for waxing, never use it on clothes.) After you ski, always dry your skis and poles with a cloth to keep them from rusting.

**To clean ski boots,** wipe them off with a damp cloth—if they are the hard-plastic variety—and remove the inner boot after each use so that both will dry properly. Wipe leather boots with a damp cloth, but avoid getting them very wet. Let them air-dry, but never near heat, which will dry out and crack leather. If your leather ski boots do get wet, remove the insoles and stuff single sheets of newspaper in them. Keep leather boots coated with a leather-waterproofing product, available from sporting goods and shoe shops.

**To clean a snowboard,** follow the instructions for cleaning and waxing skis described above. Every time you snowboard, dry your board afterwards with a cloth to keep it from rusting.

**To clean a soccer ball,** which is typically made of easy-to-clean synthetic leather, just wipe it off with a moist cloth.

**To clean your tennis racquet**—or your squash, or badminton racket—wipe it with a damp cloth. Don't get the strings wet, because moisture can ruin them. Try not to wet the leather grip either, as moisture can take away the grip's tackiness and make it slippery. Instead, wipe perspiration off with a dry cloth. If your over-grip (the material you can wrap around or slip over the grip) gets dirty, replace it.

**When washing outfits for any sport,** promptness is key. Don't leave sweaty outfits in lockers or lying in gym bags. Wash them in your washing machine without delay. Shrinkage is another big issue. You can't play well if your pants and jersey are too small. To avoid shrinkage, stick to cold-water wash cycles and air-drying instead of using the dryer. Hot dryers can also make the screen-printed numbers and team names on uniforms crack.

A spray-on fabric guard will keep pads clean and waterproof.

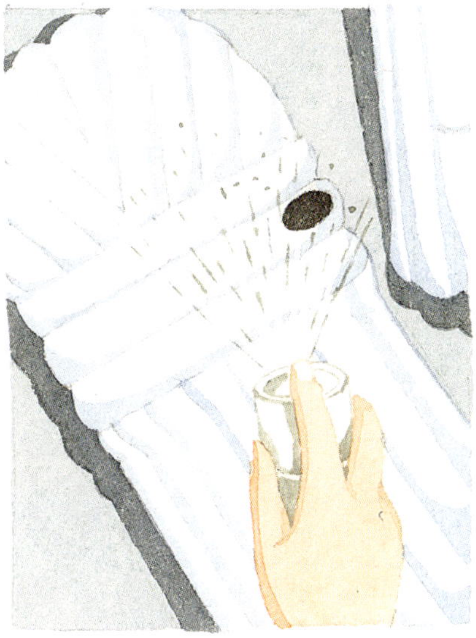

**Cricket whites** often require special care, because they tend to be covered with ball and grass stains. You can rub the stains with the ammonia and methylated spirits solution used for cricket gloves (see page 323), or sponge with a eucalyptus wool wash mix, before placing them in the washing machine.

**If you need to clean pads and protectors** for sports, such as cricket, hockey and football, surface clean them with a cloth and plain water or a very mild solution of dishwashing liquid and water. Rinse by wiping with a wet cloth. Don't be tempted to submerge pads or protectors—the water might remain in the padding and lead to bacteria growth and odours. Spray pads with a fabric-waterproofing product, such as Scotchgard (see left), to help keep them clean and less susceptible to moisture damage.

## SPRINKLERS

**YOUR LAWN SPRINKLER** SYSTEM WILL LET YOU KNOW WHEN IT NEEDS CLEANING BY SPRAYING IN AN ODDBALL PATTERN—OR NOT AT ALL—WHEN IT GETS JAMMED BY SEDIMENT OR MINERAL DEPOSITS. CLEAN IT ONCE AT THE BEGINNING OF THE WATERING SEASON AND ONCE AT THE END, AND YOU CAN REDUCE THE MISFIRING.

**Remove sprinkler spray heads** (if possible) and rinse in a bucket of water. Look for any sediment that may be clogging the nozzles. Scrub lightly with a toothbrush. Use your hose to force high-pressured water back through the holes. Since most sprinklers these days are made of plastic parts, don't use soaps, oils or solvents, which can create a build-up or degrade the plastic. If all else fails, try to loosen the sediment by gently pushing a wire into the nozzle (see below) and then test run with water. If you have a mineral build-up, wipe with or soak in a solution of 1 part vinegar to 3 parts water.

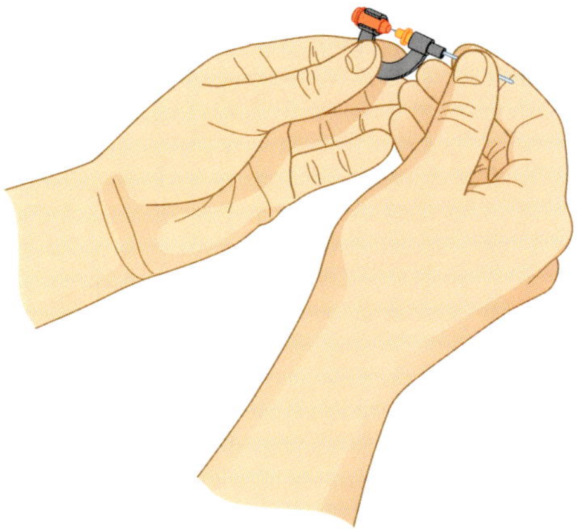

Unclog a sprinkler spray head by gently probing the nozzle with a fine wire.

### Simple solutions

#### Reducing sediments

If you are drawing the water for watering your lawn from a bore or dam, it's more likely to contain sprinkler-clogging sediment than water from a municipal system. To reduce the sediment, install an in-line filter, which you can buy from hardware shops and home improvement shops.

**Take valves apart** and clean them the same way you would the spray heads, first using water and a toothbrush and then, if that doesn't work, vinegar and water. Rinse any clogged screens in clean water.

## STAINED GLASS AND LEADED GLASS

**THE LEAD IN** LEADED GLASS REFERS TO THE MATERIAL USED IN THE CAMES—THE GROOVED METAL RODS THAT HOLD THE PANES OF GLASS TOGETHER. IF THE GLASS PIECES ARE COLOURED AND FORM A PICTURE OR DECORATIVE PATTERN, IT IS CALLED STAINED GLASS.

**Stained glass** is associated mostly with churches, but leaded- and stained-glass windows were also stylish in homes, institutions and commercial windows from about 1895 to 1925. Of course, there are also more recent examples, and craftspeople make a wide variety of beautiful ornaments out of leaded and stained glass. The following instructions for cleaning windows can also be applied to less hefty objects, such as lampshades, boxes, light (or sun) catchers and much more.

A cotton bud can get into tight corners on stained glass.

**To clean leaded or stained glass,** use plain, warm water. Wash each pane individually with a clean cloth dampened in the water. If necessary, use a cotton bud to get into corners (see above). Don't use a spray bottle, because the water will drip into the cames. Wipe dry with a clean, soft cloth or chamois cloth. Never apply much force, because you can actually bend the windows, especially if the cames are lead, which is a very soft metal. (Some cames are made of copper or zinc—but it's still called leaded glass—which are stronger.) Use only the damp cloth for cleaning the cames.

**For more cleaning power,** use 1 teaspoon of methylated spirits in 1 litre of warm water and follow the same procedure as above. If dirt or old finish remains, leave it alone. Never use common household glass cleaners, vinegar, lemon, ammonia or any kind of abrasive cleaner.

**WATCH OUT** If the glass has painting on it, don't clean it at all. Even water might damage or remove fragile paint. Painted parts of a window are usually recognisable as something like a bird or a face applied onto the glass, rather than an integral part of it. House numbers are also sometimes painted on.

## Taking the long view

Leaded and stained glass windows can last for centuries, as countless European churches show. But over time, they are subject to such ills as:

- Broken or cracked glass.
- Loosened lead around the glass.
- Broken or missing lead or solder joints.
- Deterioration of putty, glass paint or the frame that holds the window.

If you have a window that is more than 50 years old, it's a good idea to have a condition study done. Such a study will identify any problems and can be the focus of a restoration plan.

If you belong to a church with stained-glass windows and want to participate in their preservation, you could organise a group to commission such a study. To find a consultant, ask museums or large churches that have used such services. The next step would probably be to raise money—window restoration is a time-consuming and expensive project demanding professional help.

## STAINLESS STEEL

**STAINLESS STEEL NEEDS** TO BE CLEANED AND CARED FOR. IT WILL DULL OVER TIME AND PICK UP OILY FINGERPRINTS AS WELL AS MINERAL SPOTS FROM HARD WATER. BUT THE BIG ISSUE WITH STAINLESS STEEL IS IF IT GETS SCRATCHED—THE HARD, THIN OXIDE COATING THAT MAKES IT STAINLESS IS REMOVED AND THEN IT WILL RUST LIKE ANY OLD STEEL.

**WATCH OUT**

- To avoid corroding stainless steel, rinse acidic, salty or milk-based foods off stainless steel utensils that won't be washed right away.
- Never use abrasive scrubbers, such as steel wool, on stainless steel, because they will dull the finish and may even cause it to rust.

**Wash stainless steel cutlery and pots** in hot, soapy water or in your dishwasher. Scrub off stubborn food with a cloth, sponge or nylon-bristled brush, but avoid abrasives. If you're washing it in the dishwasher, be careful not to spill powdered dishwasher detergent on stainless steel—the strong powder will cause dark spots. To remove baked-on food, scrub with a paste of bicarbonate of soda and water.

**Polish stainless steel** items with a clean, dry cloth to remove hard-water spots. For stubborn spots, wipe with a cloth soaked in straight vinegar. Or you can use a stainless steel polishing product, such as Rubbedin Metal Magic or 3M Stainless Steel Cleaner & Polish. Always follow the label instructions.

**Clean stainless steel sinks and appliances** with a solution of warm water and a squirt of dishwashing liquid, using a soft cloth or sponge. Always scrub in the direction of the stainless steel grain. Rinse with a cloth or sponge and clear water. Polish dry to avoid spotting, using paper towels or a cloth. For more cleaning power, use a solution of 1 cup of white vinegar and 3 cups of water, or scrub with a paste made of bicarbonate of soda and hot water.

## STAINS

**IT'S A FACT** OF LIFE THAT STAINS HAPPEN. IT MIGHT BE A GRASS STAIN ON YOUR SON'S PANTS, RED WINE ON THE CARPET OR HOT COFFEE ON A CLEAN SHIRT. BUT STAINS DON'T HAVE TO BE PERMANENT, WHICH MEANS YOU DON'T HAVE TO THROW OUT THAT SHIRT OR LIVE WITH THAT SPLOTCHY RED CARPET.

**Stains aren't as mysterious** as some people think, and therefore not so difficult to remove. Most stains fall into one of four main stain categories: protein, oil-based, tannin and dye. The rest are usually some combination of those stain categories. By understanding what is in a stain, you can determine what will remove it. Armed with this stain-removal know-how, you can beat most stains before they beat you, with a few exceptions, of course.

Before moving on to stain-removal specifics, make sure you read the general guidelines in the box opposite. Also make sure you use the appropriate technique for the material that is stained.

There are three main categories of textiles that can be stained: washable fabrics (clothing, linens, towels), carpets and upholstered furniture. When attempting to remove stains from these three textile categories you can use the following general steps.

Use a dull knife to scrape away any solid material on the carpet.

**With washable fabrics,** one of the advantages you have (apart from the fact that you can machine wash it) is that you have access to both sides of the stain. Pre-treatment often consists of pushing the stain out from the back side of the fabric.

- Remove as much of the stain-causing material as possible by using paper towels to blot it up or scraping it with a dull knife.
- Pre-treat the stain by soaking or applying a cleaning solution. It helps to remove the stain by lightly agitating the fabric being soaked or to gently rub together the stained fabric with your hands.
- Wash in your washing machine according to the instructions on the fabric's care label.
- If necessary, repeat the preceding steps, possibly using a stronger cleaning solution.

**With carpet,** you typically have access to the top side only for stain removal. But you should never soak carpet stains, because most carpets and rugs have pads under them. Getting cleaning solutions into those pads can actually attract dirt and lead to other problems, such as mildew and glue deterioration. Try these methods instead:

- Remove as much of the stain-causing material as you can by using paper towels to blot it up or scraping it with a dull knife (see left). When blotting up a large stain, always blot from the edge of the stain to the centre to contain it.
- Avoid rubbing or pushing the stain deeper into the pile. Avoid using a circular motion, which can destroy a carpet's texture.
- Because you should never soak a carpet, spray bottles are good for

## Some general guidelines for removing stains

- Always follow the instructions on care labels. These days, most fabric items, including clothes, rugs, linens and upholstery, have care labels. Because fabrics differ in so many ways—type of material, type of weave, colour, style—their care will be different. Use the care label instructions as your baseline.
- Remove spills before they become stains. Blot up spilled liquids, scrape away solids and begin your step-by-step stain removal as soon as possible. Factors such as heat and evaporation make stains that are older than about 24 hours much harder to remove.
- To remove stains from 'dry-clean-only' fabrics, first remove as much of the stain residue as possible and then have the item dry-cleaned as soon as you can (within a day or two).
- Be patient. As effective as stain-removal know-how can be, it is often a multi-step approach, from mildest to harshest treatment. Try one tactic, and if that doesn't work, move on to a stronger cleaning solution. If you lose patience and try to jump ahead, you may make things even worse.
- It is best to test cleaning solutions on an inconspicuous part of an item, such as an inside seam or hidden corner. That way, if the fabric or fabric colours react poorly to the cleaning solution, you haven't ruined the whole thing. To test a chlorine bleach solution, mix 1 tablespoon of bleach with ¼ cup of water. Use an eye-dropper or cotton bud to apply a drop of the solution to the stained fabric. Let the garment stand for 2 minutes and then blot dry with a clean cloth.
- If a stain persists, don't put it in the dryer, because its heat could set the stain permanently. Because your first approach may not remove the stain, always check for persistent stains on items after they've gone through the wash and before they go into the dryer. If your washer cycle didn't remove a stain, pull that item out and let it air-dry. Likewise, don't iron or press something if a stain is still in it.

Spray bottles are good for squirting carpet stains (right).

Always bag your brick, or heavy object, to prevent colour transfer to the carpet (far right).

applying a light amount of water-based cleaning solution and rinse water (see above left).

- To dry patches of carpet that have been rinsed with water, lay a pad of paper towels on the spot and place a heavy weight, such as a brick, on the pad. To prevent transferring colour from the brick to the carpet, put the brick in a plastic bag or wrap it in foil (see above right). When the carpet is dry, remove the paper towels. Brush the carpet pile to restore a consistent texture.

**With upholstery,** you face the same problem you have with carpet: you rarely have a chance to get at both sides of the stain. Even if you can remove the upholstery material, most upholstery manufacturers warn against washing cushion covers separately from the cushions because of possible shrinking and other problems. The trick, as with carpeting and pads, is to remove the stain from the top side without soaking the cushion beneath. So follow the steps for removing carpet stains, listed above, to deal with your upholstery stains.

**PROTEIN-BASED STAINS** are caused by such substances as baby food and formula, creamy or cheesy foods, eggs, faeces and urine.

**For fresh protein stains,** cold water is sometimes all that you'll need to remove them. Be careful not to use hot water, because it can cook the proteins, causing the stain to coagulate between the fibres in the fabric and making it more difficult to remove the stain. For washable fabrics, soak in cold water for half an hour, put the stain under running cold water and gently rub the fabric against itself to loosen the stain. Wash in the washing machine in warm water.

**For an old or dried protein stain,** you may have to be more aggressive and take your stain-removal tactics to the next level. Soak washable fabrics for half an hour in a solution of 1 teaspoon of liquid detergent (preferably one containing enzymes—the label will say whether it has them) per 2 litres of cold water. Follow this soaking by washing the fabric in your washing machine, using warm water. Inspect the item before drying. If the stain is still there, soak the fabric an additional half-hour and then wash it again. If the stain remains after that, your only option may be to add the recommended amount of bleach to the next wash cycle, especially if the stain was caused by coloured ice-cream or baby food.

**For a fresh protein stain in carpet or upholstery,** spray with cold water and blot, repeating until clean.

**For a dried protein stain in carpeting or upholstery,** lightly apply a solution of ¼ teaspoon of mild dishwashing liquid (one that doesn't contain lanolin or bleach) in 1 litre of cold water. Apply the solution to a cloth, and use a blotting motion to work the solution into the affected area. Blot with a clean paper towel to remove the solution. Rinse by lightly spraying the stain with water and then blotting. Do this until all the suds are gone. Then spray again lightly with water. Don't blot this time. Instead, lay a pad of paper towels over the spot, put a weight on it and let it dry. (See the last step of removing stains from carpet, at the top of page 330.)

If the stain persists, repeat the procedure with a stronger solution: ½ teaspoon of liquid detergent (preferably a detergent containing enzymes) per 1 litre of cold water.

If that still doesn't completely remove the stain, moisten the stained tufts with 3 per cent hydrogen peroxide. Let it stand for 1 hour. Blot and repeat until the carpet or upholstery is stain free. No rinsing is necessary following this procedure, because light will chemically change the peroxide to water. To dry, use the method mentioned previously involving a pad of paper towels and a weight. But be careful, because hydrogen peroxide is bleach and can whiten colours.

**OIL-BASED STAINS** include those from motor oil, hair mousse, hand and suntan lotions, ointments, kitchen grease, butter, bacon, oils and salad dressing. Oil-based stains aren't as difficult to remove as most people think they are. Many pre-wash stain-removal products, such as Preen UltraLift Plus or Frend and citrus-based pre-wash stain removal sprays, contain special solvents for removing oil and grease.

**For oil-based stains in washable fabrics,** pre-treat new and old stains with a commercial pre-wash stain remover. If you don't have one of those products, apply liquid laundry detergent (or a paste made from granular detergent mixed with water) directly to the stain. Work the detergent into the stain. Immediately after pre-treatment, wash the item in the washing machine in hot water (if that is safe for the fabric

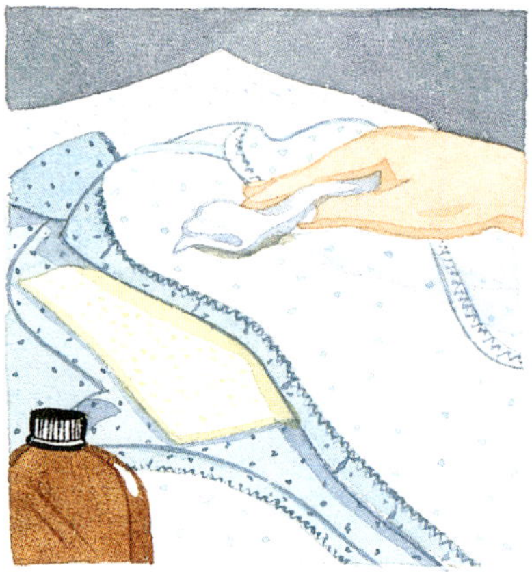

Use paper towels to absorb the cleaning fluid as you work on a stain.

and colours). Before drying the fabric, inspect it. If the stain is still evident, repeat the process until it is gone. For heavy stains, lay the stain face down on a clean, white towel (or stack of paper towels) and press a dry-cleaning solvent, such as Murlex, Woolclean Spot Dry Remover No. 2 or white spirit, on the stain, forcing it out and into the towels (see left). Repeat and then wash.

**For oil-based stains in carpets and upholstery,** apply methylated spirits to a clean, white cloth or white paper towel and blot the stain. Discard the dirty towels and repeat using fresh paper towels and metho until the stain is gone. Don't let the metho penetrate the carpet backing, as it can destroy the latex lining. If that treatment doesn't remove the stain, try the method recommended on page 331 for removing dried protein stains from carpet and upholstery.

**TANNIN STAINS** include those from alcoholic drinks, coffee or tea without milk, fruits and juices, soft drinks and wine. Most jams also contain tannins, but cherry and blueberry jams should be treated as dye stains. (See opposite page.)

**For tannin stains** in washable fabric, soak for half an hour in a solution of 1 teaspoon of liquid detergent (preferably one containing enzymes) per 2 litres of warm water. Then wash in the washing machine in the hottest water that is safe for the fabric, using laundry detergent and not soap. Natural soaps—including soap flakes, bar soap and detergent containing soap—make tannin stains harder to remove. To remove stubborn tannin stains, you may need to wash with bleach. If all the sugars from one of these stains aren't removed, they could turn brown when put into the dryer, as the sugar will caramelise.

## Tracking down mystery stains

You don't always have the luxury of knowing what caused a stain, as anyone who has children can attest. So how do you handle a mystery stain?

Start by using your senses to pick up clues: how the stain smells, what colour it is and where it is on a garment. For example:

- You typically find food stains on the front of clothes.
- Black grease, the kind you find on cars and other heavy machinery, often turns up on pants and skirts at the level of your car door latch.
- Colours can be misleading. For instance, old dried blood can be black, not red.

If you can't figure out what caused a stain, use trial and error to remove the stain. First off, avoid washing unknown stains in hot water, which will set protein-based stains, such as egg or blood. Try the mildest method first and if that doesn't work, you will have to become more aggressive in your treatment:

- Soak in cold water, which just might remove a protein-based stain.
- If that doesn't work, pre-treat by rubbing with liquid laundry detergent and then wash with either warm or hot water.
- If that doesn't work, try spraying with a pre-treatment product or blotting with dry-cleaning solvent.
- Still no luck? Time for the bleaches, beginning with oxygen (all-fabric) bleach. Use a diluted chlorine bleach soak as a last resort.

## Old and new

If a stain has dried, sometimes you can make it 'fresh' again by simply lubricating it with glycerine (from a pharmacy). Rub the glycerine into the stain to saturate it. Leave it for 10 minutes, then treat the stain as a fresh stain.

**For tannin stains in carpet or upholstery,** lightly apply a solution of ¼ teaspoon of mild dishwashing liquid and 1 litre of water. Use a blotting motion to work the solution into the affected area. Blot with a clean paper towel to remove the solution. Rinse by lightly spraying with water and blotting to remove excess water. Do this until all the suds are gone. Then spray lightly with water again, but don't blot. Instead, lay a pad of paper towels down, weight it and let it dry. If the blemish persists, repeat the procedure using a solution of ½ teaspoon of liquid detergent (preferably one containing enzymes) per 1 litre of water. If that doesn't completely remove the stain, moisten the tufts in the stained area with 3 per cent hydrogen peroxide. Let it stand for 1 hour. Blot and repeat until the stain has disappeared. No rinsing is necessary following this procedure. To dry, lay down the weighted pad of paper towels mentioned above.

**DYE STAINS** include those from blueberries, cherries, grass and mustard. Dye stains can sometimes be difficult to remove. After all, dyes are usually meant to stick. They're what colour our clothes.

**For dye stains in washable fabrics,** pre-treat with a commercial pre-wash stain remover. Or apply liquid laundry detergent directly to the stain, work the detergent into the stain and rinse well. Next, soak the fabric in a diluted solution of oxygen bleach (you will find the words 'oxygen', 'sodium percarbonate' or 'chlorine-free' on the label), following the instructions on the packaging. Wash, and then inspect the item to see whether the stain is still there. If so, try soaking the entire garment in a solution of chlorine bleach and water (following the instructions on the bleach container). But be careful, because bleach can drastically alter colours and weaken fabric.

**For dye stains in carpet or upholstery,** good luck. You may have to call a professional cleaner or, in the case of a solid-coloured carpet, cut the stained part out and patch it with clean carpet. But before you go that far, try the procedure described above for tannin stains on carpet or upholstery.

**COMBINATION STAINS** contain both oils or waxes and dyes. They are commonly divided into two categories:

- Group A combination stains include those from lipstick (see page 334), eye make-up (mascara, eyebrow pencil, eyeliner, eye shadow), furniture polish and shoe polish.
- Group B combination stains include chocolate, gravy, hair spray, face make-up (foundation, powder, rouge), peanut butter and tomato-based foods.

To remove these stains, you first must remove the oily or waxy portion, and then you can try to remove the dye. As with any tough stain, your success is not guaranteed. But by following the steps below, you do stand a chance, especially if you get to the stain while it's fresh.

**For washable fabrics with stains in Group A,** apply a dry-cleaning solvent, such as Murlex or Woolclean Spot Dry Remover No. 2. Next, rub with a liquid laundry detergent and scrub in hot water. This should remove the oily or waxy part. Then wash, using a laundry detergent and an oxygen bleach. Inspect before drying. If the stain persists, try washing with chlorine bleach.

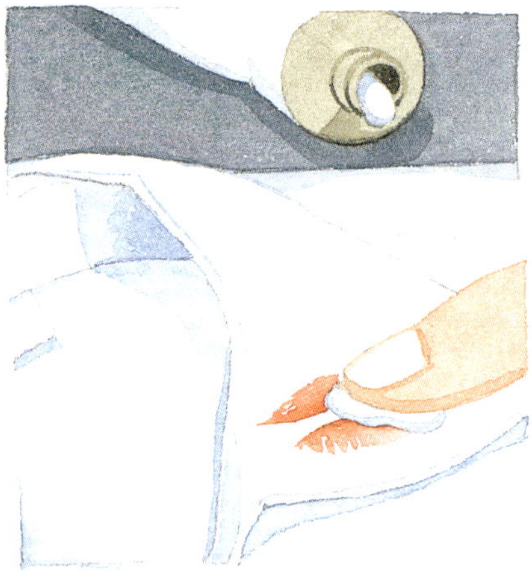

Rub toothpaste on collars stained with lipstick. Then wash as usual.

**For washable fabrics with stains in Group B,** skip the dry-cleaning solvent. Rub the stain with a liquid laundry detergent and wash in the washing machine in the hottest water possible for the fabric. If that doesn't work, try first the oxygen bleach and then, if that fails, the chlorine bleach.

**For combination stains in carpets and upholstery,** also begin by removing the oily or waxy part first. Apply methylated spirits to a clean, white cloth or white paper towel and blot the stain. Discard the dirty towels and repeat using fresh paper towels and metho until the stain is gone. Don't let the metho penetrate the carpet backing, as it could destroy the latex lining.

If the methylated spirits treatment doesn't work, try the next step:

- Lightly apply a solution of ¼ teaspoon of mild dishwashing liquid (one that doesn't contain lanolin or bleach) and 1 litre of water. Use a blotting motion to work the solution into the affected area. Blot with a clean paper towel to remove the solution. Rinse by lightly spraying with water and blotting. Do this until all the suds are gone. Then spray again lightly with water. But instead of blotting this time, lay a pad of paper towels down, put a weight on it and let it dry.
- Finally, if that doesn't completely remove the stain, moisten the stained tufts with 3 per cent hydrogen peroxide and let it stand for 1 hour. Blot and repeat until the stain is gone. No rinsing is necessary following this procedure. To dry, use a pad of paper towels and weight.

**OTHER STAINS** not in the categories already mentioned include stains produced by perspiration, glue, paint, mud and nail polish.

**Treat deodorant and perspiration stains** as you would dye stains. The aluminium or zinc salt build-up from deodorants can make them particularly stubborn.

**To remove glue,** begin by scraping off whatever you can with a dull knife (rubbing ice on it first to harden it). If the glue is white school glue, such as PVA, treat it as you would a protein-based stain, which means no hot water—the hot water could cook the proteins. If it is model-aeroplane glue, treat it as an oil-based stain. If the glue won't come out, place the stain face down on absorbent paper towels. To force the stain out, blot the back of the fabric with a cloth moistened with dry-cleaning solvent.

**Treat acrylic paint while it is wet.** Soak the fabric in cold water and then wash it in cold water with laundry detergent. If the paint has dried, even for as little as 6 hours, treat it as you would a Group A combination stain (see opposite page).

**Remove oil-based paint when it is wet, too.** Spot treat with paint thinner or turpentine and a sponge or cloth until the paint is loosened and as much of it is removed as possible. Then, before it can dry, wash in hot water and detergent.

**Handle mud as you would a protein-based stain,** with one exception: it's always best to wait until mud has dried before cleaning it. Once it has dried, scrape off the excess solids and then follow the protein-stain procedures (see page 330).

If a rust stain remains after removing the mud, a solution of lemon juice and salt will sometimes remove it. Sprinkle salt on the stain, squeeze lemon juice on it and put the item in the sun to dry. Make sure you test the lemon juice first, since it can bleach some fabrics. Don't use chlorine bleach, as it makes rust stains permanent.

**To remove nail polish,** blot with a clean cloth moistened with acetone or nail-polish remover until the nail polish is gone. If possible, lay the stain face down on white paper towels and blot from the back side to force the stain out the way it came in. Don't ever be tempted to use acetone or nail-polish remover on acetate, triacetate or modacrylic fabrics, as it will dissolve these fabrics.

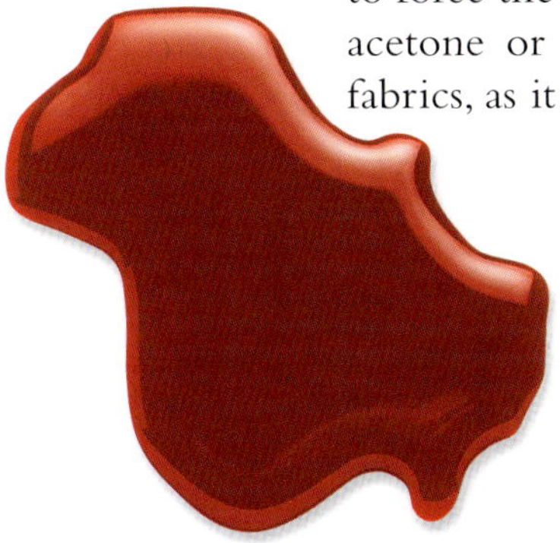

**Yellowing of a fabric** can occur for several reasons: not enough detergent in a wash cycle, too much detergent, insufficient wash temperatures, colour transfer from other items while washing or a fabric's loss of artificial whiteners. Your best bet for restoring the original brightness and whiteness is to wash with the proper amount of detergent and bleach. First, try oxygen bleach. If that doesn't work, try a cycle with chlorine bleach.

# STAIRS AND STEPS

**YOU'RE RACING THROUGH** THE VACUUMING AND THEN YOU GET TO THE STAIRS, WHICH CAN BE A CLEANING NIGHTMARE, ESPECIALLY IF THEY ARE CARPETED. SUCH AN AWKWARD UPWARD PROCESSION OF SMALL SURFACES, SO MANY DUST-FILLED CORNERS! AND THEN THERE'S THE DANGER FACTOR—TRIPPING OVER THE CORD WHILE BOTH HANDS ARE BUSY JUGGLING THE VACUUM CLEANER AND ITS HOSE. WHAT CAN YOU DO?

**Use vacuum cleaner savvy.** If you don't have one already, investigate whether it is possible to buy an extension tube for your brand of vacuum cleaner. There are extenders for upright and canister vacs. Added to your existing 2 metres or so of hose, these extenders will allow you to leave the heavy vacuum cleaner on the ground floor while cleaning the entire staircase (see below).

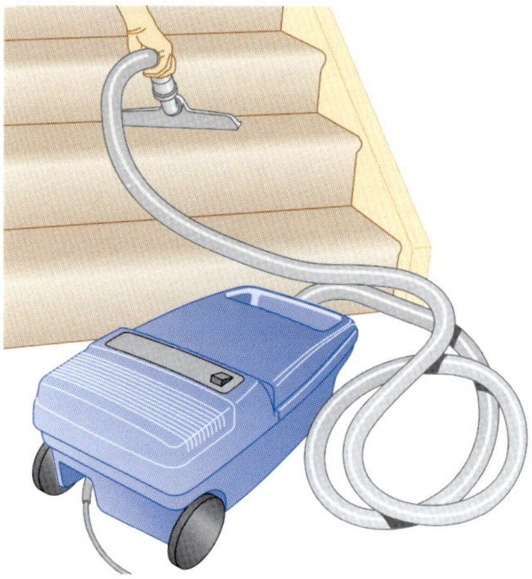

Invest in an extra length of vacuum hose to make cleaning the stairs much easier.

**For carpet-covered stairs,** it is sometimes possible (depending on your brand of machine) to buy a turbo tool, which is also a relatively inexpensive (and well worth the money) add-on for your vacuum cleaner. Powered by the incoming airflow (hence the name turbo), these attachments act like small beater bars to help loosen and pull up hairs, lint and dirt from carpet pile. But because they don't need a power cord to rotate, they can be attached to extension hoses. Or you could go out and buy one of the new, reasonably priced compact vacuum cleaners made especially for stairs. These are hand-held and have long cords that are made to reach up a flight of steps.

**Clean stairs from bottom to top.** That way, you don't grind dirt into the carpet or spread it around on hardwood floors. After cleaning the broad stair treads, use a vacuum crevice tool to get into the cracks along the wall and where the vertical riser meets the tread. Periodically, vacuum the carpeted risers.

# STEREO EQUIPMENT

**CLEANING STEREO EQUIPMENT** USUALLY MAKES PEOPLE SHUDDER. IT MIGHT SEEM COMPLICATED, BUT IT'S NOT REALLY—AND IT IS IMPORTANT TO KEEP YOUR STEREO CLEAN, BECAUSE DUST AND LINT CAN DAMAGE THE FINE ELECTRONIC PARTS. THE FOLLOWING CLEANING APPROACH IS EASY AND DOESN'T INVOLVE GETTING INTO THE GUTS OF THE MACHINERY.

**Clean the front panels** with a soft cotton cloth and glass cleaner. (First, make sure all components are off.) Don't spray the glass cleaner directly onto the equipment. Instead, spray it on the cloth and gently wipe the cloth on the panel. For sensitive areas, such as around the panel controls and buttons, dust with a small, dry paintbrush (see below). Don't apply cleaner to these areas, since it could seep into the controls. The paintbrush is also a good hedge against accidentally changing your control settings.

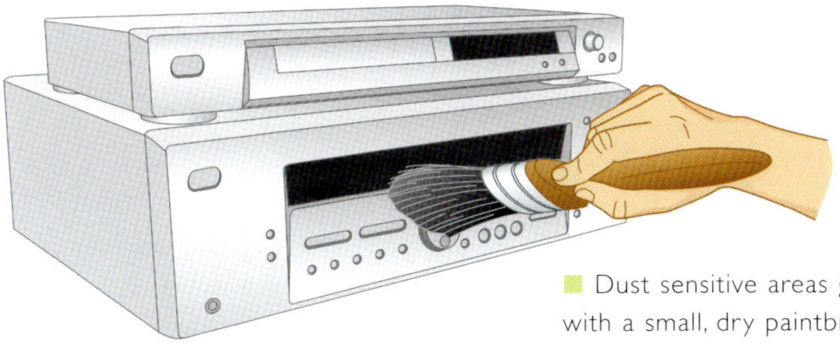

Dust sensitive areas gently with a small, dry paintbrush.

**To clean the component's chassis**—that is, the sides and top—use a soft cloth that is either dry or lightly misted with glass cleaner. Don't wet the cloth, since any residue left on the chassis could collect dust and lead to corrosion. Never spray anything directly onto the chassis. Wipe away from, not towards, the vent holes to avoid pushing dust into the innards of the stereo.

**Dust the back of the unit,** where the cable jacks are, with a dry paintbrush. Don't use cleaner around this sensitive area. If you must remove cables to access the rear, label the cables beforehand with masking tape or pre-printed stereo component labels, which are sold at audio shops. But be forewarned, as many components store data for user settings, clocks and timers, and this memory can be lost when the component is unplugged from the electrical outlet.

**Wipe cables down** with a cloth misted with the same cleaner you used on the panels. Be careful not to pull any cables out.

*See also:* • CASSETTE PLAYERS • CD PLAYERS AND CDS • DVD PLAYERS

## STICKERS

**THESE DAYS, GUMMY** HARD-TO-REMOVE STICKERS AND PRICE TAGS ARE PLASTERED ON ALMOST EVERY NEW PRODUCT, FROM TOILETS TO TOYS TO INDIVIDUAL GRANNY SMITH APPLES. STICKERS ARE CONVENIENT FOR THE SELLER BUT CAN BE FRUSTRATING FOR THE BUYER.

**For stickers with water-soluble glue,** the kind that must be dampened before applying, soak the sticker in a basin of warm water until the glue dissolves and the sticker comes off. If you can't soak it in water, soak a towel in water and apply that to the sticker.

**To remove pressure-sensitive adhesive labels** (those that are peeled from a backing and then pressed into place, such as the stickers that come on glassware and the name tags you get at school functions), start by peeling as much of the label off as possible. Then rub the remaining adhesive off with your fingers the way you would 'thumb-roll' rubber cement into small pellets. Scrape off any difficult adhesive with your fingernail or a dull knife. Sticky residue can be lifted with a citrus-based solvent gum remover, such as De-Solv-it or Big Kev's Goo Remover.

**If the adhesive is old or dried out,** you may have to resort to a different method. Depending on the type of material the sticker is stuck to, try removing it with warm, soapy water or a 50:50 solution of vinegar and warm water. You might also try eucalyptus oil, WD-40 or acetone (or an acetone-based nail-polish remover—that's the kind that smells like bananas).

Before you move onto the nastier sort of solvents, such as lacquer thinner or rubber cement thinner (which can sometimes damage surfaces), give the citrus-based ones a go. Not only do they smell much nicer but they almost always work.

**If the pressure-sensitive adhesive label is on wood,** blot with methylated spirits or heat with a hair dryer to remove.

## STONE

**STONE IS ONE** OF THE MOST DURABLE MATERIALS ON EARTH. MOST OF IT HAS BEEN HERE FOR THOUSANDS—EVEN MILLIONS—OF YEARS. BUT DURABLE IS ONE THING; CLEAN AND SCRATCH-FREE IS ANOTHER. EVEN TOUGH STONE CAN BE SCRATCHED BY EVERYDAY GRIT AND DAMAGED BY SOME OF THE MOST COMMON HOUSEHOLD SUBSTANCES, INCLUDING VINEGAR.

**Sweep or dust stone often** to remove sand and dirt from flat surfaces, where particles can be ground down by shoe soles, furniture or pots and pans. The grit can scratch the stone. Dust using either a vacuum cleaner; or for floors, a dry dust mop (see right); or a clean, dry rag for benchtops and tables. Wipe up spills immediately to avoid staining.

Dry mopping a stone floor regularly prevents grit damage.

**To clean a stone benchtop,** first try using only warm water. Wipe it off with a soft cloth or sponge. Let caked-on food soak a bit before wiping. You should be able to remove spills, crumbs, sauces and other substances this way. If not, add a little dishwashing liquid to the water. Rinse the stone benchtop well with clean water, because leftover soap can leave a film or cause streaking. Avoid stronger cleaning products, such as bath and tile cleaners and scouring powders. These can stain or scratch your stone benchtop. Never use vinegar, lemon juice or other acidic cleaners on marble, travertine or limestone. The acid will eat away at the calcium in the stone.

**To remove stains,** keep it simple and be patient. Most stone stains are solid residue jammed in between the crystals of the stone after the liquid that carried the stain has evaporated. The trick is to put the solid back into solution so it can be removed. You must first determine whether your stain is water-based (for example, from spilled grape juice) or oil-based (salad dressing).

- If the stain is water-based, pour hot water (from the tap, not the kettle) onto the stain and let it stand for a few minutes. Wipe away the excess water. Stack 6 millimetres of paper towels on the stain and saturate with hot water. Cover with a piece of plastic and a flat, heavy weight, such as a cast-iron skillet or a book (careful not to ruin the book). Let it stand for about 10 hours. (Do it overnight and you won't have to worry about anyone moving it.) Next, throw away the paper towels, and the stain should go with them.
- If the stain is oil-based, follow the same procedure as above, only instead of water, use acetone (but don't heat). After the 10 hours is up, throw away the paper towels and wash the stain. In both cases, let the spot dry and then observe. If some of the stain is still present, repeat with hot water or more acetone.

**Sweep patio stone regularly** to remove leaves and sticks, which can stain and hold mould-growing moisture. Once a year, give your patio stone a more thorough cleaning using Tricleanium Ultra Concentrated Cleaner or CRC Hydroforce (both available from hardware shops) following the package instructions. Use a stiff-bristled brush (a long-handled one will be easier on your back and knees) to scrub the patio. To remove barbecue grease, tar, tannins and other stains from stone, use a specialist product, such as Liquid Magnet, a concrete cleaning product available from hardware shops.

**EXPERT ADVICE**

**OLD STONE**

If you are the custodian of centuries-old stone flagging or other stone surfaces, they will no doubt be marked with the signs of wear and tear over the years. While you will never get them pristine again, this is now part of their charm. However, you can often protect them from further damage with an appropriate sealer. Speak to a stone supplier—they know all the tricks. Or if you live near an old stone church, ask the vicar what is used to clean and protect the floor.

*See also:* • BENCHTOPS • PATIOS

# STOVES

**AS WITH OVENS,** THERE'S A VERY IMPORTANT REASON TO KEEP YOUR STOVE CLEAN: IT REDUCES THE RISK OF FIRE FROM OIL, GREASE AND OTHER FOOD SPILLS. THE TRICK IS TO STAY ON TOP OF THE FOOD SPILLS AND SPLATTERS—NOT LET THEM BUILD UP AND HARDEN INTO SOMETHING THAT WILL MAKE YOU GROAN WITH CLEANING DREAD.

Clear your non-removable clogged burner caps with a sewing needle.

**Wipe your stove after you cook,** every time. This may sound unnecessary and over the top, but those few minutes of prevention will save time in the long run. Use a clean, moist sponge or cloth to remove crumbs and oil. Wipe the control panel. Do it while the oven is still warm, and the job will be even easier. For more stubborn spatters and spills, use a solution of dishwashing liquid and warm water or a 50:50 solution of vinegar and warm water. Never use abrasive scrubbers such as steel wool on your stove.

**Periodically give the parts a more extensive cleaning.** Wash burner drip plates and other removable accessories (but not electric burner coils) either by hand in the sink or by running them with your next dishwasher load (if the owner's manual for your stove says they are dishwasher safe). Carefully remove control panel knobs (usually by pulling straight out) and clean around the knobs' bases. Wash the knobs in hot, soapy water, rinse and dry before replacing them.

**If your stove doesn't have a sealed stovetop,** periodically lift up the stovetop (like lifting the bonnet of a car) and clean beneath it. This is an important, often overlooked way to cut down on potential cooking fires. Follow the owner's manual instructions for lifting the top without damaging it. Then clean the grease build-up with a sponge and soapy water or a 50:50 solution of vinegar and warm water. Rinse with clean water and a sponge.

**For electric stoves,** you need to periodically wipe spilled food from the coils once they have cooled. Remove the coils to make the job easier. Use a damp rag and soapy water or a vinegar solution to clean off more stubborn food.

**For gas stoves,** periodically remove and clean burner caps (also called burner heads) and grates. Wait until they have cooled. Use a damp rag and soapy water or a vinegar solution for stubborn food. For any stuck-on food, put the burner caps (if they are removable), grates and drip plates in a plastic bag with a small bowl of ammonia. Seal it and let it stand overnight. The ammonia fumes will loosen the food and grease. Follow up by cleaning the burner caps with soapy water, rinsing with fresh water and air-drying.

If the burner caps aren't removable and get clogged with food, clear them with a sewing needle (see left). If the flame pattern remains jumpy, let the cap cool and clean again with the needle. Repeat until the flame pattern is consistent.

**For ceramic or glass stovetops,** clean often but with great care. These stovetops are easy to clean, but they are also quite sensitive. Never use anything abrasive, including plastic brushes or scrubbing pads, unless they are recommended by the manufacturer. Don't use harsh-cleaning chemicals on ceramic or glass stovetops—wipe with water or soapy water instead. You can use a ceramic cleaner and polish, such as Rubbedin Cooktop Magic (see www.rubbedin.com.au for distributors). Typically, a drop or two will do. Spread it over the stovetop and polish dry with a dry cloth or paper towel.

**For the tough, cooked-on, yellow-brown deposits** that build up on porcelain enamel stovetops, try these tips:

- Moisten a paper towel, add a squirt of dishwashing liquid and squeeze the towel to distribute the detergent. Lay the towel over the deposit and leave it for 10 minutes. Then gently remove the softened gunk with your fingernail or a nylon scrubber, being careful not to scratch the surface. If needed, follow up with a squirt of a degreaser, such as Spray n' Wipe, or an orange oil cleaner, such as Citro-Clean Multi-Purpose Cleaner or Mr Muscle Orange Energy.
- Use a cleaner designed specifically for stovetops, such as Rubbedin Cooktop Magic (see www.rubbedin.com.au for local distributors).

## STUFFED TOY ANIMALS

**STUFFED TOY ANIMALS** TEND TO SPEND A LOT OF TIME ON FLOORS MINGLING WITH DUST MITES OR SNUGGLING UP WITH CHILDREN, WHO UNINTENTIONALLY RUB WHATEVER FOOD AND GRIME THEY HAVE ON THEIR HANDS INTO THE FAKE FUR. BECAUSE OF THE VARIETY OF STUFFING MATERIALS AND ACCESSORIES, SUCH AS CLOTHING AND RIBBONS, CLEANING THEM CAN BE TRICKIER THAN SIMPLY TOSSING THEM IN THE WASHING MACHINE.

**Periodically dust your stuffed toy animals** to keep them fresh, allergen free and looking their best. Use your vacuum cleaner's brush attachment to remove dust. Make sure you don't suck up any loose buttons or clothing accessories. Preen the fake hair with a clean hair-brush and then vacuum again to lift whatever the brush loosened. (So that you won't get dirt and hair-product residue on the toys, buy a brush that you use only for this purpose.) To remove pet hair and lint, use a lint roller (see below).

For a quick and effective clean, use a lint roller to pick up pet hair and lint.

Simple solutions

### Playtime

For a quick and easy way to dust and freshen plush toys, throw them into a dryer and tumble on the lowest setting for 10 minutes. To remove odours from your favourite stuffed animals, add a scented dryer sheet when you tumble them in the dryer.

**To remove light dirt,** just lightly clean the surface. Wipe with a damp cloth, trying not to get moisture into the stuffing. Follow up by preening with a hairbrush.

**To remove juice and other spills on a stuffed animal**—shake it furiously. Shake it outside or in a bathtub, to keep the liquid from splashing onto anything else. This will remove some of the liquid without smearing it into the fur—or worse, the stuffing. Blot up as much remaining liquid as you can with paper towels. Never rub. Wet with a cloth or sponge. Blot again. Rinse the cloth or sponge. Repeat this procedure until the spill is gone.

**For deeper cleaning,** start by reading the care label sewn into the seam. Machine washing is OK for some stuffed animals, such as those filled with most synthetic fibres, but it can ruin others, such as those filled with Styrofoam or that have cardboard stiffeners. The same goes for drying—for some stuffed toys, a dryer is fine, but other toys are stuffed so tightly that they will mildew or will never dry out.

**If your toy isn't machine washable,** surface-clean using a solution of warm water and mild dishwashing liquid. Rub gently with a cloth or sponge dampened in the solution, making sure you don't soak the filling. Rinse the toy by wiping with a cloth or sponge dampened with clear water. To maintain a consistent look to the surface, clean the whole stuffed toy and not just one spot. Air-dry and then preen with a hairbrush.

**If the care label says it's OK to wash,** tie the stuffed toy up in a cloth bag, such as a laundry bag or pillowcase (but not a mesh bag), to protect the fur. It's OK to put several toy animals in the bag, as long as they fit loosely and aren't too big for the washing machine. Wash in cold water using a mild detergent on a gentle cycle. Don't use bleach or fabric softeners. And then put the whole bag in the dryer and tumble on the machine's gentlest setting.

## SUEDE

**SUEDE IS LEATHER** WITH A SOFT-NAPPED FINISH. IT IS ONE OF THE TRICKIEST MATERIALS TO CLEAN; AS TOUGH AS SUEDE MAY SEEM, IT IS EASY TO RUIN. IF YOUR SUEDE IS DIRTY, THERE ARE A FEW TRICKS TO CLEANING IT. ABOVE ALL, BE CAREFUL AND PATIENT. IF YOUR SUEDE IS NOT DIRTY, DON'T GO ANY FURTHER UNTIL YOU'VE SPRAYED IT WITH A SPECIALIST WATERPROOF PROTECTOR, SUCH AS WAPROO WATER AND STAIN PROTECTOR.

**Brush your suede regularly** to remove dirt and restore the nap. When you are going to put it away for a while, brush the item with a suede brush, available from shops that sell leather goods or shoes. Do it gently and in a slow, circular motion. If you don't have a suede brush, use a clean, dry kitchen sponge.

**If you stain your suede,** the best thing to do is blot up as much of the stain as possible and then take the item to a professional cleaner who has experience cleaning leather and suede. However, a couple of exceptions to this rule are:

- For grease or oil stains, cover the stain with a small pile of cornflour or talcum powder (see below). Let it stand overnight. By morning, the powder might have absorbed the stain.
- Remove dried water marks by brushing lightly with a suede brush or clean, dry sponge.

**WATCH OUT** Don't get perfume, hair spray or any other cosmetic products containing alcohol on your suede. They can make the colours run. For the same reason, never use a liquid or solvent-based spot remover on suede, unless it is specifically manufactured for suede. Your blue suede shoes might wind up blotchy. Elvis would never forgive you.

Remove oil stains from suede by covering them with cornflour or talcum powder.

# SWIMMING POOLS

**NO POOL IS** MAINTENANCE-FREE. THESE DAYS, MANY POOL OWNERS USE ADVANCED POOL-CLEANING SYSTEMS, SUCH AS AUTOMATIC UNDERWATER VACUUMS, PUMPS AND FILTERS. BUT AS SWIMMING POOL EXPERTS LIKE TO SAY, THESE AUTOMATED SYSTEMS ARE MEANT TO KEEP A CLEAN POOL CLEAN. LET THE ALGAE AND POOL GRIME REALLY BUILD UP, AND YOU'LL END UP SPENDING HOURS SCRUBBING BY HAND. SO THE TRICK TO KEEPING POOL CLEANING TO A MINIMUM IS TO STAY ON TOP OF IT, EVEN IF YOU HAVE AN AUTOMATED SYSTEM.

**Spend at least 5 minutes every day with your pool.** Walk around it, picking up debris near the edge and making sure the water is clear and not cloudy—a sign of improper pH levels. Any time you see more than five or six leaves or sticks, use a long pole and net to scoop them up (see below). Although an automatic vacuum system will pick up the occasional leaf or twig, its main job is cleaning dirt. Too many leaves can clog the system.

A daily scooping will keep your pool clean and help the filter work more efficiently.

**Keep up the chemical regimen.** Maintain your pool with the manufacturer's recommended dosage of chlorine, which kills bacteria and germs. Use an algicide—not chlorine—to reduce algae. After rains, watch for algae blooms, especially mustard algae, which are present in the air. If you have a Gunite pool (a type of sprayed-on concrete finish), be careful about using a copper-based algicide, which can stain the Gunite. Read the label—algicides containing suspended copper are typically OK to use on Gunite.

**Clean skimmers and filters regularly.** Do it once a week, and more often if needed. (See 'Expert advice' box, on opposite page.)

**Periodically 'sweep' the surface.** Walk around the pool's edge, scooping up debris with the pole and net as you go. Empty the net occasionally to keep leaves from falling back into the pool. When you've finished the edges, net the middle by stretching the net out, letting it fall upside down in the water, and dragging it back towards you. Repeat this while making your way around the pool. Do this once a week or as needed.

**Clean the sides using a long-handled pool brush.** Starting at the top of the pool wall, make one smooth motion downwards with the brush (see above, on opposite page). When you reach the bottom,

★★★
EXPERT ADVICE

SKIMMER DANGERS!

It's the job of the pool skimmer, those little round baskets along the sides of pools, to catch debris. Sometimes that debris is less than savoury and can be downright dangerous. Don't stick your hand into a leaf-filled skimmer basket that you can't see. At the very least, you might encounter scummy leaves, dead insects, frogs, even drowned rodents. But in funnel-web areas you can also grab hold of a spider—with disastrous consequences. They have an amazing ability to stay alive in the skimmer basket for long periods. Even if a funnel-web appears drowned, do not touch it. If your skimmer basket does not have a handle, lift it with a hook made from an old wire coat hanger.

bring the pool brush back to the top and do it again, after you've moved over one brush width. Continue until you've circled the pool once. Do this once a week or as needed.

**Once a week, scrub the tile** using a pool-tile cleaner and a tile brush, available at pool supply shops. Use as little cleaner as possible to keep the product from filling your pool with suds. To avoid damaging the tiles, use a soft nylon pool brush, and only use a harsher brush if there's a real problem, such as black mould.

Scrub tiles weekly to keep them clean and algae free.

**Vacuum the pool floor,** once you have brushed the sides and cleaned the tile, to remove dirt and debris. (Make sure all sediment has settled.) Begin by netting up large debris. Then attach your vacuum head and hose to your extended pole. Work your way around the pool, vacuuming towards the main drain. To fill your vacuum hose with water (which you must do before vacuuming), hold the end up to your pool's return water jet until it is full. This way, you won't have to laboriously dip and raise the hose to fill it.

# TABLE LINENS

**BECAUSE OF THE** FOOD STAINS THEY SO EASILY ACCUMULATE, MOST TABLECLOTHS AND CLOTH SERVIETTES ARE, THANKFULLY, MACHINE WASHABLE. BUT SIMPLY TOSSING DIRTY OR STAINED TABLE LINENS INTO THE WASHER MAY NOT BE ENOUGH TO KEEP THEM LOOKING CRISP AND FRESH. A FEW TRICKS OF THE TRADE WILL HELP.

**Wash table linens before stains set.** After spills or big, messy dinner parties, wash them in a washing machine as soon as possible, following the manufacturer's recommendations on the care label. Pre-treat stains with a commercial spot remover. For best results, don't let the pre-treatment dry before washing.

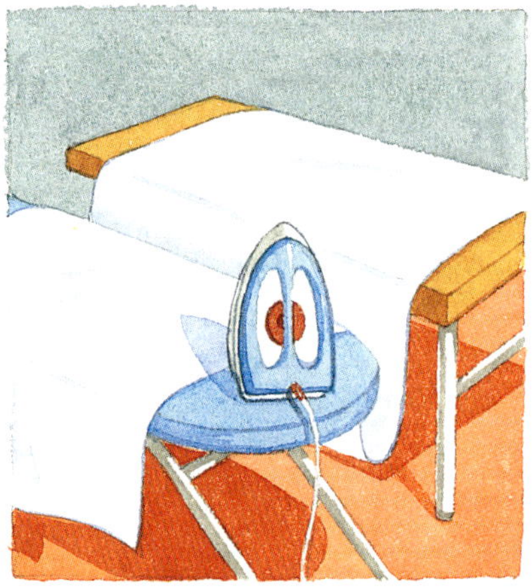

Drape a long cloth over a table to keep it clean when ironing.

**When ironing tablecloths,** cut down on the creasing by placing a table next to your ironing board. Let the tablecloth hang over the table but don't let it drag on the floor (see left).

**If your table linens have lace,** make sure you can wash the lace in a washing machine. Some lace you can't, as it might shrink considerably when washed in water.

- If the lace is not washable, have it dry-cleaned.
- If it is washable—and luckily, most table linen lace is—wash it gently. The safest technique is to hand wash it in warm water with a squirt or two of dishwashing liquid.
- If it is machine washable, wash it in a mesh bag or pillowcase tied at the top. This prevents the lace from snagging.
- To keep the lace from wrinkling, which it will do in a tumble-dryer, air-dry it, laying it as flat as possible.
- When ironing, make small, gentle circular motions with your iron to avoid stretching the lace out of shape.

# TAPESTRIES

**EVEN THOUGH TAPESTRIES** ARE HUNG ON WALLS THEY STILL NEED REGULAR CLEANING. IF IT'S AN ANTIQUE TAPESTRY THAT NEEDS CLEANING, PLAY IT SAFE AND TAKE IT TO A PROFESSIONAL—A TEXTILE RESTORER OR A DEALER IN ANTIQUE TAPESTRIES OR ORIENTAL RUGS.

**Periodically dust your tapestry** using your vacuum cleaner with its upholstery attachment. If possible, leave the tapestry hanging and gently vacuum it in place. This will save the time and hassle of having to take it down and rehang it. Depending on the conditions in your home (how much dust you have), do it once or twice a year.

**If you need to spot-clean a tapestry,** make a soapy shampoo by mixing ½ teaspoon of dishwashing liquid in 1 litre of warm water. Whip up a head of suds by squeezing a sponge in the solution. Before you commence, test the tapestry's colour-fastness by rubbing a cotton bud dipped in the suds on an inconspicuous corner of the tapestry. If the colour holds, then continue. Using as little water as possible, scoop the suds off the top, applying them sparingly with a sponge to the tapestry surface and gently rub. Before the suds dry, lightly rinse

each area as you go with a clean, damp sponge. Make sure you remove all the suds, or the residue will cause the textile to soil faster.

**For a deeper cleaning,** you will need to have the tapestry dry-cleaned by a professional. For the best possible results, do your homework and make sure the drycleaner has experience cleaning the type of tapestry you own.

**To remove any wrinkles or creases,** gently iron the back of your tapestry with a steam iron on a medium setting. If you must iron the front, lay a thin towel on the tapestry to protect the fibres from the hot steam as you iron.

It takes a lot of work to create a tapestry. Using a professional cleaner may be the safest way to clean and protect this piece of decorative art.

## TAR

**TAR ON YOUR** CAR'S UPHOLSTERY OR RUGS CAN BE FRUSTRATING. BUT BEFORE IT STARTS TO NIGGLE TOO MUCH, TRY REMOVING THE TAR WITH THE FOLLOWING CLEANING STEPS.

**WATCH OUT** If you are using methylated spirits to remove tar on an upholstered cushion or carpet, try not to let the metho soak into the stuffing or backing material. It can destroy the bonds of certain synthetic materials.

**Firstly, try to remove as much tar as possible** by scraping with a spoon or dull knife. Remove further tar residue by blotting with a clean, dry paper towel.

**Next, blot off the remaining tar** with methylated spirits on a paper towel. Repeat several times, using clean paper towels each time with more freshly applied metho.

If the tar stain still remains, the next step is to try a soapy solution of warm water and a squirt of dishwashing liquid. Put a small amount of the soapy solution on the stain and work it in by blotting with a paper towel. Rinse by spraying lightly with clean water. Dry the area by stacking paper towels on the stain and weighting them down with a flat, heavy weight, such as a brick.

**Tar can also be dissolved by eucalyptus oil,** dry-cleaning fluid, such as Murlex or Woolclean Spot Dry Remover No. 2, or a citrus-based solvent, such as Big Kev's Goo Remover. However, test first for colour-fastness in an inconspicuous spot.

## TARPAULINS

**WE THROW UP** TARPS TO PROTECT OUR TENTS, BOATS, LAWN MOWERS, WOOD AND OTHER THINGS FROM THE ELEMENTS. AS A RESULT, TARPS TAKE A BEATING, CATCHING BIRD DROPPINGS, DIESEL SMOKE, SAP AND DUST. CLEANING YOUR TARP CAN HELP IT DO ITS JOB LONGER.

**There are two main types of tarps:**

- The heavy-duty vinyl tarps you see covering boats and party tents.
- The garden variety lightweight polyethylene tarps, which come in blues and greens and browns and appear to be woven.

It's a good idea, when cleaning your tarp, to use a long-handled industrial brush to save your back.

**To clean heavy-duty vinyl tarps,** scrub the tarp with a nylon-bristled brush, a solution of dishwashing liquid and water, and lots of elbow grease. Lay it out on a freshly hosed-off driveway or clean parking lot. To make the job easier on your back, scrub the tarp with a long-handled industrial push broom (see left). For stubborn stains, add vinegar (1 cup of white vinegar per 4 litres of water) to the soapy water.

**Clean polyethylene tarps the same way,** but expect to clean them less often. Because of their chemical make-up, polyethylene tarps don't attract dirt as readily as vinyl.

## TAXIDERMY

**YOU'RE PROUD OF** YOUR TROPHY. THAT'S WHY YOU HAD IT PRESERVED. SO YOU WANT TO KEEP IT LOOKING AS GOOD AS THE DAY IT CAME HOME FROM THE TAXIDERMIST, OR PERHAPS FROM THE ANTIQUE SHOP, IF YOU FOUND AN OLD SPECIMEN.

**Don't touch the animals.** A taxidermic specimen isn't made for manhandling. Often it contains insecticides to prevent moths, larvae and other organisms from setting up house and feasting on it. So inspect it regularly for signs of damage from these pests. But avoid touching it. Besides leaving damaging skin oils on the piece, you might expose yourself to insecticides or even to toxic heavy metals such as arsenic and mercury, which may have been used in preserving it.

**Dust is another enemy of a taxidermic specimen.** It can find its way into fur and feathers and be quite difficult to dislodge. And when you do dust, leaking toxins can migrate into a dust cloth or become airborne. Besides stirring up heavy metals, you could send asbestos flying, if the modelling compound used to construct parts such as facial features contains asbestos, as some antique specimens do.

**For a thorough cleaning, call a professional.** Unless you know that your taxidermic specimen was preserved without dangerous toxins—perhaps because you requested it be done without them—realise that even minimal cleaning involves risks. Experts recommend that specimens be cleaned by a professional every 10 years or so. That's the lowest-risk way to get the job done.

Simple solutions

## Location is the key

If you want to preserve a stuffed creature, find a position away from tobacco smoke, fireplaces, heat ducts, airborne grease, the oil from human hands and direct sunlight (which will fade the fur or feathers). It needs to be a dry area, to ward off mildew. If possible, keep your stuffed animal in a self-contained display case (available from taxidermy supply houses and sometimes from antique shops).

If you know your specimen is free of these toxins, or you have decided to give it a quick once-over regardless, gingerly dust fur-bearing trophies with a barely damp, soft cloth, following the natural direction of the fur. Wipe only the fur: even slightly dampened skin will begin to stretch, and fats in the wet skin can begin to turn rancid. For birds, use a feather duster, working from the bill or beak back, following the natural direction of the feather pattern.

**To keep those eyes bright,** apply glass cleaner or a mix of 1 part white vinegar to 4 parts water to a small patch of clean cloth and wipe onto the glass eyes. Baby oil, applied similarly, will bring back the lustre of horns and tusks. In either case, keep the cleaner away from fur, feathers and skin, to prevent any damage to these fragile areas. And avoid getting any solvents on specimens, particularly on preserved fish—they'll dissolve the fish's lacquer finish.

# TELEPHONES

**YOU USE THE** TELEPHONE EVERY DAY. SO DO THE OTHER MEMBERS OF YOUR HOUSEHOLD, AS WELL AS FRIENDS. WITH ALL THE PEOPLE WHO REACH OUT AND TOUCH YOUR TELEPHONE RECEIVER, YOU CAN BET IT NEEDS AN OCCASIONAL CLEANING AND DISINFECTING.

**Simply spraying it with disinfectant won't do.** Your phone is an electronic instrument with intricate wiring and receiver and speaker holes that you don't want to block up. Follow the ironclad electronics-cleaning rule of applying cleaner (or disinfectant) to a cloth and using the dampened cloth to wipe the phone clean.

**To simultaneously clean and disinfect a phone,** use methylated spirits. Pour a little onto a cleaning cloth and wipe the entire phone, paying particular attention to the receiver and receiver bed (see below). Wait a few minutes and then buff with a dry cloth.

**You can also clean your phone** first and then follow up with a disinfectant. But make sure you pick an all-purpose cleaner that's

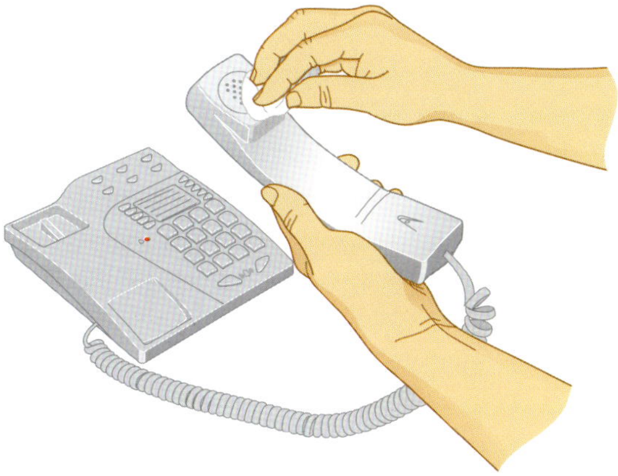

Use methylated spirits to clean and disinfect your phone.

gentle or labelled safe for plastics. (You won't want a cleaner that contains strong solvents like those used to clean petroleum or tar—they'll damage the phone.) For a natural, plastics-friendly cleaner, use 1 tablespoon of borax in 3 cups of water.

Follow the cleaner with a disinfectant such as Dettol, dabbed onto a rag or cotton pad. Leave the disinfectant on the phone surface for 5–10 minutes. Then buff with a dry cloth.

An alternative disinfectant to use is a strong, germ-killing mouthwash, such as Listerine.

**Perhaps the easiest option for cleaning and disinfecting** your telephone is the pre-moistened towelette made specifically for telephones and sold in office supply shops. Towelettes are the more expensive way to go, but worth it, as they are certainly effective and easy—just wipe and throw away.

## TELEVISIONS

**TELEVISIONS ARE DUST** MAGNETS. DUST IS ATTRACTED BY THE STATIC ELECTRICITY ON THE TV SCREEN AND WILL COVER THE SCREEN WITH A MINUTE GREY FUZZ. BEFORE YOU START TO CLEAN YOUR TV, UNPLUG IT FIRST, PARTICULARLY IF YOU NEED TO USE A WET CLEANER.

**To clean a TV screen,** you first need to identify the type of screen you have. Only standard tubes and plasma screens can be wiped with a wet cleaner as described below for the TV's case. Liquid crystal display (LCD) screens—which include not only LCD TVs but also projection TVs with digital light processing (DLP) screens—should be wiped clean with a clean, dry cotton cloth. Consult your owner's manual for what the manufacturer suggests. If the TV came with a cleaning kit, use its cleaner and cloths.

**To clean a TV's case**—or to clean a tube or plasma screen that allows liquid cleaner—slightly dampen a soft cotton cloth with your chosen cleaner. (Pick a non-fraying fabric, as this will avoid having ragged ends that could catch in the ventilation slits.) Glass cleaner or methylated spirits make good cleaners because they will evaporate quickly. Or you can make up your own cleaner—a solution of 1 part liquid fabric softener to 4 parts water. After dipping the cloth in the solution, wring it out, so it's just barely damp, never dripping, and then wipe down the television. Never apply liquid cleaner directly to your screen or casing—the drips could damage the electronics. Buff the screen afterwards with a dry cloth (see above right).

Simple solutions

### Cut down the dust

You can reduce the dust-attracting static electricity on your TV's screen by wiping it with CRC antistatic wipes, or an antistatic dryer sheet such as Fluffy, or alternatively spraying Statique Antistatic Spray onto a cloth and wiping the TV screen.

For that extra shine, buff the screen with a dry cloth after cleaning.

**Some other ways to clean your TV:**

- Simply wipe the screen with an electrostatic dust cloth (available from computer shops, and some supermarkets).
- Dust the body of the TV case with a dry cloth, or clean the case with a solution of 1 part neutral-pH cleaner (such as liquid hand soap) to 3 parts water.

## rules of the game

TUBE TACTICS

- Pull the plug out before you clean.
- Identify the type of screen you have, as some don't take well to liquid cleaners.
- Never spray any liquid directly onto the television or its screen. Spray cleaner onto a cloth to slightly dampen it and then use the cloth to wipe it.

## TENTS

**TODAY'S HIGH-PERFORMANCE** TENTS ARE CERTAINLY NOT CHEAP, SO KEEPING THEM CLEAN IS A WISE CHOICE. BY DOING SO, YOU'LL KEEP ZIPPERS WORKING LONGER AND PROLONG THE LIFE OF YOUR TENT'S WATERPROOF COATING.

**After a camping trip,** shake out loose dirt and wipe the floor and fly, using a soft sponge and warm tap water. Let the tent dry completely before storing. Grit and sand can wear down the inside of the zipper slider (the metal part you slide to zip and unzip the tent), causing it to stop working properly. (If the slider fails—allowing the zipper to open behind the slider—work the slider back to the beginning. Then use a pair of pliers to pinch one rear corner of the slider and then the other, so that the slider's upper and lower parts grip the zipper track better.)

**Keep zippers lubricated.** Use a specialty zipper-lubricating product, such as Selleys Ezi Glide (see right),

To keep zippers on tents working well, use a lubricant.

The best tent to take on a camping trip is one that is clean, waterproof and has zippers that work.

**WATCH OUT** After washing a tent, make sure that the seams, which stay damp the longest, are thoroughly dry before storing it. Moisture can cause mildew and mould to grow. Mildew can work its way in between the waterproof coating and the tent fabric, loosening and separating the coating from the fabric as it spreads.

a cleaner and lubricant available from hardware and camping shops. Paraffin wax or candle wax will also help—some campers even use lip balm! Don't, however, use petroleum-based products.

**Occasionally clean your tent more thoroughly.** Set it up outside and lightly spray it with a garden hose. Mix up a mild solution of water and a gentle fabric cleaner such as Softly. Use a sponge or soft cloth to gently wipe the tent clean. Rinse well, but don't saturate the tent material. Let the tent dry in indirect sunlight.

**To clean mildew from a tent,** wash the tent with soapy water (as detailed above) and then wipe it out with a solution of 1 cup of salt, 1 cup of concentrated lemon juice and 4 litres of hot water. Don't rinse the tent, just let it air-dry. To help prevent mildew, always store your tent in a cool, dry place, and store it loosely in a large cotton bag or box (rather than its own stuff bag), so that air can circulate.

**If the waterproof coating starts to peel** because of mildew or any other cause, reapply a waterproofing compound. Look for the appropriate waterproofing product at your local camping shop.

**To remove sap or tar from your tent,** try cleaning it off with eucalyptus oil and a clean cloth. If this doesn't do the trick, you can try a small amount of kerosene. Make sure you test first on an inconspicuous part of the tent.

Simple solutions

## A useful barrier

To keep your tent clean, always use a ground cover beneath it. And just as important, the ground cover will help keep the tent's floor—and you—drier.

## THERMOS FLASKS

**THERMOS FLASKS ARE** NOT NEW, BUT THEY'RE JUST AS AMAZING AS THE DAY THEY WERE INVENTED, FOR THEY KEEP YOUR COFFEE HOT AND YOUR VICHYSSOISE COLD. THERMOS FLASKS ARE LESS EXCITING WHEN IT COMES TO CLEANING THOUGH. SOME YOU'RE NOT SUPPOSED TO SUBMERGE; MANY HAVE NECKS TOO NARROW TO ACCESS WITH BRUSHES. SO HOW DO YOU CLEAN THEM?

**Clean thermos flasks after each use** with hot, soapy water. Scrub them with a bottlebrush, if possible (see right). Then rinse well and air-dry. Try not to get water between the outer casing and the inner insulating flask.

**For the stubborn or hard-to-reach stains,** fill the thermos with hot water, drop in two denture-cleaning tablets and let it stand overnight. In the morning, rinse the thermos with clean water and allow to air-dry.

**If your thermos has taken on a nasty odour** that regular washing does not overcome, pour in a few tablespoons of vinegar or bicarbonate of soda. Fill the thermos the rest of the way with hot water and let it sit for half an hour. Then pour the solution out, rinse and air-dry.

Use a bottle-brush to thoroughly clean your thermos after each use.

## TIES

**PER SQUARE CENTIMETRE,** TIES ARE CERTAINLY THE MOST VALUABLE GARMENT IN A MAN'S WARDROBE, ESPECIALLY FOR MEN WHO LIKE A NICE TIE. IT'S EASY TO RUIN A TIE, THOUGH—EASY FOR YOU AND EASY FOR A DRYCLEANER WHO IS NOT SO EXPERIENCED IN CLEANING TIES.

**Have a silk tie professionally cleaned** once or twice a year, depending on how often you wear it. Clean a visibly dirty or stained tie immediately. Look for a drycleaner who's experienced in cleaning silk ties. Ask how they 'finish' the tie after cleaning it. Ties should not be pressed—they should be rolled and reshaped with steam. If you are trying a new drycleaner, don't give them your best ties first.

**To refresh a tired-looking silk tie,** you can try a little steam. You can hang the tie in a steamy bathroom. Or wrap a damp cloth over the sole plate of your iron and pass the steaming iron over the tie without actually touching it (see below).

When steaming your tie, don't let the iron actually touch the tie.

**For extra protection,** spray on a specialised fabric guard and avoid tie-threatening situations, such as soup bowls and tomato sauce sachets.

**WATCH OUT** Never put water (or soda water) on a tie to remove a stain, as you might just create a larger water stain. Besides, water won't remove oil-based stains, such as salad dressing and gravy.

**If you do spill something on your tie,** blot away the excess using a clean, white cloth or serviette and then take the tie to a drycleaner as soon as possible. Stains, and especially food stains, tend to set after 24–48 hours. Never try to rub the stain out. You might rub the colour from the fabric, especially if it's silk.

## TILES

**CERAMIC AND VINYL** TILES—TWO VERY DIFFERENT MATERIALS—ARE RELATIVELY LOW-MAINTENANCE, EASY-TO-CLEAN SURFACES. HOWEVER, BOTH TILES CAN SCRATCH. TO PREVENT THIS, IT'S IMPORTANT TO KEEP THEM DIRT-FREE.

**For regular cleaning of floor tiles,** of both ceramic and vinyl, sweep with a broom or vacuum. Trapped dirt and sand are highly abrasive and can cause lasting damage to matte and glossy finishes. If you vacuum, avoid using the machine's beater bar (for carpets), which can permanently damage tile finishes.

**Once a week, clean floor tiles** by going over them with a damp mop. Again, this goes for both ceramic and vinyl tiles. Damp mopping removes stubborn, smeared-on dirt. Never use excessive amounts of water with vinyl tiles, since the water can seep under the tiles and damage the glue. Avoid soapy or oily cleaners, as they can leave a dull film. If anything, add a splash of vinegar to the mop water. An alkaline-based, all-purpose cleaner, such as Handy Andy, is also effective. Or use a specialty tile floor cleaner, such as Vinyl Magic or Pledge One Go, available from hardware shops and home improvement shops. Follow the manufacturer's instructions.

Avoid soapy or oily cleaners when wiping down ceramic wall tiles.

**For ceramic wall tiles,** wipe them regularly with a damp sponge. As with floor tiles, avoid soapy or oily cleaners. Add a splash of vinegar to the water, or use a commercial bath-and-tile cleaner. Another alternative is to add 1 capful of methylated spirits to 4 litres of water in a bucket and wipe down the tiles using a sponge or clean, soft cloth (see left). Never use abrasive scrubbers or cleaning products, such as scouring powders. These can scratch glazed tiles, dulling the finish and making them more susceptible to dirt.

**To keep grout clean,** it's best to do it regularly so that the scum and mildew don't have a chance to get a foothold in the porous surface. Indeed, it's a good idea to clean grout after you shower, while it's still steamy moist and the soil has been loosened. Mix together ¼ cup of vinegar with 4 litres of water and scrub the grout with a toothbrush or nylon-scrubbing pad. For more cleaning power, go over it once with a degreaser, such as Orange Power Shower or bath and tile cleaner, which will loosen the germ-harbouring soap scum, and then with a

solutions

## What a heel

You can remove black heel marks from tile floors using methylated spirits. Dip a clean, white cloth in some metho and rub the black heel mark off the tile.

## Tough measures for grimy grout

For really grimy grout that stubbornly resists standard cleaning methods, try a solution of chlorine bleach and water.

Make sure the area you're working in is well ventilated, and wear rubber gloves. Then mix together a cup of bleach and 2 litres of water in a bucket. Using a toothbrush or nylon-scrubbing brush, scrub the dirty areas then let the solution soak for 10–20 minutes before rinsing with clean water. Rinse a second time—again with clean water, not the water you used in the first rinse—and wipe the area dry with a clean cloth. You can also spray on a ready-mixed commercial product, such as Selleys RMK Rapid Mould Killer.

After the grout dries thoroughly, apply a silicone sealer (available from home improvement shops) to reduce future maintenance. Grout manufacturers generally recommend resealing grout joints twice a year to prevent staining. However, you can skip this step if the joint is filled with epoxy grout.

disinfectant all-purpose spray, to kill the germs themselves. Let your cleaning products do the work for you. Too much scrubbing grinds the grime in deeper. Spray or wipe each product on and leave it on for several seconds. Wipe it down with a clean, wet sponge to rinse off the cleaning solution. If you must scrub, use a long-bristled brush that is not too stiff (you don't want to wear down the grout) or use an old toothbrush. Steel wool is too abrasive. If the grout is really grungy, see the 'Tough measures for grimy gout' box above.

*See also:*
• FLOORS

## TIN

**TIN IS SILVERY** WHITE WITH A BRILLIANT LUSTRE. IT IS USED AS A DECORATIVE PLATING AND TO PROTECT METALS FROM RUSTING. YOU SEE IT OFTEN ON MEXICAN CRAFTS AND INEXPENSIVE KITCHENWARE. BE CAREFUL NOT TO SCRATCH IT WHEN CLEANING. IF YOU DO, YOU'LL INVITE RUST.

**Dust decorative items regularly**. Use a feather duster for pieces with lots of detail. Or wipe with a dry or slightly damp rag.

**Wash tin in a solution of mild dishwashing liquid** and warm water and a soft cloth. Don't use abrasive scrubbers or cleaners, because they may scratch through the tin plating.

**To remove rust on tin,** rub it with superfine steel wool (0000). Once the rust is gone, wash the tin in the soapy solution. Rinse well and dry completely. To prevent rust from returning, apply a thin coat of paste wax—an auto-wax, for instance.

# TOASTER OVENS

**TOASTER OVENS TYPICALLY** NEED A BETTER CLEANING THAN TOASTERS. MANY PEOPLE DO MORE THAN JUST TOAST BREAD IN THEIR TOASTER OVENS—THEY MAKE TOASTED SANDWICHES DRIPPING IN CHEESE, JUICE-OOZING FRUIT PIES AND EVEN GRILL SMALL GREASE-SPATTERING CHICKENS.

**The outside of the toaster oven** can be kept clean by regularly wiping it with a damp cloth. Add a splash of vinegar or a squirt of dishwashing liquid to the wash water for added cleaning power. The control buttons may pull off to make cleaning the control panel easier. Check your owner's manual.

**Every week or two,** depending on use, empty the crumb tray, which, in most toaster ovens, is removable. Some even have doors underneath for removing the crumbs that fall past the tray. If you'll be opening this trapdoor, make sure you unplug the unit first. Wash the removable tray. Most trays are thin aluminium and may not be dishwasher safe. Read your owner's manual to find out. If you're unsure, hand wash the tray in warm, soapy water.

**Clean the oven** soon after messy toaster-oven cooking sessions. Let the oven cool, unplug it and then remove any oven trays or racks. Clean trays and racks in hot, soapy water. Wipe the inside of the oven with a damp cloth. If you're lucky, your toaster has a non-stick surface on the inside, and baked-on food will come right off. Carefully lift up the heating element (if possible) and clean under it.

**For stuck-on food,** try a moist plastic or nylon scrubber. Never use anything abrasive, such as steel wool. You'll scratch the smooth surface, which will make food stick worse next time. If the plastic scrubber fails, put a small bowl of full-strength ammonia inside the unplugged oven with the door closed. Leave overnight and then remove the ammonia. The fumes will loosen the food. Wipe the inside again and let the oven air out before using.

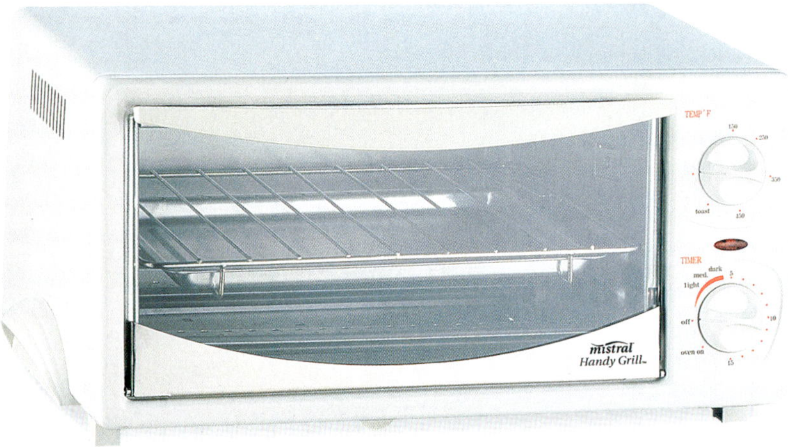


For the best cooking results, make sure your toaster oven is clean.

## TOASTERS

**YOU'RE BOUND TO** GET CRUMBS IN THE TOASTER DURING THE TOASTING PROCESS. MAKERS ARE AWARE OF THIS AND DESIGN THEIR APPLIANCES FOR EASY CLEAN-UP.

Use a clean, dry toothbrush to remove crumbs from the toaster.

**Empty the crumbs out of your toaster** once every week or so, depending on how much you use it. Toasters are designed for easy crumb removal. Some toasters have slide-out crumb trays; others have hinged doors that allow you to empty the crumbs. No matter what kind of toaster you have or what sort of mechanism it has for crumb removal, always unplug the toaster before cleaning it.

**If you can't get them all out,** try disintegrating them with heat. Run the toaster empty on the hottest setting two or three times. (This is also the principle behind self-cleaning ovens.)

**For those hard-to-remove crumbs,** use a clean, dry toothbrush, (not the one you use to scrub grout—a new one) or an old, clean paintbrush. Again, be sure the toaster is unplugged. Loosen the crumbs with the brush and then brush them out (see left). Turn the toaster upside down and shake. Make sure you do it gently, as you don't want to damage the heating element.

**Wipe down the outside of the toaster** with a damp cloth. Wipe around the control knobs. Add a dash of vinegar or squirt of dish-washing liquid to the cleaning water for more cleaning power. For stainless steel toasters, polish with a stainless steel polish, available from supermarkets and home improvement shops.

## TOILETS

**WE ALL HAVE** THEM, AND WE ALL HAVE TO CLEAN THEM. APART FROM A NATURAL AVERSION, MOST PEOPLE ARE NOT EFFICIENT AT CLEANING THEIR TOILETS. AND MANY ARE STUMPED BY THOSE STUBBORN RINGS LEFT AROUND THE BOWL.

**To clean a toilet,** work from the top down. Start with the tank, move to the seat, clean inside the bowl and then clean the base. Doing it this way will help you focus. Moreover, the dirtiest part of the toilet—and hence the last place you want your cloth to touch—is the base, where the dust and urine dribbles settle.

**For everything but the bowl,** use a dry cloth (old nappies work well) and a spray-on bathroom cleaner, preferably one that contains ammonia. Spray the cleaner on the toilet surface and wipe it off with the cloth. Keeping the cloth dry makes it easier to wipe everything up.

Simple solutions

### Ring around the bowl

For stubborn rings around the toilet bowl, use a pumice stone, available from pharmacies and specialist bath-product shops. (Pumice stones are the same product you use to rub corns off your feet.) Keeping the stone wet, rub it on the ring until it's gone. This works for old rings as well. It will not scratch white vitreous china, which is what most toilets are made of, but it will scratch fibreglass, enamel, plastic and other materials.

Wet it, and you'll be chasing that moisture around, wringing and re-wringing the cloth, so it's important to change cloths when one becomes soaked with cleaner. Avoid sponges, which work OK but can absorb—and transfer—micro-organisms. (You wash your cloths after each use, but do you wash your sponges? See 'Disinfecting your kitchen sponges', on page 423.)

**Clean the bowl** with a rounded bowl brush and cleaner. Avoid brushes with metal wire, since the metal can scratch the toilet bowl.

**To clean around the hardware** that holds the seat to the toilet and the toilet to the floor, use a grout brush or an old toothbrush.

## TOOLS

**IN THE OLD** DAYS, TOOLMAKERS DATED THEIR TOOLS—CARVING THE YEAR INTO THE WOODEN BLOCK OF A PLANE, FOR EXAMPLE—IN THE EXPECTATION THAT THE TOOLS WOULD LAST FOR GENERATIONS. THE SAME IS TRUE TODAY. IN THIS DISPOSABLE WORLD WE LIVE IN, A WELL-BUILT TOOL IS ONE OF THE FEW GOODS MEANT TO LAST. LUCKILY, MOST DON'T NEED MUCH IN THE WAY OF CLEANING.

**The most basic goal with hand tools,** especially those made of wood and metal, is to keep them dry. If a tool gets wet, wipe it dry. If it gets sweaty or dusty, clean it with a damp cloth and then wipe it dry with another cloth. Water must be removed, as it can quickly rust a saw blade and warp a wooden level.

**Keep retractable measuring tapes** free of dirt, sand, dust and other debris. These foreign objects can scratch the Mylar coating on the metal tape. Once it is scratched, the metal tape will rust. Frequently wipe the tape clean with a dry cloth. Don't use a wet cloth—and don't let your tape get wet. Moisture will find its way into the spring mechanism and will rust it. To remove tar and glue from the tape, use methylated spirits or mineral turpentine. Avoid harsher solvents, which can melt the protective coating.

*See also:* • POWER TOOLS • GARDEN TOOLS

**WATCH OUT** Avoid oiling most tools (garden tools are the exception), since the oil could get on the handle, causing the tool to slip, which is potentially very dangerous.

# TOYS

**CLEAN YOUR TOYS** SO THEY LOOK GREAT AND ARE FREE OF BACTERIA. MOST TOYS THESE DAYS ARE MADE OF EASY-TO-CLEAN PLASTICS. THE MAIN ISSUE IN CLEANING TOYS IS TO NEVER USE ANYTHING TOXIC. EVEN IF YOUR CHILD NO LONGER CHEWS ON TOYS, HANDS WILL WIND UP IN THEIR MOUTHS.

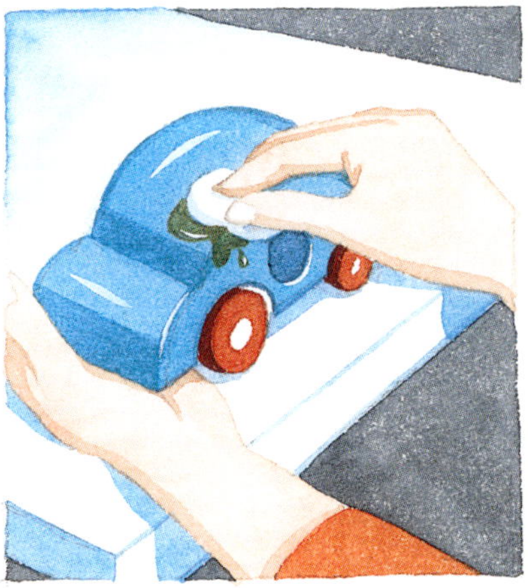

Don't saturate wooden toys with oil when cleaning them—wipe them clean.

*See also:*
• STUFFED TOY ANIMALS • DOLLS

**Wash toys regularly** to keep them clean and bacteria-free. Wash rubber and plastic toys with warm water combined with a squirt of dishwashing liquid. Wipe clean with a soft cloth or sponge. Be careful of painted-on features, such as faces, numbers or other designs, as these could rub off. Dry with a cloth or air-dry. For bigger plastic toys, such as plastic wagons and plastic playhouses, use a hose, a bucket of soapy water and a soft-bristled scrubbing brush.

**Wipe down metal toys,** such as tractors and cars, using a damp cloth. Water leads to rust, so avoid soap (since suds require rinsing) and don't submerge such toys. If a metal toy or a toy with metal parts does get wet, dry it immediately with a hair dryer to avoid rust. If there are batteries, beeping sounds or blinking lights, don't wet the toy. Water will ruin the circuitry.

**Clean wooden toys** with a mild solution of a neutral cleaner, such as Howard Clean-A-Finish Wood Soap and water. (Follow the manufacturer's instructions for amounts.) Use a cloth or soft-bristled brush. Don't soak or submerge the wooden toy. Instead, dip the cloth or brush in the soapy water and wipe the toy clean. Rinse with a clean cloth and plain water. Dry with a clean, dry towel. If the toy is scratched, splintered or chipped, or if the water has raised the grain (making the wood feel rough), lightly sand it with fine sandpaper once the toy has dried.

**If a wooden toy has a natural, oil-based finish,** reapply small amounts of oil to keep the wood conditioned (see left). Since toys often wind up in children's mouths (wooden baby chew toys are expressly meant for this purpose), use a food-grade vegetable or paraffin oil. Allow oil to penetrate for about an hour and then wipe off the excess.

It is especially important not to clean wooden toys with harsh chemicals, because wood absorbs and harbours such chemicals.

**Clean Barbies and similar dolls** by wiping with a cloth and water mixed with a little dishwashing liquid. Wash hair with baby shampoo. (A drop of hair conditioner will soften the hair.) Don't use any heat source, such as a hair dryer, to dry the hair, as that will turn it frizzy. Instead, comb the hair out, starting from the bottom and working up to remove tangles. Let the doll air-dry.

# TYPEWRITERS

**NOT MANY OF** YOU WILL STILL HAVE A TYPEWRITER. HOWEVER, A TYPEWRITER IS DEPENDABLE AND STILL USEFUL FOR PERSONAL LETTERS, APPLICATIONS, LABELS AND OTHER NEEDS. BUT DOES ANYONE REMEMBER HOW TO CLEAN ONE?

**You need to dust your typewriter regularly** to keep dust and lint from settling between the keys. You can use a vacuum cleaner with an upholstery attachment to suck the dust out (see below), or the reverse—a can of compressed air, available from office supply shops—to blow it out. Or you can brush between the keys with a small, dry paintbrush.

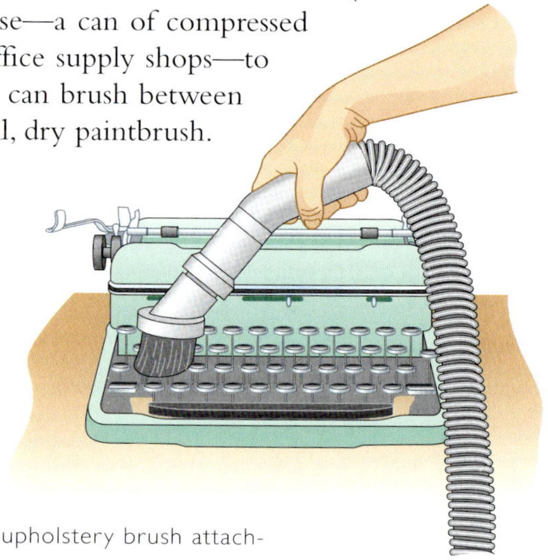

A vacuum upholstery brush attachment will remove any dust and debris from between the typewriter keys.

**Wipe the case and body of the typewriter** with a clean, lint-free cloth lightly moistened with a commercial window cleaner (the emphasis here is on lightly moistened). You don't want to risk letting liquid drip into the body of the typewriter, especially if it is an electric typewriter. Wipe the key tops, buttons and bars. Fight the urge to use paper towels, since they might tear and leave little pieces of paper stuck in the mechanism.

**To clean beneath the keys,** wrap the same cloth around the end of a letter opener and gently work it between the keys.

**Wipe the black roller,** known as the platen, with the same cloth. It is likely to have ink on it (especially if you have children who like to press the keys without paper in the machine). The ink may or may not come completely off. Don't worry. A little leftover ink is better than trying to remove it with an ink stain remover that contains alcohol, which will dry the platen out and make it brittle. You want it to remain soft and slightly pliable. The ammonia in the glass cleaner will help condition the platen.

**Have your typewriter professionally lubricated** every so often. Don't try to do it yourself. You might do more harm than good.

## UMBRELLAS

**UMBRELLAS DON'T GET** VERY DIRTY, WHICH IS FORTUNATE, BECAUSE THEY'VE GOT TO BE AMONG THE MOST AWKWARD THINGS IN THE WORLD TO CLEAN.

**To clean your regular umbrella,** just let the rain do the job the next time it showers. To prevent mould and mildew, open the umbrella and allow it to dry thoroughly before you put it away. If you really want to clean it more thoroughly, open it up, spray it with a hose and then scrub gently with a sponge dipped in warm water with a squirt of dishwashing liquid. Rinse and, again, dry thoroughly.

**To remove dirt and bird poo from a patio umbrella**—which is usually made of either vinyl or a coarse fabric, such as canvas—spray it with a garden hose. Then scrub it with a nylon-bristled brush dipped in a bucket containing a sudsy solution of warm water and dishwashing liquid. Rinse by spraying the umbrella with the hose.

**Protect a patio umbrella's metal rods** by polishing them with car wax. Wax also makes the metal easier to clean in the future. Following the manufacturer's instructions, lightly wax the metal. Take care not to get the wax on the umbrella covering, as it can stain fabric and make a mess of vinyl mesh.

**If your umbrella has wooden parts,** condition and protect them with wood oil, rubbed in with a clean, soft cloth. Again, take care not to spill it on the canvas.

## UPHOLSTERY

**UPHOLSTERY POSES A** CLEANING CHALLENGE, SINCE IT ALMOST ALWAYS COVERS SOME SORT OF PADDING—BE IT COTTON BATTING OR FOAM RUBBER. EVEN WHEN UPHOLSTERY MATERIAL CAN BE REMOVED FROM THE PADDING, IF THE UPHOLSTERY SHRINKS, IT MAY NOT FIT BACK ON THE CUSHION. SO YOU NEED TO CLEAN WITHOUT SOAKING THE PADDING BENEATH.

**Vacuum upholstery regularly** to remove dust and the dust mites it harbours. Use an upholstery attachment with a gentle brush end, so you don't damage the upholstery material, and use the crevice tool attachment for nooks and crannies. If your upholstered piece is stuffed with feathers, do not vacuum it unless it is lined with a down-proof ticking. Otherwise, you might suck the feathers out while you're cleaning. If you don't have any vacuum-cleaner attachments, brush the dust away with a soft-bristled brush at least once a month. Dust, when it's moistened or ground in, can stain upholstery.

**For more thorough cleaning,** or to remove stains, your upholstery will need washing. First, check the upholstery manufacturer's suggestions on the care label instructions. This label will tell you whether you should use a water-based shampoo, a dry-cleaning solvent or neither of the two. Next, pick an inconspicuous spot on the upholstery and pre-test whatever cleaning technique is recommended. If there is shrinking, bleeding or running colours, contact a professional cleaner. If not, you can assume it's safe to clean it.

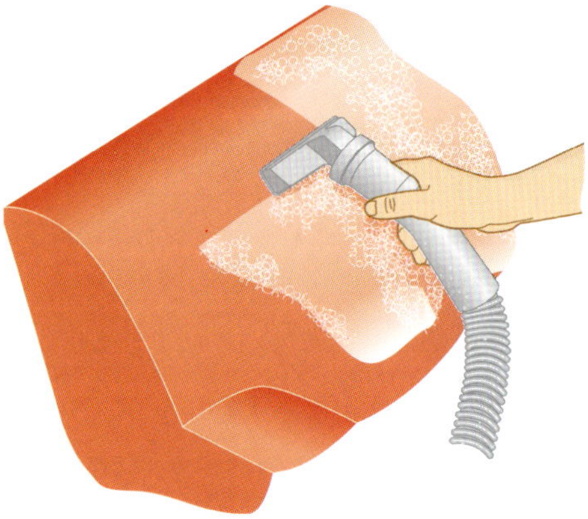

A commercial foaming shampoo should be perfectly dry before you attempt to vacuum it off upholstery.

**If shampooing is allowable,** use as little moisture as possible. You don't want to wet the upholstery's stuffing, because it dries very slowly and can attract dust mites and mould. Clean using suds only. The easiest method is to use a foaming commercial shampoo in an aerosol can. Follow the instructions on the can, which typically will tell you to allow the foam to stand until dry and then to vacuum it off (see left).

**To make your own upholstery shampoo,** mix ½ teaspoon of dishwashing liquid per 1 litre of warm water. Make suds by squeezing a sponge in the solution. Scoop the suds off the top, applying them sparingly with the sponge to the upholstery. Rub gently in the direction of the fabric's grain. Rather than letting the suds dry as you would a commercial shampoo, work on a small area at a time, lightly rinsing each area as you go with a clean, damp sponge. Again, avoid soaking the fabric. Make sure you rinse out all of the suds from the fabric, or the residue will cause the fabric to soil faster.

**If the fabric calls for dry-cleaning only** and the upholstery is portable, have it professionally cleaned. If, however, you are cleaning a stain—or if the upholstery is part of a large piece of furniture—you can do it yourself, using a commercial dry-cleaning solvent, such as Murlex or Woolclean Spot Dry Remover No. 2. Don't pour the solvent on the stain. Instead, moisten a clean, white cloth with the solvent and use that to draw the stain out. Blot repeatedly—never rub. Rubbing can stretch or damage the texture of the fabric. Always use solvents sparingly and in a well-ventilated area. And don't use them on upholstery filled with latex foam rubber padding, because the solvent can dissolve the padding.

## Upholstery stain-removal basics

To find out what solution you should use to remove a stain—what takes out chocolate or grease, for example—see 'Stains', on page 328. Meanwhile, here are some general tips for removing stains from upholstery:

- Remove as much of the stain as you can by blotting with paper towels or scraping with a dull knife. When blotting up a large stain, always blot from the edge of the stain to the centre to contain it.
- Avoid rubbing or pushing the stain deeper into the upholstery.
- Since you never want to soak an upholstered cushion or piece of furniture, trigger spray bottles are good for lightly applying water-based cleaning solutions as well as the rinsing water.
- To dry upholstery that has been rinsed with water, lay a wad of paper towels on the spot and place a weight, such as a brick or the telephone directory, on the pile of paper towels. (Put the brick in a plastic bag or on a piece of foil to prevent colour transfer from the brick to the upholstery.) Allow the upholstery to dry and then remove the paper towels.

# VACUUM CLEANERS

**A DECENT VACUUM** CLEANER IS AN INVALUABLE CLEANING TOOL, BUT ONLY IF IT IS OPERATING EFFICIENTLY. VACUUM CLEANERS DON'T NEED MUCH ATTENTION, BUT THEY WILL ONLY GIVE OPTIMUM RESULTS IF YOU KEEP THEM IN OPTIMUM CONDITION, BY KEEPING THE BRUSHES AND PIPES UNCLOGGED AND THE FILTERS CLEAN.

**Whether your vacuum uses a bag system or not,** make sure that you empty the dust and dirt from the cleaner frequently, and certainly always before you put the vacuum away. Full bags or dust compartments don't draw as well, making you—and the cleaner—work harder to pick up the dirt.

**If the plastic attachments,** such as the crevice tool and upholstery brush, are looking a bit grubby, give them a gentle wash in warm water and dishwashing liquid.

**Check to see if the brush attachments** on your vacuum are clogged with dust, lint and pet hair. If they are, their efficiency is considerably reduced. Use the vacuum itself to suck as much debris as you can from the brush, but if any still remains, work it out from between the bristles with an old comb.

**The upholstery brush attachment** can often get very clogged. After removing as much dirt and fluff as you can, give it a gentle wash in warm water and mild dishwashing liquid. Shake it out and let it dry thoroughly before reusing or storing.

**Most vacuum cleaners** these days have some kind of filter system, from the expensive and efficient HEPA (high efficiency particulate air) filters—which are especially beneficial to asthma and allergy sufferers—to simpler kinds. But whichever type you have, remove it and either replace it, or clean it, frequently, following your manufacturer's instructions. If the air smells 'stale' when you vacuum, add a couple of drops of your favourite essential oil or eucalyptus oil to the disposable filter before you start vacuuming.

**Check the tubing of your vacuum** for blockages every so often, especially if the sucking seems sluggish and the dust canister is not full. Sometimes a gentle squeeze and rap will dislodge the blockage, but if it doesn't, detach the tube from the machine and gently probe it with the end of a long cobweb broom.

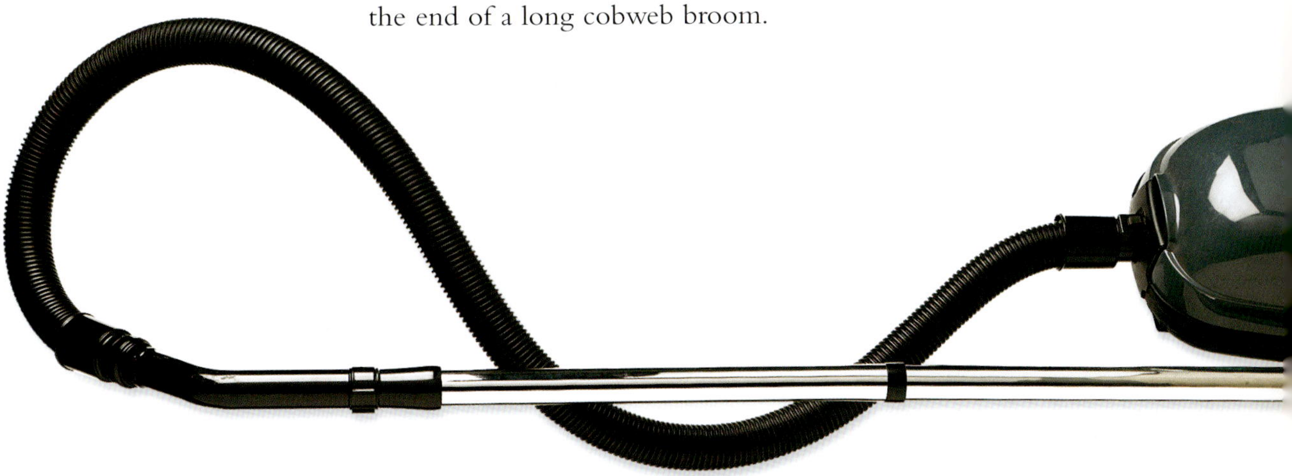

## VASES

**DIRTY VASES NOT** ONLY LOOK BAD, BUT THEY ALSO REDUCE THE LONGEVITY OF THE CUT FLOWERS YOU KEEP IN THEM. THE RESIDUE IN VASES, INCLUDING GROWTH SUCH AS ALGAE, PLUGS UP THE STEMS OF WATER-DRINKING FLOWERS AND CAUSES THEM TO DRY UP QUICKER.

**The easiest way to clean vases** is to scrub them with hot, soapy water and a bottlebrush. Rinse well after washing, to remove traces of detergent, and allow them to dry completely before storing.

**To remove white mineral-deposit stains** from the inside of vases, swirl a mixture of rock salt and vinegar around inside the vase (see below). The salt will gently scour the surface while the vinegar breaks down the deposits.

Swirl a mixture of white vinegar and rock salt in a vase to remove white mineral deposits inside it.

Simple solutions

### Oh, those narrow-necked vases

If you can't get to the inside of a vase to clean it with with a bottlebrush, fill the vase with hot water and add a couple of denture-cleaning tablets (available from the toothpaste section of supermarkets), and let it stand overnight. Rinse well and dry.

## VCRs AND VIDEOTAPES

**AS WITH ANY** ELECTRONIC GEAR, THE CLEANER YOU KEEP YOUR VCR, THE BETTER ALL THOSE LITTLE PARTS WILL WORK—AND THE LONGER THE PIECE OF EQUIPMENT WILL LAST. THAT SAID, IT'S NOT NECESSARY TO OPEN UP YOUR VCR FOR INTERIOR CLEANING. YOU CAN CAUSE MORE HARM THAN GOOD. THE INSIDE RARELY NEEDS CLEANING IF YOU KEEP THE OUTSIDE CLEAN. THE ONLY INTERIOR PART YOU NEED TO CLEAN IS THE PLAYBACK HEAD—WHICH YOU DO WITH A HEAD-CLEANING TAPE.

**Clean the front panel** with a soft cotton cloth and glass cleaner, such as Windex or Mr Muscle. (First, turn off the VCR.) Don't use paper towels, as they can tear and shed lint. And don't spray the glass cleaner directly onto the unit. Instead, spray it on the cloth and gently wipe the cloth on the panel. For sensitive areas, such as around the panel control knobs and buttons, dust with a small, dry paintbrush. Don't apply cleaner to these areas, since it could seep into the controls. This way, you won't accidentally change your control settings, either.

**To clean the chassis of the VCR**—that is, the sides and top—use a soft cloth either dry or lightly misted with glass cleaner. Don't wet the cloth, since any residue left on the chassis could collect dust and lead to corrosion. You should never spray anything directly onto the chassis. Wipe away from vent holes (not towards them) to avoid pushing dust into the workings of the VCR.

**Dust the back of the unit,** where the cable jacks are, with a dry paintbrush. Don't use cleaner around this sensitive area. If you must remove the cables to access the back, be forewarned: many units store information for user settings, clock and timers, and this memory can be lost when the unit is unplugged from the electrical outlet.

**WATCH OUT** Avoid machines that are designed to clean video cassettes. Because these particular devices sometimes involve rewinding machines, they often damage the tape by stretching it.

**Wipe cables down** with a cloth misted with the same cleaner you used on the panels. Be careful not to pull cables out.

**Clean the playback head periodically**—once every few months, depending on use, or when the playback quality indicates a problem. If you rent a lot of videotapes, you may need to clean more often, since rental tapes bring with them dirt and debris picked up from all the other VCRs they've been played in.

Use a good-quality, dry head-cleaning cassette ('dry' because the liquid that sometimes comes with head-cleaning cassettes may not evaporate completely before another tape is inserted, which can worsen the situation by attracting grime from the tape to the playback head). And that could lead to an expensive service call. Make sure you read your owner's manual first. If your VCR incorporates an automatic head-cleaning system, the manufacturer may recommend that you not use any kind of head-cleaning tape.

**If you need to clean a videotape's case,** carefully wipe it with a damp cloth. Make sure you don't wet the tape itself or the tape path. Remove any labels or adhesives that are coming off. Labels that fall off are one of the biggest causes of tape jams.

*See also:*
• CAMCORDERS

## rules of the game

STEP-BY-STEP
VCR CLEANING

- Turn off the VCR.
- Spray glass cleaner on a soft cloth and gently wipe the front panel.
- Dust control knobs and buttons with a small, dry paintbrush.
- Clean the sides and top with a soft cloth (dry or lightly misted with glass cleaner, such as Windex or Mr Muscle).
- Dust the rear of the machine with a dry paintbrush. Wipe cables with a cloth lightly misted with a glass cleaner.
- Clean the playback head with a good-quality, dry head-cleaning cassette. First, check your owner's manual.

## VELCRO

**WHEN VELCRO GETS** 'DIRTY'—MEANING THE TWO SIDES GET CLOGGED UP WITH LINT AND FUZZ BALLS—IT STOPS WORKING. WHEN THAT VELCRO IS ATTACHED TO A PAIR OF SANDALS OR A HANDBAG, YOU MIGHT BE TEMPTED TO GET RID OF THE SANDALS OR HANDBAG, BUT DON'T. IT'S EASY TO FRESHEN VELCRO UP SO THAT IT IS AS GOOD AS NEW AGAIN.

**To remove lint from the bristly side of Velcro,** use a fine-toothed comb (see below). Gently comb out the lint and hair and stray threads. If possible, submerge the Velcro in water while combing.

Running a fine-toothed comb along Velcro will get it looking—and sticking—like new again.

**To remove lint from the soft side of Velcro,** use the sticky side of duct or electric tape the way you would use a lint roller.

**To keep Velcro fresh,** seal the two parts together when it's not in use or while machine washing. If you need to, buy extra Velcro tape from a fabric or craft shop and use that to seal the Velcro.

**If worst comes to worst,** instead of throwing away that shoe or handbag, replace the Velcro. Shoe repairers and tailors will often do the job for very little cost.

## VENTILATION SYSTEMS

**AIR QUALITY IS** A BIG ISSUE THESE DAYS. ALLERGIC REACTIONS AND ILLNESSES CAUSED BY HOUSEHOLD DUST AND MOULD MAKE IT EASIER FOR DUCT-CLEANING COMPANIES TO SELL THEIR SERVICES. HOWEVER, FEW, IF ANY, HOME OWNERS NEED TO CLEAN THEIR VENTILATION SYSTEMS ON AN ANNUAL BASIS, AS SOME CONTRACTORS SUGGEST. HAVING THE DUCTWORK CLEANED MIGHT ACTUALLY MAKE MATTERS WORSE BY DISLODGING DUST AND MOULD.

**The most important thing** you can do is prevent dust and moisture from building up. And if you do determine that your ducts need cleaning, you should hire a reputable service provider. (See the 'Choosing an air-duct cleaning service' box on the page opposite.)

**Keep your system clean** by using high-quality filters and changing them at least twice a year, in the spring and autumn. If they become clogged, change them more often. Not only does that excess dust fill the air, but it also makes your air handler work harder, raising power bills and shortening the life of the motor.

**Vacuum your house often** and use a high-efficiency HEPA-filtered vacuum cleaner. The more often you vacuum, the less potential dust there will be to get into your ventilation system. The HEPA system keeps the vacuum cleaner from sucking up dust and then blowing it back into the air, which results in dust particles circulating. As a part of your vacuuming routine, make sure you also vacuum your ventilation system's vents. (See 'Vents', on the page opposite.)

### Do your ducts need cleaning?

Determining whether your ductwork needs to be cleaned is fairly straightforward. Clean ducts if:

- There is substantial visible mould growth inside the duct itself.
- You know that the ductwork has been infested with rodents or insect pests.
- The ducts are clogged with excessive dust or debris, or if particles are actually released into the home from your supply registers.

If none of these conditions is present, it's not necessary to have your ductwork cleaned.

**Control moisture**—the essential ingredient for biological growth—by repairing any leaks or water damage in your ducting system. Make sure the ducts are properly sealed and insulated in non-airconditioned spaces, such as attics and crawl spaces. This will prevent moisture from condensing inside the system.

**If your ductwork does need cleaning,** hire a reputable professional. This is one of those jobs that is impossible without the right equipment and know-how. The pros typically hook the entire duct system up to a high-powered vacuum and then use special tools to snake around the ducts, loosening dust and debris. It can be expensive, so take your time in choosing the right contractor.

## Choosing an air-duct cleaning service

There are plenty of opportunists out there making big bucks off the fear stirred up by stories about illness and allergies related to mould. These cunning contractors may charge exorbitant fees for a duct-cleaning job that is both shoddy and unnecessary. What's worse, they may leave your home's air quality worse than it was before they began tinkering with your ducts.

If you have determined that you really do need your ducts cleaned (see the 'Simple solutions' box, above), take these steps to ensure that you get your money's worth for a job well done:

- Talk to at least three contractors. Get written estimates. Compare their services. Check references. If they make any claims about mould or dust as a reason your ducts need cleaning, ask them to show you the evidence. Ask how they will protect you and your pets from contamination while cleaning. Check any licences or certifications they say they have.
- Beware of the cleaner who makes broad claims about duct cleaning being good for your health. Those claims have not been proven, unless there is a serious amount of particulate matter being fed back into the air you breathe, or in special circumstances, such as, say, in the case of rodent or insect pest infestation. Certainly steer clear of any cleaner who recommends duct cleaning as a regular part of maintaining your home heating and cooling system.

# VENTS

**AN IMPORTANT PART** OF YOUR VENTILATION SYSTEM ARE THE VENTS AT THE END OF THE DUCTWORK. VENTS TYPICALLY HAVE ANGLED LOUVRES TO KEEP LARGE DEBRIS FROM GETTING INTO THE SYSTEM, BUT THEY COLLECT LINT AND DUST AND NEED TO BE CLEANED REGULARLY, WHICH IS NOT HARD TO DO.

**Vacuum the outside of the vent often,** as part of your regular vacuuming routine. It will cut down on dust and lint build-up considerably. Use an upholstery brush, which helps loosen dust (see below).

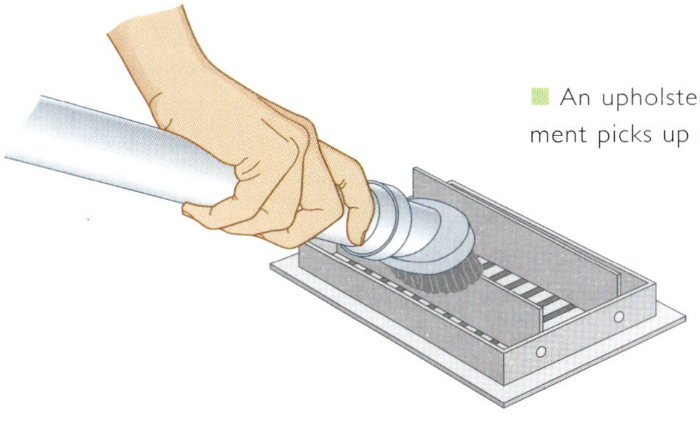

An upholstery brush attachment picks up dust on a vent.

**At least twice a year,** remove registers and returns and clean both sides of them. Try cleaning them with the vacuum. If that does not completely remove the dust, wipe them with a moist dust cloth. If you replace filters behind your returns more often than twice a year, clean the return vents every time you remove them.

## VINYL

'VINYL IS FINAL', THE SAYING GOES, MEANING NO MORE PAINTING FOR A VINYL-SIDED HOUSE. BUT PAINTING IS ONLY PART OF MAINTENANCE, AND CLADDING IS JUST ONE OF THOUSANDS OF USES FOR VINYL.

**WATCH OUT** When cleaning vinyl, avoid harsh solvents and cleaners. They may cause the vinyl to become brittle.

**To wash vinyl cladding,** if your local water restrictions permit, use a garden hose attached to a long-handled car-brush attachment and water. Such brushes are available from hardware, discount and automotive shops. If the cladding is especially dirty, use the car brush to apply a cleaner consisting of ½ cup of powdered laundry detergent, ¼ cup of Tricleanium Ultra Concentrated Cleaner or sugar soap (both available from hardware and paint shops), and 4 litres of water. If mildew is a problem, substitute 2 litres of chlorine bleach for 2 litres of the water. Strain the cleaner through an old sock to remove any lumps.

Apply the cleaner with the brush (you can detach it from the hose for this part, if you want), working from the bottom up. Allow the cleaner to sit for a few minutes. Rinse with clear water from the top down before the detergent solution dries (otherwise you'll end up with streaks on your cladding). Vinyl cladding should be washed every 12–18 months, depending on the climate and presence of air pollutants.

**To clean cladding more thoroughly,** use a pressure washer rated at about 2500 psi (pounds per square inch). Cover any electrical outlets and wear safety goggles. Move methodically from side to side from the bottom up, reversing direction for the rinse cycle.

**To clean aluminium cladding,** see 'Aluminium', on page 55.

**To clean articles made of vinyl,** there are several cleaners you might want to try:

- A little dishwashing liquid in warm water.
- A solution of 4 litres of water and 2 tablespoons of borax, available from the laundry section of supermarkets.
- Mild cleaners such as Earth Choice Multi-Purpose spray or detergents specially formulated for car washing.
- For mould and mildew, 1 part white vinegar to 2 parts water.

**To keep vinyl soft and pliable,** rub a bit of petroleum jelly (Vaseline) into the surface and then buff with a soft cloth (see left). Or use a vinyl cleaner and conditioner, which is readily available from hardware and automotive shops.

Petroleum jelly will help to keep your vinyl items soft and pliable.

# VOMIT

**CLEANING UP VOMIT** IS A JOB NO ONE RELISHES, BUT FEW CAN AVOID THE TASK FOREVER, AND CERTAINLY NOT PARENTS AND PET OWNERS.

**On a floor or other hard surface,** dump clean, clay-based kitty litter onto fresh vomit. It will absorb most of it and can then be swept up. Follow by wiping with a damp sponge or cloth. If you don't have any litter, use bicarbonate of soda or cornflour.

**If the vomit is old on a hard surface,** scrape off as much as possible with a putty knife, kitchen knife or spatula. Wash the surface with a little undiluted dishwashing liquid applied to a sponge or cloth, then rinse and dry. If the vomit's acid has eaten away wax or an underlying finish, renew it with a spot application.

**To clean vomit from a carpet or upholstery,** lift off any solids with paper towels and then sponge with cool water. Follow by saturating the spot with plenty of bicarbonate of soda, which will absorb the liquid, neutralise the acid and wipe out the odour. Allow the soda to dry, then vacuum. Sponge the stain with a solution of 1 teaspoon of dishwashing liquid in 1 cup of cool water. Rinse and blot dry.

**To clean clothing, bedding or table linens,** flush fresh mishaps with cold water. Hold the item under the tap with the soiled side down. Don't use hot water—it will cook the protein and make it harder to remove. For dried vomit, scrape off any solids and then soak in cold water, using an enzyme pre-soak, for several hours. For both new and old stains, follow by rubbing a little undiluted liquid laundry detergent into the stain and washing in warm water with detergent. If any stain remains, soak again in the enzyme or use chlorine bleach on white fabrics or oxygen bleach on coloured ones. If possible, dry on a clothes line rather than in a tumble-dryer.

*See also:*
• PET CLEAN-UP

## WADING POOLS

**BECAUSE CHILDREN, AND** SOMETIMES A DOG OR TWO, ARE THE MAIN USERS, WADING POOLS CAN BECOME REALLY FILTHY.

**After each day's use,** empty the pool and hose it out to prevent it from becoming a germ or mosquito incubator. Store it under cover, upside down or propped on its side against a fence (see below left).

**To remove scum from the sides,** clean with a sponge or cloth dipped in a solution of ¼ cup of bicarbonate of soda in 4 litres of warm water. Or wash with a solution of 1 tablespoon of dishwashing liquid in 4 litres of water, then rinse clean with a hose.

Lean a wading pool on its side after each day's use, to allow it to dry.

### When someone poos in the pool

Sooner or later it will probably happen, despite your best efforts at prevention. If it does, immediately remove all children from the pool and encourage them to wash themselves thoroughly with soap and water. Chlorine in the water from your tap dissipates quickly, so a wading pool can become a rich medium for the growth and spread of germs. Even small amounts of faecal matter can cause problems and make children very sick if the germs get into their mouths.

As for the wading pool, here's what to do in case of an accident:

- Pour the contents into a bucket and flush them down the toilet.
- Wash the pool with a solution of 1 part chlorine bleach to 99 parts water (about 1 cup for every 22 litres).
- Allow to air-dry.

Take these precautionary steps to minimise the risk of transmitting illness:

- Don't let children use the pool if they have diarrhoea, open sores or rashes, or if they are not toilet-trained.
- Encourage children to go to the toilet before they get in the pool.
- Insist that all children using the wading pool take frequent toilet breaks.

## WAFFLE IRONS

**MOST WAFFLE IRONS** THESE DAYS HAVE A NON-STICK SURFACE, BUT SOME PEOPLE STILL PREFER UNCOATED SURFACES BECAUSE OF THEIR BETTER HEATING QUALITIES.

**To clean a waffle iron with a non-stick surface,** wipe it with a damp cloth while the iron is still warm (but not while it's hot). Use a clean, dry brush, such as a pastry brush, to remove bits of food and crumbs from all the nooks and crannies.

**A waffle iron without a non-stick surface** needs to be seasoned before it can be used the first time and will need reseasoning whenever sticking becomes a problem or it doesn't release waffles easily. To season a waffle iron, follow these steps:

- Brush a generous amount of fat, such as unsalted butter or peanut oil, on the grids.
- Heat the iron until the grids start to smoke.
- To absorb the fat, cook a waffle and throw it away.

**To clean a seasoned waffle iron,** wipe with a damp cloth. If that doesn't do the trick, try one of these solutions:

- If the iron has removable plates, take them out and wash them in a solution of dishwashing liquid and hot water. Scrub with a nylon scouring pad if necessary.
- If the plates are not removable, use an old, clean toothbrush dipped in the dishwashing liquid solution to clean the grids, then rinse thoroughly with a damp cloth.

Repeat the seasoning process whenever you scrub the grids.

**To clean the outside of a waffle iron,** wipe it with a damp cloth. If you need extra cleaning power, add a few drops of dishwashing liquid to the cloth, but don't use an abrasive cleaner or scrubber. Never immerse the iron in water, unless the instructions for your machine specify that immersion is OK.

## WALL COVERINGS

**THE MOST COMMON** WALL COVERING IS WASHABLE WALLPAPER, WHICH IS TREATED WITH VINYL FOR EASIER CLEANING. BUT MANY OTHER COVERINGS EXIST, INCLUDING DELICATE PAPERS; FABRICS, SUCH AS COTTON, LINEN, SILK, RAYON, HESSIAN AND VELVET; AND COVERINGS MADE FROM GRASS, REEDS, HEMP, CORK OR LEATHER. THEY GENERALLY ARE NOT WASHABLE, ALTHOUGH SOME GENTLE CLEANING METHODS ARE UNLIKELY TO HARM THEM.

**To determine whether wallpaper is washable,** wet an inconspicuous area with a solution of a little dishwashing liquid and water. If the paper absorbs water or darkens, or if the colours run, it's not washable and the cleaning solution will damage it.

**To clean washable wallpaper,** use one of the three cleaning solutions recommended in the 'Walls' entry, on page 372. Follow the instructions in that entry, while taking heed of these precautions:

- Don't flood the surface with water, overwet the seams or edges, or leave water on for more than a minute.
- Don't scrub unless the manufacturer says the covering is scrubbable.
- Don't use harsh, abrasive cleaners.

Simple solutions

### Smudged wallpaper?

- To remove fingerprints and smudges from wallpaper, try an art gum eraser (available from office supply shops), or Chux Magic Eraser (available from supermarkets), for hard surfaces.
- To remove greasy spots, make a paste of cornflour and water. Apply to the spot, let it dry and then vacuum it off.
- To remove wax, heavy crayon or grease, hold a double thickness of paper towels on the spot and go over it with a warm iron.

**To clean other wall coverings,** vacuum regularly, using the upholstery brush attachment. Another acceptable cleaner is an old-fashioned product called wallpaper dough, which is sometimes available from hardware, paint or wallpaper shops. It is very similar to Play-Doh, so if you can't find the original, you can use a white or light-coloured Play-Doh instead. Roll the dough into a ball and then roll it over the dirty area on the wallpaper. When the dough ball becomes dirty, knead the dirty part back into the middle, make a new ball and then continue. You can also use white bread in the same way.

## WALLS

**MARKS APPEAR ON** WALLS FROM TWO MAIN SOURCES: DIRT THAT COMES OFF PEOPLE'S HANDS AND DIRT THAT COMES FROM AIR-BORNE PARTICLES. HOW OFTEN YOUR WALLS NEED WASHING WILL DEPEND LARGELY ON THE HANDS AND QUALITY OF THE AIR THAT COME INTO CONTACT WITH THEM. IF YOU HAVE A FIREPLACE, YOUR WALLS WILL SHOW IT. IF YOU HAVE CHILDREN, YOUR WALLS WILL HAVE GRUBBY FINGERPRINTS AND OTHER MARKS ON THEM FROM TIME TO TIME.

**To dust walls,** a lamb's wool duster works well. Or wrap a microfibre dust cloth or clean, white cloth around a broom and dust with that. It's handy for higher places and for ceilings (see below).

Wrap a cloth around a broom, or another long-handled implement, so that you can get at hard-to-reach areas.

**To remove spots,** rub gently with an art gum eraser, available from arts and crafts or office supply shops, with a Chux Magic Eraser, or with a paste made from bicarbonate of soda and water. Use mineral turpentine or white spirit on grease and WD-40 (all available from hardware shops) on crayon marks. Use methylated spirits on ink or felt-tip pen marks. (Apply cleansers to the cloth, not the wall, and test on an inconspicuous area first.)

**Three cleaning solutions** for washing walls that are painted or covered with vinyl paper include the following:

- One cup of borax (available from supermarkets) and 2 tablespoons of dishwashing liquid in 4 litres of warm water.
- One cup of ammonia (available from supermarkets), 1 teaspoon of dishwashing liquid and 4 litres of water.
- If you're washing before applying new paint, a good cleaner to use is sugar soap, available from hardware and paint shops.

Keep the cleaning solution in one bucket and plain water for rinsing in another bucket. To protect the floor, use a drop sheet.

**To keep water from running down your arms** when they're raised, use this trick: wrap rags around your wrists and hold them on with rubber bands.

**To clean the walls,** wash with one of the solutions mentioned in 'Three cleaning solutions', on page 372, using a natural sponge, available from hardware shops, or a white cloth. Follow the guidelines in the 'Rules of the Game' box, below, for applying the cleaning solution. Reach the high points by standing on a sturdy stepladder that is tall enough that you won't need to stand on the upper two steps.

## rules of the game

WORK YOUR WAY UP

- Apply cleaning solution over a small area at the bottom of the wall.
- Wash, using circular strokes.
- Rinse thoroughly with plain water.
- Dry freshly washed part of wall with a towel.
- Move up the wall to clean the next area.

*See also:* • PAINTED SURFACES • WALL COVERINGS

# WASHING MACHINES AND DRYERS

**EVERY NOW AND** THEN YOU NEED TO CLEAN THE WASHING MACHINES AND DRYERS THAT DO SO MUCH CLEANING FOR YOU. FORTUNATELY, IT'S EASY TO DO—AND THESE MACHINES EVEN HELP TO CLEAN THEMSELVES OCCASIONALLY.

**To clean the exteriors of your washing machine or dryer,** you don't have to do a lot. The most common spots are blotches of spilled laundry detergent, fabric softener or bleach. They're all designed to respond best to warm water, so wipe them up with a cloth dipped in a solution of warm water and mild dishwashing liquid, which will get rid of dirt and dust, too.

**To clean a washing machine's interior,** open the washing machine and wipe down the inside of the door using the same solution of warm water and mild dishwashing liquid on the cloth that you used on the exterior. Use an old toothbrush to clean the crevices of the moulded frame around the door. If you have a removable bleach dispenser cup, take it out to clean it. If it's built in, clean it as thoroughly as you can, using a pipe cleaner, if necessary. The rest of the interior of your washing machine gets a pretty good cleaning every time you use it, but if you have a heavy build-up of lint, detergent scum and calcium deposits, you can give it a run with a product called Rubbedin Washing Machine Magic, which should solve your problems, although it's not suitable for front loaders.

Simple solutions

### Keep your dryer's duct clean

If you keep your dryer's filter clean but it still isn't as efficient as it used to be, the duct ushering the air outside may be blocked, if you have a ducted machine. Detach the duct from the back of your dryer and clean it out. (Do this once a year as a matter of habit.) Make sure the vent cover on the outside of your house is clean and in place. (Replacements are available from home improvement shops.) This should prevent rodents and birds from taking up residence in your vent and really slowing down the airflow.

**If your washing machine develops a musty odour,** you can easily cure it by wiping out the inside with bicarbonate of soda, then running the machine through a wash cycle without any clothes in it. Use the hottest temperature setting available and a medium or high water level. While the washing machine is filling, pour in a bottle of white vinegar. As a preventive measure, follow this routine once a year.

**When cleaning a dryer,** the first task is to clean the filter. Dryers work by heating air, drawing it across your wet clothes to sop up the moisture, and pushing the soggy air outside through a vent. So the name of the game is air traffic control. If that airway gets clogged up, your dryer won't be able to do its job, and your power bill will skyrocket needlessly. So clean the filter before or after every load of clothes.

**Cleaning a dryer filter** is quite straightforward. Most dryers have a removable filter made of metal or plastic. Pull the filter out of the dryer, hold it over a garbage bin, then scrape the little blanket of lint off the filter with your hand. If some of the lint won't come free, take the filter to a sink and clean it in a solution of warm water and a squirt of mild dishwashing liquid.

If you discover crayon marks inside your dryer, run the dryer empty for 5 minutes to heat it up and soften up the marks. Then wipe them away with a cloth dipped in a solution of water and dishwashing liquid.

## WASTEBASKETS

THE DETAILS OF CLEANING WASTEBASKETS VARY ACCORDING TO THE MATERIALS THEY'RE MADE OF, BUT THE BEGINNING IS ALWAYS THE SAME: REMOVE THE WASTE MATERIALS.

**To clean a wastebasket made of a natural material**—such as cardboard, paper, wicker, straw or wood—use a vacuum cleaner with the upholstery brush attachment. If the basket becomes soiled, wipe it with a damp cloth or sponge. Don't use harsh cleaners.

**To clean a plastic or metal wastebasket,** wash it with a solution of ¼ cup of bicarbonate of soda or borax (available from the laundry section of supermarkets) in 4 litres of warm water. Use a cloth, a sponge or, for more challenging dirt, a stiff brush. Rinse and then dry with a soft cloth.

Simple solutions

### Less wasteful waste handling

Using a liner makes cleaning a wastebasket so much easier. But buying new plastic bags is completely unnecessary when households are usually awash in perfectly reusable plastic and paper bags from supermarkets and shops.

Nor is it necessary to change the liner each time the basket is emptied, unless the garbage is food or anything moist and sloppy. For dry garbage, just empty the liner into the main garbage bin, then put it back in the wastebasket.

**Clean the kitchen wastebasket** at the same time you're mopping the kitchen floor, just by mixing up your cleaner-and-water solution in the wastebasket itself instead of in a bucket. During the 10–15 minutes it takes to mop the floor, the dirt in the wastebasket will be loosening. When you pour out the mop water, give the interior of the wastebasket a once-over with a stiff brush, rinse with running water and then dry with a cloth.

## WATCHES

**SALT WATER IS** ONE OF YOUR WATCH'S BIGGEST ENEMIES, AND IT'S EXPOSED TO IT CONSTANTLY FROM YOUR SWEAT. OTHER CONTAMINANTS INCLUDE SKIN OILS, DIRT AND SUBSTANCES SUCH AS LOTIONS AND INSECT REPELLENTS. ONLY EVER ATTEMPT TO CLEAN THE BAND AND THE OUTSIDE OF THE WATCH—LEAVE THE INNER WORKINGS FOR A PROFESSIONAL.

**For daily cleaning,** wipe the band and watch with a damp cloth, then with a clean, dry cloth.

**For more extensive cleaning,** remove the band by releasing the pins on both sides of the watch.

- Clean a leather band with saddle-soap, then follow up with a quick buffing using a clean, dry cloth.
- Wash a fabric band with a bit of dishwashing liquid and water, rinse in clean water and then lay flat to dry.
- Clean a metal band by soaking it in a solution of dishwashing liquid and water, then use an old toothbrush to scrub it. Rinse thoroughly in clean water and dry with a soft cloth.

**Check the crystal** (the transparent face plate) and have it replaced immediately if you notice any damage to it or to the face of the watch, which indicates moisture has entered. A jeweller can also buff out scratches in a plastic crystal.

**To store your watch,** keep it in an individual compartment in a jewellery box or wrap it in a piece of soft cloth (see below left).

**To clean the inner workings,** take the watch to a professional. Mechanical watches (the kind you have to wind) need an overhaul about every two years, and analog quartz watches (with hands and batteries) need one every three to five years, just about when you need to replace the battery anyway. Digital watches, which have no mechanical works, don't need an internal cleaning, although you will eventually need to replace the battery.

Wrap your watch in a soft cloth for storage, to protect it from scratching.

## WATERBEDS

**WATERBEDS ARE EASY** TO KEEP CLEAN, ESPECIALLY IF YOU USE A MATTRESS COVER THAT CAN BE REMOVED AND WASHED.

**To wash the mattress itself,** wipe it off with a damp cloth or sponge. You should not have to do that very often.

**To clean the water inside the mattress,** you need to use a special conditioner made for waterbeds and sold at waterbed shops. The conditioner keeps bacteria, algae and other slimy undesirables from growing inside. It also bursts noisy bubbles and conditions the vinyl of the mattress. Follow the instructions provided by the manufacturer, but a general recommendation is to add conditioner every year. There is no need to change the water for the sake of cleanliness, but you will have to empty it to move the bed.

## WATER FEATURES

**WHETHER YOU'RE TENDING** A LARGE FOUNTAIN, OR JUST THE SMALL ONE ON YOUR PATIO, THE SAME RULE APPLIES: WATER FEATURES HAVE TO BE CLEANED PART BY PART.

**Wash your water feature periodically** with a solution of 1 part bleach to 10 parts water to help inhibit algae.

**In hard-water areas,** to prevent any mineral deposits from forming on bowls, the motor shaft or other parts of the pump (which could cause it to fail), always use distilled water, rainwater or dehumidified water in the water feature. If your water feature is so big that using distilled water is not a practical solution, you can treat the water with a mineral deposit inhibitor, or another product recommended by your local water feature or garden shop.

**To remove any mineral deposits**—should they develop despite all your best efforts—you'll first need to know what material your water feature bowl is made of.

- Some materials, such as resins and copper, are soft and should always be cleaned with a cotton rag.
- Slate can be cleaned with a soft-bristled brush—but don't use soap. Slate can be porous and if the bowl absorbs soap, your water feature could turn into a bubble bath.
- Other water feature bowl materials can be cleaned with an abrasive sponge and white vinegar or a mineral deposit cleaner, such as CLR Calcium Lime Rust Remover, which is available from hardware shops and home improvement shops.

If your preventive maintenance is working, you may need to clean your water-feature parts only once a year. If you're getting mineral deposits, you'll have to clean the parts more frequently—likewise if you're not using a water-treatment product. In general, you should sterilise your water feature after you clean it and before you reassemble it by dipping all parts, including the pump, in the mild bleach solution mentioned above (1 part bleach to 10 parts water).

**To clean the fountainhead,** you need to know what it's made of:

- Most moulded fountainheads are cast from a polyester resin mixed

Simple solutions

### If you want to see the coins at the bottom

To combat slime and algae in a fountain, a bit of preventive maintenance will go a long way. A water treatment product will keep the green stuff at bay and yet is safe for birds, pets and plants (not always for fish, though). You typically add a few drops to the fountain each week. Treatment products are available from fountain and garden shops.

with fillers such as powdered marble. These materials are strong, however, they do scratch easily, so the best way to clean them is with warm, soapy water and a soft sponge. Before using tile cleaners or other acids on a cast resin fountainhead, make sure you check it by putting a few drops of the cleaner on the bottom of the fountainhead and scrubbing it a bit with a toothbrush.

- When cleaning concrete or natural stone, make sure you never use an acid cleaner. Dishwashing liquid or bleach mixed with water, plus a scrubbing brush, will do the trick instead.
- Clean slate as described above for removing mineral deposits.

**To clean a water-feature pump,** first check to see how well it's working. Most pumps have some sort of inlet strainers or screens to ensure that small pebbles and other debris don't get into the pump and jam or damage it. Watch the water flow in your water feature. If you notice it's slowing down, clean the pump before it clogs entirely, overheats and burns out. (Then you'll have to replace it.)

With indoor pumps and simple outdoor pumps you can follow the instructions that came with the pump to learn how to take it apart and reassemble it. If your pump has an adjustable flow, take note of the setting when you remove the pump for cleaning, in case you inadvertently change it. Once you have the pump apart, clean it with warm water, dishwashing liquid and an old toothbrush. Dip the parts in a bleach solution and reassemble it.

The more complex, industrial-type water features are trickier to clean and should be entrusted to a professional.

## WATER STAINS

**IT SEEMS IRONIC** THAT THE MOST ABUNDANT CLEANER, WATER, IS ITSELF CAPABLE OF LEAVING ONE OF THE TOUGHEST STAINS TO REMOVE.

**To treat furniture with a white water stain,** remedies abound. If one of the solutions following doesn't work, another one probably will. In all cases, unless otherwise noted, rub with a cloth dipped in the cleaner, going with the grain of the wood (see below). Then buff with a clean cloth and apply your regular furniture polish.

Always rub a timber surface in the direction of the grain.

- The best (although, the most expensive) method is to use a product called Howard Restor-A-Finish. This is a wipe-on, wipe-off process for restoring the finish on most wood furniture without the need to strip, re-stain and re-polish. An alternative is Briwax Furniture Cleaner.
- A 50:50 mix of bicarbonate of soda with white toothpaste (make sure it's not coloured or gel).
- Mayonnaise—let it sit for an hour.
- Petroleum jelly—let it sit for a day.
- A solution made from a little hot water with a few drops of clear ammonia added to it.
- A solution of equal parts of vinegar, boiled linseed oil and turpentine, the latter two available from hardware and paint shops.
- Paste wax applied with superfine steel wool (0000), both available from hardware and homeware shops.

If none of the above solutions works, re-finishing may be the only way to get rid of the water stain.

**To treat furniture with a black water stain**—if Howard Restor-A-Finish doesn't work—there's probably only one remedy. You'll need to strip off the finish and bleach the wood. Chances are, if the wood has such a stain, the finish is already next to non-existent, so removing it shouldn't be too difficult. Use a paint and varnish remover, available from hardware and paint shops. Let the piece dry; then treat it with oxalic acid bleach, available from hardware shops. Follow the instructions on the labels of these products.

**To treat water stains on painted walls or ceilings,** use a mixture of ¼ cup of chlorine bleach in 1 litre of warm water. If several applications don't work, you'll need to repaint. But first apply a sealant so the stain won't bleed through. Talk to someone at your hardware shop about a sealant that is appropriate for your situation.

**To treat water stains on a carpet or upholstery,** you can try a 50:50 solution of water and white vinegar. Wet a cloth with the solution and gently blot the surface. If this doesn't work, your best bet is to call a professional.

## No watertight answers for cloth

Water stains on washable cloth are water soluble to some extent, especially when recent. But detergent doesn't help much, because the water stain isn't dirt; it's caused by a change in the fibres. Bleach can help, but caution is needed. Chlorine bleach can damage fibres and leave a residue. Don't use it on items that you care about.

- To treat stains on washable cloth, use a colour-safe bleach, which is not chlorine-based. Treat the whole item, not just the spot. Use ¼ cup per litre of water, and rinse several times.
- For fragile antique items, wash in a solution of 1 teaspoon of Orvus WA Paste per 4 litres of distilled water. Look for Orvus at museum suppliers, or try a heritage preservation web site, such as www.zettaflorence.com.au. Rinse in distilled water until the water runs clear. For especially valuable or precious items, you will need to consult a professional conservator.
- For unwashable items, such as those made of wool or silk, you're probably stuck with the stain. Because it's caused by water, dry-cleaning won't help.

# WAX

**WHEN YOU BURN** CANDLES, INEVITABLY SOME WAX WILL SPILL. ONE WAY TO MINIMISE DAMAGE IN ADVANCE IS TO BURN ONLY WHITE CANDLES. THE DYE IN COLOURED CANDLES, ESPECIALLY RED ONES, COMPOUNDS THE PROBLEM.

**To remove white wax from carpeting or upholstery,** use the fire-and-ice approach.

- Put some ice cubes into a plastic bag and place it on the wax for a few minutes to make the wax more brittle (see below left).
- Scrape off the wax with the dull side of a table knife.
- Use a hair dryer on *High* to soften the remaining wax.
- Scrape again.
- Put paper towels or white rags over the wax and iron over the area. Keep moving a clean area of the towels or rags onto the spot.
- Use dry-cleaning solvent, such as Murlex or Woolclean Spot Dry Remover No. 2 (available from hardware shops). Test first on an inconspicuous area, and if OK, blot a little into the remaining wax stain.

Ice cubes will harden the wax for easier removal (see right).

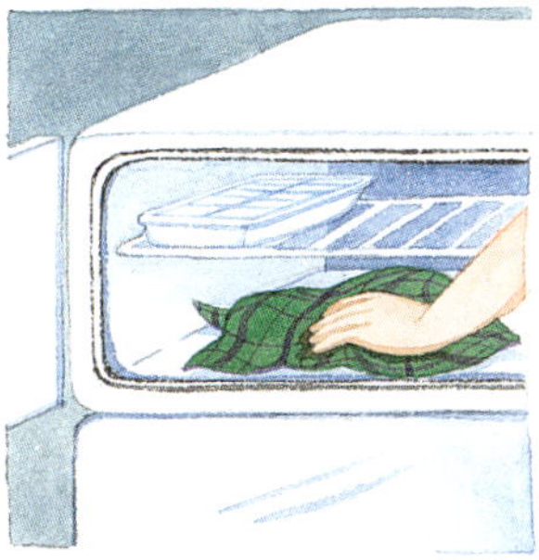

Place a wax-stained tablecloth directly in the freezer, or into a plastic bag and then in the freezer, to harden the wax (see far right).

**To remove white wax from table linens or clothing,** use the above methods, with these changes:

- Put the item directly in the freezer, or into a plastic bag and then in the freezer, for half an hour before scraping (see above right).
- On washable items, once you have removed as much wax as possible, saturate the final stain with a solution of 1 part methylated spirits to 2 parts water and let it sit for half an hour. Rinse and then wash in the washing machine. Send non-washable items to the drycleaner.

**For coloured wax, skip the ironing.** The heat will only help set the dye. Instead, try this:

- After freezing and scraping, use mineral turpentine or white spirit, available from hardware and paint shops, on the rest of the wax. Test first and work on only tiny areas at a time, blotting with a rag. Some dyes may not be removable, so stop before damage is done.
- Treat washable colour-fast fabrics with bleach, following instructions on the package, then wash.
- For fine rugs or upholstery, consult a professional.

**To remove wax from dishes and glass,** heat with a hair dryer and wipe with a cloth. Then keep wiping and polishing with used fabric softener sheets.

Simple solutions

## Wax-free wood

The birthday party ended with your elderly aunt blowing out all of the candles—and wax all over your beautiful mahogany table. But, take heart—wax comes off fairly easily from wood surfaces.

- If you get at the wax while it is still warm, wipe up all you can with a clean cloth.
- If the wax has hardened, soften it with a hair dryer set on medium and then wipe.
- Remove the last bits with a cloth dampened with mineral turpentine.

# WEDDING DRESSES

**UNLESS YOUR WEDDING** DRESS IS WASH-AND-WEAR, NEVER TRY TO CLEAN IT YOURSELF. GRANTED, A LOT CAN HAPPEN BETWEEN THE ALTERATIONS AND THE ALTAR, AND IT USUALLY HAPPENS WHEN YOU'RE DRESSED AND READY TO WALK DOWN THE AISLE. BUT IF YOU HAVE AN EMERGENCY KIT FOR THOSE LAST-MINUTE ACCIDENTS, A SPILL WON'T SPOIL YOUR DAY.

Iron on the wrong side only with a handkerchief as a pressing cloth.

**To fix a last-minute stain,** don't use spot cleaner on your dress. If you're lucky, it might remove the spot, but it also will damage the fabric. If you're going to use hair spray, apply it before you put on your dress. Nothing dulls beading like hair spray.

- If clumsy feet leave scuff marks along the bottom of the dress, mark over them with a piece of white chalk.
- Accidental spots or spills? Talcum powder will disguise them. Just sprinkle some talc on the spots and let it absorb the moisture.
- Whether a little dribble or a major spill has marred your dress, soda water is your best friend. It will help to treat any spills or spots immediately—they will only be more difficult to remove later on. Depending on where the stain is located, you might have to undress and then re-dress. Working from the inside out, use a man's dry handkerchief to blot up as much of the stain as possible. Make sure you dab, not rub. Then wet the handkerchief with the soda water and, again from the inside, dab, don't rub.

**If the dress needs a final touch-up,** press only on the inside of the dress. And don't use steam. If the fabric hasn't been pre-washed, steam can create spotting or a colour change. Place a dry handkerchief between the iron and the dress (see left). (You don't want to use a towel, because terry towelling can leave lint.) Then press in a downwards direction. Don't move the iron back and forth—it destroys fibres. Press one area, then move the cloth to another.

**When the honeymoon is over,** don't put off taking your dress to the drycleaner. You might want to hand it down to someone or even sell it, and without the proper care, your once-priceless wedding dress will become yellow and useless to anyone else.

**First, take off any removable trim and shoulder pads.** Then search for the spots and stains that happened without you knowing at the reception. Dry-cleaning usually removes the obvious—make-up, grass stains, food spills—but you may also find some invisible spills (champagne is a classic) that show up later. If you can remember where they are, give the drycleaner an indication of their location. Otherwise, when your dress is preserved and stored, the champagne stains will be, too.

**When you store your dress,** don't put it in plastic or expose it to sunlight. Instead, ask the drycleaner to wrap your dress in acid-free tissue and store it in an acid-free box. This is the best way to slow the ageing process.

### EXPERT ADVICE

#### A SLICK WAY TO SAVE THE DAY

It's inevitable. Your aunt, who wears too much make-up, will make her way—rouged, lip-sticked and powdered—towards you and your wedding dress. And she'll probably smudge you with a kiss or a hug just before pictures are taken. Just in case something like this does happen, go prepared. Drycleaners use a formula they call 'paint-oil-grease' because that's what it removes. But if there's no time for dry-cleaning—the photographer is waiting—take a can of WD-40 (nothing else!) and spray a very light mist of the lubricant on a cloth. Then dab—don't rub—with the cloth to remove the make-up stain.

## WHEELCHAIRS

**REGULAR CLEANING AND** MAINTENANCE WILL ENSURE BETTER PERFORMANCE AND LONGER LIFE FOR YOUR WHEELCHAIR.

**To clean a wheelchair,** wash the frame, wheels, tyres, seat and back with warm water and a little dishwashing liquid. Apply with a clean cloth or sponge, rinse with plain water and dry with a clean cloth. But don't get water in the wheels or castor bearings. This kind of cleaning should be done about once a month. For daily cleaning, wiping with a damp cloth is usually sufficient.

**To clean the castor axle bolts,** remove the bolt, wipe crud away with a cleaning cloth and put back the bolt. This spot tends to collect hair, string and other debris that will make the chair harder to propel.

**To clean the axles,** remove the wheels and wipe the axles with a clean cloth containing a few drops of oil (whatever oil is recommended by your owner's manual). This area, which can accumulate mud and dirt quickly, should be cleaned once a month or more.

**To clean between users,** disinfect the chair with a disinfectant cleaner, available for the purpose from surgical supply shops.

## WICKER, RATTAN AND BAMBOO

**WICKER REFERS TO** SOMETHING MADE OF ANY OF SEVERAL NATURAL MATERIALS THAT ARE BENT AND WOVEN TOGETHER. THE MOST COMMON ARE RATTAN (A SOLID-CORED VINE OF A CLIMBING PALM), CANE (THE BARK OF LARGE RATTANS), REED (SWAMP GRASSES OR RATTAN CORE), BAMBOO (A LARGE GRASS WITH A HOLLOW CORE), WILLOW AND TWISTED PAPER FIBRE. WICKER COMES IN MANY FINISHES: FROM NATURAL TO OIL, VARNISH, SHELLAC OR PAINT. SYNTHETIC VERSIONS OF WICKER ARE ALSO MADE FROM RESIN, PLASTIC OR FIBREGLASS. THE DIFFERENT MATERIALS REQUIRE DIFFERENT CLEANING TECHNIQUES.

**When cleaning synthetic wicker,** you can be aggressive. This is the only wicker that should be allowed to remain outdoors. If water restrictions allow, clean it with a garden hose using a cloth or sponge, or scrub with a stiff brush and a solution of a little dishwashing liquid in water. Rinse with the hose and dry with a clean cloth.

**To clean natural-fibre wicker,** keep the pieces free of dirt with a vacuum cleaner, using the brush attachment. Other useful tools are a toothbrush, a stiff paintbrush and a pencil-sized dowel sharpened in a pencil sharpener. Wipe the wicker with a damp cloth or sponge, but undertake more extensive wet cleaning cautiously. Consult an expert before doing any major cleaning or re-finishing of antique pieces. To find an expert, check with antiques dealers or on the Internet.

**To wash most natural-fibre wicker,** use a solution of a little mild soap—dishwashing liquid or Softly, for example—in warm water. Wipe with a cloth or sponge wrung out in the solution. Rinse with a

### Pressure clean

You can actually wash some wicker in the car wash, if you can find one that doesn't think you're crazy! Don't even think about it for antiques, bamboo or paper-fibre pieces. But it won't hurt synthetic wicker, and it can make short work of removing paint from painted pieces before re-finishing.

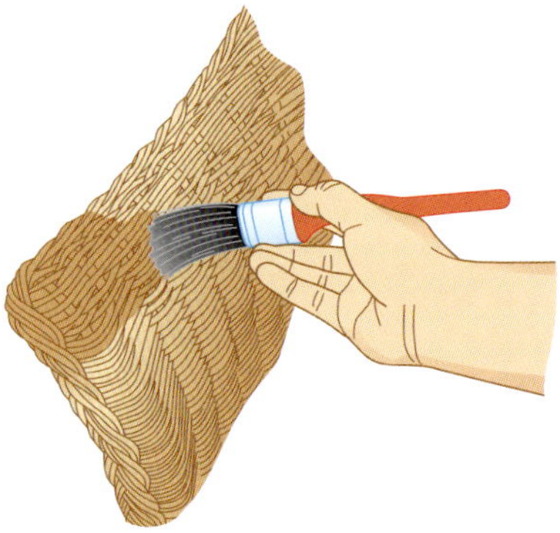

Apply mineral turpentine and linseed oil to wicker to prevent cracking.

garden hose and dry quickly—in the sun or with a hair dryer or fan. Don't sit on the furniture for two or three days, because you could stretch the fibres and cause them to sag.

**Some exceptions to hosing down are** bamboo or twisted-paper wicker. Instead, clean these with a sponge dampened with soapy water, followed by a sponge dampened with clear water. Wipe dry.

**To treat for dryness and cracking,** you can use 1 part turpentine to 2 parts boiled linseed oil on all natural-fibre wicker, except for bamboo. Apply with a clean paintbrush, using as much solution as the wicker will absorb (see left). You could also use a wood product, such as Howard Orange Oil or Pledge. Wipe off any excess with a cloth and let it dry for three or four days. For bamboo, you should apply a thin coat of liquid or paste wax periodically.

## WIGS

**WIGS ARE MADE** OF SYNTHETIC MATERIALS, HUMAN HAIR OR EVEN A COMBINATION OF THE TWO. SYNTHETIC WIGS ARE EASIER TO CARE FOR BUT NOT AS VERSATILE WHEN STYLING. FOR EXAMPLE, HEAT, SUCH AS IN A CURLING IRON, CAN RUIN SYNTHETIC WIGS. WHEREAS HUMAN HAIR WIGS CAN BE PERMED, COLOURED AND CURLED WITH A CURLING IRON OR HEATED ROLLERS.

**To wash a wig,** follow these steps:

- Gently straighten the hair with a comb.
- Run water—cool to lukewarm, not hot—into a pan large enough to immerse the wig.
- Dissolve about 1 tablespoon each of shampoo and bicarbonate of soda in the water.
- Swish the wig around in the solution.
- Rinse well in cool water.
- Dissolve 1 tablespoon of hair conditioner in a pan of fresh water. Swish the wig in the solution, then rinse.
- Lay the wig on a towel and roll it up to remove as much water as you can. Don't wring!
- Remove the wig from the towel and gently shake it out. Use your fingers to loosen the fibres, but don't try to remove tangles with a comb or brush while the wig is wet.
- Set the wig on a bottle or some other tall item to dry.

If you need to clean make-up from the front of the wig's cap or hair area, make a paste of bicarbonate of soda and shampoo. Apply the paste during the shampooing process with an old toothbrush and scrub gently. Then follow the rest of the instructions, as above.

Simple solutions

### Compressed air for hair

Yet another use for compressed air is to blow away loose dirt from your wig between washings. Set the wig on its stand and hold the can upright so it doesn't spew out propellant. Separate the layers of hair and blow away!

# WINDOWS

**SO MUCH HAS** BEEN PRINTED ABOUT THE FASTEST AND BEST WAY TO CLEAN WINDOWS THAT YOU MAY BE FEELING CONFUSED. THE TRUTH IS, LOTS OF THINGS WORK.

**Here are a few simple hints** that apply to most windows:

- Clean the windowsills and frames before the glass. Vacuum to remove loose dirt before wiping with a damp cloth.
- Start at the top of the window and work down. This will avoid dripping water onto clean windows.
- Don't clean windows in direct sunlight. The cleaner will dry before you can wipe it off, creating streaks.
- Make your drying strokes go up and down on one side of the window and back and forth on the other. That way it is easier to tell which side the streaks are on.
- Your drying technique and materials affect the final appearance more than the kind of cleaner.

Now let's move on to the contentious part.

**The cheapest way to clean a window** is to use plain water and newspaper. Apply the water with a sponge or window wand, available from hardware shops. Dip the wand into a bucket of water, picking up just enough to wet the window without drenching it. Then scrunch up the newspaper a bit and rub the window until it's dry.

This method, besides being inexpensive, is also environmentally friendly. The disadvantage is that it no longer works quite as well as it used to, since the composition of printer's ink has changed from the solvent-based ink of the old days. And quite a lot of newsprint these days is coloured. The ink from the newsprint will get on your hands (you can wear rubber gloves) and can soil the non-glass window parts. Nonetheless, it's so cheap, it's still worth a try. Paper towels also work but are expensive and wasteful. A chamois cloth works as well, too.

## Double the fun for double-hung

Many double-hung windows—that's the most common type of window—are now made so they can be tilted inwards for cleaning. But if you don't have that kind, you can still clean both sides from inside the house—provided both upper and lower windows move fully, as they're supposed to. Here are instructions for reaching the outside of both windows—you can figure out the inside for yourself.

- Pull the top window all the way down. (It will be on the outside.)
- Reach through the window opening to clean the top part of the outside. Wash the window, then wipe.
- Raise both windows all the way to the top.
- Reach through the opening to clean the bottom part of the outside.
- Lower the inside window enough to reach the outside window and push it all the way to the bottom.
- Reach through the opening to clean the top part of the inside window.
- Raise the outside window all the way to the top and lower the inside window as much as possible while leaving room for your arm to pass through the window opening.
- Reach through the opening to clean the bottom part of the inside window.

## Cleaning windows

1 Draw the squeegee across the windowpane from the top.

2 Now draw it vertically downwards, sticking close to the edge of the pane.

3 Slightly overlap each vertical down-stroke across the width of the pane.

**Using a squeegee to clean windows** is the method preferred by many people, including most professional window cleaners. If it's your choice, buy a good squeegee with a removable rubber blade so that it can be replaced as it wears. The main disadvantage of a squeegee is that it's impractical on small panes of glass. When using a squeegee, technique is very important.

- First, wet the squeegee.
- Draw it across the top of the pane (see 1, above).
- Start the squeegee at the bottom edge of that swath and draw it down one side of the glass to about 5 centimetres from the bottom of the window (see 2, above).
- Repeat this step, overlapping each stroke as you work your way across the window (see 3, above).
- Draw the squeegee across the bottom of the pane, and wipe the squeegee on a cloth between strokes.
- Use a clean cloth to wipe the window edges, if necessary.
- On very large windows, it is best to wash and dry the top half, and then proceed to the bottom half.

**For added cleaning power on dirty glass,** here are some good formulas to try:

- For grease or hard-water deposits, use 1 cup of white vinegar in 4 litres of water, plus a squirt of dishwashing liquid.
- For grime, grease or smoke, you can use ½ cup of clear ammonia in 2 litres of water.
- For tough window cleaning jobs, use 2 cups of methylated spirits and 2 tablespoons each of clear ammonia and dishwashing liquid. This formula requires rinsing after cleaning.
- For the toughest jobs, use automotive rubbing compound, available from hardware and automotive shops, following the instructions on the can. It does take a lot of time, so you aren't likely to use this for general-purpose cleaning.

*See also:*
• GLASS

# WOKS

**A WELL-SEASONED** WOK HAS THE EQUIVALENT OF A NON-STICK SURFACE AND WILL REQUIRE ONLY LIGHT CLEANING.

**To clean a new wok made of carbon steel** (the authentic kind), begin by removing the temporary protective coating applied by the manufacturer. Scrub the wok inside and out with dishwashing liquid and steel wool and rinse with hot water. If some coating remains, fill the wok with water and boil it until the coating dissolves. Empty the water and scrub again with steel wool and detergent.

**To season a new wok,** after washing it as described above, follow these few simple steps:

- Set the wok down on a burner and heat it until a few drops of water sprinkled into the wok do a mad dance (see 1, below). As it heats, the wok will change colour.
- When it turns black, dip some scrunched-up paper towels into sesame oil. Hold the wad in a pair of tongs and wipe the oil over the inside of the wok (see 2, below).
- Turn the heat down to low and let the wok sit on it for 15 minutes. If the surface looks dry, wipe with another thin coat of oil.
- Turn the heat off and let the wok cool.
- Repeat the oiling and heating process once more before you use the wok for cooking.

**To clean a wok after cooking,** wipe it out with a paper towel or damp cloth. Scrubbing a seasoned wok or using a detergent will ruin the carefully cultivated patina, but if you do need to scrub or wash with detergent, the good news is that the wok can be re-seasoned as described above. Similarly, if a wok gets rusty, just follow the steps for cleaning and seasoning a new wok.

**To clean an electric wok,** follow the manufacturer's instructions, which will vary depending on what kind of surface the wok has and whether it is immersible in water.

Seasoning a new wok

1 The hot wok should make a few drops of water sizzle.

2 Wipe the wok out with paper towels and sesame oil.

# WOOD STOVES AND HEATERS

**WHETHER IT'S A** FUEL STOVE, A POTBELLY STOVE OR OTHER WOOD HEATER, KEEPING YOUR WOOD-BURNING STOVE CLEAN ISN'T ONLY A MATTER OF CLEANLINESS. IT'S ALSO A VITAL MATTER OF SAFETY. EVERY YEAR WOOD STOVES ARE RESPONSIBLE FOR FIRES THAT DESTROY HOMES AND KILL PEOPLE, AND ONE COMMON CAUSE IS IMPROPER DISPOSAL OF ASHES.

**To dispose of ashes safely,** remove them with a metal ash shovel and place them in a tightly covered metal bucket. No plastic shovels, no paper bags, no cardboard boxes—no substitutions! Then take the bucket outside and let it sit for a couple of days to ensure that the harmless-looking ashes aren't still harbouring any embers. For final disposal, add to garden soil or sprinkle on the lawn so the potassium and other minerals in the ash are absorbed. This is the cleaning job that needs to be done whenever the ashes are 8–10 centimetres deep.

**Cleaning a stovepipe or flue** is another job you may have to perform several times during a season. If your flue is removable, disconnect it from the chimney and from the stove when the fire is out. Take the stovepipe outside and shake it into a metal bucket to remove the soot and creosote. If there are stubborn clumps of residue, use a stiff-bristled brush. If your flue is not easily removable, or you would rather not remove it, you can use a chimney and flue cleaner, such as Rubbedin Soot-Loose (available from some supermarkets and barbecue shops, or see www. rubbedin.com.au for distributors), which loosens soot and creosote deposits when it is used as instructed.

**To ensure the cleanest operation of your stove,** burn hardwood (eucalyptus, for example) that has been seasoned for a year. Burn a hot fire for at least half an hour every week during winter. If you are unsure of the meaning of hot in this context, you can buy a stovepipe thermometer from a wood stove dealer to tell you.

**To clean the outside of the stove,** vacuum when there is no fire, using the small brush attachment. For dirt that vacuuming won't remove, wipe the surface of enamelled stoves with a damp sponge. On stoves made of cast iron, plate steel, sheet metal or a combination of these materials, use a stove polish, such as Dr Lakeland's Cast Iron Stove Polish (available from hardware shops and wood-heating specialists or see www. rubbedin.com.au for distributors). Balled-up waxed paper, used on a warm stove, also shines these finishes. Rust or other heavy dirt may be cleaned from a cold stove with fine steel wool and WD-40, which is available from hardware shops.

**To clean glass doors,** follow the instructions in your owner's manual. A mixture of water and a little ammonia will remove smoke, but check your manuel to make sure the glass doesn't have a protective coating, which might be damaged by the ammonia. There are also specialist products, such as Rubbedin Hot Glass Cleaner (see www. rubbedin.com.au for distributors), that are specially formulated for removing soot, tar and creosote from wood stove windows and doors.

**WATCH OUT** If your flue or chimney is neglected or very dirty, don't rely on chemical cleaners to clean it completely. However, it's OK to use those cleaners, especially if you have used them regularly and have done so since your stove was new. They will certainly reduce some of the soot and creosote, causing it to flake and fall. But, for a heavy encrustation, they won't get rid of it all and could give a false sense of security.

The only way to get rid of heavy soot and a build-up of creosote is by mechanically brushing and scraping. If you are in any doubt, have an annual inspection and cleaning, if necessary, by a chimney sweep. Look in the *Yellow Pages* for listings.

**Other stove parts that need periodic cleaning** are baffles, smoke shelves and catalytic combustors. These stove parts increase the efficiency of your stove and reduce pollution. They're often located near the spot where the stovepipe or flue meets the stove. Your owner's manual will tell you if your stove has one or more of these parts and will explain how to clean them.

## WOODWORK

**WOODWORK USUALLY GETS** DIRTY FASTER THAN WALLS AS IT'S THE EDGING AROUND DOORS AND WINDOWS THAT MOST OFTEN COMES INTO CONTACT WITH DIRTY HANDS. YOU WILL PROBABLY FIND YOURSELF CLEANING THE WOODWORK MORE OFTEN THAN THE WALLS, BUT FORTUNATELY IT TAKES UP A LOT LESS AREA THAN WALLS.

**For routine cleaning,** vacuum skirting boards, dado rails (the waist-level moulding on walls that prevents chairs from marking the walls), wainscoting and architraves (the framework around doors and windows) with the small brush attachment. Dust the top surfaces of this woodwork periodically with a microfibre cloth.

**To wash woodwork,** use a solution of a little dishwashing liquid in warm water (see below). Apply with a wrung-out sponge or rag and then rinse with plain water. If the gloss has been dulled, follow by rubbing with a cloth that has a tiny amount of furniture polish on it. This works on both painted and urethane surfaces.

A solution of dishwashing liquid and water on a sponge will remove most marks from dirty woodwork.

**To clean heavily soiled areas,** apply a little undiluted dishwashing liquid directly to the sponge or cloth. Rub the dirty area of woodwork and rinse with plain water.

**To prepare the surface for new paint,** wash with a solution of sugar soap and water, following the manufacturer's instructions for the particular concentration of sugar soap you are using. Wear rubber gloves and rinse afterwards.

**To clean woodwork that has a varnish or shellac finish,** use a solvent-based (not water-based) wood cleaner, available from home improvement shops and hardware shops. It is both a cleaner and a wax in one product. Apply it with a cloth and buff afterwards.

# YELLOWED TEXTILES

**YELLOWING, PARTICULARLY OF KNITS, IS CAUSED BY A NUMBER OF FACTORS, INCLUDING AGE, IMPROPER STORAGE AND REPEATED EXPOSURE TO DIRECT SUNLIGHT. HOWEVER, NOT ALL YELLOWED TEXTILES CAN BE RESTORED TO THEIR ORIGINAL WHITE COLOUR, AS SUNLIGHT ACTUALLY CAUSES A CHEMICAL CHANGE IN PURE-WOOL FIBRES. BUT IT'S STILL WORTH TRYING A COUPLE OF GENTLE PROCESSES.**

**If you have baby shawls and knitted garments that have yellowed,** try soaking them in a bucket of lukewarm water with a cup of bicarbonate of soda. Let the garments soak for an hour or so, then wash them in a wool-safe product such as Softly or a eucalyptus woolwash, making sure to keep the temperature of both the washing and the rinsing water lukewarm. Roll in a towel to remove excess water, then dry flat, in the shade.

**If the yellowing is stubborn,** you could try soaking one test knit (not the antique shawl) in Dylon Run Away for Whites or in Napisan, following packet instructions. Rinse well and dry flat in the shade. Whilst neither of these products is recommended for use on wool, it's worth a try if the clothes are otherwise unusable.

**Sometimes yellowing occurs in fabrics, such as linen table-cloths,** cotton Marcella bedspreads and nappies, that have been washed and packed away. How you approach this problem will depend on the fabric that has yellowed. Cotton fabrics and cloth nappies will respond to a good soak in a nappy product, such as Napisan. If the problem is more severe, the items can be bleached, but make sure you follow the manufacturer's instructions.

**Simple solutions**

### Natural remedy

Try your grandmother's remedy for yellowed linen tablecloths and serviettes. Crush egg shells roughly and tie in a calico cloth. Boil the cloth with the yellowed linen for 15–30 minutes, then wash as usual.

**Linen tablecloths can also be bleached,** but before you get out the bleach bottle, try this gentler method. Dissolve a cup of cream of tartar (from the baking section of the supermarket) in a bucket of water and soak the cloth overnight. Wash as usual. Yellowed nylon curtains also respond well to the cream of tartar treatment.

**Yellowed lace needs to be treated with caution,** especially if it is old and fragile. First try gentle washing and then drying the lace in the sun. If that doesn't work, soak the lace in a weak solution of hydrogen peroxide, then wash gently.

## ZIPPERS

**THERE ARE TIMES** WHEN YOU SHOULD CLEAN A ZIPPER WHETHER OR NOT THE ITEM IT FASTENS NEEDS A CLEAN. FOR EXAMPLE, THE ZIPPERS IN TENTS, SLEEPING BAGS, LUGGAGE, WETSUITS, FISHING GEAR, JACKETS AND BOOTS MAY NEED SEPARATE ATTENTION NOW AND THEN.

**To clean zippers in items that can be washed,** wash the item with water and a detergent that is suitable for the fabric. Close the zipper before putting the article into the washing machine. When ironing, make sure you protect the zipper by closing it and covering it with a cloth. Excessive heat from the iron can damage or destroy nylon, plastic and polyester zippers.

**To make the slider work more smoothly,** rub a candle along the zipper teeth and move the slider up and down several times to work in the wax. A white candle works best, so you don't smear any dye around. Wipe off any excess. This treatment will counteract the damage done by detergents and bleach to the factory-applied coating that keeps zippers slippery.

**To clean the zippers on large articles**—such as tents, backpacks, wetsuits, suitcases and boots—first unzip the zipper. Remove any loose dirt from the teeth with a toothbrush. To wash the zipper, dip the toothbrush in a solution of a little dishwashing liquid and warm water. Rinse with plain water and leave the zipper open until it has dried. Lubricate the teeth with a candle (see below). A special zipper lubricant, such as Selleys Ezi Glide (available from hardware shops) can be used. It is a dry, non-oily lubricant that works not only on zippers, but also on curtain tracks, sticking windows and sliding doors.

An ordinary, white candle will make a zip slide easily.

# 3 cleaning crises

# Cleaning crises

No matter how careful you are, somehow something always manages to spill on the floor, your clothes, the furniture and just about every other surface in the home. The most important thing is to attack the spill as quickly as possible, thereby improving your chance of cleaning it off without leaving a stain or nasty odour behind.

## ANIMAL URINE, POO OR VOMIT ON FLOOR OR CARPET

**Remove the urine, poo or vomit as soon as possible.** Stash a crisis kit containing the following items in your broom cupboard or laundry: paper towels, plastic grocery bags (for disposing of solids and used paper towels), a sponge and an enzyme-based cleaner (available from pet shops). Start by removing any solids, then blot up as much of the liquid content as possible. Soak the accident site in the enzyme cleaner and rinse away residue with plain water to avoid leaving any fragrant clues that might draw your pet back to use the same spot.

## BABY URINE, POO OR VOMIT ON CLOTHES OR UPHOLSTERY

**First try cold water,** which might be all you'll need to remove any of these protein stains if they're fresh. Don't use hot water, since it can cook the proteins, causing the stain to coagulate between the fibres in the fabric. Soak washables in cold water for half an hour, run the stain under cold tap water and then gently rub the fabric against itself to loosen the stain. Then launder as usual in your washing machine, using warm water. For carpet or upholstery, spray with cold water and blot with a clean cloth or paper towels. Repeat until the stain has gone. If residue remains, soak the accident site in enzyme cleaner. Wash and rinse according to product instructions.

## BERRY STAINS ON CLOTHING OR TEA TOWELS

**Berry stains are considered dye stains, and they're tough.** For washable clothes and tea towels, pre-treat the stain with a spray-on stain remover, or apply liquid laundry detergent directly to the stain. Work the detergent in well, then soak the fabric in a diluted solution of oxygen bleach (identified as 'all-fabric' or 'percarbonate' on the label—follow package instructions). Machine wash. For dry-clean-only clothes, blot a dry-cleaning solution, such as Murlex or Woolclean Spot Dry Remover No. 2, on the stain with a clean, white towel.

## BIG PARTY MESS TO CLEAN UP

**Gather cups, bottles and glasses first.** As you do this, look for spills and address them straight away. Empty the cups, bottles and glasses in the kitchen sink, toss rubbish into a garbage bag and put the empty glasses on the benchtop. Fill your dishwasher and start the first load. Next, gather up the rest of the party garbage, starting in the outer rooms, working your way towards the kitchen. The goal is to centralise the clutter. Dust and vacuum, again working your way towards the kitchen and clean the kitchen last. Take the garbage out as soon as bags are filled and tied (to prevent accidental leaks and bad odours).

## BLOOD ON FABRIC OR CARPET

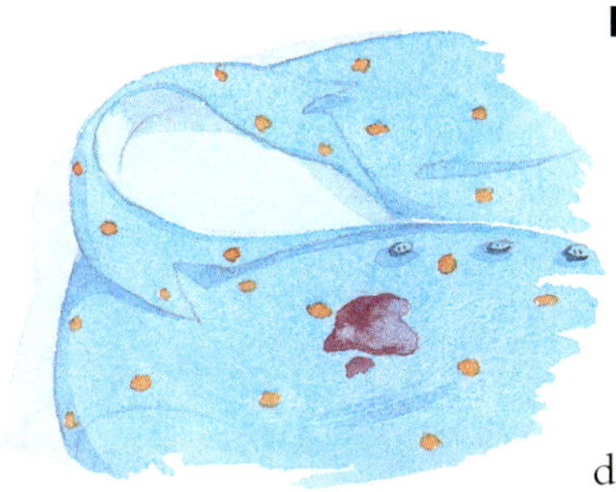

**If it's fresh, cold water should be all you'll need** to remove this protein stain. Don't use hot water, since heat will cook the proteins, causing the stain to coagulate between the fibres in the fabric. Soak washables in cold water for half an hour, run the stain under cold tap water and gently rub the fabric against itself to loosen the stain. Launder in warm water. For carpet or upholstery, spray with cold water and blot with a clean, white towel (white, so there's no chance of dye transfer), repeating until clean.

## CANDLE WAX ON FABRIC OR CARPET

**If the wax is still soft, blot up the excess with a paper towel.** If it's hard, gently scrape the excess with a dull knife. Next, lay a plain brown bag or white paper towel (no dyes or printing inks) over the wax and run a hot iron over the paper. The heat will melt the wax and the paper will absorb it. Continue by moving the bag or paper towel around to unsaturated sections until all the wax is absorbed. Remove residue by blotting with a dry-cleaning solvent, such as Murlex or Woolclean Spot Dry Remover No. 2. Test on an inconspicuous spot.

## CHEWING GUM ON UPHOLSTERY, CARPET OR HAIR

**Use ice to remove chewing gum from a variety of places:** clothing, upholstery, carpet and hard surfaces. Simply rub the ice on the gum until it freezes and hardens. To avoid water drips, put the ice in a plastic bag before rubbing it on the gum. Scrape away

the hardened gum with a dull knife. If residue remains, remove it by blotting with a dry-cleaning solvent, such as Murlex, or a citrus-based solvent, such as De-Solv-It. Always test the solvent first on an inconspicuous spot. For gum in your hair, apply a few drops of baby oil, eucalyptus oil or peanut butter to the gum and knead it until it's soft. Keep pulling away bits of gum until it's gone, then shampoo.

## COFFEE ON CLOTHES

**For washable fabrics, soak for half an hour** in a solution of 1 teaspoon of liquid laundry detergent (preferably one containing enzymes) for every 2 litres of warm water. Then launder in the washing machine with the hottest water that is safe for the fabric, using laundry detergent, not soap. Natural soap—including soap flakes, bar soap and detergent containing soap—makes tannin stains harder to remove. To remove stubborn tannin stains, you may need to wash with bleach. If all the sugars from one of these stains are not removed, they could turn brown in your tumble-dryer, as the sugar is caramelised by the heat.

## COOKING ODOUR PERMEATING THE HOUSE

**Open the windows and turn on a fan** to get fresh air circulating. Next, wipe surfaces with a degreaser, such as Handy Andy, to remove the particles and grease deposited by the smoke. Clean walls and other surfaces close to the stove. Because heat rises and is drawn to cool areas, concentrate on wiping windows and window trim, light fittings and high-up cupboards.

A quick fix for cutting out cooking odours is to mix ¼ cup of vinegar in 1 litre of water and boil on the stove. The rising warm air will carry the odour-neutralising vinegar particles to the surfaces on which the smoke and grease have settled.

## COOKING OIL SPLATTERS ON STOVE, BENCHTOPS OR CLOTHES

**First, the stove and benchtops.** Wipe oil from benchtops and the stove with paper towels. Then wipe surfaces with a moist sponge and a solution of dishwashing liquid and warm water or a 50:50 solution of vinegar and warm water. Check underneath the stovetop (if it's not sealed—follow owner's manual instructions) and wipe up oil there to prevent a cooking fire.

For oil on clothes you must dry-clean—blot the grease with a paper towel dampened with acetone-based nail-polish remover. (Do not use it on acetate, as acetone will dissolve the fabric.) For washable clothes, use a commercial pre-wash stain remover, such as Preen or Frend, or a liquid laundry detergent. Work the detergent into the stain and immediately after pre-treatment, launder the item in hot water (as long as that is safe for the particular fabric and colours).

## FELT-TIP MARKER ON FRIDGE, BENCHTOP OR FURNITURE

**First, try wiping the marks off with a paper towel** or dry cloth. Depending on the surface and whether the marker ink is still wet, you may be able to remove the mark. If not, you can try wiping with a clean cloth moistened with methylated spirits. If that doesn't work, try mineral turpentine or kerosene. But be careful, as these solvents are all flammable. Test them first on an inconspicuous corner of the material.

## FLEAS IN CARPET

**Vacuum the carpet,** concentrating on areas frequented by your pet and under seats and sofas. Also vacuum upholstered furniture in the vicinity. Wash any removable throw rugs or pet bedding. Ask your vet or at a hardware shop for a low-toxic spray to help kill any remaining fleas and prevent reinfestation. Once the carpet has dried, vacuum again. Vacuum often for the next two weeks. Don't leave the vacuum bag in the machine when you've finished; remove it and tie it up tightly in a plastic bag, so that the fleas will not spread. Dispose of the bag in an outside garbage bin.

## GARBAGE BAG SPILL ON CARPET

**Quickly pick up large solids** and put them in a new bag or garbage bin. Clean up any small solids, such as coffee grounds or dirt, with a vacuum cleaner. Blot up liquids with paper towels. If there are stains remaining, do your best to figure out what they are and then address each one using the appropriate stain-removal technique. (See 'Stains', on page 328.) For big spills, work from the outer edge of the spill to the centre to contain the mess.

## GLASS BROKEN IN CROWDED ROOM

**Leave someone near the spot to warn others.** Go and get a small cardboard box (or a bucket), a pair of work gloves and a dustpan and broom (for hard floors) or a vacuum cleaner (for carpets). Wearing gloves, pick up the big pieces and put them in the box or bucket. On a hard floor, inspect in a wide circle around the crash site for pieces that may have flown further afield. (Ask guests to check their pants' cuffs and shoes, in case any shards landed there.) Next, sweep or vacuum. Vacuum the carpet several times to make sure you have removed all tiny shards. Empty the vacuum bag when finished. Transfer the glass from the bucket to a box. Seal the box and put it in the garbage bin. (The box will protect anyone handling the garbage.)

## GLUE SPILLED ON FURNITURE OR SOFA

**Start by scraping up whatever you can using a dull knife.** If the glue is white PVA glue, treat it as you would a protein-based stain (see page 393), which means no hot water—the hot water can cook the proteins. Instead, spray the spot with cold water and blot with a clean cloth, repeating until clean. If it is model glue or craft glue, blot it with a cloth moistened with a dry-cleaning solvent, such as Murlex or Woolclean Spot Dry Remover No. 2, or methylated spirits.

## LIPSTICK ON CLOTHING

**Lipstick contains both an oily or waxy base and dyes.** You must first remove the oily or waxy part and then you can try to remove the dye. For washable fabrics, begin by applying a dry-cleaning fluid, such as Murlex or Woolclean Spot Dry Remover No. 2. Next, rub with a liquid laundry detergent and scrub in hot water. This should remove the oily or waxy part. Then launder in your washing machine using a laundry detergent and an oxygen or all-fabric bleach.

## MUD WALKED IN ON RUG

**Mud wreaks havoc on a rug.** But don't despair, let the mud dry first and you'll have a better chance of getting it out. If the mud is ground in, brush it to the surface, then get up as much as you can with a dull knife. After that, vacuum. If you still see muddy paw- or footprints, mix ¼ teaspoon of dishwashing liquid with 1 cup of warm water and blot the solution onto the rug with a clean, white towel. Use another damp towel to rinse and remove soap.

## MUSTARD ON CLOTHING

**Mustard is a dye stain.** For washable clothes and towels, pre-treat with a commercial stain remover. Or apply liquid laundry detergent directly onto the stain. Work the detergent in well. Next, soak the fabric in a diluted solution of oxygen bleach (identified as 'all-fabric' or 'percarbonate' on the label—follow instructions on the packaging). Launder in your washing machine. For dry-clean-only clothes, blot with dry-cleaning fluid on a clean, white towel.

## NAIL POLISH ON FURNITURE, FLOOR OR CARPET

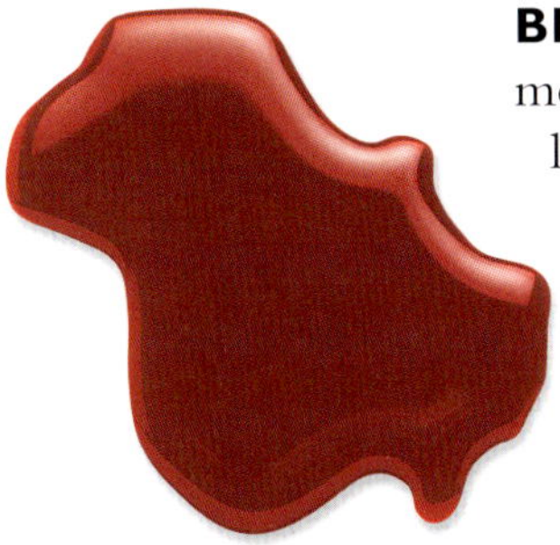

**Blot up excess with a paper towel.** Then blot with a cloth moistened with acetone-based nail-polish remover. Be careful not to let the nail-polish remover seep into a carpet's latex backing. To remove the nail-polish remover, mix a solution of 1 squirt of mild dishwashing liquid (containing no bleach or lanolin) with 1 litre of water. Wipe the wood or work the solution into the textile with a clean towel. Draw the solution back out by blotting with a dry paper towel. Rinse by lightly spraying with clean water and then blot the water up with fresh paper towels.

## OIL AND GREASE ON CLOTHES

**Blot up as much as you can with a paper towel** or carefully scrape solids up with a dull knife. For clothes that can only be dry-cleaned, blot the grease with a paper towel dampened with acetone-based nail-polish remover. (Don't use acetone on acetate, because it will dissolve the fabric.) For washable clothes, spray with a commercial pre-wash stain remover or use a liquid laundry detergent. Work the detergent into the stain. Immediately after pre-treatment, launder the item in your washing machine using hot water (if that is safe for the particular fabric and colours).

## PAINT DRIPPINGS ON FLOOR OR CARPET

**Start by blotting up as much dripped paint as possible** using paper towels. If it is acrylic paint, spray with clean water and blot. Repeat until you've removed as much paint as possible. If it is oil-based

paint, blot with a clean cloth or paper towel moistened with paint thinner or turpentine, refreshing cloths or paper towels repeatedly. If vestiges of the paint remain on the carpet, moisten the tufts with 3 per cent hydrogen peroxide and let that stand for an hour. Blot with a clean paper towel to absorb excess moisture.

## PEN INK ON YOUR POCKET

**Remove the pen and put it in the garbage.** Remove the item of clothing, making sure not to smear the ink stain on anything else. Place the stain face down on white paper towels. (Put plastic beneath, to keep the ink from bleeding through and staining the surface you're working on.) Blot with a cloth moistened with methylated spirits, forcing the stain into the paper towels. If that doesn't work, try mineral turpentine or kerosene. Be careful, because these solvents are flammable. (Test them first in an inconspicuous corner of the material.) Rinse with water and launder in your washing machine.

## ROTTEN SMELL FROM UNKNOWN SOURCE

**Follow your nose.** First, try to isolate the odour. Is it in a particular room? Is it wafting up from under the house? Is it a dead animal smell, a pet accident smell, a musty mould smell, a cooking odour? Use deductive reasoning; if it's in the kitchen and smells like rotten food, check the refrigerator, sink and the garbage bin. Look under cupboards or appliances for dropped food. If it's a musty odour, such as mould or mildew, check the sink drain or refrigerator drip pan. Look under the house for damp or mildew. Look for dead rodents. Here's how to handle a few common odour problems:

- For a kitchen with lingering cooking smells, wipe down all hard surfaces near the stove with a degreaser such as Handy Andy, including windows, light fittings and cupboards. Wash curtains and tea towels.
- To clean and deodorise your sink, pour in ½ cup of bicarbonate of soda followed by ½ cup of white vinegar.
- To deodorise your refrigerator, throw out any old food, wipe down the interior and place an open box of bicarbonate of soda at the back of one of the shelves to absorb any remaining odours.

## SCORCH MARKS ON FABRIC

**Bad scorch marks cannot be removed.** Try laundering the fabric in your washing machine using bleach, if that is safe for the fabric. If not, soak in all-fabric bleach and hot water and then launder.

## SEWAGE BACKING UP THROUGH DRAINS

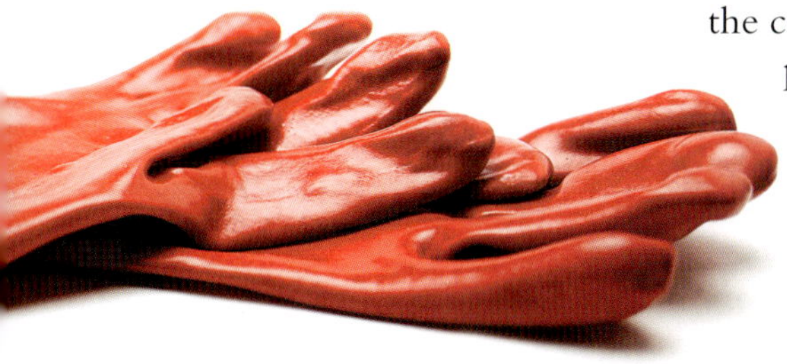

**Firstly, avoid using any toilets, sinks, bathtubs or showers** in the house until the backup is corrected. And avoid direct contact with the contamination. (You may need rubber gloves and boots.) If you are part of a municipal sewerage system, contact the local council authority. They should send someone to diagnose the problem—and clean it up if it was their fault. If it's your fault, call a plumber or correct the backup using a plumber's eel to clear the blockage. Clean up the mess using a wet vac and mop to remove the spillage. Mop the floors and wipe the walls with a heavy-duty cleaner and disinfectant. Then clean plumbing fixtures. Finally, call a professional to steam clean your carpets and rugs (the easiest and most effective approach), or do it yourself by renting or buying a steam cleaner (also known as a hot water extraction machine), following the instructions that come with the machine.

## SMOKE FROM A FIREPLACE

**When smoke from the fireplace comes into the house,** first make sure there is no chimney fire. Check for a loud roaring sound or sparks in the chimney. If it's a chimney fire, call the fire brigade. If it's not, then chances are your chimney is not drawing properly. Open a door or window on the windward side of the house to help the chimney draw. To clear out existing smoke, open more windows and doors on the windward side and use fans to circulate the air. If the smoke smell lingers, wash the curtains and clean the upholstery. (Rugs should be OK, as smoke rises.) Wipe all exposed metal in the room with a degreaser spray, such as Handy Andy, since smoke seeks out cool surfaces. (The acidic soot can etch metal.)

## SMOKE FILLING THE KITCHEN

**Firstly, turn off the oven or stove.** Contain the smoke by closing the doors to other rooms. Open the windows and turn on fans to help circulate air. Next, wipe surfaces with a degreaser, such as Handy Andy, to remove the particles and grease deposited by the smoke. Clean the walls and other surfaces close to the stove. Wipe the windows and window trim, light fittings and high-up cupboards. Later, wash the kitchen curtains and exposed tea towels.

To get rid of the smoke odour quickly, combine ¼ cup of vinegar with 1 litre of water and boil on the stovetop. The rising hot air will carry odour-neutralising vinegar particles to the surfaces on which the smoke and grease settled.

## SUNTAN LOTION ON CLOTHING

**Blot excess lotion with a paper towel** or carefully scrape up the excess with a dull knife. On washable clothes, spray the stained area with a commercial pre-wash stain remover. If you don't have that sort of product on hand, apply liquid laundry detergent directly to the stain and work it in. Immediately after pre-treatment, launder the item in your washing machine in hot water (if that is safe for the particular fabric and colours). With dry-clean-only clothes, blot with a paper towel dampened with acetone-based nail-polish remover. (Acetone will dissolve acetate, however, so don't use it on that fabric.)

## TAR ON SHOES

**Remove as much of the tar as possible by gently scraping** with an old spoon. Remove further residue by blotting with a clean, dry paper towel. Next, apply methylated spirits to a paper towel and blot or gently rub. Repeat several times using clean paper towels with freshly applied metho. If any tar remains, try wiping with a sudsy solution of warm water and a squirt of dishwashing liquid. Put a small amount on a cloth and gently blot or rub. Rinse by spraying lightly with clean water and wiping dry.

## WASHING MACHINE, TOILET, BATHTUB OR SINK OVERFLOWING ONTO FLOOR

**This—along with bathing the dog—is why you keep those old towels around.** The first thing to do is turn off the water source and open any drains. Then grab as many old towels as you possibly can and toss them onto the pooling water to soak it up. (Have a bucket or empty washing basket on hand to collect the water-soaked towels in.) With another towel or several smaller rags, contain the water by soaking it up from the outside, moving towards the centre. Mop or use a wet vac and then allow the floor to dry, using fans if necessary.

## WATER OR ALCOHOL STAIN ON FURNITURE

**If it's a fresh stain,** soak up any excess water or alcohol with a paper towel and then rub the spot vigorously in the direction of the grain with the palm of your hand or a cloth dipped in furniture polish. If it's an old, dry stain, you'll need an abrasive and lubricant combination. Use a few drops of paraffin or baby oil with rottenstone (a fine abrasive available from hardware shops) sprinkled on top or apply a paste wax with a very fine grade of steel wool (such as 0000). You could even use cigarette ash and mayonnaise. No matter what combination you use, rub gently with the grain using a clean, dry cloth.

## WINE ON CARPET

**Blot up as much of the wine as you can with paper towels.** For large spills, work from the outside in, so as to contain the spill. Next, lightly apply a solution of ¼ teaspoon of mild dishwashing liquid and a litre of water. Work the solution into the affected area. Blot the stain with clean paper towels to remove. Rinse by lightly spraying with water. Then blot to remove excess water. Do this until all suds are gone. Then spray lightly with water and don't blot. Instead, lay a pad of paper towels down, put a weight on the pad and let the towels dry. If the stain persists, moisten the tufts of the carpet fibre with 3 per cent hydrogen peroxide. Let that stand for about an hour, then blot with clean paper towels.

## WINE ON TABLE LINEN

**Regardless of the type of wine,** if the fabric is washable, soak it for half an hour in a solution of 1 teaspoon of liquid laundry detergent (preferably one containing enzymes) for every 2 litres of warm water. Then launder in your washing machine using the hottest water that's safe for the fabric and laundry detergent, not soap. Natural soap—including soap flakes, bar soap and detergent containing soap—makes tannin stains harder to remove. To remove stubborn tannin stains, you may need to wash with bleach. If all the sugars from one of these stains are not removed, they could turn brown in a tumble-dryer, as the sugar is caramelised.

# 4 tools of the trade

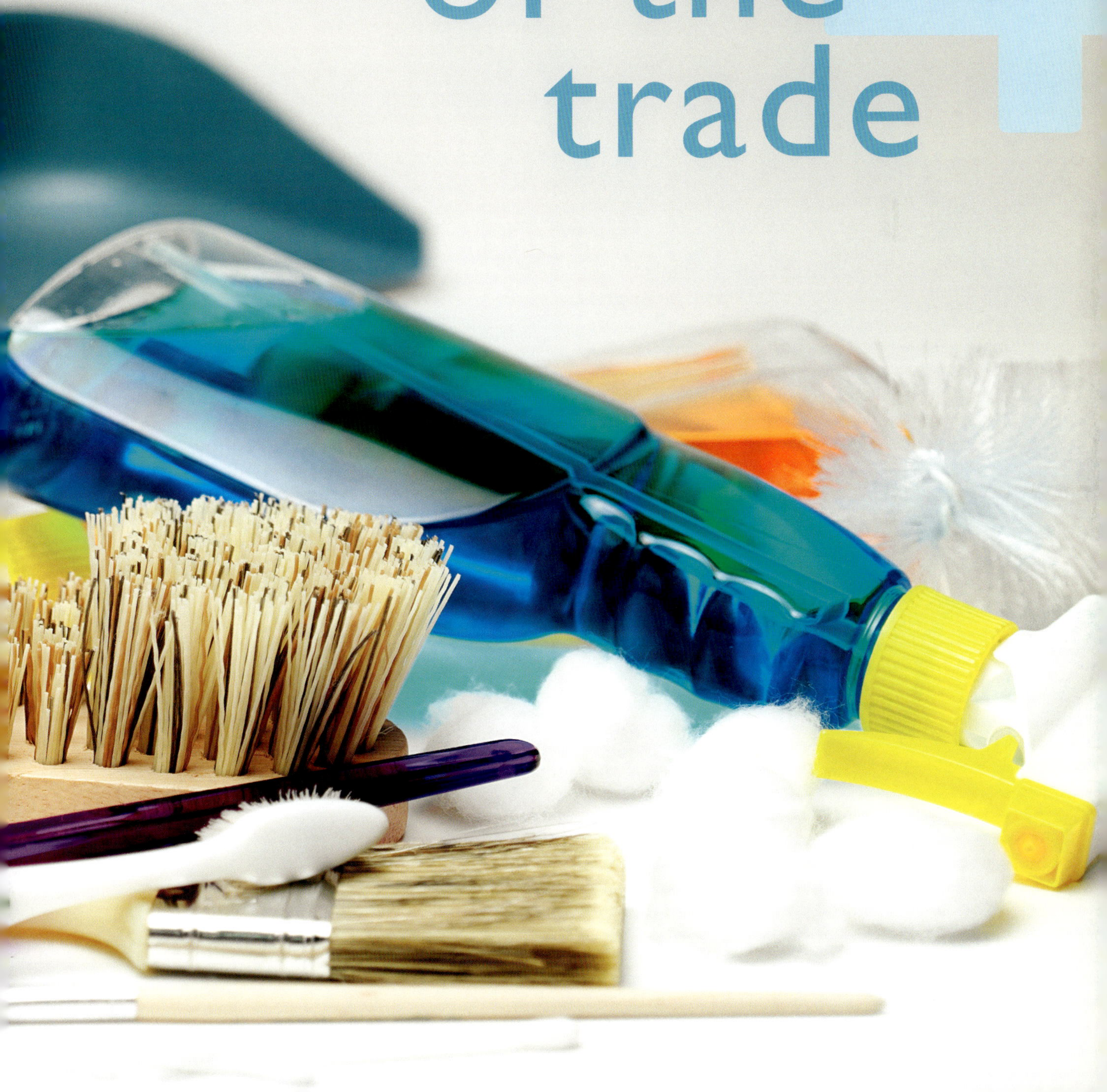

# Tools of the trade

## ABRASIVE CLEANERS

Using abrasive cleaners is a mechanical process. Abrasive cleaners are made of particles, usually minerals, that scratch off the offending grime with friction created when you rub. The finer the particle, the less abrasive the cleaner; the coarser the particle, the more abrasive the cleaner. Many abrasive cleaners, which come in powdered and liquid forms, also contain cleaning chemicals such as detergent or bleach.

**Use a full-strength abrasive cleaner**—a scouring powder, such as Ajax—to wear off dirt, stains, tarnish and hard-water deposits. Rub across the surface of the item with a sponge or brush and then rinse.

**Use a mild abrasive cleaner,** such as Jif, for cleaning sinks, tiles, showers, baths, toilets and benchtops. Follow package instructions. Be careful not to rub too hard. Even mildly abrasive cleaners can scratch and damage hard, smooth surfaces, making them rough and difficult to clean in the future.

**A pumice stone,** the same abrasive block you use to file away corns on your feet, will help remove a particularly stubborn toilet bowl stain.

**Scrubbing pads,** ranging from nylon mesh to steel wool soap pads, also work by abrasion.

**Some common household compounds** can be used instead of commercially prepared abrasives:

- Bicarbonate of soda is a mild abrasive. Sprinkle it on the item to be cleaned or make a paste by adding water to bicarbonate of soda until it's a bit thicker than toothpaste. Bicarbonate of soda can be used to scour pots and pans, ovens, and also drip pans.
- Toothpaste (regular white, not gel) can remove water marks in sinks and clean tarnish on silver. Coat the silver with toothpaste, run it under warm water, work it into a foam and then rinse it off.
- Salt is abrasive. Reach for the salt shaker if you have a spill in your oven. With the oven still warm, wet the spill lightly and sprinkle on salt. When the oven cools, scrape away the spill and wash the area clean.

**Abrasives can be found** in supermarkets, home improvement shops and hardware shops. They include all common scouring powders.

## ABSORBENTS

Absorbents do their cleaning by sucking up liquids or gases. They're particularly handy for wet, messy situations such as food spills, oil spills, pet accidents, vomit and blood. Absorbents include such household products as bicarbonate of soda, baby powder, cornflour, kitty litter and table salt as well as commercial products. Not all absorbent products are granular, pour-on materials, of course. Paper towels and cloths soak up spills and messes by absorption, too.

**Common absorbents and their uses** include these:

- Paper towels are great for removing spills, especially from the floor.
- Washable cotton cloths (old cotton T-shirts and nappies, for example) are also great for spills and are more economical.
- Microfibre cleaning cloths, which can absorb several times their own weight, are great for general cleaning.
- Bicarbonate of soda in the box, tucked in a corner of your refrigerator, is a good absorber of food odours. Out of the box, bicarbonate of soda is good for absorbing grease around a stove or spills in an oven—even for cleaning vomit. Just add bicarbonate of soda until the liquid solidifies, then scrape it off.

**Don't overlook these handy absorbents:**

- Salt absorbs grease spots on carpet. Immediately pour salt on the grease to absorb it and prevent staining. Vacuum off.
- Kitty litter (the clay type) works well on outdoor oil spills. In addition, it can be used to solidify very small quantities of paint and other liquids, or to line the bottom of your outdoor barbecue drip tray.
- Sand or soil also works well for oil spills outside or in a garage.

**Commercial granular absorbent products** are the favourite solution of school cleaners when someone vomits on any surface.

---

NOTE: *For laundry products, see Chapter 5, Advice on laundry, p. 26.*

**Absorbent products are available** from supermarkets, home improvement shops, hardware shops and specialist cleaning suppliers.

## ACIDIC CLEANERS

Acid is the opposite of alkali (or base) on the pH scale, with 0 indicating extreme acidity, 7 neutrality and 14 extreme alkalinity. Each point that you move away from neutral pH 7 is ten times more alkaline or acidic. So you don't need to go far from pH 7 to get a strong cleaner. Some common acids include lemon juice (citric acid), vinegar (acetic acid), hydrochloric acid and phosphoric acid.

**Common uses for acidic cleaners** include removing rust stains, mineral deposits and stains on grout, as well as unclogging pipes. Read product labels and use extreme caution when using acidic cleaners. Otherwise, you risk damaging finishes and injuring yourself. A rundown of acidic cleaners at various pH levels follows.

**Hydrochloric acid** (pH 0) is the strongest acid and is used in extreme cases of hard-water deposits, lime and rust, most often in the toilet bowl. A cleaner with 9 per cent hydrochloric acid has a significant amount of acid in it and could etch surfaces and burn skin. Wear gloves and eye protection and follow instructions. If the label says the product merely 'contains' hydrochloric acid, it's probably fairly diluted and mild.

**Phosphoric acid** (pH 2 to 4) is milder than hydrochloric and can be used on bathtubs, sinks and tile to dissolve mineral deposits, rust stains and mildew. Cleaning agents with phosphoric acid are fairly gentle on metal trims of shower doors and on taps if you rinse thoroughly after cleaning. Be aware that phosphoric acid doesn't really 'clean'. It etches surfaces, and if you use it too frequently, you could dissolve the grout around your tile.

**Vinegar and citric acid** (pH 2 to 4) and other acids in this category work well for frequent cleaning. They're commonly used on glassware, teapots and coffeepots, and other common kitchen items.

For washing clothes, add 1 cup of white vinegar to the final rinse to eliminate soap residue. Vinegar breaks down uric acid, so it's especially good for babies' clothes. To get wool and cotton blankets fluffy, add 2 cups of white vinegar to the rinse water.

Lemon juice is a good acid for removing stains on clothing, such as berry stains. It acts like bleach, which makes it good for cleaning chopping boards and benchtops. To remove a stain on a benchtop, squeeze on fresh lemon juice, let it sit for 45 minutes, sprinkle on bicarbonate of soda and rub with a sponge. Then rinse out the sponge and wipe again. (Do not use lemon juice on marble benchtops.)

**Take precautions** when using acidic cleaners:

- Don't use vinegar if you add chlorine bleach to your rinse water. The mixture will produce harmful vapours.

- Don't use vinegar on wooden floorboards.
- Don't let acidic cleaners sit too long on metal fixtures, or they'll damage the chrome.
- Don't use acid on stone (including granite and marble) or concrete—both materials are alkaline and will dissolve with acid.

**Buy acidic cleaners** at local supermarkets, home improvement shops and specialist cleaning suppliers.

## AIR CLEANERS

The air in a home can be improved in a number of ways, but all approaches to doing it fall into these two broad categories:

- Chemical products that attack the sources of odours or mask odours.
- Air-cleaning devices and filters that pull irritants out of the air.

**Disinfecting cleaners** don't clean the air directly, but they do eliminate the source of odours. To destroy mould or bacteria that generate a bad odour, just spray the surface where the offending microbes are growing with a traditional disinfecting cleaner, such as Pine O Cleen. New sprays that have recently hit the market claim to kill odour-causing bacteria actually in the air and to neutralise other nasty smelling particles.

**Air fresheners** don't really eliminate odours—they just cover up the smell. They come in spray and time-release forms. A spray, such as Glade, can mask an unpleasant odour by simply using it in the area with the offending odour. A time-release air freshener—a wick, solid cake or saturated wood block—has a longer freshening effect. Air fresheners of

either kind are most commonly used in bathrooms and kitchens.

**The filter** that's part of the typical reverse-cycle, forced-air heating and cooling system does the crucial job of removing irritants from the air in your home. Everyday filters should be changed once a month during prime heating and cooling seasons. These inexpensive disposable filters remove less than 10 per cent of the particles in the air. If you upgrade, a medium-efficiency filter for your airconditioning system will cost a little more, but will trap 20 to 50 per cent of the particles in the air.

**A stand-alone air-filtering appliance** should be considered for heavy-duty air cleaning. Such units filter air in a variety of ways, but for all-around removal of airborne particles, high-efficiency particulate air (HEPA) filters are a great choice, particularly for people with allergies. They trap particles in fine, disposable filters and are rated at 60 to 95 per cent efficiency. Electrostatic precipitators also do a good job of trapping particles, and their filters are reusable.

**Buy chemical air fresheners** from supermarkets and hardware shops. Air-filtering systems are available from department stores, home improvement shops, hardware shops, discount shops and some medical supply companies.

## ALCOHOL

Alcohol is an effective solvent for cleaning and eliminating stains, and it kills germs, too. The most common disinfectant sprays, for instance, contain up to 79 per cent ethyl alcohol.

**Alcohol comes in several forms.** Alcohol is an organic compound consisting of hydrocarbons. It's a colourless liquid, has a mild odour and is highly flammable. Common forms are isopropyl alcohol, available from pharmacies (often called rubbing alcohol, used for massages and as an antiseptic) and ethyl alcohol, or ethanol (the stuff in alcoholic drinks and a common ingredient in cleaning products, mouthwash and hair sprays). Methylated spirits is ethanol that contains a small amount of poisonous methanol, or wood alcohol, making it unfit for consumption. It's also an antiseptic and is commonly used to thin or remove paint and varnish, and to remove greasy smudges from surfaces.

**Use alcohol-based cleaners** when you need a solvent that evaporates quickly. They are especially suited to cleaning glass because they clean and quickly vanish without leaving streaks. They are also useful for cleaning telephones and the keyboards of computers, calculators and such. Apply alcohol to electronic items with a cotton bud.

Alcohol is handy for eliminating oil-based stains in carpets and upholstery, for removing hair spray from mirrors, and for dissolving ink, lipstick, crayon and other stains.

**Be careful** with alcohol on some finishes. Alcohol can soften plastic and paint, so don't leave alcohol-based cleaners on these surfaces for too long.

**A word of warning**—methylated spirits is undrinkable. Rubbing alcohol is toxic, too. Drinking even a few millilitres of these alcohols can blind you, put you in a coma or even kill you. Keep this stuff out of reach of children.

**Where you buy alcohol cleaning products** depends on what type they are. Alcohol-based cleaners and disinfectants are available from supermarkets, specialist cleaning suppliers, home improvement shops, discount shops and hardware shops. Isopropyl alcohol is available from pharmacies. Methylated spirits can be found on the paint thinner shelf in hardware and home improvement shops.

## ALKALI CLEANERS

Alkali cleaners are at the opposite end of the pH scale from acidic cleaners. (See page 405.) Any cleaner above pH 7 (neutral) is considered an alkali. Most multipurpose cleaners have an alkali base because alkali cleaners neutralise acid, and most spills and stains are acidic.

**Common uses for alkali cleaners** include degreasing and removing heavy soil. They're also good for washing windows and dealing with coffee and tea stains. Alkali cleaners include dishwashing liquid; mild detergents (the wool detergent Softly is pH-neutral); all-purpose cleaners, such as Spray n' Wipe; and glass cleaners, such as Windex and Mr Muscle. The more aggressive degreasers, oven cleaners, caustic soda drain openers and wax strippers are also alkali-based products.

Here's a rundown of various alkali cleaners. The higher the pH number, the more caustic the cleaner is.

**The mildest alkali cleaners** (pH 8 and pH 9) include dish-washing liquid and bicarbonate of soda—the Swiss Army knife of the cleaning world. In a solution with water (2 tablespoons of bicarbonate of soda per 1 litre of warm water), bicarbonate of soda cleans hard surfaces such as glass, tile, porcelain, stainless steel, chrome and fibreglass. For cleaning up heavier soil, sprinkle bicarbonate of soda on a damp sponge and rub.

**Moderate alkalis** (pH 9 to pH 11) include all-purpose degreasers, such as Spray n' Wipe; borax, which boosts the cleaning power of laundry detergent; sugar soap, for cleaning painted surfaces, porcelain and tile; ammonia, a general cleaner, grease cutter and wax stripper; soaps; scouring powders; and window cleaners.

**The strongest alkalis** (pH 12 to pH 14) include caustic soda (used in drain openers and oven cleaners), garage floor degreasers, carpet shampoos and washing soda (for extra cleaning power in the laundry).

**Some cautionary notes** about alkali cleaners:

- Strong alkalis can damage skin and fabrics. They also corrode and darken aluminium. Wear hand and eye protection when handling the stronger alkalis.
- Most alkalis, except bicarbonate of soda, are toxic if swallowed.
- To remove an alkali residue from a surface you have already cleaned, rinse the surface with a solution of 2 tablespoons of vinegar in a litre of water, then wipe dry.

**Alkali cleaners are available from** in supermarkets, specialist cleaning suppliers, home improvement shops and hardware shops.

## ALL-PURPOSE CLEANERS

All-purpose cleaners are just what their name implies—they do a wide variety of cleaning jobs. Most of them are moderately alkaline, meaning they're superb grease cutters.

**The big advantage of all-purpose cleaners** is that you don't have to keep a lot of specialty cleaners around the house. Don't assume, however, that your all-purpose cleaner disinfects. Check the label if you're hoping to kill germs as well as clean.

**You can use all-purpose cleaners** safely on most surfaces and fabrics—benches, cupboards, walls, floors, and patio and outdoor furniture. They will even remove fingerprints. It's best to test an all-purpose cleaner on an inconspicuous part of the item you're cleaning before you squirt it over the entire object. Because many all-purpose cleaners have a relatively high pH, they may cause colours to run. They can also damage wood finishes.

**Citrus-based cleaners,** such as Spray n' Wipe Orange Force and Citro Clean Multi-Purpose Cleaner, are increasing in popularity. Use them on clothes, carpets, grout, shower curtains, garbage bins, decks, toilets, the kitchen and stains. They will remove gum, tar and grease, and they smell pleasant.

**All-purpose cleaners can be bought** almost anywhere—supermarkets, home improvement shops, specialist cleaning suppliers and discount shops. They're more economical if you buy them in concentrated form, because you're not paying for the water.

## AMMONIA

Ammonia is made up of nitrogen and hydrogen, so it's a gas; one that's suspended in water. Ammonia is an alkali booster (by itself, it's not a cleaner) that helps detergents with degreasing, stripping wax and removing soil.

**Many common cleaners** use solutions that are 5 to 7 per cent ammonia. If you have a container of household ammonia, it's actually mostly water, and the ammonia content is 5 to 10 per cent. Cloudy ammonia has a detergent added.

**Cloudy ammonia** works well on stove rings, grilling trays, floors, ceramic tiles and stainless steel. A bowl of ammonia left in the oven overnight will loosen burned-on grease and grime—just wipe it off in the morning. Ammonia is also a feature ingredient in commercial window cleaners.

**Take extra care** when working with ammonia:

- Keep the area well ventilated. Evaporating ammonia fumes will make your toes curl—if it doesn't make you sick.
- Never mix ammonia with chlorine bleach, which creates poisonous chlorine gas.
- Ammonia can darken aluminium and discolour some fabrics, so proceed carefully.

Ammonia is available from supermarkets, home improvement shops, specialist cleaning suppliers and most discount shops.

## BATHROOM CLEANERS

Bathroom cleaners are designed to eliminate soap scum and mildew on bathtubs, tiles, showers and grout. It's a good idea to use bathroom cleaners that disinfect—that is, kill germs. Not all bathroom cleaners are disinfectants, so always check the label. In general, these are tough cleaners for a tough job, so wearing rubber gloves is usually a good idea.

**All-purpose cleaners,** such as Orange Power Shower, bath and tile cleaner, or Pine O Cleen Bathroom Power Foam, are the best choice for cleaning the whole bathroom. Look for a product that will attack germs and soap scum at the same time.

**Acidic bathroom cleaners,** such as CLR Bathroom & Kitchen Cleaner, handle everyday cases of soap scum nicely. Cream cleansers also work, but are slightly abrasive and could scratch surfaces, especially stainless steel. First just try white vinegar mixed in equal parts with water. If you need something stronger, pick up phosphoric acid in a 20 per cent concentration from a specialist cleaning supplier. For the worst cases of build-up, use it full strength. Otherwise, dilute it to 2 parts water and 1 part phosphoric acid. Apply with a damp sponge or cloth and then rinse thoroughly.

**Commercial toilet bowl cleaning products** are numerous and widely available. But you may not even need a special cleaner, because bicarbonate of soda or non-chlorine scouring powder will often do the job. Put the bicarbonate of soda or cleaner on a sponge or on the surface you want to clean, then scrub and rinse. To remove stains from toilet bowls, pour in ¼ cup of borax and let it sit for at least 30 minutes—overnight is better. Scrub the bowl well and then flush.

**Bathroom cleaners can be bought** almost anywhere, including supermarkets, home improvement shops, discount retailers and specialist cleaning suppliers.

## BICARBONATE OF SODA

It can't sing and dance, but this venerable white powder is still the most versatile substance around. Bicarbonate of soda is known by various names, including sodium bicarbonate, carb soda, baking soda (in the US) and—for those of you who stayed awake during chemistry lessons—$NaHCO_3$. These non-toxic crystals act as a chemical cleaner, double as a scouring powder, neutralise odours, keep your drains unclogged and are handy for putting out grease or electrical fires. (Sprinkle it on dry.) And bicarbonate of soda is also used in baking.

**The cleaning uses of bicarbonate of soda** are myriad. Here's just a sampling:

- For regular cleaning on hard surfaces, pour a bit of bicarbonate of soda on a damp sponge or cleaning cloth and wipe. Follow up with another clean, damp sponge or cloth to remove any residue.
- To remove surface stains in the kitchen or bath, pour out enough bicarbonate of soda to cover the stain and add just enough water to make a paste. Let the paste stay on the stain for several minutes, then scrub with a sponge and wipe it away.
- To help remove oil and grease stains from clothing, add ½ cup of bicarbonate of soda to the wash.
- To keep your kitchen sink unclogged, pour ½ cup of bicarbonate of soda down the drain each night, followed by warm water. Do the same thing for other drains in your house once a week.

**The odour-killing powers of bicarbonate of soda** are equally famous. There's a good chance you have an open box in the back of your refrigerator right now. Here are a few more dry applications:

- Sprinkle bicarbonate of soda on carpets, rugs and even car mats. Let it stand for 15 minutes and then vacuum it up.
- When you're changing the kitty litter, sprinkle some bicarbonate of soda in the bottom of the cat litter tray and then a little bit more on top of the new kitty litter (unless your brand of kitty litter already includes bicarbonate of soda).
- Pour bicarbonate of soda into ashtrays to control the stench of old cigarette butts.

**Bicarbonate of soda also soaks up odours** when it's dissolved in water. Pour 4 tablespoons of bicarbonate of soda into 1 litre of warm water. Use the solution to:

- Rinse your mouth to get rid of garlic breath.
- Deodorise a stinky plastic container. Fill it with the solution and let it sit overnight.

- Soak a nappy that smells like ammonia because of urine.

**Bicarbonate of soda is readily available** from supermarkets and discount retailers.

## BROOMS

Vacuum cleaners have tended to take away many of the cleaning duties once performed by brooms. But there are still plenty of times when a broom will do a superior job. Besides, they're easier to haul out than a vacuum cleaner and, of course, they don't require electricity.

**Brooms come** in two basic styles:
- Push brooms, with a head measuring 45–120 centimetres wide. These are good for sweeping hard outdoor surfaces, such as garage floors, patios and footpaths.
- Traditional kitchen brooms, with the narrower head. These are better for interior use on hard floors.

**What a broom is made of** is important. While most brooms today have synthetic bristles, there are still plenty available with natural bristles, including corn, straw and horsehair. Flagged bristles are split at the ends to make the bristles thinner and better able to pick up dirt. Non-flagged bristles are thicker and better for sweeping up larger sized particles and rubbish (pebbles, broken glass or china and that sort of thing). Some brooms have both types of bristles—flagged bristles on the outside and non-flagged bristles on the inner row. These brooms can sweep up pebbles and fine dust at the same time. For sweeping inside the house, softer nylon bristles are a much better alternative, because they won't scratch the floor.

**If you store your broom** by standing it on its bristles, the bristles may curl, giving you less than perfect sweeping or brushing action. Therefore, it's better to hang up your broom. Many models come with a loop on the handle for just this purpose. If necessary, drill a hole in the handle and make a loop for it, or use the hole to hang the broom on a nail. There are also broom and mop holders you can attach to a wall for storing.

**The best place to purchase a broom** is from specialist cleaning suppliers, which usually carry a large selection. Supermarkets, hardware shops, discount shops and home improvement shops also sell a variety of brooms.

## BRUSHES

There's a special brush out there for just about anything you'd ever want to give the brush-off—everything from dirt to mildew, barbecue grime to benchtop crumbs. They can be used dry (to remove surface dirt from irregularly shaped objects) or wet (to work in conjunction with cleaners).

Make sure the brush you're using won't damage the object you're attempting to clean. Brush bristles can be made of soft hair, synthetics, natural fibres or metal (most commonly stainless steel or brass).

Brushes fall into the following main categories:

**Kitchen brushes** include these:
- Oven brushes for cleaning the racks and the sides of the oven. (Best on stainless steel ovens; painted enamel and chrome will scratch.)
- Scouring brushes for use on pots and pans.

- Scrubbing brushes for use on floors and grout.
- Benchtop brushes, which originally were used in shops to sweep crumbs from the counter. Now they're typically sold as a set with a dustpan.
- Bottlebrushes, for scrubbing inside tight spaces.

**Floor brushes** include these:
- Hand-held brushes that have stiff bristles.
- Deck brushes (similar to the hand-held brushes, but with poles in them).
- Carpet-spotting brushes (pole-mounted brushes for removing spots on carpets).

**Specialty brushes** include:
- Automotive brushes
- Tile brushes, which are small-headed brushes with fine bristles for cleaning tile and grout
- Window brushes
- Wire brushes for tough jobs, such as cleaning barbecue grills
- Cobweb brushes, with extension handles for reaching the ceiling
- Vacuum cleaner brush attachments, for a gentle touch when you're suctioning up dirt from upholstery or airconditioning vents and the front grilles of appliances that readily trap dust
- Paintbrushes, which can be adapted to cleaning purposes. For instance, they're great for dusting between the pleats of fabric-covered lampshades.

**Personal hygiene and grooming brushes** include:

- Old, used toothbrushes and nail-brushes that you've recruited for other purposes—cleaning around taps, for instance.
- Whisk brushes used for removing lint, dirt and dust from clothing.

**Brushes can be bought** from supermarkets, hardware shops and home improvement shops.

## BUCKETS

You know what a bucket is, of course, but are you sure you know how to use one?

**The problem with buckets** is that they can redistribute dirt and germs on the floor that you're trying to clean. For example, when you mop the bathroom floor, you mop up the grunge, and when you put the mop back into the bucket, the dirt and germs get distributed throughout the water. Then you mop another section of the floor, spreading those germs all around.

**The solution** is to purchase a bucket with two chambers for holding liquid, plus a wringer for squeezing your mop. Rinse water goes in one side of the bucket, and cleaning solution in the other. After the first round of mopping, place the mop in the rinse water and then squeeze it through the wringer to remove the dirt. Then dip the mop back into the cleaning solution and mop some more.

**Two-compartment buckets** typically come on rollers, which help if you hate all that lifting (4 litres of water weighs about 4 kilograms). When you're

purchasing a bucket for mopping floors, make sure it's wide enough for your mop to fit inside, and get one with measurement marks on the inside so you can tell how much water you've poured in.

**You can buy buckets** from supermarkets and discount shops, but for one with two compartments you may have to visit a home improvement shop or a specialist cleaning supplier.

## CADDIES

When it's time to clean, you don't want to waste time tracking down supplies. A sturdy cleaning caddy will hold and organise your cleaning products and cloths, and as is outlined out in Chapter 6 of Part One, it is an essential part of an organised cleaning system. For tips on what supplies to put in your cleaning caddy, see pages 44–45.

**The design of a caddy** is something you need to pay attention to. Look for one that has dividers in it, so you can separate smaller items from larger ones. The individual slots also enable you to separate items you use less frequently, so they will be less likely to fall out when you reach for the cleaners used most often. Caddies with higher side walls also prevent your cleaners from disappearing overboard.

Make sure your caddy has a handle mounted in the centre, and arrange your products so the caddy is well balanced. Spend an extra dollar or two on a caddy with a rubber-coated handle, which is easier to carry when fully loaded.

**The material a caddy is made from** is also important. Avoid wooden caddies, since wet wood will warp and is a breeding ground for mildew. Rubber, vinyl-coated wire or plastic caddies are better alternatives, but avoid cheap, flimsy plastic that will crack.

**Caddies can be bought** from home improvement shops, larger supermarkets and discount retailers.

## CARPET DEEP-CLEANERS

Not too long ago, buying your own deep-cleaning carpet machine was a silly proposition. It was easy to over-wet your carpet with them, running the risk of encouraging mildew and some models didn't heat the water well enough to do a good cleaning job. Some new models have overcome those problems, but you still would be wise to weigh the alternatives before deciding to invest in another vacuum-cleaner-sized appliance that will take up storage space.

**A professional cleaner** is still likely to do a better job of cleaning your carpet than you can do by yourself with a home unit. Then again, you could pay for a home unit with the money you'd spend on a pro for just a visit or two.

**Renting a deep-cleaning unit** is economical, but hauling the gear from the shop back to your house and then back to the shop again is a hassle, and it's hard to know what condition your rental unit will be in until you come to use it.

**If you decide to buy a unit,** shop around to see what you actually need and how much you can afford to pay. The more expensive home machines include such features as dials that automatically adjust the amount of cleaner dispensed based on whether you're cleaning a low- or high-traffic area; an on-board heater that gets the water several degrees hotter than your hot-tap water; a self-propelled feature (if you have a self-propelled lawn mower or vacuum cleaner, you'll appreciate this feature); and a powered hand tool attachment made especially for cleaning small spaces, such as stairwells and around toilets or built-in furniture.

**Deep cleaners work** by forcing a heated cleaning mixture into the carpet, then sucking about 90 per cent of the liquid back out—and with it grime and embedded dirt. (They are sometimes called steam cleaners, but they actually use hot water, not steam.) Even the best vacuum cleaners can't reach the dirt at the base of a carpet, so periodic deep cleaning is important. Every 6–18 months ought to do it. (However, deep cleaning is not a suitable regular treatment for all carpets. One hundred per cent wool carpet can undergo shrinkage, so check with the manufacturer before deciding to use a water treatment.) Deep cleaners come in upright models as well as those squat canisters with a hose attachment.

**Consider storage and manoeuvrability** when shopping for a deep cleaner. The units can weigh up to 10 kilograms and have nozzle widths of up to 35 centimetres for full-sized models.

**Drying time** varies from about 4 to 6 hours, depending on the thickness of the carpet and underlay.

**Carpet deep-cleaners are available** from discount retailers, department stores and home improvement shops.

## CAR POLISHES

There's a big difference between polishing a car and waxing one. Polishing adds brilliance. Wax provides protection. And if you polish your car at least once a month, you'll probably eliminate the need to wax.

**Before you polish,** though, the car must be clean, or you'll rub tiny particles of dirt into the finish and create noticeable scratches. Clean the exterior with car wash solution rather than dishwashing liquid—detergents draw oil out of the car's paint, which accelerates oxidation and makes the paint look cloudy.

After the car has been cleaned and is free of bonded contaminants such as tree sap and insect residue, it's time to polish. The role of polish is to condition and nourish the paint and give the paint finish a deep, wet-look shine.

Done properly, polishing adds brilliance and makes a car as smooth as glass before you wax. The paint is rejuvenated, and unlike the wax build-up you can get from over-waxing, polishing only improves the paint finish with each use.

**The key to proper polishing** is using clean cloths. Have several cloths (100 per cent cotton or microfibre) on hand and constantly rotate the area of cloth you use so you're not pushing the residue you've already removed right back into the paint. When there are no more totally unused areas on the cloth, switch to a clean one.

Another benefit of polish is that if you've just had your car painted and you have been instructed not to wax it for three months, you can still polish, since polish doesn't inhibit the curing process.

**Spray-on polishes** are the easiest to apply, but there are trade-offs: They aren't as good at rejuvenating an oxidised finish, and their shine doesn't tend to last as long.

**Liquid and paste polishes** require more elbow grease, but the effect is more durable. But if the label of a polish tells you to keep the product away from rubber and plastic trim on your car, take heed. Such polishes will leave permanent, unsightly streaks on the trim.

**Car polishes are widely available,** but you'll find the best selection at automotive shops. Even the more specialised or expensive polishes made by industry leaders, such as Meguiar's, are relatively inexpensive and worth investing in.

## CLEANING CLOTHS

Cleaning cloths were once a simple proposition—pull out some clean, 100 per cent cotton rags and get to work. But newer products are improving on the traditional standby, and they score considerable points for effectiveness and ease of use.

**Microfibre cloths** are taking off in the cleaning world, due to interwoven fibres that are ten times finer than silk. They grab and trap dust and pull it off the surface you're cleaning, without scratching. They're great for cleaning computers, CDs and TV screens—any surface that's especially vulnerable to scratching.

**Use microfibre cloths** for dusting and polishing household surfaces, or combine them with cleansers, polishes or water for an unlimited number of household tasks. Because they absorb several times their weight in fluids, they're particularly adept at streak-free cleaning.

**Cleaning microfibre cloths** is easy, too. Shake them out when they're filled with dry dust and machine wash them when they look especially dirty. Also available in mitts, the cloths can be used and washed up to 500 times (lasting about two years under normal use) before losing effectiveness. When washing microfibre cloths, though, avoid using fabric softener or bleach, including softener sheets in the dryer. Also avoid drying them with towels, since lint from the towels will stick to the microfibres. Some microfibres are treated with cleaning solutions and should not be washed, such as microfibre jewellery cleaning cloths that remove tarnish and polish precious metals.

**Cotton cloths** still make great cleaning aids. Old T-shirts are a top choice. Old socks are also handy, because you can wear them like mittens and just use your hands to dust. If you don't want to give up your cotton cloths, just make sure you wash them between uses.

**You can buy microfibre cloths** in supermarkets, home improvement shops and automotive shops. They are more expensive and less widely available than cotton cloths, but compared to one-use disposable wipes, they're very economical.

## DISHWASHERS

When shopping for a dishwasher, the first order of business is finding a model that cleans thoroughly and fits your budget. And since the whole point of a dishwasher is to ease the burden of hand washing, it makes sense to find a model that doesn't require a lot of rinsing of dishes before you load them in.

**Water and energy use** are major considerations when you shop for a dishwasher. Look for features that will reduce water use, such as booster heaters and smart controls. Ask the sales staff how many litres of water the dishwasher uses during different cycles. Dishwashers that use the least amount of water will also cost the least to operate.

With rising water and energy costs, consumers also need to consider the dishwasher's energy rating—the greater number of stars on the efficiency rating sticker, the more energy-efficient (and therefore cost-saving) the appliance.

**The cost of a dishwasher** varies enormously from a basic unit to a sleek, deluxe model that makes no more noise than a pot of boiling water and has adjustable heat settings that can handle everything from fine crystal to the grungiest pots and pans.

**Check a machine's noise level.** Today's open architecture, in which kitchens are connected to family rooms and entertainment areas, increases the importance of finding a model that isn't noisy. Ask the sales staff to explain the decibel level of the unit you're considering. High-end models have a decibel level in the low 40s (about as loud as quiet conversation), while less expensive units are in the middle to high 50s (comparable to the noise in an average office).

**What else do you get with a high-end model?** One of the Rolls Royces of dishwashers is made by Miele Inc., a German company founded in 1900. Each model features three spray arms, which provide more thorough cleaning compared to the one spray arm in less expensive dishwashers. Miele also doesn't have an exposed heating element. This internal heating, as it's called, is more energy efficient and adds to the appliance's longevity (20 years compared to 8 to 10 years for lower cost units). Internal heating provides a greater range of heating temperatures, from a low of about 46 °C for china and crystal to 76 °C for pots and pans. The internal heating feature also prevents the melting of plastic parts

that may fall to the bottom of the dishwasher during a wash cycle.

Design and craftsmanship are other considerations. You'll pay more for a stainless steel model with a cutting edge design and the latest technology.

**Dishwashers are sold** at appliance shops, home improvement shops, discount merchandisers and most department stores.

## DISHWASHING DETERGENTS

You have two choices when it's time to do the dishes: load them into the dishwasher or wash them by hand.

Let's look first at the easier method. Newer dishwasher models (those manufactured in the last five years) tend to work well even if you don't rinse the food off first. And rinsing agents can eliminate the water spots and film that used to make it necessary to rewash some glasses by hand before using.

Automatic dishwashing detergents come in three forms: powdered, gel and tablet. All of them are effective, so let personal preference be your guide.

**Powdered formulas** have been around the longest and are still generally the least expensive to use. The newer products—gels and tablets—offer some added benefits in certain situations, though. Powders can turn to grit if your dishwater doesn't get hot enough (60 °C) to dissolve all the powder.

**Dishwashing gels** dissolve more quickly than powders or tablets and so begin cleaning dishes faster. Gels are also a good choice if you live in a humid climate, where powders have a tendency to cake.

**Tablets** offer the convenience of eliminating the need to measure, since each tablet is formulated to clean one load.

**Rinse products** prevent spotting and filming by lowering the surface tension of the water, causing it to sheet off dishes. They also enable dishes to dry faster when left to air-dry or when you use the energy-saving function on your dishwasher. Rinse agents come in liquid and solid forms. Liquids may be used only in dishwashers with a built-in rinse reservoir. Solid forms are made to attach to the upper dishwasher rack, where they dissolve slowly during the various cycles.

**Hand dishwashing products** are among the gentlest detergents available and can also be used to wash everything from delicate clothing to the family dog. Dishwashing liquids work by loosening grime and suspending it until it can be rinsed away. When the suds disappear, so does the cleaning action, so you'll need to add more detergent. If you buy a cheap brand that gives out quickly, you'll just have to use more, which is not a bargain at all.

**Dishwashing liquid innovations** include hand care ingredients such as vitamin E, aloe vera and aromatherapy-inspired scents added to the liquid.

**Never use hand dishwashing liquid** in your dishwasher, because the suds and foam it produces can inhibit the cleaning process in the machine. Always use automatic dishwashing detergents, which are specially formulated for dishwashers and produce little or no suds.

**Dishwashing detergents are available** from supermarkets and discount retailers.

## DISINFECTANTS

Disinfectants are designed to kill germs on surfaces, including bacteria and viruses that spoil food, create unpleasant odours and cause illness. Some products clean as they disinfect, so read the label if you're looking for a dual-purpose disinfectant. A product that does both will advertise that benefit.

**Disinfectants contain** microbe killers, which show up on the label as pine oil, quaternary ammonium compounds or phenols. Disinfecting cleaners also contain surfactants (surface-active agents) to remove various soils.

**When choosing a disinfectant,** checking the label is especially important. Depending on the formulation and active ingredients, disinfectants may be designed to kill:

- Bacteria that cause intestinal illnesses, such as *E. coli* and salmonella
- Staphylococcus; kinds of bacteria that cause skin infections
- Fungi that cause athlete's foot
- Viruses, such as rhinovirus, which is the most typical cause of the common cold.

**For disinfectants to work,** follow the package instructions to the letter. That usually means letting the disinfectant sit on the soiled surface for at least 10 minutes to kill bacteria. Many people use diluted household chlorine bleach as a disinfectant and stain remover. Make

sure you follow label instructions and dilute accordingly.

It's a good habit to daily clean and disinfect the areas where you prepare food. Moist surfaces, such as sinks and toilets, are also germ breeding grounds and should also be cleaned daily if someone in the family is sick or especially vulnerable to infection.

**Be careful not to reinfect an area** you've just cleaned by using a dirty cloth or sponge. If you clean a surface with disinfectant but then wipe with a contaminated cloth, you're simply redepositing germs on the clean surface. Some people prefer using paper towels after disinfecting, since you throw away the contaminants. Paper towels are a more expensive way to clean, though. Cloths and sponges work as well, if not better, as long as you launder them with chlorine bleach and allow them to dry thoroughly between uses.

**Disinfectants are available** from supermarkets, home improvement shops and discount retailers.

## DISPOSABLE WIPES

Disposable wipes have taken the cleaning world by storm in recent years, generating the most growth in the household cleaning marketplace because of their convenience.

**The appeal of disposable wipes** is understandable. In terms of convenience, it's hard to beat a pre-treated product that you toss after a single use. The popularity of wipes is driven by what's known as the three E's of consumer product value—they're effective, efficient and expedient.

**Some of the latest wipe products** include these:

- Disposable cloths treated with dishwashing liquid—you simply add water for a sudsy cleaning cloth.
- Specialty wipes for disinfecting surfaces such as toilets, sinks and benchtops. (In such cases, disposing of germs along with the cleaning cloth is an attractive feature.)
- Furniture wipes to clean and shine wood.
- Both dry and pre-moistened floor wipes, which are attached to easy-to-use floor sweepers and specially designed mops.

**Dry disposable wipes** rely on an electrostatic charge to attract dust. Disposable mitts, also electrostatically charged, make quick work of dusting surfaces like wood, ceramic and vinyl. The dust sticks to the mitt instead of becoming airborne.

**Disposable wipes are widely available** from supermarkets, home improvement shops and discount retailers. Obviously, it's more expensive to use a disposable wipe that lasts for only one use. But if you're a convenience-driven consumer, you'll probably think it's worth the price you pay.

## DRAIN CLEANERS

Drain cleaners come in four varieties—acids, alkalis, oxidisers and enzymatics—and their job is to get rid of blockages in drains, most commonly in kitchens and bathrooms.

Compared to mechanical drain cleaners, chemical and enzymatic cleaners are easy to use, but chemical cleaners also have the potential to harm the user if instructions aren't followed exactly. Enzymatic cleaners have a slower, biological reaction and therefore are more safe to use than chemical cleaners.

**Acids and alkalis** are the most popular of the drain cleaners for removing blockages of hair, grease, soap and other wastes. Some of these drain cleaners, particularly the faster-acting ones, cause bubbling that can splash harmful chemicals back out of the drain. So stand back once you've poured the drain opener in. Never use muriatic acid (a dilute form of hydrochloric acid) to clear drain blocks. It's a highly dangerous substance.

**Oxidisers** are effective on organic blockages. These chemicals react with and combine with the blocking material, breaking it up and disintegrating it (rather than dissolving it).

The majority of commercial cleaners, such as Drano, are a combination of caustic (alkaline) and oxidising components, meaning the cleaners work in two ways.

**Enzymatic drain cleaners** are slower-acting as they consume or digest waste blockages, but they're easier on your pipes than acids, caustics and oxidisers (which is more of a concern with old plumbing). They're also thought to do less harm to septic systems.

**Prevent drain clog-ups** in your kitchen sink with this once-a-month treatment using household products: pour 1 cup of bicarbonate of soda around the kitchen sink drain opening. Rinse the bicarbonate of soda into the drain with 1 cup of hydrogen peroxide. The bubbling and fizzing action helps to clear away the residue clinging to your pipes.

**Drain cleaners are available** from a variety of places—supermarkets, discount shops, hardware shops, home improvement shops and plumbing supply shops.

## DUSTERS

Feather dusters and lamb's wool dusters have taken a back seat these days to microfibre dusters, which can get into cracks and crevices, attracting soil and speeding your dusting chores.

**Microfibre dusters** are the cutting edge in technology. Their interwoven fibres are ten times finer than silk, making them good at snagging dust without scratching. For dusting, washing or spot cleaning, microfibre dusters are easy to use and their heads can be removed and tossed in the washing machine when you're done. (But don't use bleach or fabric softener to wash them.)

**Feather dusters,** on the other hand, may still have their place in your broom cupboard. While feather dusters have a reputation for just spreading dust around the room, they are great for dusting in hard-to-reach areas, such as inside a lamp, in the pleats of a fabric lampshade and in the corners of ceilings where cobwebs collect. Feather dusters blow the dust off the object you're cleaning, allowing you to then vacuum or wipe the dust up.

**Lamb's wool** creates a lot of static, which attracts dust. These dusters are typically good on skirting boards, ceilings, ceiling fans and blinds. Lamb's wool is not a good choice for objects that are heavily blanketed with dust.

**Dusters are available** from supermarkets and cleaning suppliers.

## DUSTPANS

The marrying of dustpan and broom is a match that goes back 100 years, and it's still popular today. Dustpans are useful little household tools consisting of a flat pan with a tapered edge and a handle. You use a small brush, or 'broom', to sweep dust and debris into the pan.

**Get a plastic dustpan.** Originally constructed of heavy metal, dustpans came with a brush about 30 centimetres long with 5–7 centimetre-long natural bristles. Today's dustpans are usually plastic or rubber vinyl with plastic handles and acrylic brushes. Soft plastic dustpans are popular because they won't break, so if you drop them no damage is done—to the pan or the floor. If you drop a metal pan, it can scratch your floor's finish, and the pan's edges may bend or curl. Plastic dustpans won't rust, either.

**A tight pan-to-floor seal** is important. Dustpans often have a rubber, tapered edge to create a tight seal with the floor so dust won't go underneath the pan when you brush dirt into it. Some other styles have a plastic edge. Both types work well, but the rubber edge may not last as long as the plastic.

Even with a good pan-to-floor seal, it's doubtful you'll be able to collect all floor dirt with a single sweep. Even if no dirt escapes under the dustpan's edge, the finest dirt often collects in a line along the edge. This is easily remedied by sweeping, moving your dustpan back a few centimetres and then sweeping again.

**Use dustpans indoors and out,** although you might want to have one for each area. It's not a good idea to put a dirty outdoor dustpan down on a clean indoor floor. Dustpans for outdoors are larger, with pans available in metal or plastic.

**You can buy dustpans** from supermarkets, hardware shops, convenience stores and home improvement shops. If you prefer to have a dustpan on a long handle, try a specialist cleaning supplier. Dustpans often come with a hand-held broom, but if yours doesn't, make sure the broom you buy is shorter than the width of the dustpan, so you won't be sweeping dust around the sides of the pan instead of into it.

## ENZYME DIGESTERS

Although you might not have heard of them, enzyme digesters are chemicals, created by micro-organisms, that eat away organic matter. So they're effective on organic stains—in other words, such unpleasant things as urine, vomit, faecal matter, protein stains and the equally unpleasant odours that are associated with those things.

**Use enzymes** around the toilet and flooring to keep your bathroom smelling fresh by digesting soil, spills, bodily oils and bacteria. You'll also find enzymes in drain openers and in carpet, upholstery and laundry products. Enzymes are safe for septic systems and can also be used in garbage disposal drains. Enzymes are temperature sensitive, so don't use them with hot water. Disinfectants will also render them ineffective. Once you open an enzyme digester, it has a short shelf life.

**Enzyme digesters come** as a powder that you activate with warm water, triggering their eating frenzy on organic matter. If you've ever cleaned spilled milk from a carpet, only to have the odour return days later, you need to use an enzyme product. Most cleaners mask the odour but don't remove the organic source of the stain.

**When treating a carpet stain** with an enzyme cleaner, first soak up as much of the stain as possible with old bath towels. (Use a wet vac if there's a lot of volume.) Apply the enzyme according to the package instructions. Pour it over the stain and make sure the enzyme penetrates to the underlay. If it doesn't, you're wasting your time—the stain and odour will remain. Keep the carpet wet while the enzyme is 'eating' the stain. It's a good idea to cover the area with plastic and place weights on the edges until the recommended time is up. Then rinse with ½ cup of distilled white vinegar per 4 litres of water. Rinse a second time with plain water.

**Enzyme digesters make a great laundry pre-soak** that eats away at organic stains before you run garments through the wash. Use warm water in the soak, according to the package instructions (the exception being blood, which requires cold water). But be careful, as enzymes will eat away at animal fibres, including silk and wool.

**To purchase enzyme products,** pet shops and your local vet are your best bet, or you could ask at a plumbing supply shop, as enzymes are often used to help regulate a smelly septic tank. You can also try typing 'enzyme digesters' into your search engine on the web, as a number of these products can be bought in domestic quantities by Internet mail order.

## FLOOR-CARE PRODUCTS

Floor cleaners, polishes and finishes are not interchangeable. Floor cleaners, as the term implies, remove dirt. Floor polishes remove scratches because they're slightly abrasive. And floor finishes finish the job—they seal and protect the cleaned surface. While some people call the finishing stage 'waxing', real wax isn't used anymore on the most popular kinds of modern flooring. Various polymers have replaced it.

**What does your floor's manufacturer recommend?** Each manufacturer has recommendations for cleaning and protecting their products, so always check the manufacturer's instructions and follow them. As a general rule, you want to remove all dirt from your floor before you apply the appropriate protective finish. Otherwise, you'll end up with a shiny, dirty floor. If you don't have the cleaning instructions from the manufacturer, here is a general rundown of the products you'll need. Always read any product's label to make sure it's OK for the floor you're working on.

**For vinyl floors,** start by cleaning with a mild detergent or all-purpose cleaner such as Handy Andy. After rinsing, apply a water-based floor polish and finish according to the package instructions. You can find one-step, clean-and-polish products, but you probably won't be as happy with the results. This same approach works for asphalt and rubber flooring. Solvent-based paste wax will also shine vinyl flooring (it requires buffing) but shouldn't be used on asphalt or rubber.

**For wood floors,** a commercial product such as Pledge Wood Magic will do nicely on a modern polyurethane finish. Floors with an old-fashioned lacquer, varnish or shellac finish need the protection of wax, such as Durosil Paste Wax. Some waxes are designed to clean and wax floors of a particular hardwood colour, so check the label.

**For ceramic tile floors,** a general household cleaner such as Handy Andy will do a good job. Specialised tile-cleaning products also are available. Avoid abrasive cleaners. Grout is easier to clean when it has been treated with a silicone sealer.

**Floor-care products are available** from supermarkets, home improvement shops, hardware shops or specialist cleaning suppliers.

## FURNITURE WAXES AND POLISHES

When you apply a wax or polish to your wood furniture, you're not beautifying the wood itself—you're beautifying the finish on the wood. Use either polish or wax—not both. If you put polish on wax, it will just puddle. Polishes don't offer as much protection as wax—they're meant to be a quick way to put sparkle in a dull-looking finish.

**Furniture waxes**—be they paste or liquid—are made from combinations of synthetic and natural waxes. The synthetic element is paraffin, distilled from petroleum and other sources. The natural elements include beeswax and carnauba, a vegetable extract. Avoid waxes that contain toluene, a solvent that has a paint-thinner smell.

**The way wax works** is to provide a barrier against moisture seeping into the wood of your furniture. This barrier also speeds your cleaning because you'll be able to remove marks and dust more easily. Before you wax, check the manufacturer's instructions. Generally, gloss or semi-gloss furniture can be waxed. If your furniture has a satin or flat finish, wax may give it a random, messy-looking sheen.

**To apply wax,** rub it on thinly with a clean, cotton cloth. Then let it sit for several minutes (check the label for precise timing), then buff it with another clean cloth.

**When you choose a wax,** consider your furniture's colour. If you have light furniture, pick a neutral tone; for mahogany, use clear or a reddish brown wax for richness; for cherry, use walnut or brown; for oak, use a chocolate brown to yellow. For pine furniture that doesn't have much of a finish, beeswax on its own is a good choice; after buffing, it produces a unique soft glow.

**Furniture polishes** often contain paraffin (mineral oil); mineral spirits, such as turpentine; perfume (scents such as lemon or orange oil); and dye, to give them the colour of lemon or orange. Not all furniture polishes use mineral spirits, which thins the paraffin to make the polish easier to use.

**Common paraffin-based polishes,** such as Clean 'N Shine and O'Cedar, are sold in bottles or aerosol cans and are easy to apply. However, some experts frown on polishes, saying they collect dust and create a dirt-and-oil mix on the furniture being polished.

**Polishes that act as revivers** contain fine abrasive pumice in the polish formula and don't contain paraffin. They clean and protect the surface and are really more like a wax than a polish.

**Polishes that contain silicone** produce a nice shine but can make refinishing the furniture more difficult in the future. Look for products that say they're silicone-free (Clean 'N Shine or Kiwi Marveer, for instance).

**Waxes and polishes can be bought** wherever cleaning products are sold—supermarkets, discount shops, hardware shops and home improvement shops.

## GARBAGE BAGS

Splits in clothing can be hard to handle, but splits in garbage bags are another story altogether. These polyethylene bags for garbage are not exactly complex equipment. Still, there are a number of features to consider.

**Pay attention to thickness** if you want a bag that won't split under a heavy load. Thickness is measured in millimetres. Heavy-lifting bags are 2.5–3 millimetres thick. The plastic bags you haul home from the supermarket are, by comparison, only about 0.5–1 millimetre thick.

**Think colour.** Garbage bags advertised for kitchen use are usually white and are 0.5 millimetres or less in thickness. White bags make the appearance of cleanliness and freshness. Dark-coloured bags, 1.5–3 millimetres thick, are designed for outdoor or commercial use. For cost-saving reasons, garbage bags used in commercial settings are generally reused (after their contents are poured into a master garbage container) until they start to smell or stains become noticeable.

**The bags' tying method** is also something to consider. Some bags have built-in drawstring ties. These bags cost a little more but make a neat, quick fastener. Other bags have plastic, notched wrap fasteners or twist ties like those that secure freezer bags. These bags often come on a roll and are torn off along a perforated line. Still other bags have a handle cut out of the bag. The bags that tend to cost the least have no tie at all; you have to secure them by making a knot with the top edge of the bag.

**If you have to tie your own garbage bag,** make simple overlapping knots, as commercial cleaners do. Pull the garbage bag from the bin and shake the contents so they settle to the bottom. Next, take one corner with the left hand and the opposite one with the right hand, pull the corners to the centre and tie a tight reef knot across the top of the garbage. Then take the other two opposing corners and tie a second reef knot. These right-over-left and left-over-right knots allow you to pick up the bag and carry it without spilling the contents.

**Garbage bags are readily available** from supermarkets and discount shops. Thick garbage bags can be bought from home improvement shops, specialist cleaning suppliers and hardware shops.

## GLASS CLEANERS

Commercial glass cleaners contain either ammonia or alcohol. They clean dirt, smears and grease and can be used on surfaces other than glass, such as Formica and laminate—but not on Corian or marble.

**The composition of a glass cleaner,** such as Windex, is a mix of ingredients: detergents or surfactants to dissolve dirt and grime; fragrances; ammonia, an alkaline cleaner; colouring; alcohol, to remove filmy residues and prevent streaks; and solvents, to dissolve oily films.

**Choose a glass cleaner** that does not contain phosphorus, which has a tendency to smear glass. Those popular citrus cleaners may not be the best choice for your home's windows either, since they often contain a solvent called limonene, which can damage wood and vinyl frames. Some glass cleaners are formulated specifically to prevent dripping.

**Homemade glass cleaners** are not only cheap and effective but are also easy to put together. Here are two such concoctions:

- For general cleaning, in a bucket mix 2 squirts of a mild dishwashing liquid (preferably one that does not contain phosphorus), ½ cup of methylated spirits and 4 litres of warm water.
- For cleaning up smeary glass, in a 1 litre spray bottle mix ⅓ cup of distilled white vinegar, ¼ cup of methylated spirits and enough distilled water to fill the bottle.

**When you're using glass cleaners** to actually clean glass, do it in the morning or early evening—not during the day, when the sun's rays will be heating the glass. Hot glass causes whatever window cleaner you're using to dry quickly, and you're more likely to have a problem with streaking.

**Glass cleaners are available** from supermarkets, discount shops, hardware shops and home improvement shops. Home improvement shops also sell money-saving concentrates.

## HYDROGEN PEROXIDE

Hydrogen peroxide is an oxidising agent, similar to bleach, that removes colour and sanitises surfaces. Many products that promise to brighten or whiten clothes contain hydrogen peroxide. Use it with care. Peroxide is made of two parts hydrogen and two parts oxygen, and it's the extra oxygen molecule that turns plain water into a potent oxidiser. You can purchase hydrogen peroxide in concentrations ranging from 3 per cent to 50 per cent.

**Peroxide is a germ killer** as well as a substitute for bleach. It's a potent enemy of salmonella and *E. coli* bacteria. To kill these germs, spray 3 per cent hydrogen peroxide on a benchtop or chopping board, for example, followed by a squirt of white distilled vinegar. Then rinse with fresh water.

Other uses for hydrogen peroxide abound. Here are a few examples:

**For removing carpet stains,** 3 per cent hydrogen peroxide is a good choice. Pour the peroxide on the spot, wait 30 minutes, then blot it up with paper towels. Rinse with ¼ cup of white vinegar mixed with 1 litre of water, blot, rinse again with plain water and blot once more. Test on an inconspicuous spot first.

**To fight mould in bathrooms,** 30 or 35 per cent peroxide, mixed 50:50 with water, is effective. Spray it on, wait an hour and spray again. Don't rinse. If mould remains, spray again in two days. Don't use hydrogen peroxide on coloured grout.

**Brighten your laundry whites** by adding ½ cup of 30 per cent peroxide, 2 cups of 3 per cent peroxide or 1 cup of 6 per cent peroxide to your wash.

**To remove yellow underarm stains,** pour 3 per cent peroxide directly on the stain, let it sit for several hours and then rinse.

**Remove red dye stains** caused by ice-blocks, punch or cordial with 3 per cent peroxide poured directly on the spot. Wait for 30 minutes and then rinse thoroughly.

**You can buy** 3 per cent hydrogen peroxide in some supermarkets and pharmacies. Beauty salons and pharmacies carry 6 per cent peroxide, medical supply shops sell 30 per cent and health food shops carry both 35 per cent and 50 per cent, which is considered food grade.

## METAL POLISHES

Commercial metal polishes remove tarnish (oxidation) and create a burnish, or shine, when you apply some elbow grease. Read labels to find a polish suited to the specific metal you want to clean up. (You won't be as happy with a general-purpose metal polish.) Metal polishes typically do their job through mild abrasion combined with chemical cleaners.

**Metal polishes come** in liquids and creams. Convenient polishing cloths that are lightly saturated with polish are also available.

**How often you polish** an item depends on how often the item is handled. Every time you handle a metal piece, you transfer acid from your hands to the item, which translates into oxidation.

**To apply polish,** use a cotton T-shirt or lint-free cotton cloth. Then use a terry towelling cloth to remove any excess and a microfibre cloth to buff the polish on the metal. Make sure you remove as much of the residue of the polish as possible afterwards, as the chemicals can damage metals over time. To reach nooks and crannies, use an old toothbrush. Some metal polishes contain strong chemicals, so always wear rubber gloves and work in a well-ventilated area.

**Metal polishes are available** from hardware shops, supermarkets, home improvement shops and specialist cleaning suppliers.

## MOPS

Back in simpler times, mops came in two varieties—string or sponge. Now the choices include sponge, cotton string, terry towelling, disposable towelettes (electrostatic or pre-moistened), and microfibre.

**Mops are used** to clean floors in two ways—dry-mopping or wet-mopping. To dry-mop, microfibre mops and the disposables (Swiffer, for instance) are good choices because they easily snag dirt and dust. If you have heavier or coarser dirt near entrances, you may need to do a quick sweep first with a dustpan and broom. To remove dried-on grime from a surface, wet-mopping is the way to go.

Here's a rundown on the five types of mops:

**Cellulose sponge mops** are made from open-cell foam and are good at cleaning vinyl floor coverings. To use a cellulose sponge mop, dip it in a bucket of floor cleaner and warm water, wring out the excess moisture and then start mopping. A sponge mop is also good for stripping and waxing a vinyl floor, but not for use on hardwood or marble flooring. The head of your sponge mop will need to be replaced—how often depends on frequency of use.

**String mops** are usually 100 per cent cotton (although some contain polyester), with strings 30–45 centimetres long. In 1893, Thomas Stewart, an American, patented a string mop with a clamping mechanism worked by a lever to wring out water. Today's string mops can be used indoors or outdoors. They're good for cleaning garage floors and decks, tile and linoleum floors, and uneven surfaces of granite flooring. But string mops are not the ideal choice for hardwood or marble floors, because they hold a lot of moisture, which can damage those surfaces. You can extend the life of the mop by machine washing and drying the cotton head, if your mop has a removable head.

**Towel mops** use ordinary terry towelling cloth secured with a holding device. Towel mops can be used wet on all floors, you can replace the towels easily when they become soiled, and you can wash and dry them. Among the many towels on the market, the heavy-duty hand towels will give you the best results. In addition to floor cleaning, you can use towel mops to dust cobwebs and clean ceilings.

**Disposable towelette mops** are a recent arrival on the market. They're available dry or with pre-moistened disposable pads or wipes. Just place them on the swivel head and start mopping. When the towelette is soiled, replace it with a fresh one. Some models come with a spray bottle that holds cleaning fluid. You simply pull a trigger on the handle and the cleaner is sprayed on the floor in front of the mop. These mops are convenient and easy to use, but the replacement towels can be expensive.

**Microfibre mops** are another relatively new thing. They are made of microscopic synthetic fibres that act as hooks to latch on to dust, dirt and grime. They can hold several times their weight in water. The fibres are lint free and non-abrasive. The lightweight mops can be used on all floor types. To use the mop, dip the microfibre head into the cleaning solution and wring it by hand, leaving it damp. Wipe the floor, but don't put the mop back in the bucket. Change the mop head after mopping each room.

Microfibre mops use far less water and cleaning solution than conventional mops because the mop head is changed frequently. Four litres of cleaner-and-water solution can clean up to 22 rooms. Although microfibre mop heads cost more and have to be laundered separately from other rags, they last for years and prove cost-effective over time.

**When buying a mop,** you can pick up a sponge, string or disposable towelette model from most supermarkets, discount retailers, hardware shops and home improvement shops. Terry towelling mops are available from department stores, discount retailers and home improvement shops. Microfibre mops are available from discount retailers, some supermarkets and specialist cleaning suppliers.

## OILS

Oils used on natural wood surfaces or leather make them look healthy. Most oils for wood or leather are extracted naturally from animals, seeds or the peel of citrus fruits. Oils should never be used on stone, which is porous and will absorb the oil, producing dark spots in the stone. If you want to use oil on wood or leather, test it first on an inconspicuous spot. Some commonly used oils are listed below.

**Citrus oil (orange, lemon and grapefruit),** such as Howard Orange Oil Cleaner and Polish, will help restore the finish on wood that has been neglected or has faded. Citrus oil penetrates to moisturise and condition wood. They are often combined with a chemical cleaner. Apply lightly, putting the oil on a cloth and then wiping onto the furniture or woodwork. Oil has a tendency to streak if you apply too much. Wait for about 30 minutes for the oil to dry.

**Pine oil** is a general cleaner and disinfectant for floors, benchtops and bathrooms. It comes from the turpentine family and has a distinct aroma. To use, dilute it in a spray bottle or in mop water according to the package instructions.

**Tung oil and linseed oil** are good for natural wood, tabletops, wood panelling and wooden floors. Some brands have dyes in them, so they act like a stain. Linseed oil is also good for protecting outdoor furniture. Both tung oil and linseed oil can combust spontaneously, so be very careful not to leave oil-soaked rags lying around the house or in a garbage bag. Hang oily rags outside to dry thoroughly before you dispose of them in an outdoor garbage bin. Or dispose of them in a sealed metal container outside in a shady spot.

**Neat's-foot oil,** which is a light yellow colour, is obtained from the feet and shinbones of cattle. It's a great conditioner for leather (boots, saddles and those sorts of things), keeping the leather soft.

**To use an oil,** apply it with a cloth, let it soak in for about 5 to 10 minutes and buff or polish it dry, using circular motions. Cotton towels, nappies or old T-shirts are great for this job.

**You can buy** citrus oil and pine oil products anywhere home supplies are sold—supermarkets, hardware shops, home improvement shops and discount retailers. Tung oil and linseed oil are available from specialist cleaning suppliers and hardware shops. Neat's-foot oil is available from saddleries, hardware shops, shops that sell leather goods, and shoe repair shops.

## OVEN CLEANERS

These are among the strongest—and most toxic—cleaners available to home owners. Most contain a strong cleaning alkali, usually sodium hydroxide or potassium hydroxide. This caustic soda, or lye, converts fats to soapy, water-soluble compounds that wipe away easily.

**Oven cleaners come** in aerosol sprays, liquids, pastes and powders and are usually thick so that they can stick on the vertical walls of an oven. They are toxic and can cause deep burns and blindness if they come into contact with skin or eyes. If swallowed, oven cleaners can be fatal. Don't use oven cleaners on self-cleaning ovens, which break down fats and other food with high heat instead of chemicals.

**Take care with all oven cleaners.** Wear rubber gloves and protective goggles and work in a well-ventilated area. Never spray commercial oven cleaner on a hot oven, electric elements or oven lights—heat can make it even more caustic.

**Oven cleaners are available** from supermarkets and discount retailers.

## PAPER TOWELS

Professional cleaners use paper only for quick clean-ups, such as emergency spills. It would be a major waste of trees to go through an entire roll of paper towels cleaning a bathroom, for instance. And since paper towels are major lint producers, they leave behind a paper trail on mirrors and windows, and whenever you attempt any serious scrubbing with them.

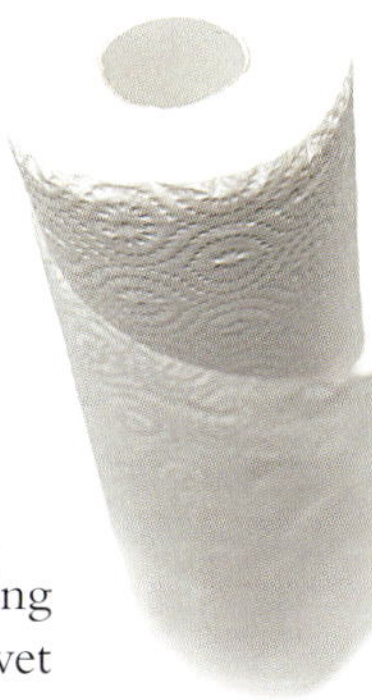

**For emergency or messy wipe-ups,** paper towels are a great convenience, but they've got to be within arm's reach to be truly convenient. Keep paper towels around for juice spills, pet accidents and wiping up anything (such as wet paint or cooking grease) that might ruin a rag or ruin anything in the same washing load with it. Keep a roll in the kitchen, another in the garage or shed (they're great for wiping oil and grease off hands), and another in the laundry for bleach and liquid detergent spills.

**Paper towels are available** from supermarkets and discount retailers. As long as you've got the room to store them, buy in bulk to save money. They won't go off, and you'll eventually use them. And skip the decorative prints, since the printing inks can occasionally bleed, which means you'll have yet another stain to remove.

## RUBBER GLOVES

When it comes to household cleaning, safety is essential. Gloves are important for protecting your hands when using harsh cleaning chemicals or working with hot water. In addition to protecting your hands from injury, gloves help to keep hands soft and smooth.

**When selecting protective gloves,** you can get ones made of either rubber or soft plastic polymers. The level of protection depends on how permeable they are, which typically depends on thickness. The thicker the glove, the more protection it provides.

- For general household use, standard latex washing-up gloves are fine. (Choose a latex substitute if you are allergic to latex.)
- For using paint strippers and solvents, you'll need a thicker glove. The thicker the glove, however, the bulkier and clumsier it will be.

**Replace gloves** before they wear out and can't protect you. Signs that suggest your gloves need replacing include staining or colour change; softening, swelling or bubbling; stiffening or cracking; and, of course, leaking as a result of puncture.

**Disposable gloves** are available in bulk containers. If you reuse your disposable gloves, make sure you wash them well with warm, soapy water. Let the outside dry and then reverse them, letting the inside dry. When the inside is dry, turn them right side out again and sprinkle a little bit of talcum powder inside them to stop the rubber sticking.

**Rubber gloves are available** from supermarkets, discount shops, hardware shops and home improvement shops.

## SEALANTS

Grime is toughest to remove when it gets a foothold in most materials. When things like food spills and mildew get lodged in the fibres of a sofa cushion, the grains of wood in a deck, or the pores of ceramic tile grout, they can remain there permanently. To prevent grime from taking up long-time residence, scientists have devised sealants—for textiles, grout, wood, brick and concrete—to block pores, making surfaces less susceptible to staining and easier to wipe clean.

**Fabric sealants** come in two varieties—fluorochemical sealants, such as Scotchgard and Teflon, and silicone sealants. Silicone sealants work only against water-based spills, such as juices; any spill containing oil can penetrate the sealant. Silicone sealants can even trap oily stains, making them harder to remove. Some upholstery comes presealed. If the sealant wears off, reapply it or have a professional reapply it. Before reapplying a fabric sealant, be sure to clean the fabric well and remove all cleaning residue. Otherwise the sealant will not bond properly.

**Brick and concrete floor sealants,** like fabric sealants, add a protective layer to floors, making cleaning easier. Always clean and prepare a floor surface well before applying a sealer. Reapply when signs of wear appear.

**Wood sealants** also protect against scratching and water damage. They come in the following varieties:

- Penetrating sealers seep into the grain of the wood and keep dust and dirt from doing the same.
- Surface coating sealers—polyurethanes, shellacs and varnishes—form a protective layer over the wood surface. The most popular surface sealant is polyurethane, which is durable and relatively easy to use. Polyurethane sealers are either oil- or water-based, and they come in a variety of finishes, from matte to high gloss.

**Grout sealants** combat what has traditionally been one of the toughest things in the house to clean. This sealant, available from homeware and hardware shops, is easily applied with a sponge paintbrush and prevents oil, dirt and mildew from staining grout lines.

**Fabric sealants are available** from supermarkets, discount shops and shops that sell carpets and soft furnishings, as well as through professional cleaning companies. Sealants for hard surfaces are available from hardware, paint and home improvement shops.

## SOAP

Apart from plain water, soap may be the oldest known cleaner. During the excavation of ancient Babylon, archaeologists found a soaplike material in clay cylinders dating back to 2900 BC. According to ancient Roman legend, soap got its name from Mount Sapo, a place of animal sacrifice. Rain mixed the melted animal fat with wood ashes and washed it down to the clay soil along the Tiber River, where women washed clothes. The women found that the mixture removed soil from clothes far better and more easily than plain water.

**The way soap is made** has not changed since then. Animal or vegetable fats are still treated with a strong alkali, such as sodium or potassium. Soap differs from detergent, which is a synthetic product, first made in 1916 in response to a shortage of soap-making fats. Both contain 'surface-active' agents, or surfactants, which reduce the surface tension of water and soil, in effect loosening the soil, dispersing it in water and holding it in suspension until it can be rinsed away.

**Soap is used** these days almost solely for personal skin and body care. In most other cleaning endeavours, synthetic detergents have almost completely replaced natural soaps, especially for washing dishes and clothes by machine. In hard water, soap is not as effective as detergent, and it forms a curd or soap scum that can ruin clothes and stain tubs and sinks.

**Don't use soap on tannin stains,** such as ones produced by coffee, fruit or jam, if you can avoid it. Soap tends to make the stain harder to remove.

**Soap is widely available** from supermarkets, pharmacies, department stores and discount shops.

## SOLVENTS

Water is the universal solvent, since it can be used to dissolve many different substances, from dirt to blood to certain paints. In cleaning terminology, however, solvent refers to liquids other than water that are used to dissolve things water can't dissolve. Water can't dissolve grease, for instance. Working on the principle that 'like dissolves like', you'd need a non-water-based solvent, such as mineral turpentine, to dissolve grease.

**Common cleaning solvents** include acetone (found in many nail-polish removers), methylated spirits and eucalyptus oil, as well as petroleum-based chemicals, such as mineral turpentine, naphtha, kerosene and dry-cleaning fluids.

**Cleaning uses for solvents** typically include removing greasy or oily substances, cleaning materials that can be harmed by water (for instance, spot-cleaning dry-clean-only fabrics), and removing special finishes, such as decals, wood finishes, oil-based paint and waxes.

**Solvents are a last resort,** to be used for the few things that water and detergent won't clean. Solvents tend to be strong, aggressive cleaners. Although many solvents can be dangerous to inhale and dangerous if they make contact with your skin or eyes, they vary in their degree of toxicity.

**Always take safety precautions** when using solvents.

- Solvents are highly flammable. Never use them near open flames, including pilot lights and sparks.
- Always ventilate the area in which you are working.

- Wear the proper gear, including chemical-resistant gloves, long-sleeved shirts and long pants, protective eyewear and, depending on the solvent, a ventilator.

**Solvents are widely available** from hardware and home improvement shops.

## SPONGES

Household cleaning sponges, typically made of cellulose, are great for absorbing liquids, and they hold lots of cleaning solution. For that reason, sponges are fast and efficient cleaning tools. But they are also a breeding ground for bacteria. The key to using sponges is to understand their limitations and to avoid cross-contamination.

**Plain cellulose sponges** are well suited to bathrooms, where being able to wipe moisture off walls, benchtops, basins, bathtubs and showers is handy. But keep them in the bathroom. Don't use the bathroom sponge in the kitchen, where germs can spread. Don't use a toilet sponge on the benchtop where you store your toothbrush. Let a sponge dry between each use. Throw sponges away after a few weeks.

**Abrasive kitchen sponges** are designed for dishwashing. These might be wrapped in a lightly abrasive mesh or backed by more heavily abrasive scrubbing pads. Use common sense when cleaning with sponge abrasives. They will scratch Teflon-coated pots and pans, stainless steel sinks, benchtops and the like. And kitchen sponges are just as apt to provide a breeding ground for bacteria. Keep them as clean as possible and throw them out after a few weeks of use. Even if you don't use sponges on a regular basis, keep them around for spills.

**Natural sponges**—the brown, irregularly round ones—have been used for thousands of years for bathing and household cleaning. Although synthetic sponges, introduced in the 1940s, now have the lion's share of the market, natural sponges are still used for bathing, cleaning and a number of industrial applications ranging from printing to surgery.

A natural sponge is actually the skeleton of a sea animal. There are more than 2000 species of sponge in the ocean, but these three are mainly used commercially:

- Sheep's wool or sea wool sponge: the softest, longest lasting and most absorbent type of sponge.
- Yellow sponge, which is a slightly stiffer variety.
- Grass sponge, which has finer pores and is more delicate.

Natural sponges are considered a renewable resource. They can regenerate themselves from fragments. When divers harvest them off the sea floor, they're careful to leave the root so that the sponge has the chance to regrow.

**Disinfecting your kitchen sponges** regularly is important. Moist sponges are notorious for harbouring bacteria. You may think you're cleaning, but you're really slathering a layer of germs all over your sink, benchtops, appliances and kitchen table with that infected sponge. Here are three ways to disinfect those squishy sponges. First, rinse your sponges completely to remove any food particles. Then do one of the following:

- Toss them into the top rack of your dishwasher.
- Put them in a microwave oven for 30 seconds. (Careful—they get hot.)
- Pour 4 litres of water into the kitchen sink, add ¾ cup of chlorine bleach and soak your sponges for about 10 minutes.

**Sponges are widely available** from supermarkets, discount shops and home improvement shops—the cellulose variety, that is. For natural sponges, try at paint, hardware, home improvement and bath and beauty shops.

## SPOT REMOVERS

The supermarket shelves are lined with spot and stain removers. While the number of different ingredients in spot removers is mind-boggling, these products basically fall into two main categories—wet and dry.

**Wet spot removers** are water soluble. These typically contain a concentrated laundry detergent and work best on food stains, such as drink spills and tomato sauce. But some wet spot removers also contain secondary solvents, such as alcohol and mineral spirits, to boost their stain-removal power and make them more effective on greasy stains.

**Dry spot removers** contain chemical solvents, including some that drycleaners use. (Liquid is still involved. The 'dry' part means that water isn't used.) These are best for dry-clean-only fabrics as well as greasy or oily stains.

**Carpet and upholstery spot removers** are specially designed for use on those materials. They are sometimes foamy, since low-moisture vacuumable foams are typically better for textiles with pads or cushions beneath.

**A word of caution:** Make sure you always use the right spot removal product for the right job. To make sure the material you're cleaning is colour-fast, pre-test the product in an inconspicuous corner or seam. Always follow the manufacturer's instructions carefully.

**Spot removers are widely available** from supermarkets and discount shops.

## SPRAY BOTTLES

Spray bottles can be time- and money-savers. Not only do they allow you to mix your own cleaning solutions—or buy bulk containers of your favourite commercial cleaners—but they also make applying cleaning solutions much easier and more exact than simply pouring them on. Even when you're just using water—for instance, if you need to lightly wet a carpet stain—spray bottles do a great job.

**To find good spray bottles**—ones that are more durable and have a larger capacity—drop into a specialist cleaning supplier. These professional-grade squirters will have more pumping power, making your work easier.

**When using spray bottles,** the most important rule is to label them. Some bottles come with white rectangles on the side intended for labelling with a permanent marker. Don't pour in your bleach solution thinking you'll label it later. Do it straight away to avoid future confusion—and possible safety issues. And to avoid contaminating nearby surfaces, use the appropriate nozzle setting for the job you're doing. Use a tighter stream for smaller areas, such as toilet seats, and a wider mist for larger areas, such as large bathroom mirrors.

**A warning:** if you're using a harmful cleaning chemical, such as bleach, in a spray bottle, avoid making the mist too fine. It will aerosolise the chemical, making it easier to inhale or get in your eyes.

**Spray bottles are available** from supermarkets, home improvement shops, discount retailers and specialist cleaning suppliers.

## SQUEEGEES

Cleaning pros rely on squeegees. Anyone faced with cleaning smooth surfaces—such as windows, mirrors and tile—should too. They are quicker and more effective at removing cleaning solutions and the dirt those solutions loosen. They don't streak; they don't leave behind lint, as paper towels do; and they're not as messy as newspapers.

A 23–30 centimetre-wide squeegee is the right size for glass cleaning. Any bigger, and it will be unwieldy. Any smaller, and it won't cover enough surface area. (You can have a smaller, secondary squeegee for smaller, divided windowpanes.)

**Buy a good-quality model** that will work well and last. Get one with a high-quality (pliable and flexible) wiping blade. Cheaper squeegees have hard-rubber blades. When they split or have a nick in them, they leave a line of water behind, meaning you have to work twice as hard or buy a new one.

**When using a squeegee,** keep a dry towel in your other hand, and wipe the squeegee on the towel after each swipe. For how to clean a window with a squeegee, see 'Windows', on page 383.

**Small bathroom squeegees** are available for wiping down wet shower recess walls, thus preventing soap scum build-up.

**Squeegees are available** from hardware, discount and home improvement shops.

## STEEL WOOL

Steel wool is a specialty cleaning product and should never be used for general cleaning purposes. Even the finest steel wool is abrasive and can scratch (and ruin) many surfaces. That said, steel wool can be extremely useful for removing the most stubborn grime and for doing it without harsh chemicals.

**Steel wool comes** in grades that range from ultra-fine (grade 00000) to extra coarse (grade 4). Traditionally, it has been used to remove baked-on food from pots and pans. Some brands have soap already embedded in the pads for convenience. But with the ubiquity of non-stick cooking surfaces, it is less important to keep those woolly balls under the kitchen sink these days. Besides making surfaces look bad, when steel wool scratches something, it creates a surface that attracts stains and rust. Use steel wool as a last resort or on surfaces that you don't mind scratching.

**Steel wool is available** from supermarkets, hardware shops, discount shops and home improvement shops. Look for ultra-fine steel wool at restoration shops and antique dealers.

## TOILET CLEANERS

Commercial toilet cleaners tend to be strong and acid-based. Often they contain hydrochloric acid for eating away at stubborn stains and mineral deposits—those rings that seem cemented to the toilet bowl. And often they are of a thick consistency, which helps them stick to the wall of the toilet long enough to do their job properly.

**For regular toilet cleaning,** hydrochloric acid is probably overkill. The less you use it, the safer you are and the less chance you have of damaging some nearby surface with an accidental spill or drip. Try a mild detergent or bath and tile cleaner or look for a product with a milder acid, such as phosphoric acid.

**If a toilet bowl is grungy**—you haven't cleaned it in a while or your household water is hard or contains excess iron—you may need a stronger cleaning product. Or, for an entirely chemical-free approach, use a pumice stone (the same product you use to rub coarse skin off your feet). Keeping the stone wet, rub it on the ring until it's gone. This works for old rings as well as recent ones. Pumice will not scratch white vitreous china, which is what most toilets are made of, but it will scratch fibreglass, enamel, plastic and other materials.

**Here's a tip:** apply your toilet bowl cleaner and then go and clean the bathtub or the basin. Come back to the toilet 5 minutes later, when the cleaner has had plenty of time to loosen the grime.

Toilet bowl cleaners are widely available from supermarkets, discount shops and home improvement shops. Pumice stones are available from pharmacies and supermarkets.

## VACUUM CLEANERS

Flick through this book and count the number of times a vacuum cleaner is called on for in a particular cleaning job, and you'll quickly get tired of counting. A good vacuum cleaner is a key cleaning tool for any home owner, both for routine dust and dirt removal and for emergency situations, such as broken glass and upturned pot plants.

**Choosing a vacuum cleaner** is more confusing than ever, since the differences between canister and upright vacuums have been blurred. What used to be a matter of floor type—upright for carpets, canister for bare floors—is now just a matter of personal preference. The good news is that the similarities and overall improvements in quality in most vacuum cleaners these days, makes it hard to go wrong when choosing a new model.

In addition to uprights and canisters, there are also wet and dry vacuum cleaners and hand-held cleaners, each with its own functions and features. Generally speaking, some features are marketing gimmicks, whereas others are genuinely useful.

**Features to consider** when buying a vacuum include the following:

- The on-board tools, such as crevice and upholstery tools, extension wands, and nozzles with rotating bars, are essential for non-floor cleaning duties (curtains and upholstered furniture, for instance).
- Manual pile adjustment is important not only for better dirt retrieval when you're vacuuming carpets, but also for better carpet protection, since the 'standard' setting on many beater bars can destroy a carpet's fibres and wear out the vacuum cleaner's motor.
- A gauge alerting users when the bag is full improves efficiency. (Full bags don't draw as well, making you work harder to pick up the dirt.)

**Filtration systems** are among the best features to find their way onto vacuum cleaners in recent years. These systems improve air quality by capturing tiny particles that otherwise would be blown back into your home in the machine's exhaust. The machines with the best filters, known as high efficiency particulate air (HEPA) filters, are expensive to buy and to replace—but for people with asthma or allergies, they are extremely beneficial. Some manufacturers claim their machines have 'microfiltration' systems. Although these might not be true HEPA filters, they may be an improvement over the standard, filterless vacuum cleaner. If you want to buy a filtering machine, it's worth doing your homework. Check the results of tests done by organisations such as the Australian Consumers Association, the non-profit organisation that publishes *CHOICE* magazine.

**More gimmicky features** include dirt sensors, which alert you to how much dirt is passing through your vacuum cleaner, not how much dirt is left in a rug. These devices are unnecessary and can be misleading. Vacuum manufacturers these days also like to brag about power, usually in the form of number of amps or suction amps. Amps measure electric current, not a machine's ability to clean. More important, though, is how one machine stacks up to another in real tests, those you read about in consumer magazines and those you experience while 'test-driving' a vacuum cleaner in the shop, which is something you should do before spending hundreds of dollars on a machine.

Here's a look at the various styles available:

**Upright vacuums** were once the clear choice for homes with lots of carpets because of their powerful rotating 'beater bars', but not any-more. Although, while canister vacs these days also come with beater-bar attachments, uprights are still easier to operate on carpets and easier to store when you're finished. They are taller and often self-propelled, reducing the amount of stooping and pushing required to vacuum a carpeted room. And because they often come with a hose and assorted attachments, they are versatile. If your house is filled with carpeting, an upright will be faster and more efficient. If your house has a mix of carpet and bare floors, it's a toss-up.

**Canister vacuums** are usually the better choice if your house has mostly bare floors or if you have lots of curtains, upholstery and window blinds to vacuum. These models have a built-in hose, plus attachments, usually including a powered nozzle with a beater bar. Canister machines are easier to carry around the house and up the stairs. But they are typically more awkward to store, since they take up more floor space than uprights. An added convenience when it's time to put away your canister vacuum is the button-operated retractable cords that come with most canister models, instead of cords you have to manually wrap around the machine for storage.

**Wet and dry vacuums** tend to be powerful, less expensive workhorses. Sometimes known as shop vacs, these special canister machines are notable for being able to safely pick up water—unlike other vacuums. They are most at home in garages and around outdoor living areas, where they're useful for sucking up everything from sawdust to smelly water leaks. Generally speaking, the more you spend, the more reliable the machine will be and the more extras it will include.

**Hand-held vacuums** are portable battery-operated machines. Ever since the introduction, years ago, of the DustBuster, hand-held vacs have been hugely popular. Most are quite powerful and surprisingly inexpensive. But since they have limited battery power—often less than 10 minutes at a shot—they are useful only for quick jobs, such as spills and cleaning up toddler crumb trails. Today, they come with more and more features and attachments, including better filtration systems (which may or may not be necessary for the kinds of jobs they tackle). As with full-sized machines, don't get tempted by useless extras. When buying, stick to the basics—brand reliability, warranties and battery power.

**If you have stairs to clean,** instead of buying a separate, smaller vacuum cleaner made for stair-cleaning, outfit your existing machine with the appropriate extras, if you can. First, buy an extension tube (usually 3–4 metres long), which will allow you to leave your machine on the ground floor while you clean the entire flight of steps. You can buy extension tubes for both uprights and canister vacuums.

For carpet-covered stairs, buy a turbo tool. Powered by the incoming airflow (hence the name turbo), these attachments act like small beater bars to help loosen and pull up hairs, lint and dirt from carpet pile. But because they do not need a power cord to rotate, they can be attached to extension hoses. They are much lighter than motor-driven beater-bar nozzles.

**Vacuum cleaners are available** from department stores, discount shops and home improvement shops.

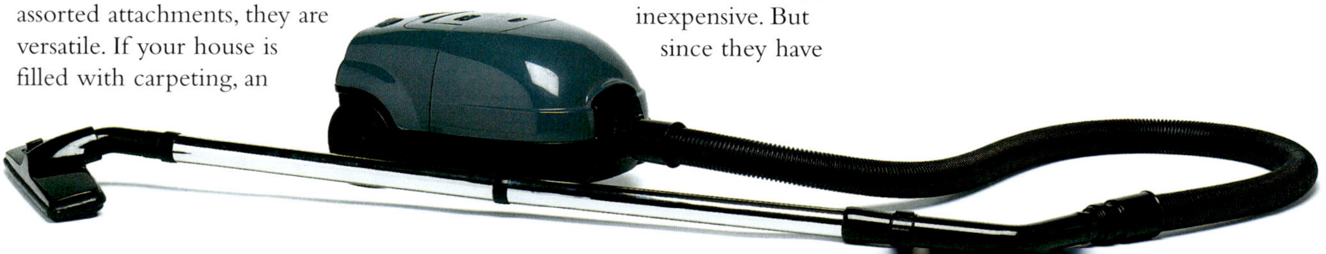

# Index

## A



## B

## C

## E



## F

## G



## H

## I



## J



## K



## L

## V



## W

# Picture credits

The pictures in *How to Clean Just About Everything* were supplied by the people and agencies listed below. All photographs not listed are the copyright of Reader's Digest.

## Photographs

**26** *bottom* Courtesy of Miele Australia Pty Ltd. **32** *bottom* Courtesy of Miele Australia Pty Ltd. **58** *bottom* Photodisc. **59** *top left* Corel Corporation. **64** *centre* Photodisc; *bottom* Courtesy of Edmonds Pty Ltd. **74** *bottom* Photodisc. **80** *bottom right* Photodisc. **82** *bottom* Photodisc. **103** *bottom* Courtesy of Eurogem Australia. **112** *bottom* Photodisc. **113** *bottom* Inmagine Stock Photography. **115** *bottom* Inmagine Stock Photography. **137** *bottom* Inmagine Stock Photography. **151** *centre* Photodisc. **154** *centre* Photodisc. **156** *centre* Photodisc. **177** *bottom* Photodisc. **181** *bottom* Courtesy of Polivac International Pty Ltd. **184** *bottom* Photodisc. **206** *bottom* Inmagine Stock Photography. **207** *bottom* Photodisc. **209** *centre* Photodisc. **223** *bottom* Science Gallery/OSF/Auscape. **261** *bottom* Photodisc. **290** *bottom* Photodisc. **291** *bottom* Inmagine Stock Photography. **323** *all top left & bottom left* Photodisc. **325** *top left & bottom right* Photodisc. **347** *centre* Margaret Heldon. **356** *bottom* Courtesy of Mistral International Pty Ltd. **369** *bottom* Photodisc. **392** *bottom* Photodisc.

## Illustrations

**Stephen Pollitt** 38, 53, 54, 59, 61, 69, 70 *top*, 73, 77, 79, 83, 87, 89, 90, 94, 95, 96, 101, 110, 111, 116, 120 *bottom*, 128, 130, 134, 136, 146, 150, 159, 162, 165, 166, 170, 174, 178, 189, 197, 202, 203, 209, 210, 211, 216, 218, 219, 226, 228, 229, 231, 234, 235, 238, 242, 248, 254, 261, 265, 275, 278, 283, 284, 287, 290, 292, 295, 296, 298, 299, 300, 301, 302, 303, 306, 314, 315, 317, 320, 324, 326, 327, 336, 337, 340, 349, 353, 354, 357, 360, 362, 367, 372, 377, 382, 384, 385.
**Sue Ninham** 8, 9, 13, 16, 18, 21, 22, 23, 27, 34, 37, 41, 43, 46, 49, 55, 57, 60, 62, 65, 66, 67, 68, 70 *bottom*, 71, 74, 81, 82, 85, 92, 100, 113, 119, 120 *top*, 121, 124, 126, 127, 132, 133, 135, 138, 139, 140, 141, 142, 147, 148, 151, 154, 156, 161, 168, 171, 175, 176, 182, 183, 184, 186, 190, 193, 196, 199, 207, 221, 224, 233, 237, 240, 244, 246, 257, 258, 259, 268, 272, 285, 288, 293, 304, 305, 307, 308, 310, 311, 312, 316, 319, 323, 325, 329, 330, 332, 334, 338, 341, 344, 345, 346, 348, 351, 359, 364, 366, 370, 374, 379, 380, 387, 393.

## HOW TO CLEAN JUST ABOUT EVERYTHING

**Writer** Jeff Bredenberg

**Consultant, Australian and New Zealand edition** Georgina Bitcon

**Project Editors** Liz Connolly, Don Earnest, Kathy Gerrard

**Designer** Donna Heldon

**Picture and Prop Researchers** Victoria Williams, John Pryce-Jones, Andrew Crighton, Joanna Collard

**Photographer** Michal Kaniewski, Ad Libitum

**Illustrators** Sue Ninham, Stephen Pollitt

**Proofreader** Tim Learner

**Indexer** Diane Harriman

**Production Controller** Janelle Garside

## READER'S DIGEST GENERAL BOOKS

**Editorial Director** Elaine Russell

**Managing Editor** Rosemary McDonald

**Art Director** Sue Rawkins

*How To Clean Just About Everything* is published by
Reader's Digest (Australia) Pty Limited
80 Bay Street, Ultimo, NSW 2007
GPO Box 4353, Sydney, NSW 2001
www.readersdigest.com.au

First Australian and New Zealand edition 2005


National Library of Australia Cataloguing-in-Publication data:
How to clean just about everything.

Includes index.
ISBN 1 876689 03 X.

1. Cleaning. 2. House cleaning. 3. Housekeeping.
4. Cleaning compounds. I. Reader's Digest (Australia).

648.5

Prepress by Sinnott Bros, Sydney
Printed and bound in China by Everbest Printing Co Ltd.

We are interested in receiving your comments on the contents of this book.
Write to: The Editor, General Books Editorial,
Reader's Digest (Australia) Pty Limited,
80 Bay Street, Ultimo, NSW 2007
GPO Box 4353, Sydney, NSW 2001
or email us at bookeditors.au@readersdigest.com

To order additional copies of *How To Clean Just About Everything* call 1300 303 210 (Australia) or 0800 540 032 (New Zealand) or email us at customerservice@au.readersdigest.com

Concept code US 4513
Product code 041 3104